Richard G. Dumont, Ph.D.

D0886880

Richard G. Dumont, Ph.D.

Class, Conflict, and Mobility

Chandler Publications in
ANTHROPOLOGY AND SOCIOLOGY

LEONARD BROOM, *General Editor*

SOCIOLOGY

CHARLES M. BONJEAN, *Editor*

HT
609
.L64

Richard G. Dumont, Ph.D.

Class, Conflict, and Mobility

Theories and Studies of Class Structure

Joseph Lopreato
The University of Texas at Austin

Lawrence E. Hazelrigg
Indiana University

WITHDRAWN

CHANDLER PUBLISHING COMPANY
An Intext Publisher
SAN FRANCISCO • SCRANTON • LONDON • TORONTO

Tennessee Tech. Library
Cookeville, Tenn.
340376

Library of Congress Cataloging in Publication Data

Lopreato, Joseph.
    Class, conflict, and mobility.

    (Chandler publications in anthropology and sociology)
    Bibliography: p.
    1. Social classes.   2. Social mobility.
3. Job satisfaction.   I. Hazelrigg, Lawrence E.,
joint author.   II. Title.

HT609.L64   301.44   72-152048
ISBN 0-8102-0429-0

COPYRIGHT © 1972 BY CHANDLER PUBLISHING COMPANY

ALL RIGHTS RESERVED

LIBRARY OF CONGRESS CATALOG CARD NO. 72-152048

INTERNATIONAL STANDARD BOOK NO. 0-8102-0429-0

PRINTED IN THE UNITED STATES OF AMERICA

To the
KARLS
and the
VILFREDOS
and the
GEORGES
and the
BENJAMINS
—for one reason or another.

Contents

Tables

Preface

Social stratification, broadly defined, is one of the oldest and most researched areas of sociology. As a focus of scholarly quests for knowledge of the social, it antedates the Christian calendar by more than a millennium certainly, probably by much more. Indeed, it is quite difficult to imagine that early man could have puzzled for long over the nature and meaning of his social being without having apprehended at least some of the issues that we include today within the topical domain of social stratification. For such issues are inescapably central to an understanding of social organization; the coin of social order is inscribed on the one side with differences and particles, and on the other side with similarities and the whole.

The ensuing corpus of informed observation, speculation, and theorizing with regard to matters of social stratification has grown immensely rich with insight. The corpus of thought in this single topical division of sociology comes close to comprising the entire field within its divisional boundary. We do not offer here or in the text proper a review of this extensive literature, in the manner of attending directly to insights generated by the long line of scholars from Aristotle, Plato, and Lao-tzu to Harrington, Hobbes, Locke, Rousseau, and the like. Rather, we begin with the accumulated knowledge of the mid nineteenth century, and in Europe. For purposes of contemporary investigations and formulations in social stratification, this period is of predominant importance: the middle 1800's, when the great social-philosophical synthesis of Karl Marx appeared.

Bernard Shaw once remarked, in specific reference to the exploitation of labor, that it "is easy to show that Mill and Cairnes and Sidgwick knew it and said it, but the fact is that the average pupil of Marx never forgets it, while the average pupil of Mill and the rest never learns it." Obviously Marx built upon the contributions of a large number of predecessors—a fact which he readily acknowledged. But, to use the idiom of the present day, he "got it all together," and in a most impressively creative and powerful way. Without discounting the evident value of those prior contributions upon which he built, it must be said that it is the work of this scholar that most persistently informs, directly or indirectly, recognized or not, the greater bulk of subsequent endeavors in the study of social stratification. Indeed, the issues elucidated, sharpened, and invigorated or re-invigorated by Marx are still today *fundamental* issues of social structure.

To be sure, when we look into the stratification literature that has appeared since Marx, we do find important theoretical contributions by a number of scholars. In our view, especially noteworthy contributions include the works of Vilfredo Pareto, Max Weber, Ralf Dahrendorf, and, together with Wilbert E. Moore, Kingsley Davis. Still, these scholars were concerned in one manner or another with the complex set of issues that revolve around the basic dynamics of class structure—particularly, the dynamics of class consciousness, conflict, and social mobility—just as Marx had been before them. No one of them could escape the influence of Marx's monumental construction.

This book is an effort, first, to state comprehensively and (where necessary) clarify the theories of class structure and stratification put forth by Marx and the aforementioned "post-Marxian" scholars, and second, to apply to a particular body of data some of the insights and propositions generated in those theories. Accordingly, the volume is divided into five parts. Part I presents the theories of Marx, Pareto, Dahrendorf, Weber, and Davis and Moore, in that order. Part II consists of five chapters, of which the first offers a conceptual analysis of class consciousness and the next four make empirical applications of that analysis. Part III consists of two chapters on job satisfaction and alienation, wherein Marx's statements on the subject are examined closely, and partly in conjunction with elements of the Davis-Moore theory. Part IV, devoted to the study of social mobility, begins with an examination of rates and measures of vertical occupational mobility and continues with four chapters on various correlates of mobility. Finally, Part V contains one chapter, in which Dahrendorf's work is examined critically with a view toward determining not only the extent of its empirical validity but also the degree to which it constitutes a theoretical bridge between Marx and one of Marx's keenest interpreters and critics, Pareto.

The research data that we utilize in all but the first part of the volume are from Italian society of the mid nineteen-sixties. Thus, in one sense this is a book about class structure, class consciousness, and social mobility in Italy. But we have intended more than that. We have made an effort to transcend the reality of the specific case and to address ourselves to issues that are pertinent to industrial society in general. Our aim has been not merely to write a book about aspects of social structure in Italy (although there is considerable value in that) but also to construct a volume that will prove useful to social scientists and teachers who are concerned with a systematic examination of theories of stratification and with their applications to class structure in industrial society.

Various organizations and institutions have given financial support to this study. Fulbright scholarships for research in Italy granted to the senior author in 1962–1964 made the basic field work possible; we are deeply indebted to the Fulbright program and to Dr. Cipriana Scelba, the Italian executive director in Rome, for their generous help. The Social Science Research Council provided the funds to carry out a survey from which our data are drawn. The National Science Foundation made available the funds needed to carry the study through to its final stage. The University of Texas Research Institute added research and clerical assistance. We are deeply grateful for the generosity of these agencies.

Acknowledgments to individuals are now traditional forms, in the same manner that a tip of the hat used to be. Such is not here the case, for we owe a clear and substantial debt to more persons than we can mention. Leonard Broom, Janet Chafetz, Lewis Coser, Carlo Genelletti, Elton Jackson, Frank Jones, Lionel Lewis, Luigi Lombardi Satriani, and Richard Simpson have read all or parts of the book in manuscript form and offered generous and helpful suggestions. Professor Pierpaolo Luzzato Fegiz and his staff at the DOXA public-opinion institute in Milan were invaluable in their criticisms and suggestions when field work began through their facilities; then more, throughout the endeavor they mustered their highest competencies enthusiastically and at generous cost.

A number of other persons contributed long hours of conscientious and diligent work as research assistants. In this connection, we are especially grateful to Ambretta Dobrilla and Vito Spadone, who coded the interview schedules, and to Marilyn Bidnick, Patricia Bullock, Janet Chafetz, and Sue Keir, who at various times during the project performed constructive, and often creative, research tasks.

Many other persons gave lavishly of their time in typing various drafts of the manuscript, reading proof, and assisting with the construction of indexes. Our greatest debt here is to Carolyn Lopreato and JoAnne Hazelrigg, without whose aid and encouragement the job of preparing this volume would have been much less pleasant. And sincere thanks are due to Helen Litzler and her girls in the office of the Sociology Department of the University of Texas— Judy Frank, Beverly Molder, Barbara Pickett, and Sherry Villemez—for cheerful help, often beyond the call of duty.

Bill Parker, of Chandler Publishing Company, took on the job of editor with genuine interest. He added logic and content, as well as form, to our efforts, and we are sincerely happy that he worked with us.

Finally, some sections of Chapters 13, 15, and 17 appeared in preliminary form in several journal articles. For permission to use these materials, we are grateful to the *American Journal of Sociology,* the *American Sociological Review,* the *Journal of Conflict Resolution,* and *Social Forces.*

Happy is he who has escaped the tempest at sea and found harbor. Happy is he who has risen triumphant over his toils. In one way or another one man outstrips another in the race for wealth and power. And a thousand others are cherishing a thousand hopes; some result in happiness for mortals and some fail. But I call blessed the man whose life is happy day by day.

Euripides, *The Bacchants* (The Chorus)

By this, recalling the Old Testament
    near the beginning of Genesis, you will see
    that in the will of Providence, man was meant

to labor and to prosper. But usurers,
    by seeking their increase in other ways,
    scorn Nature in herself and her followers.

Dante, *The Inferno* (Canto XI)

INTRODUCTION

By all accounts, social stratification has clearly become one of the chief substantive "specialities" of the sociological enterprise. Even a cursory review of the discipline's major journals, for example, will reveal a startling growth in the relative number of materials devoted to the area. Understandably, of course, the greatest increment followed closely upon that series of economically and socially catastrophic events known in the aggregate as the Great Depression. Between 1930 and 1940, the incidence of journal articles concerned with issues of stratification more than doubled certainly, and perhaps even tripled.

This growth ought to have happened, for the study of social stratification deals with issues that pervade, indeed are at the heart of, the whole sociological enterprise. One could also justifiably argue that it is a scientifically opportune growth, for in this time of increasing academic specialization social stratification constitutes a most natural antidotal bridge between the entirety of sociology and many of its sister disciplines—philosophy, anthropology, economics, political science, history, psychology.

The pervasiveness of the social-stratification perspective is easy enough to understand. Social stratification is unique in laying emphasis on an idea about the social existence that is central to nearly all scholarly social pursuits. It is the idea, lifted to the level of an epoch-making formula by the theorists of the social contract, that social living *is* social participation in a written or unwritten, spoken or understood contract bearing with it *a cost for a profit*. Social stratification explicitly points to the fact that some participants in the social contract bear a high cost while receiving niggardly profits, whereas quite the opposite holds true for other participants. In this sense, social stratification renders relevant, theoretically not merely ideologically, the idea of distributive (in)justice in society—an idea that is compelling to the human mind, whether for reasons humane or selfish, in many of its social conceptions.

The concern with issues attendant on social stratification is very old. But our interest in this volume concentrates on only the major and most timely theoretical issues together with some of their empirical relevancies; accordingly, we shall make no effort here to follow a growing convention and direct attention back to the Greek philosophers; nor will we attend to the subsequent literature that ranges from the Bishop of Hippo to Ibn-Khaldun, Thomas Aquinas, Giordano Bruno, and others. We shall instead point out that by the eighteenth century, problems of the economic-industrial order and of political consciousness had reached such a point that an intellectual renaissance was manifested in philosophy and history, a renaissance at whose center can be found a number of interesting assumptions about the nature of man and his institutions and about the malleability of both. In the school of thought wherein the great Turgot and Condorcet were central, one finds the linked assumptions (1) that man is a rational being and (2) that the world, including the social, is susceptible of rational alteration; thus, man's institutions can be deliberately, progressively, and decisively molded by man to make them better serve his needs. Not at all surprisingly, sociology was born of and nursed by a program of thought and action that had its roots in such assumptions.

Unfortunately, the problems of the political and economic existence that had been manifested in bitter form to the rationalists of the seventeenth and eighteenth centuries did not wither with the advance of industrialization and urbanization—rather, they were exacerbated by this advance and developed in pace with it. By the mid nineteenth century the capitalist, moralist, and utopist Robert Owen could demonstrate—to the astonishment of none but the insentient—that women and children, ill or well, were toiling in the mines of Britain and the sweatshops of all Europe for ten, twelve, or more hours a day to earn wages barely equal to self-sustenance at best.

Within this milieu the monumental figure of Karl Marx stood forth and creatively cast seeds that were to have an enlightening epochal significance, both within purely intellectual endeavors and within the frame of practical politics. The student of social stratification must be struck by the ubiquity of Marx's influence: he can hardly find a major theoretical statement that lacks the mark of his theory of classes. It has even been said that much of sociology is an attempt to answer the arguments of the nineteenth-century "revolutionaries" in general and of Karl Marx in particular—a "debate with Marx's ghost."

We cannot accept in full measure this dramatic characterization, but it is certainly undeniable that the recent history of social stratification as a subject matter of social science must be read with Marx firmly in the wings. One of the chief aims of this book is to present stratification theory in a fashion that is historically coherent and permits valuable heuristic uses as well. Accordingly, we have chosen to focus on certain major theories, each of which is surrounded by a variety of controversies of both substance and approach. In addition to the theory presented by Marx, which is our point of departure, we have selected four others. The first is by Vilfredo Pareto, who represents and to some extent summarizes the argument of an entire school of thought sometimes referred to as the "elite school," which in its essential elements appeared at the turn of the century. Although essentially a Marxian scholar himself, Pareto takes exception with various elements of Marx's analysis. Two of these are especially crucial and are here mentioned in anticipation of a more detailed treatment.

Under the influence of the French Era of Enlightenment and of the French revolutionaries, Marx tended to assume that man is a rational being; indeed, his theory, particularly the future-seeing aspect of it, cannot be comprehended unless this assumption is clearly understood and held in mind. By contrast, the assumption of *non*rationality is central in all of Pareto's sociology. Nonrationality, in turn, has implications for a second assumption found in Marx: the perfectibility of social institutions, and especially the possibility of so arranging institutions that the political existence would not spell out (as Marx claimed it had up to his time) the exploitation of one class by another. Pareto's position was that—given the nonrational *and* self-seeking nature of social action, and excepting the temporary ameliorations of social situations engendered by periodic revolution—in the long run the lion's share of the good things in life would always be appropriated by those holding the near-monopoly of power, those located in what Pareto conceived of as the *inevitable* "governing class."

These crucial differences of perspective between Marx and Pareto—and we should here emphasize parenthetically that, given such differences, there are still a great many similarities in these scholars' historical analyses—can be relatively clearly defined by contrasting the Marxian eschatology with its Paretian counterpart. A child of the French Enlightenment philosophers and, through them, of the Augustinian *procursus,* Marx fits essentially in the Judeo-Christian tradition with its imagery of the "arrow of time": of human history as an inevitably consummative linear progression toward the state of "perfection." Pareto, on the other hand, does not concern himself with what may be called, properly speaking, "final things," but instead picks up elements of the older Greek imagery of "Ixion's wheel" and the notion of cyclical movement: the sense in which everything changes and yet everything remains the same. The membership of the governing class may change, either gradually or abruptly, says Pareto, but the fact of a governing class is forever constant. This vigorous break with the centuries-long dominant tradition of progress and perfection may in part explain why Pareto's sociology was diagnosed in Western democracies, particularly in the United States, as having an "antidemocratic" bias.

A recent theory by the German sociologist Ralf Dahrendorf is closely related to both Marx's and Pareto's formulations. As we shall later see, Dahrendorf intends a supersedure of Karl Marx, which is allegedly necessitated by a number of "post-Marxian" developments in industrial society, developments that have rendered invalid many aspects of the Marxian theory. In the process, he combines rather effectively elements of Pareto with elements of Marx; while laying stress on conflict between classes dichotomously viewed, he focuses not on economic factors to explain this conflict but on political factors, specifically the distribution of authority in what he terms (following Weber) "imperatively coordinated associations." Moreover, while the conflict is between the "haves" and the "have-nots"—between those who hold authority-endowed positions and those who are excluded from them—the contention is between "classes" composed of individuals who appear to have individual ends in view, not group ends. Relatedly, the resolution of "class conflict" is deemed only a temporary phenomenon, and indeed Dahrendorf purposefully eschews the idea of conflict resolution in favor of the notion of conflict "regulation." Hence, whenever and wherever one finds imperatively coordinated associations—and they will be found at all times and places—one can expect to find also at least the makings of class conflict.

One of the best-known responses to Marx's theory was given by Max Weber in the early part of this century. Although too much has been made of certain differences between these scholars, a few divergences are indeed important. First, it may be fairly said that Weber reacted to the Marxian argument against the German idealists as being somewhat excessive. Whether he recognized Marx's polemical stance as mere tactic is debatable; in any case, Weber took issue with Marx's apparently extraordinary emphasis on the role of economic factors in social conflict and change, although he was sometimes at pains to show what Marx had in fact never denied, namely, that the products of man's thought could be influential upon the material conditions of existence. Second, in what was again mostly a shifting of emphasis, Weber stressed that the economic variable consists not solely of economic factors but also of the *economically relevant* and the *economically conditioned,* and that the stratification of historical societies is not unidimensional but multidimensional, based on "status groups" and "parties" as well as on "class."

Weber was less concerned than Marx with the results of capitalism as an economic institution, except insofar as he dealt with it from the vantage point of his most famous "ideal type," bureaucracy. Much more than Marx, he tended to be descriptive of phenomena of social stratification—which means that, whereas Marx took a futuristic stance with respect to social evolution, and emphasized what he called the laws of social-economic development,

Weber put himself in the position whereby he could more accurately describe systems of inequality at particular times and places. To this extent Weber, like Pareto, could emphasize the factors which increasingly differentiated people, namely the proliferation of interests in society, rather than those which under some conditions could bring them together. This point stands out most sharply in Weber's treatment of class. In contrast to Marx, who constructed a descriptive scheme of classes simply as preparatory to his analytic scheme of classes, which in turn became the key tool for his analysis of social conflict and change, Weber devoted the greater part of his time to constructing the analytic scheme —essentially the same as Marx's—which he then used as a descriptive device.

The final statement of stratification theory to be treated in this book was formulated more than a quarter of a century ago by the United States sociologists Kingsley Davis and Wilbert E. Moore. Their formulation represents, on the one hand, the most radical modern challenge to the Marxian synthesis and, on the other, a reversion to what might be considered the earliest modern theory of stratification, that held implicitly or explicitly by the classical economists. The basic problem that Davis and Moore pose concerns the inevitable cause of social stratification broadly viewed, that is to say, of social stratification in universal form. In effect, their position is that social stratification as a variable system of social inequality is inevitable because the needs of society are many and heterogeneous and because not all of the participants in the social contract contribute equally to the fulfillment of those needs. Without here elaborating the point, it should be noted that the Davis-Moore challenge to Marx's theory consists in their postulate that those positions which on balance contribute most to the fulfillment of societal needs also must convey the highest rewards for their incumbents—thereby leading inevitably to a system of inequalities.

Social stratification is a very broad and highly diverse area of study. Hence, the serious student has literally hundreds upon hundreds of theoretical issues confronting him—some major, others merely nuance. Our firm conviction is that the issues posed by Marx and the other scholars just mentioned are still *the critical issues* of social stratification, and indeed of *contemporary industrial society,* notwithstanding the massive bulk of sociology that has accumulated over the years.

On the one hand, stratification theory concerns itself with the processes of class formation and identity, which in Marx's theory appear under the label of *class consciousness.* These are the *associative* dynamics of social stratification. On the other hand, there are the *dissociative* processes of stratification, which may be subsumed under the general label of *social mobility.* Mobility plays a central role in all of the five theories in question as a process that is antithetical to class consciousness, in the sense that it refers to the circulation of people from one class to another, people who bring with them fragments of previous and now extraneous ideologies and thereby make their classes of destination ideologically heterogeneous and politically disorganized.

Accordingly, we have organized the materials that follow into five principal sections. The first, Part One, affords presentations and critical discussions of the five above-identified theories of social stratification. Part Two applies aspects of those theories to survey data from Italian society, which provides the empirical setting for the entire volume. This Part consists of five chapters dealing with the conceptualization and assessment of class consciousness. Part Three comprises two chapters and continues our interest in class consciousness by focusing on issues of satisfaction and alienation in the work setting. Part Four addresses questions of vertical social mobility—rates and comparisons, education and migration factors, political "consequences," and a series of other social-psychological correlates. Part Five, finally, consists of a single chapter which treats comparatively Marx's theory and Dahrendorf's theory, in view of the latter's intended supersedure of the former.

METHODOLOGICAL NOTE

The data on which the empirical sections of this volume are based consist of information obtained from a sample of 1,569 Italian male family heads. No claim is made here that Italian society is representative of "other" societies according to any set of criteria that one might wish to invoke. Some, of course, would argue that, since Italy is divided into an industrialized half and another half that is essentially agricultural but in the process of development, sociological studies of that country are apt to be relevant to most societies today. We are not inclined to push this argument. Rather, our intent is to illustrate and, where plausible, show the empirical validity of some basic issues of social-stratification theory viewed comparatively in terms of a single body of empirical data.

The universe of potential sample members was restricted to family heads inasmuch as the family is considered the proper unit of analysis in studies of social stratification (a woman and her children assume the class position of the family breadwinner, usually the husband and father), and to *male* family heads in order to avoid the nuisance of a very small number of women in the sample.

At the time of the study, 1963–1964, the resident population of Italy comprised approximately 14 million families. Little of an official nature was known about the particular construction of the total Italian population. The number of resident families by region of the country was available from the 1961 General Census, but data pertaining to the geographic distribution of families with male heads of household, the occupational composition of male heads of household, and similar other questions were not available from official sources.

An appropriate alternative source of detailed information was afforded by recent surveys conducted by DOXA, the Institute for Statistical Research and the Analysis of Public Opinion, a nongovernmental research organization with headquarters in Milan. In particular, DOXA had conducted during the early part of 1963 a survey of 16,000 families in order to examine questions of style of life and consumer behavior. These families were selected through a complex series of procedures designed to insure maximum representation of the entire population of families. After dividing all inhabited localities in the country according to several levels of population size and selecting a total of 625 localities as representative of all size levels and regional variations, a total of 6,000 voting districts or polling places were randomly selected from the 625 localities. These, in turn, constituted the base for purposes of drawing at random 16,000 names and addresses. In order to avoid attributing too much weight to those families with a higher than average number of adults (or voters), and in order to include in the sample at least a portion of those families who had moved only recently and were not contained in the voting lists, the 16,000 interviewees of the final sample were not those whose names were actually drawn from the voting lists but those families residing in dwellings in closest proximity to the formally selected families.

In this fashion, DOXA constructed a large sample that promised the highest possible representativeness and permitted the collection of various types of detailed data. The resulting information guided construction of the present sample. First, the age and occupational composition of male family heads was determined for each of three categories of community size (less than 10,000, 10,000 to 100,000, more than 100,000), cross-classified by three broad geographical regions (northern, central, and southern Italy). Second, the male family heads were divided according to "zone of residence within the community" (city, periphery, hamlet, isolated homestead). These procedures permitted the isolation of 90 homogeneous areas, arranged by five categories of community size and zone of residence for each of the 18 district regions of Italy, exclusive of Sardinia. The 90 areas included a total of 122 localities.

Interviewees were selected according to the "purposive-stratified-sample" technique. Each of 144 interviewers was instructed to find a certain quota of interviewees on the basis of the following parameters: (1) age of the interviewee (up to 34 years, 35–44, 45–64, 65 or above); (2) occupation (eight categories); (3) zone of residence (city, isolated homestead or hamlet up to two kilometers from the city, isolated homestead or hamlet more than two kilometers from the city).

DOXA has carried out various surveys utilizing both this method of sample construction and the random-sample technique. The results show that the two yield near-identical information, provided that particular care is taken to stratify the sample according to zone of residence—as well as sex, age, and occupation—since this variable, like the latter, correlates rather strongly with variations in custom, style of life, and attitude.

The number of interviews originally scheduled was 1,650. Of these, 1,569 were completed, for a rate of 94 percent. The remaining 6 percent of the interviews were not completed for the following reasons: (1) personal difficulties of the interviewers, such as sickness, about 1 percent; (2) absence of particular categories of interviewees in particular communities, about 2 percent; (3) impassable roads, about 2 percent.

Interviewing took place between December 10, 1963, and January 15, 1964. The 144 interviewers were selected from among those who in recent years had most diligently and competently participated in DOXA surveys, especially those of a sociological nature. The work of 46 interviewers, 32 percent of the total, was checked through second visits to the interviewees in order to ascertain the accuracy of completed schedules. No irregularities were discovered.

Before being finally chosen for use, each question in the interview schedule was tested and retested many times on various localized groups of people and once on a small nationally scattered sample. The coding of answers given by interviewees to interview questions that were not structured and precoded was based on a detailed examination of 25 percent of the completed interviews. The interview schedule employed may be found in Appendix I.

PART ONE

Theories of Class Structure

I

KARL MARX: CLASSES, CONFLICT, AND CHANGE

From time to time in the succession of intellectual developments, a figure arises whose work marks a giant stride toward a master synthesis whereby a new era of thought is commenced. In the area of social stratification, Karl Marx (1818–1883) reached deeply into the legacies of the past and cast a bright light forward which—though dimmed by a multitude of now instructive, now garrulous controversies—still today informs the principal stream of knowledge and research.

Among the virtues of Marx's work, three are outstanding and remain unmatched today. In the first place, despite the fact that their substance must be gleaned in patches and shreds from his numerous writings and those of his lifetime collaborator Friedrich Engels,[1] Marx produced theories that explain institutionalized social inequality and related phenomena.

In the second place, his thought does not obscure, as countless others have done, the plain facts of human *conflict* and social *change* that surround systems of inequalities. Indeed, Marx's theories will not make sense unless they are viewed primarily as explanations of human conflict and of the

---

[1] No distinction is made in this volume between Marx and Engels, and we often have both scholars in mind, although reference may conveniently be made to Marx alone. However, it should be noted that Engels, especially in his later works (such as *Dialectics of Nature*) engaged occasionally in certain reinterpretations of Marx, particularly in regard to the relationship of consciousness to material conditions. (See Hodges, 1965.)

social change that both produces and follows that conflict.

Finally, Marx had no sympathy for the too-often-revered value of keeping scientific work untouched by human passion. A scientist, philosopher, moralist, and humanist all at once, Marx could never operate fully on one phase of his skill in absolute isolation from the others. In this blending he elevated to a new zenith the civic *engagement* of the social philosophers of eighteenth- and nineteenth-century Europe in general and of revolutionary France in particular. Marx stressed the incontrovertible fact that systems of social inequalities both express and determine human injustices. In keeping with the philosophy of the social contract, he viewed man's participation in social institutions as acts of exchange intended to favor the fulfillment of human needs. Hence, for Marx, the truly relevant questions about social arrangements were: How well do they fulfill human needs? Do some individuals and classes pay a higher cost than others in their social participation and exchange?

ALIENATION IN CAPITALIST SOCIETY

Marx was keen to the most fundamental question: What is the human state of well-being? On the basis of the answer he produced, he was able to argue that "capitalist" society is a society of dehumanized, "alienated" men. Marx conceived of man as a spiritual entity characterized by the "principle of movement." The essential human property was a powerful dynamic impelling man to ever greater stages of creativity, self-awareness, and self-fulfillment.

The arena for this spiritual unfolding of the individual was his work situation. As Fromm (1961:16) has noted in interpreting Marx, "Labor is the expression of human life and through labor man's relationship to nature is changed, hence through labor man changes himself." It was in the act of transforming nature, through his work, that man developed his spiritual and social being to the limits of his capacities. Labor was the self-expression of man, the conveying expression of his physical and mental powers; the product of labor represented reflections of man's abiding efforts toward self-realization. Work—free and genuine activity—was not therefore merely a means to an end; it was the end itself: the most basic process of the evolving self. (See Schaff, 1965: Chapter 1.)

It follows that when man[2] is forced to engage in highly segmented activities that have no meaning to him, and whose direction, quality, and quantity are thoroughly predetermined for him, he is mutilated in the most vital part of the self. He is a maimed stranger to himself—he is *alienated*. His alienation is all the more crippling when the products of his work—the reflections of his

---

[2]Strictly speaking, Marx's concern in his discussion of alienation was with the worker, not with man in general. Nevertheless, it could be proven that his argument was broad enough to apply to all men at work. Accordingly, in this volume we make no assumptions about the relative applicability of the alienation concept in a population.

activities toward self-fulfillment—become the property of another and are then used as an instrument of power against the creator himself. Let Marx be heard in some detail in his own words:

> We shall begin from a *contemporary* economic fact. . . . The *devaluation* of the human world increases in direct relation with the *increase in value* of the world of things. Labor does not only create goods; it also produces itself and the worker as a *commodity,* and indeed in the same proportion as it produces goods.
>
> This fact simply implies that . . . the worker is related to the *product of his labor* as to an *alien* object. For it is clear on this presupposition that the more the worker expends himself in work the more powerful becomes the world of objects which he creates in face of himself, the poorer he becomes in his inner life, and the less he belongs to himself. It is just the same as in religion. The more of himself man attributes to God the less he has left in himself. The worker puts his life into the object, and his life then belongs no longer to himself but to the object (Marx, 1844:95–96).

> What [specifically] constitutes the alienation of labor? First, that the work is *external* to the worker, that it is not part of his nature; and that, consequently, he does not fulfill himself in his work but denies himself, has a feeling of misery rather than well being, does not develop freely his mental and physical energies but is physically exhausted and mentally debased. . . . His work is not voluntary but imposed, *forced labor.* It is not the satisfaction of a need, but only a *means* for satisfying other needs. Its alien character is clearly shown by the fact that as soon as there is no physical or other compulsion it is avoided like the plague. External labor, labor in which man alienates himself, is a labor of self-sacrifice, of mortification. Finally, the external character of work for the worker is shown by the fact that it is not his own work but work for someone else, that in work he does not belong to himself but to another person (Marx, 1844:98–99).

A careful examination of Marx's manuscript on "Alienated Labor" (1844:-93–109) reveals that, although *self-alienation* is the crux of the affliction in question, there are several different expressions of the phenomenon. These include the alienation of man from (1) his productive activity, (2) the products of that activity, (3) other men, and (4) his species-being. All are expressions of man's alienness to his natural self, and therefore of man's alienation from nature, since man is a creature of nature. And all are expressions of a social *and* a psychological alienation, since man is naturally both social and psychological.

The first three expressions hold particular importance for our research in later chapters. The fourth—*alienation of man from his species-being*—perhaps can be understood best as the culmination of all other expressions of self-alienation, raised to a higher level of abstraction, such that man in all his activities is thoroughly separated from his natural being, the nature of the species, and set against it. In those odd moments when the glimpse of a human consciousness briefly reappears, he feels totally *strange* in the world.

Alienation of man from his creative labors and from the resulting products can be treated in conjunction with each other, inasmuch as the latter follows from the former, as an *alienation of production.* Given forced, highly frag-mented, and hence meaningless labor, Marx argued, man experiences a pro-found sense of impotence and lack of worth. He is forced to sell his potentially creative labor—the only social power he has—to another in order to acquire the conditions of sustenance, and in doing so he relinquishes the products of his labor, which incorporate part of his own being, to the control of others. Labor thus externalized is dissatisfying, boring, and tiresome. The process of work, which if true to man's nature would express and indeed enhance his creative powers, instead stagnates into a tragic *tedium vitae.* Such expression of alienation today informs many studies of job dissatisfaction.

Alienation of man from man may be properly viewed as an injurious social consequence of the alienation of production. In Marx's brand of anthropology the creative, whole, and nonalienated man is one who is free from all taint of domination; his sense of freedom is inextricably tied to his sense of being morally and functionally on a par with his fellowmen. But in the alienation of production, one man also becomes another man's master. As Petrović (1967:83) has so aptly put it, "as the worker alienates the products of his labor, his own activity and his generic essence from himself, so he alienates another man as his master from himself."

The language of Marx's argument appears too recondite in our era of technologically impregnated ideas. Nevertheless it is possible to extract from it certain empirically relevant propositions, some of which will be useful as broad guides to our research in subsequent chapters. On the basis of the argument regarding alienation of production, for instance, we should expect that *job dissatisfaction increases* (1) *as the monotony of work increases,* (2) *as the exercise of control over one's work and its products decreases,* and (3) *as the exploitation of one's work and its products by others increases.* In these proposi-tions, job dissatisfaction as one operational definition of alienation is properly conceptualized as the dependent variable.

Conversely, from Marx's discussion of man's alienation from man, proposi-tions in which job dissatisfaction is the independent variable follow. For exam-ple, *as job dissatisfaction increases,* (1) *resentment against those in power increases,* (2) *generalized perceptions of distributive injustice increase,* (3) *a tendency to view interclass relations as dominated by conflict increases,* and (more generally) (4) *class consciousness increases.*

The Thesis of "Two Marxes"

Marx's early, emphatic work on alienation did not come to the attention of scholars until recent years. At the same time, the enduring focus on aliena-tion in his later works (for example, *Capital*) can rather easily go unnoticed within a complex economic discussion, wherein the term "alienation" gives way to less philosophical terminology. As a result, after having grown accustomed to judging Marx's thought in terms of a raw economic determinism, many have endeavored to show that there were *two* Marxes, so to speak—a "young" Marx and an "old" Marx (see Bell, 1962).[3] It was only while Marx was still a young man, according to the argument, that he was interested in such a humanistic topic as alienation. Feuer (1966:37, 39), otherwise a keen student of Marx, has argued, for example, that Marx "rejected in his maturity the concept of alienation" and that "the alienationist trend" is an effort to "restore the ethical consciousness to Marxism" after the Stalinist era of utter contempt for all ethical considerations. Feuer's second point is reasonable. But even if perfectly accurate, it fails to prove the thesis of "two Marxes." As for his first point, there is much to show that the "mature Marx" did not reject the concept of alienation.

We would maintain that scholars of Marx the moral philosopher have welcomed the opportunity to discard those crude and thoughtless interpretations of Marx's "materialism" that are so well represented by the following note:

The economic theories of *Das Kapital* are no longer an active challenge to us. But its philosophy, which elevates the triumph of matter over spirit to the category of a historical necessity, continues to haunt the world like a spectre, just as in 1848 Marx said it would (Levitsky, 1965:xxi-xxii).

Without entering the controversy in detail (see Schaff, 1965), it is worth noting the work of several scholars who have sought to show that "far from abandoning the concept in his later years, Marx refined it and treated it as an objective process" (Irving Zeitlin, 1967:45). Zeitlin has cogently demonstrated that Marx's chief and undying concern was to define the price that the machine-dominated worker must pay in freedom, creativity, skill, and reflective powers.

Another scholar (Petrović, 1967), arguing that the importance of the alienation concept in Marx's later works has often been overlooked by scholars because it is used "implicitly rather than explicitly," has described the entirety of Marx's thought as "revolutionary humanism." After comparatively examining three of Marx's major works written over the course of forty years *(Economic and Philosophical Manuscripts, Sketches for the Critique of Political Economy,* and *Capital),* Petrović concludes that the three works "possess a basic unity, even an essential identity." The fundamental idea in the "young" *Economic and Philosophical Manuscripts* is that man is maimed in his essentially free, creative being by capitalist society and that the real conditions will necessarily develop in that society for a struggle in favor of a de-alienated "free community of free men. And this is also the guiding idea of the *Sketches for the Critique of Political Economy* and of ["old"] *Capital"* (Petrović, 1967:

---

[3]A similar effort was made by the Stalinists, who undoubtedly found Marx's pronounced humanism most embarrassing in their zealous destruction of individual freedom (see Schaff, 1965).

42–43). Whether these latter works include the term "alienation" is irrelevant; the basic content of their arguments is the same, despite the different terminology.

Marx's aim was not to "elevate the triumph of matter over spirit," but, on the contrary, to show the way to a state of social affairs in which the material interest would cease to be the dominant one. His unfailing focus on phenomena of alienation was unavoidably tied to his emphasis on the individual as the basic unit of social analysis. All too often today, social science obliterates the true social being with supernormative arguments. We read everywhere that "in order for a society to survive," it must fulfill X conditions; that attacks against "core values" are "dysfunctional for the social structure"; that Y arises because "society" has certain needs; that men engage in X behavior because it is "expected" of them. Over 125 years ago, Marx fully understood the danger of reifying "society" and "culture," and of losing sight of the real acting human being. Consider the following passage:

> It is above all necessary to avoid postulating "society" once again as an abstraction confronting the individual. The individual *is* the *social being*. The manifestation of his life—even when it does not appear directly in the form of a communal manifestation, accomplished in association with other men—is therefore a manifestation and affirmation of *social life*. Individual human life and species-life are not *different things,* even though the mode of existence of individual life is necessarily either a more *specific* or a more *general* mode of species-life, or that of species-life a more *specific* or more *general* mode of individual life (Marx, 1844:130).

Marx's focus on alienation was a natural result of his sensitivity to the fact that social structures do not always respond to human needs, and of his belief that man is infinitely perfectible, and social structures are capable of profound alteration. Marx's theory of classes is above all a theory of the changes that will—and, as he saw it, must—happen before society can create the conditions for the free and unalienated man.

THE SOCIAL CLASSES

More specifically, Marx's theory of classes represents an analysis of the industrial society of his time in terms of the interaction of its economic and social organizations, their particular form, and the forces driving the society as a changing entity. What he saw in "capitalist society," however, bore the clear markings of past conditions and demanded accordingly a historical perspective. The major process underlying the unfolding of human history was what he termed a continuous "class struggle" accompanying the very struggle for existence.

> The history of all hitherto existing society is the history of class struggles.
> Free man and slave, patrician and plebeian, lord and serf, guild master and journeyman, in a word, oppressor and oppressed, stood in constant opposition to one another,

carried on an uninterrupted, now hidden, now open fight, a fight that each time ended either in a revolutionary reconstitution of society at large or in the common ruin of the contending classes (Marx and Engels, 1848:7).

According to Marx, history may be conveniently divided into several major periods, each of which is characterized by a predominant economic organization and mode of production. Based on each mode of production, in turn, is a particular class structure. He distinguished four major modes of production: the Asiatic, the ancient, the feudal, and the bourgeois. Each featured a particular type of class relations and exploitation. The Asiatic mode, for instance, produced the subordination of all workers to the state, while the ancient, the feudal, and the bourgeois were characterized, respectively, by slavery, serfdom, and wage earning.

The basic attribute of each mode of production was the appropriation of the wealth of society by a few individuals as private property. This alleged fact kept the classes constantly in a state of covert, and often overt, conflict with each other.

Such antagonism, according to Marx, was becoming increasingly evident in modern industrial society, which was "more and more splitting up into two great hostile camps, into two great classes directly facing each other: bourgeoisie and proletariat"—namely, the "modern capitalists, owners of the means of social production and employers of wage labor," and "wage laborers who, having no means of production of their own, are reduced to selling their labor power in order to live." The major factors underlying this polarization of the classes included the competitive nature of the bourgeoisie and the continuous transformation of the "instruments of production." Unlike all earlier industrial classes, which were characterized by the conservation of traditional techniques of production, the bourgeois class was distinguished by "constant revolutionizing of production, uninterrupted disturbance of all social conditions, everlasting uncertainty and agitation" (Marx and Engels, 1848:7–10).

The Forces and Relations of Production

However, the bourgeoisie, which in the heart of feudal society had "played a most revolutionary part," subsequently resisted all attempts to change existing economic and social relations. In consequence, "The weapons with which the bourgeoisie felled feudalism to the ground are now turned against the bourgeoisie itself" (Marx and Engels, 1848:13). This statement presents the inherent "contradiction" of capitalist society.

Specifically, the contradiction refers to the dialectical tension between what Marx termed the "forces of production," which may be conveniently thought of as all the forces representative of a society's wealth potential, and the "relations of production," which consist of "property relations" or, roughly, the distribution of control over that wealth and the people who produce it.

Because the success of capitalist enterprise necessarily depends on competition for profit through technological innovation, investment, and the minimization of production costs, as capitalism produces more and more wealth it inevitably generates an increasing polarization between those who control the wealth and those who produce it. In one process, extreme competition within the bourgeoisie leads to proletarianization—that is, the progressive decline of weaker and poorer capitalists—and thus to the concentration of capital "in a few hands." In another, the cost of production is minimized both by depressing the level of wages directly and by charging to the helpless workers the cost of innovation and investment. These twin processes of *proletarianization* and *pauperization* generate conflicts which eventually lead to the downfall of the bourgeois class structure. In this sense, then, the conditions for the destruction of capitalist society are to be found in the womb of that very society. The "oppressed" workers, according to Marx, will inevitably organize themselves to bring into harmony the productive forces and the relations of production.

Etiologically, this argument clearly states that changes in the economic structure of society are followed by changes in the social structure of the society, with or without the resistance of the ruling interests. Marx argued:

Modern bourgeois society with its relations of production, of exchange, and of property, a society that has conjured up such gigantic means of production and of exchange, is like the sorcerer who is no longer able to control the powers of the nether world whom he has called up by his spells. For many a decade past, the history of industry and commerce is but the history of the revolt of modern productive forces against modern conditions of production, against the property relations that are the conditions for the existence of the bourgeoisie and of its rule . . . (Marx and Engels, 1848:12–13).

Moreover, "a change in men's productive forces necessarily brings about a change in their relations of production" (Marx 1847:122). And again:

Social relations are closely bound up with productive forces. In acquiring new productive forces men change their mode of production; and in changing their mode of production, in changing the way of earning their living, they change all their social relations. The handmill gives you society with the feudal lord; the steam-mill, society with the industrial capitalist (Marx, 1847:109).

What Are the Social Classes?

What constitutes a class for Marx? On this question, he was more than usually complex, and as a result has left puzzled even the keenest interpreters of his ideas. Marx postponed the systematic presentation of his theory of classes until death was ready to put an end to his career.[4] But even if he had completed his work, it is unlikely that he would have left us a legacy without confusion. The problem is that Marx, the social historian and economist, was

---

[4]The last chapter of Marx's *Capital* bears the title "The Classes." It breaks off, however, after only several paragraphs.

keenly aware of the great heterogeneity of social and economic structures and the diversity of interests represented in them. But Marx the model builder, profoundly keen in perceiving phenomena of social conflict and change—and yet driven by a political utopia which he held dear above all else—was inevitably led to a simplified, analytical conception of the class structure. As a result for Marx, a simple definition of class is not possible, nor quite desirable, because his conception of class logically varies with his changing conception of the complex social structure as a whole.[5] To ask Marx for a simple definition of class amounts to asking for his analysis of the changing capitalist socio-economic system in general (Ollman, 1968:580). If, however, a rough definition must be essayed for convenience, the following may be taken as an approximation to original intent: *A class is a group of people holding a common relationship to the means of production, to the political-power structure, and to the ideas of the time, a relationship which necessarily brings it into conflict with* some *other group having divergent ideas and different interests with respect to the economic and political structures.* This statement presents the basic notion of class that runs as a unifying thread through all of Marx's criteria of class division. As Ollman (1968:578) notes, " 'Who is the enemy?' is a question that can be asked whenever Marx uses 'class.' "

Tied to the difficulty of defining class is the question of the number of classes identifiable in Marx's sociology. Bukharin (1925:282–284) was able to distinguish between such different class types as basic classes, intermediate classes, transition classes, and mixed-type classes. Again, as skilled a student of Marx as Ossowski (1963:83) could argue that the works of Marx and Engels contain at least six distinctive conceptions of the structures of contemporary capitalist societies.

According to Marx, in "the earlier epochs of history" one could find almost everywhere "a manifold gradation of social rank" and "a complicated arrangement of society into various orders." In the Middle Ages, for instance, he distinguished the "feudal lords, vassals, guild masters, journeymen, apprentices, serfs; in almost all of these classes, again, subordinate gradations" (Marx and Engels, 1848:7). Even for his time, on those occasions when Marx succeeded in restraining his dynamic approach in favor of a descriptive one, he rarely failed to take into account at least "the three big classes" of his time.

The owners merely of labour-power, owners of capital, and land-owners, whose respective sources of income are wages, profit and ground-rent, in other words, wage-labourers, capitalists and land-owners, constitute the three big classes of modern society based upon the capitalist mode of production (Marx, 1867, III:885).

---

[5]Bendix and Lipset (1966:7) are probably a bit hasty in stating that "A social class in Marx's terms is any aggregate of persons who perform the same function in the organization or production." This "functional" conception of the classes is indeed present in Marx, but it is only one of several conceptions.

In this scheme, it may be noted, the classes appear to be determined by the relation to different kinds of property, namely, industrial capital and landed property. Accordingly, we have a class comprising the propertyless and two classes of owners. Although, vis-à-vis the poor man, both owning classes could be considered as one, Marx chose here to consider landowners and capitalists as two separate classes because, just as bourgeoisie and proletariat were in contention about the society-to-be, so the bourgeoisie and the landed aristocracy were mutually antagonistic with respect to the society-that-was. Thus, in his analysis of the antagonism between the Legitimists (faithful to the pre-industrial Bourbon House) and the Orleanists (oriented toward large-scale industry) in mid-nineteenth-century France, Marx argued that what kept "the two factions apart" was "their material conditions of existence, two different kinds of property, it was the old contrast between town and country, the rivalry between capital and landed property." Although it was not advisable always to treat landowners and capitalists as two separate classes, it was often fruitful, for "Upon the different forms of property, upon the social conditions of existence, rises an entire superstructure of distinct and peculiarly formed sentiments, illusions, modes of thought and views of life" (Marx, 1852b:47).

The "owners merely of labour-power," consisting of industrial workers and agricultural workers, in a sense also represent different classes, or at least two factions of one class; in so far as they have relations to two different forms of property, they are bound to have divergent economic interests. Marx, however, usually chose to disregard this fact in favor of two others. In the first place, both categories of workers were poor, powerless, and exploited—and hence were held together, theoretically at least, by the "interest" of remedying a common disadvantageous situation. In the second place, under the pull of advancing industrialization, the peasants were more and more moving to the cities, and thus becoming entirely one with the industrial workers.

A second and more frequent trichotomous scheme in Marx's work concerns the recognition of a major class, the petty bourgeoisie, as intermediate between the bourgeoisie and the proletariat. In this scheme, the focus is on varying relations to only one type of property, namely, that type characteristic of industrial society, which is for all practical purposes the true object of Marx's analysis.

Marx (1850:63) defines the petty bourgeoisie, sometimes referred to plurally as the "middle strata," as consisting of "keepers of cafés and restaurants, *marchands de vins,* small traders, shopkeepers, handicraftsmen, etc." Functionally speaking, they represent various types. Bober (1927:105–106), who has done an exhaustive inquiry into this issue, divides Marx's middle strata into the *small producers* who themselves work while also employing some labor; those employed in the *circulation of commodities,* like wholesalers, shopkeepers, real-estate dealers, and other such middlemen; *salaried persons working in factory and office,* that is, those who "command in the name of capital," such as supervisors, foremen, bookkeepers, and clerks; and the *ideological* branch, consisting of such professionals as physicians, lawyers, newspapermen, clergy, and such state servants as civil workers, military personnel, and the police.

In so far as sociological *description* of actual society was concerned, Marx deemed even the trichotomous scheme quite insufficient to do justice to the reality of the case. Thus looking at the society of his time, he considered it necessary at times to single out such other classes as the *peasantry* and the *Lumpenproletariat,* which latter he defined as mischievous people "without home or tie" and "without a definite trade, vagabonds" (Marx, 1850:50). Indeed, Marx's writings are replete with references to the detailed and hetero-geneous nature of the stratification system of an actual historical society. In his articles on *The Class Struggles in France (1848 to 1850),* for instance, he (1850) pointed to the "mass . . . of the nation . . . standing between the proletariat and the bourgeoisie" and singled out several scores of different classes, or strata, and interests.

These, however, were for Marx mere "subdivisions of classes" or "transi-tion classes," and further social development would determine their disappear-ance. Hence, the fact that remaining "middle and intermediate strata" obliterated the lines of his theoretical demarcation "is immaterial for our analysis" (Marx, 1867, III:885). The society of his time appeared to be simpli-fying class divisions, in the sense that it was "more and more splitting up into two great hostile camps, into two great classes directly facing each other: bourgeoisie and proletariat" (Marx and Engels, 1848:8). Marx's class di-chotomy, therefore, pointed to the direction in which capitalist society was seen developing.[6] Far from wishing to describe in detail an existing state of society and all factors that accounted for that state, his chief concern was with isolating "certain laws" of social development and the forces inherent in that development[7]—which is to say that Marx's theory was *dynamic* and *analytical* rather than *static* and *descriptive* (Dahrendorf, 1959:19).

What we have said about the social classes implies that, when applied to the conditions of his time, the class dichotomy can properly be viewed as a

[6]This interpretation does not preclude another offered by Ossowski (1963:83), according to whom the class dichotomy referred to the major classes participating in the dominant (capitalist) form of production. Accordingly, the dichotomy was intended to characterize society with regard to its dominant form of relations of production, while more detailed schemes reflected the actual social structure.

[7]Geiger (1969:92) notes in this connection that Marx did not, strictly speaking, view the society of his time as being dominated by "the class principle." Marx merely saw and described the "tendency toward the abolition of the then structural lines" and erroneously predicted a develop-ment toward the pure (dichotomous) class structure. This point is interesting, but it obviously overstates the case. While it is best to avoid playing games with words, it is nonetheless more exact to state that Marx saw the society of his time as in fact being dominated by the class principle *in the making.*

methodological idealization—the sort of heuristic device which in the discipline is sometimes thought to have been unique to Max Weber but which is in fact a venerable tool of all science (Lopreato and Alston, 1970). Marx was intimately familiar with the idealization strategy in theory construction; the fact that Galileo's law of falling bodies, for instance, applied to the hypothetical situation of a complete vacuum was methodologically very significant for him. Thus, in the preface to the first German edition of *Capital* (1867, I:8) he mused most learnedly:

> The physicist either observes physical phenomena where they occur in their most typical form and most free from disturbing influence, or, wherever possible, he makes experiments under conditions that assure the occurrence of the phenomenon in its normality.

For Marx's purposes of examining the capitalist mode of production and related phenomena, England represented the "classic ground"—the "ideal type," other people would say. But even here, where "modern society is indisputably most highly and classically developed in economic structure," "the stratification of classes does not appear in its pure form. Middle and intermediate strata even here obliterate lines of demarcation everywhere (although incomparably less in rural districts than in the cities)" (Marx, 1867, III:885). In sum, then, when we observe Marx operating with the dichotomous class model, it should be understood that, in keeping with his reliance on the logic of the methodological idealization, he is deliberately at work in a sort of "experimental" situation. Practically speaking, this work method means that in his theory of classes he first focuses on the dominant (industrial) mode of production. And, second, he temporarily thinks away all relations of production other than those between the "owners of capital" (the bourgeoisie) and the "owners merely of labour-power" (the proletariat). The model, he felt, was all the more justifiable and fruitful because capitalist society appeared to move in the direction of a situation isomorphic with the model. By the same token, the frequent employment of more detailed schemes of analysis indicates Marx's awareness of the necessity to take into account "real conditions" whenever an actual historical situation (such as the class struggles in France) had to be examined.

Property, Power, and Influence

The basic condition underlying a given mode of production, and hence the constituent element of classes, is *property*. Property, however, must be understood in a special sense. Specifically, it must be viewed as "private property," as the control by a minority, the capitalists, of the wealth of an entire nation. In this sense, "social power becomes the private power of private persons" (Marx, 1867, I:132), and the institution of private property results in subjection of the masses to a small minority for their very existence.

But matters do not end here, for economic power also determines political power.[8] Writing at a time when property in fact determined to a large extent the legal inclusion or exclusion of the individual in the political affairs of his community, Marx could with little exaggeration argue that "The executive of the modern state is but a committee for managing the common affairs of the whole bourgeoisie" (Marx and Engels, 1848:9).

Moreover, according to Marx, control of the means of production produces control also over the ideas that mold the character of a period. On the capitalist form of organization is built a whole *superstructure* of sentiments, modes of thought, and conceptions of life that would further the class interests of the bourgeoisie. Thus:

> The ideas of the ruling class are in every epoch the ruling ideas: i.e. the class, which is the ruling material force of society, is at the same time its ruling intellectual force. . . . The individuals composing the ruling class . . . among other things rule also as thinkers, as producers of ideas, and regulate the production and distribution of the ideas of their age . . . (Marx and Engels, 1845–1846:39).

This statement, which was, as Bottomore (1966:78) points out, scarcely an exaggeration at the time of Marx's writing, meant a number of things. Joseph Kahl (1953:2) has an excellent brief interpretation of it, and we shall defer to it:

/ The ruling class, through law and propaganda, would create a whole superstructure of community life that would further its class interests. Thus the rules of property, the laws of family life and inheritance, the schools, and even the churches, were shaped for the benefit of the few who had power. Naked economic interest need not always be in evidence, for the rationalizations of men are devious and wondrous. Through their power even a slave can be made to accept slavery and fight for his master.   /

CLASS CONSCIOUSNESS AND THE REVOLUTION

We have depicted the social situation which in Marx's theory the proletariat is called forth to rectify. But how? One thing is sure: before society as a whole can change, the working class itself first must change. Specifically, it must transform itself from a simple statistical category (merely a group of people with theoretically common interests) to a real class, that is, to a political community able and willing to engage in concerted action against the enemy class. This transformation of the working class Marx saw as inevitable.

Economic conditions had first transformed the mass of the people of the country into workers. The combination of capital has created for this mass a common situation,

---

[8]Sidney Hook (1955:26–27) makes the following interesting point which goes to support Marx's position here: "A dominant economic class may not at any given moment be the dominant political class, but unless it becomes such, its economic interests and the functioning of society as a whole are subject to continuous frustration." The tendency toward the type of situation described by Marx would seem to be a powerful force.

common interests. This mass is thus already a class as against capital, but not yet for itself. In the struggle . . . this mass becomes united, and constitutes itself as a class for itself. The interests it defends become class interests (Marx, 1847:173).

But how, specifically, does a "class-in-itself" *(Klasse an sich)* become a "class-for-itself" *(Klasse für sich)*? Or, rewording the same question, how does a class develop class consciousness? An answer to this question leads directly to Marx's concepts of *revolution* and *classlessness*. It also discloses Marx's theoretical reduction of a multiplicity of classes and strata into the basic dichotomy between bourgeoisie and proletariat. Among the conditions which would be necessary and, as a whole, sufficient for this phenomenon, the following are outstanding: alienation, demographic concentration and communication, equalization of skills and wages, pauperization, proletarianization, and political organization.

Alienation

First must be mentioned the set of factors which, as previously noted, Marx subsumed under the alienation concept even though, as we have argued, the term "alienation" was not always employed. We may recall the following important passages from Marx:

It is a result of the division of labour in manufactures, that the labourer is brought face to face with the intellectual potencies of the material process of production, as the property of another, and as a ruling power (Marx, 1867, I:361).

Moreover,

within the capitalist system . . . all means for the development of production transform themselves into means of domination over, and exploitation of, the producers; they mutilate the labourer into a fragment of a man, degrade him to the level of an appendage of a machine, destroy every remnant of charm in his work and turn it into a hated toil . . . they transform his life-time into working-time, and drag his wife and child beneath the wheels of the Juggernaut of capital. . . . It follows therefore that in proportion as capital accumulates, the lot of the labourer, be his payment high or low, must grow worse (Marx, 1867, I:645).

And again,

Owing to the extensive use of machinery and to division of labor . . . it is only the simplest, most monotonous, and most easily acquired knack that is required of [the workman]. . . . Masses of laborers, crowded into the factory, are organized like soldiers. As privates of the industrial army they are placed under the command of a perfect hierarchy of officers and sergeants. . . . The more openly this despotism proclaims gain to be its end and aim, the more petty, the more hateful, and the more embittering it is (Marx and Engels, 1848:14).

There are in the above passages a number of very interesting ideas, all of them concerned with losses endured by the worker of a type that bears little or no resemblance to economic loss. In the first place, a feeling of impotence and meaninglessness in the worker grows directly with "the intellectual potencies of the material process of production." The guiding intelligence of the work process is the workshop as a whole—not man the thinking and feeling animal, forever predisposed toward creative activity and self-realization. The workers, therefore, are converted into mere "parts" of the "engine" that is the workshop. In short, man can find himself, his spiritual potential, only in work; yet he is degraded to the point of performing tasks that to him have no reason, no meaning. The minuscule tasks of the assembly line have no subjective meaning in the conceptualization of the whole; the worker "can fit them into no larger scheme"; they yield "products alien to his own designs" (Becker, 1968:129–130).

It follows, in the second place, that the over-all intelligence of the work process represents "the property of another" and presents itself "as a ruling power," thus negating the very sense of freedom that is associated with man's need for self-fulfillment.

It follows, in the third place, that the laborer feels mutilated into "a fragment of man." His work loses "all charm"; it becomes "hated toil," for nothing but physical, unthinking exertion is required of the worker.

Finally, in the way of a theoretical statement, Marx is obviously arguing that the more marked "the despotism" of the machine and the greater the sense of meaninglessness and impotence in the worker, the greater his bitterness, and the higher the chance that he will learn to express his disaffection within the context of the politically organized interests of his class. In short, the tendency toward class consciousness grows with increasing alienation (or job dissatisfaction). More specifically, *the probability of class consciousness increases (1) as a feeling of powerlessness on the job increases; (2) as a sense of being exploited increases;* and (3) *as the monotony (unskilled nature) of the job increases.*

Demographic Concentration and Communication

With the continued development of industry the proletariat increases in number and at the same time "becomes concentrated in greater masses, its strength grows, and it feels that strength more" (Marx and Engels, 1848:16). The physical concentration of laborers in the factory facilitates *communication* and, therefore, the *visibility* of their common lot and interests. It also provides the workers, assembled in apparent common "misery," with a sense of courage and a collective purpose. Again, therefore, the hypothesis follows from Marx's argument that the greater the concentration of workers, the greater the chance of communicating their common dissatisfaction, the greater the visibility of their common class interests, and the greater the chance that they will pursue those interests within the context of the common class as a political group. More simply, *the probability of class consciousness grows with the rise in urbanism and industrialization of localities,* so that the workers in urban industrial centers are more likely to be class conscious than their rural counterparts.

Marx's argument makes possible other hypotheses, still more specific: that

(1) *alienation* and (2) *class consciousness are more prevalent among workers recently arrived on the industrial scene* (for example, rural migrants) *than among those reared in an industrial setting.* He almost admiringly argued that "the bourgeoisie, historically, has played a most revolutionary part." It tore asunder the feudal system and hence led society one step closer to "the good society." In the process, however, it put an end to all "patriarchal, idyllic relations," and "left remaining no other nexus between man and man than naked self-interest, than callous 'cash payment.' " It "resolved personal worth into exchange value." "In one word, for exploitation, veiled by religious and political illusions, it has substituted naked, shameless, direct, brutal exploitation" (Marx and Engels, 1848:9–10). Clearly, then, Marx recognized a certain advantage, from the individual's viewpoint, to living in the country. Hence, the shock of the industrial order was that much more unbearable at the first contact with it, when the relative loss of freedom and of at least paternalistic relations with the employer were still fresh; a particularly marked bitterness could be expected from the newly arrived in the urban setting.

This point is not always clearly understood, and students of class consciousness tend to mistakenly equate the long-range politicization of the working class as a whole with the politicization over time of the individual worker. John Leggett (1968:69), for instance, would seem to misinterpret Marx when he attributes to him the "assumption" that workers who are seasoned "throughout their work lives to the harsh realities of industrial capitalism would have a higher degree of class consciousness than those who had but recently migrated from rural areas." Quite to the contrary, Marx merely argued that the conditions of class consciousness for the working class as a whole matured with the natural development of the capitalist mode of production. He also recognized that during this process workers would succeed in wresting some important concessions from the bourgeoisie. These concessions would not, Marx erroneously felt, undermine seriously the class struggle; but we may be reasonably sure that he also felt that the ensuing economic security would somehow render less virulent the class spirit of the most secure workers. By definition, the inexperienced new arrivals would initially profit least from improved economic conditions at the same time that they would experience the loss involved in the uprooting from a customary, and less "naked, shameless . . . exploitation."

Equalization of Skills and Wages

A third set of conditions facilitating the rise of class consciousness in the working class consists of a tendency in the capitalist mode of production to eliminate distinctions in work roles and to equalize wages. Specifically,

The various interests and conditions of life within the ranks of the proletariat are more and more equalized, in proportion as machinery obliterates all distinctions of labor and nearly everywhere reduces wages to the same low level (Marx and Engels, 1848:16).

This alleged fact had the effect, according to Marx, of reducing any remaining economic and idiosyncratic differences that would otherwise tend to undermine the overriding common class interest of the workers.

Pauperization

In addition to the equalization of work tasks and wages, Marx seems at times to have postulated a tendency in capitalist society toward a decrease in real wages. "In proportion . . . as the repulsiveness of the work increases, the wage decreases" (Marx and Engels, 1848:14).

Marx was not always clear on this point, but we believe Bottomore (1966:22n) to be correct in arguing that the reduction in wages referred only to a decline relative to the rising profit of the bourgeoisie—in short, that the capitalists received progressively more from the increasing wealth of the nation. The capitalist mode of production, according to Marx, had an inherent tendency to yield to the worker only the bare means of subsistence required for himself and for the propagation of his species. (See *Wage Labour and Capital,* in Marx and Engels, 1955, I:79–105.)

The full import of Marx's argument must be appreciated against the background of his theory of surplus value and exploitation. In this connection, Marx distinguishes between two major types of economic exchange, the "direct barter" of products and a type of exchange through the "money-form." In the first instance, "each commodity is directly a means of exchange to its owner, and to all other persons an equivalent" (Marx, 1867, I:88). In the second case, the use of money (the "universal equivalent") as an instrument of exchange introduces the element of "circulation" (the middleman, who buys in order to sell dearer, thus giving rise to profit, on the one hand, and to exploitation, on the other). "M—C—M' is therefore in reality the general formula of capital as it appears prima facie within the sphere of circulation," where M = money, C = circulation, and M' = the initial amount of money plus a surplus—the profit (Marx, 1867, I:155).

But what makes profit possible? Briefly, the exploitation of the worker. Excluded as he is from control over the means of production, the only commodity the worker has for exchange on the market is his own work-energy. "The capitalist epoch is therefore characterised by this, that labour power takes in the eyes of the labourer himself the form of a commodity which is his property; his labour consequently becomes wage-labour" (Marx, 1867, I:170n). The question arises, what economic value does the worker get from his labor power? Marx argued that the value of labor-power is the value of the means of subsistence necessary to the laborer—plus something else. Marx (1867, I:172) puts it thus:

The labour-power withdrawn from the market by wear and tear and death must be continually replaced by, at the very least, an equal amount of fresh labour-power. Hence the sum of the means of subsistence necessary for the production of labour-power must include the means necessary for the labourer's substitutes, *i.e.*, his children in order that this race of peculiar commodity-owners may perpetuate its appearance in the market.

In order to modify the human organism, so that it may acquire skill and handiness in a given branch of industry, and become labour-power of a special kind, a special education or training is requisite. . . . The expenses of this education (excessively small in the case of ordinary labour-power), enter pro tanto into the total value spent in its production.

Theoretically, that is, in order to insure his survival, his eventual replacement by his offspring, and the proper training on the job, a man should work P number of hours per day. However, something intervenes that makes him work more, and this results in surplus value.

The fact that half a day's labour is necessary to keep the labourer alive during 24 hours, does not in any way prevent him from working a whole day. Therefore, the value of labour-power, and the value which that labour-power creates in the labour-process, are two entirely different magnitudes; and this difference of the two values was what the capitalist had in view, when he was purchasing the labour-power (Marx, 1867, I:193).

What Marx does is to distinguish between "necessary labour-time," which refers to that portion of the working day during which the worker produces enough to sustain himself and his family as well as to pay for the wear and tear of tools, and "surplus labour-time," which consists of the remainder of the working day. In the first case we have "necessary labour," while the latter yields "surplus labour." The "surplus" produced during the "surplus labour-time" constitutes "surplus value" and represents the capitalist's profit. "The rate of surplus-value is therefore an exact expression for the degree of exploitation of labour-power by capital, or of the labourer by the capitalist" (Marx, 1867, I:218).

Proletarianization

As we have suggested, the increasing exploitation, and thus pauperization, of the masses is due, in large part, to "the growing competition" within the bourgeoisie itself which "during its rule of scarce one hundred years, has created more massive and more colossal productive forces than have all preceding generations together" (Marx and Engels, 1848:12). This bourgeois competition would also result in the *proletarianization* of certain strata, and thus facilitate the spread and growth of a class spirit. In capitalist free competition, Marx argued, the poorer and less powerful capitalists are ruined by the richer and more powerful. The classes and strata intermediate between capitalists and proletarians are worn thin. Recognizing a principle widely developed among critics of *laissez-faire* economics (see Ward, 1897) and later embodied in antitrust laws, Marx took recourse to what he called "the immanent laws of capitalistic production," whereby "one capitalist always kills many," leading to "the centralization of capital." The result is that "Along with the constantly diminishing number of the magnates of capital . . . grows the mass of misery, oppression, slavery, degradation, exploitation; but with this too grows the revolt of the working-class, a class always increasing in numbers . . ." (Marx, 1867, I:763). In short, on the basis of Marx's argument regarding proletarianization, which in one sense pertains to the phenomenon known today as downward social mobility, it is possible to hypothesize that *the probability of class consciousness is directly associated with downward social mobility.*

Political Organization

Among the various sets of conditions that would insure the development of the working masses from a *Klasse an sich* into a *Klasse für sich,* none was more important, nor more inevitable, than the political organization of the workers. The alleged transformation of the proletariat from a mere statistical category to a political community would follow several stages.

With its birth begins its struggle with the bourgeoisie. At first the contest is carried on by individual laborers, then by the workpeople of a factory, then by the operatives of one trade, in one locality, against the individual bourgeois who directly exploits them. They direct their attacks not against the bourgeois conditions of production, but against the instruments of production themselves; they destroy imported wares that compete with their labor, they smash to pieces machinery, they set factories ablaze, they seek to restore by force the vanished status of the workman of the Middle Ages (Marx and Engels, 1848:15).

Initially, the laborers "form an incoherent mass scattered over the whole country and broken up by their mutual competition" (Marx and Engels, 1848:15). Their unity, such as it is, is not so much the result of their own active motives as it is the consequence of the motives of the bourgeoisie which, in order to attain its own ends, is "compelled to set the whole proletariat in motion" against the enemies of the bourgeoisie. Marx's idea here is that the proletariat is used by individual capitalists as a lever in their own competition against others more or less of their own kind. For a while, then, the proletarians engage in battle not their chief enemies, "but the enemies of their enemies," namely, "the remnants of absolute monarchy, the landowners, the non-industrial bourgeois, the petty bourgeoisie" (Marx and Engels, 1848:15–16). But all the while they are also gaining a political education.

Soon, the workers "begin to form combinations" (trade unions) against the industrial bourgeoisie, initially for the immediate purpose of keeping up the rate of their wages. Gradually, however, the immediate economic purpose becomes a class purpose, and in this the organization of the bourgeoisie itself is a powerful cause.

Large-scale industry concentrates in one place a crowd of people unkown to one another. Competition divides their interests. But the maintenance of wages, this common interest which they have against their boss, unites them in a common thought of resistance—*combination*. . . . If the first aim of resistance was merely the maintenance of wages, combinations, at first isolated, constitute themselves into groups as the capitalists in their turn unite for the purpose of repression, *and in face of always united capital,* the maintenance of the association becomes more necessary to them than that of wages. . . . In this struggle—a veritable civil war—elements necessary for a coming battle unite and develop. Once it has reached this point, association takes on a political character (Marx, 1847:172–173—second emphasis added).

The positive effect of bourgeois organization on proletarian unity is described even more explicitly by Marx (1850:33) in his articles *The Class Struggles in France (1848–1850),* wherein he argues that revolutionary advance made headway by the creation of a united counterrevolution. In fighting against this greater threat "the party of revolt first ripened into a real revolutionary party."

The political organization of the proletariat is further enhanced by the concrete aid of certain bourgeois elements who desert their class interests. Specifically,

in times when the class struggle nears the decisive hour, the process of dissolution going on within the ruling class, in fact within the whole range of old society, assumes such a violent, glaring character that a small section of the ruling class cuts itself adrift and joins the revolutionary class, the class that holds the future in its hands. Just as, therefore, at an earlier period, a section of the nobility went over to the bourgeoisie, so now a portion of the bourgeoisie goes over to the proletariat, and in particular a portion of the bourgeois ideologists, who have raised themselves to the level of comprehending theoretically the historical movement as a whole (Marx and Engels, 1848:17).

Such enlightened "bourgeois ideologists," Marx himself included, were of course the "communists." They served several major functions. In the short run, they clarified for the various sections of the working class their common interests, and they presided over the "formation of the proletariat into a class," the "overthrow of the bourgeois supremacy," and the "conquest of political power by the proletariat" (Marx and Engels, 1848:20). In the long run, they prepared the political and economic grounds for the advent of the classless society.

Implicit here is Marx's concept of revolution. At times he described the overthrow of bourgeois rule as a sudden and violent overthrow. But revolution as the "brutal *contradiction,* the shock of body against body" was considered only the "highest expression" of the revolutionary movement and not, it would seem, altogether inevitable (Marx, 1847:174–175). Contrary to common belief (see Dahrendorf, 1959:130), revolution for Marx did not have to be "the sudden and rapid upheaval of a social structure," but might be merely a series of proletarian assertions and capitalist concessions. It was entirely conceivable for Marx that a series of strikes, riots, tensions, and disorders of all sorts would result in concessions to the workers which would increase their political power so much that the fatal blow to bourgeois society would be as simple and painless as plucking a ripe pear.

That Marx's concept of revolution does not necessarily postulate violent insurrection and sudden change is best attested by his willingness to consider the attainment of universal suffrage an important revolutionary step. Marx's concept of revolution is, therefore, linked with his concept of man as an individual capable of gaining political power and using it rationally according to the interests theoretically attributable to his class as a whole. Remarkable testimony of this point may be found in the following statement from a discussion of working-class activity in Britain (Marx, 1852a).

We now come to the *Chartists,* the politically active portion of the British *working class.* The six points of the Charter which they contend for contain nothing but the demand of *Universal Suffrage,* and of the conditions without which Universal Suffrage would be illusory for the working class; such as the ballot, payment of members, annual general elections. But Universal Suffrage is the equivalent of political power for the working class of England, where the proletariat forms the large majority of the population. . . . The carrying of Universal Suffrage in England would, therefore, be a far more socialistic measure than anything which has been honoured with that name on the Continent. Its inevitable result, here, is *the political supremacy of the working class.*

Twenty-three years later, however, in 1875, Marx showed considerable impatience with the people who drafted the Gotha program (on which the two German socialist parties had been united), because they were willing to pursue their revolution within the context of existing institutions. According to Marx (1875:128), the political demands of the program contained

nothing beyond the old democratic litany familiar to all: universal suffrage, direct legislation, popular rights, a people's militia, etc. They are a mere echo of the bourgeois People's party, of the League of Peace and Freedom. They are all demands which, in so far as they are not exaggerated in fantastic presentation, have already been *realized.* Only the state to which they belong does not lie within the borders of the German Empire, but in Switzerland, the United States, etc.

In general, this much can be said of Marx's concept of revolution: it was meant to refer to a radical alteration of existing bourgeois society but *not* necessarily to a sudden, violent, and rapid upheaval. However, as Marx grew older, he also became increasingly impatient with the pace at which desired changes were effected, and his revolutionism often reflected his contempt for what as early as 1852 he had termed "parliamentary cretinism" (Marx, 1852b:114).

THE CLASSLESS SOCIETY

The victory of the proletariat in its epochal struggle against the bourgeoisie was to result in the classless society—the free community of free and unalienated individuals. Much has been made in the literature of the fact that Marx never took the time to spell out the classless society, and indeed the concept is necessarily vexing to anyone who demands to be given a clear view of the communist millenium ahead. The problem is that Marx, consummate artist of the dialectical method, deliberately refused to lay down an exhaustive set of specific objectives. He had no "ideal type" of future society, and none was desirable. For, although one could point in general terms to what was welcome in human development, none could even guess the range of possibilities of human amelioration. Hence, Marx could argue:

Communism for us is not a condition that is to be established nor an ideal to which reality must adjust itself. We call communism the actual movement which abolishes present conditions. The conditions under which this movement proceeds result from those now existing (cited in Mannheim, 1936:126).

The classless society, therefore, was to be the good society in the making. As Mannheim (1936:126) notes in his penetrating discussion of this question, "It is not the task of political thought to set up an absolute scheme of what should be. Theory, even including communist theory, is a function of the process of becoming."

The Abolition of Private Property

Marx's unwillingness to describe the *minutiae* of the classless society does not mean, however, that it is not possible to outline in broad terms the basic principles of that society. The first, quite clearly, is the abolition of private property. Marx held that class antagonisms arose with the rise of private property—specifically not such property as personal effects, a domicile, or a garden plot, but wealth capable of being used as an instrument of power over others, as "a social power capable of being monopolized." This type of property, in turn, seemed to Marx to have arisen from conditions of economic scarcity, as a result of economic insecurity and the attendant struggle for existence. The technological creativity of modern society, however, had now developed productive forces to such an extent that a more rational production would make possible an economy of abundance, thereby removing the cutting edge from the struggle for existence.

In this economy, the control over the means of production and the distribution of wealth would be in the hands of a collective agency. But how would such mechanism effect what the German socialist Ferdinand Lassalle had termed "fair distribution"? On the assumption of a forthcoming economy of abundance, Marx's answer (1875, especially 117–119) makes some sense. The individual worker "receives a certificate from society that he has furnished such and such an amount of labor" after deductions for "the common funds," and with this certificate he draws from the public store items of consumption equal in value to the value created in his own labor time.

Marx recognized the difficulty inherent in the fact that there are individual differences in needs and in contributions to the collective enterprise. For instance, "one man is superior to another physically or mentally, and so supplies more labor in the same time, or can labor for a longer time" (Marx, 1875:118).

Further, one worker is married, another not; one has more children than another, and so on and so forth. Thus, with an equal performance of labor, and hence an equal share in the social consumption fund, one will in fact receive more than another, one will be richer than another, and so on. To avoid all these defects, right instead of being equal would have to be unequal (Marx, 1875:119).

For Marx, however, these defects constituted real problems and would produce "inevitable" difficulties only for a limited time—"in the first phase of communist society as it is when it has just emerged after prolonged birth pangs from capitalist society." "In a higher phase of communist society," when various communist virtues (like equality between "mental and physical labor") have developed and "the springs of collective wealth flow more abundantly," the society will then be able to institute and follow the principle of "From each according to his ability, to each according to his needs!" The notion of unequal distribution would then be irrelevant, for there would be enough of everything to go around to satisfy eveybody's needs.

The Abolition of the State

Another major feature of communist society is the abolition of political power in the traditional sense of the expression. The following statement is specific in this respect:

When, in the course of development, class distinctions have disappeared and all production has been concentrated in the hands of a vast association of the whole nation, the public power will lose its political character. Political power, properly so called, is merely the organized power of one class for oppressing another. If the proletariat during its contest with the bourgeoisie is compelled, by the force of circumstances, to organize itself as a class, if, by means of a revolution, it makes itself the ruling class and, as such, sweeps away by force the old conditions of production, then it will, along with these conditions, have swept away the conditions for the existence of class antagonisms and of classes generally, and will thereby have abolished its own supremacy as a class (Marx and Engels, 1848:29).

This eventuality, of course, is more easily stated than achieved, as "communist" history has shown so far. Marx held that the total abolition of classes—namely, the abolition of all institutionalized social inequalities—would be possible only after a period of revolutionary transformation of vanquished capitalist society. During this period, the proletariat would be "the ruling class," and "the state can be nothing but *the revolutionary dictatorship of the proletariat*" (Marx, 1875:127).

By this rather abstruse notion, Marx meant a period of intense transformation in which the victorious proletariat would, forcefully if necessary, see to it that the intended aims of the classless society were carried out and solidly instituted. Engels (Marx and Engels, 1955, I:485) gave the Paris Commune as an example of the dictatorship of the proletariat. That would seem to mean that the dictatorship should be interpreted as revolutionary activity producing such measures as universal suffrage; a popularly and frequently elected body subject to easy recall; suppression of the standing army and police; and elective and revocable judges (Marx and Engels, 1955, I:473–485). It would also include such measures as a heavy progressive income tax, abolition of all right of inheritance, the institution of a national bank, equal liability of all to work, free education for all children in public schools, and abolition of child labor (Marx and Engels, 1848:28–29).

It may be noted, therefore, that Marx did not envision the abolition of all public authority, but merely the abolition of "political power" viewed as the power of one class over another. In effect, he called for the rise of an administration on the part of men of knowledge and skill who truly worked for the public good and who could easily be replaced by others of equivalent or superior skill. It is at this point that Marx most clearly reveals his debt to French revolutionary doctrine, which tended to regard politics, or the state, as a phenomenon not only secondary to the economic and social institutions but also susceptible to all manner of abuse. Consequently, as Aron (1965, I:116) notes, Marx "presented political power as the expression of social conflicts. Political power is the means by which the ruling class, the exploiting class, maintains its domination and its exploitation."

The Equality of All Labor

A third major characteristic of the classless society concerns the economic value of human labor. "However . . . productive power may vary, the same labour, exercised during equal periods of time, always yields equal amounts of value" (Marx, 1867, I:46). This feature of the classless society is perhaps the most crucial. Rejecting a widespread notion of the differential functional importance of occupations (which, as we shall see in Chapter V, constitutes the cornerstone of Kingsley Davis and Wilbert E. Moore's theory of social stratification), Marx argued that X hours of work are equal in value to X hours of work, whether the work involves organizing and directing production, teaching school, or tediously operating an industrial machine. For him, all work activities were equally important to the well-being of the collectivity. In this very essential sense, all men were indeed equal, even though they might perform different functions in society.

Free Circulation of Talent and Skill

A final feature of the classless society is a good complement to the preceding one; at the same time it represents one of the most enlightened conceptions of

Western civilization. It concerns what may be termed the *free circulation of talent and skill* in society. In Marx's scheme of the "good society," there is place for a system of guaranteed minimum subsistence which would not only provide man with freedom from economic insecurity but would afford him also, and especially, a chance to escape tedium at work by developing varied skills and seeking self-fulfillment in various occupations. In short, Marx rejected the division of labor insofar as it hindered a free diversification of skills in the individual worker. In the existing division of labor, he argued,

each man has a particular, exclusive sphere of activity, which is forced upon him and from which he cannot escape. He is a hunter, a fisherman, a shepherd, or a critical critic, and must remain so if he does not want to lose his means of livelihood; while in communist society, where nobody has one exclusive sphere of activity but each can become accomplished in any branch he wishes, society regulates the general production and thus makes it possible for me to do one thing to-day and another to-morrow, to hunt in the morning, fish in the afternoon, rear cattle in the evening, criticize after dinner, just as I have a mind, without ever becoming hunter, fisherman, shepherd or critic (Marx and Engels, 1845–1846:22).

If this exuberant but engaging notion is added to the previous point concerning the equality of all human labor, we have a conception of functional differentiation *without invidious differential rewards and without permanence.* The classless society, so conceived, does not seem so mysterious after all—nor so startling. It was not long ago that the principle of unemployment compensation was still in the realm of utopias; so, too, was the eight-hour work day. Child labor was in the nature of things. And economists proved "scientifically" that it was in the best interest of all to have an army of jobless and impoverished people. Marx's position is obviously predicated on the pious assumption that in the wondrous boat that is the human condition all men are truly equally worthy. To be sure, such a conception may be adjudged by some to be sociologically unrealistic; but it has never been proven false. Nor would our "sacred" mores countenance such proof.

SELECT COMMENTS

It seems to be an established tradition that no treatment of Marx is complete without a lengthy critique of his thought. The criticisms advanced from all quarters against Marx are truly legion. Some are well taken; others are thoroughly unfounded. Some instruct the reader; others completely mislead him. And again, some are constructive and pertinent; others are totally irrelevant. We shall not follow this approach, for our purpose is primarily to carve out from Marx's work—as well as from that of others to come, who are clearly related to him—an area of sociological knowledge that casts light on a major part of the human existence and that is useful in organizing the research data to be treated in subsequent parts of this book. We would fall short of our intentions, however, if we failed to make a few critical observations regarding particularly problematic aspects of Marx's thought and the controversies that surround them. (See Birnbaum, 1968.)

The Progressive Worsening of the Workers' Conditions

One set of criticisms frequently leveled at Marx maintains that he erred in predicting certain changes in the conditions of the working men in capitalist society. He predicted, for instance, that the skills of the workmen would be gradually reduced to a common low level. The middle strata, moreover, would gradually fall to the rank of the proletariat and join it in its mean conditions. These two events, it will be recalled, were considered crucial in stimulating the full formation of the proletarian class.

Quite clearly, neither event has come to pass. Indeed, the very opposite has happened. The middle class everywhere in industrial society has actually grown greatly in size, thereby providing a sort of "demilitarized zone" standing formidably between bourgeoisie and proletariat. Again contrary to Marx's prediction, the heterogeneity of skills in blue-collar jobs has so increased that they encompass the highly skilled engineer-type workers as well as the highly unskilled. (See Dahrendorf, 1959: Chapter II; Geiger, 1969:91–104.)

The validity of a related prediction allegedly made by Marx is more problematic. All too often, Marx is reproached for having erroneously predicted the increasing pauperization of the working class. Aside from the fact, previously noted, that Marx probably saw increasing pauperization among the masses only in relation to the increasing wealth of the industrialists, another question must be taken into account that closely bears on the issue at stake. Sociologists are very familiar with an interesting phenomenon that goes under the name of the "self-fulfilling prophecy" (Merton, 1968: Chapter XIII). "If men define situations as real," stated the great American sociologist W. I. Thomas, "they are real in their consequences." Begin by assuming that women —cooks by connubial ordination—are incapable of the culinary refinements found in the best restaurants, then keep them out of the kitchens of such restaurants, and you will surely be correct in the ingenious observation that there are no great female chefs. The road to the conclusion that "they just haven't got it" is a short one. The theoretical possibility remains, however, that they "*would* have it" *if* they were not barred from the kitchens of the best restaurants.

It is truly amazing that, in assessing the historical validity of Marx's prediction, his most bitter critics and his warmest sympathizers alike invariably fail to consider the possibility of the counterpart to the self-fulfilling prophecy— the "suicidal prophecy." According to Merton (1968:477n), the suicidal prophecy "so alters human behavior from what would have been its course had the prophecy not been made, that it *fails* to be borne out. The prophecy destroys itself." Let a mechanic tell a client that he is going to kill himself because the brakes in his automobile are deficient, and the "moribund" driver is likely to have his brakes repaired—and thereby kill nothing but the validity of the mechanic's prediction.

The monumental task of documenting in detail Marx's influence on the labor and political movements of human society remains to be done. Nevertheless, it is evident that the force of his ideas has energized many popular actions designed to wrest concessions from those who live in the halls of economic and political power. Many employers, for instance, have been induced to "mend their ways," thereby invalidating the very prediction that made amelioration possible in the first place. It may well be, in short, that Marx has been to society what fever is to the human organism. Through his signal, modern man may have been enabled to prevent, or at least to rectify, some of the most mutilating illnesses of industrial society. Children of seven years no longer slave in coal mines. Governments today are more often responsive to public needs, and attentive to public opinion when they propose to enact laws and initiate actions that may have momentous consequences for future society. By how much, one may ask, do these altered circumstances result from the power of Marx's doctrine? How much of the present "affluence," leisure, and "contentment" of the working masses would not exist, were it not for the revolutionary humanism of Karl Marx? Raymond Aron (1965, I:138) is wise in his warning that "One ought not draw any premature conclusions from the fact that the death of capitalism was not theoretically demonstrated by Marx, for regimes have a way of vanishing without having been condemned to death by theorists." It is of more than passing interest to note at this point that Engels, in the Introduction to Marx's (1850:27–28) *The Class Struggles in France (1848–1850)*, recognized dramatically the practical force of revolutionary ideology. "The irony of world history," he argued, "turns everything upside down. We, the 'revolutionaries,' 'the rebels'—we are thriving far better on legal methods than on illegal methods and revolt. The parties of order, as they call themselves, are perishing under the legal conditions created by themselves."

Surely, the capitalism of today bears little if any resemblance to the capitalism of the mid nineteenth century. It behooves the critic of Marx to investigate the historical influence of Marx's thought and political prowess no less attentively than their historical validity. For more than a century, the Marxian legacy has provided the stage on which the political, legal, and intellectual drama of the modern world is enacted. Ossowski (1963:69) justly observed in such connection that "If one measures the significance of a theoretical work by the scope of its social consequences, one must regard the Marxian system as one of unusual importance." Throughout the industrial world and beyond, trade unions and political parties are organized on that system or on some interpretation of it. Thinkers and men of action in search of a new order have been reared on the ideas contained in that system. Everywhere political movements have opposed or championed the belief that economic and social justice is prevented by the inevitable laws of the capitalist society. Demands are made by parties and unions representing the working masses, and concessions made, more or less reluctantly, by those whom they oppose.

In the United States of America, the country of the most affluent working class in the world, the men who in 1882 organized the American Federation of Labor wrote in the preamble to its constitution an echo of the *Communist Manifesto:*

A struggle is going on in all the nations of the civilized world between the oppressors and the oppressed of all countries, a struggle between the capitalist and the laborer, which grows in intensity from year to year.

The present constitution of the AFL-CIO no longer speaks of struggle, capitalism, and oppression, but of "our way of life and the fundamental freedoms which are the basis of our democratic society." It is easy, of course, to pronounce this change a glaring example of the failure of Marx's predictions regarding pauperization. It would be more scholarly and more fruitful, however, to consider the influence that the political spirit of 1882 had on the labor movement in the United States and on the way of life which that movement has produced for the American worker. The history of the labor movement in the United States, as elsewhere, is not one of management-labor harmony and orderly collective bargaining, but one of tremendous clashes, strikes, and riots that only in recent decades have given way to relative harmony, order, and well-being.

One perforce wonders how much poorer, more "solidary," and more embittered the working people would be today without the struggles and collective demands of the past. Writing about Great Britain, Strachey (1956:137–138) concluded after a careful examination of the evidence that up to 1939 there had been little or no redistribution of the national wealth in favor of the working masses, either through trade-union pressure or through budgetary changes. The wage earners' standard of life had merely risen in step with the rise in the total national income, their share remaining about constant. Similarly, Meade (1964:27) has shown for the period 1911–1913 to 1960 that the distribution of wealth continues to be "extremely unequal," not only in the value of property holdings but also in the personal incomes yielded by property. For 1959–1960, "no less than 75 percent of personal property was owned by the wealthiest 5 percent of the population," in contrast to 79 percent in 1936–1938, and at least 92 percent of all property-derived personal income (before taxes) went to the wealthiest 5 percent (thus the rich enjoy a higher yield on their property). Such findings lead to arguments of the sort put forth by Strachey (1956:150–151):

All this is evidence that capitalism has in fact an innate tendency to extreme and ever-growing inequality. For how otherwise could all these cumulatively equalitarian measures which the popular forces have succeeded in enacting over the past hundred years have done little more than hold the position constant? Is it not clear that, if the workings of the system had not been continuously modified, it would have produced just that ever sharper polarisation which Marx diagnosed as its essential tendency?

Economic Determinism

A second major criticism of Marx's thought holds that for Marx the cause of all things social is to be found in the economic world. A particularly crude interpretation to this effect was made by Gaetano Mosca (1939:439), who argued:

The economic factor would . . . be the sole and exclusive cause of all the material, intellectual and moral changes that occur in human societies, and all other factors should be regarded not as factors but as mere effects and consequences of the economic factor.

Marx, of course, does state that the division of the classes, and the social processes which flow therefrom, are determined by men's relations to the means of production. Moreover:

As individuals express their life, so they are. What they are, therefore, coincides with their production, both with *what* they produce and with *how* they produce. The nature of individuals thus depends on the material conditions determining their production (Marx and Engels, 1845–1846:7).

It is entirely too hasty, however, to focus on statements of this kind and from them draw conclusions like Mosca's. For a detailed scrutiny of Marx's whole argument reveals variables that bear no relationship to economic factors, except in a very broad sense of the word. The argument is stated in terms of such factors as competition, conflict, industrialization, consciousness of kind, and work dissatisfaction, as well as the relations to the means of production. For Marx, what is grossly termed "the economic factor" represented *the major differentiating factor* in a complex set of interdependent factors—one which could be seen ultimately asserting itself over the others if one were interested in ultimate causes. The point was made clearly by Engels in a famous letter to Joseph Bloch written in London in 1890. Engels argued:

According to the materialistic conception of history, the *ultimately* determining element in history is the production and reproduction of real life. More than this neither Marx nor I has ever asserted. Hence if somebody twists this into saying that the economic element is the *only* determining one he transforms that proposition into a meaningless, abstract, senseless phrase. The economic situation is the basis, but the various elements of the superstructure—political forms of the class struggle and its results, to wit: constitutions established by the victorious class after a successful battle, etc., juridical forms, and even the reflexes of all these actual struggles in the brains of the participants, political, juristic, philosophical theories, religious views, and their further development into systems of dogmas—also exercise their influence upon the course of the historical struggles and in many cases preponderate in determining their *form*. There is an interaction of all these elements. (Cited in Feuer, 1959:397–398.)

The fact is that Marx was not interested in ultimate causes, except for polemical reasons. If he stressed the fundamental influence of the economic factor, it was because, first, this factor is manifestly crucial to an understanding of human affairs and, second, the philosophers and historians against whom he argued tended to consider it irrelevant.

The economic determinism of Karl Marx, properly understood, amounts to little beyond a biological truism to the effect that, as Marx and Engels (1845–1846:16) put it in *The German Ideology*,

the first premise of all human existence, and therefore of all history, [is] that men must be in a position to live in order to be able to "make history." But life involves before everything else eating and drinking, a habitation, clothing and many other things. The first historical act is thus the production of the means to satisfy these needs, the production of material life itself.

For Marx, this simple fact had important social consequences which scholars before him had not deigned to treat exhaustively. He therefore used his argument as a primary weapon against the philosophical abstractionism of the "German ideology" prevailing at the time. In the process, he often deliberately exaggerated. In the same letter to Bloch referred to above, Engels clarified the matter as follows:

Marx and I are ourselves partly to blame for the fact that the younger people sometimes lay more stress on the economic side than is due to it. We had to emphasize the main principle vis-à-vis our adversaries, who denied it, and we had not always the time, the place, or the opportunity to give their due to the other elements involved in the interaction. But when it came to presenting a section of history, that is, to making a practical application [such as the class struggles in France], it was a different matter and there no error was permissible. Unfortunately, however, it happens only too often that people think they have fully understood a new theory and can apply it without more ado from the moment they have assimilated its main principles, and even those not always correctly. And I cannot exempt many of the more recent "Marxists" from this reproach, for the most amazing rubbish has been produced in this quarter, too . . . (cited in Feuer, 1959:399–400).

Beyond this, there is another point that needs to be emphasized. Those who, like Mosca and countless others, have argued that in Marx's thought only economic factors may be properly treated as causes of change are unfortunately unaware of the fact that Marx had a fairly mature understanding of what today is termed "system analysis." Specifically, if it is true that the economic structure of society was seen by Marx as determining the "superstructure" (the world of ideas, values, and attitudes), it is equally true that this superstructure in turn produced changes in the economic structure. Thus, it was the capitalist mode of production and the "contradiction" therein that produced the necessary and sufficient conditions for the rise of class consciousness. But as class consciousness developed, this in turn reacted on the mode of production and the entire economic system, causing radical transformations therein. The immediate cause of the revolution, for instance, was not the mode of production but class consciousness—a set of factors patently of a social-psychological nature.

The Concept of Man and the Classless Society

The most monumental error in Marx's thought is his failure to accept the fact—so well recognized by established religion, for instance—that man is by nature a fallible and "sinful" animal. And he is likely to be that, whatever the form and content of his community. Human nature is much less easily changed than social structure.

Marx erred in his expectation that the proletariat would make revolution as the representative of the entire society and reach for the millennium in the name of all. He was abysmally wrong in failing to understand that human beings can *invent* needs to maintain a situation of scarcity—that man is a self-seeking animal. The universal and full satisfaction of basic human needs, like food and clothing, is certainly conceivable, but needs that begin in the realm of "luxuries" are forever in the making and, *by definition,* out of the reach of the masses who covet them. After all, we have "leisure classes" whose predilection is "conspicuous consumption" (Veblen, 1899). Marx was still alive when in New York City people of great wealth were giving parties at which guests smoked cigarettes wrapped in $100 bills.

Relatedly, Marx argued that the ruling ideas of an epoch are the ideas of the ruling class, but he failed to realize that the proposition would apply regardless of the form of society. For instance, what, short of continuous revolution, would prevent the ruling council of the proletariat, during the period of its dictatorship, from consolidating its rule and imposing its ideas on the governed? Yet, according to Marx in one of his worst moments, one of the first things that the victorious proletariat should do during its dictatorship was to confiscate the property "of all emigrants and *rebels*" (Marx and Engels, 1848:28—emphasis added). Marx intended this mandate to apply to the bourgeois rebels, but, as the history of revolutions amply shows, there are various kinds of "rebels," including former "companions in arms" in the revolution. One wonders whether, in this "reactionary" stance, Marx intuitively recognized that any ruling group will have to develop a doctrine of its own and *make it acceptable* to the governed, if it is to retain its power and provide the degree of political and social stability required by the very idea of "order." In the process, however, one ruling class replaces another and, as Pareto will put it later, history turns out to be "a graveyard of aristocracies." The Paretian vision is less pleasant than the Marxian but, alas, more in keeping with the known facts of world history to this point.

The most damning example to oppose Marx's thought is the "new class" which Djilas (1957) finds in present-day societies that call themselves "communist." To be sure, these societies do not flow at all from Marx's vision of the future society. Yet they are the only polities produced by the ideology that most directly dips into the holy water of Marx's thought. Djilas shows that the state did not, as expected, wither away. "The reverse happened." "This new class, the bureaucracy, or more accurately the political bureaucracy, has all the characteristics of earlier ones as well as some new characteristics of its own" (Djilas, 1957:38). At a maximum, the new class of communist bureaucrats is more brutal and all-embracing than other ruling classes. At a minimum, it is simply "a new ruling and exploiting class."

In sum, it may be said that Marx did not pay sufficient attention to the psychological dimensions of participation in what was once termed "the social contract." He did not recognize the true strength of the will to power, the striving for social recognition and superiority, *the self-seeking of status-seeking* —in short, he did not recognize the ever-present concern with matters of social honor. Weber and Pareto will later make this concern central to their thinking on systems of inequalities, and our data will uphold much of their argument.

Unfortunately, such criticisms of Marx (and many other strictures that are possible) often obscure the true value of his epoch-making thought. Leonard Reissman (1959:44) was wisely to the point when he argued that "Marx should be read today with understanding rather than with misplaced pedantic precision." Marx's contributions to social thought and the human condition are legion and enormous. Consider these: He isolated in the phenomena of alienation, inauthenticity, and boredom the malignancy that gnaws at the social fiber and at the human heart. His thought informs and inspires a large body of modern theory in the social and moral disciplines. His doctrine, however interpreted, sets the stage for the foremost political drama of our time. His figure is truly monumental for having retrieved the relevance of the majority —the masses—for the study of society. Before Marx, the study of man was replete with histories of the aristocracy, of the bourgeoisie, of battles and wars, and of the loves and hatreds of the likes of Lucrezia Borgia; Marx, the true father of sociology, gave explosive birth to the study of the common man.

The American sociologist Albion Small once suggested that Marx was to social science as Galileo was to physical science, for Marx was unique and imaginative in emphasizing the incessant influence of economic factors on human ideas and beliefs. Marx, moreover, introduced into social science a sensitivity to a phenomenon of the human world analogous to that of parasitism in biology. As Feuer (1959:xiv) notes, "Just as there are organisms which live off the bloodstream of others and contribute no labor of their own, there are likewise those who in the social world take something for nothing." Marx found social parasitism in capitalist exploitation.

Again, Marx's thought contains the most sweeping and pervasive theory of social change available to us today; his hopeful view of the world clearly helped him in this accomplishment—he made the point dramatically in the last of his *Theses on Feuerbach* as follows: "The philosophers have only *interpreted* the world, in various ways; the point, however, is to *change* it" (Marx, 1845:245).

Finally, Marx unmistakably identified class conflict as a major form of "stress" in the social system, and thus as a chief source of change in society. Better still, he identified the constructive and ameliorative role of conflict in society. This is Marx's everlasting sociological virtue: "No antagonism, no progress. That is the law that civilization has followed up to our days" (Marx, 1847:61).

II

VILFREDO PARETO: CLASSES, CONFLICT, AND ELITE CIRCULATION

One of the first great sociologists to address themselves critically but constructively to Marx's famous synthesis was Vilfredo Pareto (1848–1923), an Italian aristocrat who brought to sociology an ample reserve of knowledge in history, philosophy, the classics, and economics, in addition to formal training in mathematics and physical science.

SELECT CRITICISMS OF MARX

Pareto's work in social stratification, best described as a theory of class exchange or mobility, is predicated on the assumption, among others, of the paramountcy of the nonlogical element in human affairs. He argued that Marx, however incisive and brilliant at points, offered a theory that "beat the well-worn path that leads to logical conduct." As such, the theory took the easy road, for

If we assume that certain conduct is logical, it is much easier to formulate a theory about it than it is when we take it as non-logical . . . in order to organize a theory of non-logical conduct we have to consider hosts and hosts of facts, ever extending the scope of our researches in space and in time, and ever standing on our guard lest we be led into error by imperfect documents (Pareto, 1916:262).[1]

Like many other scholars, moreover, Marx was not satisfied with discovering what is. He was "anxious to know, and even more anxious to explain to others, what *ought* to be."

Pareto wrote approvingly of Marx's emphasis on the class struggle. "The struggle of some individuals to appropriate the wealth produced by others," he argued, "is the great factor dominating all human history" (Pareto, 1896–1897:117), and the class struggle is "a real factor," the signs of which can be found "on every page of history." He disagreed with Marx, however, in arguing that the class struggle is not confined to Marx's two classes—the proletariat and the bourgeoisie. On the contrary it occurs "between an infinity of groups with different interests, and above all *between the elites contending for power*" (Pareto, 1902–1903, I:117–118—emphasis added).[2] Thus, people in the same occupation naturally tend to group together. In many countries, the makers of sugar have acted in concert to exact tribute from their fellow citizens. Shipowners unite to get shipping bounties; the retailers combine to do in the big shops by taxes; shopkeepers with fixed premises join together to hinder street sellers; entrepreneurs in one region unite to exclude those of another region; "organized" workers agree to take jobs away from "nonorganized" workers; the workers of one country try to exclude from the "national market" the workers of another country; the workers of one town, to keep out those of another (Pareto, 1902–1903, I:118–119—our paraphrase).

Elsewhere, not content with Marx's own passing distinctions, Pareto (1916:2231) emphatically contends that the term "capitalist" has been defined too narrowly, and that

Writers have confused and persist in confusing under the term "capitalists" (1) owners of savings and persons who live on interest from property and (2) promoters of enterprise—"*entrepreneurs.*" That confusion is a great hindrance to an understanding of human society. In reality those two sorts of "capitalists" often have interests that are different. Sometimes indeed they are diametrically opposed and stand in even greater conflict than the interests of the classes known as "capitalist" and "proletarian."

These two types of "capitalists" he terms *rentiers* and *speculators* (Pareto, 1916:2233–2235, 2313). *Speculators* are individuals whose incomes are basically variable and depend upon "the person's wide-awakeness in discovering sources of gain." Among them will be found business promoters, *entrepreneurs,* stockholders in industrial and commercial corporations, owners of real estate in cities (where building speculation is rife), landowners—on a similar condition that there be speculation in the lands about them—stock-exchange

---

[1]Pareto's major writings are organized into numbered paragraphs or sections. Following convention, throughout this volume the number after the year of the present publication will refer to the section number.

[2]All translations into English from this source are ours.

speculators, and bankers who make money on governmental, industrial, and commercial loans; also, all persons depending upon such people—lawyers, engineers, politicians, working people, clerks. "In a word, we are putting together all persons who directly or indirectly speculate and in one way or another manage to increase their incomes by ingeniously taking advantage of circumstances" (Pareto, 1916:2233).

The *rentiers* comprise persons who have fixed or virtually fixed incomes. Among them are persons who have deposited their savings in banks or invested them in life annuities; people living on incomes from government bonds, corporation bonds, or other such securities; owners of real estate and lands in places where there is no speculation; small farmers; many working people; clerks, depending upon such persons and in no way depending upon speculators.

These two categories of people represent quite different interests and mentalities. Where the speculators are primarily responsible for change, for economic and social progress, the *rentiers,* on the contrary, are a powerful element in stability. In general, they are secretive, cautious, timid souls, mistrustful of all adventure—"not only of dangerous ventures but of such as have any remotest semblance of not being altogether safe" (Pareto, 1916:2313).

Conflicts of a noneconomic nature are also of great moment. Differences in such factors as nationality, religion, race, and language are often more productive of conflict than economic differences; by the same token, similarities in these respects frequently overshadow the possible effects of class divergences. Pareto (1902–1903, I:118) noted that in his own day the struggle between the Czechs and the Germans in Bohemia was more intense than that between the proletariat and the bourgeoisie in England.

Parcto was particularly skeptical about Marx's idea of a classless society. After chiding "socialists" for naively believing that a new elite of politicians will keep their promises better than those who have preceded them, and after quoting from the *Communist Manifesto* the statement defining the proletarian movement as being in the interest of the immense majority, Pareto continues to point out that unfortunately this *true* revolution, which is to bring men an unmixed happiness, is nothing but a mirage that never becomes a reality. It is similar to the golden age of the millenarians: forever awaited, it is forever lost in the mists of the future; it invariably eludes its devotees just when they think they have it (Pareto, 1902–1903, I:61).

The idea of a classless society, a society without a ruling class, was merely a case of wishful thinking, for "it is always an oligarchy that governs" (Pareto, 1916:2183). Ignoring exceptions, which are few and short-lived,

one finds everywhere a governing class of relatively few individuals that keeps itself in power partly by force and partly by the consent of the subject class, which is much more populous. The differences lie principally, as regards substance, in the relative proportions of force and consent; and as regards forms, in the manners in which the force is used and the consent obtained (Pareto, 1916:2244).

It is illusory even to think that a class of people who succeed in driving away from power an older class will be interested in acting in favor of the collective utility. In reality, "the sole effect of their action is . . . to gain control of the power and to impose on the [governed] a yoke which is often more severe than" the previous one (Pareto, 1902–1903, I:36). It is not that those who publicly proclaim justice, liberty, and equality are always hypocrites. They may very well be in earnest about their ideals during the period of their ascent to power. More often, however, they do not declare their true intentions because they "would be defeated before the battle" (Pareto, 1896–1897:156). In any case, whatever their intentions during the period of their ascendancy, they, like all men, have deeply entrenched selfish interests which eventually and invariably assert themselves over the public ideals and good. This skepticism permeated much of Pareto's thinking. In a 1921 letter to a friend, from whom he had received an antisemitic book, he wrote:

Have you become antisemitic? Once, if I do not err, you were Dreyfusard. There are those who accuse the Jews of all manner of evils; others so accuse the Masons; still others accuse the clericals (once they were called Jesuits), or the militarists, the Social- ists, the reactionaries, and so forth. The only truth in all this is that men are inclined to form cliques in order to seek an advantage at the expense of others (Pareto, 1960, III:281–282).[3]

Society represents a vast array of groups, each of which tries to get hold of the goods produced by others, and such a condition would in all probability survive radical changes such as the abolition of private property. It is this sort of thinking that leads Aron (1960:208) to state that "The elite theory of a Pareto is better adapted to the interpretation of revolutions which claim to follow Marx than is Marxism." According to Pareto, private property will inevitably emerge again after its abolition. However perfectly the rules may be thought through for the distribution of consumers' goods, these rules will have to be applied by human beings, and their actions will reveal both their qualities and their defects. If today there are judges who decide always against the people of a given class and in favor of those of a certain other class, there will very likely be "distributors" in a future society who will divide the pie in such a way as to give a very little piece to A and a very big piece to B (Pareto, 1902–1903, I:129).

Not only was Pareto skeptical of the possibility of ever abolishing private property, but he also doubted the possibility of ever substantially changing the distribution of wealth among the classes, that is, of diminishing the inequality of incomes. Although he eventually departed somewhat from his original position, nevertheless in his law of the frequency distribution of income, widely known in statistics and economics as "Pareto's Law," he argued that the income frequency distribution is largely unchanging, and that the only way to

---

[3]The translation into English is ours.

change it, however slightly, and to diminish the inequality of incomes is through increased production (Pareto, 1906).[4] In respect to this law, the course of events has been remarkably favorable to Pareto. Strachey's argument, referred to in Chapter I, concerning the difficulty of the British working classes in holding their own despite all their militancy, is especially worthy of note in this connection.

The working classes in general in Western society have moved a few notches up the economic ladder, in consequence of an interlude of capitalist prosperity. But this fact of absolute improvement does not seem to warrant the conclusion that class differences have significantly diminished, not even under the conditions of welfare capitalism. The movement has been under capitalism's own terms. In examining this question, Kolko (1962:39; see also Meade, 1964) has concluded to the contrary that welfare capitalism "has not changed the nature of income inequality, nor raised the standard of living of the lowest income classes above what it would have reached if they had not been subjected to Federal taxation."

In short, for Pareto social and class inequalities were unavoidable, and societies would always be so arranged that some would be on top, rich, commanding and exploiting, while others—the vast majority—would be at the bottom, poor, governed and exploited. Nothing could express the substance of Pareto's position on this question better than that famous commandment which the donkey Benjamin read from the barn of *Animal Farm* to his fellow animals: "All animals are equal but some animals are more equal than others" (Orwell, 1946:123).

It can be easily surmised that, like Marx, Pareto too had a theory of exploitation (he preferred the term "spoliation"). Societies characterized by private property, "which is to say just about every society known up to the present," offer two essentially different means of acquiring wealth. One is to produce it directly or indirectly through the work and services of one's own capital; the other is by appropriating the wealth so produced by others. These two ways have been employed at all times, and it would be foolish to believe that it will be different in the future. Social movements generally develop along the line of least resistance. The direct production of economic goods is often very arduous, whereas the appropriation of the goods produced by others is at times extremely easy (Pareto, 1902–1903, I:115–116).

The irony is that spoliation is not a simple result of the exploiter's greed. It is in part made possible also by the unshakable apathy of the masses. It is a curious circumstance, Pareto argued, that "men often act with much more energy in appropriating the wealth of others than in defending their own." Consider the proposal in a nation of thirty million to levy one dollar per year on each citizen and to distribute the total to thirty individuals. According to

---

[4]For a detailed discussion and application of Pareto's Law, see Macaulay (1922).

Pareto, those who hope to gain a million will work night and day for the success of the proposal; the despoiled will be much less active—after all, their loss is only one dollar (Pareto, 1902–1903, I:128). Spoliation seldom meets with resistance on the part of the despoiled. Limitations on it come rather from the spoliators themselves who, in virtue of the losses spoliation inflicts on the entire society, often discover that they "end up by losing more than they gained" (Pareto, 1896–1897:116).

The power of the spoliators is great because it does not depend on their wealth alone. Thus, Pareto (1896–1897:120) argued that

> Wealth is not the only basis of the strength of the spoliators: they use many other means, and cunningly make recourse to the most worthy things and those intrinsically most useful to society. The maintenance of order and security being the most pressing need of society, they make use of it and glibly deploy it as a pretext in order to ensure the success of their operations. Spoliation has also been given the sanction of religion and morality. In the eyes of the dominant class, the things most abominable are those which may threaten its power, and often enough they manage to get those subject to them to accept this viewpoint. The thing most indispensable to men, after morality, is justice: hence at all times the dominant class has sought to make justice serve its ends.

RESIDUES, CLASSES, AND ELITE CIRCULATION

Pareto's general position on the question of systems of inequality can best be understood in relation to his theory of "sentiments" or "residues." He begins his sociology by raising the fundamental question concerning what impels human beings to action. In asking this, he resembles many other fathers of sociology who have sought to single out what are severally known as the basic "forces," "wishes," or "needs" underlying human behavior. In Pareto's work these forces are referred to as "sentiments." Their causal presence in human behavior can be inferred by observing men in action and by studying their verbal behavior. Once inferred and catalogued, the sentiments are referred to as "residues." The fundamental characteristic of sentiments is that they do not correspond to any determined, conscious, or logical mental states, but rather to forces which are largely premotivational and automatic—mere reflexes of social, indeed in some cases possibly even biological, forces.

Sharing One's Property with Others

A few of the fifty-two basic sentiments classified by Pareto are of special importance for his argument on systems of social inequalities. The first one concerns what he (1916:1149–1152) termed the sentiment of "sharing one's property with others." This sentiment, though forever straining to manifest itself, is actually very weak and rare in its pure form, tending rather to appear as a compound wherein personal interests predominate. Considering the case of those few individuals in the ruling class who at any given time appear to side with the subject class, Pareto classifies them into five types, as follows. In the first type he places persons who "assume leadership of the subject classes to attain some political, financial, or other advantage." In this case, the underlying sentiment of sharing one's property with others is clearly dominated by a self-seeking goal. In days gone by, according to Pareto, violence was the only recourse of such individuals, a fact which, interestingly enough, tended to limit their number. But nowadays, when revolutions are no longer necessary, due to the institution of the ballot, their number has vastly increased.

The second type comprises persons who, without assuming leadership of the masses and "with an eye to their interests, tie the donkey where the 'boss' directs." For instance, "under the Restoration in France, the 'level-headed young man' went to mass; under Louis Philippe he read Voltaire; under the Second Empire he found it highly praiseworthy to say that he was 'uninterested in politics.' " In Pareto's own time, financiers and industrialists had discovered that it was profitable "to abet the Socialists."

In the third type may be found those "who are *sincerely inclined* to give something to others because they *instincitvely feel* that they will receive more than they give. They give away a sparrow in the hope that he will come home a capon" (emphasis added).

The fourth type consists of " 'intellectuals,' defective in energy, knowledge, and good sense, who take the declamations of the types named above seriously." These are "few in numbers," and "some who might seem to belong among them really belong to the other types."

Finally, in the fifth type may be found a few "individuals of energy, knowledge, and good sense who propound social and 'solidarian' doctrines out of a sincere desire to share their goods with others." However, it is not easy to find examples of them. For instance, at first blush one might consider the early socialist and sociologist Saint-Simon as an example of this type. He was rich, and died poor and friendless. However, he squandered his wealth in pleasure seeking, and in his friendless poverty he was comforted by "his pride in being a Messiah, the founder of a new religion."

Sentiments of Superiors and Inferiors

A second class of sentiments directly relevant to Pareto's theory of classes is what he (1916:1153–1159) termed "sentiments of social ranking (hierarchy)." In an interesting anticipation of a major assumption of "the functional theory of stratification," to be discussed in Chapter V, Pareto argued that such sentiments are so widespread that it would seem indeed that no human society at all complex could survive without them. He distinguished between two subclasses of them: "sentiments of superiors" and "sentiments of inferiors."

Sentiments of superiors are "sentiments of patronage and benevolence,

supplemented oftentimes by domineering sentiments, or sentiments of pride."
Sentiments of inferiors, in turn, are sentiments of "subordination, affection,
reverence, fear." Pareto considered these "indispensable" to "the ordering of
human societies." They are "manifestations of the sense for authority," which
is so widespread in human beings that it can be found even in anarchists. The
sense for authority shows various degrees of intensity, running from simple
admiration to outright deification, but it is common in all walks of life to accept
as given and inalienable the authority of a person who has some real or
imaginary symbol of superiority. Consider the reverence, still common everywhere, of the young for the old, of the poorly educated for the learned, of the
woman for the man, of the novice for the expert. As we approach class
phenomena, we find the reverence, or at least the awe, of the poor for the rich,
the mere citizen for the politician, the worker for the successful businessman,
the subject for the sovereign, the plebeian for the noble. When Queen Elizabeth
II of Great Britain journeyed to the republican United States a few years ago,
the masses, the various grades of dignitaries, and the television public in
general produced a festivity on the scale of a national holiday. Independent-
minded workmen in industry strain hard to catch a glimpse of the firm's
president when he walks in full retinue down the hallway. Throngs of
humanity from all walks of life converge on airports, public squares, or
auditoriums to have a peek at the politician, hear his fatuous chatter, and,
glory of all glories, to touch his hand. So powerful seems to be the veneration
of authority that many individuals previously hostile to a particular politician
melt into a rapturous purr after shaking hands with him or merely receiving
his wave of the hand.

What is even more interesting is that the sentiment of veneration for authority is quite independent of the actual qualities of the "superiors." People are
entirely capable of venerating the monarch in the abstract at the same time that
they hate their actual sovereign. Once an agglomerate of relations has grown
up, an abstraction often develops and persists in time. The sentiment of authority, once it has developed, often becomes disengaged from the person and
attached to such symbols of authority as the monarchy, the presidency, the
priesthood, wealth, or the like. This phenomenon, Pareto (1916:1157) further
notes, explains "the importance for those in authority of 'keeping up appearances'—'prestige,' the outward semblance of superiority." Appearances reinforce the masses in their inclination to accept the status, and hence the
legitimacy, of superiority.

Sentiments of Equality in Inferiors

The third and most important set of sentiments strictly relevant to Pareto's
argument on social stratification consists of what he somewhat ironically
termed "sentiments of equality in inferiors" (Pareto, 1916:1220–1228). At

close inspection it develops that this sentiment "is often a defence of integrity on the part of an individual belonging to a lower class and a means of lifting him to a higher." He may talk of the interests of his social class as a whole rather than of his own personal interest, because "that is a fashionable mode of expression" and because he is not aware of the difference between his real and his apparent purposes.

In examining carefully the sentiment we are discussing, Pareto is struck by an interesting contradiction between two tendencies in human behavior, namely, what might be called the need for aristocracy and the need for equality.

On the one hand there is a tendency to make the largest possible number of persons share in the advantages that the individual asks for himself. On the other, there is a tendency to restrict that number as far as possible. The contradiction disappears the moment we consider that the tendency is to admit to the advantages all whose cooperation helps one towards obtaining them, so that their introduction yields more in profits than it costs; and to exclude all who do not help, or help less effectively, so that their participation costs more than it yields. Similarly, in a war it is a good thing to have as many soldiers as possible for the fighting, and as few as possible for the division of the spoils. Demands for equality almost always conceal demands for privileges (Pareto, 1916:1221).

A similar observation was recently made by Lenski (1966:44) as the "first law of distribution," namely, that "men will share the product of their labors to the extent required to insure the survival and continued productivity of those others whose actions are necessary or beneficial to themselves."

In short, the sentiment of equality in inferiors reveals a person's need for a society unhindered by class obstacles in order that he may improve *his own* social condition; however, once the successful person has reached his desired goal, the need for equality and classlessness ceases to operate, and the need for aristocracy, for a class-structured society protected by hindrances against the less fortunate, takes over. "People agitate for equality to get equality in general, and then go on to make countless numbers of distinctions to deny it in the particular. Equality is to belong to all—but it is granted only to the few" (Pareto, 1916:1222).

The heart of his argument in the present connection is disclosed most colorfully by the following passage in which Pareto (1916:1227) argues that the so-called sentiment of equality is really mostly selfish interest—that is, the appeal to equality is really a rationalization (a "derivation" in Pareto's terminology) concealing an individual aim in mind:

The sentiment that is very inappropriately named equality is fresh, strong, alert, precisely because it is not, in fact, a sentiment of equality and is not related to any abstraction, as a few naïve "intellectuals" still believe; but because it is related to the direct interests of individuals who are bent on escaping certain inequalities not in their favour, and setting up new inequalities that will be in their favour, this latter being their chief concern.

Dimensions of Stratification

So much then for this question concerning the presence in society of sentiments that make social inequality inevitable. Pareto's next argument is that
sentiments are not evenly distributed in society; nor are they of equal intensity
in the various social classes and strata. In general, they vary with occupation.
Along that line, Pareto grants, Marx's theory of "economic determinism"
might be linked with the theory of residues (or sentiments) by correlating the
residues with economic status; and as far as it goes such a correlation would
undoubtedly be sound. However, Pareto argues (by emphasizing Marx's economic determinism beyond what, as we have shown, is warranted by Marx's
thought), Marx's theory goes wrong in isolating economic status from other
social factors toward which in fact it stands in a relation of interdependence.
It goes wrong, further, in envisaging a single relation of cause and effect,
whereas there are many such relations, all functioning simultaneously (Pareto,
1916:1723–1727).

First to formally introduce the concept of system into sociological analysis,
Pareto was naturally very favorable to the idea of interdependence among
strategic factors of social inequality (see Henderson, 1935). One seeking to
stratify a population could take a host of characteristics into account, such as
income, education, occupation, skill in influencing politicians, skill in the
political administration, and the like. In short, there are many "hierarchies of
ranks" in society, and they are all interdependent. For instance, a wealthy man
has a good probability of becoming a powerful political figure, just as a politician is likely to enrich himself or to become much richer than he was before
he entered politics.

If it is true that there are various and interdependent dimensions of social
stratification, it is equally true, however, that they are not necessarily equal in
their reciprocities. For any given individual, there need not be what in more
recent years has come to be known as "status consistency." According to
Pareto, "The same individuals do not occupy the same [equally high or equally
low] positions" as we move from one dimension to another.

Pareto's point here is intended to emphasize the necessity of distinguishing
analytically among the various factors relevant to social stratification. Beyond
this emphasis, his argument, like Weber's later, does not substantially damage
Marx's position. Indeed, Pareto grants Marx the point that the economic,
social, and political dimensions are of prime importance for a study of class
structure and change. Moreover, while retaining his insistence on the interdependence of such factors, Pareto concedes the extreme power of the economic factor and points out that

if men should be ranked according to the degree of their influence and political and
social power, then in most societies, to some extent at least, men would occupy in this
figure a position corresponding directly to their position in a figure representing the

distribution of wealth. The classes called *superior* are also generally the richest (Pareto, 1902–1903, I:8).

Elite Circulation

There are various social classes and strata in society, and they are not entirely distinct even in countries where a caste system prevails. One major reason for this fact is that there is at all times a great deal of mobility between the classes. Indeed, "in modern civilized countries circulation among the various classes is exceedingly rapid" (Pareto, 1916:2025). This circulation or mobility is not always readily evident because it is very often concealed by several factors. It is only by studying history over a long period of time—for example, for several centuries—that one can perceive the general direction and the major lines of this movement (Pareto, 1902–1903, I:34). When this study is done, it shows that members of the lower strata of society rise to the higher strata, first flourish there, and then fall into decadence, are annihilated, and disappear. This circulation of elites is one of the principal movements of history, and it is essential to take it into account if we are to understand great social movements (Pareto, 1902–1903, I:15). It is not, however, the only one. Pareto warns that we must not fall into the common error of claiming that all change is explained by a single cause. Social evolution is extremely complex, and to seek to reduce its "several main currents" *(plusieurs courants principaux)* to a single one "is a rash enterprise" *(est une entreprise téméraire)* at least for the time being (Pareto, 1902–1903, I:41).

"In order to have it the more manageable," Pareto reduces the great variety of social classes and strata into two major classes and isolates one of the principal dynamic elements in society in the struggle of the less privileged against a small minority dominating society. Unlike Marx, he focuses on the political structure rather than on economic factors; hence, his basic classes are a *governing class* and a *governed class.* Moreover, again quite unlike Marx, the struggle is not between the governing class and the governed masses as a whole but usually between the governing class and select members, "the elite," of the governed class who seek to replace it.[5]

Pareto's argument here is methodologically impeccable, but unless the reader uses the utmost care he can easily misinterpret it (Lopreato and Alston, 1970). Bottomore (1964:42), for example, is unnecessarily confused when he reproachfully asks whether Pareto's "circulation of elites" refers to "a process in which *individuals* circulate between the elite and the non-elite, or to a process in which *one elite* is replaced by another." The answer is emphatically the latter, but we must take the liberty of continuing to term "elite" those skidding members of the governing class who are no longer really elite in the

---

[5]Struggles between sections of the governing class also occur and are important, but Pareto pays little specific attention to them.

sense of being best fit to govern. Pareto argues that often members of the governing class are also members of an elite *when they first come to power*. At this point, governing class and governing elite are rather congruent. Soon, however, the governing class begins to lose its elite character.

The problem is that Bottomore, like many others, confuses Pareto's concept of "elite" with that of "governing class," and "non-elite" with "governed class." In Pareto, however, the governing class is synonymous with the elite only in the hypothetical case of totally free circulation or mobility of talent. In the absence of totally unhindered mobility, the governing class contains members of the non-elite as well as of the elite, just as the subject class contains members of the elite as well as the bulk of the non-elite. Hence, the circulation of elites refers to a process in which part or all of a governing class that may have once been an elite is replaced by another elite which has been part of the governed class. To emphasize: "elite circulation" regards the downward movement of a previous elite and the concomitant upward movement of another. Given the particular composition of the classes, the movement is also between the governing class and the governed class.

As Aron (1960:203–204) has noted, for Pareto, in contrast to Marx, the problem was not to eliminate class inequalities—which Pareto deemed impossible in any case—but to insure that the most competent persons would rise to the highest positions. Hence the emphasis on the elite concept. Fundamentally, the circulation of elites occurs because those who govern are often incompetent, while among those who are governed there are cases of high competence with a will to power strong enough to propel them to the top. This difference is the basic source of the social dynamics which interested Pareto. He therefore had to devise a concept of elite which made it possible to distinguish what is from what would be if social justice and social wisdom were at a maximum. He did so by establishing what in the methodology of theory is sometimes referred to as an "idealization." The following passage clearly tells the story:

> Let us assume that in every branch of human activity each individual is given an index which stands as a sign of his capacity, very much the way grades are given in the various subjects in examinations in school. The highest type of lawyer, for instance, will be given 10. The man who does not get a client will be given 1—reserving zero for the man who is an out-and-out idiot. To the man who has made his millions—honestly or dishonestly as the case may be—we will give 10. To the man who has earned his thousands we will give 6; to such as just manage to keep out of the poor-house, 1, keeping zero for those who get in. . . . For chess-players we can get very precise indices, noting what matches, and how many, they have won. And so on for all the branches of human activity (Pareto, 1916:2027).

Pareto's next step is to make a category (a class, loosely) of the people who, in terms of the above hypothetical scale, could be shown to have the highest indices in their branch of activity, and to that group he gives the name of "elite." Further, inasmuch as he is interested mainly in political processes, he divides this category into two types: "a *governing élite*, comprising individuals who directly or indirectly play some considerable part in government, and a *non-governing élite,* comprising the rest" (Pareto, 1916:2032). Next to these types—the result of an idealization—he places the "real" categories of governing class and subject class, both of which can in principle be isolated by simple enumeration. But we must bear clearly in mind that the two sets of concepts are not interchangeable. Indeed, it is the lack of congruence between the phenomena to which they refer that, according to Pareto, provides one of the chief dynamics of the social system.

Perhaps in consequence of a deficiency in formal scientific training among social scientists, one encounters but rarely an adequate understanding of Pareto's formal argument. Thus, Pareto's idealization of the elite has led many a sociologist to interpret Pareto in ideological terms and attribute to him a hostility toward both modern democracy and socialism. The charge would be entirely irrelevant if social science were concerned more with the scientific payload of arguments and less with gossip. Pareto's approach clearly spells out the assumption that social discontent and disorder are due to the fact that people are not always found in positions which are warranted by their talent and skills. His use of the idealization is designed precisely to allow him to demonstrate the injustices in society and the social dynamics that ensue therefrom. On this objective he is extremely clear.

In the concrete, he argues, there are many exceptions to correspondence between the quality of the position occupied and the talent and skill required by that position. Such exceptions are blatant within the governing class for the reason, among others, that "some of the labels—the label of wealth, for instance—are hereditary. . . . Wealth, family, or social connexions also help in many other cases to win the label of the *élite* in general, or of the governing *élite* in particular, for persons who otherwise hold no claim upon it." Moreover, in societies where the social unit is the family, "the label worn by the head of the family also benefits all other members" (Pareto, 1916:2035–2037). In short, some members of the ruling class either continue in or "have found their way into that exalted company without possessing qualities corresponding to the labels they wear" (Pareto, 1916:2035).

If all these "deviations from type" were of little importance, they might be disregarded. As a matter of fact, such deviations are many, and "we are therefore required to make a special study of them" (Pareto, 1916:2038–2040). Specifically,

we must pay special attention (1), in the case of one single group, to the proportions between the total of the group and the number of individuals who are nominally members of it but do not possess the qualities requisite for effective membership; and then (2), in the case of various groups, to the ways in which transitions from one group to the other occur, and to the intensity of that movement—that is to say, to the velocity of the circulation (Pareto, 1916:2043).

Circulation depends on a variety of factors. In the first place it depends on "the supply of and the demand for certain social elements"; when a country is at peace, for example, it does not require many soldiers in its governing class. On the other hand, when the country is in a state of warfare, many soldiers are necessary, and it is precisely the failure to make this type of adjustment that has been one of the causes in the collapse of many aristocracies, or ruling classes.

A second cause of circulation concerns a question that has received considerable attention in recent studies of social mobility. It refers to the transformation of a nonindustrial and noncommercial society into an industrial and commercial one. The greater the development, the greater the mobility, regardless of the form of stratification. In this connection Pareto makes a statement that is rather precocious for his time. He distinguishes between what in recent years has sometimes been termed *forced* mobility and *free* mobility and points to the necessity of assessing rates of mobility in a given society within the framework of a *full-equality model*. He (1916:2046) notes:

> We must not confuse the state of law with the state of fact. . . . There are many examples of castes that are legally closed, but into which, in point of fact, new-comers make their way, and often in large numbers. On the other hand, what difference does it make if a caste is legally open, but conditions *de facto* prevent new accessions to it? If a person who acquires wealth thereby becomes a member of the governing class, but no one gets rich, it is as if the class were closed; and if only a few get rich, it is as if the law erected serious barriers against access to the caste.

We shall return to this question in more detail in Chapter XIII.

The third major cause of mobility concerns the fact that fertility rates among the governing class are usually not high enough to insure self-perpetuation. This deficiency is all the greater if, for one reason or another, a society and its governmental functions are expanding. The governing class must then be replenished with elements rising from the governed class.

A fourth, and perhaps most important, cause of mobility concerns the varying distribution of sentiments in the social classes. With time, a governing class loses the cultural, moral, and intellectual qualities that in the period of ascendancy endeared it to the masses. That is, a "degeneracy" develops in the members composing it. If we hypothesize a society in which at some point position in the governing class is justified by a corresponding capacity, it inevitably happens that "as time goes by, considerable, sometimes very considerable, differences arise between the capacity and the label" (Pareto, 1916: 2052). Hence, "aristocracies can subsist only by the elimination of these elements [the degenerate] and the rise of new ones" (Pareto, 1902–1903, I:9–10). If one of those movements—elimination of the degenerate and rise of the new —comes to an end, or worse still, if both come to an end, the governing class "crashes to ruin and often sweeps the whole of a nation along with it." One of the most powerful causes of change in the political fiber of society is the accumulation of superior elements in the governed class and, conversely, of inferior elements in the ruling class.

A mere lag in elite circulation may have the effect of considerably increasing, on the one hand, the number of degenerate elements within the class at the helm and, on the other, the number of elements of superior quality within the subject class. In such case, the social equilibrium becomes unstable; the least shock, whether from within or from without, destroys it. A conquest or a revolution overturns everything, brings to power a new elite, and establishes a new equilibrium (Pareto, 1902–1903, I:11).

For Pareto, in consequence of class circulation, the governing class is always in a state of continuous change. Differences in the rate of transformation provide us with a clue to the sorts of social movements that societies as a whole experience. For instance, revolutions come about because of too slow a circulation of elites, which permits the accumulation in the ruling class

of decadent elements no longer possessing the residues suitable for keeping them in power, and shrinking from the use of force; while meantime in the lower strata of society elements of superior quality are coming to the fore, possessing residues suitable for exercising the functions of government and willing enough to use force (Pareto, 1916:2057).[6]

Concerning this question of "force," Pareto has some very interesting remarks to make. First, he argues that a mere handful of citizens, if inclined to use strong means, can force their will upon public officials who are not so inclined. Second, to prevent or resist the forceful tactics of such individuals, the governing class often resorts to "diplomacy," fraud, corruption. Making reference to Machiavelli's famous categories, Pareto (1916:2178) argues that "governmental authority passes, in a word, from the lions to the foxes." A governing class is very difficult to overthrow if it is adept in turning the flank of the obstacle it cannot demolish in frontal attacks. It is especially difficult to overthrow when it successfully absorbs most of the individuals in the subject class who show those same talents and might therefore become the leaders of the disgruntled masses. Third, however, "in the long run the differences in temperament [that is, sentiments] between the governing class

---

[6]Pareto's discussion of the use of force has caused some discomfort to many social scientists because they have understood Pareto to condone the use of force at all costs. The reaction is indefensible. It is unfortunate but true that many cringe and have irrational reactions at the mere thought of force in society. For Pareto, as for all other "Machiavellians," force is a social phenomenon like many others. He does not call for the use of force; he merely isolates it as a mechanism capable of *slowing down* the downfall of a governing class *and* as something that to one degree and form or another all governments actually employ (Lopreato and Ness, 1966). Moreover, the Italian term *forza* does not carry the connotations of the English term *force*. *Forza* is more appropriately translated by the English "strength" or "might" than by "force" in its usual connotation of violence. Thus Pareto (1902–1903, I:37) warns: "One must not confuse violence with force. Violence often accompanies weakness. . . . Trajan was strong but not violent; Caligula was violent, not strong."

and the subject class become gradually accentuated." "When that difference becomes sufficiently great, revolution occurs" (Pareto, 1916:2178–2179).

Very peculiar things happen to declining elites. Pareto puts it thus:

> When an elite declines, we can generally observe two signs which manifest themselves simultaneously:
> 1. The declining elite becomes softer, milder, more humane and less apt to defend its own power.
> 2. On the other hand, it does not lose its rapacity and greed for the goods of others, but rather tends as much as possible to increase its unlawful appropriations and to indulge in major usurpations of the national patrimony (Pareto, 1901:59).

"Humanitarians" is the label that, sarcastically and scornfully, Pareto applies to a declining elite. And he emphasizes their greed and corruption. Note the following:

> Our ruling class is insatiable; as its power wanes, its fraudulent practices increase. Every day in France, in Italy, in Germany, in America, it demands new tightenings of duties, new provisions to safeguard trade, new obstacles to commerce under the pretext of sanitary provisions, new subsidies of every kind. In Italy, under Depretis, the government used to send soldiers to mow the fields of landowners who refused to pay the wages requested by free mowers; today this fine practice is being renewed. . . .
> Such is the method of despoiling the poor, applied by our foremost "humanitarians." Congresses against tuberculosis are fine, but it would be even better not to steal the bread from those who starve and it would also be preferable, either to be a little less "humanitarian," or to respect the property of others a little more (Pareto, 1901: 69–70).

CONCLUDING COMMENTS

Pareto's reception into sociology in the United States, which dates from the depression years of the 1930's, has been marked by an extraordinary degree of turbulence. His actual, though largely hidden, influence has been great through the works of such scholars as Talcott Parsons and George Homans and their students. But on balance, until very recently at least, reactions to his sociology have been passionately hostile, if not always consistent with one another, and fundamentally authoritative, if seldom well-informed by knowledge of the target. Accusations have ranged from "sterile biologism" to "sterile mechanism," from hatred of democracy to hatred of socialism, from plagiarism to demonic creation. And, most curious of all, Pareto has been branded as sympathizer, supporter, and/or intellectual godfather of modern fascism. This reputation—or, rather, series of reputations—stands in ironic contrast to Pareto's international prestige in economics.

A number of factors were undoubtedly at play in this important though still underwritten chapter in intellectual history and the sociology of knowledge. Perhaps the foremost concerns the way in which Pareto—as compared with some of his illustrious predecessors—dealt with the market model of society.[7]

A full market society inherently generates class divisions in the distribution of rights and privileges; not all individuals have equal access to and equal control over the range of market utilities, including their own labor, existent at any given time. Yet, as a child of the bourgeois-democratic revolution, a market society requires for its own justification the postulation of equality— an equality of *individual* rights and *individual* opportunities. This contradiction, still characteristic of mid-twentieth-century market society, was recognized by Pareto, just as it had been recognized by Marx. It was not so clearly recognized by many of the theorists and interpreters of the bourgeois-democratic revolution—John Locke, John Stuart Mill, Thomas Jefferson being examples—whose works became cornerstones in the political edifice of Western democracy. Pareto's analysis of the full-market society differs from their analyses in the sense that he stripped the justificatory postulate away and examined what lay beneath as the fundamental character of the society. This much Marx too had done, only in much broader terms. But whereas Marx attempted to resolve the contradiction by discarding the market society, thereby allowing the reintegration of the postulate of equality into a model of "natural" society, Pareto would not discard it. This colossal skeptic refused to accept the postulate, *under any conditions*, as anything more than a rationalization (derivation). Marx once stated that religion is the opium of the masses. Pareto came very close to saying that egalitarianism was the opium of the masses. In consequence, he left the social body uncomfortably naked, and just at a time when the cover of whole cloth was psychologically most needed.

We shall now conclude this chapter by presenting a few propositions which are either explicitly stated by Pareto or are logically derivable from his argument. They will be useful to us in interpreting the research findings reported later in this book. The following appear to be of special importance.

Given the circulation of personnel (that is, mobility) between the upper stratum of society and the lower strata:

1. By virtue of inherited privilege, the downwardly mobile will most often skid to adjacent strata.

2. By virtue of the postulated struggle between the governing class and the nongoverning elite, the upwardly mobile originate in the middle strata of the social structure, where elite talent can be more easily developed into appropriate skills.

3. In view of the postulated struggle between the governing class and the nongoverning elite, class conflict will be greatest between those in the highest

---

[7]This model is critically distinguished by two postulates: (1) each individual is the sole and free proprietor of his own utilities, including his own (alienable) labor; (2) each individual seeks to maximize his own self interests, but some have more skill and talent than others.

reaches of an authority structure and those who partake in a lesser degree of the distribution of authority.

4. Likewise, given the veneration for authority which Pareto finds in the masses, antagonism against those in positions of authority on the part of the masses is likely to occur less frequently than it occurs among those who are closer to those positions.

5. In view of the search for status and privilege which Pareto attributes to man, the political behavior of the socially mobile will resemble the political behavior of the "superior" and the privileged strata.

6. Moreover, given the self-seeking nature of man, an apparently proletarian political orientation, if found among the socially mobile, is induced by selfish rather than by classlike interests.

III

RALF DAHRENDORF: AUTHORITY STRUCTURE AND CLASS CONFLICT

Ralf Dahrendorf (1929—), at the time of this writing secretary of state in the Foreign Ministry of the Federal Republic of Germany, recently offered a theory (1959: *passim*) of social classes which constitutes an interesting blend of Marxian and Paretian elements. As such, it may be viewed as an attempt to bring Marx up to date and to reconcile Marxian thought with what is usually known as "elite theory." In the process, it also represents an endeavor to revive or in any case to strengthen (see also Dahrendorf, 1958) interest in problems of social conflict, which especially in United States sociology have been rather neglected in recent decades. Although Dahrendorf has since expressed some criticism of his own previous work on class and class conflict— indeed, has said that "the class theory of conflict is not so much wrong as irrelevant if applied to conflict, *and to the striking absence of conflict,* in the contemporary world" (1967a:14; emphasis added)—we shall focus here on his 1959 presentation, *Class and Class Conflict in Industrial Society.*[1] This volume continues to be quite influential in sociological circles, and it will be helpful

---

[1]As the above quotation indicates (see also Dahrendorf, 1967b; 1968), Dahrendorf has moved progressively away from the "class theory of conflict," a movement with perceptible beginnings in his best-known *Class and Class Conflict in Industrial Society.* Indeed, in his study of German society (1967b) he deliberately eschewed the use of class as an explanatory variable of any importance.

to us in our analysis of research findings later in our book. In view of Dahrendorf's self-criticism, however, we should make clear at the very beginning that our concern will be not so much with the amount of conflict we may be able to isolate from the perspective of Dahrendorf's theory but with the tenability of Dahrendorf's conception of the class structure.

Dahrendorf cogently argues that most of the efforts that have passed as studies of social class are in fact studies of social strata and are directed to problems of social status, social ranking, and style of life. Such studies usually yield highly complex pictures of social differentiation and stratification, but they say little or nothing about structurally induced conflict and the dynamics of social structure. For Dahrendorf (1959:76),

Class is always a category for purposes of the analysis of the dynamics of social conflict and its structural roots, and as such it has to be separated strictly from *stratum* as a category for purposes of describing hierarchical systems at a given point of time.

Societies are historical entities and therefore "require the motive force of conflict—or, conversely, because there is conflict, there is historical change and development."

Conflict, it may be noted, performs many important social functions. Some concern the relative stability and vitality of societies and groups; for instance, conflict often results in an at least temporary removal of the disagreements and dissociating elements of a society, thereby reestablishing social unity. Moreover, as Coser (1957; see also Coser, 1956) puts it, "the conflict between vested interests and new strata and groups demanding their share of power, wealth and status, have been productive of vitality." Other functions of conflict pertain to the *structural transformation* of society; it is these that Dahrendorf finds most important for class analysis. Indeed, he rejects such a view of conflict as Coser's (which allegedly shows conflict only as a "tolerable" process that fosters rather than endangers the stability of social systems) in favor of a position represented by Dubin (1957), who holds that "continuing group conflict" represents "an important way of giving direction to social change."

SOCIAL CHANGES SINCE MARX'S TIME

In his concern with conflict as a force of structural change, Dahrendorf's starting point is naturally Marx's work. After a useful attempt to envision Marx's unwritten chapter on class theory,[2] Dahrendorf proceeds to winnow the sociological from the ideological and philosophical elements in Marx's thought and to examine in some detail those developments taking place in industrial societies over the past century which, largely unimagined by Marx,

---

[2]For two other attempts, see Geiger (1949) and Bendix and Lipset (1966).

have prevented an historical validation of his theory.[3] For our purposes, a brief mention of a few of these will suffice.

Decomposition of Labor

For Marx, it may be recalled, the downward leveling of the skills of the proletariat was a necessary condition for that intensification of the class struggle which was to lead to a radical societal reorganization. By contrast Dahrendorf notes that, far from being a homogeneous aggregate of equally unskilled and impoverished people, the working class of today comprises three different and discrete major groups of workers: (1) a growing stratum of highly skilled workers who increasingly have much in common with both engineers and white-collar employees; (2) a relatively stable category of semiskilled workmen "with a high degree of diffuse as well as specific industrial experience"; and (3) a declining stratum of totally unskilled laborers consisting of either beginners in industry, such as former agricultural laborers and immigrants, or semiunemployables (Dahrendorf, 1959:48–50). On a key reminiscent of both Weber and Pareto, Dahrendorf then continues to argue that this situation presents

a plurality of status and skill groups whose interests often diverge. Demands of the skilled for security may injure the semiskilled; wage claims of the semiskilled may raise objections by the skilled; and any interest on the part of the unskilled is bound to set their more highly skilled fellow workmen worrying about differentials (Dahrendorf, 1959:51).

Decomposition of Capital

The "decomposition of labor" has evolved in pace with a parallel process within the class of capitalists of old: "the decomposition of capital." When Marx wrote, the typical capitalist was simultaneously the sole owner of the enterprise, its chief manager, and, what is even more important, the absolute arbiter of all matters that related to the enterprise. No longer does this relationship hold. During the past century, the phenomenon of the joint-stock company, already perceived by Marx, has developed so rapidly that today more than two-thirds of all companies in highly industrialized societies are of that type, while their property exceeds four-fifths of the total property in economic enterprises. Moreover, the stock of such companies is dispersed rather widely, so that the enterprise owned and run by a single individual, or even by a single family, is no longer the prevailing pattern of economic organization (Dahrendorf, 1959:42).

The upshot of this development has been what has come to be known as

---

[3]For a detailed discussion of these developments, see Geiger (1949), to whom Dahrendorf surely owes a great debt. A brief excerpt in English from Geiger's book may be found in Geiger (1969:91–104).

"the separation of ownership and control," whereby the economic organization of today is composed increasingly of "capitalists without function" (stockholders) and "functionaries without capital" (the managers).[4] This development has implications concerning the etiology of class conflict. For Dahrendorf, once control is separated from ownership, private property (so critical a variable in Marx's scheme) loses its analytical value. It is Dahrendorf 's contention that a supersedure of the Marxian theory of classes is possible if the exercise of or the exclusion from authority, rather than the possession or nonpossession of private property, is taken as the criterion of class formation. This, Dahrendorf suggests, would have been the more logical arrangement even in Marx's scheme, for the authority associated with legal ownership of property is what produces the relations upon which Marx's theory of class formation is built. Property is only one of several possible forms of authority, and authority is therefore the more general social relation. Wherever there is property, Dahrendorf argues, there is authority, but not every form of authority implies property (Dahrendorf, 1959:136–137).

Dahrendorf's argument against Marx is not predicated on logical grounds alone. He emphasizes that societal conditions have changed since Marx's time and that these changes demand a sociological reorientation in the theory of classes. Not only was the "capitalist society" of the mid nineteenth century

---

[4]Although this separation, or "decomposition of capital," as Dahrendorf refers to it, has not been without consequence, its importance has been overstated on occasion, especially by James Burnham (1941) and to some extent by Dahrendorf himself. As far as he goes, Dahrendorf may be reasonably accurate. But he tends to make too much of this simple diffusion of stock ownership by assuming an inordinately sharp and uniform division between management and *all* stockholders. The number of stockholders in the United States, for example, is quite large and is steadily increasing. But the great majority of them are very small holders and are far removed from the locus of operation. As Berle and Means (1932) demonstrated in their classic study, in 1929 the 200 largest nonfinancial corporations in the United States exercised *legal* control (actual control was even greater) of 58 percent of the reported net capital assets of all nonfinancial corporations. Moreover, within these 200 corporations, relatively small groups of active stockholders exercised effective control: in 44 percent of the 200 corporations, control was by management without material stock ownership; in 23 percent, by minority stock ownership; in 21 percent by minority or managerial groups through a variety of legal devices (Berle and Means, 1932:94). To assume that "management," owning or nonowning, in these largest corporations was somehow significantly independent of the small groups of active shareholders is curiously naive. Within limits, conceded, management is free to run the corporation as the managers see fit; but the limits are telling: continuation of a satisfactory profit margin for the minority of active stockholders, and only incidentally for the other holders too.

The situation since the Berle and Means study can hardly be interpreted as more "democratic" or reflective of a greater "decomposition of capital." Indeed, roughly two-thirds of all privately owned stock is held by the top one percent of families in the United States. Put differently, 500 corporations control about two-thirds of the entire United States nonfarm economy, and within each of the 500 a small minority of stockholders exercise ultimate authority. "Since the United States carries on not quite half of the manufacturing production of the entire world today, these 500 groupings—each with its own little dominating pyramid within it [and many of them with shared memberships]—represent a concentration of power over economics which makes the medieval feudal system look like a Sunday school party. In sheer economic power this has gone far beyond anything we have yet seen" (Berle, 1957:14; see also Lampman, 1962; Meade, 1964).

characterized by the "union of private ownership and factual control of the instruments of production" (Dahrendorf, 1959:40), but in addition the lines of industrial and political conflict were superimposed. This coincidence, so central to Marx's theory, no longer exists in what Dahrendorf terms "post-capitalist" society. Thus:

The opponents of industry—capital and labor—met again, as bourgeoisie and proletariat, in the political arena. . . . It is one of the central theses of the present analysis that in post-capitalist society industry and society have, by contrast to capitalist society, been dissociated. Increasingly, the social relations of industry, including industrial conflict, do not dominate the whole of society but remain confined in their patterns and problems to the sphere of industry. Industry and industrial conflict are, in post-capitalist society, institutionally isolated, i.e., confined within the borders of their proper realm and robbed of their influence on other spheres of society. In post-capitalist society, the industrial enterprise is no longer the model after which all other relations are fashioned (Dahrendorf, 1959:268).

Accordingly, given the particular role of economic institutions in present-day society, class conflict is best seen as arising out of a dispute over the distribution of authority in a given authority structure.

The New Middle Class

The above two post-Marxian developments in industrial society—the decomposition of labor and of capital—are perhaps the weightiest both in assessing the failure of Marx's theory of social classes to be validated by historical circumstances and in understanding the particular direction taken by Dahrendorf's attempted "supersedure" of Marx's theory. A few others, however, must also be mentioned. In addition to the changes experienced in the ranks of Marx's two basic classes, industrial society has also given rise to an entirely new social stratum, the "new middle class." At the time of Marx's death, only about one in twenty members of the labor force were employed in white-collar occupations; the corresponding ratio today is one in every five and is rising. What is even more noteworthy, however, is that this middle stratum was born divided into two segments with clearly divergent orientations (Dahrendorf, 1959:56). On the one hand, there are the "bureaucrats," such as the postoffice clerk, the accountant, and the executive who share "the requisites of a ruling class." These are oriented toward management and account for two-thirds of the new class. On the other hand, there are those persons employed as salesgirls and such other employees in tertiary industries who more closely resemble the class of industrial workers. Hence, the emergence of large numbers of salaried employees represents extension of both of the older classes of bourgeoisie and proletariat. What is more important, by these extensions both classes have become even more complex and heterogeneous than they would have been by virtue of their "decomposition" alone. "By gaining new elements, their unity has become a highly doubtful and precarious feature" (Dahrendorf, 1959:51–57).

Citizenship Rights

Among the other developments in industrial society, one concerns changes in what Marshall (1950; 1965: Chapter IV) has termed the "civil, political and social" parts of "citizenship," defined as "a status bestowed on those who are full members of a community. All who possess the status are equal with respect to the rights and duties with which the status is endowed." Citizenship is a "principle of equality," and as such it has naturally been "at war" with the capitalist class system, which is manifestly a system of inequalities (Marshall, 1965:92–93).

The drive toward equality, which has been in progress for some 250 years, has accelerated since Marx's time and has produced the following citizenship rights: *civil*—liberty of the person; freedom of speech, thought, and faith; the right to own property and to conclude valid contracts; and the right to justice; *political*—the right to participate in the exercise of political power, as a member or elector of such institutions as parliaments and councils of local government; *social*—the whole range of rights, from the minimal right to a modicum of economic welfare and security to the maximal right to share fully in the social heritage and to live the life of a civilized being, partaking of the opportunities of such institutions as the educational system and the social services (Marshall, 1965:78–79).

What effect, we may now ask, have these popular achievements had on the probability of class struggle as envisioned by Marx? Marshall (1965:127) cogently answers that "Status differences can receive the stamp of legitimacy in terms of democratic citizenship provided they do not cut too deep, but occur within a population united in a single civilization; and provided they are not an expression of hereditary privilege." In short, as Dahrendorf (1959:63–64) himself puts it, "There can be little doubt that the equalization of status resulting from social developments of the past century has contributed greatly to changing the issues and diminishing the intensity of class conflict."

The Legalization of Class Conflicts

The intensity of class conflict has been diminished also because these citizenship rights have led to what Dahrendorf, following Geiger, refers to as "the institutionalization of class conflict." According to Geiger, the tension between capital and labor is now recognized as a principle of the very organization of the labor market and, therefore, as a "legal institution of society." Once recognized, the strategies, weapons, and techniques of the class struggle are brought under control. Hence,

The struggle evolves according to certain rules of the game. Thereby the class struggle has lost its worst sting, it is converted into a legitimate tension between power factors which balance each other. Capital and labor struggle with each other, conclude compromises, negotiate solutions, and thereby determine wage levels, hours of work, and other conditions of work (Geiger, 1949—translated and quoted in Dahrendorf, 1959:65).

It is interesting to note that as early as 1875 Marx himself was aware of, and in effect warned against, the danger of legal compromise on the part of the workers in their struggle against the capitalist system. In his famous critique of the Gotha program, Marx lashed at the Lassalle-dominated German socialist party's preoccupation with striving "by all legal means for the *free state—and—*socialist society." For Marx (1875:123–126), in view of the fact that the state was "an organ superimposed upon society," the use of "legal means" was tantamount to accepting the state as given and failing to convert it into an organ "completely subordinate" to society.

The essential point for Dahrendorf is that, given the legalization of conflicts, "Instead of a battlefield, the scene of group conflict has become a kind of market in which relatively autonomous forces contend according to certain rules of the game, by virtue of which nobody is a permanent winner or loser" (Dahrendorf, 1959:67).

Mobility Opportunities

Finally, underlying all the above developments, and in part reflecting them, has been a change of truly epochal value. Dahrendorf discusses it under the heading of "social mobility." He argues that, while in the Marxian analysis mobility was merely a short-lived symptom of either the consolidation or the breakdown of capitalist society, in postcapitalist society social mobility has become one of the crucial properties of its very structure. To be sure, Dahrendorf is not being perfectly faithful to Marx's position, for, as we have seen, Marx considered a third kind of mobility, major and enduring: the absorption of "intermediate classes" into the proletariat. Dahrendorf is justified in noting, however, that study after study of social mobility shows industrial societies to have rather large percentages of class turnover from one generation to another; they also have rather comparable rates of such mobility (see Lipset and Bendix, 1959; Miller, 1960:1–89).[5]

What is the end result of this phenomenon? Dahrendorf (1959:60) provides a cogent answer, as follows:

Where mobility within and between generations is a regular occurrence, and therefore a legitimate expectation of many people, conflict groups are not likely to have either the permanence or the dead seriousness of caste-like classes composed of hopelessly alienated men. And as the instability of classes grows, the intensity of class conflict is bound to diminish. Instead of advancing their claims as members of homogeneous groups, people are more likely to compete with each other as individuals for a place in the sun.

---

[5]For a more recent study questioning Lipset and Bendix' comparison of the United States with other countries, see Blau and Duncan (1967).

In conclusion of this section, it may be seen that the conditions of an exacerbated form of class conflict perhaps no longer exist. Class conflicts, however, have not been eliminated entirely. According to Dahrendorf (1959:-60), where intense class conflict is not possible, "group conflicts assume a somewhat milder and looser character than class struggles of a Marxian type." Conflict for him need not be violent and intense, but can express itself in numerous milder forms. This position, in effect, makes it possible to revitalize the concept of class conflict now that class explosions seem to have a low probability of occurrence.

In keeping with this position, Dahrendorf takes issue with scholars who would distinguish between "conflict" and such related phenomena as "competition," "tension," "contest," and the like. For him the term "conflict" refers to disputes, contests, competitions, and tensions, as well as to more formidable types of social antagonism. The differences among them refer to differences in the "intensity" or the "violence" of conflict as the general term for social antagonism. Dahrendorf (1959:135, 209) states:

All relations between sets of individuals that involve an incompatible difference of objective—i.e., in its most general form, a desire on the part of both contestants to attain what is available only to one, or only in part—are, in this sense, relations of social conflict. . . . Conflict may assume the form of civil war, or of parliamentary debate, or of a strike, or of a well-regulated negotiation.[6]

DAHRENDORF'S THEORY OF CLASS CONFLICT

So much then for Dahrendorf's critique of Marx's theory. His next step is to attempt the formulation of a theory of his own to replace the older one. Mere criticism or even clarification of another's theory is not sufficient; of what use, he asks (1959:72–73), is the remark found in many a research report that its results refute one thesis or another of Marx's work, if the progress of science stops at this early point?

---

[6]Raymond Mack (1965:391) takes issue with this position, arguing in favor of what he feels is a necessary distinction between "conflict" and "competition." According to him, the latter concept refers to "the act of striving for some object that is sought by others at the same time, a contention of two or more persons or groups for the same goal," while conflict refers to "opposition or antagonistic struggle, the aim of which is the annihilation, defeat, or subjugation of the other person or group." More specifically, while in competition the chief objective is the same goal or "scarce object," in conflict the chief objective is "the injury or destruction of the opponent." Mack argues his point well. In general, however, his distinction adds to the confusion of already numerous sociological logomachies. Human acts designed to *injure and destroy* an opponent are probably few, even when the defeat of the other is an end in view. To use his own example, the racer who makes conflict out of competition and "pokes his foot between the other fellow's legs," so as to beat him to the tape, is not necessarily interested in the injury of the opponent but in slowing him down. "Conflict" would seem to be quite adequate as a general concept referring to striving for scarce goods, although we should indeed distinguish among the means that are used to achieve that goal.

We shall make no effort in this volume to present and confront the entirety of Dahrendorf's formulation. Our concern with it goes only as far as the applicability of the survey data to be treated in later chapters will allow, and only in so far as the theory addresses itself directly to Marx's formulation. Nor shall we make an effort in this chapter to treat Dahrendorf's theory critically; the whole of our last chapter is devoted to that task.

What Dahrendorf does is to shift the focus from the economic sphere of society, which largely attracted Marx's attention, to social structure in general, and specifically to those social structures wherein a relation of control and submission obtains. He is led to this focus by the considerations already encountered, especially those concerning the separation of ownership and control. His thesis (1959:172–173) is that "the distribution of authority in associations is the ultimate 'cause' of the formation of conflict groups [or classes], and . . . the cause of the formation of two, and only two, conflict groups." The associations in question are "imperatively coordinated associations," that is, associations within which "some positions are entrusted with a right to exercise control over other positions in order to ensure effective coercion" (Dahrendorf, 1959:165).

Dahrendorf conceives of authority (following Weber, he says) as the "probability that a command with a given specific content will be obeyed by a given group of persons." For him, authority is "dichotomous." The authority structure in any imperatively coordinated association is divided into two "sides." Thus he could argue above that in the associations of his concern there are two, and only two, social classes. He is not interested in the question of whether some individuals in a given association have more or less authority than others. The important distinction for him—and herein resides, as we shall see in Chapter XVII, the heart of his theoretical troubles—lies between those who have any degree of authority at all and those who have none whatsoever. However difficult it may be to identify the borderline between "domination" and "subjection," in every association there is a "plus-side" of authority consisting of those who participate *to any degree* in its exercise, and a "minus-side" comprising those who are *completely subjected* to it. This is not to say that there is no difference between superiors who have a great deal of authority and those who have merely a little authority. "But such differentiation, while important for empirical analysis, leaves unaffected the existence of a border line somewhere between those who have whatever little authority and the 'outs' " (Dahrendorf, 1959:173).

Dahrendorf next attributes to the two classes divergent "objective" interests, namely,

interests in the maintenance or modification of a *status quo.* Our model of conflict group formation involves the proposition that of the two aggregates of authority positions to be distinguished in every association, one—that of domination—is characterized by an interest in the maintenance of a social structure that for them conveys authority, whereas the other—that of subjection—involves an interest in changing a social condition that deprives its incumbents of authority. The two interests are in conflict (Dahrendorf, 1959:176).

Stated otherwise, these objective interests may be seen as "role interests," that is, "*expected* orientations of behavior associated with authority roles in imperatively coordinated associations" (Dahrendorf, 1959:178—emphasis added). From the point of view of the individual, these role interests are

latent interests, i.e., undercurrents of his behavior which are predetermined for him for the duration of his incumbency of a role, and which are independent of his conscious orientations. As such they can, under conditions to be specified presently, become conscious goals which we shall correspondingly call *manifest interests* (Dahrendorf, 1959:178).

By contrast to latent interests, manifest interests are "psychological realities." They refer to the actual will or desire of persons "directed toward some goal." "In this sense, manifest interests are the program of organized groups." In short, as Dahrendorf (1959:178–179) points out, the manifest interests are similar to Marx's notion of "class consciousness."

It is important to bear in mind that until the latent interests are converted into manifest interests, the aggregates of authority positions do not constitute classes in the real sense of the word; that is, they do not form "conflict" or "interest groups." To be sure, being united by a common characteristic (either participation in or exclusion from the exercise of authority), they are "more than mere masses or incoherent quantities." At the same time, however, they do not constitute real classes; they are at best "potential classes," corresponding to Marx's *Klasse an sich*. They constitute "quasi-groups." Only under certain conditions, which we shall examine shortly, will quasi-groups be converted into conflict groups.

To summarize in Dahrendorf's (1959:183–184—emphasis added) own words:

In every imperatively coordinated association, two quasi-groups united by common latent interests can be distinguished. Their orientations of interest are determined by possession of or exclusion from authority. From these quasi-groups, interest groups are recruited, the articulate programs of which defend or attack the legitimacy of existing authority structures. In any given association, two such groupings are in conflict. *This model of conflict group formation is as such complete and suffices for all purposes of theoretical analysis.* In principle, little need be added to it, and what additions are required are in the nature of refinements.

Classes, therefore, are "social conflict groups the determinant (or *differentia specifica*) of which can be found in the participation in or exclusion from the exercise of authority within any imperatively coordinated association" (Dahrendorf, 1959:138). The groups are in conflict in the sense that they defend or seek to alter the existing authority structure. More specifically, the interests of the group endowed with authority yield values and activities which seek to establish and support the legitimacy of its rule. By contrast, the interests of the group excluded from the exercise of authority constitute a threat to the legitimacy of that rule. That is why Dahrendorf (1959:176) suggests that "Empirically, group conflict is probably most easily accessible to analysis if it be understood as a conflict about the legitimacy of relations of authority."

The question now remains, what are "the conditions," referred to earlier, under which latent interests become conscious goals or manifest interests, resulting in class formation? Dahrendorf specifies three broad sets of such "structural conditions of organization." The first concerns "technical conditions of organization," relating to such Malinowskian notions as "a charter, certain norms, a personnel, and certain material requisites." Briefly, as a minimal requirement, for an organized interest group to emerge out of a quasi-group, "there have to be certain persons who make this organization their business, who carry it out practically and take the lead" (Dahrendorf, 1959:185). The argument here is reminiscent of Marx's notion of the political cadre, the "communists," as one of the conditions for the transformation of a *Klasse an sich* into a *Klasse für sich*.

"Political conditions of organization" are the second category of conditions that must be satisfied for interest-group organization to be possible. To put the point in a negative statement: Conflict groups allegedly cannot organize themselves where "a plurality of conflicting parties is not permitted and their emergence [is] suppressed by the absence of freedom of coalition and by police force," as in the totalitarian state (Dahrendorf, 1959:186). This is a perplexing conception which implies a number of rather odd suggestions. Two are particularly worthy of note. In the first place, Dahrendorf seems to be arguing, against the wisdom of history, that a people can be permanently tyrannized. Thus, where for Marx the class consciousness and rebelliousness of the masses grew in proportion with the "oppression" they suffered, for Dahrendorf the inverse relation is true. Secondly, and relatedly, when all is said and done, the irony implied by Dahrendorf's position is that class conflict is possible within "democratic" societies, but *not* within "totalitarian" ones. Accordingly, his theory might be termed a "middle-class theory" of capitalist or Western "industrial tensions" rather than the theory of class conflict that it was designed to be. Moreover, on this basis Dahrendorf finds himself making common theoretical cause with his sociological archenemies the "functionalists," who are accused from all directions of being unable to cope with "endogenous" change in society. For if class conflict is impossible in totalitarian states, then a major source if not the chief source of internally produced structural change is eliminated.

The third and last factor of class formation refers to the "social conditions of organization," which concern the ease of communication in the society and the topological and ecological dispersion of the members of quasi-groups. Again on a Marxian key, Dahrendorf suggests that where the dispersion is great and communications difficult, the formation of an organized interest group is most unlikely. Although Dahrendorf apparently fails to recognize that communications may be difficult for *political-cultural* as well as natural-technological reasons—and in both "democratic" and "totalitarian" societies —he does rightly point out that the significance of this factor has steadily diminished in industrial societies, characterized as they increasingly are by a highly developed system of visual as well as audio communication (Dahrendorf, 1959:187).

In addition to these sets of variables, which may tend either to facilitate or to avert the emergence of interest groups and class conflict, Dahrendorf singles out two other crucially important factors: the multiplicity of associational life, and social mobility.

The fact of being simultaneously a member of a multitude of associations probably mitigates one's identification with any one particular membership group, according to Dahrendorf (1959:191): "It appears that the factual weight of an individual's belongingness to different associations within the ensemble of his social personality also influences the intensity of his solidarity with any one conflict group to which he belongs."

However, it must be clearly borne in mind, Dahrendorf (1959:213–215) continues, that the conflict-generating dichotomy of positions of authority holds for specific associations only—although among these is society itself, viewed as a political association. The conflict possibly arising between the two classes within a given association does not necessarily correspond to the conflict arising in another association. Accordingly, theoretically at least, any given society can have twice as many classes as it has associations. But in fact this extreme scattering of conflicts and conflict groups rarely occurs. Empirical evidence shows that different conflicts are often "superimposed" in society, "so that the multitude of possible conflict fronts is reduced to a few dominant conflicts." Considering, for instance, the three associations of state, industry, and the church, "It is more probable that the workers of industry are at the same time mere members of the church and mere citizens of the state." Superimposition of conflicts, in turn, positively influences the intensity of conflict. "When conflict groups encounter each other in several associations and in several clashes, the energies expended in all of them will be combined and one overriding conflict of interests will emerge."

Although we have previously encountered the argument, it is worth re-emphasizing Dahrendorf's (1959:222) point that the rise and intensification of class conflict is undermined by occupational mobility:

There is an inverse relation between the degree of openness of classes and the intensity of class conflict. The more upward and downward mobility there is in a society, the less comprehensive and fundamental are class conflicts likely to be.

Unfortunately, Dahrendorf does not specify the exact role that mobility plays in undermining class conflict. It is not clear, for instance, whether, in terms of the psychology of social mobility, there is any difference between actually experienced mobility and mobility that is only vicariously experienced. If the focus is on rates of mobility—that is, on a societal rather than a personal phenomenon—it is not, strictly speaking, possible to distinguish between individuals or groups in terms of classlike behavior in association with mobility. A little reflection at this point would suggest that the *perception* of mobility in society might be even more destructive of class conflict than the actual experience of mobility itself. A more precise and formal restatement of Dahrendorf's position on the relation of mobility to class conflict might be as follows: (1) *the better the opportunities for mobility in a society, the higher the probability that the citizenry will perceive such opportunities;* (2) *the higher the perception of opportunities for mobility in one's society, the lower the likelihood that one will engage in classlike behavior;* (3) *therefore, the better the opportunities for mobility in a society, the lower the chance of classlike behavior among its membership.*

CONCLUSIONS

In conclusion, a number of interesting propositions, either stated by Dahrendorf himself or logically derivable from his argument, can now be listed for purposes of later research:

1. Conflict between classes is determined by the varying relations to the distribution of authority in associations.

2. Relations to an authority structure are dichotomous in the sense that one either has or does not have authority; that is, the class structure is dichotomous —hence to the extent that social conflict is observed within either of the classes, it is not of a classlike nature.

3. To the extent that the dichotomous authority and class structures are experientially real in a population, a dichotomous class image of society can be expected.

4. Those deprived of authority in a given association are both less acquiescent to the imperative control of the association and more likely to view it as illegitimate than those exercising authority functions.

5. Those who either consider themselves upwardly mobile or readily perceive opportunities for upward mobility are less likely to engage in classlike behavior than those who either consider themselves socially stationary or are less optimistic about mobility opportunities in society.

6. By extension of this logic, moreover, those who have actually experienced mobility (especially the upward kind)—and hence are most likely to perceive mobility opportunities—are less likely to engage in classlike behavior than those who have not experienced mobility.

IV

MAX WEBER: CLASS, STATUS, AND PARTY

We have deferred the presentation of Max Weber (1864–1920), perhaps the best known of all students of stratification, because Pareto, in the essential elements of his work, came chronologically before Weber. At the same time, Dahrendorf's emphasis on dichotomous class formation and authority structures is decidedly a synthesis of Marxian and Paretian theories. Like Pareto and Dahrendorf, however, Weber must be viewed as moving in the Marxian orbit. Indeed, perhaps more than any other major sociologist, this scholar engaged in what Salomon (1945:596) has termed "a long and intense dialogue with the ghost of Karl Marx." Almost the entirety of Weber's work may be considered an effort either to answer Marx's arguments or to pursue the issues and problems posed by him.

WEBER VERSUS MARX IN THE LITERATURE

A curious fact about Weber is that among students of social stratification he has quite varying reputations. By and large, in the United States, he is deemed the most important theorist and consequently the most influential source of ideas in this area.[1] His name is also almost certain to pop up whenever

---

[1]An interesting exception is provided by Oliver Cox (1950:227), who argued at the other extreme that Weber's position is "too generalized and inconsistent to be of any considerable value as a source of fundamental suggestions in understanding the phenomena" of social stratification.

Marx's work is considered. In the hasty and usually unwarranted comparisons that invariably ensue, Marx typically emerges as the inferior of Weber. Marx's theory is generally presented as a "monistic, economic view" (Barber, 1957:-224) of social structure that is "too simple and sweeping to fit the facts of the system of *social* classes" (MacIver and Page, 1959:362). It represents a vast oversimplification of the historical process presented in "glib and superficial" terms (Kahl, 1953:5).

By contrast, Weber's contribution to social stratification is usually characterized as "great." Even as Marxian a scholar as C. Wright Mills (1959:52n) could feel justified in saying that Marx "is quite unfinished and much too simple about classes; he did not write a theory of classes, although Max Weber finished one version which . . . Marx would have liked." The consensus on this question, however, is not unanimous. Lenski (1966:18), by contrast, holds that Weber "never developed a systematic theory of stratification."

Some of the condemnations of Marx's thought are well justified. Reissman (1959:55), for instance, is correct in arguing that Marx did not give adequate attention to the psychological consequences of class for individuals; and Veblen (1899) and Pareto, among many others, long ago had made analogous observations. As has been noted, Marx undoubtedly underestimated the "psycho-economic" (Feuer, 1959:xvi) dimension of human behavior: the selfishness, the striving for social success and recognition, the need for superiority.

Often, however, criticisms of Marx tend to be indiscriminate. The following statement, for example, is puzzling in its unfavorable comparison of Marx to Weber:

The hard structure of a stratification system as well as the dynamics that propelled it could be accounted for more parsimoniously and could be handled with greater analytical ease by Weber's analysis than by that of Marx (Reissman, 1959.57).

Again, it is not possible to agree with Kahl (1953:7), whose otherwise excellent textbook has helped train many students of social stratification, when he proposes that "Weber took Marx's notion of class and broke it into three components. He showed how they tended to coalesce, but not in any mechanical and automatic way." In what follows we hope to show that Weber did less to Marx's concept of class than Kahl suggests.

In contrast to United States students of social inequality, their European colleagues place generous stress on Marx's theory and tend to underestimate the contributions of Weber. Thus, in his volume on *Prestige, Class and Mobility,* Svalastoga (1959) refers to Weber mostly for his exquisite manner of rigorously defining sociological concepts—his taxonomy. And the same can be said of Dahrendorf himself. An outstanding exception is provided by Bottomore (1966:24), who holds that Max Weber was "the first to present a comprehensive alternative to Marx's theory." This scholar, however, is really uncertain about the value of Weber's work, for only a few pages later (34) he argues that the criticisms of Marx's theory, which include Weber's work and others mainly based on Weber's thought, "do not amount as yet to a comprehensive new theory, which can take the place of that which Marx proposed. They provide, rather, a more or less systematic inventory of the outstanding problems" of social stratification.

It is not unlikely that ideological differences operate among scholars to produce comparative assessments of Marx and Weber. European students tend to be concerned with problems of conflict and structural change in society. Furthermore, their approach to systems of institutionalized inequality tends toward deliberately simplifying relationships, their class schemes being employed as heuristic constructs rather than as descriptive devices. "Class" is a methodological tool which facilitates the study of major cleavages and their attendant changes in society. In this approach, Marx's theory—or some variation thereof—is manifestly important.

By contrast, students in the United States are inclined to emphasize descriptive aspects of social stratification. Additionally, they are most frequently concerned with questions of prestige, social distance, consumption patterns, and the like, while problems of conflict tend to be overlooked. Weber's work here is especially relevant because, as we shall see, he placed heavy emphasis on precisely such phenomena.

There is a certain irony in these differences. United States culture, heavily influenced by elite and managerial ideology, is a powerful obstacle to the recognition of the various problems of class inequalities. As a result, sociologists in the United States neglected for a long time the analysis of class phenomena (Reissman, 1959: Chapter I). When they finally were led to a recognition of them—probably under the influence of the Great Depression and the end of a "frontier psychology" which depicted a highly fluid society —they took the concept of class too seriously and with a certain misunderstanding. Eager to demonstrate the presence or absence of classes, they set out with might and main to find them—or to miss them. The result was a sort of theoretical compromise: what they found were many, but not clearly definable, classes. The difficulty of delineation was apparently due to the fact that men and their groups were unequal not merely along one social dimension, but along a plethora of dimensions: wealth, prestige, ethnicity, religion, and even manners, to mention but a few. The "discovery" was made, moreover, that, far from seeking common action based on similar economic conditions, men were ever so eager to make and sustain all sorts of social distinctions. Lost was Marx's important lesson that pointed toward events such as the great social reforms of the 1930's as structural changes resulting from conflict between the privileged and the underprivileged—whatever the degree of consciousness of kind among the latter. One suspects that "only in America" was it possible for a young sociologist (who has since developed rare theoretical acumen) to inquire whether "social classes" were "statistical strata or social groups" (Lenski, 1952).

Little wonder, then, that United States students of social stratification have produced a great number of community studies where the prestige gradient could easily titillate one's taxonomic imagination. By contrast, studies of conflict, tensions, and social change were largely neglected until recent times. In this neglect, Weber's position on social stratification has unwittingly been a powerful influence.

To the ideological harmony between Weber's approach and the background of "the American character" can be added another factor to explain Weber's popularity in the United States. Although his statements on social stratification are many and strewn throughout his many brilliant works, his basic, though not "definitive," position is neatly presented in only a few pages (Weber, 1921–1922, II:926–939). By contrast to Marx's monumental and widely scattered theory, it can be apprehended with relatively little effort. Understandably, people whose interest in Marx's work is secondary do not have the time to engage in a detailed analysis of it.

THREE ORDERS OF SOCIAL STRATIFICATION

While Weber's general sociology is informed by a skillful application of the historical method, his work on social stratification is more restricted in scope. It represents a modest attempt to demonstrate the shortcomings of what seems to be a predominantly economic analysis and to fill in some of the details of a descriptive approach, which Marx's dynamic and analytic approach had by necessity de-emphasized.

The central point of Weber's argument is that social stratification is a reflection of the unequal distribution of power. Whatever the form of a system of stratification, a person's standing in it is determined by his power, namely by "the chance of a man or of a number of men to realize their own will in a social action even against the resistance of others who are participating in the action" (Weber, 1921–1922, II:926). Since power can be expressed in more than one way—that is, since it derives from different kinds of resources—a system of stratification presents more than one dimension according to which a man has a standing. This point concerning the multidimensionality of stratification was recognized by Marx and explicitly made by Pareto. Weber, however, was the most emphatic about it; indeed, it represents the shell into which the entirety of his argument on social stratification is deliberately fitted.

It is Weber's contention that an individual is simultaneously a member of three different "orders" of stratification and that, while these are very often superimposed, they sometimes work at cross purposes. Typically, however, the relationship among them is one of interdependence and functional correlation. They are (1) *the economic order,* which refers to "the way in which economic goods and services are distributed," and which features "classes," who hold "economic power"; (2) *the social order,* which refers to "the way in which social honor is distributed in a community between typical groups participating in this distribution," and features "status groups"; and (3) *the legal order,* which seems to refer to the distribution of "political power" and to a medium through which individuals or groups may work in order to enhance their chances to reach their aims, such as economic power and social honor; this order features "parties" (Weber, 1921–1922, II:926–927).

Classes

Weber's most extended discussion of class is found in the older part of *Wirtschaft und Gesellschaft,* in a rather discursive treatment of the "distribution of power within the political community" (Weber, 1921–1922, II:926–939). This section is host to a number of insights into his conception of class. But Weber did not intend it as a definitive statement. That was to come later, as one chapter in an intensive terminological and conceptual analysis designed to complement (and precede) the far-ranging historical materials of Part II. As with Marx's corresponding chapter, death interrupted completion of Weber's planned work. In consequence, the "definitive statement" remains nothing but a series of notes which Weber had recorded for later use (1921–1922, I:302–307).

This circumstance has left much of what Weber did say about class rather confusing. Try as one might, a systematic, internally consistent conceptualization of class will prove elusive if every phrase or sentence is taken at face value. Too much of the connective tissue of a fully worked-out explication is missing. For one thing, the major categories of his taxonomy of class (1921–1922, I:302–307) do not seem to be differentiated according to a uniform set of criteria. For another, definitions of the content of specific classes are not always clear, a problem that shows up most clearly when Weber (1921–1922, I:303) identifies slaves as constituting a particular class at one point in his analysis but explicitly rejects such identification elsewhere (1921–1922, II:928), stating that slaves constitute a status group "in the technical sense of the term."

Still more confusing is his inconsistent use of the fundamental concept of "property." In offering a definition, Weber (1921–1922, I:44) follows conventional usage from economics: "property" consists of appropriated rights ("advantages") as they describe the *relational* component of the market situation. It pertains to the utilization of "goods" and "services" for economic ends. "Goods" refers to material objects, including other human beings (slaves), while "services" refers to labor skills. (Weber also loosely refers to a residual category, neither "goods" nor "services," but consisting of such things as "good will.") But when Weber discusses the notion of class, "property" is often restricted to the popular sense of the material object itself. For instance, he (1921–1922, I:303; II:927) refers to people who "make a living from their property *or* their acquired skills" and to people who *"being propertyless,* have nothing to offer but their labor or the resulting products . . ." (emphases added). In speaking thus, he has seemingly removed human labor from the category of property relations, and therefore cannot logically entertain the possibility of an *alienated* human labor.

If one looks beneath the surface of confusion, however, and ignores some of the inconsistencies of detail, the outlines of a more or less coherent conception of class can be recorded. In many respects, it is quite similar to Marx's conception.

Beginning on a Marxian key, Weber contends that the basic distinction in all class situations is between property and the lack of property, between "owners" and "non-owners." Having specified these categories, he, like Marx, then points out that within each there are historically dissimilar classes, differentiated "on the one hand, according to the kind of property that is usable for returns; and, on the other hand, according to the kind of services that can be offered in the market" (1921–1922, II:928). Ignoring his apparent juxtaposition of the generic (property) to the specific (services), we perceive that Weber as well as Marx envisions a number of classes in historical society, the interests of which are often divergent in all directions.

On the basis of these differentiations—first, between those who have property and those who lack property; second, within each of those—Weber is led to his famous taxonomy of class, the major types being (1) "property classes," (2) "acquisition classes," and (3) "social classes." Some of the more superficial confusion surrounding this taxonomy has undoubtedly stemmed from Weber's use of the generic "property" as a designator of a particular type; it can give the impression that somehow the acquisition classes have nothing to do with property, which is of course contradictory to his prior statement that property or the lack thereof is the basic distinction in *all* class situations.

Before proceeding with our explication of Weber's taxonomy, we should review his own descriptions. A class is a *property class,* says Weber (1921–1922, I:302–304), when its members' "class situation" "is primarily determined by property differences." Logically, property classes can be "positively privileged" (composed of owners) or "negatively privileged" (composed of non-owners). Within each of these categories, in turn, further types can be isolated. The negatively privileged property classes may consist of (1) those who are themselves the objects of ownership (that is, slaves; although, as noted above, Weber earlier denied that slaves could constitute a class, and correctly so); (2) the "declassed," who are excluded from the economic process (again, it is unclear how these constitute a *class*); (3) debtors; and (4) "paupers." Similarly, positively privileged property classes, who typically live from property income, may be divided in terms of the specific source of income, that is, in terms of their specific property rights. Such rights may be in human beings, in land, in mines, in fixed equipment such as plant and machinery, in ships, and so on. The primary significance of positively privileged class (whether property or acquisition, for that matter) lies in the ability of the class members to "monopolize" various kinds of "opportunities" and "privileges"—for example, the executive positions in business or the privileges of socially advantageous kinds of education.

Between the positively and negatively privileged property classes stand various "middle classes" *(Mittelstandklassen)*. This term gives recognition to the fact that its members neither monopolize privileges nor completely lack property. In part the reference here is to what is commonly termed "the old middle classes"; but only in part, for Weber states explicitly that some of these people "in between" may be entrepreneurs and some may be proletarians—a new class structure is wedging in to replace the old. But we are now getting ahead of ourselves; let us turn to the second of Weber's major "types of classes."

The *acquisition class* consists of people whose class situation is determined primarily by opportunities for the exploitation of services in the market. The opportunities concern largely the supply and demand of special skills. Where these skills are rare and the demand for them is high, we have "positively privileged" acquisition classes. These classes include entrepreneurs of various types: "merchants, shipowners, industrial and agricultural entrepreneurs, bankers and financiers." Under certain circumstances, members of the "liberal" professions, with privileged positions resulting from their abilities or training, and "workers with monopolistic qualifications and skills" also belong to positively privileged acquisition classes. The services they provide on the basis of their rare and especially valuable skills yield for them a certain monopolistic control in the market (Weber, 1921–1922, I:304). Conversely, people whose skills are in great supply are negatively privileged members of the acquisition class. These include the "*laborers* with varying qualifications," which Weber divides by the well-known labels of "skilled, semiskilled, unskilled" (Weber, 1921–1922, I:304).

As in the case of the property classes, intermediate between the positively and negatively privileged acquisition classes are the "middle" classes. These include "self-employed farmers and craftsmen," frequently officials in private or public employment, workers "with exceptional qualifications," and practitioners of the "liberal professions," who had been previously classified—under "certain circumstances"—as members of the positively privileged acquisition classes.

The *social class* comprises the third major type in Weber's taxonomy of classes. Weber gives this type very little attention, defining it simply as "the totality of those class situations within which individual and generational mobility is easy and typical." As such, this type of class bears a strong resemblance to the "status group," soon to be discussed. He singles out four major varieties or subtypes of social classes, which, in terms of the various relevant factors of stratification taken together, show a high degree of internal homogeneity—hence his stress above on the facility of mobility within the class. These are, first, "the working class as a whole"; second, the "petty bourgeoisie," such as small shopkeepers and proprietors of small handicraft workshops; third, "the propertyless intelligentsia and specialists" or people with special technical training; and, fourth, "the classes privileged through property and education" (Weber, 1921–1922, I:305).

As was noted earlier, Weber's taxonomy invites considerable confusion of interpretation, at least in part because of the extremely abbreviated manner in which it is presented. In order to interpret it adequately, one must bear in mind that Weber's foil is the Marxian analysis of class structure and the development of capitalist society. Thus, his first step is an economic-historical analysis of the transition from feudalism to the full market society. In its essentials, his analysis parallels Marx's. Both employ substantially the same model, and from that model both generate substantially similar class schemes as representative of the end-points of the model—one for the feudal society, the other for capitalist society. For Marx, they are the landowner class versus peasant class and the capitalist class versus wage-earner class, respectively. For Weber, they are the positively versus negatively privileged property classes and the positively versus negatively privileged acquisition classes, respectively. The distinction *within* each correlative set is between property and the lack of property. Both scholars agree that this variable can be empirically represented as a continuum, and therefore both entertain the existence of various "middle" classes or strata; but for the convenience (and power) of analysis, both agree that these intermediate variations in property may be ignored.

The historical dimension of the model—that is, the distinction *between* the correlative sets of classes—concerns not property versus lack of property but rather how appropriated rights are utilizable in the market situation. "Class situation," says Weber (1921–1922, II:928), "is . . . ultimately market situation." And "the effect of naked possession *per se* . . . is only a forerunner of real 'class' formation," a point that is entirely clear in Marx himself. One's class, therefore, is historically determined not only by the *amount* of property but also by the mode of property *utilization,* that is to say, by the manner in which appropriated rights of goods and services can be used for economic gain (see Weber, 1921–1922, II:927–928). Thus, Weber's property classes, and Marx's correlated landowner and peasant classes, are distinguished by a situation in which appropriated rights are used for "rent income" (by *rentiers*). Weber's acquisition classes, and Marx's correlated capitalist and wage-earner classes, are distinguished by a market situation in which appropriated rights are used for "profit making" (by *entrepreneurs*).

The class schemes engendered by Marx and Weber in their economic studies of particular societies constitute one order of description and analysis. Another class scheme, which can be recognized as composing a different (more abstract) order of description and analysis, was devised by both Marx and Weber as applicable to investigations of the dynamics of social change across the historical dimension specified by their model. Here, however, Marx and Weber significantly diverge. The class schemes which they had developed for their economic analyses of the feudal and capitalist societies were static idealizations, particular to the two idealized stages of socio-economic development. Marx, in order to demonstrate the dynamics of class as the propeller of human history, formulated in addition an idealized class scheme that was bound to neither particular stage of development but could commonly apply to both. Stringently following the dialectic as a heuristic, he constructed this scheme in terms of the isomorphic dichotomies of exploiter-exploited, ruler-ruled, oppressor-oppressed. Because he was most concerned with the capitalist era as the historically fructiferous stage, he usually concretized this general dichotomy in terms of bourgeoisie and proletariat.

Weber constructed an analogous class scheme, the "social classes," but it differs importantly in both content and usage. Because Weber did not consider as plausible Marx's postulation of a corporate class consciousness (due to the great heterogeneity of interests within objective classes, a point we shall later discuss), he could not adopt Marx's powerful heuristic of dialectically opposed self-conscious "class communities" as a vehicle for the analysis of social change. Thus, Weber's "social classes" tend to be synthetic of class and status-group criteria (for instance, the distinctions of education and technical training; or the scale and degree of economic "independence" of members of the petty bourgeoisie or *Kleinbürgertum*), and are therefore more detailed than the corresponding class scheme in Marx.

Status Groups

Weber's discussion of the various types and subtypes of classes represents an interesting specification, if not amplification, of Marx's position—and, as will be seen in the next section, also a sobering challenge to the postulated type of class action that was so central to Marx's theory. Weber's principal correction of the Marxian conception of class, however, is found in his discussion of "status" *(Ständische Lage),* the second of the three orders of stratification singled out by him.

In this order, like Pareto, Weber can focus on the psychological dimension of stratification that, as already noted, Marx had largely neglected.

In contrast to the economic order, which consists of classes of people holding in common certain economic interests, the social order comprises "status groups" *(Stände)*—groups of people who share a specific "style of life." Whereas the class situation of an individual concerns his portion of control over commodities on the market, his "status situation" pertains to his share of the "prestige" or "social honor," which "may be connected with any quality shared by a plurality" (Weber, 1921–1922, II:932)—a mode of living, a formal process of education, the prestige of birth, an occupation (Weber, 1921–1922, I:305–306).

Weber came by the concept of status group early in his career. In his studies of the stock exchange and farm labor in eastern Germany, he had noted that such groups as *Junkers,* industrialists, and civil servants displayed a subculture that was sometimes independent of their economic status. To contract a "good marriage," for instance, was not wholly a question of securing a wealthy spouse; it was also a matter of marrying someone who was not beneath one's *Stand* (status group). This *status*-consciousness indicated to Weber that the collective actions of groups could not be understood in economic terms alone. It was also necessary to know the social and psychological idiosyncrasies of each group—its style of life, in Weber's terminology (Bendix, 1960:104–105).

The behavior of men in the flesh—not those men wishfully imagined by Marx—shows that where economic equality exists, men often take recourse to less tangible factors (such as "culture," "taste," family lineage, the type of clothes worn on the job) in order to set one another apart. Indeed, Weber held, it is easier to make common cause on such esoteric bases, and to create a feeling of community as well, than on the basis of common economic interests. The search for status and honor, the need for social superiority, the desire to be distinct—all are very powerful human qualities. Status equals seek one another and maintain free interaction among themselves. At the same time, they jockey for recognition from their social superiors *and* they limit interaction with those inferior to themselves. The irony is, in short, that the consciousness of kind which Marx saw as a tendency of class was in fact a tendency toward the association of *socially exclusive* groups and the dissociation of broad classes economically conceived. Implicitly or explicitly, the emphasis on status groups is one of the chief corrective thrusts made into Marx's thought by Weber as well as by Pareto.

Classes, as we shall see again, are not communities, according to Weber, though they are possible bases for communal action. By contrast, status groups usually represent communities, namely, collectivities wherein continuous and intimate relationships are to be found. Prestige evaluations and judgments of social honor require generally accepted standards of evaluation and more or less intimate knowledge of those who receive such evaluations. This fact clearly puts some serious limitations on the size of a group of social peers. Perhaps for this reason, status groups tend toward exclusiveness and closure. They tend to monopolize both the opportunities and the symbols conferring honor upon them in order to keep those symbols meaningful and to maintain the social distance separating them especially from inferior groups. If everybody could join the Daughters of the American Revolution, it could hardly be an honor to belong to such an organization.

The goal of exclusiveness can be achieved through legal means, such as laws controlling expenditure for items of consumption, or merely through custom and convention. In all cases, the natural tendency of status groups is in the direction of becoming a caste, which in Weber's work may properly be viewed as the "ideal type" of the status group. "All the obligations and barriers that membership in a status group entails also exist in a caste, in which they are intensified to the utmost degree" (Weber, 1920–1921:39–40). Status distinctions in a society wherein status groups are set apart to such extreme degree are guaranteed not only by laws and conventions but also by rituals. According to Weber (1921–1922, II:933),

This occurs in such a way that every physical contact with a member of any caste that is considered to be lower by the members of a higher caste is considered as making for a ritualistic impurity and a stigma which must be expiated by a religious act. In addition, individual castes develop quite distinct cults and gods.

Given Weber's definition of classes and status groups, what then is the causal relation between the two? Weber was not unaware of the fact that status distinctions could be reflections of class distinctions. In the long run, he pointed out, property is recognized as a status qualification "with extraordinary regularity." "But status honor need not necessarily be linked with a class situation. On the contrary, it normally stands in sharp opposition to the pretensions of sheer property" (Weber, 1921–1922, II:932). Witness the difficulty encountered by the *parvenu* in his search for recognition from the old-established, often less wealthy, members of exclusive circles. Again, propertied and propertyless people can often belong to the same status group, as the case of rich nobility and impoverished aristocracy can attest.

The important point Weber wishes to make is that there is no necessary correspondence between class status and social status. Nor is social status always determined by class status. Indeed, if a relationship does exist between them—as in fact between any combination of all three orders of stratification—it is likely to be one of interdependence. Thus, "every definite appropriation of political powers and the corresponding economic opportunities tends to result in the rise of status groups, and vice versa" (Weber, 1921–1922, I:306).

Among the reasons suggested by Weber for the fact that status honor can influence the class situation, one is particularly worthy of note.

Social honor can adhere directly to a class situation, and it is also, indeed most of the time, determined by the average class situation of the status-group members. This, however, is not necessarily the case. Status membership, in turn, influences class situation in that the style of life required by status groups makes them prefer special kinds of property or gainful pursuits and reject others (Weber, 1920–1921:39).

It may be seen that in his dialogue with Marx, Weber's discussion of the status order has an extreme importance. As Bottomore (1966:25–26) has noted, stratification by prestige affects Marx's class conception in two important ways. First, it interposes between Marx's two major classes a range of status groups which bridge the gulf, so to speak. Second, it suggests a social hierarchy of a continuum of status positions, based on a wide variety of factors, that is incompatible with the formation of class camps in profound conflict with each other. The relations between status groups are relations of avoidance or emulation, not of conflict. The upshot of all this is a formidable check on the growth of the type of class consciousness which was envisioned by Marx. We shall return to this question shortly.

Parties

Weber's discussion of the third order of social stratification, the legal order, is both scanty and somewhat confusing. The argument seems to be predicated on the assumption that man is a power-seeking being—and for understandable reasons. The attainment of "legal" power naturally facilitates the maintenance or acquisition of status and class privileges. Aggregates of people communally oriented toward the acquisition of power constitute "parties." Whereas for Marx, however, a party was the class grown aware of itself, for Weber, parties might represent status groups, classes, and other groupings in society as well. "In principle, parties may exist in a social club as well as in a state." Moreover, the goal of party action is not necessarily a "cause" directed at a class utility, to use Pareto's terminology. It can also be "Personal sinecures, power, and from these, honor for the leader and the followers of the party. Usually the party aims at all these simultaneously" (Weber, 1921–1922, II:938).

Party actions are always directed toward a goal that is pursued in a planned manner.

Parties are, therefore, only possible within groups that have an associational character, that is, some rational order and a staff of persons available who are ready to enforce it. For parties aim precisely at influencing this staff, and if possible, to recruit from it party members (Weber, 1921–1922, II:938).

Weber, it may be seen, stresses the competitive aspect of human behavior. Parties exist in a house of power. They are formed or joined by people who would influence the administrative structures and functions of their milieu in order to obtain privileges and to *realize their own will* even against the resistance of others. The aim pursued could be any number of things. It might concern economic or class interests, such as securing a favorable tariff, or status interests, such as obtaining zoning statutes favorable to maintaining intact an "exclusive" residential area. Again, the goal might pertain partly to status interests and partly to class interests; sometimes it concerns neither, as when a religious group such as the Amish endeavors to keep "outside" the larger society.

It follows that one's position in the legal order—one's potential for influencing administrative structures and functions—clearly influences one's class (economic) position and one's status position. Indeed, party action is often aimed at enhancing such positions. It is equally true, however, that the "staff" enforcing the "rational order" (the administrative personnel) may be more easily influenced by the wealthy and prestigeful than by those who are less fortunate in these respects. Hence, the legal order is influenced, in turn, by the economic and social orders. There is a systemic relationship among them— the three orders are mutually influential. The causal reciprocity, however, does not obtain inevitably. "Not all power," for instance, "entails social honor." Weber points to "the typical American Boss" as an example of a politically powerful individual who "deliberately relinquishes social honor" (Weber, 1921–1922, II:926).

Clearly, Marx's emphasis on the economic factor meets here with sound admonition for greater analytical precision. At least three dimensions of social stratification are worth close consideration, not one. Usually, the three are mutually dependent, but sometimes they are in fact independent of each other. What remains to be done obviously is to determine, if at all possible, whether the mutual dependence among the three orders, when it exists, is entirely symmetrical. Is one of the three orders more powerful in influencing the others? And if so, under what conditions? For Marx, the economic order was the one "ultimately" asserting itself, though *not* the only significant order. It was most powerful at all times, but especially in periods of rapid economic expansion and industrialization. Weber seldom gave answers to these and like questions, and when he did, he tended to agree with Marx. We shall have to return to this issue in the final section of the chapter.

In conclusion of this section, we may more specifically note a few interesting theoretical effects of Weber's argument. As in Pareto's analysis, but more systematically, Weber's emphasis on multiple and not always perfectly congruous dimensions of stratification clearly indicates the possibility, increasingly examined in recent years, that an individual holds inconsistent or discrepant statuses and that the *discrepancy* is associated with special types of behavior —a radical political orientation, for instance. We shall examine this question in Chapter XV. Again, Weber's entire argument has the effect of showing that *men are power-seeking beings;* they tend to pursue goals for selfish, not altruistic, reasons, imposing their will on others if they can have their way. Add to this the proposition, clearly derivable from Weber's discussion, that *men are also status-seeking beings,* and the Paretian argument recurs, perhaps more forcefully, that class consciousness and then classlessness, as conceived by Marx, are goals which, like a chimera, may be forever pursued but never reached. We should expect to find interesting support for these propositions in the remaining parts of the volume.

CLASS CONSCIOUSNESS

The issue of class consciousness or class action has been touched on various occasions. This is now a good place to pursue it somewhat more systematically. The generally negative relation of the social and legal orders to class consciousness has already been briefly treated. We need only repeat here that the search for power is a selfish phenomenon; it is, moreover, directed toward influencing authority structures, not toward their radical transformation; finally, we might add that it tends to be predicated on considerations of immediate relevance and value rather than on long-range and abstract goals such as equality and justice. Similarly, the search for prestige is paradoxically a phenomenon that is *dis*sociative in the very act in which it is *as*sociative: it presents a situation in which "birds of a feather flock together" in order to maintain social distance from others; in the process, the actual unity that can theoretically exist on an economic or class basis is undermined.

Weber's treatment of classes is equally indicative of the powerful obstacles existing in the way of concerted class action. His argument is that " 'classes' are not communities; they merely represent possible, and frequent, bases for social action" (Weber, 1921–1922, II:927). Indeed, as Hodges (1964:50) notes, for most members of a class, "parallel material circumstances must eventually give rise to parallel styles of life." Hence, classes tend to change in the direction of status groups, with all that this transformation entails in the way of undermining what Weber termed "organized class activity" by large masses of disparate though related economic statuses.

One important effect of Weber's conceptualization of class is to greatly increase the number of class interests existent on the market. Consider in this connection the following statement:

Associations of class members—class organizations—may arise on the basis of all three types of classes [property, acquisition, social]. However, this does not necessarily happen. "Class situation" and "class" refer only to the same (or similar) interests which an individual shares with others. In principle, the various controls over consumer goods, means of production, assets, resources and skills each constitute a *particular* class situation. A *uniform* class situation prevails only when completely unskilled and propertyless persons are dependent on irregular employment (Weber, 1921–1922, I:302).

Given the plethora of class interests, the possibility of massive concerted class action is not very considerable. The fact, moreover, that some persons (like those completely unskilled) are in a strictly identical class situation does not lead automatically to organized activity. Concerted action within the class is hindered by various factors. There are intellectual differences that undermine a common economic interest. Not all members of the class are constitutionally qualified for concerted action to an equal degree. The membership may or may not expect "promising results" from class action. Moreover, the concerted pursuit of objectively common interests is linked "to the extent of the contrasts that have already evolved, and is especially linked to the transparency of the connections between the causes and the consequences of the class situation" (Weber, 1921–1922, II:929).

Elsewhere, Weber (1921–1922, I:305) considers factors that favor organized class activity in the Marxian sense of the term. They include (1) the *similarity of class situation* for large masses of people; (2) the technical possibility of being easily brought together, in other words, facility of communication and-/or physical concentration of workers; and (3) leadership directed to readily understandable goals, which generally are "imposed" or "interpreted" by persons, such as the *intelligentsia*, who do not belong to the class in question. To these three echoes of Marx's own argument, Weber adds a fourth and crucial one, which we have already encountered in connection with Dahrendorf's discussion of "the separation of ownership and control": "Class-conscious organization succeeds most easily against the immediate economic opponents (workers against entrepreneurs, but *not* against stockholders, who truly draw 'unearned' incomes, and also *not* in the case of peasants confronting manorial lords)" (Weber, 1921–1922, I:305).

These factors or conditions are not, as the fourth one clearly shows, easily satisfied. The massive class as conceived by Marx is therefore likely to be continuously fragmented into numerous smaller classes and numerous status groups, with the result that class action, though possible especially on a small scale, is unlikely on a Marxian level.

WEBER AND MARX REVISITED

However inadequate and poorly coordinated with the course of historical events, Marx's work on social classes constitutes a theory, an attempted explanation of the development and conceivable resolution of a particular type of social inequality. Hence, it is above all a theory of social change—an area of knowledge that is still today scarce in social science. By contrast—despite the previously noted contention by Mills that Weber finished one version of a theory which Marx, who allegedly did not have one, "would have liked"—Weber did not have a theory of stratification at all.

Above all, *in his specific statements on stratification*, Weber showed little interest in the changes registered by social structures.[2] Rather, he addressed himself largely to the question, "How does a given society look at a given point in time?" In so doing, Weber treated us to a largely morphological analysis, while Marx had engaged in the analysis of the dynamics of class inequalities. Whereas Marx endeavored to present a "big picture" of class divisions, class relations, and social change, Weber, like many others of Marx's critics, focused

---

[2]Which is not to say that he was not interested in social change. His famed study (1904–1905) of the development of capitalism is a milestone as a study of social change.

on the details of really or potentially divergent interests and values to be found in social hierarchies and their varying dimensions.

Interesting enough, however, on those occasions when Weber addressed himself to the problem of social change, he emphasized, like Marx, the "class situation." The statement below clearly reveals this fact, in addition to inviting consideration of the fact that, while Marx wrote at a time when society was in the throes of the industrial revolution, Weber took pen in hand at a time of relative industrial stability.

When the bases of the acquisition and distribution of goods are relatively stable, stratification by status is favored. Every technological repercussion and economic transformation threatens stratification by status and pushes the class situation into the foreground. Epochs and countries in which the naked class situation is of predominant significance are regularly the periods of technical and economic transformations. And every slowing down of the change in economic stratifications leads, in due course, to the growth of status structures and makes for a resuscitation of the important role of social honor (Weber, 1921–1922, II:938).

The analysis here is quite Marxian, with one reservation: there is an implication in it that is quite at odds with Weber's usual penchant for reversible propositions. It is not the class formation that produces social change, Weber seems to argue, but technological and economic change that produces the class formation. In this case at least, Marx had been much more explicit in stating a reciprocal relationship. For the development of classes produced economic transformation just as this transformation enhanced the development of classes.

Contrary to widespread belief, Weber had little intention to complete Marx's theory of classes, far less to supersede it. He felt much more obliged to "the great thinker's" work than do most contemporary sociologists. Despite the thunderous reception given to his work, he appears to have seen himself more in the role of the devil's advocate than in the role of Marx's substitute —perspicaciously, even if fleetingly, uncovering social complexities hidden in the huge intellectual heap left behind by the Marxian synthesis. The only role that Weber truly cherished for himself was that of demonstrating the inadequacy of a pure economic determinism. In this he was successful, more or less, but his argument was with the "vulgar Marxists," by and large, not with Marx himself.

In a manner of speaking, Weber was an economic determinist in his own right. He was greatly appreciative of the centrality of the economic factor in human affairs. There was, however, an important difference of strategy between Marx and himself. Where Marx had used the very term "economic" as a big umbrella to cover a broad range of culture, Weber parceled the concept into three sharp analytical distinctions. In introducing to the public the famous journal *(Archiv für Sozialwissenschaft und Sozialpolitik)* that just after the turn of the century he edited with some friends in Munich, Weber observed:

Like the science of social-economics since Marx and Roscher, our journal is concerned not only with economic phenomena but also with those which are "economically relevant" and "economically conditioned." The domain of such subjects extends naturally . . . through the totality of cultural life (Weber, 1904:65).

Thus, the phenomena of the stock exchange and the banking world, for instance, are *economic phenomena*. Other phenomena, though not exclusively economic in nature, may have consequences which are of interest from the economic point of view. In his famed *The Protestant Ethic and the Spirit of Capitalism* (1904–1905), he tried to show, for instance, that the rise of bourgeois capitalism, as Marx had defined it, required not only certain changes in production technology and in class structure but required also a transformation in values concerning the nature of work and the utilization of profit. The ethic of the ascetic branches of Protestantism, Weber argued, favored diligence at work and a rational utilization of profit. In short, ideas, even the otherworldly ideas of religion, have the power to produce change in such profoundly secular areas as the economic structures of a society. Such aspects of culture are *economically relevant* phenomena. Finally, there are noneconomic, but economically influenced, aspects of culture, such as "the social stratification of the artistically interested public." These Weber termed *economically conditioned* phenomena (1904:64–66).

Such distinctions clearly made possible a more detailed view of culture and provided Weber with multiple perspectives from which to look causally at culture. In so doing, however, he did not really damage Marx's position. Nor did he really add very much beyond what was logically implicit, if not entirely explicit, in Marx's thought and in much of the thinking before him, since him, and surrounding him.

As we have suggested, Marx's conception of classes, and indeed his entire theory, was presented in the form of scientific idealizations. Weber himself was among the first to note that

Marxian "laws" and developmental constructs—insofar as they are theoretically sound —are ideal types. The eminent, indeed unique, *heuristic* significance of these ideal types when they are used for the *assessment* of reality is known to everyone who has ever employed Marxian concepts and hypotheses. Similarly, their perniciousness, as soon as they are thought of as empirically valid or as real . . . is likewise known to those who have used them (Weber, 1904:103).

In short, if we are to take Weber seriously (and those of us who take him in earnest on other grounds should do so here, too), formulation and causality in Marx's thought must be judged for their heuristic value. In so far as causal relationships are concerned, Marx's heavy emphasis on the economic factor was a deliberate strategy of oversimplification. Its aim, so to speak, was to invite and encourage elaboration. It must be noted, however, that scientific simplification is usually made in order to give guidance to the *empirical* part of inquiry. Weber's addition—some say "correction," others "supersedure"—

to Marx was largely speculative or classificatory. But, one might argue, Marx himself or another genius like him might have done likewise had he not deliberately simplified matters for heuristic purposes. The net balance of Weber's contribution must, therefore, remain a fascinating question mark.

Beyond this, a question arises concerning the value of the "functional correlation" approach suggested as a desideratum in Weber's multidimensional perspective. The major issues here are two: One concerns the ideas of "functional interdependence" and "multiple causation"; their value for analysis can hardly be overestimated. The other pertains to the question of whether the strategy of multiple causation, specifically the tendency to state "reversible" rather than "deterministic" propositions, can be put to formal use. If not, it is a strategy of empty words.

It is easy enough to emphasize interdependence, as both Pareto and Weber so freely did; it is even desirable. But the concept merely complicates mental images and is of little or no scientific value at all unless its logic can be formally implemented in actual research. Marx had emphasized the "economic" factor because he assumed that work and making a living were the central aspect of man's existence. However, to say that the economic factor determines an entire superstructure is not necessarily to say that there is no reciprocal relationship between the two. It may merely mean, according to the logic of system analysis, that in the set of system reciprocities, the economic factor has the greatest weight. As Sidney Hook (1965:58) suggests with respect to Pareto's own method of functional correlation, in the absence of an experimental situation that makes it possible to assign specific causal weights to the system (mutually dependent) variables, to say merely that there is a reciprocal relationship among variables is no better (and it may be worse) than to say less ornately that X determines Y.

What is further worthy of note is that the moment the researcher leaves the realm of methodological finesse to enter the world of actual research, he—whether Marx, Weber, or Pareto—tends to drop the idea of functional correlation in favor of a more convenient deterministic analysis. Thus, in his essay on social stratification, Weber seemed to be permanently committed to reversible propositions. When, however, he engaged in explanation, as in *The Protestant Ethic and the Spirit of Capitalism,* he too found it handy to seek out a *major differentiating factor,* the "Protestant Ethic." In the essay on stratification, Weber could never go wrong because he stated a methodological desideratum rather than theoretical propositions. In the brilliant essay on religion and capitalism, he may have gone wrong, at least in part; nevertheless, he attempted an explanation of a phenomenon—and the explanation was largely in deterministic terms.

The excessive emphasis on religious values grew out of Weber's polemical stance in relation to Marx, whose economic determinism had somewhat deemphasized the role of ideas in historical events. Weber's intention was to show that the economic factor could be fruitfully treated as a dependent variable as well as an independent one. Modern man, he argued, was "unable to give religious ideas a significance for culture and national character which they deserve." He fully realized, however, that "it would also further be necessary to investigate how Protestant Asceticism was in turn influenced in its development and its character by the totality of social conditions, especially economic." Indeed it was

not [his] aim to substitute for a one-sided materialistic an equally one-sided spiritualistic causal interpretation of culture and of history. Each is equally possible, but each, if it does not serve as the preparation, but as the conclusion of an investigation, accomplishes equally little in the interest of historical truth (Weber, 1904–1905: 183).

The problem is that the influence of economic conditions on Protestant asceticism was *not* investigated by Weber. Nor can he be easily excused for his failure to investigate merely on the grounds that he really had no intention to substitute one type of one-sided explanation for another. Poppycock grinds no flour. Weber's actions necessarily speak louder than his words, and it would, therefore, seem that by his own standards they accomplished "little in the interest of historical truth." What remains is the type of one-sided analysis that Weber found so misleading in Marxian thought. Weber's failure to practice the method of functional correlation and his overemphasis of a "spiritualistic causal interpretation," admittedly for illustrative and polemical purposes, were all the less excusable when one considers that, as was noted in our first chapter, Marx had overemphasized the economic factor in order to correct German idealism, which had neglected economic factors.

In conclusion, one is tempted to wonder what gives rise to the uncritical glorification of Weber's contribution to social stratification, and conversely to the usual aversion to Marx's theory, in the writings of United States sociologists. Are these valuations based on judicious, scientific decisions, or do they display ideological aspects of these scholars' thought? That Marx failed to present a complete, coherent, and everlastingly valid theory of stratification goes without saying. But the tendency among these sociologists to dismiss that theory in favor of Weber's simple and not always very fruitful efforts to clarify and specify the theory does justice neither to Marx nor to Weber, and still less to the science of society.

We suspect that the facile and uncritical recourse to Weber betrays an ideological aversion to the ideological aspects of Marx's theory. The recourse to brilliant Weber, in a manner which Weber himself would not have condoned, possibly alleviates the scientific guilt, so to speak, induced by our aversion. The fable of the redeeming hero is of all periods of social thought.

V

KINGSLEY DAVIS AND WILBERT E. MOORE: FUNCTIONAL IMPORTANCE AND SOCIAL INEQUALITY

The fifth and final theory of stratification to be considered here has been the focus of heated controversy for about a quarter of a century. In 1945, Kingsley Davis (1908—) and Wilbert E. Moore (1914—) published "Some Principles of Stratification." Then in 1948, Davis republished the theory in amended form in a volume on general sociology. It is this latter version that we should rely on for our purposes, all the more so since Davis has shown some impatience with critics who prefer the less comprehensive 1945 joint statement. However, in view of the substantial similarities between the two constructions, we shall often have to treat the 1948 rendition as a joint effort.

THE THEORY

Unlike the formulations presented so far, the Davis-Moore theory is not concerned with the delineation of classes and the specification of conflict bases. Rather, it addresses itself to the *universal causes* of social stratification, that is, the organization of "unequal rewards attached to different positions" in society. It is a theory that endeavors to explain the universality of social stratification *whatever* its particular form in time and space.

Davis and Moore begin by noting that, barring very small primitive communities, no society can be found that is unstratified. At the same time, the form of stratification varies remarkably from one society to another. Accordingly, a full analysis of stratification phenomena would require two different approaches: one to explain the *universal features* of stratification, the other to explain its *variable features.* Davis and Moore deliberately address themselves only to the former.

A search for the fundamental causes of social stratification yields what the authors term "the functional necessity of stratification." Any society, they argue, must insure that its members will occupy the positions of its social structure and will be *induced* to perform the demands of those positions. Every society must solve "the problem of motivation at two levels: to instill in the proper individuals the desire to occupy certain positions and, once in these positions, the desire to perform the duties attached to them" (Davis, 1948:366). By and large, "the proper individuals" are those best qualified for given positions and most diligent in the performance of their duties.

Davis and Moore note that the roles associated with the various positions in society are not equally "pleasant." Nor are they equally important to "social survival" and equally dependent "on the same ability or talent." If they were, there would be little or no problem of social placement, for it would make no difference who got into which positions. Inevitably, then, in view of the variability of positions in terms of the above factors,

a society must have some kind of rewards that it can use as inducements and some way of distributing these rewards differently according to positions. The rewards and their distribution, as attached to social positions, thus become a part of the social order; they are the stratification (Davis, 1948:367).

In short, a society allegedly satisfies the need for a competent discharge of functions, a need inherent in its various social positions, by developing a system of unequal rewards. The specific principles underlying the distribution of rewards will be touched upon shortly. For the moment, we may note that Davis and Moore isolate three major kinds of rewards that a society has at its disposal: the *economic incentives,* contributing to "sustenance and comfort"; the *esthetic incentives,* contributing to "humor and diversion"; and the *symbolic incentives,* which contribute to "self respect and ego expansion." While there is some question about the authors' intended meanings, these probably refer roughly to income (or purchasing power), to diversion, and to esteem and prestige. Such rewards are "built into" each position and consist of the "rights" and "accompaniments or perquisites" associated with the position. "In any social system all three kinds of rewards, as well as others, must be dispensed unequally as between different positions" (Davis, 1948:367).

Now, if the rights and perquisites inherent in positions are, or must be, unequal, then "the society must be stratified, because that is precisely what stratification means."

Social inequality is thus an unconsciously evolved device by which societies insure that the most important positions are conscientiously filled by the most qualified persons. Hence every society, no matter how simple or complex, must differentiate persons in terms of both prestige and esteem and must therefore possess a certain amount of institutionalized inequality (Davis, 1948:367–368).

Determinants of Rank

Davis and Moore isolate two factors that determine differential rewards and thus the differential "rank" of different positions.

In general those positions convey the best reward and hence have the highest rank which (a) have the greatest importance for the society and (b) require the greatest training or talent. The first factor concerns the relative functional contribution of the position as compared to others; the second concerns the relative scarcity of personnel for filling the position (Davis, 1948:368).

In short, the relative rank of social positions, and therefore of their occupants, is determined by their value to social survival and by the difficulty of filling the positions in terms of the talent and training which they require. Generally speaking, the greater the functional importance of a position and the greater the difficulty in filling it, the greater the rewards that inhere in that position and, hence, the greater the status of its occupants. It cannot be emphasized enough, however, that the rank of a position is the result of the *combined* operation of both determinants. While both functional importance and scarcity of personnel are necessary to determine the relative rank of a position, neither is in itself sufficient. For instance, if a position is easily filled, that is, if there is no scarcity of personnel, it need not be abundantly rewarded even though it may be functionally very important; only sufficient rewards are needed to insure that it is competently filled. On the other hand, if it is both important and hard to fill, "the reward must be high enough to get it filled anyway." Again, if it is unimportant but hard to fill, it will probably be dropped altogether (Davis, 1948:368).

Unfortunately, Davis and Moore have not provided much help for the difficult task of establishing the functional importance of a given position. In their 1945 statement, however, they did suggest "two independent clues," namely, "(a) the degree to which a position is functionally unique, there being no other positions that can perform the same function satisfactorily; (b) the degree to which other positions are dependent on the one in question" (1945:244n). Then again in a statement replying to a criticism (Tumin, 1953a) of the 1945 article, Davis (1953:395) proposed another "rough measure" of functional importance. He suggested that in wartime, for instance, decisions must be made that give first priority to certain industries and occupations for capital equipment, labor recruitment, raw materials, and the like. Note that Davis is now making a concrete effort to put teeth in the highly abstract notion of "social survival" employed elsewhere. Survival here equates with winning the war. In times of war, when the political life of a society is at stake, the military establishment would seem to be a reasonable societal representative to establish the priorities of productive activities.

Concerning the scarcity-of-personnel variable, Davis and Moore argue that ultimately there are only two ways in which a person's qualifications with respect to a position come about, namely, through talent or inherent capacity and through training. The two are closely tied together, but the scarcity of personnel may often lie primarily in one or the other rather than equally in both. For example, some positions require such high degrees of talent that the persons to fill them are rare in the first place. Other times there is no scarcity of talent, "but the training process is so long, costly, and elaborate that relatively few can qualify."

Theoretical Qualifications

It should be clear by now that Davis and Moore do not claim that actual social conditions fit their theory exactly. The theory represents "a high degree of abstraction, because there are obviously other aspects of society which in actuality affect the operation of the [reward] element" (Davis, 1953:394). Practically speaking, this acknowledgment means that some people occupying certain positions only apparently possess the skills required by those positions —or in any case are not the best qualified for them. The full validity of the theory rests on the assumption of an unhindered competitive order in society, that is, the "full-market" model of society (see MacPherson, 1962).

The theory as presented so far, then, carries with it some major qualifications and clarifications. Two are especially important. The first is that the theory concerns "the system of positions, not the individuals occupying those positions." It is one thing, the authors argue, to ask why different rewards attach to different positions, and quite another to explain why certain individuals rather than others get into those positions. The second pertains to the phenomenon of mobility, which allegedly has received most of the theoretical attention in the discipline. The former question—why different positions carry different rewards—is, however, "logically prior" to the other question, and with this question Davis and Moore claim to be concerned.

It can now be shown that, with respect to their first qualification, the authors are not entirely consistent with the basic logic of the theory. The problem lies in the admixture of structural and social-psychological variables. Recall their previous argument that a system of stratification arises because, given the variability of functional exigencies and human talent, every society must "solve the problem of motivation." They refer to this as presenting "the functional necessity of stratification." Under the circumstances, it is impermissible to rescue the theory from the discomforts of imperfection that every theory must suffer by proposing that they are concerned with the system of positions, and not with the manner in which individuals come to occupy those positions. If the logic of the theory as a whole is predicated on the assumption that differential rewards are required in order to instill the proper motivation among human individuals, the question of whether the "right" individuals move into the "right" positions is one that the authors cannot disregard. The proper functioning of societal arrangements depends on the proper motivation of personnel, and that manifestly concerns the manner in which individuals come to occupy given positions. The proper way, the theory clearly implies, is for individuals to occupy positions because they possess the requisite skills.

The second qualification to the validity of the theory modifies the "full-market" model's assumption of free and unhindered competition. The "functional necessities responsible for stratification," Davis notes, "do not operate to the exclusion of all other functions. There are certain additional functions, equally necessary, which have the effect of limiting and guiding stratification." This point is indeed crucial. The presence of the family and the functions that it discharges require that stratification be somehow accommodated to this institution. "Such accommodation takes the form of status ascription." It is well known that every child initially inherits the status of his parents. Consequently, even in highly competitive societies, there is an initial family endowment that assists or hinders the individual in the acquisition of adult positions.

Family organization impedes to a degree the operation of the stratification system in the idealized fashion that the Davis-Moore theory conceptualizes. Nevertheless, as they point out, there is always some competition in any society, including so-called caste societies, and to this extent "it is still possible to [partially, they should have said] explain on the basis of functional importance and scarcity of personnel the general hierarchy of positions."

The presence of additional "functional necessities" in society gives Davis and Moore a clue to the explanation of differences in stratification between societies. Such differences are attributable to whatever factors affect the two basic determinants of stratification—functional importance and scarcity of personnel. By the same token, the universal presence of certain structures and functions in human society explains the fact of "an underlying similarity in the kind of positions put at the top, the kind put at the middle, and the kind put at the bottom of the scale" (Davis, 1948:371).

An Example

Davis cogently illustrates the manner in which positions come to achieve their rank. Take religious leaders, for instance. Religion is such that,

Through the worship of the sacred objects and the beings they symbolize, a powerful control over human behavior is exercised, guiding it along lines sustaining the institutional structure and promoting the ultimate values and ends (Davis, 1948:371).

If this interpretation of religion is correct, Davis continues, it is easy to see why in every known society those persons who are in charge of religious activities tend to enjoy greater rewards than ordinary members.

> There is a peculiar relation between the duties of the religious official and the special privileges he enjoys. If the supernatural world governs the destinies of men more ultimately than does the real world, its earthly representative, the person through whom one may communicate with the supernatural, must be a powerful individual. He is a keeper of sacred tradition, a skilled performer of the ritual, and an interpreter of lore and myth. He is in such close contact with the gods that he is viewed as possessing some of their characteristics. He is, in short, a bit sacred and hence free from some of the more vulgar necessities and controls (Davis, 1948:371).

In view of the great importance of religious leaders, one wonders why they do not get entire control over their societies. There are several reasons for this. In the first place, Davis notes, the amount of technological competence necessary for the performance of religious duties is small. In other words, the scarcity-of-personnel variable is so weak that it undermines the influence of functional importance. Secondly, and relatedly, given the small amount of technical competence necessary for the performance of religious duties, the priest can never be free from vulgar competition. The competition is facilitated by the fact that genuine contact with the supernatural can never be demonstrated strictly. For this reason, priestly prestige is highest where membership in the profession is rigidly controlled by the priestly guild itself, thus creating "an artificial scarcity." Again it is the vulgar competition which explains, at least partly, special practices such as elaborate devices, rituals, special diet, celibacy, and the like. Finally, in view of the priest's role as alleged mediator of contact with the transcendental, pertaining to extrascientific phenomena, the priest's status may be expected to vary inversely with the degree of scientific technology and rationality in society.

However, even in technologically advanced societies, religious leaders as a category tend to occupy prestigious positions because even in such societies "some system must exist for the integration of ultimate values, for their ritualistic expression, and for the emotional adjustments required by disappointment, death, and disaster" (Davis, 1948:373).

Social Mobility

One final note about the content of the theory concerns social mobility. Mobility is crucial to its validity. In the ideal case described by the theory, the occupancy of positions in any generation is established on the bases of talent and of motivation to undergo the appropriate training rather than on the bases of inherited privilege and of related factors. Hence, the fact does not escape Davis that even in so-called "closed systems" there is always a certain amount of upward and downward mobility. The reasons are many. Consider the case of caste India. Any such attempt to institutionalize absolute social inequality cannot escape the inherent contradiction whereby the very scale of values or standards by which one stratum is judged better than another motivates people to try to improve themselves with reference to these standards; in so far as they succeed, the community is bound to recognize their achievement by giving them more or less prestige (Davis, 1948:384).

Traditional Hindu culture places a high value on the seclusion of women, knowledge of the sacred lore, celibacy of widows, and purity of diet. It follows that any group which is able to improve its performance in conforming to these standards, such as a caste or even a family, will also improve its social status, whether within the same caste or across castes (Davis, 1948:382). By the same token, anyone relaxing the observance of rules and ideals will lose status. In this connection, Davis (1948:383) then grants a major point to Marxian theory by stating that since the observance of most of the rules is costly, "the more successful the caste is in an economic sense the more it can improve its conformity"—and thus, we might add, its social status.

Competition cannot be wholly eliminated, Davis insists, not only because "absolute inequality" is internally inconsistent but also because it is "incompatible with basic societal needs." One of these needs allegedly is some degree of social change. And this change, in turn, implies social mobility. Davis, a population expert, offers the following demographic explanation:

The moment there is social change there is also social mobility, for two reasons: (a) Any society, simply by the interaction within its structure, generates internal frictions that inevitably lead to a change of the structure. (b) The external conditions in which the society lives, and to which it must adjust if it is to survive, are constantly changing.

If, for example, we wished to have each caste and subcaste performing its own unique occupation and occupying the same rung generation after generation, a uniform rate of population replacement would be necessary in every caste. But the very notion of caste implies that there are different caste customs, and some of these customs will unavoidably affect fertility and mortality. This being true, some castes will expand in population and others will contract. For those that expand, some new occupations must be found because the caste members would be crowded out of employment in the old. For those castes that contract, replacements from other castes must be found because otherwise the necessary occupation would not be practiced. Differences in natural increase therefore prevent absolute immobility (Davis, 1948:384).

CONTROVERSY AND CRITICISM

A rather large and heterogeneous literature has developed around this, one of the most controversial theories of the sociological enterprise. Unfortunately, however, the smoke has been far out of proportion with the roast. While the battle of words has raged for a quarter of a century, only too few efforts have been made to subject the theory to empirical test. In general, the discipline has found the theory too abstract for purposes of deriving from it empirically relevant propositions. A few years ago, Arthur Stinchcombe (1963) did suggest a number of "empirical consequences" or empirically testable "derivations" of the theory. For instance, noting that the functional importance of positions can vary in time as well as in space, Stinchcombe rediscovered the testable propositions, long ago advanced by Pareto, that "in time of war the abilities of generals become more important than in time of peace," and hence the rewards of generals rise in relation to other elites. But to our knowledge, empirical studies have continued to be conspicuous by their absence (see Lopreato and Lewis, 1965).

The first major attack on the Davis-Moore theory appeared some five years after Davis published his 1948 modification. In both his original critique (1953a) and his reply to Davis (1953b), Tumin raises several interesting questions, some of which have had a pronounced impact. First, he doubts the validity of the assumption that certain positions in any society are functionally more important than others. Second, he wonders whether there are not other types of rewards significant enough to human beings to warrant consideration by the theory. Third, he takes issue with the assumed inevitability of social stratification, when the latter is viewed as a system of differentials in prestige and esteem. And, fourth, he criticizes the assumption that social stratification is positively functional to "social survival."

The last point is somewhat irrelevant to the main thrust of the Davis-Moore theory, but it is sociologically pregnant and will be treated in more detail in a later section of this chapter. The third point is incidental to the essentials of the theory, but since it has been the focus of much controversy, we shall explore it momentarily. The first two points, on the other hand, constitute the main thrust of Tumin's attack.

There is no way to demonstrate, Tumin argues, that the engineers of a factory are functionally more important to the continued operation of that factory than are the unskilled workers. And, as far as he goes, he is probably right. But he neglects to consider the variable of scarcity of personnel, which plays a crucial role in the theory as a condition to the postulated explanatory power of "functional importance." Tumin does question the role of scarcity in the theory, basing his argument on ascriptive processes in society, but in so doing he ignores Davis's 1948 modification. Even more to the point, he does not consider the scarcity variable *in relation to* functional importance; that is, he neglects the Davis-Moore postulate of functional importance as a sufficient explanatory variable *only in conjunction with* scarcity of personnel. Nevertheless, as we shall see below, there is evidence to show that functional importance, though it is taken as the basic variable by Davis and Moore, is far weaker in its causal weight than is scarcity of personnel. In this sense, then, Tumin is at least heuristically justified in raising doubts about the value of functional importance to the theory as a whole.

With respect to the criticism concerning types of rewards, Tumin proposes that in addition to the kinds of rewards or inducements considered by Davis and Moore, there are "alternative motivational schemes," such as "intrinsic work satisfaction" or what Veblen termed "instinct for workmanship." Tumin (1953a:391) wonders whether "the allocation of differential rewards in scarce and desired goods and services is the only or the most efficient way of recruiting the appropriate talent" for given positions. Whether there are additional types of inducements available for effective performance in given positions is undoubtedly a question that is both legitimate and possibly fruitful for theoretical development. That men can be induced to work effectively on all sorts of jobs for exclusively intrinsic rewards like "joy in work" is, however, a possibility for which the annals of "productive labor" provide little if any support. Moreover, the question of relative "efficiency" among varying ways of recruiting the appropriate talent for given positions is entirely irrelevant to the Davis-Moore theory, which does not state that "society" *never* fails to provide the "right" incentives.

On the matter of inevitability, Tumin argues that while stratification has been universal heretofore, it does not follow that it is inevitable. Focusing on the dimension of esteem and prestige, he claims that

no systematic effort has ever been made, under propitious circumstances, to develop the tradition that each man is as socially worthy as all other men so long as he performs his appropriate tasks conscientiously (Tumin, 1953a:392–393).

It is perhaps for this reason that, in his study of Puerto Rico, Tumin allegedly finds a widespread spirit of *dignidad,* namely a

belief that all men are ultimately equal and equally worthy of respect, regardless of temporary or even enduring differences in their material standard of living, in the formal power they exercise, or in the prestige which their occupations and educations evoke (Tumin with Feldman, 1961:18).

One suspects that there is a big sociological heart at work here. It is only unfortunate that the heart often makes one see what the mind would not concede. Elsewhere, Tumin (1953a:392) suggests that

the only items which any society *must* distribute unequally are the power and property necessary for the performance of different tasks. If such differential power and property are viewed by all as commensurate with the differential responsibilities, and if they are culturally defined as *resources* and not as rewards, then, no differentials in prestige and esteem need follow.

One wonders if Tumin is talking about the *human* animal.

The fact is that efforts have been made, in as "propitious" circumstances as one can hope for, to develop a tradition of universal *dignidad.* The kibbutzim of Israel are surely a case in point. By original intent and by initial structuring, the kibbutz emphasized a complete equality in the life of the collective. But despite a continuation of equalitarianism in *economic* rewards, a two-rank stratification of "managers" and "workers" gradually emerged. According to Rosenfeld (1951; see also Spiro, 1956), these strata resulted from a general recognition of the need for ability in leadership positions. Given the pioneering, closely circumscribed conditions of the kibbutz, satisfaction of that need was of crucial importance. But by virtue of those same conditions, ability was relatively scarce. This gap between supply and demand had two immediate consequences: (1) it put a premium of personal status on those who exhibited the greatest competence in leadership roles; and (2) it undermined the originally desired "institutionalized principle of an alternating chairmanship" (Dahrendorf, 1959:221). Those who demonstrated the most ability not only gained an added factor of esteem; they also came to be elected over and over again to managerial positions. Eventually, through a transformation in social consciousness, the locus of superior status shifted from the person (esteem) to the position (prestige). Rosenfeld (1951:768) concludes, therefore—with direct reference to the Davis-Moore argument—that in the Israeli collectives the question of "how certain individuals get into [certain] positions" is more fundamental than the question of "why different positions carry different degrees of prestige." In the kibbutz, it would seem, some people had an initial advantage of power, based at least in part on resources of knowledge and skill. In consequence, "managerial positions gained high prestige because of the initially high prestige [esteem] of the persons who became elected to fill them." Furthermore, evidence suggested that factors of social inheritance were beginning to operate. The offspring of "managers" enjoyed slightly superior qualifications for special training and higher education, and "some of the 'halo effect' of parents does fall on their children" (1951:773–774). Such evidence does great damage to Tumin's argument against the alleged inevitability of social stratification.

Beyond this, however, it can be shown that while inevitability is indeed postulated by Davis and Moore, it is an incidental, secondary aspect of the theory and does not merit the attention given to it by Tumin, among others. What is crucial to the Davis-Moore argument is the explanation of a system of stratification, *when and where it exists.* The theory must be approached with a view to the falsity or truth of its critical statements, whether these are stated explicitly or implicitly.

Another sociologist, George Huaco, has attempted a "logical analysis" of the Davis-Moore theory and found that the "problematic core of the theory lies in the postulate that different positions have unequal functional importance for the preservation or survival of the society" (Huaco, 1963:803). For him, "unequal functional importance is a complete unknown"; and as presented by Davis and Moore, "it cannot serve as a legitimate explanation for 'unequal rewards' " (Huaco, 1963:804).

Bear in mind that the concept of functional importance is conceptualized by Davis and Moore in purely structural or "systemic" terms. That is, the functional importance of a given position is allegedly determined not by actual members of a society but by the "functional necessities" of the society as a whole. There is, in short, a certain reification of the concept of society in the theory. One is led to imagine an entity existing over and beyond individual human beings that regulates their affairs and determines, in terms of its own needs, the importance of their activities. This peculiar notion flows from a sort of classical-economics model that underlies the entirety of the Davis-Moore theoretical structure. The basic problem is, ironically, that these scholars do not seem to be sufficiently appreciative of the fact that a society is a highly stratified and heterogeneous affair and that some individuals and groups in it may have the power, legitimate or otherwise, to define "functional necessities" and to impose on others the standards for the assessment of functional importance. Marx and Pareto, it may be recalled, had clearly understood this point. More recently, George Homans has restated the issue briefly but forcefully. It is not "society" in the abstract that rewards its members, Homans (1967:67) properly argues; it is the members of society—*people*—who confer rewards upon one another. Some of them, moreover, are in a position not only to receive the greatest rewards for their activities, but they are also "in a position to take them—and this is one reason why they are important."

Gerhard Lenski (1966:102–112) cogently makes an analogous point in an illuminating discussion of hunting and gathering societies, wherein "the central fact of life" is the absence of any appreciable economic surplus. In such societies, functional importance (as measured, for instance, by industry in food procurement) and personal ability and skills have a marked tendency to determine such rewards as power, privilege, and prestige. Hence, both intergenerational and intragenerational mobility is very high, for these societies "lack certain things which facilitate the transmission of advantage from one generation to the next." The lack of wealth, for instance, makes it impossible to transmit one major form of advantage from father to son. Competition and actual contribution to the needs of the group are important avenues of achievement. In this respect, the more advanced societies "differ greatly," for they exhibit class-based subcultures that make it possible for the more privileged to transmit special advantages to their children. The power of the parent, in short, often determines the "rewards" of the child, not the functional importance of the child's position, even though this may be high indeed. It would seem that the greater the division of labor in society, the greater the degree of institutionalized and self-perpetuating inequality.

The point is remarkable also for its affinity to one made over a century earlier by Karl Marx, who in turn was borrowing from Adam Smith:

the very different genius which appears to distinguish men of different professions, when grown up to maturity, is not so much the *cause* as the *effect* of the division of labour. In principle, a porter differs less from a philosopher than a mastiff from a greyhound. It is the division of labour which has set a gulf between them (Marx, 1847:129).

A few sociologists have made an effort to operationalize the functional-importance variable (see Simpson and Simpson, 1960; Lopreato and Lewis, 1963). The latter team has argued (1963; 1965) that, despite the structural conception of functional importance, the variable is fundamentally social-psychological in nature and can be articulated only in social-psychological terms. The problem here is of the same nature as that encountered in a previous context when Davis and Moore were found arguing that theirs is a theory of the causes of differential rewards accruing to positions rather than a theory of how different individuals get into those positions. Our contention then was that the basic logic of the argument invited a social-psychological perspective in view of the theory's emphasis on motivation, and that the question of the manner in which individuals come to occupy social positions cannot be entirely avoided. An analogous problem now arises in connection with the relationship between functional importance and prestige as one of the possible rewards inherent in positions.

According to Davis and Moore, social position P has functional importance Q on the basis of its contribution to some unspecified need or state X of the "society." Contribution, and hence functional importance, are abstractly conceived. If, however, we accept the argument that functional importance (in combination with scarcity of personnel) is the "cause" of rewards like prestige, something very odd happens to the abstractionism of Davis and Moore. Prestige is manifestly a social-psychological phenomenon. It is human beings in the flesh that confer prestige on each other, not the abstract agent that is "society." Hence, we must necessarily conclude that actual human beings define the functional importance of social positions; otherwise, they would be unable to confer upon each other the "correct" amount of prestige. And so it happens that a strictly societal variable turns out to be really a psychological one—or at least, it can be legitimately operationalized in psychological terms.

All this implies that functional importance can be understood only in terms of the social values existing in a society at a given time. Davis and Moore would have been well advised to consider carefully Parsons's (1953) approach to stratification, wherein the concept of social values performs a central etiological role. Earlier still, the great French sociologist Emile Durkheim (1897:249) had argued quite emphatically that

there is a dim perception, in the moral consciousness of societies, of the respective value of different social services, the relative reward due to each, and the consequent degree of comfort appropriate on the average to workers in each occupation. The different functions are graded in *public opinion* and a certain coefficient of well-being assigned to each, according to its place in the hierarchy (emphasis added).

Lopreato and Lewis (1963) have found evidence in support of Durkheim's and Parsons's positions and have further suggested that in the Davis-Moore scheme there is a variable that fairly adequately represents social values. It is the variable of prestige as a type of social reward. In a study relating four of the Davis-Moore variables—skill (or scarcity of personnel), imputed[1] func-

---

[1]Presenting a sample of interviewees in two United States communities with a list of 24 occupations, the researchers asked: "Please indicate which you think are the most *necessary* and

tional importance, prestige, and economic reward—in terms of the variables' indices on 24 occupations, they found that prestige was consistently more highly correlated with the other three variables than was any other. Moreover, using the statistical technique of partial rank correlation, they found that when functional importance was partialed out, the relationship between pairs of the other variables hardly diminished, indicating that functional importance contributed little or not at all to the correlation between the two variables. If, for example, the variables of skill and prestige were correlated without partialing out the possible influence of functional importance on these two variables, the correlation was .77. When the effect of functional importance was controlled, the correlation was reduced only slightly to .69. Conversely, when prestige was partialed out, the correlation between pairs of the other variables was greatly reduced, indicating in effect that the correlation between the two variables was to a large extent due to the effect of prestige on them. For instance, when functional importance and economic reward were correlated without controlling for prestige, the correlation was .45. On the other hand, when the influence of prestige was controlled, the correlation was reduced to .06. Lopreato and Lewis, therefore, were led to conclude that while scarcity of personnel (or skill) could properly be treated as an independent variable, functional importance, as they assessed it, was in fact dependent on prestige, or the social values that this factor represented.[2]

From the vantage point of the Davis-Moore theory, it would seem to us that men in the flesh tend to behave in a circular fashion. They first look at a given position and assess the amount of prestige that attaches to it. If the prestige is high, then they tend to view the position as having high functional impor-

---

which the least necessary for the life of this community. That is, what occupations do you think contribute most to the maintenance of this community, so that if they were withdrawn things would be pretty much disrupted? Which contribute the least?" Five possible choices, from "very necessary" to "actually harmful," were given as alternatives.

[2]In a recent paper, which represents a mathematical formalization of the Davis-Moore theory in part from the vantage point offered by Lopreato and Lewis (1963), Kenneth Land (1970) offers support for this finding. The Lopreato-Lewis study has also been partially replicated by Edward Harris (1964). Exploring the association between a nationally derived scale (the Duncan Socio-Economic Index) of socioeconomic status and the variables of prestige, economic reward, skill, and functional importance as these were measured in the Lopreato-Lewis restricted-sample study (1963), Harris found that the substantial conclusions of the Lopreato-Lewis study could not be altered and that "The generality of prestige has been demonstrated regardless of how prestige is measured." A second paper by Harris (1967) compares "different conceptions of 'functional importance'" and finds that the Lopreato-Lewis measure provides the highest correlation in combination with other conceptions.

In another connection, Lewis and Lopreato (1963) found that when the functional importance of certain occupations was varied by comparing, for instance, educational to gambling occupations in a college town (Amherst, Massachusetts) and in a gambling town (Las Vegas, Nevada), no variation in prestige was noted between the two communities. In both, educational occupations were much more prestigious than gambling occupations, indicating in effect that the statistically demonstrable functional importance of gambling occupations in Las Vegas was counteracted by social values of a national character.

tance; if the prestige is low, the functional importance is deemed correspondingly low. Hence, the actual mechanisms that yield given amounts of prestige for social positions remain to be examined. Perhaps Homans's previously mentioned idea, essentially rooted in Marxian and Paretian sociology, might well be a good starting point: those in society who have the most power also "take" the highest rewards.

In what is surely one of the most fruitful if not the most known efforts to modify the Davis-Moore theory, Richard Simpson (1956) has proposed to abandon completely the "value-laden concept of 'functional necessity' " in favor of a more neutral "demand-supply" scheme of analysis. In effect, the suggestion emphasizes the etiological import of the scarcity-of-personnel variable. Simpson proposes that, in general, the greater the demand for the services inherent in given positions the higher will be the rewards attached to them. Likewise, the more limited the supply of desired services the higher will be their rewards. In the manner of the scientist who sets out to account for actual cases that depart from idealized ones, Simpson then continues to isolate factors that affect the supply and demand of position holders and their services. Those that affect demand include cultural values, technology, and power to reward. For instance, the cultural values of a deeply religious society constitute a high demand for priests and are likely to reward them highly. Factors that affect the supply of position holders include such things as the talent and training required for positions, the power to restrict the supply of personnel, and labor mobility. Thus, physicians who depress the number of openings in medical schools are affecting the supply of medical services by creating an artificial condition of scarcity.

In addition to factors that directly affect the supply and demand of personnel and their services, and therewith the rewards attached to positions, a number of other factors indirectly influence those rewards. Examples are custom and the "halo effect." Among secretaries, for instance, a halo effect is often at work in the sense that they tend to be ranked according to the ranks of their bosses, whatever the skills required of them. Similar transmissions are often at work between parent and child and between older sibling and younger sibling.

The Davis-Moore theory has been attacked on many fronts. Walter Buckley (1958) has argued, among other things, that if the theory is anything at all it is a theory not of stratification but only of some aspects of "social differentiation and hierarchical organization." The theory, Buckley maintains, is not about more or less permanent "strata" or other groups of people but about a hierarchy of individual social positions. What is perhaps far worse, according to Buckley (see also Buckley, 1959: 84–86), the theory does not account for social inheritance, and Davis and Moore neglect the connection between scientific generalization and empirical data.

Davis (1959:82–83) has failed to respond effectively to Buckley, but it can be shown that while Buckley's argument generates a number of interesting points, the two major points noted above are not well taken. It is true that the 1945 Davis-Moore article does not account for social inheritance; but the 1948 version of the theory—which antedated Buckley's article by a decade—does recognize the phenomenon of status ascription as a factor which impedes to varying degrees the mobility of the most qualified persons into the most important positions.

Similarly, Buckley's charge that the Davis-Moore theory is only a theory of social differentiation rather than one of social stratification, while true in a sense, is also irrelevant. What Davis and Moore attempted was an explanation of the *universality* of social stratification within an analytically pure achievement order. Hence, they took social stratification as given and sought to pinpoint its fundamental causes, *whatever its particular form in time and space.* To be sure, a more complete theory will have to take into account the specific variations across time and space in terms of cultural values, historical legacies, economic institutions, and the like. But there is nothing in the history of science to suggest that all of these factors should have been accounted for by one or even two scientists in a single effort. In this sense, Davis (see 1953; 1959) is fully justified in his frequent complaint that critics have been too much concerned with verbally disproving the theory and too little concerned with modifying or replacing it.

In a paper originally published in 1962, the Polish sociologist Wesołowski offers a somewhat more relevant critique of the Davis-Moore theory. He (1966:64) contends that the core of the theory "is the hypothesis concerning motivation"—that is, the question of why a person would "bother to train himself to fill" an important position that requires costly preparation, unless it also provides greater incentives. After examining the difficulty of interpreting positional "importance," he then takes issue with the Davis-Moore assumption that prestige and material advantage are universally ranked as the primary "end-values" in the social consciousness, while authority and education are assumed to be secondary, instrumental values. Wesołowski argues that it is entirely possible—and is at least *approximated* concretely in some societies (Poland, Norway)—that education and authority act as central motives for the occupation of important positions. As an example from his own society, he points out that "neither in earnings nor in prestige is [the factory foreman] superior to those under his authority. But the very fact that a foreman does have people under him is one of the assets of such a position . . ." (1966:67). Thus, he concludes that while "the whole situation is hypothetical" and in need of research "on the strength of various motives on the choice of social positions," one could argue that "if there is any functional necessity for stratification, it is the necessity of stratification according to the criterium of authority and not according to the criterium of material advantage or prestige" (1966:68–69).

One of the more carefully weighed reviews of the two decades of controversy surrounding the Davis-Moore theory is given by Huaco (1966). Generally speaking, we concur with his major points of criticism with regard to both the theory and its critics. There are two important exceptions, however. The first concerns his negative appraisal of power as an explanation of high-reward positions. Huaco (1966:227) contends that, while power is unquestionably a major determinant of ascription, it is less "effective in accounting for the inequality of rewards attached to positions." In clarifying this argument, he cites the "well-known historical example" of the Aryan invasion as the "origin of the Hindu caste system." This "power event," he continues, tells us "why the high-reward positions of priest and warrior were occupied exclusively by members of the conqueror group," but "it does *not* explain why both the conquerors and the conquered alike . . . should have regarded the roles of priest and warrior as high-reward positions." As far as he goes, Huaco is probably correct. But in seeking a genetic explanation, he has overlooked an important point: namely, the possibility that as individuals supply new demands, or old demands in more effective ways, they (1) become powerful and (2) gain in esteem. As these new relationships are gradually institutionalized, the locus of reward shifts from the person (esteem) to the position (prestige). Power is not an exclusive determinant, since it in turn is influenced by factors of supply and demand; but it is a major determinant. If you utilize resources to supply a new demand X, whatever that may be, you immediately become powerful—in degree according to the intensity of demand and to your monopoly of necessary resources—and in return you receive esteem, as well as other rewards, perhaps. Only later does the institutionalized *position* of "X supplier" appear, and, assuming the continuation of appropriate supply-demand ratios, become a high-reward position.

Our second exception to Huaco's discussion concerns his treatment of scarcity. In summarizing the "remaining fragments" of the Davis-Moore theory that "seem to hold considerable promise" (1966:237–239), he states that "differential scarcity of qualified personnel is a cause of *the range* of unequal rewards attached to different positions." Then, on the assumption that supply and demand of qualified personnel can vary at least in part independently of each other, he generates a four-cell table of logical possibilities from dichotomies of the two variables. One of these cells (high supply—high demand) he labels "mature industrial society"; another (low supply—low demand) he labels "traditional society," and of the latter he asserts that "here it makes little or no sense to speak of a differential scarcity of personnel." But Huaco has again overlooked essential points. First, scarcity is not only a matter of gaps in observer definitions; it is also a matter of gaps in cultural definitions (see Stanley, 1968). Second, while the traditional society may be characterized by a paucity of both need for and supply of highly qualified personnel in comparison with the mature industrial society, *within its own context* the "low" demand may still be greater in magnitude than the "low" supply, either by observer definitions or by cultural definitions, or by both. In such case, it makes a great deal of sense to speak of a differential scarcity of personnel.

The Idealized Nature of the Theory

While most critics have contributed good insights for an eventual formal modification and elaboration of the Davis-Moore theory, many have also created more confusion than is perhaps salutary for any scientific theory. The basic difficulty lies in the virtually general failure to understand a particular methodological aspect of the theory.[3] Our contention is that, like Pareto's theory of elite circulation, the core of the Davis-Moore theory must be viewed in the form of a "theoretical idealization" (Lopreato and Alston, 1970). A theoretical idealization is a proposition stated in the form of a "law" claiming universal validity under certain *ideal* conditions. For instance, Galileo's law for falling bodies states that all falling bodies will accelerate at uniform rate *provided* that the bodies be freely falling; that is, the law applies only to bodies moving in a hypothetical medium totally devoid of resistance.

While Davis and Moore may not have been aware of the particular character of their work, the end result of their efforts is an unmistakable application of a strategy of theory construction that has proven most successful in the older sciences. The central aspect of their theory basically states that a *person's social position, as defined in terms of the rewards attendant upon his occupational activities, is determined by the contribution made by those activities to a desired state X (integration, prosperity, or the like) of that person's society.* In the best scientific tradition, Davis and Moore then go on to argue that their statement is valid *provided* that (1) free competition in the labor market exists, and (2) the supply of personnel for given occupations meets exactly the demand for it. In the absence of the first condition, a certain amount of inherited privilege will produce a discrepancy between rewards received and "functional importance" of position. Similarly, either an excessive or an inadequate supply of personnel for a given position will artificially alter its functional importance, with the result that its incumbents will receive either excessive or inadequate rewards. (See Lopreato and Alston, 1970.)

We submit that much of the discussion that has wastefully surrounded the Davis-Moore theory would have been avoided if the authors had presented their work as a theoretical idealization, or if the rest of us had understood it as such. Interested students could then have directed their energies more fruitfully toward solving remaining problems concerning the operational

---

[3]The outstanding exception is Richard Simpson (1956), who, after stating what appear to him as the most tenable propositions of the theory, goes on to single out some of the major conditions that to some unspecified degree interfere with the validity of those propositions.

clarity of functional importance, the possible requirement of additional qualifying statements, and the like.

Given applicability of theoretical idealizations to hypothetical cases only,
logical strategy requires the introduction of additional statements of theory
whose function is to account for discrepancy between actual situations and the
hypothetical ones that the idealizations describe. The strategy, in other words,
is to state a universally applicable law and then explain systematically those
actual cases which exhibit behavior inconsistent with the law. A theoretical
idealization is a *focal point of a research program whose execution enhances the
probability of producing systematic and cumulative theory.* The job of cumulative research and theory construction does not, however, fall to one or even
a few individuals but usually, and more fruitfully, to a scientific discipline as
a whole. Sociology might have been much better off if most of the critics of
the Davis-Moore theory had understood the theoretical demands made on
them by that formulation.

UTILITIES AND DISTRIBUTIVE INJUSTICE

Before concluding this chapter, we should return to Tumin's (1953a) discussion of the Davis-Moore theory and examine in some detail the fourth of his
criticisms previously noted. Davis and Moore make the assumption that stratification is positively functional to social survival; Tumin disputes that argument by offering a number of adverse "provisional assertions." While these are
somewhat irrelevant to the intent of the Davis-Moore theory, they are nonetheless potentially very fruitful for an understanding of social stratification as a
whole and are worth reporting in full:

(1) Social stratification systems function to limit the possibility of discovery of the
full range of talent available in a society. This results from the fact of unequal access
to appropriate motivation, channels of recruitment and centers of training.

(2) In foreshortening the range of available talent, social stratification systems
function to set limits upon the possibility of expanding the productive resources of the
society, at least relative to what might be the case under conditions of greater equality
of opportunity.

(3) Social stratification systems function to provide the elite with the political power
necessary to procure acceptance and dominance of an ideology which rationalizes the
status quo, whatever it may be, as "logical," "natural" and "morally right." In this
manner, social stratification systems function as essentially conservative influences in
the societies in which they are found.

(4) Social stratification systems function to distribute favorable self-images unequally throughout a population. To the extent that such favorable self-images are
requisite to the development of the creative potential inherent in men, to that extent
stratification systems function to limit the development of this creative potential.

(5) To the extent that inequalities in social rewards cannot be made fully acceptable
to the less privileged in a society, social stratification systems function to encourage

hostility, suspicion and distrust among the various segments of a society and thus to limit the possibilities of extensive social integration.

(6) To the extent that the sense of significant membership in a society depends on one's place on the prestige ladder of the society, social stratification systems function to distribute unequally the sense of significant membership in the population.

(7) To the extent that loyalty to a society depends on a sense of significant membership in the society, social stratification systems function to distribute loyalty unequally in the population.

(8) To the extent that participation and apathy depend upon the sense of significant membership in the society, social stratification systems function to distribute the motivation to participate unequally in a population (Tumin, 1953a: 387–393).

Again, it must be pointed out that, while a more nearly complete theory of stratification must take into account its dysfunctions as well as its eufunctions, Davis and Moore cannot be faulted for failing to do it all themselves in one sitting. The reference to the functionality of social stratification is tangential to the core of the theory, but to the extent that the reference is made at all it concerns functionality to the society viewed as a historical unit.

We shall better understand the quarrel between Tumin and Davis-Moore if we note an important distinction made by Pareto between types of function, or "utility" as he preferred to term it. Pareto (1916:2131-2135) distinguished between the utility *"of* a community" and the utility *"for* a community." The utility *of* a community refers to the community survival value, its health, its power to weather threats from other communities, and the like. The utility *for* a community, on the other hand, concerns the welfare and satisfaction of its members. It is clear, then, that in "functionally" assessing social stratification, Davis and Moore were concerned exclusively with the utility *of* the society, whereas Tumin argues that they should have been concerned with the utility *for* the society as well.

However unjustifiable Tumin's position may be from the viewpoint of the intent of the Davis-Moore theory, the fact remains that it is exceedingly useful to sociology in general and to us in this book in particular. Tumin's argument sensitizes us to the simple fact that whatever the societal causes of a system of institutionalized inequalities, and however just that system may be from the viewpoint of some abstract standard of evaluation, human beings have to bear it and live by it. From their vantage point, their participation in the distribution of contributions and rewards may be too costly to themselves. To the extent that, W. I. Thomas once argued, the individual and the social definitions of a situation are not always in harmony with each other, men in the flesh may experience a sense of distributive injustice. And that feeling will not only produce human dissatisfaction but it may be expected to have detrimental consequences for "social survival" as well.

Emile Durkheim (1897:250), who understood human beings when he cared to consider them, pointed out that it would be of little use for everyone to recognize the justice of the hierarchy of functions established by public opinion, if he did not also consider the distribution of these functions just. The workman is not in harmony with his social position if he is not convinced that he has his desserts. If he feels justified in occupying another, what he has would not satisfy him.

We should note in closing, then, that by pointing out another major turn that the Davis-Moore theory could take, Tumin has in effect prodded the theory toward the humanistic tradition which reached its peak in the great synthesis of Karl Marx. When that tradition and the excellent work of Davis and Moore are brought together, a number of research propositions immediately come to mind. The following, or variations of them, will be particularly helpful to us in the analyses of subsequent chapters:

1. Incumbents of positions that yield the highest returns in income and power are the most satisfied with their productive roles, and those whose positions yield the lowest returns in income and power are the most dissatisfied.

2. Irrespective of how they define the functional importance of their productive roles, individuals who perceive the social recognition accruing to their jobs as high are more satisfied at work than individuals who perceive the social recognition accruing to their productive roles as low.

3. Like Marx's alienated man, individuals who (a) define their productive roles as having low functional importance, and (b) perceive low social recognition on that basis, will be the most dissatisfied with their productive roles.

4. The more men are dissatisfied with their jobs, the more they are dissatisfied with the broader social and political conditions in their milieu.

PART TWO   **Studies in
Class Consciousness**

VI

CLASS CONSCIOUSNESS: A CONCEPTUAL ANALYSIS

The cardinal variables of class theory are two. They refer to the two fundamental processes of class dynamics: *class consciousness* and *social mobility*. It
is no exaggeration to say that the history of any class structure is to a large
extent the history of the interplay of these two great social forces. It may be
recalled that in Marx's theory class consciousness refers to the social-psychological process underlying the transformation of the *Klasse an sich* into the
Klasse für sich. Thus, the working class is viewed as going through a series
of steps which lead to its organization into a political party powerfully situated
to engage in concerted action against the enemy class. Class consciousness, in
short, is an *associative* variable.

By contrast, social mobility is largely a *dissociative* variable. To be sure,
Marx had viewed the decline of "the middle strata" into "the working masses"
as an important factor in the political development of the proletariat. However,
in the literature that has developed in part as a reaction to Marx's extreme
thesis of proletarianization, mobility is properly seen as the crucial variable
interfering with the formation of classes. Mobility bears an interesting conceptual relationship to migration: it abstracts some people from a population
(a class) and adds them to another. This process of abstraction and addition, which is everywhere continuous, keeps the social classes in a state of uninterrupted resocialization and reorganization. The remainder of this volume is basically concerned with these two processes of class dynamics, using

the body of data from Italian society to which we referred in the Introduction.

CLASS CONSCIOUSNESS: AN OVERVIEW

The strategic component of class formation in Marx's theory of class conflict is class consciousness. Conceived as a synthesis of complex social and psychological processes, class consciousness was for Marx the keystone in the bridge between an estranged past in human history and a positive, unmediated humanistic future (see Petrović, 1967:160–163). It was simultaneously the natural outcome of man's alienated state in capitalist society and the essential condition for a revolutionary proletariat—and thus the signal of the new society. Despite its strategic position in class theory, however, class consciousness has remained one of the most neglected concepts of social stratification. It is today about where Marx left it nearly a century ago. The legacy is undernourished.

Marx most certainly gave close attention to the processes which would allegedly lead to full class consciousness and conflict: unhindered capitalist competition, increasing exploitation and alienation, greater densities of workplace and residence, pauperization and proletarianization, political organization, and so on. Marx's interest was keenest precisely in the historical process of societal reorganization—both those of the past and, especially, those of the future, as they could be envisioned given the economic organization of his own time. His was a theory of what would happen tomorrow, given the conditions of today. But for all that, Marx said very little about the specific social-psychological stages that in the social consciousness were to bridge the gap between his own time and yesterday's tomorrow. In short, the problem of different stages in the formation of a self-conscious, politically active class—for example, of getting from consciousness of class to class consciousness as an organizational form—is an unasked question in Marx's theory.

As the discussion in Chapter I made apparent, class consciousness in the full sense of the concept refers to a state of mind in which the individual identifies with a given class *(Klasse an sich)* to the point of adopting its interests as his own and engaging in concerted action within that class against the interests of another. This state of mind, in fully developed form, typifies the politically active conflict group or "community of fate." Analysis of this complex phenomenon should focus on the developmental conditions that lead to and are ultimately incorporated by the end state of class action. The object of sociological investigation cannot be, properly speaking, the complete array of events, persons, and places that collectively and idiosyncratically constitute an instance of class action but, instead, the dynamics that create a *situation* of class action. As Stinchcombe (1965:169) has noted in a related context, "Rather than explaining the occurrence of revolution, a sociological theory ought to . . . explain the occurrence of a 'revolutionary situation.' " So it is with class consciousness.

For purposes of subsequent discussion, we shall view class consciousness as a phenomenon in the process of becoming, so to speak. Fully matured class consciousness as Marx sometimes spoke of it is a highly tenuous, inherently unstable situation, and thus seldom lasts for more than short periods of time, if it ever exists. For this reason, and also because of the practicalities of conducting scientific research in the face of open class conflict, the data of class consciousness are difficult to capture except in retrospect through the eyes and memory of former participants or through the documentary reconstructions of social historians. What *is* possible is to analytically isolate and identify some of the stages that in the broad social consciousness may eventually culminate in class action (see Geiger, 1949: Chapter VI). While we cannot under any but the most highly unusual circumstances directly examine the self-conscious "class-as-corporate-group," we can study categories of people who are *conscious of class* to varying degrees. In order to do so, however, it is of crucial importance that we first distinguish the person who is only vaguely aware of social differences from the person who seems willing to energetically hoist the banner of class action, and other individuals who represent intermediate stages in the formation of class consciousness from each of these. These distinctions we shall undertake in the present chapter.

Before turning to this conceptual analysis, however, some introductory comments are in order. Although the phenomenon of class consciousness received its most famous exposition in Marx's work, it was not entirely unknown to pre-Marxian scholars. In an apparent reference to the late eighteenth century, John Millar (1803:338–339) records some observations which, but for matters of linguistic style, might well have come from pages of Marx's notebooks:[1]

From the progress . . . of trade and manufactures, the state of a country . . . is gradually changed. As the inhabitants multiply from the facility of procuring subsistence, they are collected in large bodies for the convenient exercise of their employments. Villages are enlarged into towns; and these are often swelled into populous cities. In all those places of resort, there arise large bands of labourers or artificers, who by following the same employment, and by constant intercourse, are enabled, with great rapidity, to communicate all their sentiments and passions. Among these there spring up leaders, who give a tone and direction to their companions. The strong encourage the feeble; the bold animate the timid; the resolute confirm the wavering; and the movements of the whole mass proceed with the uniformity of a machine, and with a force that is often irresistible.

In this situation, a great proportion of the people are easily aroused by every popular discontent, and can unite with no less facility in demanding a redress of grievances. The

---

[1]Although Marx did not cite Millar in any of his works, he does occasionally refer to Adam Smith, who was both mentor and colleague to "the forgotten Scot." On the possibility of a direct influence on Marx, see Meek (1954).

least ground of complaint, in a town, becomes the occasion of a riot; and the flames of sedition spreading from one city to another, are blown up into a general insurrection.

The point of Millar's observations, of course, has to do with the transformation of the eighteenth-century political economy of Europe, not with the conditions of a proletarian revolution. Nevertheless, his description of some of the changes in industrial society, brief as it was, eminently presaged a more famous declaration that was to appear a half-century later.

As a specific term, class consciousness may be subsumed within the more general category of "group consciousness." Other forms of this generic concept include nationalism, racism, familism, and religious-group consciousness.[2] The common denominator of these otherwise diverse phenomena is an awareness on the part of those concerned that they are members of a *distinctive group*. They think of themselves as forming a collectivity separate and apart from the rest of a larger aggregate, with interests that are peculiar to themselves. On this basis they are often capable of taking cooperative action in furtherance of their own collective interests and in opposition to the interests of nonmembers.

The several variants of group consciousness differ most fundamentally in the basis on which that awareness of common interests and membership is constructed. In nationalism, it is in the notion of the nation-state and "national interest." In racism, it is in the notion of innately superior and inferior categories of people, separated according to skin color or some other convenient fiction. In Marx's class consciousness, it is in the awareness of common membership in a distinct community of *economic* interests. There is a "type of mind," as Briffault (1936:52–53) put it, "an ideology, corresponding to the economic situation" of groups of people, and the "specific characters of those types of mind and of their contents" vary according to the relationship of each group of people to the means of production in society. Thus, Briffault continues (in a patently Marxian vein), recent history has revealed the existence of three types of mind, or "class mentalities": those of the ruling landowning aristocracy, of the trading "middle class" or bourgeoisie, and of the servile proletarian class.

The key element in the formation of such types of mind is not simply the "objective facts" of one set of economic interests in opposition to another, as an external observer might define them. Also involved are the class-conscious individual's *own* perceptions of those interests. Briefs (1937:51) states in his account of the proletariat, "To be a proletarian . . . is . . . to have a characteris-

---

[2]Typically, only the "negative" aspects of these forms of group consciousness are recognized, especially today in the case of racism. But to the extent that any one of them has a positive or constructive aspect, they all have. That aspect lies precisely in the anchorage they provide for the cooperative *intragroup* pursuit of common interests and goals. When we see one form as constructive and "good," and another as destructive and "bad," we are merely revealing our ideological biases—and, thereby, as Marx taught, we reveal in which set of interests we think we are winning and in which we think we are losing.

tic mental 'set,' a predisposition to react to one's given environment" in closely circumscribed ways. The emerging proletarian's perceptions of his own interests are continually formed and reformed in the light of a growing realization that other people share a similar fate of exploitation and oppression, that Talleyrand's world of "shearers and shorn" is suddenly upon them. This sense of separation from the comfortable world of the bourgeoisie, and of lacking an honorable place in the social scale, has profound subjective consequences. Through a transvaluation of moral standards, Briefs continues to note, the feeling of worthlessness and numb subjugation to conditions both vile and servile become a powerful source of proletarian pride. The dialectical nature of human experience inevitably produces, as a correlate of the sense of social distance and separation, a contrasting sense of worth and solidarity, a "fellow feeling that comes with the realization that all who have a common lot face a common fate" (Briefs, 1937:90). Thus, given sufficient conditions, the individual gradually may merge his own interests and identity, along with those of his similarly situated fellow men, into the corporate identity of a self-conscious and politically vital class.

The extremes of class consciousness—a vague awareness of social differences versus a readiness to participate politically in group action—imply a contrast between two conceptions of human experience: at the one extreme a phenomenal, passive consciousness of concrete events; at the other a reflexive consciousness of socially situated and meaningful action. In the first, the individual has no clear image of the arrangements of society or of his place within them. His is the instantaneous, often disjunctive experience of day-to-day existence. While he may well engage in "disruptive" actions—riots, protests, sedition—he does so for reasons other than commitment to an ideologically anchored consciousness-of-kind ideal. He behaves according to the objective forces that impinge upon him, but without awareness of them as identifiable and possibly manageable forces. He has not yet objectified them in his own consciousness as manifestations of a shared class legacy and "destiny." Consequently, he often reacts to external stimuli in ways that are compatible with, or even beneficial to, the theoretical class enemy, thereby seemingly demonstrating a "false" consciousness.[3]

By contrast, the individual endowed with reflexive consciousness has converted his disjointed experiences into an ideologically coherent and supported image of the social structure, and he has located himself and significant others

---

[3]"False" consciousness is closely tied to Marx's analysis of alienation, estrangement, and reification. Historically, Marx argued, man has endowed his creations with powers superior to himself and with an existence separate from his own. Through this objectification of part of his being, man becomes something less: his creations become alien to him; he becomes a stranger to himself, to his fellow men, to his species-being. His consciousness of reality is "false." Even the materialist conception was a negative conception for Marx, although he recognized it as a necessary starting point in the analysis of human history, since it negated man's freedom of being (see Petrović, 1967).

within it. His constructed image is both retrospective, since it posits a history of causes, and prospective, because it promises specific solutions. In the case of the class-conscious proletarian, the causes and solutions pertain to a social order that is deemed obsolescent because it is highly damaging to his (and his class's) best interests. Unlike the person who moves about with only individuated pictures of concrete occurrences in his mind, the class-conscious individual has differentiated his role from the roles of an opposing group's membership because of conflicting expectations and obligations. He has developed affiliations and loyalties to a network of persons who occupy role relationships similar to those in the opposing class.

His image of the social order is reflexive also in the sense that it shapes his future relations with others. An act of creative imagination has been performed, whereby the role of being-a-proletarian has been lifted out of the dust of daily labors and enshrined. The collective result of numerous such creations is the proletariat, whose emotive core harbors sentiments of destructiveness with regard to the social world-that-is and promises to become a compelling force of change toward a better world-to-come.

Either of these two conceptions of human experience can be applied as an idealized approximation to an objectively demarcated "working class." Marx, for the most part, employed the latter conception—that of reflexive experience —thereby revealing his own optimism about the "uniform proletarian pigment"[4] of the body of labor. His implicit faith in the rational faculty of mankind led him to the conclusion that each worker *could* perform that creative transformation of individuated concrete experience into purposive corporate action, and that he *would* do so (Marx, 1847:146–147). In contrast to this superb faith, Lenin, like Weber and Pareto, more often confined himself to a conception of the workers which went little beyond the level of individual phenomenal experience—and in this difference Lenin proved to be the more realistic revolutionary. He was less optimistic about the worker's capabilities, and accordingly proposed more clearly than Marx the necessity of a cadre of leaders who, as "midwives" to the revolution, were to commit the imaginative act *for* the bulk of the workers and thus provide the proletariat with its ideological justification for existence (Lenin, 1902).

For Marx, the indelible experience out of which the self-constructed consciousness of kind would eventually arise was that respect-spoiling profanation of roles forced upon *all* sections of the laboring class.

The bourgeoisie has stripped of its halo every occupation hitherto honored and looked up to with reverent awe. It has converted the physician, the lawyer, the priest, the poet, the man of science into its paid wage laborers (Marx and Engels, 1848:10).

---

[4]This descriptive phrase, which well summarizes one conception of the proletariat, was coined by Heinrich Herkner (1911) during the 1911 Nürnberg conference of the *Vereins für Sozialpolitik*. Herkner, however, utilized the phrase somewhat facetiously when, during discussions of the "Problems of Worker Psychology," he argued that "further consideration of a uniform 'proletariat' " is useless.

The product, and indeed the very essence of human labor, was wholly dena-
tured by the forced dependence of man-the-creator upon man-the-ruler. What
remained from this profanation, Tawney (1920:12–13) later observed, "was
private rights and private interests, the materials of a society rather than a
society itself."

So long as the worker remains dependent upon the organizational arrangements and resources of a ruling class for the satisfaction of his needs and
desires, the ruling class will be to that degree materially free of need for the
worker's consent. If the worker cannot meet his needs from other sources, that
fact of scarcity enables the ruling class to control the flow of satisfactions,
without courting the consent and compliance of subordinates (see Stinchcombe, 1965:181–182).[5] In short, the workers as a *Klasse an sich* stand in an
intense and increasingly alienative relationship of dependency to the ruling
class.

Continuation of that state of dependency is necessary to the full development of a proletarian class consciousness. Without the dependency, the worker
either remains in a perniciously disjunctive state of alienation or, if the ruling-
class monopoly of resources and satisfactions is otherwise altered, he may lapse
into the preemptive consciousness of status distinctions. This reveals the extreme tenuity of class-consciousness formation. Only at the full fruition of class
consciousness—the political *Klasse für sich*—are the chains of dependency
completely broken.

At the same time, however, some lessening from a condition of *total* dependency, if such has persisted, is necessary before the aggregate of workers
can change from their current standing as a class-in-itself to the class-for-itself.
Otherwise, it will be denied the resources out of which a political organization
is built—for example, secure channels of communication; the capacity to
recruit, and then protect, a competent leadership; and, above all, an eman-
cipated will to power. As Marx noted, many of the building blocks are potentially available as unintended outcomes of the increased concentration of
workers in factories, homogeneous neighborhoods, mutual-aid societies, and
the like. But until the workers are allowed the possibility of discretionary
activities in workplace, neighborhood, and aid society, alternative sources of
need satisfaction remain inaccessible.

As the aggregate of workers moves progressively closer to consciousness of
itself as a community of fate, the basis of its dependency on the ruling class

---

[5]This dependency partially accounts for the conservative tendency of labor unions in pluralistic
societies (such as the United States) today. To the extent that the worker can satisfy his needs
through union activity and thereby become somewhat independent of the company, management
is dependent upon the subordinate employee. The employee, in turn, is freed from the "restrictive
covenant" of monopolistic company demands and sources of need satisfaction—freed, that is, to
engage in the practice of invidious status distinctions. The success of the labor-union movement
ironically impedes the development of *class* consciousness by terminating "prematurely" the
strong dependence of the individual worker on the possessing class and by promoting the development of status consciousness (see Perlman, 1922; Blackburn and Cockburn, 1967).

is altered. When it is a *Klasse an sich,* its dependency is predicated on the functional interdependence of *individual* worker and superior; the superior is dependent upon the subordinate's labor, and the subordinate is dependent upon the superior's wage payments. With the formation of the *Klasse für sich,* however, dependency has shifted from an individual to a group basis and from a material linkage of functional interdependence to complete segmentation. However tenuously, each class now stands materially alone; each has its own resources, its own separate political organization. The only connection remaining is the dependency of moral antithesis, which characterizes all conflict groups in one degree or another.

DIMENSIONS OF CLASS CONSCIOUSNESS

It is evident that the notion of class consciousness raises some complex issues of conceptualization. Perhaps in part because this notion is intrinsically synthetic of factors both social-structural and psychological in nature, and in part because it refers to intensely dynamic phenomena, social scientists have not done full justice to it. *In particular,* the problem of class-consciousness formation has escaped systematic analysis at both the purely conceptual and the empirical level, with the result that our knowledge of it has advanced very little beyond the scattered observations, and sometimes misconstructions, of Marx's would-be interpreters.

In an eminently readable, scholarly account of *The Making of the English Working Class,* E. P. Thompson (1963:10) defines class consciousness as "the way in which [class] experiences are handled in cultural terms," and then goes on to observe that

If the experience appears as determined, class-consciousness does not. We can see a *logic* in the responses of similar occupational groups undergoing similar experiences, but we cannot predicate any *law.* Consciousness of class arises in the same way in different times and places, but never in *just* the same way.

Perhaps Thompson's nomothetic pessimism is exaggerated. Yet there is undeniably a truth to what he is saying: the phenomenon is, as we have called it, a process of becoming, and it is an exceedingly sensitive "becoming." It is keenly historical and subjective, a "fluency which evades analysis if we attempt to stop it dead at any given moment and anatomise its structure" (Thompson, 1963:9). Still, as sociological observers we must abstract and categorize the phenomenon to some degree, even though in doing so we violate the historical-personal continuity of its instantiation. To be honest within our epistemological limitations, we can (as was cautioned earlier) attempt theories only of a *situation* of class consciousness and not of particular instances of it.

Where Thompson's definition is in need of further specification for analytical purposes, the great majority of those offered in the literature are simply narrow operational guides for the conduct of specific researches. They fail to illuminate or even suggest the logical intricacies of the phenomenon. This practice is surely understandable; but it is acceptable *only if* the researcher is cognizant of the fact that he *is* studying only one or a few aspects of the class-consciousness process—usually what is known as "class awareness" or the ability to identify classes in society. Unfortunately, however, the definitions employed often overlook or even obscure the complete meaning of class consciousness. When they do so, the claims of evidence far exceed what is justified by the research data. Lionel Lewis (1965:325) aptly summarizes the practice when he concludes that many who are interested in the investigation of class consciousness in the United States study only the question of "class identification and at times seem barely cognizant of the possibility that class consciousness can mean more than this."

One of the major difficulties intrinsic to a comprehensive analysis of class consciousness stems from the existence of multiple bases of stratification in society, a topic on which, as was previously noted, we owe much particularly to Max Weber. When viewed as a set of abstractions in the black-and-white of a printed page this multiplicity appears to be quite easily divisible, but he who attempts concrete application finds a veritable entanglement of crisscrossing relationships. As Runciman (1966:42) warns by reference to Weber's three "orders," "there is nothing very novel in the emphasis on either status or power as against economic class. What is difficult is to *retain* the tripartite distinction throughout all discussion of social stratification and the feelings of relative deprivation to which it gives rise" (emphasis added).

It may be recalled from Chapter IV that Weber identified three analytically distinct orders, or bases, of stratification: *class,* denoting relations to the means of production of market goods; *status,* denoting the principle of consumption as represented by special "styles of life"; and *party,* denoting communal action oriented toward the acquisition and use of "social power." Weber's taxonomy introduces the distinction of *types,* as opposed to degrees, of social consciousness. There is a type of consciousness corresponding to each of the three orders. The difficulty of treating these phenomena in a single, consistent scheme of analysis stems from the circumstance that, as a society grows in complexity, the likelihood that a given individual will hold an equivalent position in all three orders steadily diminishes. Concomitantly, the likelihood that he will experience his power, prestige, and class position as congruent with one another also diminishes. When we speak of "class" consciousness, therefore, the first question we must raise is, is it *class* consciousness, *status* consciousness, or *power* consciousness? And, further, how are the three interrelated?

The first of these types of consciousness is the least problematic experientially, inasmuch as an individual can rather easily assess his objective economic position in his group. The third is considerably more complex, simply because an individual engages in relationships of power and influence in a wide array of role-sets, "parties," and cliques. For this reason, he can less easily weigh his over-all power vis-à-vis other individuals and groups. Furthermore, unlike class, wherein factors of social inheritance often lend a high degree of stability, power is more nearly a function of individual skills and talents and is thereby open to frequent change in its relation to particular social environments. Power in the sense of accessible resources (Blalock, 1967:110) is, beyond question, closely related to class position: the son of a hod carrier has from the very beginning less access to the important resources of power than does the son of a corporation president. But the actual implementation of accessible resources is in the last analysis a matter of individual capabilities and sentiments. An incipiently self-conscious working class will remain impotent until it consists of men who can wisely deploy its accumulated potential.

The remaining type of consciousness—status consciousness—is even less manageable than power consciousness, since the individual has multiple group memberships and identifications, each of which bears a different amount of social honor, but not all of which give access to important resources of social power. Because of this multiplicity of ties and the potential for cross-pressures of loyalty and obedience, the consciousness of status stands in a critical relationship to the fully developed *Klasse für sich*. An understanding of the latter presupposes some understanding of the former.

Fundamentally, status consciousness refers to the common human tendency to stress aspects of social experience that block the formation of corporate consciousness along economic and political cleavages. It does not necessarily preclude awareness of class differences in society or even the identification with one class or another; it may even enhance such awareness or identification under certain conditions. People generally consider themselves to be status equals to the extent that they share a common class experience and situation. But since this is neither automatic nor omnipresent, as Orwell's naval commander and his grocer illustrate, status consciousness suggests behavior that is antithetical to full class consciousness in two crucial respects. First, the status-conscious person openly seeks social superiority for himself rather than an equality for all. Being basically anti-egalitarian, despite possible claims to the contrary, he pursues satisfaction of "the need for equality" in that special self-centered sense which Pareto so trenchantly described. The goal is not to win equality for all but to achieve first status among equals. Second, the person who is status-conscious pursues social superiority as an individual rather than as the member of a collectivity. To be sure, he often seeks or demands superior status—that is, prestige and honor—because of membership in a certain group, whether it be religious, occupational, racial, or of some other kind. But he nevertheless invariably acts for his own personal gain rather than in the name of a collective goal.

Status consciousness is manifested in various hues and textures. There are the simple ingratiators and the aggressive "status seekers"; the arbiters of etiquette and fashion; the tradition-bound and the snobbish; the amateur genealogists with their mail-order coats of arms (and often without the ability to distinguish the sign of bastardy from the sign of legitimacy). In their effect on the dynamics of class structure, however, they may be considered as one: a single force of *social emulation for personal gain.* They have in common the desire to fortify the cultural barrier separating themselves and a few select others from the great unclean masses; or, if they have not yet "arrived," they emulate the behavior of those more privileged than themselves. Blalock (1959: 243) has drawn a composite picture of this emulator:

He is careful to learn the proper etiquette and to join the right organizations. . . . He has a high respect for status, defers to his superiors, and expects those beneath him to do likewise. . . . He learns to know the status system in his community and can readily evaluate the relative standings of various civic, social, or religious organizations. He takes pride in knowing members of the elite, either personally or vicariously. In short, [he] lives and acts as though status considerations are of the utmost importance. They are to him the essence of social interaction.

Whatever identifications the status seeker may make with his models of "success," they are often by intent only temporary since today's "models" are but passing landmarks along the long road to ultimate "position." Once their particular skills and demeanor have been learned, the models lose all usefulness. Yet in this very temporariness of reference-group identifications the status emulator's predisposition to do the bidding of those above is reinforced. Not only the circumstance that some people *are* "successes," but also the subjective expectancy of his own ascent impels the status emulator to engage in actions that disrupt actual class interests. To state it otherwise, status consciousness thrives on social mobility, real or perceived, a matter on which we shall focus in Chapter XV.

Weber's distinctions concerning the bases of stratification should sensitize us to different types of consciousness as phenomena in addition to possible variations of degree in class consciousness. We have implicitly taken the position that the economic and political orders have their counterpart in Marx's theory of classes, though in modified form. They will be treated accordingly in subsequent discussion and analysis of the formation of class consciousness. The status dimension has no explicit counterpart in Marx's theory, but it was indirectly discussed by Marx during his scattered observations regarding the conditions underlying class consciousness. Since status consciousness reflects behavior that is contradictory to the corporative awareness that was so central to Marx's thought, a discussion of the conditions of the latter is by inversion a discussion of aspects of the former.

The point must be reiterated that, by and large, Marx conceived class consciousness as a peak in class development, as a state of mind pervading an entire class (the proletariat) such that it is ready and willing to engage in battle against another class (the bourgeoisie) for the reorganization of economic, political, and social structures. Without presuming to resolve all difficulties surrounding the notion of class consciousness, we propose to distinguish in the remainder of this chapter some different aspects of human awareness that are involved in the formation of class consciousness. As an inherently dynamic phenomenon, this formative process is manifested in different degrees of social awareness. We suggest that a minimum account of those dynamics must entail consideration of the following: (1) *social perceptivity,* or the awareness of differences in individual skills and distributed rewards in society; (2) *class awareness,* or the identification of crystallized economic and political interest groups in society; (3) *dimensional awareness,* or conceptions of the factors underlying class divisions and membership; (4) *class placement,* or self-location of the individual within a subjectively conceived class structure; and (5) *class solidarity,* or the congruence of location and image with interests, as represented by a comparison of objective and self-assessed positions and by expressions of unity in ideas and needs with other members of the self-assessed class. Although these five aspects of class-implicated consciousness are not entirely exhaustive of the intricacies of class-consciousness formation, they encompass reasonably well the wide range of human experiences and cognitions that enter into it.

Social Perceptivity

As men begin to contemplate their own places in the scheme of things and compare them with those of others, their perceptions of social differences gradually grow more acute. In the terms of Davis and Moore's theory of stratification, they become aware of the fact that people do not all possess the same skills or perform the same tasks, and that as a result of those differences the "rewards" of prestige, pecuniary remuneration, and the like are also unequally distributed.

These initial cognitions, which we designate as *social perceptivity,* comprise a minimal foundation for the further development of class consciousness. If awareness of social differentiation fails to develop beyond this stage, the conflict that Marx saw as an integral property of the social consciousness in capitalist society could never come about. Such would be the case, for instance, if the unequal distribution of rewards were considered equitable because of a corresponding lack of equality in the "functional importance" of the various positions in society. Davis, as we concluded in Chapter V, never advances this assumption of equity, although his argument does not effectively combat the temptation to assume that he does. Ironically, the assumption of equity is more germane to the Marxian theory of classes, and in particular to Marx's discussion of the terminal or "communist" society. Marx argued that in the new society there would be, not a perfect equality, but a perfect equality of oppor-

tunity, and that the distribution of rewards would follow the utilitarian principle of "from each according to his ability, to each according to his needs." At
any given time, then, one could expect to find an equitable inequality of reward
distribution and enjoyment.

One could additionally expect to find an equitable inequality in the uneven
distribution of authority. Writing in the Italian *Almanacco Repubblicano* in
1874, Engels (1874) argued—against the anarchists of the time, and in a key
strongly anticipating the later elite theories (especially Michels, 1914)—that
authority relations are inevitable to social organization. In the complex industrial enterprise, "the will of the single individual will always have to subordinate itself, which means that questions are settled in an authoritative way."
Industrial production, because of its scale, would be quite impossible without
some regimen of superordination and subordination to ensure the efficient
utilization of human energy and material resources. A factory engine, to put
it simply, knows nothing about human needs, human feelings, or human
sensitivities; it can only aid in the satisfaction of material human needs, but
only at some cost of subjection.

The principle which renders logical in Marx's theory the assumption of
justice within a context of unequal distributions of authority and reward is the
principle of individual freedom of destiny. Such distributions are not stagnant
and class-bound but fluid, individually based, and socially imperative. The
worker is a fully developed being. Consequently, the different social functions
performed by him are but so many alternative, equally humane modes of
activity. With his various skills, he may be today in a position of authority,
tomorrow a plain machine operator. Since his talent is given free rein of
development and expression, social differentiation never appears permanent or
absolute. In principle, the entire range of differentiation can be experienced
within the occupational career of a single individual.

But the principle applies to a society that was to be (or, is still to come?).
In historical society, the unequal distribution of authority and reward has often
indeed appeared unjust, absolute, and at times even permanent to various
categories of people. As the faintest expression of *in*equitable inequality, social
perceptivity is the individual's diffuse recognition of dirt in the porridge; how
it got there and how it can be gotten out are questions he has not yet effectively
conceived, or at least answered.

Yet, where belief in the possibilities of individual ascent within the structure
is strong, moral judgments of equity and inequity may come to naught. Since
perceptions of social differentiation are individually anchored in the first place,
if the beholder is convinced by a prevailing "success ideology" that *any* man
can succeed if only he tries, those differences may be deemed wholly legitimate.
This possibility is especially likely when conviction is occasionally "validated"
by instances of visible success. If then one's porridge is dirty, it is one's own
fault.

When combined with the success ideology of possessive individualism, namely, the ideology which holds that each person is a free agent and wholly responsible for his own successes and failures (see MacPherson, 1962), individual social mobility in industrial society leads to a consciousness of status and is a counterforce to the class-consciousness potential of social perceptivity. The important distinctions in life become matters of prestige and style of life; and the individual looks upward to emulate his betters in the hope that he may one day be at least like them. The objective fact of class situation remains, despite the circulation of membership implied by individual mobility (see Schumpeter, 1951). But its existence is greatly obscured, and the reality of the possessive market society as a necessarily class-divided society is easily ignored (see MacPherson, 1962: Chapter VI). Invidious comparisons of status seem quite legitimate, in contrast to the odiousness of class, because success in prestige and consumptive style is allegedly free of all ascriptive influence and is therefore compatible with the doctrine of individual freedom. But although class position may be ignored by the status emulator, it still exerts a strong influence on his "destiny." For the hidden outcome of his continued subscription to the success ideology of possessive individualism is the continued dominance of a monopolistic, largely self-perpetuating *possessing class,* through deception, chicanery, and fraud (Pareto, 1916:2178).

Class Awareness

Almost every study of class structure at one point or another examines the question of whether a population is aware not merely of broad social differences but also of the existence of groups which represent more or less permanent crystallizations of such differences. Whereas social perceptivity refers to the recognition, however vague, that people are not all equal, class awareness consists in the added perception that certain clusters of people have life chances, interests, and attitudes enough in common as to constitute distinct "communities of fate."

These group crystallizations are usually perceived in such descriptive terms as "the working class," "the poor," "the rich," "the industrialists," "the powerful," or in such broad spatial terms as "upper class," "middle class," and "lower class." In general, it would seem that the probability of finding the fully developed class consciousness (or the material for its eventual development) is greater where class awareness follows descriptive lines (see Marx and Engels, 1845–1846:74–75). There is already implicit in the descriptive class label some notion of antagonism—"I am poor; he is rich"—or at least the corporate feeling of consciousness-of-kind. In contrast, the spatial label more readily connotes invidious comparisons of prestige and "social importance" and an individualistic ideology of achievement and success. "Upper class" would simply not ring true in the battle songs of labor, such as the following, circa 1886 (quoted in Adamic, 1931:62):

Toiling millions now are waking—
   See them marching on;
All the tyrants now are shaking,
   Ere their power's gone.

Chorus:

Storm the fort, ye Knights of Labor,
   Battle for your cause;
Equal rights for every neighbor—
   Down with tyrant laws!

The notion of class awareness is deceptively simple and straightforward. As Landecker's (1963) discussion of "class structure consciousness" implicitly reveals, it is difficult to disentangle class awareness from the closely related stages of dimensional awareness and class placement when they are viewed as dynamic components of a total process of conceptual formation. It would seem logical that class placement should presuppose an awareness of class structure and of the factors or dimensions that delimit one class from another. But this simple reasoning begs the question of how the individual becomes aware of classes in the first place. Can we safely presume a sequential ordering among these three aspects of class-structure consciousness?

Elizabeth Bott (1957:162ff) has treated this question in some detail in her study of the family and its social network. Conceptualizing class as a reference group, she reminds us of the central Marxian principle that life determines consciousness: "People do not experience their objective class position as a single, clearly defined [entity] . . . except . . . when classes act as corporate groups. . . . the ingredients, the raw materials, of class [conceptions] are located in the indivdual's various primary social experiences." In other words, the individual creates a conception of class structure out of his experiences in "actual membership groups and social relationships both past and present."

There are three steps in the creation of a "class reference group," according to Bott. First, the individual internalizes the norms of his primary-group memberships (work associates, friends, family, neighborhood associates)— together with some hazy notions about the society at large—each of which has its own relational network of power, privilege, and prestige. Second, he engages in a conceptual reduction of these "relatively unconnected and often contradictory norms to a common denominator," thereby manufacturing a general notion of his own position in society. Finally, he projects his conceptual feat back onto society as a whole, and this becomes his conception of the class structure.

Two comments of a critical nature should be made regarding Bott's analysis. First, the heterogeneity specified in the second step, though qualified by the author, is still more problematic than her discussion would suggest. Depending upon situational conditions, the norms may be *more or less* unconnected and contradictory. If, for example, objective circumstances are such that the *Klasse an sich* exhibits high concentration and density of workplace and residence, has access to a common set of external channels of communication, and uniformly suffers restrictions in the choice of voluntary memberships, the norms of the various component groups of the *Klasse an sich* are apt to be quite connected and compatible—even mutually reinforcing. Such a linkage is likely despite the fact that very few if any of the component groups will encompass all or even most of the persons comprising the *Klasse an sich*. In such case, the individual can construct with greater facility a conception of the class structure which is shared by a great many others. And, to continue the example, his conception will more likely be described in dichotomous terms of "they and we."

The second comment refers to the last of Bott's three steps, discussion of which she terminated too soon and thereby possibly misleadingly. Her point that the individual is an active agent in the process of creative imagination is well taken. But once he has projected his creation back onto the larger society, it becomes objectified and reified to some extent. The reified conception then ceases to be under the control of its creator; it turns back upon him and works its influence *as if* it had an independent existence. In this way, conceptions of class structure, depending on their content, can either facilitate or impede the development of the *Klasse für sich* as an organizational form.

Bott's analysis of this complex and largely unconscious mental process of internalization, conceptual reduction, and objectification nevertheless suggests of its own merits the difficulty of the chicken-and-egg question which we posed a few moments ago in connection with consideration of the temporal relationship between class awareness, dimensional awareness, and class placement. Certainly class placement would seem to be highly unlikely without available conceptions of the class structure as points of anchorage. Yet, in creating those conceptions, the individual unavoidably gains some impression of his own class location. In sum, consideration of these complex mental processes, as with Mead's "social self," entails as a propaedeutic device the postulation of relationships of simultaneous reciprocity between man and his creations.

The customary method of isolating class awareness is to simply ask interviewees such questions as: "Are there social classes?" "How many social classes are there?" "What are the social classes?" But questions of this sort have the disadvantage of leading the respondent into a class description of the social order when he might otherwise report an image painted in different colors. Bott's argument—that, while people have direct experiences of distinctions in power, privilege, and prestige, they do not usually experience their class situation as a single clearly definable relational network—means that any simple verbalization of classes may represent little more than a convenient and temporary synthesis that is apt to change at the slightest stimulation of new social experience. Thus, if even approximately consistent and reliable documentation of a population's class awareness is to be accomplished, the interviewer must avoid any untoward suggestions that could trigger an otherwise nonsalient class response. A question such as "What are the important groups in X society?" might be preferable to any of the customary questions, one of which could then be used as an additional probe later in the interview.[6]

Empirical studies of class awareness are much more numerous than comparable investigations of social perceptivity. Most of them report the existence of a rather sizable minority of people who either do not know "what the classes are" or deny their very existence. Responses such as these can probably be interpreted as indication of a lack of class awareness among a certain proportion of the population, although it is almost certain that at least some of those classified as "class-unaware" are merely unable to articulate verbally their class conceptions in the interview situation.

Willener (1957:161) reports from his study of French Switzerland that as many as one in five of his subjects had no clear class image of their society. Popitz and associates (1961:233) report the same proportion from their study of 600 employees of the various foundries and smelting plants located in Germany's Ruhr industrial district. Similarly, Mayntz (1958:84ff.) found in a community study of Euskirchen—an industrial city of about 18,000 inhabitants at the time—that one-fifth of the total sample could not give an answer (or a classifiable answer) to the question, "Here in Euskirchen there are certainly different levels *(Schichten)* of people that are more or less clearly discernible from each other. How many such levels are there, in your opinion, and what would you call them?" Of all interviewed, 1 percent did not answer the question in any fashion; 2 percent denied the existence of any distinctions; 3 percent gave nonrelevant answers; and 14 percent answered with "I don't know" or a similar reply. Svalastoga (1959:179) reports that about 20 percent of his 1,844 sample members denied the existence of class differences and another 6 percent didn't know or didn't answer. Finally, in his report of a 1962 statistical survey of England and Wales, Runciman (1966:153, 158) notes that, when asked a question on self-placement ("What social class would you say you belonged to?"), 17 percent of the 1,415 sample members gave "Don't know," "None," or unclassifiable answers.

Evidence on class awareness in the United States generally parallels that for Europe. Kahl and Davis (1955) found in their study of 219 men in Cambridge, Massachusetts, that a total of 23 percent either had no conception of a class order, or denied the existence of classes, or had difficulty in describing the classes. Haer (1957) reports that of 320 white adults in Tallahassee, Florida, 8 percent said that classes did not exist, and another 12.5 percent failed to answer the interview question. Again, in their Paterson, New Jersey, investiga-

---

[6]Hammond (Oeser and Hammond, 1954:265), for example, used this procedure in his study and found that very few respondents gave nonclass answers. Approximately one-tenth of the total sample required prompting by the customary "What are the social classes?" question, and of these more than three-quarters persevered in their original replies or denied the existence of classes.

tion of the attitudes of 95 textile workers toward the class structure, Manis and Meltzer (1954) discovered that nearly all—90 of the 95—replied in the affirmative when asked if there were social classes in their community. However, when asked, "When you think of the entire country, how many classes do you think there are?" 24 of the 95 workers, or 25 percent, replied that they did not know.

One of the earliest statistical surveys of class awareness in the United States was Richard Centers's (1949:76ff.) now famous study of a national sample of 1,097 white males, conducted in 1945. Although his data more properly belong under the rubric of class placement, they show that approximately 1 percent of his respondents did not believe in classes and another 1 percent did not know enough about the class structure to locate themselves within it. Many scholars (among them Llewellyn Gross, 1949; Case, 1955; Gordon, 1958: 193-202) have since noted many shortcomings in Centers's research procedures, the more important of which we shall detail later in this chapter. For the moment we merely draw attention to Neal Gross's (1953) comparison of results obtained by use of an open-ended question with those obtained by the Centers question, which required respondents to state whether they belonged to the upper class, the middle class, the working class, or the lower class (see also Svalastoga, 1959:176). Gross's findings cast considerable doubt on the utility of the Centers question, "even" in the United States where the foregoing spatial labels are allegedly most applicable in the age of "working-class affluence" and "the end of ideology" (see Bell, 1960; Lipset, 1959, 1964; Waxman, 1968; and below). On the Centers question, only 1 percent denied the existence of class, or said that they did not belong to any class; 2 percent replied with "don't know"; 5 percent responded in terms of other class labels; no one, apparently, failed to respond in any fashion. Gross's open-ended question, on the other hand, yielded the following comparable proportions: "no classes" or "don't belong to a class," 14 percent; "don't know," 20 percent; a class other than any mentioned by Centers, 15 percent; "no response," 5 percent. Both sets of figures apply specifically to the absence of perceived self-locations in the class structure, only a component of which represents class unawareness as such. But this component was probably at least 14 percent of the total sample on the open-ended question, in contrast to only 1 to 3 percent on the Centers question.

In contrast to these investigations from Europe and the United States, several studies have revealed notably higher rates of class awareness elsewhere in the world. In the Australian research of Hammond (Oeser and Hammond, 1954:270-271), only 10 of the 129 sample members from the Greater Melbourne area demonstrated a lack of awareness when confronted by both an open-ended and then a probe question. Similarly, results from a 1962 pilot survey in Melbourne (Davies and Encel, 1965:34–35) indicate that about 11 percent of the 150 respondents saw "no class differences" when asked a question that gave "a *maximum* chance to decline." (See also Davies, 1967; Broom, Jones, and Zubrzycki, 1968).

The evidence from Puerto Rico published by Tumin with Feldman (1961:143ff.) discloses surprisingly high rates of class awareness for that predominantly agricultural society. Using what might be termed an open-ended definitional approach ("What do you understand by the term 'social class'?"), the authors found that 90 percent of a sample of 1,000 cases gave answers which could be subsumed under three major definitions of class. "The other 10 per cent fell principally into the category of 'doesn't know what the term means,' " although a "tiny minority" denied the existence of classes, and 2.5 percent had to be classified as "miscellaneous." Even more striking is the finding that when asked "How many classes are there?" 94 percent specified a definite number, and the remaining 6 percent did not know, denied the existence of classes, or gave no information.

In summary of the above-cited studies, it should be noted that there were important differences in the manner in which the interview questions were constructed. First, some of the results (such as those of Centers, Runciman, Neal Gross) are based on questions that, strictly speaking, pertain to self-placement. Second, of those questions that *directly* related to class awareness, some were demanding in the sense that they asked not simply about the *existence* of classes but about their *number* and/or the *names*. Further, some of the class-awareness questions asked about class structure in a given city or region, while others specifically focused on an entire nation. Such differences in question construction could account for variations in the rate of class awareness. Indeed, as we have seen, variations are found when results from open-ended and structured questions on self-location are compared. However, the rather limited comparisons that we have been able to make regarding different constructions of questions specifically about class awareness do not reveal systematic variations in the rate of class awareness.

Table VI:1 organizes the results from seven studies (percent "class-aware"; last column) according to two major characteristics of the interview questions: first, whether they asked only about the existence of classes (as, "Are there social classes in ——?") or about the number and/or names of classes (as, "How many . . ."; "What are the social classes in ——?"); second, whether the questions were regionally (including city) or nationally focused. Excluding the Manis and Meltzer regional question, which yielded a high frequency of positive responses probably because of an exclusively working-class sample, the proportions "class-aware" ranged from 72 to 82 percent at least, and perhaps to 86 percent depending on the exact figure from Neal Gross's study. But about as much variation occurred *within* the categories of the table as occurred *between* them.

TABLE VI:1. FREQUENCY OF CLASS AWARENESS BY CHARACTERISTICS OF
INTERVIEW QUESTION, SELECTED STUDIES

Characteristics of Interview Question	Country, Source	Sample	Positive Response (percent)
Existence of Classes:			
Regional	United States[a]	95 males	95
National	Denmark[b]	1,466 males	72
National	United States[a]	95 males	75
National	United States[c]	320 white males	79
National	Australia[d]	1,925 males	81
Number/Names of Classes:			
Regional	Germany[e]	692 males	80
Regional	United States[f]	935 heads of household	81–86
Regional	United States[g]	219 males, age 30–49 only	82
National	Denmark[b]	1,466 males	81

[a] Manis and Meltzer (1954:31).
[b] Svalastoga (1959:179, 185).
[c] Haer (1957:118).
[d] Broom, Jones, and Zubrzycki (1968:217).
[e] Mayntz (1958:84ff).
[f] Neal Gross (1953:402).
[g] Kahl and Davis (1955:323–324).

Dimensional Awareness

Class awareness probably anticipates, as a third aspect of class consciousness, a conception of the factors that account for class differentiation: that is, it anticipates what we term dimensional awareness. In general, the person who is aware of the existence of classes is also cognizant—albeit sometimes only faintly—of the dimensions along which classes are constituted, whether they are primarily wealth, occupational activity, authority, or some combination of these and others.

Dimensional awareness can fruitfully be examined in conjunction with another notion, closely related: "images of society." In recognizing factors that separate (or alternatively connect) individuals as participants in an opportunity structure, the person implicitly constructs with some degree of clarity a mental picture of his society's class differentiation. In a manner of speaking, a person's image of society can be thought of as a correlate of his dimensional awareness, and together they add content to his awareness of class.

Theoretically, these distinctions may seem to be neatly demarcated stages in the mental process of creative imagination. In practice, they seldom are.

They overlap each other, and they jointly blend into class placement. A person may be aware of certain factors that divide or unite people into more or less privileged categories of opportunity, but still lack the ability to single out those categories as discrete classes. Or the person may name a number of classes, and even locate himself in one of them, without becoming explicitly aware of the criteria that underlie the divisions of membership. Finally, for one who enumerates a series of classes and then proceeds to place himself in "the working class," the fundamental criterion of class division would seem to be occupation. But this in itself may mean very little. What, after all, does it mean to be a "worker"? In what sense, for example, is the blue-collar worker different from one who *works* as consultant on labor-management relations to the president of a large corporation? For that matter, in what sense does "blue-collar worker" designate a homogeneous category of human activity?

The point of this line of thinking is that determining dimensional awareness and associated class images, as well as determining their relationship to class awareness on the one side and class placement on the other, requires the collection of highly detailed information from people who do not always have the ability (or the patience) to express themselves adequately in an interview situation. The few studies that have been addressed to these topics have suffered greatly from such limitations and, probably for this reason as much as for any other, have yielded divergent conclusions.

Centers (1949:91) concluded from his national survey that the most important criteria of class division in the United States were (in addition to occupation, which was not included in the prepared list of alternatives): beliefs and attitudes, mentioned by 47 percent of his respondents; education, 29 percent; family background, 20 percent; and money, 17 percent. In contrast, Kahl and Davis (1955:324) report that their respondents overwhelmingly considered "income and/or style of life" the most important factor (mentioned by 61 percent). Occupation was selected by only 8 percent, and "morals" by 9 percent of the 219 men in the sample, with the remaining choices scattered among education, family background, and "innate ability." Further, 16 percent said that *no* single criterion could be considered most important. The studies by Haer (1957:118) and Manis and Meltzer (1954:32) both confirm Kahl and Davis's finding that the economic factors of income or wealth were predominant, though the proportions reported were somewhat smaller (51 and 47 percent respectively). But Haer's research, like Centers's work, also shows that factors of belief and attitude were frequently used (by 41 percent) in determining the class membership of people.

For England and Wales, Runciman's (1966:158–159) data show that by far the most important criterion for his sample was occupation. (See also Butler and Stokes, 1969:70.) When asked "What sort of people do you mean when you talk about the middle [or working] class?" nearly half replied in occupational terms.[7] Attitudinal and behavioral descriptions ranked a poor second (about one in seven), with income or wealth following closely behind. Factors of education, family background, and authority were apparently seldom mentioned.

Still another ordering of the factors of dimensional awareness is suggested by Hammond's (Oeser and Hammond, 1954:283–284) Melbourne data. On a question pertaining directly to class placement, and with a closed list of eight factors from which to choose, 36 percent of the respondents selected education as most important, 26 percent selected income, 19 percent selected family background, and only 18 percent selected occupation. Another 18 percent said that one's associates constitute an important factor in determining class membership, and the remaining choices were more or less equally dispersed among prestige, power, and beliefs. The more recent Melbourne data (Davies and Encel, 1965:35), however, indicate that nearly half of these newer respondents were of the opinion that "class is primarily a matter of money."

Turning now to the evidence on images of society, the pattern is surprisingly clear in one respect. Various investigations tend to concur that the number of classes most commonly perceived is three. Kahl and Davis (1955:324) discovered the trichotomous view more than four times as often as the dichotomous, more than twice as often as the tetrachotomous, and more than eight times as often as all remaining class images combined. In Paterson, New Jersey (Manis and Meltzer, 1954:32), 54 percent of those holding a class image of the country as a whole distinguished three classes, 35 percent saw two, and 11 percent saw four or more. The Puerto Rican data (Tumin with Feldman, 1961:147) are quite similar. Davies's (1967:6) Melbourne survey uncovered the following proportions: dichotomy, 24 percent; trichotomy, 43 percent; tetrachotomy, 12 percent; pentachotomy, 6 percent; six or more classes, 1 percent; and 13 percent of the respondents failed to answer, or supplied "miscellaneous" answers.

Moving to the European studies, we find that while Bott (1957) does not give specific figures, it seems clear from her discussion of the depth interviews that the most commonly perceived class order was trichotomic. A survey by Martin (1954), and by inference also the Runciman (1966) survey, support Bott's British evidence on this point.

Similarly, Mayntz's (1958:85ff.) Euskirchen research discloses for that city a preponderance of trichotomous images of society. Of 692 respondents, 46 percent perceived three levels *(Schichten);* 16 percent perceived four; 15 percent, five; 18 percent, six or more; and only 4 percent perceived two. Popitz (Popitz and others, 1961) does not provide a statistical summary, but from his discussion of the interview protocols and his typology of societal images the

---

[7]These proportions are drawn from a reclassification of the data of Tables 2 and 3 in Runciman (1966:158-159).

trichotomous conception appeared to be the most prevalent among his foundry workers. Svalastoga (1959:185) reports 53 percent for the trichotomous, 15 percent for the dichotomous, 7 percent for the tetrachotomous, and 3 percent for five or more classes; 22 percent did not answer, or gave "miscellaneous" answers. Finally, in his Milan study of 1,010 men and women, Pagani (1960: 107–108) found that of the 810 who perceived a class order, 51 percent held a trichotomous view, 34 percent distinguished only two classes, 10 percent saw four, and 5 percent recognized five or more.

There is no need to further document the fact that, where national or at least urban populations are concerned, the most prevalent image of society consists of three classes when *spontaneous* responses are elicited.[8] But we may properly ask, to what is this uniformity due? Does a trichotomous conception of the class structure more nearly do justice to the realities of class inequality, or does it merely represent a convenient and facile solution to a very complex problem of conceptualization? Clearly, a simple answer to these questions is not possible. However, two sets of circumstances would seem to favor a trichotomous conception over any other.

The first concerns a simple question of perception. In all historical societies the distribution of economic, political, and occupational functions has revealed to all but the most insensitive that "some have too much" and "others have too little"; that some are "rich," while others are "poor"; that some obviously occupy positions of political authority and rule, whereas others are bereft of authority and are governed; that some have to work for others, while a few put the rest to work. It is the recognition of these facts, one can well imagine, that underlay the utilization of a class dichotomy in Marx's theory of classes and in most other theories of class conflict as well. The same set of circumstances probably explains the fact that the dichotomous image is fairly common in the social consciousness of people everywhere. In a rich analysis of cultural themes gathered from philosophy, mythology, folklore, and religion, Ossowski (1956; 1963) documented an appreciable tendency throughout human history to conceive the system of social relationships in dichotomic terms. According to this scholar (1956:16), the dichotomous view of differentiation belongs to that small category of archetypal images which impose themselves on the human imagination uninterruptedly throughout the course of the centuries.

But while real, these dichotomous conceptions oversimplify reality in the minds of most. The trichotomous image of the class structure usually asserts

---

[8] By contrast, in small communities awareness of the stratification system is usually more detailed. Since the number of relationships to be comprehended at once is relatively small, more direct knowledge of the collectivity is possible. This fact, plus the research techniques typically employed in community studies, encourages minutely graded descriptions of the social structure. See, for instance, Warner and Lunt (1941); West (1945); Hollingshead (1949); Lenski (1950); Lopreato (1967b).

itself over the simple dichotomy because the distinctions and antagonisms which may inhere in the class dichotomy are at work in more than just one dimension of the social structure. The fundamental division is not merely between ruler and ruled, rich and poor, or employers and employees. These three distinctions, plus others that could be mentioned (the good and the bad, the intelligent and the stupid, and so on), are operative simultaneously in the social consiousness, fading and overlapping into each other. It often happens that, having initially constructed a two-division model of social reality, people reconsider and re-examine reality in a more analytical stance. As Ossowski (1963:32) again notes, in highly differentiated societies, "the sharp dichotomic division between those on top and those at the bottom is usually found to conflict with everyday experience." It is a simple fact that the rich and the poor, the rulers and the ruled, the employers and the employed are not equally rich or poor, not equally powerful or submissive, not equally independent or dependent. There are always gradations of wealth and poverty, legitimate authority and submission, work dependence and independence.

Under these circumstances, dichotomous first impressions of class structure tend to give way in moments of deeper reflection to a multistep conceptual arrangement. In principle, such arrangement lends itself to the sort of detailed gradation that both Pareto and Weber suggested in their critiques of Marx. The human mind, however, is not capable of infinitely complex abstractions. This limitation is manifest in all aspects of the social existence. The concept of "goodness," for instance, in principle lends itself to subdivision after sub-division, *ad infinitum.* But most people are "good," "bad," or simply "all right." By the same token, in assessing one another's height, most men do not use a yardstick but judge differences in broad terms: individual X is "tall," Y is "short," Z is "about average." In brief, social reality, which often appears at first sight in the form of a dichotomous cleavage, upon further scrutiny reveals itself to be complexly arranged. However, the capacity to abstract systematically from this complexity and to do justice to it is limited in the human animal. Probably for that reason, some studies of class consciousness find that people in the upper strata, whose power of abstraction has usually been trained by higher education, tend to perceive more class divisions than do those in the lower strata who on the average are less well educated. For the same reason, perhaps, the trichotomous view of society, so close to the simple dichotomy, is the most popular. And, too, that is why one can find without difficulty examples of societies in which, as Ossowski (1963:39) ob-serves, "within the same class milieu, dichotomous and trichotomous percep-tions of the same society are interchangeable, according to the situation."

The second set of circumstances which favor a three-division image of the class structure concerns the human reluctance to place oneself either at the top or at the bottom of the social scale. A person's description of the class structure of his society is thus influenced by his own perceived place within it. Furthermore, inherent in the concept of class structure is, practically if not theoretically, the notion of invidious comparison. To be wealthy, powerful, independent, and the like, is "better," most persons would agree, than to be poor, powerless, dependent, and the like. In consequence of this elemental circumstance, many persons who are objectively classifiable at the top of the scale feel obligated to perform an act of humility (or strategic modesty) and place themselves not quite at the top, and certainly not at the bottom, but somewhere in the middle. Similarly, at the other end of the scale, few will forgo the need for recognition and admit to being at or even near the bottom of the heap. A diligent search by almost any individual will in fact reveal that there are any number of others who are lower than he is in one respect or another. Hence, most persons find themselves somewhere in the middle. Given the aforementioned limitations in abstractive capacity, the complex range of social gradations is reduced to three convenient divisions, wherein most people will avoid placing themselves in the hauteur of the top or in the humility of the bottom.

Any given population may be in substantial agreement on the *spatial* dimensions of the class structure, but their images of that structure may still exhibit significant variations of substance. Depending on which criteria of class division are considered most central, the content of a person's image may be anchored in occupational, economic, or any number of other differentiating factors. This circumstance is of central importance to studies of social stratification. The time is past when students of stratification set out with great alacrity to demonstrate the holy truth (or, depending on their ideological predilections, the diabolical naiveté) of Marxian thought. And nearly all would now agree that ruminations about "upper classes," "middle classes," and "lower classes," together with all their splintering fractions, have very little to offer in understanding class structure. At most, these playful geometrics are simply a vague reminder that social differences exist and can in principle be arranged into a continuum of innumerable gradations. Gone also is the day when students made their fervent attempts at demonstrating the absolute validity of one class conception as opposed to another. Today's more sober student spends his energies better in determining the variety of class conceptions extant in a given population and the degree to which these images enable us to infer behavioral dispositions and tendencies toward distinguishable types of class action.

Having digested this proclamation of a turn of events in the sociological enterprise, the reader might expect to find, quite justifiably, a profusion of recent investigations into the dynamics of class conceptions and societal imagery. The record shows that only a few exist. One of the earliest, and also most fruitful, is found in Elizabeth Bott's work. On the basis of her interview data, Bott (1957:174ff) concluded that all of the images displayed by her 20 London families could be fitted into four broad models: (1) the *two-valued power model;*

(2) the *three-valued prestige model;* (3) the *many-valued prestige model;* and (4) the *mixed power and prestige model.*

The two-valued (dichotomous) power model consists of images of society in which the emphasis is on opposition and conflict. Use of such imagery, according to Bott, is "a logical consequence of using the ideas of power, conflict, and opposition, since two units represent the smallest number required for a conflict." The logic of this statement is a little startling, for the fact that two units is the smallest number required for a conflict does not preclude the possibility of conflict among multiple units. As we shall see in a later chapter, there is a general inclination in the literature to assume that dichotomous class images are necessarily expressive of social conflict, while more detailed images are indicative of basic harmony. Both assumptions are more myth than fact. In any case, Bott's study showed that the two-valued power model was used by very few individuals, all of whom were members of the working class.

The three-valued prestige model was used by people who placed themselves in the middle class. They generally spoke of a sequence of "upper," "middle," and "working," with two or three subdivisions in the middle class. The notion of conflicting interests between classes was missing; instead, emphasis seemed to be placed on within-class similarities which would facilitate informal interaction and friendship. Weber's "social class" seems to loom large here. The women in particular stressed manners, accent, taste, and social acceptability; their husbands more often spoke of occupation and income. Bott contends that the use of a three-valued model is "a logical consequence of thinking in terms of prestige." In order to conceptualize prestige, one must represent "one's equals, one's superiors, and one's inferiors." True. But it does not follow that all three-valued models are a "logical consequence" of thinking in prestige terms; they may also derive from power conceptualizations of the social structure, as we have argued, and will later show.

The many-valued prestige model was employed by people who placed themselves in the working class but felt some incompatibility with it. Typically, these were manual workers who identified intellectually and culturally with "the educated and professional class of people." By multiplying the number of classes, they presumably avoided the self-effacing effort of placing themselves in the "common" or "average" class, which would have been the natural outcome of a trichotomous model.

Finally, the mixed power and prestige image could consist of any number of classes and was used mainly by "intellectuals" who were inclined to explain the existence of a class system in terms of economic power. In the course of their conversations, however, they revealed shifting conceptions. At times, for instance, they spoke of such questions as status and skill in terms of equality, superiority, and inferiority, so that the researcher could easily perceive "traces" of a "prestige framework."

Hammond's (Oeser and Hammond, 1954:264–265, 273) research in Melbourne suggests a series of models which, aside from some differences in definition and criteria, are similar to Bott's. The most prevalent conceptions revealed by the 118 individuals who demonstrated an awareness of class were what might be termed trichotomous prestige images and trichotomous power-prestige composite images. These two types accounted for three-quarters of the sample. The dichotomous economic-power model, represented by such expressions as "the capitalists and the workers," applied to only 12 percent of the images. Davies (1967:28, 90) suggests a different series of models for his 1962 Melbourne data based mainly on the respondent's choice of class labels (for example, "middle," "working," "ordinary") and imputed size of class.

Willener in Switzerland and Popitz in Germany each found six different models of class structure among their respective samples. Willener's (1957:153, 206–208) subjects saw society in terms of *economic, occupational,* and *political* categories, as well as in terms of *prestige, class struggle,* and a *dichotomy of dependence.* The author observes, moreover, that these six broad models could be reduced to two basic images according to whether they emphasized phenomena of "class" or phenomena of "strata." These two terms—class and stratum—imply greatly divergent conceptions of social inequalities. Strata, or statistical levels, call forth an image of continuity or the lack of deep cleavages; classes suggest antagonistic groupings. Willener found that the idea of struggle (or the lack thereof) was more or less pronounced among his sample members according to their positions in the social structure: the " ' inferior' categories" responded predominantly in terms of class, whereas the " 'superior' categories" more frequently spoke of strata.

In Germany, Popitz (Popitz and others, 1961:233–242) distinguished among six class images: (1) *static order;* (2) *progressive order;* (3) *dichotomy as collective fate;* (4) *dichotomy as individual conflict;* (5) *reform of the social order;* and (6) *class struggle.* Of the 438 interview protocols that exhibited classifiable images, the two most commonly employed were those of progressive order (34 percent)—which, according to Popitz, implied satisfaction with the rate of economic growth and development, and which was prevalent among the younger workers—and dichotomy as collective fate (also 34 percent)—which implied passive acceptance of the power dichotomy as "part of life." The image of dichotomy as individual conflict was held by 14 percent of the workers, and the image of class struggle or revolutionary change accounted for only 1 percent of the 438 descriptions (see also Svalastoga, 1959: 177–178). As in French Switzerland, these six types of imagery were also reducible to the more basic division of dichotomy versus hierarchy, and, again, the former was typical of blue-collar workers, while the latter was usually produced by white-collar employees.

Finally, Mayntz (1958:89ff.) developed a series of four pure models and four mixed models from an analysis of the spontaneous expressions emitted by the

692 sample members naming the various levels *(Schichten)* of society.[9] As presented, these models are of different analytic value from those developed by Bott, Willener, and Popitz, since they directly reflect the substantive factors of class division that loomed most important in the respondent's mind. The four pure models, in order of preference, were the *occupational* model (38 percent), the *prestige* model (23 percent), the *income* model (8 percent), and the *educational* model (less than 1 percent). Nevertheless, these and the composite constructions can be combined with Mayntz's data on the spatial dimensions of respondent imagery in such a way as to more nearly parallel the previously examined models.[10] When this is done, we find that the most frequent image fits what might be called a many-valued occupational model (28 percent), and the next most common fits a trichotomous prestige model (17 percent).

Class Placement

Throughout these pages, we have noted the difficulty of *empirically* separating the analytical distinctions of class awareness, dimensional awareness, and class placement. In many respects, they appear to occur simultaneously in the human consciousness; indeed, in some of the investigations just reviewed (Mayntz, for example), evidence regarding the first two of these components was extracted from the same short question. In order to complete our examination of this tightly bundled conceptual package, we turn now to the literature on class placement.

Assessment of class placement has been traditionally attempted in one of two ways. By one method, respondents are presented with a list of class labels, which the researcher may or may not have discovered through prior observation of the respondents, and are asked to indicate "to which of these social classes" they belong. The best-known example of this technique is the research by Centers, who asked his respondents to state whether they belonged to an "upper class," a "middle class," a "working class," or a "lower class." Although the method is highly suspect, it has become so deeply entrenched in the sociologist's repertoire that it cannot be overlooked.

The major weaknesses of this technique are, first, the use of a forced-choice question and, second, the combination of spatial and descriptive terminologies. With respect to the first point, it is obvious that when confronted by the restrictions of a forced-choice question, the interviewee may feel some obligation to make a response simply in order to abide by the everyday rules of

---

[9]The list of the various expressions used is in Table 14, Mayntz (1958:88). The most frequent included "the workers," "simple workers," "the working stratum *(Stand)*," and the like, for a total of 61 percent; and "the middle stratum *(Stand)*," 44 percent. Only 4 percent chose expressions like "capitalists," and only 8 percent employed such terms as "working class *(Klasse)*" and "the proletariat."

[10]Computed from Table 15, Panel A, and Table 16 (Mayntz, 1958:96, 98).

common decency and cooperation. But in this cooperation, the spontaneity of his imagery has been dampened; one cannot determine to what extent his answer reflects his own cognitions and evaluations and to what extent it simply reflects a set of labels temporarily imposed upon his mind from without. As for the second limitation of the Centers question, a label such as "middle class" bears connotations that are entirely different from those implicit in the term "working class." The former leaves indefinite the range of differences to be encompassed; the latter is usually specific in suggesting an aggregate of predominantly blue-collar workers. Moreover, the term "working class" sometimes carries notions of corporate feeling, exploitation, and conflict, while the term "middle class" usually reveals more than anything else a concern for status distinctions and comparisons.

Spontaneous self-classification, the second and preferred method of assessing class placement, is predicated on the assumptions—inescapable in any given historical period—that the class structure is experienced differently by different people and that, to the extent that we are interested in determining how the various conceptions influence human behavior, all class models are partially true. As Kahl (1953:181) recommends, we must therefore go to the public with a flexible question that allows "*the respondents to choose both the model and their position within it.*" Llewellyn Gross (1949:418) makes a telling point when he argues against Centers that, "if class identification is an integral part of the thought and action patterns of most people," we should be able to elicit "the appropriate responses from the interviewee by *recall* rather than by recognition." The spontaneous-recall technique demands that the individual dip into his *own* well of historical reality and divine the waters accordingly.

As with any of the levels of awareness considered in this chapter, class placement may be viewed in variable terms. It is probably at a minimum when a person is only vaguely cognizant of self-location. Conversely, it reaches a maximum when this capacity is accompanied by a clear recognition of the class position of others, which in turn means (1) the awareness of sharing the same class position with certain others and (2) the awareness of *not* sharing the same class position with *all* others, that is, a feeling of separateness and social distance.

The distinction we have made between class awareness and self-placement is not common in studies of class consciousness. Frequently, the simple class-awareness stage is altogether skipped, and the interviewee is expected to manifest his cognitions of class through direct self-location. Whether the interview schedule is a structured one, as in Centers's study, or an open-ended one, the researcher demands that his respondent indicate the class to which he thinks he belongs. The result may be more a researcher's artifact than an accurate reflection of the person's thought. The two aspects of class consciousness admittedly fade into one another; nevertheless they should be distinguished for analytical purposes, and the research design ought to mirror this distinction.

TABLE VI:2. PATTERNS OF CLASS PLACEMENT FOR SELECTED COUNTRIES, BY TYPE OF INTERVIEW QUESTION

Type of Question, and Country	Self-Classification					No Response; Don't Know	Total
	Upper Class	Middle Class	Working Class	Lower Class	Other Response		
Structured							
Australia I[a]	2	50	47	*	—	1	100
Australia II[b]	1	49	44	4	—	2	100
France I[a]	6	44	46	*	—	4	100
France II[c]	10	30	36	19	—	5	100
France III[d]	3	34	33	18	11	1	100
Germany I[a]	3	52	41	*	—	4	100
Germany II[e]	2	42	53	2	—	1	100
Great Britain I[a]	2	35	60	*	—	3	100
Great Britain II[f]	1	32	67	*	—	—	100
Italy[a]	4	54	42	*	—	—	100
Mexico[a]	2	45	51	*	—	2	100
Netherlands[a]	4	33	60	*	—	3	100
Norway[a]	1	43	45	*	—	11	100
United States I[a]	4	42	51	*	—	3	100
United States II[g]	3	43	51	1	1	1	100
United States III[h]	4	36	52	5	—	3	100
United States IV[i]	1	35	60	2	—	2	100
United States V[j]	2	42	45	3	6	2	100
United States VI[k]	5	43	47	3	—	2	100
United States VII[l]	1	66	31	1	—	—	99
United States VIII[m]	2	61	34	2	—	1	100

Unstructured

							Total
Australia[b]	1	49	34	4	—	12	100
Denmark[n]	0	34	20	4	35	7	100
England and Wales[o]	2	40	40	*	17	—	99
France[c]	8	23	27	8	16	19	101
Germany[p]	1	46	20	1	33	—	101
United States I[j]	1	31	11	3	15	39	100
United States II[k]	1	52	14	2	13	18	100
United States III[q]	2	43	6	2	12	35	100
United States IV[r]	—	21	50	5	23	2	101

* The "Lower Class" label was not considered.

[a] Buchanan and Cantril (1953:13).

[b] Broom, Jones, and Zubrzycki (1968:219).

[c] Rogoff (1953b). *Note:* "Upper Class" was originally designated "Bourgeoisie"; similarly, "Lower Class" was "Peasant."

[d] Special tabulations supplied by Mattei Dogan from his French survey data collected in 1968 ($N = 3,300$). *Note:* "Other Response" includes "Proletariat" (4 percent), "Petty Bourgeoisie" (4 percent), and "Other class" (3 percent).

[e] Reported in Centers (1949:225, n.1).

[f] Kahan, Butler, and Stokes (1966).

[g] Centers (1949:77). *Note:* Refers to the 1945 survey.

[h] Centers (1949:77). *Note:* Refers to the 1946 survey.

[i] Eulau (1956).

[j] Neal Gross (1953).

[k] Kahl and Davis (1955).

[l] Tucker (1968:510). *Note:* "Middle Class" was originally divided into "Upper Middle," "Middle," and "Lower Middle."

[m] Hodge and Treiman (1968:536). *Note:* "Middle Class" was originally divided into "Upper Middle" and "Middle."

[n] Svalastoga (1959:181). *Note:* "Middle Class" includes "Upper Middle," "Middle," and "Lower Middle"; "Lower Class" includes that label plus "The Small Ones."

[o] Runciman (1966:158). *Note:* Original replies were to an open-ended question, but were then collapsed to a three-category scheme. Also, the "No Response; Don't Know" percentage includes "Other Classes" and "No Classes."

[p] Mayntz (1958:103). *Note:* Figures calculated from Table 17; "Middle Class" includes both *Stand* and *Klasse.*

[q] Haer (1957:119). *Note:* Tallahassee data.

[r] Manis and Meltzer (1954:33).

It sometimes happens that a person is *not conscious of his consciousness of class.* Having spontaneously described the class structure, he then fails to consistently locate himself within it. Having mentioned classes A, B, and C, as representative of the class structure of his society, he then proceeds to locate himself in class D. Shifts such as this occur because conceptualizations of social structure are anchored in a great variety of actual experience, and the stimuli of the interview situation may evoke any combination of those experiences and, therefore, varying perspectives on class structure.

We turn now to some empirical studies of class placement, most of which have already been cited in previous contexts. In reviewing this literature an important caution must be observed.[11] Meaningful comparisons of class-placement data across particular studies must take into account differences in the occupational composition of juxtaposed samples. This warning, which applies in some degree to the previously considered stages of awareness, must be heeded for both intrasocietal and cross-societal comparisons. In the latter case, for example, we should not be surprised to find that proportionately more people of a predominantly agricultural society place themselves in a "peasant" or "farmer" class than do the inhabitants of an advanced industrial society. With this in mind, then, the following review should be interpreted as primarily a benchmark for our later analysis of the Italian data.

To avoid taxing the reader's forbearance with yet another lengthy narration of findings, the pertinent data have been conveniently arranged in Table VI:2. Apart from the above warnings, and given our control for the type of interview question ("structured" versus "unstructured"), these data can be considered as approximately comparable.

Considering the forced-choice data first, one finding stands out in particular: nearly everyone eschewed self-placement in either the top or the bottom. Excluding the data from Rogoff's study (France II) and those from Dogan's study (France III), no more than 5 to 6 percent of the various samples, and

---

[11]Another caution, of considerable import, must be given due emphasis—even though (indeed, *because*) little more than recognition is presently possible. And that concerns the problem of imputation and meaning equivalence, not only in the above data but throughout the chapters of Part II. In any study of class consciousness, but especially in those based on standard sample-survey techniques of data collection, and especially also when crosscultural (whether intersocietal or intrasocietal) comparisons are attempted, it is a matter of the greatest importance to attend to questions of semantic equivalence or variability with respect to the several class terms employed. Stated in the abstract, this caution seems perfectly obvious, of course: the researcher must not assume uncritically an equivalence of meaning structures when numerous interviewees respond to the same question with apparently common terminologies—he cannot assume that "middle class," for example, has identical meanings to all who employ it. Nevertheless, in the actual practice of social research this and related problems of imputation have been evidently less than obvious, in view of the extremely meager attention they have received in investigations of class awareness, imageries, self-placements, and the like. For a good illustration of some aspects of the problem, see London and London's (1966) analysis of the Harvard Project on the Soviet Social System; their findings are germane to a good deal more than that particular instance of survey research.

usually fewer, chose either "upper class" or "lower class." Our categorizations of Rogoff's and Dogan's data are somewhat misleading, moreover, since the original response alternatives in each study were "bourgeoisie" rather than "upper class" and "peasant" rather than "lower class." Certainly we cannot assume semantic equivalence in the case of either pair; "peasant," for instance, probably is a less onerous term than "lower class."

In view of the diversity of populations represented, the distributions shown in the top panel of the table (Structured) might well be considered impressively uniform. When only three class labels were offered the interviewees, the range of variation in the frequency of middle-class self-placements was from 32 to 54 percent; for working-class self-placements, from 41 to 67 percent. These are large ranges, certainly, but if only two countries are excluded from the list (Great Britain and the Netherlands) they are reduced to only 12 and 10 percentage points, respectively. For the United States alone, where in all but the Buchanan and Cantril study (United States I) a four-class scheme was submitted to the respondents, six of the eight samples yielded very similar distributions. The seventh and eighth, reported by Tucker and by Hodge and Treiman, respectively, are the newest sets of data, and the greater frequencies of middle-class self-placements recorded by these national surveys (1963 and 1964, respectively) may be indicative of historical change in both objective social structure and in subjective conceptions of, and self-locations within, that structure. They may also simply reflect differences in research procedure.

Schreiber and Nygreen's (1970) review of results from several nationally based United States sample surveys conducted between 1945 and 1968 revealed no over-all decline in the rate of working-class self-placements (structured-question data, mostly from employed white males aged 21 and over). There were noticeable fluctuations from study to study, but results from 1964, 1966, and 1968 surveys conducted by the Survey Research Center paralleled Centers's 1945 data and the data from a 1946 survey by the American Institute of Public Opinion. Slightly over one-half of the interviewees in each case considered themselves working-class, and slightly over two-fifths chose a middle-class label (see also Lane, 1965).

Studies which employed an open-ended question highlight the difficulty with which the sociological content of such expressions as "the middle class" can be interpreted. Three comparisons from the table are instructive. The studies by Rogoff for France, by Kahl and Davis for Cambridge, Massachusetts (United States II), and by Neal Gross for Minneapolis, Minnesota (United States I), each contain, for a single sample, data that were obtained from both structured and open-ended questions. When juxtaposed, these sets of findings indicate that popular usage of self-placement expressions like "middle class," and especially "working class," is considerably less prevalent than a structured question alone would have us believe. Moreover, "other" responses and "don't know" or "no answer" responses are greatly more frequent in the unstructured situation than in the structured one. Neal Gross, for instance, found that when presented with a closed list of four labels, 87 percent of his respondents chose either "middle class" or "working class" self-descriptions. But when previously asked an open-ended question on class placement, the corresponding proportion was only 42 percent, with 15 percent selecting "other" expressions and 39 percent naming no class or not responding. To complicate matters even more, there is no assurance that a self-styled middle-class respondent to an unstructured question will not shift to a working-class designation on a closed question. In the structured situation the researcher gets rather what he asks for, and then he faces the ungodly task of determining what it all means.

Some of the diversity of evidence displayed in the second panel of Table VI:2 (unstructured) may be attributed to differences in the composition of samples. Although rigorous controls cannot be inserted in these studies, a few observations may be tendered. Most of the investigations (among them Runciman, Mayntz, Svalastoga, Neal Gross) have demonstrated that, while far from perfect, there is a fairly strong positive correlation between occupational position and self-placement. An internal comparison of Neal Gross's findings shows that among the 249 respondents drawn from a high-rent area of Minneapolis, 45 percent placed themselves in the middle class, and only 1 percent chose a working-class designation. Conversely, of the 197 people drawn from a low-rent residential area, only 10 percent considered themselves to be members of the middle class, while 15 percent selected the working-class label. Mayntz's sample was composed mostly of high-manual and low-nonmanual occupational positions; moving up the scale from low- to high-manual and from low- to high-nonmanual occupations, the proportions choosing the working-class designation were 59, 38, 6, and zero, respectively. Finally, Manis and Meltzer's 95 interviewees were mostly skilled craftsmen or operatives, and all were members of the local textile union. It is not surprising, then, that this study reports the highest percentage of working-class self-placements.

To summarize briefly: When no restrictions were placed on the interviewees' choice of expressions, a great variety of self-designations were produced, and the pattern of responses was not altogether uniform from society to society. In some countries, labels with strong affective meanings were more frequent, while in others the relatively neutral spatial designations were typical. The 8 percent in Rogoff's study who labeled themselves as members of a "bourgeois" class, for example, cannot be matched by comparable groupings from either the United States or Great Britain.

An intriguing question has yet to be answered: What accounts for the relative cross-societal consistency displayed by the structured-question data? The above discussion has suggested two possible answers, but neither is entirely satisfactory. The fact that the interview question *was* closed is irrelevant in a sense, because *approximately* the same question was asked in *approxi-

mately the same way in all nine countries. Nor can intrasocietal evidence of a correlation between class placement and occupational position provide the answer, since that would involve the patently unfounded assumption of similar occupational structures in all nine countries. To take just one comparison from the table, one-quarter of Mexico's economically active population in 1950 (the census date nearest the time of the study) was employed in nonmanual occupations; this fraction contrasts with almost two-fifths for the United States (1950). And yet these two countries show roughly the same pattern of class placement: excluding the United States survey data for 1963 and 1964, in each case about two-fifths of the respondents identified with the middle class. In short, if class placement corresponded closely to the occupational structure of a society, we would undoubtedly observe more disparate findings than those reported in Table VI:2.

A third possible answer to our query lies in the nature of the alternative class labels that were presented to the sample members. All but one of these labels are purely spatial designations, and the exception ("working class") may acquire similar characteristics from association with the others. An overriding trait of spatial labels is their relativity. Since they are in large measure devoid of any solid anchorage in immediate human experience, they do not *necessarily* apply to any specific occupational groupings. Rather, they are free to shift from one application to another, according to external circumstances. Since "upper," "middle," and "lower" levels can be perceived in any system of ranking, all divisions of labor and distributions of reward can be graded in such fashion. Thus, people in a given country may define a certain range of the occupational structure as constituting the "upper," "middle," or "lower," regardless of how it compares with that of some other country. This argument is admittedly conjectural, and we have no way in which to test it with the data of Table VI:2. But if the conjecture should be empirically supportable, it leads to an interesting ramification, namely, that people throughout the Euro-American world closely agree on what proportions constitute "upper," "middle," and "lower" despite the fact that in appearance these labels lack concrete anchorage.

Class Solidarity

The fifth stage in the formation of class consciousness refers to what Briefs (1937:90) so well depicted as a "fellow feeling that comes with the realization that all who have a common lot face a common fate." In keeping with Marx's theory of class conflict, class solidarity may be defined more specifically as the manifestation of common attitudes, beliefs, and behavior in economic and political matters among persons who share particular life chances in the economic and political orders of their society.

An essential component of Marx's theory, it may be recalled, was the individual recognition of class interests. Such interests, according to that theory, are predicated in the economic situation of the *Klasse an sich*. As certain structural conditions of society develop, the people who in the aggregate comprise a *Klasse an sich* gradually recognize their common lot with respect to those particular interests, and the consequence is "a force that unites into groups people who differ from one another, by overriding the differences between them" (Marshall, 1965:180).

Class solidarity implies the complementary sentiments of *intra*class cama-raderie and worth, on the one hand, and *inter*class resentment and antago-nism, on the other. This complementarity describes the peculiar dependency that all conflict groups not only endure, but in fact celebrate. Thus, given Marx's focus on the asymmetry of power relations, interclass antagonism from the worker's standpoint is dependent on individual recognition of common interests and on a shared sense of exploitation at the hands of a more powerful and privileged class. In turn, the intraclass camaraderie can reach full propor-tions only in the heat of interclass hostilities. It is in this sense that class solidarity represents a predisposition to aggressively engage in a course of action designed to promote the interests of one's own class and to destroy those of another.

Class solidarity should not be confused with *class action* proper, however. Marx (1852b:47) was only too explicit in arguing that we must distinguish between what a man thinks and says and what he is and does. Hence, as DeGré (1950:177) correctly notes, class consciousness as class action can be delineated only through a historical-structural analysis of actual human events. Even in its most extreme, militant form, class solidarity represents only the *view* that class conflict is the inevitable outcome of antagonistic class interests, a *predis-position* to take up arms against the opposing class (see Leggett, 1968). In the concrete exigencies of human life, many factors may intervene to prevent this predisposition from terminating in corporate class action (see Rosenberg, 1953). For one, the realities of such a venture entail not mere inconveniences but profound sacrifices. The risks are immediate and potentially very great; but the rewards are long-term and highly problematic. It is well short of disparage-ment, then, to judge that many people simply lack the political courage re-quired by such an undertaking. And for many others, the provenience of their courage lies in circumstances so extreme that they very rarely discover it. In short, there is an inertia to human nature by virtue of which solidarity with "one's class" *tends* to remain at the theoretical or sentimental level.

Furthermore, it cannot really be argued that the best way to assess class solidarity is to study common class action, for one cannot assume that histori-cal instances of what may be deemed class action invariably bear witness to the presence of solidarity in the social consciousness of the participants. While the inference is probably justifiable in many instances, it may also happen that for some individuals participation reflects not solidarity with the class but merely a belief that such participation is the most effective method of reaping *individual* advantages. Pareto (1916:1220), it may be recalled, judged this "soldier of fortune" sentiment to be widespread: an individual talks of his class interests instead of his personal interests because it is a fashionable mode of expression and because it is frequently very profitable in its consequences. Italian skidders, as we shall see in Chapter XV, come quite close to manifesting precisely this type of behavior.

The class-action approach also poses certain practical problems for the researcher. To begin with, appropriate settings for the conduct of investigation are not common; nor are they commonly accessible to the statistical techniques of social-science research. Secondly, sites of class action are not among the safest locations for the staid researcher with his interview schedules and note pads in hand. For these as well as other reasons, then, we propose an alternative method of obtaining large quantities of information relevant to class solidarity: Ask the individual about his feelings toward various class phenomena. Although this method has some disadvantages in comparison to a more direct approach, especially those disadvantages which stem from possible disparities between reported attitude and actual behavior, it does offer one important advantage (aside from researcher longevity). It allows us to single out a stage in the formation of class consciousness which, although constituting a predisposition toward class action, may or may not actually terminate in it.

Class solidarity has been all too often neglected in studies of class consciousness. The neglect has been so pronounced, in fact, that a literature of findings comparable to those we have reviewed for some of the previous stages simply does not exist. The record shows instead that studies of the class-consciousness process typically exhaust themselves with considerations of class placement: what kind of self-placement the subject makes; what descriptions or imageries he uses; how his self-placement compares with his objective position in the social structure.[12] In view of this poverty, we shall have to content ourselves with a brief examination of empirical studies that are for the most part only collateral to our interest in class solidarity.

In his investigation of Lasswell's (Lasswell and Kaplan, 1950:25) concept of "political perspective"—that is, "a pattern of identifications, demands, and expectations"—Eulau (1956) paid particular attention to questions of consistency between self-placement and objective position in the social structure. His

---

[12]A brief exception is found in Svalastoga (1959:181, 184). Of the 64 percent of the 1,466 males in his sample who said that they belonged to "a definite social class," nearly half (49 percent, or 460 respondents) answered "No" when asked, "Do you think that the —— class [respondent's class] has interests which are counteracted by the other classes?" Of the 44 percent who answered "Yes," most (27 percent, absolute) gave what Svalastoga called a "non-aggressive specification"; 12 percent gave an "aggressively formulated specification," and 5 percent gave no specification.

major aim was to determine "whether those similarly identified in terms of class are also similar in political" perspective. Cross-tabulating objective class position and self-placement for a national sample of 1,132 Americans, Eulau distinguished among working-class consistents (workers self-assessed as workers), middle-class consistents (middle-class people classifying themselves as middle-class), middle-class affiliates (workers classifying themselves as middle-class), and working-class affiliates (middle-class persons classifying themselves as workers). On the basis of this scheme and various research questions, Eulau discovered that regardless of their objective positions in the social structure those identifying with the working class preferred to see themselves as Democrats, whereas those identifying with the middle class saw themselves as Republicans (see also Eulau, 1962).

A number of other investigations have similarly demonstrated the influence of self-assigned class on political perspective (these include Runciman, 1966: 170–187; Nordlinger, 1967:163–175; Butler and Stokes, 1969:76–80; Soares, 1967:487–489; Dogan, 1967; Hamilton, 1967; Davies, 1967:54–65). Runciman, for instance, found that "the relationship between self-rated 'class' and party preference . . . makes so much difference to Labour or Conservative support that it reverses the direction" of the original class-politics linkage. While a variety of personal attributes—including income, age, education, sex, and social origin—exerted in varying degrees an independent influence on the relationship of self-placement to party preference, none could explain it away. Thus, Runciman concludes, "the way in which people see their location in the social hierarchy is, irrespective of the actual degree of inequality to which they are subject, a major influence on their propensity to radicalism."

Such findings, unfortunately, tell us little in a positive way about class solidarity. They do little more, in fact, than once again substantiate W. I. Thomas's (1923:42) famous dictum concerning the self-fulfilling consequences of subjective definitions of the situation. At any given time (short of Marx's imminent revolution, at least), a person of objectively defined middle-class position may judge himself to be of the working-class (or the reverse), may on that basis make some identification with his self-assessed class peers, and yet may or may not demonstrate a solidarity of interests with them. In one sense, of course, he cannot do so by definition, for his objective class interests are what they are regardless of what he thinks they might be. As Marx and Engels (1844:53) put it, "The question is not what this or that proletarian, or even the whole of the proletariat at the moment *considers* as its aim. The question is *what the proletariat is,* and what, consequent on that *being,* it will be compelled to do." In the subjective definitions of his situation, the person may identify with the interests of a class not his own and therein show some manner of "solidarity"—behave as a "working-class Tory," for example. But this identification—whether accountable in terms of status striving, economic satisfaction, deference, ignorance, or some other scheme of explanation[13]—is not representative of a "false" *class* solidarity in the sense characteristic of the *Klasse für sich*.

An assessment of class solidarity requires information beyond what is given by the kind of scheme Eulau, Runciman, and others employed. If nothing else, it requires at least a simple, direct query concerning expressions and feelings of unity toward one's class. Data of just that sort will be examined in Chapter X. But Eulau's approach can still be used fruitfully as a summation of the first four levels in the development of class consciousness. This, with the addition of information about class solidarity as we conceive of it with our data, may represent the closest approximation to full class consciousness that can be attempted away from the fire of class action proper. We shall return to these matters in Chapter X.

A second body of literature which is pertinent to the question of class solidarity in many respects, and which has gained notable popularity in recent years, concerns an alleged "end of ideology." Briefly put, the thrust of the argument has it that we have witnessed in recent history the "exhaustion of political ideas" and a concomitant decline in the ideological content of political institutions and activities. (See for example, Aron, 1957; Bell, 1960; Lipset, 1964; Shils, 1955.) Thus, Lipset (1959:406–407) contends—on a surprisingly ideological key—that "the fundamental political problems of the industrial revolution have been solved," and that, since disparities in wealth have declined, the necessity of ideology has also declined "within stable democracies." The deceptions of what pass as democracies are apparently rather complete.

No doubt the structural changes that have taken place in Western society over the last several decades have wrought important consequences for class behavior. In part, these consequences have stemmed from the reflexive influence of Marxian thought itself. By every objective measure the working classes of the twentieth century, encouraged in part by Marxian doctrine, have won concessions that produce an increased sense of well-being and, to that extent, undermine the resentments and antagonisms which were current and foreseeable when Marx wrote. But the deradicalization of a particular social movement does not in itself spell an end of ideology. Even in deradicalization, change is typically achieved under an ideological façade of nonchange.

To speak of the end of ideology and of depoliticization in contemporary society is somewhat ambiguous, for the term can refer to at least three different phenomena (Himmelstrand, 1962:83–90): (1) a development toward ideologi-

---

[13]A number of authors (among them Butler and Rose, 1960; Abrams, 1964) have suggested the status-striving explanation for the "working-class Tory" phenomenon. However, Runciman (1966:144–145) concludes from his data, and Nordlinger (1967:168) concurs, that this explanation is inappropriate. According to these authors, rather than identifying with the middle-class culture in the hope of one day becoming a member of it, the working-class Tory is simply expressing his satisfaction with the current order of things and does not want to encourage anyone to rock the boat, so to speak.

cal consensus, which in any case harbors potential internal fissures; (2) the decreasing salience of ideological statements, which could be more a matter of changes in rhetoric than anything else; and (3) the weakening impact of ideologies, which may reflect nothing more than a trough in an ocean of change. What purport to be scientific generalizations about the end of ideology and depoliticization are suspect if for no other reason than that the proposition is about change, and the data that have been applied to it are singularly lacking in a longitudinal perspective. (See LaPalombara, 1966a; Allardt, 1964; Littunen, 1964.)

Considering all the evidence available, including that which comes from simply being in the world, contemporary industrial society would seem to be filled with a *greater complexity* of ideological cleavages and conflict than was nineteenth-century society. Many of the bases of social cleavage are re-emerging as clearly visible and active forces only after a period of relative quiescence (see Janowitz and Segal, 1967; Aron, 1968). The foremost examples include "race," concretized as skin color, and nationalism. Others, such as the much-discussed gap between the "have" and the "have-not" nations in economic development, and the "conflict of generations" (Feuer, 1969), are appearing in dramatic terms for perhaps the first time in the social consciousness. It is indeed the case that the classical age of bourgeois ideology, and with that the classical age of a proletarianized wage-earner ideology, has lost its efficacy (see Bendix, 1956). But the resolution of class conflict is yet to come. Classes have not ceased to exist; neither has class conflict come to an end; neither, moreover, is there no element of exploitation in class relations today. At most, and possibly only for the moment, one can say that "classes as entities construed by their members as massive, on-going and necessarily opposed realities are . . . but quasi-groups, capable certainly rapidly of becoming internally structured and self-conscious, but only intermittently existent as responses to a variety of precipitating causes" (MacRae, 1958:270). Ideologies and consciousness of class have lost their monopoly of conflict and cleavage—if they ever truly had it; today's complexly interwoven network of cleavages and conflicts responds not only to class but also to other phenomena such as generational differences, race, and nationalism. Perhaps it is an unwitting participation in the last of these three phenomena that leads many scholars into presumptuous proclamations about the end of ideology.

Whether notions about the end of ideology are themselves curiously ideological, the point of our concern is something different. To the extent that MacRae's judgment is sound, class solidarity is generally lacking in contemporary class relations. Whatever the objective inequalities of power and economic position, experiences of relative deprivation resulting therefrom are translated into a consciousness of social cleavages apart from those classical cleavages of class. The "working-class Tory," for various possible reasons—deference to "one's betters" or to "national interest," reaction to an implied racial threat, or simple concern for the perquisites of status—prefers an expression of political support for a party that has not been allied in any positive way with the working-class movement. These, however, are empirical questions, not to be answered as a convenient extension of this or that ideology (LaPalombara, 1966a), and we shall treat them accordingly in Chapter X.

SUMMARY

Class consciousness, to recapitulate briefly, can be conceived both as a process of becoming and also as an end state of class action. Societies of different times and places differ in the distinctness of class boundaries, in the range of social inequalities, and in the cleavages of class interests. What was true of nineteenth-century England or France would not be equally true of mid-twentieth-century Italy or the United States; nor would the latter pair be equivalent in all respects. By the same token, class consciousness as a formative process may be viewed in variable terms, whether it concerns the prevalence of class consciousness or concerns its content and emotional charge (Ossowski, 1963:140). In seeking to assess the range of contents and emotional charge that span the formation of class consciousness, we have found it convenient to begin with a simple generalized form of awareness of social differentiation and thence trace it through the intermediate stages of class awareness, dimensional awareness, class placement, and finally class solidarity.

We have repeatedly emphasized throughout the foregoing pages that for Marx and the revolution, there could be no leaping of the abyss in two jumps. Class consciousness was the fully constructed bridge, an organizational event through which man becomes most intensely a *zoon politikon* (a politicized animal). As such, it calls for a historical-structural analysis of class action, whereas the components we have outlined are abstractive of the participants' "theoretical" awareness of class—that is, of their contemplation of class rather than their direct action to support a class initiative. However, there begins in simple awareness a negation of that distinction accorded by Greek, Stoic, and Christian philosophers to the *vita contemplativa* versus the *vita activa.* Class awareness is at least a beginning of class consciousness, an early stage in a sequence and process whereby theory and practice become fused. Thus, even though we cannot make adequate use of a structural analysis of class action, our investigation of class awareness, dimensional awareness, class placement, and sentiments of class solidarity—predominantly "theoretical," perceptual evaluations by our subjects—is far from being irrelevant to it.

One final point should be mentioned before turning to that investigation. Theoretically, the concept of class consciousness is applicable to any class, although this point is often neglected in discussions of the subject. We usually read only of "working-class consciousness." But class in its psychosocial dimensions inherently involves class consciousness and political interests and practice; consequently, we can speak of a class-conscious bourgeoisie as well as a class-conscious proletariat. By the very history of the phenomenon, one demands the other. Marx made this fact the focal point of an equilibrium analysis in his discussion of *The Class Struggles in France (1848–1850)*.

To take what might be deemed an extreme illustration, the new elite groups of emergent West African nationalism have constituted an identifiable "middle" class situated between an imperialist ruling elite and the ruled tribal mass. (See Wallerstein, 1967:498–499; Lloyd, 1966.) As such, and despite the persisting influences of tribal stratification systems and an imperfect congruence of class and ethnic groupings, they have developed "a reasonably marked class consciousness, in the sense that they realized they had a set of economic interests, separate from that of the European ruling elite and . . . the African peasant masses. They acted on this realization and created political associations to pursue these class interests." Accordingly, our concern in the empirical analyses of the following chapters will be with not only a working class, proletarianized or otherwise, but also with a variety of other economic interest groups.

VII

CLASS STRUCTURE AND IMAGES OF SOCIETY

The empirical literature reviewed in the preceding chapter has produced a range of broad expectations for the analysis of our survey data.[1] We should expect, for example, that from a fifth to a third of the sample members will be unaware (or, at least, incapable of expressing awareness) of class structure; that the majority of those who show class awareness will have made some conceptualization of its content and of the factors underlying class division; that most of the class-aware will succeed in locating themselves within the self-defined class structure, albeit not always consistently with their theoretically appropriate class interests; that only some, perhaps fewer than half, of those who make self-assignments will express sentiments of unity or solidarity with their self-assessed class peers. Moreover, we should expect that the trichotomous images of society will be most prevalent, particularly those three-valued conceptions that stress elements of honor or prestige.

Despite the bulk of the available literature, however, we are given little or no basis for anticipating *specific* patterns in the distribution of class-implicated social consciousness. Aside from a few tenuously reconstructed inferences, the literature offers very little with regard to such questions as: How many of those who are class-aware are also aware of dimensional factors? Are the class-unaware respondents also unaware of social differences broadly speaking?

---

[1]The reader is referred to the Introduction for our discussion of the sample.

What proportion of those who demonstrate awareness at one level of conceptualization also demonstrate awareness at higher levels? Is class placement typically made within the framework of self-stipulated conceptions of class structure, or is there considerable shifting, as Bott has suggested? How prevalent are the socially "unaware"—that is, people who express no visualization of major differences in society, including differences of class?

Tᴀʙʟᴇ VII:1. Tʜᴇ Pʀᴇᴠᴀʟᴇɴᴄᴇ ᴏғ Sᴏᴄɪᴀʟ Cᴏɴsᴄɪᴏᴜsɴᴇss

A. Social Perceptivity

"In your opinion, are there strong social differences in Italy?"

Yes	1,202	76.6%
Yes, but they are diminishing	84	5.4
No	121	7.7
Other answer	13	0.8
Don't know; no answer	149	9.5
Total sample	1,569	100.0%

B. Class Awareness

"Nowadays, there is frequent talk of social classes. In your opinion, what are the social classes in Italy?"

Named specific classes	958	61.1%
There are various classes (but didn't specify)	21	1.3
There are no classes	20	1.3
Other answer	3	0.2
Don't know; no answer	567	36.1
Total sample	1,569	100.0%

With Probe Added:

("By social classes we usually mean social categories that differ from one another in terms of importance, power, style of life, wealth, privileges, etc. Tell me please, what social classes are there in Italy?")[a]

Named specific classes	1,275	81.3%
There are various classes (but didn't specify)	28	1.8
There are no classes	32	2.0
Other answer	3	0.2
Don't know; no answer	231	14.7
Total sample	1,569	100.0%

C. Dimensional Awareness

"To decide whether a given person belongs to your class, what single factor do you have to consider most? That is, by what in particular can you recognize a person belonging to your class?"[b]

Named a specific factor	1,395	88.9%
Don't know; no answer	174	11.1
Total sample	1,569	100.0%

TABLE VII:1. (*continued*)

D. *Class Placement*

"In which of these classes would you put your own family?"[c]

Named a specific class	1,276	97.9%
Don't know; no answer	27	2.1
Total	1,303	100.0%
Inapplicable[d]	266	
Total sample	1,569	

E. *Class Solidarity*

"You said you belong to the —— class. Do you feel a sense of unity with that class? That is, do you think that your needs and your ideas are similar to or different from the needs and ideas of other persons in your class?"

Yes, similar	958	75.1%
No, different	227	17.8
Don't know; no answer	91	7.1
Total	1,276	100.0%
Inapplicable[e]	293	
Total sample	1,569	

---

[a] The probe was asked of those 567 respondents who replied to the initial class-awareness question with "don't understand" or "don't know," who gave no answer, or who otherwise did not respond. The distribution shown here gives results which are inclusive of the probe question.

[b] This question was asked of the entire sample, regardless of the respondent's answer to the class-awareness question.

[c] This question followed immediately after the probe question on class awareness and was asked of all respondents who named specific classes (either spontaneously or under probe) plus the 28 respondents who said "there are various classes" but did not specify them either on the initial or the probe question.

[d] These people did not manifest an awareness of class on the spontaneous question in B, above, nor even on the follow-up probe question.

[e] These people did not name a specific class in response to the question on placement (D, above). Of these, 266 were naturally not asked the class-placement question since they were not aware of class in the first place.

These and similar other questions are the concern of the remaining chapters of Part Two. In the present chapter, following a brief discussion of the interview questions and the distributions of responses elicited by them, we consider the kinds of "class maps" of social structure articulated by the respondents— the number of classes perceived, the various contents of class imagery, the relationship of different images to theoretically objective class structure, and the like. In Chapter VIII, analysis focuses on the perceived dimensions of class division and on the self-locations or identifications made within participant-defined class structure. Chapter IX turns to a consideration of the relationship between structural conditions of existence, including observer-defined class position, and the distribution of consciousness, taking into account important questions of the consistency or uniformity of respondent conceptualizations.

Chapter X continues this chain of analysis by focusing on the link between class structure in the social consciousness and the politically relevant
class attitudes and interests of the respondents. Among other things, we examine further the distinction between "effective" and "false" consciousness.

THE PREVALENCE OF SOCIAL CONSCIOUSNESS

The interview questions used to elicit information for each of the levels of
social consciousness are conveniently organized in Table VII:1, along with
appropriate response categorizations and associated frequencies for the total
sample. We shall make some general comments and conclusions about these
questions and the responses they engendered before getting into a detailed
analysis of patterns and internal consistency.

Social Perceptivity

In surveys of social stratification the researcher almost invariably seeks
knowledge of the stratification system without first determining whether his
interviewees have even conceptualized their experiences in the simple terms of
broad social differences. A notable exception is S. S. Sargent (1953:23), who
argues that a "necessary first step . . . is to discover whether or not class is
a significant variable in people's thinking" by inquiring into their perceptions
of "important *differences*" in society. Usually, the investigator moves straight-
away into questions of class awareness and identification, and either through
the use of a prepared list of class labels or through inclusion of the word "class"
in an "unstructured" question, the interviewee is subtly (but to an unknown
degree) guided by the mental categories of the interviewer. Given the
popularity of the word "class" in everyday vocabularies, it is likely that many
respondents succumb to the subtle guidance and give class descriptions where
they otherwise would not.

In anticipating a question on class with one on social perceptivity, the
present study has sought a more nearly accurate assessment of the degree to
which people see important differences in the distributions of such class-
relevant factors as talent, authority, and rewards. As Table VII:1 shows, such
perceptions were widespread. Over four-fifths of the respondents perceived
"strong" differences along dimensions unspecified and totally of their own
imagination, so to speak. A small number of these, just over 5 percent of the
total sample, admitted the presence of strong differences but judged them to
be on the wane. This judgment probably is a recognition by particularly
fortunate individuals of recent advances in Italy in economic development, job
opportunities, and a variety of legal and social enactments that have been
beneficial to the population as a whole.

Class Awareness

The initial question on class awareness can be considered a fairly rigorous one, especially in comparison with many previous measurements (such as one which leads to equating lack of awareness with the failure to respond to a prearranged list of class labels). It is probably more rigorous in the following respects: First, in order to be defined as "class aware," the respondent had to give not merely the vague reference to the existence of classes that 21 of the 1,569 sample members made on the initial question; rather he had to name *specific* classes. Second, the question asked about classes on a *national* level, rather than leaving interpretation of the scope of the query to the respondents. Whether some interviewees actually projected regionally specific class conceptualizations to the country as a whole we cannot determine.

The information gained from a question on class awareness can be organized from a number of perspectives: the presence or absence of awareness; the detail of conceptualization; the type of class imagery employed. In time, each of these perspectives will be examined, but for the moment we are concerned only with the first.

The data of Table VII:1 are striking in their demonstration of the difficulty with which some people conceptualize the class order. Whereas 82 percent of the respondents asserted the existence of strong social differences in their society, only 61 percent could express those differences, without prompting, by naming specific classes. Thirty-six percent manifested no conception, or no clear conception, of class structure, either by refusing to answer the question altogether or by explicitly stating that they did not know what the classes might be. Slightly more than 1 percent denied the existence of a class order ("There are no classes"; "We are all equal"; "There is only one class"; "I don't believe in classes"). Another 1.5 percent gave a variety of answers that ambiguously alluded to the notion of class but failed to specify classes clearly enough to warrant inclusion in the "class-aware" category. The 61 percent who responded positively to the interview question, on the other hand, held a class image lucidly enough to describe it according to one of several models that will be discussed later in this chapter.

On the whole, these data justify a statement made by Barber (1957:197), who, after summarizing past studies of class awareness, concluded that "there is a considerable amount of either ignorance or vague knowledge about the system of stratification." Or, as Dahrendorf (1959:288) somewhat impatiently put it, a great many people "get along with a minimum of reflection on matters beyond the immediate horizon." Considering analogous findings from most other countries, it may seem that such people are especially numerous in Italy; but one must remember that the present data are the result of a less structured question on class awareness than most others. As we cautioned on a previous occasion, intersocietal comparisons of the distribution of social awareness can be very misleading unless variations in research techniques are controlled. It is also pertinent that awareness of class is linked with variations in occupational structure. Agricultural occupations, which tend to hamper class awareness, are relatively more numerous in Italy than in such other countries as the United States, Germany, and Great Britain (see Dogan, 1967:141–142).

Failure to answer the initial question on class awareness does not constitute, strictly speaking, conclusive evidence that class awareness was nonexistent. In some cases it may mean nothing more than the absence of linguistic tools necessary to the articulation of what is necessarily a complex conception. In others it may indicate an inability to conceive of a *national* class structure, because of restricted life experience, and an unwillingness to generalize local class structure to the nation as a whole. Moreover, from the perspective of class theory the acid test of class awareness ultimately consists in the phenomena that accompany the mature stages of class-attitude formation and class action.

In part for these reasons, and in part for purposes of comparison with studies based on a more structured question, the interview schedule contained an informative probe designed in part to ascertain the extent to which people can be nudged into class verbalizations. Immediately after the unstructured question on class awareness, those respondents who expressed unawareness were asked the probe question, as shown in Table VII:1. Of the 567 sample members who had failed to answer the spontaneous question, 231, or 41 percent, persisted in their original responses. Another 2 percent denied the existence of classes, and 2 percent made vague references to unspecified classes. It is remarkable, however, that a total of 56 percent did produce specific class images under the conditions of guidance.

Dimensional Awareness

As has been noted, an important but often neglected consideration in any analysis of class structure and social consciousness consists of the dimensions along which people distinguish one class from another. An individual may demonstrate an awareness of class and yet be unable to formulate particular criteria of division. In such case, consciousness of class is still rather vague and uninspired by conflicts of politicized interest, either because the individual has not yet identified the bases of conflicts or because the conflicts are relatively weak to begin with. On the other hand, if a person has made some discovery of the criteria of class division, it is important that we learn what they are, for they will tell us something about his conception of the particular distribution of "good things" in his society. Inductively, such knowledge will tell us what experiences make up homogeneous *class* groupings and what meaningfully differentiates these from groups of people who are predominantly status-conscious. Deductively, it will tell us what attitudes and actions may be expected from various categories of people, and what structural conditions underlie the distribution of those attitudes and actions. Consequently, when we examine the respondents' class imageries, the range and content of the dimensions of class will have to be treated in some detail.

At present, our task is restricted to the simpler determination of what proportion of the respondents could cite the factor which best defined class division and membership. As Table VII:1 reveals, the entire sample was asked this question, whether or not respondents had shown class awareness. The stress on the single factor was intentional for two reasons: first, to facilitate analysis; second, to provide a maximum of clarity in the factors utilized by the respondents.

Nearly nine of every ten sample members named a specific factor. The first impression one gains from this finding is of inconsistency between it and the comparable datum on class awareness. Whereas only 81 percent had identified a class structure, 89 percent now profess to know what criteria underlie class membership. The discordance can be accounted for by two circumstances. In the first place, the finding reflects once again the ease with which some people can be led into an otherwise nonsalient class conception of the social order. The mere circumstance that the interview question contained the phrase "your class" was sufficient to induce some who were otherwise class-unaware to think in "class" terms. Second, however, a good part of the inconsistency (nearly two-thirds) may represent a uniquely authentic pattern of awareness. The people here in question perceived strong social differences, were aware of important factors underlying those differences, and could even locate themselves within the context of the differences. But apparently they did *not* conceptualize them in terms of class, although they were willing to go along with the interviewer's vocabulary. We shall return to these respondents in Chapter IX.

Class Placement

The question on class placement was spontaneous in the sense that the interviewee was in a position to choose among class expressions suggested by himself. The responses provide our primary data for the analysis of placements and identifications. Inasmuch as most investigations have relied on a structured list of class labels, however, we also included in the interview schedule a forced-choice question. Data resulting from this probe are purely supplemental to our present concerns and are treated in a short section in Chapter VIII.

As panel D of Table VII:1 indicates, the class-placement question was asked of only those respondents who had demonstrated earlier in the interview an awareness of class. Against that standard, 98 percent were able to locate themselves in a specific class. It would seem, then, that once a person succeeds in conceptualizing a class structure, he has little or no trouble in finding his own place in it: only 27 of the respondents to the question could not do so. For purposes of later analysis, we will treat both these 27 respondents *and* the 266 of whom the class-placement question was not asked as incapable of making a self-location. The rationale for this latter inclusion is quite simple: since those 266 persons showed no conception of a class structure, we could not expect them to locate themselves within a presumably "nonexistent" social space.

Class Solidarity

Responses to the last of the five interview questions represented in Table VII:1, perhaps more than those to any of the others, should be regarded as crude approximations to the phenomenon considered. The core of class solidarity is emotive as well as cognitive—a root sentiment of common experience, common feeling, and common fate, as well as a simple verbal expression. It is extremely difficult to capture all of this in the verbalization of survey research. Thus, here more than in any other section of our analysis, the tenuity of statistical-survey methods becomes most hauntingly apparent and the need for critical instruments of historical-structural analysis most strongly felt. We shall try to provide some of these tools along the way, but we must be ever mindful that we are operating at a *dispositional* level, not at the level of a fully matured class consciousness.

For the present we restrict ourselves to the question of whether expressions of class solidarity were given or not; hereon, the striking finding from Table VII:1 is that 958 interviewees, or 75 percent of the 1,276 who were able to locate themselves in a particular class, stated that they did feel a sense of unity with that class. A few of these (12) qualified their replies by noting that their needs were similar but their ideas were different, and one individual stated the reverse qualification. Another 29 respondents gave a "yes, more or less" reply. But the remaining 916 interviewees gave a simple, unencumbered "yes." On the other hand, nearly 18 percent of those who had located themselves within the self-defined class structure replied with a precise "no" to the question of solidarity. Considering the nature of the question and the problems of measurement noted above, this is probably a fairly accurate indication of their actual feelings. Finally, 7 percent of those who had made a self-placement either failed to answer the question or gave "don't know" answers, and 293 of the sample members were not asked the question, since they had not assigned themselves to a class in the first place.

Ignoring for the moment problems of consistency between verbalization and actual sentiment, we find it significant that three-quarters of the people who identified themselves as members of a particular class also proclaimed some feeling of unity with that class. This information gives us a good basis for examining, among other things, the interconnections between self-assigned class membership and objective economic situation, between what is usually referred to as "false" consciousness and "effective" consciousness. Assuming that those people who named a specific class as their own and then proclaimed sentiments of unity with it were actually manifesting appropriate psychological identifications, we must then take Marx at his own method and examine the experiences which determined that consciousness. Moreover, it is not sufficient, as Geiger (1949:123 ff) correctly observes, to answer questions of "false" consciousness solely on the basis of an observer model of class structure, which is itself necessarily ideological. "Differences in the class consciousness of members of the same class are facts that simply exist," and they are accountable in the empirical terms of concrete human experience. We shall return to this issue in Chapter X.

The five interview questions taken collectively were designed to give some semblance of theoretical order to the processes involved in the formation of class consciousness. We assume for reasons of theory, in other words, that social perceptivity comes before class awareness; that class placement presupposes dimensional awareness, class awareness, and social perceptivity; and so on. A rigorous logical ordering in the sense of mathematical scalability cannot be presumed, however. Given the complexity of the phenomena, the intentions of our investigation, and the quality of the tools of the trade, any fabrications of that sort would very likely produce only misinformation and misconstruction. Problems of consistency among the five levels of awareness will instead be handled as a matter of empirical inquiry and theoretical classification, without guidance from the rules of scalar ordering and sequence. This examination we must defer until Chapter IX, however.

IMAGES OF CLASS STRUCTURE

When individuals envision a class order, how detailed or complex does it appear to them? What criteria do they most frequently employ, explicitly or implicitly, in defining the internal cleavages of that order? (This question concerns, among other matters, Dahrendorf's disagreement with Marx with respect to the actual bases of class division.) What distinguishes individuals holding different images of society and different estimations of the salient factors of class differentiation? In pursuing answers to these and related questions, we shall examine in some detail the responses of the 958 interviewees who evinced awareness of class structure without probing from the interviewer (upper part of panel B, Table VII:1). We prefer at this point the more rigorous sample construction in order to emphasize the quality of spontaneity of conception and to maximize within current means the probability that class images were nationally based. (For purposes of brief comparison, results of the probe will be recorded in initial tables; otherwise, they are excluded from the following discussion.)

A good point of departure for our analysis is the number of classes perceived. Referring to Table VII:2, of the 958 spontaneously class-aware respondents, about 17 percent perceived a dichotomous arrangement, identical proportions saw a tetrachotomous or polychotomous scheme, and 49 percent perceived an arrangement of three classes. Respective proportions for the interviewees who were class-aware only under conditions of the probe show the same general pattern. In short, then, the trivalent conception was roughly three times as frequent as any other, a finding that is well in accord with conclusions reported in analogous investigations of other populations (such as those of Kahl and Davis, 1955; Davies, 1967:28; Tumin with Feldman, 1961: 147; Mayntz, 1958:85; Martin, 1954).

TABLE VII:2. THE COMPLEXITY OF CLASS IMAGERY

Class Structure *Perceived as:*	*Respondents Who Were Class-Aware*	
	Spontaneously	*Under Probe*
Dichotomous	17%	20%
Trichotomous	49	44
Tetrachotomous	17	19
Polychotomous	17	18
Total	100%	101%
N	958	317

Focusing on the spontaneously aware subsample, variations by objective class position were generally small and somewhat irregular, with the dichotomous images appearing most often among the semiskilled (19 percent) and unskilled (23 percent) strata of the working class. Contrary to vague suggestions in the literature, there was no consistent relationship between standing on the occupational scale and complexity of imagery. While the polychotomous conceptions were most frequent among the elite (industrialists, high government functionaries and politicians, top-level executives, university-educated professionals), nearly as many members of the petty bourgeoisie (22 percent versus 28 percent) displayed an awareness of five or more classes. Indeed, the peasants (sharecroppers, small farm owners, tenants), were not too far behind (19 percent). Although, as we shall see later, differences in educational attainment discriminate between the class-aware and the class-unaware, they did not discriminate among the various degrees of complexity of class imagery, either within the class-aware subsample as a whole or within specific categories of objective class position.

Most of the statements given by the 958 respondents as descriptions of class structure can be reduced to a half-dozen major categories, the most prevalent of which, regardless of the number of classes perceived, was an economic model, thereby providing evidence against Dahrendorf's attempted "supersedure" of Marx's formulation. Contrary to the idea that "it is difficult to construct a three-valued power model" (Kahl, 1953:179), the economic (manifestly power) model accounted for nearly a third of all the trichotomies and more than a tenth of the four-part divisions as well. Some form of a three-valued power model was the commonest image presented by our interviewees.

Rather than present a confusingly detailed cross-tabulation of images by the number and content of classes perceived (trichotomous economic, dichotomous occupational, and so forth), we have grouped the images according to a series of nine models. An examination of the occupational and educational characteristics of those persons who stressed one particular factor or complex of factors in their conceptions, as opposed to some other, did not reveal any worthwhile differences in the frequency with which they produced dichotomous, trichotomous, or more detailed images of society. Therefore, the loss of information incurred by our condensation of the original matrices is negligible. Table VII:3 reports the distribution of models for both the spontaneously class aware and the 317 respondents who were class aware only under probe conditions. In the following discussion, however, the focus is on only the spontaneously aware.

TABLE VII:3. THE CONTENT OF CLASS IMAGERY

| | Respondents Who Were Class-Aware | |
Class Model	Spontaneously	Under Probe
1. Economic	25%	29%
2. Occupational	10	12
3. Political-Ideological	12	5
4. Dependency	3	4
5. Prestige	9	6
6. Composite Power	8	14
7. Composite Prestige	6	2
8. Polychotomous Images[a]	17	18
9. Residual Images	10	9
Total	100%	99%
N	958	317

[a] Five or more classes.

1. Economic Images

The most usual linguistic representation of economic images is given by the expressions, "the rich, the poor, and those in the middle," or simply "the rich and the poor." Together, the economic images accounted for 45 percent of all dichotomies, 31 percent of the trichotomies, and 12 percent of the tetrachotomous divisions.

It is difficult to say, in reference to Marx's theory of classes, whether these economically nurtured class conceptions carry any flavor of resentment and belligerence implied in the twin notions of proletarian and capitalist interest groups. More detailed probes would possibly have uncovered an element of intense class feeling, in the theoretical sense of the term, in many instances. But available evidence suggests that for the vast majority, the unequal distribution of wealth and economic power was visualized as an unfortunate but natural fact of life, a fact that merited little more than a simple recognition of its existence and, perhaps, a faint wish that things were different. The sense of collective purpose upon which class action is predicated was missing from the spontaneous responses in all but a few cases. One respondent of singular individuality, who envisioned his society as divided into "the poor and the rich who take advantage of them," went on to add that "unfortunately there are also the Communists."

By tradition, economic class orders may be interpreted as power models. There can be hardly any doubt that in Italy, as in most other societies, those who have the purse also pull the strings. It is also quite likely that the idea of domination and subjection was an integral part of those economic images displayed by our respondents. Nevertheless, it is hardly justifiable to conclude that such images of class structure are evidence for any preponderance of class-antagonism conceptions of society. Not only are nuances of conflict entirely missing in many of the expressions used; but also, as we shall soon see, economic models were produced by occupants of bourgeois positions. It is improbable that members of the privileged class have much that is of a material nature to complain about.

2. Occupational Images

The most frequent example of occupational dichotomies, which accounted for 10 percent of all two-valued images, is given by the expression "office workers and manual workers." Occasionally the interviewees conveyed the idea through the phrase, reminiscent of the Lynds' work (Lynd and Lynd, 1929), "those who work with their heads and those who work with their hands," while others distinguished between "professionals and workers" or even between "peasants and industrial workers." This last expression was produced by two individuals: one a peasant; the other, a manual worker who was previously a farm laborer. Both cases are indicative of a phenomenon now rather general in societies undergoing industrialization: the major goal of many agricultural workers—one which may outweigh any *class* aim—is to leave the poorly yielding and excessively demanding farm for the opportunities of the city, the locus of modern civilization. Peasants increasingly see the city as a place where they can end their century-old toils and earn incomes sufficient to purchase the amenities of the modern world (Lopreato, 1967b). For them the classes that have real meaning are but two: themselves (the peasants), and those who are not peasants.

Occupational trichotomies (11 percent of all trichotomies) were expressed in a great variety of forms. Although an element of class ideology may not be lacking in all cases, most tended to emphasize some of the functional divisions of the occupational structure. Cases in point are: "professionals, workers, and farmers"; "managers, merchants, and workers"; "office workers, independent people (shopkeepers), and workers." In some instances, the ideological component of the class image was rather apparent, as in the following: "entrepreneurs, workers, and the middle stratum *(ceto medio)*." Such responses appear to be consistent with Marx's own classical description of the classes as comprising the proletariat, the capitalists, and "the middle strata."

Tetrachotomous divisions carry still further the analytical tendency inherent in the above expressions. They represent such images as: "big industrialists, salaried workers, small owners (merchants, etc.) and workers"; "professionals, office workers, owners and merchants, and manual workers." Again it must be noted that it is not possible to determine to what extent a theoretical class ideology is operative in such images. Many of them no doubt simply reflect a recognition of the multiplicity of functions in society. But a few are probably extensions of the classical dichotomy of conflict, made more complex by the existence of visibly higher rates of upward mobility, which induces a tendency to see society as a gradation of steps.

3. Political-Ideological Images

The clearest indication that at least some respondents were thinking in terms of class antagonisms is found in what we have termed the political-ideological model, which accounts for slightly more than 12 percent of all images. They appear in three degrees of detail. The dichotomies are represented by such classical expressions as "bourgeoisie and proletariat," "those who have all the power and those who have none," "the exploiters and the exploited," and "those who have to work to live and those who live without working."

In some cases, the expression of antagonism was less direct. A semiskilled worker who had declared himself a faithful Communist, for example, defined the class structure as consisting of the "capitalist class and the petty bourgeoisie." In so doing he intentionally omitted his own class. But by that very omission he gave powerful indication of the hostile character of his class experiences. There is a tendency among doctrinaire Communists to use the term "class" in a disparaging sense, as a category which incorporates evil, corruption, and suppression. The idea, of course, is squeezed from Marx's own conception of classes as phenomena destined to disappear. Historically, according to that conception, the class structure as a whole has been associated with the social evils of "exploitation," "state," and "private property"; and the dialectical tensions bottled up by that structure have led to the crystallization of two classes: one (the bourgeoisie) that is "bad" and one (the proletariat) that is "good" in the sense that it serves temporarily as an "anticlass." Because of these moralistic overtones, many rank-and-file Communists are ambivalent at best about using "class" as a self-description. The ambivalence frequently results in simple ideological ellipses of the sort we have just observed. At other times, it manifests itself in the very denial of classes.

Political-ideological trichotomies were second only to economic trichotomies in prevalence. They account for over 15 percent of all trichotomies. Almost invariably they reflect Marx's own descriptive model of classes by pointing to the "bourgeoisie, the middle bourgeoisie, and the workers." Sometimes the imagery is even more transparent in its ideological message. One respondent put it this way: "The classes are still two—three, actually. They are the filthy rich, the middle bourgeoisie, who still fail to understand what's good for them, and the proletariat."

In the tetrachotomous political-ideological divisions, which account for 12 percent of all four-valued conceptions, still greater sensitivity to the complexity of class was demonstrated. We found some recognition, for example, of a descriptive reality that at times seemed to be of some theoretical embarrassment to Marx himself. It is not always clear whether for Marx the landowners were a truly separate class, as he indicated in his last remarks in *Capital*, or whether they were merely a vanishing stratum of the *ancien régime*. This dilemma was expressed within the context of the present study by people who identified "the proletariat, the capitalist class, the middle bourgeoisie, and the latifundists."

Other respondents added a residual category which had a "false-consciousness" type of relation to the nucleus of classes. An illustration is "the bourgeoisie, the petty bourgeoisie, the proletariat, and the fools who hang around priests and politicians," the latter referring mostly to people whose religiosity led them to the centrist-traditional Christian Democratic Party supposedly against their class interests. In still other cases, the basic trichotomy was enlarged to distinguish between capitalists and managers—an image which shows keen recognition of the phenomenon of the "separation of ownership and control." A case in point is "the entrepreneurs, the managers *(dirigenti)*, the middle stratum, and the proletariat."

It may be concluded that the ideological component of class consciousness is most evident among those images that we have subsumed under the political-ideological model. Whether it excels all other class models in the conveyance of actual class antagonisms remains to be seen. But it is apparent that Marx's famous classes of bourgeoisie and proletariat provided the basic point of departure for the construction of such images. Sometimes the respondent went no further than this. At other times he inserted the middle bourgeoisie between the two major classes. And then again he occasionally added a fourth component by distinguishing, in effect, between agricultural capitalists and industrial capitalists, or between capitalists proper and mere executives of the capitalist enterprise. But in all cases the notion of an overriding tension between polar sets of interests was clearly discernible.

4. Images of Work Dependency or Political Dependency

Dependency class images concern what Ossowski (1963:30ff) calls "correlative classes," namely, aggregates whose respective positions are determined by their relationship to one another.[2] The set contains two categories of privileges and privations: those engendered in a political context and those of the work setting. Both express more directly than any other the conflict basis of Dahrendorf's theory. The political-dependency image is represented by only two respondents, both of whom produced dichotomies: "the high authorities and the people"; "the rulers and the governed." The image of work dependency is featured primarily as a dichotomy also, and it comprises nearly 16 percent of all bivalent conceptions. Typical labels included "employers and employees" and "managers and dependent workers." Only seven respondents used a trichotomous image of work dependency, represented by answers such as "the bosses, the office people, and most of the dependent people" and "the employers, their supervisors, and those who need a job."

It is possible that most of the cases included in the present model could have been subsumed under one or more of the other models. They have been kept separate, however, not only in recognition of Dahrendorf's emphasis on authority relations but also because they may contain an element of the idea of "interdependence." An individual who freely states that one class depends on another is also likely to feel that the dependence is to some extent mutual, at least in the work sphere. Such individuals may not have in mind a class structure characterized by antagonism and resentment. Such is the case, for instance, among many authority-endowed workers, as we shall note in the last chapter of the volume.

---

[2]Ossowski's term does not imply the existence of classes that are nonrelational; class is a relational phenomenon by definition. "Correlative classes" merely refers to a structure containing a number of classes, each of which "is correlated in a similar manner to some other class; for instance, the social position of the serf is determined by his relationship to the landowner, just as the position of the apprentice is determined by his relationship to the master craftsman in the guild" (p. 30). Marx's famous dichotomy of bourgeoisie and proletariat is simply a special case of "correlative classes," one in which the entire structure has been reduced to only *one* pair of opposing classes. The concept of dependency, of course, expresses most clearly the idea of correlativeness.

5. Prestige Images

The usually popular prestige image of society applies to relatively few of our sample members. It is conceivable that Italians do not think as persistently as do other nationals in the language of prestige. What is more likely, however, is that the varying prevalence of prestige labels results from our different decisions as to the meaning of such apparently spatial terms as "upper," "middle," and "lower." In classifying our data we have assumed that spatial terms appearing concurrently with descriptions of differences in occupation, wealth, or power were merely short cuts to terms concordant with such differences. An individual who saw the class structure as composed of "bourgeoisie, proletariat, and the middle group," for instance, was essentially employing the sort of description that we have subsumed under the political-ideological model. When inferences of this sort could not be made and the expressions did not constitute pure prestige images, they were kept separate, and will be treated in connection with a composite prestige model.

As expected, the most recurring prestige image was trichotomous, comprising somewhat more than 14 percent of all trichotomies and about half that proportion of all class images. It was commonly expressed through the phrase "the upper stratum *(ceto alto),* the middle stratum, and the lower stratum." In a few cases, the spatial terms "upper" and "lower" were replaced by "superior" and "inferior," the middle term remaining unchanged. A few other respondents spoke of an "aristocracy" rather than an "upper stratum."

A prestige dichotomy was used by only three respondents, and two of these gave descriptions connoting family lineage: "patricians and plebeians" and "the aristocratic stratum and the popular stratum." An interesting feature of all three cases was the tendency to lump the vast majority of people into one large category at the bottom, and accord distinction to only a small number at the very top.

Finally, among the tetrachotomous prestige divisions, employed by 16 respondents, the tendency was to split the middle term of the trichotomy as follows: "the upper stratum, the upper middle stratum, the middle stratum, and the lower stratum." The extra division strongly reflects the operation of status-striving attitudes.

6. Composite Power Images

Composites power images embrace occupational, economic, and political-ideological considerations. They appear in either trivalent or quadrivalent form, with a slight preponderance of the former, and constitute about 8 percent of all class images. An interesting example of the tetrachotomous composite is given by the expression, "the class that has the political power, the class that has the economic power, the middle bourgeoisie, and the proletariat." This respondent seems to have accomplished a splendid feat of analysis: besides taking account of Marx's "intermediate strata," he has split the bourgeoisie in such a way as to distinguish between those who control the wealth and those who hold sway over the authority structure of the society. In brief, this respondent, as well as a few others like him, has in his own way resolved the Marx-Dahrendorf dispute by suggesting that class conflict results from the operation not of one or the other factor but of both. This point will receive substantial confirmation in Chapter XVII.

A particularly revealing illustration of the trichotomous power composite model is given by the expression, "the poor, the rich, and the clergy." The principal focus is on the basic economic cleavage characteristic of Marx's class model, but the respondent also singled out the ecclesiastical power structure as a third force in the economic dynamics of Italy. In doing so, he illustrated the strong resentment of many Italians against the role played by organized religion in the politics of the nation. If it can be said, as is frequently heard, that the Catholic Church has been instrumental in obstructing the progress of Communism in Italy, it is at least equally true that for a number of Italians a vote for the Communist Party is less a reflection of ideological commitment than an indication of resentment against what is considered unnecessary meddling by the church, a meddling too often to the advantage of old interests and to the detriment of the masses. Many Italians, furthermore, are angered by a series of privileges and subsidies enjoyed by the church. While carrying out "dry runs" of a question on party affiliation in several parts of the country, we were frequently given an answer by Communist interviewees in the nature of the following remarks, made by one such respondent:

> Yes, I am a Communist, and will always be one as long as the affairs of this country are run by the eunuchs in the Vatican and by their ignorant henchmen in the provinces who are anything but Christian. They have no interest except in frightening the poor people in order to fatten up on their toils and make scandalous display of their expensive jewelry and their richly perfumed bodies. The Communists are no angels themselves—believe me, I know. But they are to be preferred by far. I would give anything to see the perennial leeches of Italy put in their place, where they belong: tilling the fields with a muzzle tightly clamped on.

Not all of those who resent the actions of the Church are so articulate; neither are they all so furious in their invective. The resentment is nevertheless there, and it adds much color to whatever class struggle may exist in the country.

7. Composite Prestige Images

Composite prestige images encompass 6 percent of all class conceptions and consist of images of society that blend prestige and powerlike phenomena. Of the latter, occupation is the most frequent factor. Most of the expressions which illustrate this set of images are trichotomous in nature; a few are tetrachotomous. Representative examples include "the upper stratum, the middle stratum, and the poor workers," "the upper stratum, the middle stratum which contains most of us, and the very needy people," "the educated classes, the rich classes, the middle classes, and the poor classes," "the very rich, the common people, the middle class, and the disinherited."

8. Polychotomous Images

We have grouped into the category of polychotomous images all images of society which contain at least five classes. It consists of 163 cases, or 17 percent of all class images and 10 percent of the entire sample. The vast majority (110) are five-valued divisions, and another 34 contain six classes. The remaining 19 cases are scattered among even more complex breakdowns. By and large, they represent distinctions so heterogeneous that to classify them separately in terms of substantive factors would result in a large number of multifactored models, each with very few cases. The following examples illustrate this diversity: "managers, big chiefs, the workers, the poor, and dishonest people"; "the capitalist class, the managerial class, the class of merchants, the class of small merchants, salaried employees, and the workers"; "employers, big merchants, middle class, artisans, peasants, the lower class, and dependent workers"; "the rich, the ignorant, the capitalists, the professionals, the poor, the workers in general, the factory workers, and the middle strata"; "peasants, workers, salaried employees, merchants, clergy, industrialists, military people, artisans, and the poor."

9. Residual Images

Finally, we come to the inevitable "residual" category, which here comprehends those dichotomies, trichotomies, and tetrachotomous divisions that did not seem to fit any of the other models. They comprise 10 percent of all spontaneously given class images and a variety of conceptions touching upon such things as religion, morality, honesty, intelligence, and luck. Some illustrative expressions are: "the lucky and the unlucky"; "the honest and the dishonest"; "working people, religious people, and the Communists"; "those who have pull, those who work honestly, and the office workers"; "the rich, the poor, the students, and the migrants"; "office workers, the clergy, honest people, and the dishonest."

CLASS POSITION AND IMAGES OF CLASS

From the vantage point of "objective" class position, that is, of observer-defined class, certain types of class imagery were more common to some classes than to others (Table VII:4). For example, the tendency to construct images based on economic criteria was inversely related to class position, ranging from a low of 6 percent among the elite to a high of 36 percent among the semiskilled workers. "The tongue licks the aching tooth," goes an old Italian proverb:

TABLE VII:4. CLASS POSITION AND CLASS IMAGERY

Class Model	Bourgeoisie			Working Class			Peas-antry	Total
	Elite	High	Petty	Skilled	Semi-skilled	Un-skilled		
1. Economic	6%	19%	19%	26%	36%	32%	27%	25%
2. Occupational	8	7	9	8	10	19	11	10
3. Political-Ideological	22	21	17	14	9	6	6	13
4. Dependency	3	3	4	5	4	2	3	4
5. Prestige	17	12	10	9	9	2	8	9
6. Composite Power	3	5	7	11	9	15	13	9
7. Composite Prestige	6	7	3	5	7	6	4	5
8. Polychotomous Images	28	17	22	16	9	15	19	17
9. Residual Images	8	9	10	5	7	4	9	8
Total	101%	100%	101%	99%	100%	101%	100%	100%
N	36	169	136	146	141	103	113	844

wealth, or rather its absence, is immediately salient to the lowly and poor; hence, it imposes itself most forcefully on their consciousness. Similarly, the tendency to visualize society in terms of the composite power model—that is, images synthetic of economic, occupational, and political-ideological factors —correlated negatively with position in the class structure. As in the foregoing case, this correlation is not unexpected. Indeed, what is somewhat surprising is the fact that the percentage differences were not greater, as both Marx and Dahrendorf would have predicted.

Not all of the relationships were so compatible with expectations. A case in point concerns the political-ideological images, which were most popular among the elite and the bourgeoisie and least used by the unskilled stratum of the working class and by the peasants. Considering the heavy stress usually put on *proletarian* rebelliousness in theories of class conflict, this distribution may seem a bit surprising. In part, the relationship can be accounted for by variations in educational attainment: conceptions stressing political-ideological cleavages were commonest among the best-educated respondents, just as the economic image was most common among the least educated; for instance, 28 percent of the university-educated held a political-ideological image of classes, in contrast to only 6 percent among those who had only an elementary-school diploma. Conversely, 33 percent of the latter held an economic image, in comparison to 11 percent among the university-educated. The sort of abstractive capacity that is called for in the creation of class images based on anything but the most immediate existential bases exists in greater abundance among the better educated. Awareness of the fact that some are rich while others are poor, that some wield a hoe while others fill sheets of paper with abstract symbols, is the simplest and least escapable form of class awareness possible. Imputations of culpability and ill-intent to the actions of others, however, involve more complex processes of abstract reasoning, a reasoning that can handle questions concerning the source of private property, the equality of man before nature, the social value of various forms of human labor, and a number of other such issues. The skills needed to grapple with questions of this sort are acquired through formal education, as well as, to some extent, through the simplified renditions offered by political sloganry. Thus, when variations in educational background are controlled, the disparities between workers and the more privileged classes in political-ideological imagery are greatly attenuated; such imagery accounted for 19 percent of the urban workers with more than the elementary-school diploma, in comparison to 21 percent of the elite, bourgeoisie, and petty bourgeoisie.

A number of factors, some of them linked to educational background, contributed to the higher frequency of political-ideological imagery among the privileged classes. In the first place, for example, the Italian Communist and Socialist Parties attract relatively large numbers of university-educated professionals and "intellectuals." Second, the linkage also reflects the political-ideological imagery of "radical rightists," as they are currently styled—rank-and-file ideologues of the neofascist and other right-wing political parties, many of whom hold top-level positions in industry, commerce, and, to an extent, in the state bureaucracy. Ironically, the "leftist" legacy of Marx has often impelled conflict theorists to overlook the political-ideological salience of the far right. Third, for reasons that will be discussed in greater detail in Chapter IX, many members of the petty bourgeoisie, especially the low-grade clerks with moderately good formal education, employed a leftist political-ideological conception of society. A sizable number of them had ascended from blue-collar families and still retained the party orientations of their parental homes; for them, the exigencies of their work situation often made such imagery particularly relevant.

In accord with a rather general conclusion in the literature (see Dahrendorf, 1959; Willener, 1957; Popitz and others, 1961; Mayntz, 1958), the privileged classes were also the likeliest to perceive society in terms of prestige differentials, such images accounting for 17 percent of the elite and 12 percent of the upper bourgeoisie. There is some evidence to suggest that this tendency may not have held for those relatively few members of the privileged classes who managed no more than five years of formal schooling, only 3 percent of whom used a prestige model in contrast to 13 percent of the better educated. The greater number of the less educated had proportionately lower incomes—in some cases even lower than the incomes of some skilled workers—and economic or even political-ideological distinctions may have therefore had a greater salience to them. Due to their low education, moreover, opportunities for future ascent were rather limited. To the extent that a prestige model of society mirrors concern for style of life, deferential behavior, and the like, the limited promise which status emulations held for these people probably dictated nonprestige conceptions of social structure.

To summarize briefly, the data are fairly clear in showing that the content of class imageries varied with location in the class structure. But the class structure is seldom uniform throughout an entire society. Instead, it typically varies in rather close conjunction with economic geography. This variation is found not only in industrial societies, in which particular industries and economic functions are concentrated in particular regions; it is also characteristic of agrarian societies, wherein the greatest differentiation is between the city—the usual habitat of the elites, the merchant classes, and the craftsmen—and the countryside with its peasantry. (See Sjoberg, 1960; Lenski, 1966.) And the variation is particularly applicable to a society such as Italy's, one half of which is industrial and the other half essentially agrarian.

Anyone traveling the length of the Italian peninsula, whether trained researcher or carefree tourist, cannot help but become aware of the existence of "two Italies." From Rome northward to Venice, Milan, and Turin lies a predominantly urban, industrial society that has had its share in the "economic miracle" of post-war European recovery. Heavy industry is concentrated in these regions, particularly in the Industrial Triangle bounded by Milan, Turin, and Genoa, and agricultural enterprises are generally mechanized. To the south, by contrast, lies the *Mezzogiorno*, historically a land of abject poverty and peasant traditions. With the possible exception of a few coastal areas and the maritime industries of the major seaports, the South as a whole remains starkly inferior in both industrial and agricultural development. Much has been written concerning the historical circumstances and present-day conditions of this rupture in the life of Italy, and there is little point in repeating here what has been said many times elsewhere. (See Lutz, 1962; Martellaro, 1965; Schachter, 1965; Surace, 1966; Lopreato, 1967b.) A few facts and figures will be sufficient.

From the time of national unification in 1861, when through the automatic nullification of regional customs protections the fledgling economy of the South was inundated by the competition of superior northern industry, the developmental problems of the *Mezzogiorno* have been continually exacerbated by various circumstances, not least of which was the early application of national economic policies dictated by northern interests. The consequence has been that the southern economy is highly commercialized, but the commercial activity depends on *external* industrialization. In a sense, unification came before the *Mezzogiorno* was capable of competing with the stronger regions of the North. As one southern observer lamented some thirty years after the birth of modern Italy, "We were still on the threshold of the Middle Ages when we were hurled all at once into the modern era" (Fortunato, 1926:204). Indeed, remnants of a medieval society can still today be perceived in aspects of the South's social structure.

Although succeeding national governments have periodically offered promises of major reform and the application of economic-development policies beneficial to the South, much less than was expected and needed has come of them. To choose a few illustrative figures: by 1963 the southern regions contained merely one-quarter of the total industrial labor force of Italy, despite the fact that about 38 percent of the Italian population lived in those regions (Istituto Centrale di Statistica, 1964: Table 11). Furthermore, nearly 60 percent of its industrial force was employed in small firms of ten or fewer persons, as compared with less than 25 percent of the North's industrial labor force (Lutz, 1962:93). Capital-investment statistics tell much the same story. During the prime years of the 1950's, for instance—when the general economy of Italy was registering substantial gains—more than three-fourths of all public investments were made in the northern regions; the proportion of private investments was even higher. Finally, whereas per capita income in 1961 was approximately $550 (U.S. equivalent) in the North, it was only $290 in the South; looked at differently, the North reaped three-quarters of the total national income (Lutz, 1962:91; Schachter, 1965: Table II).

In short, from nearly any perspective one chooses to take, the *Mezzogiorno* has at least as much in common with other underdeveloped countries as it has with Germany, Great Britain, the United States, or northern Italy itself. This applies not only in terms of the hard figures of economic growth rates, but also in the subtler distinctions of cultural tradition. The political monuments of a single Italy have yet to be fully built in the general social consciousness of the people.

The sharp contrast between industrial region and agrarian region—the latter predominatly encompassed by the *Mezzogiorno,* proportionately speaking—gives rise to perceptions of an equally sharp boundary between abundance and poverty and, concomitantly, to sentiments of relative deprivation on the part of those who are located on the unfortunate side of that boundary. It is reasonable to expect that such variations in objective class structure according to economic geography would be mirrored in the class images of our respondents. Focusing on the respondents who visualized two, three, or four classes, for example, we note that 34 percent of the northerners and 28 percent of the southerners surprisingly expressed images in economic terms. Another 14 percent of the northern residents, as opposed to 9 percent of the southerners, utilized a composite power imagery. Collectively, then, the regional difference in the rate of usage of these two types of class imagery, both of which pertain to matters of wealth and poverty, was 11 percent (48 minus 37 percent). Conversely, 20 percent of the respondents from the North, in contrast to 14 percent of the *Mezzogiorno* residents, depicted the class structure in terms of either the prestige or the composite prestige model. Similarly, the northerners were slightly more likely to employ political-ideological images (16 versus 13 percent).

The weakness of the observed relationships, as well as their unexpected nature, probably lies more in the imprecision of the regional measure of expected differences between industrial and agrarian economic geography than in the expectation itself. Neither the *Mezzogiorno* nor, especially, the several regions here denoted as "the North" are uniform in economic development, certainly, and it is entirely possible that the expected differences would emerge from a more refined contrast between industrial and agrarian economic structures. This possibility may be examined by comparing imageries according to city size. Given the generally urban locus of industrial enterprise, we should expect to find the greatest differentiation between the smallest towns, villages, and hamlets, on the one hand, and all larger communities, on the other. Also, there may have been secondary differentiations among the larger cities, reflecting in part the concentrations of heavy industry and bureaucratic decision-making centers in the major metropolitan areas.

The latter expectation is apparently not supportable by the data. Variations in imagery among the largest three categories of community size were either nonexistent or occurred at the lower end of the scale. But the first expectation

TABLE VII:5. SIZE OF COMMUNITY OF RESIDENCE AND CLASS IMAGERY

	Size of Community			
Class Model	Less than 3,000	3,001- 50,000	50,001- 500,000	Over 500,000
1. Economic	33%	24%	24%	23%
2. Occupational	6	13	8	8
3. Political-Ideological	6	12	15	14
4. Dependency	2	3	4	6
5. Prestige	1	10	10	12
6. Composite Power	23	10	5	7
7. Composite Prestige	4	7	4	7
8. Polychotomous	13	15	22	17
9. Residual	11	7	8	7
Total	99%	101%	100%	101%
N	82	440	243	170

is generally supported. Economic and composite power images, that is, those images associated most closely with peasants and the working class, were stated most often by residents of communities with fewer than 3,000 inhabitants. This tendency held in both the northern and the southern subsamples, but the relationship was stronger among the former, probably because the northern small-town and village inhabitants were in closer proximity to the relatively affluent life of large industrial cities and were therefore more keenly aware of relative disparities in wealth and poverty. Moreover, the northern small-town and village residents employed "pure" economic images (such as "the rich and the poor") more often than the composite power images (39 versus 19 percent), while the reverse was true of their southern counterparts (11 versus 37 percent). Among other things, this divergence reflects a difference in the consistency of image construction—a "pure" model versus a composite model—and the southerners, being slightly less educated, more likely used composite constructions. In part, economic and power images of society are rooted in the political education imparted by such parties as the Communist and the Socialist. These parties have been more active in the North than in the South.

Whereas the economic and composite power images were most common among residents of communities with fewer than 3,000 people, prestige and political-ideological constructions were *least* often stated in such localities. Usage of the former models was directly related to community size regardless of region (North versus South); but in the case of the political-ideological model the linkage obtained only among the northerners. Slightly over one-tenth of the southern respondents, whatever the population of their community of residence, used political-ideological terms to describe the class structure.

Despite the paucity of numbers, the data of Table VII:5 show the first consistent variation in the use of dependency images yet encountered. In part, no doubt, this direct relationship with city size is a function of the proportionately larger number of jobs in urban-industrial areas, particularly in the North, that place the worker in a situation of clear-cut work dependency, and perhaps interdependence. He depends upon his employer for a regular source of income, in exchange for his labor services, and upon his fellow workers for cooperation in the completion of task assignments. The employer, in turn, must rely upon the labor of others for keeping his plant or factory running smoothly. In the smaller towns and villages, by contrast, a greater proportion of the labor force is self-employed and self-supporting. Service occupations are fewer, factories and firms are smaller, and agricultural workers account for a larger percentage of the local body of people lacking in craft skills.

The kinds of images of society people construct vary according to the individual's location within the class structure and according to certain regional differences in the composition of the class structure. They may also vary with respect to the individual's movement through social space. In anticipation of a more specific analysis of the relationship between vertical social mobility and consciousness of social structure, which is presented in following chapters, we here examine differences of class imagery between the mobile and the nonmobile. Mobility is measured by a comparison of father's and son's occupational classes. In order to simplify the analysis, we have collapsed the three privileged strata shown in Table VII:4 into one, which we label simply "privileged class," and the three strata of the working class into one. The peasants are excluded from the sample of respondents, but nonpeasant sons of peasant fathers are retained; the assumption will be that movement from the peasantry to the working class constitutes upward mobility. Table VII:6 incorporates data for both upward mobility (columns 2, 3, and 6) and downward mobility (column 4). In examining downward mobility we are limited in the number of comparisons that may be made, owing to the small number of peasant skidders (excluded from the table). In Italy, as in industrial society in general, the boundary between agrarian and industrial occupations tends to be permeable only to upward movement.

The comparative distributions shown in Table VII:6 are best interpreted from the perspective of political socialization theory (see Hyman, 1959; Lane, 1959). Just as the upwardly mobile tend to shift their political allegiances in the direction of their class of destination (see for example, Lipset and Bendix, 1959; Lipset, 1959; Lopreato, 1967a), so they likewise readjust their conceptions of the social structure. Consider the percentage comparisons in Table VII:7—reported from Table VII:6 with the addition of the two-generation peasants—which pertain to the four most frequent "pure" models of class imagery. (The first row of symbols designates respondent's class; the second row, his father's class; PC = privileged class, WC = working class, and P = peasantry.) For each of the three blocks, we can contrast the percentage

TABLE VII:6. SOCIAL MOBILITY AND CLASS IMAGERY

	Respondent's Position					
	Privileged Class			Working Class		
	Father's Position			Father's Position		
Class Model	Privileged Class (1)	Working Class (2)	Peasantry (3)	Privileged Class (4)	Working Class (5)	Peasantry (6)
1. Economic	16%	21%	20%	42%	29%	22%
2. Occupational	9	7	8	9	8	12
3. Political-Ideological	19	22	14	11	12	10
4. Dependency	4	1	8	4	7	2
5. Prestige	11	12	12	4	7	12
6. Composite Power	5	7	8	9	8	15
7. Composite Prestige	3	7	10	8	5	9
8. Polychotomous Images	24	13	14	13	16	11
9. Residual Images	9	10	8	0	9	6
Total	100%	100%	102%	100%	101%	99%
N	196	83	51	53	170	107

Table VII:7. Social Mobility and Class Imagery

Respondent's Class: Father's Class:	PC PC	PC WC	WC WC	PC PC	PC P	P P	WC WC	WC P	P P
Economic	16	21	29	16	20	33	29	22	33
Occupational	9	7	8	9	8	16	8	12	16
Political-Ideological	19	21	12	19	14	4	12	10	4
Prestige	11	12	7	11	12	5	7	12	5

distribution of the mobile respondents with the distributions of the stable members of their origin and destination classes. In all but two instances, the data suggest that the achievers were gradually adjusting their images away from those characteristic of their former class peers and toward those of their class-of-destination peers. In some cases, in fact, the alterations had progressed to the point that newcomers were virtually indistinguishable from old-timers: witness the peasant-to-privileged-class achievers with respect to occupational images (second row of percentages in middle block), and the working-class-to-privileged-class achievers in both the political-ideological and the prestige models (third and fourth rows of percentages in left block).

The two exceptions are enlightening in their own right, inasmuch as they seem to covary with each other. Urban manual workers who came from peasant families were less likely to hold economic images and more likely to emphasize prestige conceptions than either their former or their new class peers. These two frequency variations—one for the economic image and the other for the prestige image—are approximately cross-canceling; as one image frequency increases the other diminishes. The dynamics behind this phenomenon are fairly easy to adduce. As was noted previously, manual workers and peasants alike were prone to see the social structure in essentially economic terms because of their usually immediate familiarity with some degree of material want. On the whole, the peasants' situation was objectively the more impoverished; but in a sense that is beside the point, for in the peasant's eyes the urban blue-collar world must appear as a land of relative comfort. Consequently, when he "arrives" in that world, economic matters become less salient to the peasant than to the blue-collar old-timer—and questions of prestige become much more important. In effect, the covariation reflects different reference points for social comparison behavior and attitudes.

With respect to downward mobility, and again from the data of Table VII:6, available comparisons suggest that certain changes in imagery were also linked to skidding. The most notable instance concerns the prevalence of economic conceptions of society. Whereas urban manual workers were as a whole the most likely to construct economically based conceptions, those workers who had skidded from one of the privileged classes (column 4) were considerably more inclined to express such descriptions than either the blue-collar old-timers (column 5) or those workers whose fathers were peasants (column 6). The percentage differences are among the largest yet uncovered: 42 percent for the skidders versus 29 percent for the stable workers and 22 percent for the sons of peasants. Apparently, the downwardly mobile were people who had suffered dramatic economic hardships.

With regard to the other "pure" models, the skidders were rather consistently either midway between classes of origin and destination or indistinguishable from the stationary members of their new class location. Thus, the only exception to a resocialization interpretation of the data on downward mobility concerns the distribution of economic images. It is entirely understandable that skidders should have been especially sensitive to problems of poverty and wealth. Presumably, social descent was for most if not all of these people an involuntary event, and for the greater number of them it involved some degree of material loss. Their proclivity for economic images—and also for combinations of power and prestige factors—suggests that they were "looking backward," longingly.

POLITICAL ORIENTATION AND CLASS RELATIONS

Before concluding this chapter, we may appropriately consider as correlates of class imagery two variables which are particularly germane to the preceding discussion. These are, first, the political interests and orientations of our interviewees to the various parties of Italy, and second, their perceptions of interclass relations. In exploring the relationship of these variables to class imagery, we incorporated a gross control for variations in educational attainment. It should be kept in mind that this also serves as a rough control for variations in objective class position.

Those who expressed economic conceptions of social structure were predominantly centrist in their political preferences. This finding, essentially a recurrence of a previously discovered uniformity, results from the constellation of factors associated with popular support for the major center party, the Christian Democrats.[3] Much of its support comes from the least educated, the most rural, and the poorest people of Italy.

The use of a political-ideological model, on the other hand, occurred most often among those who favored parties of the left, especially among the better-educated leftists, and next most often among those who preferred parties of the right.[4] In short, as we have noted, to the extent that political-ideological images are indicative of a marked tendency toward class conflict, such proclivities flow from both left and right. This observation is generally consistent with the logic of theories of class conflict, which, although sometimes neglectful of class belligerence from the right, nevertheless revolve around the basic notion of antithetical interests locked in a struggle for supremacy.

Finally, the popularity of prestige conceptions increased with education and with movement toward the right on the spectrum of political orientations. By and large, this variation manifests occupational differences associated with the respective party preferences. While the better-educated respondents were predominantly members of the privileged classes, many more held clerical jobs in industry, business, or government than held top-level executive, proprietorship, or entrepreneurial positions. The salience of prestige was characteristi-

---

[3] Each of the major political parties of Italy will be described in Chapter X, when we examine questions of class interests and attitudes.

[4] The majority of the rightists selected the Italian Liberal Party, which has been the traditional favorite of industrialists and entrepreneurs in Italy; the leftists were split between the Communist and Socialist Parties (see Chapter X).

cally lower among the clerical than among the top-level group; so too was the salience of rightist political sloganry and party programs. Consequently, clerical workers tended to be leftists and political-ideological in orientation, while the elite and bourgeoisie were more often rightist and more oriented toward political-ideological and prestige criteria in their class conceptions of society.

This polarity brings us to the second correlate, namely, the essentially political question of what kinds of interclass relations are portrayed by particular images of social structure. There is general agreement in the literature that dichotomous conceptions are expressive of class antagonism, while the more detailed "hierarchical" images supposedly reflect perceptions of harmony, integration, and consensus. Bott (1957:175), for example, has stated that the two-valued power model is "a logical consequence" of the ideas of conflict and opposition. In Popitz's work (Popitz and others, 1961), we have encountered a tendency to equate "dichotomy" with conflict and "hierarchy" with a sense of order and harmony. And in Dahrendorf's (1959) coverage of previous studies, the terms "conflict model" and "dichotomous image" approach interchangeability. This tendency among students of class phenomena is undoubtedly a consequence of the powerful influence still exercised by the Marxian dialectic, wherein dichotomy and conflict are inseparable dimensions.

That a dichotomous image of society necessarily reflects a conflict-laden view, and a hierarchical image a consensus interpretation, are assumptions that have never been adequately supported, however. Underlying both, moreover, is the more fundamental assumption that a contest for supremacy always involves two and only two parties. As countless historical instances testify, that assumption is patently false. Even when contending parties are manifestly two, closer scrutiny will usually reveal the existence of deep cleavages and factions within each front. Indeed, the secret of victory in such struggles is to find the sharpest break in the opponent's front before he can do so in yours. Furthermore, there are numerous examples in history of multigroup struggles which were never reduced to a bivalent contest: one was the conflict among Lutherans, Anabaptists, and the Catholic Church in Reformation Germany, no two groups of whom united even temporarily in coalition against the third.

In short, decisions to interpret experiences of conflict from such bipolar expressions as "the rulers and the ruled," or "the employers and the employed," or even "the rich and the poor," and to infer experiences of harmony and consensus from multivalued expressions such as "managers, white-collar people, and workers," or "professionals, factory workers, farmers, and the fools," are purely theoretical extensions from the dialectic of thesis and antithesis. Their correspondence to empirical observation must be demonstrated.

Table VII:8 records cross tabulations between the detail of respondents' class images, varied by education, and their perceptions of "what kinds of relations exist among the social classes." Our assumption naturally is that the class images produced reflect the respondents' visions and/or experiences of class relations. Two precautions in interpreting these data should be men-

TABLE VII:8. EDUCATION, DETAIL OF CLASS IMAGERY, AND PERCEIVED INTERCLASS RELATIONS

Perceptions of Class Relations	Education							
	Five Years or Less				Six Years or More			
	Number of Classes Perceived				Number of Classes Perceived			
	2	3	4	5+	2	3	4	5+
Amity	22%	23%	25%	20%	11%	26%	15%	12%
Hostility	53	48	34	44	40	31	32	34
Suspicion, Distance	2	2	2	3	5	2	8	4
Collaboration, Mutual Interest	5	6	12	10	15	16	15	15
Indifference	2	6	9	10	20	12	10	17
Lack of Perception	7	9	11	5	0	8	8	7
Unclassifiable	9	8	7	7	9	5	12	11
Total	100%	102%	100%	99%	100%	100%	100%	100%
N	103	263	100	86	55	196	60	82

tioned. First, the "dependent variable" measures *perceptions* of hostility, amity, and so forth, not actual behavior. Since the respondents were presumably evaluating class relations on the basis of their own personal experiences, however, their perceptions should be reasonably indicative of actual circumstances. Second, conflict and hostility are not synonymous concepts. Theoretically, they may even be conceived independently of each other (see Coser, 1956: Chapter III). Witness the feelings of sympathy and admiration sometimes held by the winning boxer for the losing opponent and, conversely, the animosity teeming in the discreet junior executive whose promotion has once again gone neglected. Still, while hostility may or may not be consummated in overt conflict, for present purposes, it can be taken as a general disposition toward conflict, much as the construct "attitude" refers to a state of readiness for action.

Looking now to the comparisons in the table, we see no clear evidence that dichotomous conceptions either monopolized the tendency to see class relations in terms of animosity or were exclusively formulated in such terms. Those respondents with dichotomous conceptions did report perceptions of hostility more often than other people, regardless of whether they were more or less educated. But the percentage differences were not exceptionally large. In short, while the extent of perceptions of hostility (in more than two-fifths of all the class-aware) shows very well that theories of class conflict continue to have relevance, it also suggests that such conflict was not linked solely to bipolar conceptions of power and privilege.

The data further reveal the importance of a third form of interclass relations, clearly distinct from relations of either consensus or conflict. A substantial proportion of the interviewees at higher levels of formal education—but also of those less well-educated persons who visualized four or more classes—perceived a relation of collaboration and mutual interest among the various classes. Describing something akin to Sumner's (1906:16–18) "antagonistic cooperation," they seemed to have identified a relationship based on conditions of potential conflict which are deliberately resolved, at least temporarily, because the contending parties find it mutually beneficial to do so. In a sense, this view is an expression of the "social contract" come true in industrial society. More mundanely, it also reflects the greater cross pressures and interdependences of an industrial order—Durkheim's "organic solidarity" of modern society.

As Table VII:8 implies, and as a direct control for class position confirms, perceptions of collaborative relations were more frequent among elements of the elite and bourgeoisie than among either the blue-collar workers or the peasants. Interestingly, this finding is well in line with numerous accounts of the efforts made by entrepreneurial classes to "interpret the exercise of authority in a favorable light" (Bendix, 1956:95–116 especially).

To return to a previous point: the assumption which links dichotomy with conflict and hierarchy with consensus and order is derived from a none too thoughtful adherence to Marx's argument that the real class conflict was between two classes, the bourgeoisie and the proletariat. Marx's bivalent scheme was essentially a heuristic in his prophetical, eschatological analysis of industrial society. When examining the actual social structure of his time, however, he entertained a more complex multidivisional model. Once the eschatological vision is cautiously excised from Marx's analysis, so that it better pertains to the circumstances of contemporary industrial society, there is no reason to assume from it that individuals who are aware of class cleavages will abstain from doing justice to the actual complexity of those cleavages. It is entirely reasonable to envision three or more classes and still define their interrelations in terms of conflict. To a proletarian at any given time, the class structure may appear to consist of "people like me, capitalists who exploit us, peasants who refuse to organize and defend their essentially proletarian interests, and others [for example, the "intermediate strata"] who play the capitalist game at the cost of their own impoverishment." Similarly, the individual who perceives only two classes and yet neither feels nor discerns antagonisms is not unusual. For many poorly educated souls the distinction between "those above" and "those below" is God-given and morally right. For others it is simply a natural circumstance, to which moral evaluations are irrelevant. In both cases, however, such people are more often interested in "enlightened inequality" than in theoretical equality. Taking their cue from Pareto, not from Marx, they are convinced that there will always be those who command and those who obey, those who have too much and those who have not enough; and instead of striving for an upheaval that will ultimately change very little, they strive to improve the beneficence of those above. There is ample evidence of this choice of strategies in our data. One of several individuals who held a dichotomous image of society and perceived amiable relations between the classes proceeded to explain that

Of course there are people who are never happy with what they have. As for me, I say "treat me half decently, give me a steady job and enough dough to feed and clothe my family, and I am content." You see, it's like this: there will always be masters and poor people. I just hope that my masters are not too greedy. Nothing more.

A comparable example is given by Manis and Meltzer (1954:33) who found that responses to an analogous question on perceived class relations could be categorized in terms of *paternalism, partnership, snobbishness* or *jealousy,* and *hostility.* The paternalistic relationship of "leaders and followers" was the most frequently stated evaluation, as represented by the following remark of one textile worker:

If the bosses would treat the working people right, they would get along all the time. It's like a dog with a bone. If you give him food, he will be all right. Just treat us right and we'll follow right along.

VIII

DIMENSIONAL AWARENESS AND CLASS PLACEMENT

In this chapter we examine data pertaining to dimensional awareness and to self-placement in the class structure. Dimensional awareness, it will be recalled from Chapter VI, concerns the recognition of factors that define class divisions and class membership. To an extent, the foregoing analysis has been informative in this regard, for the content of a person's class image gives solid clues to the manner in which he separates the classes. An economic image, for example, suggests divisions based on distinctions that somehow involve gradations of wealth—for instance: "the rich, the poor, and those who are neither rich nor poor." But class images are abstract constructions that require a certain degree of interpretation at the concrete level in order to be theoretically significant. In deciding to which class a second person belongs, an individual may interpret his imagery in a number of ways. Thus, the economic image just mentioned may be concretized explicitly in terms of the wealth or poverty of income and possessions; it may also be reduced to such tangible indicators as the manner of dress or even the kind of job a person holds—wealth or income correlates highly with mode of dress and occupational activity. Consequently, we must delve more directly than we have heretofore into the factors employed in making decisions concerning class composition.

THE DIMENSIONS OF CLASS MEMBERSHIP

In Table VIII:1 we examine the distribution of factors defining class membership for the 958 spontaneously class-aware respondents and for 317 interviewees who gave evidence of class awareness under conditions of the probe question reported in Chapter VII. The interview question is the same unstructured one used in Chapter VII to determine dimensional awareness, namely: "To decide whether a given person belongs to your class, what single factor do you have to consider most? That is, by what in particular can you recognize a person belonging to your own class?" The various factors employed by the respondents have been summarized into six major groupings; representative vernacular expressions of these grouped labels are given as footnotes.

TABLE VIII:1. THE DIMENSIONS OF CLASS MEMBERSHIP

Factors Defining Class Membership	Class-Aware Respondents	
	Spontaneous	Under Probe
Style of Life[a]	41%	44%
Occupation and Education[b]	23	18
Lowliness of Job[c]	11	21
Wealth/Poverty[d]	9	4
Character[e]	5	5
Interests[f]	3	2
Other	4	2
Don't Know	5	4
Total	101%	100%
N	958	317

[a] The way they live, dress, speak, or the like.
[b] The kind of work they do; their education.
[c] The lowliness, tediousness, hardship, or other unappealing quality of the job.
[d] Their wealth, extent of their economic sacrifices, or the like.
[e] Their morals, uprightness, honesty, and similar qualities.
[f] Their interests, way of thinking, or the like.

The criteria most often nominated by our respondents—about two of every five—fall under the rubric of "style of life"—the way people live; their tastes, dress, and appearance; their leisure-time activities, and so forth. Interestingly, this proportion was relatively stable for all but two of the class-image models dealt with in Chapter VII, which is to say that style-of-life criteria were sufficiently adaptable to allow concrete interpretations of economic, occupational, political-ideological, dependency, and composite images with more or less equal facility. The exceptions were prestige images and the polychotomous images. The latter received application in terms of style of life by only 29 percent of the respondents, which is understandable, since style of life is somewhat more resistant than other definitional factors to multiple gradations. Those respondents who held prestige images of class, on the other hand, employed style-of-life factors 56 percent of the time, which is more than 2.5 times their rate of usage of any other factor in defining class membership.

Approximately one interviewee in five cited educational attributes and especially attributes of a general occupational nature as the most important factors defining the class to which a person belongs. In such cases, questions of job qualification or training were sometimes detectable; and among those who held a dependency image of class the emphasis was on a dichotomous distinction between superior and subordinate. For the most part, however, the intent seemed to be simply a question of "what kind of work they do"—whether one is a plumber, a government employee, a farm worker, the manager of a business establishment, or other specifiable category.

A third group of interviewees, comprising about one in seven of the 1,275 class-aware respondents, also identified occupational factors, but the accent here was significantly different. The emphasis was on negative qualities of the *work situation* and of the *nature of the work* performed—not a simple matter of abstract job title but rather of how tedious, lowly, or demeaning the work was. With respect to this criterion, it may be noted, variations are quite noticeable between those who displayed class awareness unaided by a "definition" of class and those who needed such definition. Variations in distribution between the two subsamples result from a small excess of peasants and unskilled workers among those whose class awareness needed a little prodding. With few exceptions, these interviewees differentiated only two classes in society, and one of the classes—invariably their own—contained people thought to be bound to an intensely hideous job. Interestingly, this particular type of dimensional awareness came together with the dependency model of class images. Thus, disproportionate numbers of respondents with dependency images of class (19 percent) mentioned the lowliness-of-job criteria. In both subsamples, most of those who cited this type of class-distinctive factor were blue-collar workers, agricultural laborers, sharecroppers, and tenant farmers —all occupational categories that are most dependent on the largesse of employers and that are subject to some of the most demeaning features of work.

Wealth and poverty—size of income, possessions, the extent of sacrifices endured, or simple and plain "wealth"—were selected as factors by about one-eighth of the sample as a whole, but by fewer than half that many among the poorer and less educated second-round class-aware, who instead had displayed an economic or occupational imagery of class structure (11 and 14 percent, respectively).

Finally, the remaining interviewees suggested a scatter of "interests" (cited most often by those holding a political-ideological class image: 7 percent), factors of "character" (such as "honesty," "morals," "decency"), and a variety of other criteria too heterogeneous to separate into discrete categories.

What further variations in the choice of definitional factors can be related to differences in respondent characteristics? Who was most likely to choose occupational criteria, for example? Of all the control variables considered, respondent's class position accounted for the most variance. Of course, class position, as an occupational phenomenon, correlates with a number of other variables, such as educational attainment. But it is interesting to note that a respondent's educational background seems to have had less influence than his position in the class structure on his choice of class criteria. Education's greatest effect was revealed by those persons who emphasized the educational aspects of occupation—job qualifications, job training, and the like; predictably, the higher the level of schooling, the more such factors were mentioned.

The most marked variations by class position occurred in connection with the lowliness-of-job and occupational criteria (Table VIII:2). Taken together, the frequency with which these factors were selected varied curvilinearly with class position: the modal points were the elite (56 percent) and the peasantry (45 percent); the nadir of the U-shaped curve fell between the petty bourgeoisie (21 percent) and the skilled workers (29 percent).

This remarkable pattern of variation would appear to be the resultant of component *linear* relationships between class position and occupation criteria on the one hand and lowliness-of-job criteria on the other—each working cross-current to the other. Our differentiation of these components is not perfect, since, as shown in the table, the separate variations associated with the two criteria in question were less systematic than their resultant curvilinear relationship. But the data still underline our decision to treat the two sets of factors as separate categories even though they both pertain to occupational matters. Whereas the lowliness-of-job category is strongly evaluative in the information it conveys, the other category gives an impression of primarily cognitive emphasis, under which lies a somewhat less obvious concern with evaluation. "Lowliness of job" and similar expressions openly stress the *quality* of work setting and assigned task, whatever the names given them. "Occupation," by contrast, more often simply refers to occupational titles with greater or smaller degree of specificity. Frequently it also conveys evaluation, but the imputed value is presumed to be manifest in the job title or job description— as, "bank president" in contrast to "construction worker." Such labels allegedly convey enough information to enable one to ascertain another person's class position. This latter kind of occupational criterion concerned the members of the *upper* bourgeoisie. The quality of the work performed and the conditions under which it is performed were more salient to those people who were themselves engaged in lowly, tedious, and dirty work: members of the working class, particularly the unskilled urban workers and *braccianti* (farm hands), and peasants.

The only other criteria that varied systematically with class position were

TABLE VIII:2. RESPONDENTS' CLASS AND DIMENSIONS OF CLASS MEMBERSHIP

Factors Defining Class Membership	Class Position							
	Bourgeoisie			Working Class				
	Elite	High	Petty	Skilled	Semiskilled	Unskilled	Peasants	Total
Style of Life	22%	42%	48%	46%	37%	36%	35%	40%
Occupation and Education	53	29	16	17	26	16	26	23
Lowliness of Job	3	2	5	12	13	25	19	11
Wealth/Poverty	0	9	13	8	11	10	10	9
Character	8	5	7	8	4	2	1	5
Interests	6	3	2	4	2	3	2	3
Other	6	7	4	3	5	1	3	4
Don't know	3	4	5	3	3	8	5	4
Total	101%	101%	100%	101%	101%	101%	101%	99%
N	36	169	136	146	141	103	113	844

Note: This table refers to the spontaneously class-aware respondents only. Of the 958 respondents who exhibited class awareness spontaneously, 114 were not in the active labor force (students, pensioners, or otherwise unemployed), and are excluded from the table.

those subsumed by the style-of-life category—such matters as consumption style, tastes, general appearance and dress, leisure-time and recreational activities. In general, selection of these factors varied in an inverse relationship with variations in the combined occupational categories. For example, the elite most often chose the occupational sets of factors (56 percent) and least often the style-of-life factors (22 percent); among the petty bourgeoisie, the proportions were approximately reversed (21 and 48 percent, respectively); the peasants, on the other hand, were the second most likely to choose the two occupational categories and second least likely to prefer style-of-life factors.

However, the synchronization of these variations was not complete: popularity of life-style criteria tended to break into three more or less distinct clusters. The first of these, the case of the elite, has already been noted; from a purely statistical point of view, this can be accounted for by the elite's exceptionally high preference for occupational factors. Undoubtedly, these distinctions were presumed to automatically reflect the significant differences of life style as well as of wealth and quality of the work setting. The second cluster includes the semiskilled and unskilled strata of the working class and the peasants, all of whom chose life style a little over a third of the time. Indeed, if the two occupational categories are taken together, all distributions for these three groups of respondents were very much similar. In the third cluster, we see the two strata of the bourgeoisie and the skilled workers selecting style of life about equally often, and with a greater frequency than any of the other classes.

This last cluster is less homogeneous than the previous one, however: between the two strata of the bourgeoisie there are noticeable differences with respect to three sets of factors. The petty bourgeoisie were more likely to emphasize "style of life" and "wealth" and less often concerned with occupational descriptions of any sort. Their predominant interest in the first of these is partially indicative of prestige considerations; but for many of them the emphasis lay more on the haughtiness and ostentation with which people above displayed their advantages of life style than on the "positive" aspects of prestige. This inversion of emphasis probably reveals a strong element of both envy and resentment: an envy of the affluence and influence of those above, which stems from the relative proximity of certain members of the petty bourgeoisie to the loci, both major and minor, of privilege and authority; and a resentment of their own relative impotence and modest life conditions. Because they desire to participate in the privileged style of life, they cannot reject out of hand such dimensions of class membership. Instead, their envy-bred resentment seems to dictate a rejection of only the excesses, the "haughty grandeur" with which many of those above emblazon their daily activities.

CLASS IDENTIFICATIONS

In Chapter VII we saw something of the variety of class conceptions held by our sample members. Our present effort to determine self-placement in the class structure must take into account that complex range of expressions and designations. With some linguistic license, the great bulk of the data can be reasonably summarized by the tabulations shown in Table VIII:3, which for convenience shows separately the 958 respondents who were class-aware without prompting and the 317 individuals who needed some prompting. Our

TABLE VIII:3. SUBJECTIVE CLASS PLACEMENTS IN
AN UNSTRUCTURED SCHEME

Self-Assigned Class	Class-Aware Respondents	
	Spontaneous	Under Probe
Bourgeoisie	8%	5%
Middle Class	25	12
Neither Rich nor Poor	15	16
The Workers	32	43
The Powerless Poor	12	12
The Peasants	4	7
Other	3	3
Don't Know	2	2
Total	101%	100%
N	958	317

following discussion will focus on the 958 respondents as the basic working sample, but it is worth noting briefly that there was once again a rather marked difference between the two subsamples. The original class-aware respondents were about twice as likely as their prompted fellow citizens to classify themselves in the Bourgeoisie and the Middle Class.[1] In turn, what the latter lost in those respects to the former was gained in self-classification among the Workers and the Peasants. These differences again point to the more humble occupational background of the second-round class-aware respondents and to the powerful role played by formal education in the ability to verbalize complex conceptions of class structure.

Reference back to Table VI:2 will show that, with the major exception of Rogoff's (1953b) on France, our findings diverge considerably from those of

---

[1] Here and hereafter capital letters are used in names of classes to distinguish subjective class labels from objective class labels: thus *Bourgeoisie* is the self-applied label and *bourgeoisie* the objective label.

other investigations. They differ not only in the kinds of class labels employed but also in the relative frequencies of self-assignment to roughly analogous class labels. These two differences are closely interrelated, of course, inasmuch as part of any observed variation across studies is usually due to differing research decisions as to which clusters of labels belong in the same category and which specific labels should stand as representative of total categories. Regardless of the apparent simplicity with which data on spontaneous self-placement are cast by a given researcher, impressions of uniformity invariably conceal great heterogeneity of content.

In terms of coherent theoretical development, the trick, no doubt, would be to agree in advance on specific, theoretically grounded class models and then to interpret interviewee answers in terms of their degree of approximation to one or another of those models. Unfortunately, such agreement on models is currently wanting, and for reasons that go beyond possibly ideological predilections of researchers. Much of the diversity is inherent in the very fact that people simply do not conceive the range of class inequalities in society according to a single, coherent theoretical perspective. Instead, they use combinations of many perspectives without engaging in precise articulations of their interrelationships and without any effort to winnow out the inconsistencies and contradictions. No amount of energy devoted to goals of *complete* conceptual unity will yield the desired fruit from the sociological garden of actual human beings. However, there is one thing that the researcher can do in order to simplify the task of comparative analysis, and that is to make a diligent effort to specify in some detail the many sorts of self-classification that are collectively summarized by his class labels. We shall attempt to do so in what follows.

The Subjective Class Schema

Our use of the expression "Bourgeoisie" was aimed at capturing a common experiential element underlying a rather wide range of classlike expressions employed by 73 of the 958 class-aware respondents. The most common such expression was "Bourgeoisie," which recurred 32 times and supplies the name for the broader category. Another 11 classified themselves among either "the merchants" or "the shopkeepers," while still another 11 thought of themselves as "proprietors," "well-to-do" *(benestanti),* and the like. Of the remaining 19 individuals, 7 termed themselves "employers"; 5 referred to themselves as "managers" *(dirigenti);* 3 said they belonged to "the upper class"; 2 called themselves members of the "aristocracy"; and 2 termed themselves "industrialists."

The tag "Middle Class" is more problematic. It comprises 235 people, or

25 percent of the 958 class-aware respondents. Of these, the vast majority (161) referred to themselves as members of "the middle class" or "middle stratum" *(classe media* or *ceto medio).* But the temptation to assume that all such individuals conceived of the class structure in terms of gradations of prestige, which immediately comes to mind in connection with spatial terms of stratification, must be resisted. As was noted in the previous discussion of class imagery, many interviewees divided the class structure into descriptive hierarchies of economic, political, and occupational power, with one class neither high nor low in the given hierarchy. This tendency was especially marked among trichotomous class conceptions: "the rich, the poor, and those in the middle"; "the bourgeoisie, the proletariat, and the middle class"; and so on. Although many individuals represented under the present rubric of "Middle Class" properly belong there on the basis of the usual connotations of prestige differentials borne by the label, others could have been included in the Neither Rich nor Poor class or under analogous labels that might have been used.

We suspect that the strictures advanced against an uncritical acceptance of the usual connotations of the phrase "middle class" are appropriate to many other studies that utilize spontaneous self-classification data. It is quite likely that a more industrious examination of the cognitive relationship of the term to the entire class-order constructions of interviewees would alter substantially many conclusions about the prevalence of "middle-class" self-designations (see Cole, 1950). The same considerations apply to such other self-classifications as "middle bourgeoisie" and "petty bourgeoisie," which in our study contain 23 and 18 individuals, respectively, and are both subsumed by the Middle-Class label. Very likely, many of these people held an image of society harmonious with Marx's own, when on a descriptive key he envisioned the class structure in terms of a basic power cleavage and an intermediate buffer zone of middle strata.

Of the remaining 33 self-classifications included in the Middle Class, 24 were references to "white-collar" people *(impiegati)* and 9 referred to "the lower-middle class."

One of the least problematic labels in our schema is the third, the Neither Rich nor Poor. It comprises 141 individuals, or nearly 15 percent of all self-placements. Little need be said about this particular category. It, too, is a "middle-class" conception, but it differs from the preceding class in the fact that its members left no doubt that the class structure was conceivable in economic terms—trichotomously in most cases—and that they belonged to neither extreme of the class order.

These persons were probably lacking in the class resentments and antagonisms that are often associated with dichotomous power conceptions. After all, they occupy the middle ground, what Robinson Crusoe's father termed the middle state—"the best state in the world, the most suited to human happiness," exposed to neither miseries and hardships nor to wanton pride, luxury, and ambition. To the extent that their conception provides a point of reference against which to evaluate their relative blessings, they are apt to enjoy a feeling of self-conferred superiority and to consider the "system" as a whole basically sound if not altogether equitable. Marx was not sufficiently appreciative of the individualistic impulses inherent in arrangements of power—economic or political. "We are better than the Negroes," say indigent white Americans. "We are better than the farm hands," say Italian petty-farm owners. "We are better than the street beggars!" exclaim those on public relief. In short, social inquirers must take note of man's essentially individualistic approach to the material benefits of his world, of his emulative behavior, and of his tendency to evaluate the rewards and the distributive formulae of his society as comparisons rather than as absolutes. In these situations, resentment against the whole system is soothed by contemplating the conditions of those worse off.

The fourth set of self-placements was the most frequent, involving 303 individuals, or 32 percent of the 958 total. Here, too, there is little problem of interpretation and classification, but a clarification of linguistic variations is necessary. The label "Workers" actually embraces three different expressions, two of which translate directly into the English "worker." The most common was *lavoratori,* for a total of 184 cases, and the next most frequent was *operai,* with 108 individuals. The latter term is more specific than the former because it more clearly emphasizes the *manual* nature of work and suggests a degree of "we-ness" in contrast to those who command, supervise, employ, or are otherwise engaged in nonmanual positions. Both terms, however, include industrial workers as well as dependent employees in other branches of activity. The third and final type of self-classification included in the present class consists of 11 respondents who referred to themselves as "the popular class," "the common people," or simply "the people."

The closest approximation to what in many other studies is reported as "the lower class" is represented here by the series of self-designations summarized under the label, "the Powerless Poor." Encompassing 111 respondents, or about 12 percent of the 958 total, it contains a large variety of expressions. They can be conveniently subdivided into three main groups. The first, containing 78 respondents, refers to such self-descriptions as "the poor," "the propertyless" *(nullatenenti),* and "the indigent." The second group is more specifically ideological in character, but it comprises a mere 22 cases: "the proletariat," "those without economic power," "trade unionists," and "those who have to work to eat." The remaining 11 cases, comprising the third group, simply referred to themselves as belonging to "the lower class" or to "the inferior class."

The sixth and last self-assigned class in our schema—"the Peasants"—is quite unequivocal. It is also quite small, comprising only 40 individuals, even though many others are in fact engaged in agricultural work. Of the 40, 37 spoke of themselves as "peasants" *(agricoltori* or *contadini),* and 3 classified themselves as "farm hands" *(braccianti).*

We are left with 55 interviewees, 34 of whom ("other") represent a wide array of self-descriptions, expressions so heterogeneous that they cannot be organized as separate classes. For instance, 7 individuals spoke of themselves according to educational criteria: "professionals," "the educated," and so on. Another 5 classified themselves according to criteria of occupational or political dependency: "dependents," "those who obey," "the governed," and similarly. Another 3 used the term *pensionati* (pensioners). The remaining 19 used a variety of expressions, such as "the fools," "the honest," and "the clever" *(furbi).* Finally, 21 of the 55 nonclassified respondents, while previously capable of constructing a class order, were subsequently unable, and in a few cases unwilling, to locate themselves within it ("don't know"). Because of the difficulty in classifying them, these 55 respondents will not be considered in the analysis that follows.

The six classes so constructed are characterized by a considerable degree of internal homogeneity of class experiences. One indication of this fact is given by comparisons of class imagery, as in Table VIII:4. Disregarding the poorly informative polychotomous and residual images, the data show that a substantial degree of correspondence did in fact exist between the subjective class schema and the predominant class conceptions held by people self-assigned in the various classes. Thus, the Bourgeoisie most frequently conveyed a political-ideological image of society. The Middle Class looked at society in prestige terms more often than in any other terms. More telling, both the Neither Rich nor Poor and the Powerless Poor demonstrated an extreme concern for economic differentials: images of wealth and poverty were expressed more often than all other images combined. The Workers were rather evenly dispersed among four conceptions: the composite power, the occupational, the political-ideological, and the economic. This assortment makes very good sense from a Marxian perspective, for all four dimensions are intimately intertwined in the sociohistorical stance theoretically assumed by "the proletariat." Finally, the Peasants most often expressed occupational conceptions of social structure.[2] To be a peasant in Italy is not merely an economic fact; it means also to be engaged in making a living in a thoroughly contemptible manner (Lopreato, 1967b, Part I). Understandably, peasants are particularly keen to the occupational basis of class.

On a comparative key, studies of self-assigned class in some countries, notably the United States, have shown a marked preference for the middle-

---

[2]Interestingly, the self-assigned Peasants were also the most likely to hold a polychotomous image of society. This tendency contrasts with previous data which show that the peasants, objectively defined, did not so often construct such images (19 rather than 40 percent; compare Table VII:4). The difference results from the fact that most agrarians who held images less detailed than the polychotomous did not consider themselves to be peasants.

TABLE VIII:4. SUBJECTIVE CLASS PLACEMENT AND CLASS IMAGERY

	Self-Assigned Class					
Class Model	Bourgeoisie	Middle Class	Neither Rich nor Poor	Workers	Powerless Poor	Peasants
Economic	14%	14%	60%	10%	66%	—
Occupational	14	9	2	15	—	38%
Political-Ideological	22	15	5	15	11	—
Dependency	3	2	1	7	—	—
Prestige	7	24	4	3	6	18
Composite Power	4	4	4	17	7	3
Composite Prestige	3	11	4	7	1	—
Polychotomous	26	15	13	19	3	39
Residual	8	7	6	7	6	3
Total	101%	101%	99%	100%	100%	101%
N	73	235	141	303	111	40

class label as a self-description. Kahl and Davis (1955:324), for example, reported that about one-half of their subjects located themselves in some niche of the "middle class," while only 14 percent used a working-class designation. Similar results have been obtained by Tucker (1968), Haer (1957), and Neal Gross (1953). Evidence from European countries, on the other hand, has indicated that working-class descriptions are at least as popular, if not more popular, than middle-class labels (see Kahan, Butler, and Stokes, 1966; Martin, 1954; Rogoff, 1953b). The information for Italy is congenial with the latter evidence: about 32 percent of the class-aware respondents chose a working-class type of description, while 25 percent preferred to use one of the middle-class designations.

Aside from ideological differences in the way researchers interpret the sociological substance of class labels, what accounts for this divergence in findings?[3] Why should proportionately fewer people in the United States, as compared with Italy, locate themselves in a "working class"? Undoubtedly a number of factors are at play, but perhaps one major reason is that Italy contains a proportionately larger number of people engaged in manual or blue-collar occupations. During the 1960's in the United States, less than 60 percent of the urban male labor force aged 25–64 consisted of manual workers. The comparable proportion for Italy was slightly under two-thirds. Differences by agricultural employment were even greater. Whereas only 8 percent of the United States economically active population aged 25–64 worked in agricultural occupations, 25 percent were so employed in Italy (United States Bureau of the Census, 1960; International Labour Office, 1966:224).

Similar differences in the occupational composition of research samples can produce divergent conclusions. To cite an extreme illustration, Manis and Meltzer (1954:33) found that of a total of 145 self-designations (some respondents giving more than one), 52 explicitly referred to the "working class," while only 22 referred to the "middle class." For a study of the United States, this proportion of working-class self-placements is unusually high. But then it should be high, for Manis and Meltzer's sample consisted almost exclusively of textile workers engaged in manual jobs. Other samples, such as Kahl and Davis's (1955) or Haer's (1957) were more heterogeneous in this respect and, therefore, revealed smaller proportions of working-class descriptions.

Unfortunately, few studies based on occupationally representative samples have reported findings from the vantage point of sample composition. From the available data and the summary statements otherwise presented, however, there would seem to be adequate reason for expecting a general relationship between the respondent's occupational position and the kind of self-placement he makes. Martin (1954:54–55) reported a consistent reduction in the fre-

---

[3]We are assuming, of course, that once methodological differences are leveled, the divergence will only be narrowed, not extinguished. That may not be the case.

quency of middle-class self-allocations as he moved from the highest to the lowest of seven occupational categories, the sharpest break occuring at "the conventional line of demarcation" between manual and nonmanual groupings. Runciman (1966:158) shows analogous results, as do Kahan, Butler and Stokes (1966), Davies (1967:87), Broom, Jones, and Zubrzycki (1968:217ff), and Svalastoga (1959:230ff).

Our data amply confirm this relationship (Table VIII:5). Thus, nearly three-quarters of the respondents in the elite identified themselves as Bourgeoisie or Middle Class. The high bourgeoisie preferred the Middle Class. By the time we get to the petty bourgeoisie, identification with the Workers competes favorably with identification with the Neither Rich nor Poor and with the Middle Class. Skilled workers predominantly placed themselves among the Workers but revealed some leanings toward the upper reachings of the class structure. By contrast, the semiskilled and unskilled workers usually saw themselves as either Workers or Powerless Poor, but the semiskilled showed a greater tendency to glance in the direction of the middle classes. Peasants were more scattered in their choices, but they nonetheless concentrated heavily on descriptions subsumed in the lower half of the subjective class schema.

In short, most of our respondents were fairly realistic about their positions in the class structure of their society.[4] As Tumin (Tumin with Feldman, 1961:157) put it in an analogous context, if some prefer to see themselves as somewhat better off than the facts justify, others claim a slightly lower position than is warranted. By the very logic of an objective scale of class position, self-elevating tendencies are centered among the lower classes, while self-deflating tendencies occur largely in the upper classes. Thus, about 12 percent of the unskilled workers identified themselves as members of the Middle Class or the Neither Rich nor Poor, whereas a slightly higher proportion of the elite (17 percent) stated they were members of the Workers' class.

Tendencies toward self-elevation or self-deflation are not without anchorage in the personal characteristics of people. The comments in the preceding paragraph are all based on the assumption that occupation alone is a sufficient index of class position. That assumption, of course, is debatable, but even if occupation *is* a sufficient index, other personal attributes certainly influence the kinds of self-placements people make. Most such factors are relevant to the class structure in the sense that they underlie the formation of intraclass and cross-class strata in the social consciousness, a phenomenon we shall again examine in the next chapter. Consider differences in educational attainment. Respondents located in the working class as a whole rather often identified themselves as members of the Middle Class (14 percent) and occasionally as members of the Bourgeoisie (2 percent). The greater part of this self-elevation,

---

[4]Using Kendall's τ_c, a measure of rank correlation with a correction for tied cases (Blalock, 1960:319–324), the objective and subjective class schemes correlated at $+.41$.

TABLE VIII:5. OBJECTIVE CLASS POSITION AND SUBJECTIVE CLASS PLACEMENT

| | Objective Class Position | | | | | | |
| | Bourgeoisie | | | Working Class | | | |
Self-Assigned Class	Elite	High	Petty	Skilled	Semiskilled	Unskilled	Peasants
Bourgeoisie	28%	13%	14%	5%	1%	0%	5%
Middle Class	44	54	30	18	16	5	15
Neither Rich nor Poor	10	19	24	19	11	7	12
Workers	17	8	32	50	50	49	28
Powerless Poor	0	6	1	8	21	25	16
Peasants	0	0	0	0	0	13	23
Total	99%	100%	101%	100%	99%	99%	99%
N	29	158	130	136	134	99	110

however, was committed by the better-educated workers: workers with six years of education or more were twice as likely as their colleagues with five years of schooling or less to classify themselves in the Middle Class. Comparable findings obtain for other objective classes, and also for income-derived strata.

This brings us to certain problems in analyses of class identification. The set of phenomena which in sociological parlance is called "class structure" is experienced by people in a most complex and varied fashion—perhaps too complex and varied to be effectively encompassed by any single theoretical model. Kahl (1953:177; see also Cole, 1950) is certainly on the mark in arguing that "the simpler and neater the scheme, the further it is from reality." We would suggest that any scheme intended for the analysis of class structure in the social consciousness must ultimately cope with two related problems: the *evasiveness of class imagery* and the *diffuseness of class identifications.*

Evasiveness of Class Imagery

Although awareness of a class structure and self-location in that structure are closely related acts of imagination, they are nonetheless analytically distinguishable. In defense of this position, we have repeatedly pointed out that an individual may describe the class structure of his society and yet fail to place himself within it: he may either refuse entirely to assign a class position to himself or he may even locate himself, not according to the class order just constructed, but according to some other only latent in his consciousness.

Evidence of both tendencies can be found in the literature. Comparing self-placements and previously identified classes, Haer (1957:119) found that 62 percent of his respondents located themselves in one of the classes mentioned, 18 percent chose classes not previously mentioned, and 20 percent could not locate themselves at all. Even more vivid evidence of the evasiveness of class imagery is presented by Bott (1957:162ff) in her intensive study of a small sample of families in London. Notice has already been taken of her finding that class conceptualizations were tied to a variety of social experiences involving many different membership groups and frames of reference. Owing to the complexity and heterogeneity of experiences evoked by the interview situation, conceptions of class structure were constantly in flux. Depending on whether at a given moment the respondent was thinking of one category of people or another in his social circle, of one experience or another, one aspiration or another, the class system he saw was based now on family lineage, now on wealth, and then again on education, consumption patterns, or relations of dependency. As he shifted his frame of reference, so also he changed his self-classification (see also Hodge and Treiman, 1968).

Our own evidence on this matter is not as direct or as detailed as that shown by Bott. Nor can it be easily derived, given the particular system of classification employed. But insofar as it can be reconstructed from certain aspects of the data, it tends to substantiate Bott's findings. If the class structure had been experienced in a uniform and clearly describable manner, self-classifications would have been automatically in accord with the particular class images held. To some extent, however, they were not.

It could be shown, for instance, that once having described the class structure, slightly over 2 percent of the respondents presumably could not then classify themselves within it. More important still, in at least one place there is unmistakable evidence that self-locations occurred *outside* the class order previously constructed: at least 19 percent of the 160 respondents who held a dichotomous image placed themselves in classes that by definition cannot be part of a dichotomous scheme, that is, either in the Neither Rich nor Poor or in the Middle Class.

Diffuseness of Class Identifications

The idea of diffusion in class identification is implicit in the argument that both Pareto and Weber leveled against Marx at the turn of the century. Because of the complexity of economic and occupational structures in industrial society, and because of the decreasing congruity of elements thereof, sharply demarcated boundaries between internally homogeneous and mutually exclusive interest groups are, in the real world, exceedingly more difficult to construct than perhaps they once were. The multiplication of skill levels within the old class of deprived and exploited factory workers, the extension of wage and salary ranges in ways not always manifestly congruent with prevailing notions of the "functional importance" or educational requirements of specific occupations, and a number of similar other changes have made the task of formulating a coherent, inwardly consistent image of one's own class rather perplexing. As a consequence, class identifications become diffuse and undifferentiated. There is a tendency to include in one's class people from occupational categories that are both economically and socially distant.[5]

Aggregates of our respondents assigned themselves to self-constructed classes and then articulated those assignments by the use of certain class labels. To raise once again a query asked by Martin (1954:58), can we assume that these names had the same significance for all who used them? Hardly. The

---

[5]In a sense, the phenomenon we are about to examine empirically can serve as a basis for the study of *class action*. Knowing, that is, the kinds of occupational groups an individual includes in his own class gives us a basis for determining whether he is apt material for corporate, political class behavior or whether instead he is a relatively dependable defender of existing social inequalities. It is, we must caution, an approximation: the individual may not have clearly thought out the implications of his definition; and if existing inequalities are potentially painful a well-placed ideologue can sometimes do wonders in enlightening foggy thinking. Nevertheless, if person X, who works 250 days a year tending a foundry furnace in return for an annual income of $8,000, includes in his own class a large-scale entrepreneur, the chances are rather slim that he would join in a proletarian revolution.

terminology of social-class investigations, it is true, is often based on the assumption that people who share a particular linguistic expression of class structure, or even of one social class, also share a conception of the actual composition and boundaries of the classes. But we need only pose a simple question to show how fallacious that assumption can be: "Here is a list of occupational categories. Which of them do you include in your own social class?"

Eleven occupational groups were included in the list from which Table VIII:6 was made, but for the sake of convenience they have been condensed into the seven categories shown in the table. It should be noted, incidentally, that this scheme parallels the previously employed scheme of objective class structure. The category "high nonmanual" comprehends university-educated professionals, high government officials, large-scale proprietors, entrepreneurs, and managers of large firms. The category "middle nonmanual" includes semiprofessionals, proprietors and managers of medium-size firms, and middle grades of officials in state, government, and industry. The "low nonmanuals" comprise routine clerks, small proprietors and merchants and artisans with dependent workers. The remaining categories are self-explanatory.

The data should leave no doubt that each class, as spontaneously assessed, was conceived in very broad terms. An appreciable number of individuals extended the boundaries of their class far enough to include people from nearly the entire occupational spectrum. Only the self-defined Peasants, probably because of their historical tendency to think of themselves—and to be thought of by others—as a people set apart, displayed what may be judged a high degree of self-containment; in relatively few cases did they refuse to draw a clear line of demarcation between themselves and people employed in urban occupations. This self-centeredness reminds one of Marx's argument that agricultural workers tend to be social loners when it comes to the formation of a proletarian class.

The remaining classes show a rather pronounced diffuseness of self-defined composition. Thus, the self-styled Bourgeoisie were willing to include among their peers people from the lowest reaches of the occupational hierarchy. More curious still is the fact that the commonest choice in this class was directed not to individuals who were objective class peers, given the self-classification, but rather to people from the middle- and low-nonmanual strata. Obviously, the original self-assignment to the Bourgeoisie was a tenuous feeling—possibly even lacking in conviction—for many of these individuals. It was probably more often a case of wishful thinking—of the sort that is implicit in Pareto's discussion of individual self-interest and in Weber's concept of social honor— than of actual class circumstance. Such fabrication, as we shall have occasion to see later in this chapter, is often found among the upwardly mobile. Low nonmanuals whose family origins were blue-collar or agrarian, for example, often tend to identify with a class which, by their own definitions of its

TABLE VIII:6. PROPORTIONS OF SELF-ASSIGNED CLASS MEMBERS WHO INCLUDED VARIOUS OCCUPATIONAL CATEGORIES IN THEIR OWN RESPECTIVE CLASSES

Occupational Categories	Self-Assigned Class					
	Bourgeoisie	Middle Class	Neither Rich nor Poor	Workers	Powerless Poor	Peasants
High Nonmanual	22%	13%	7%	5%	3%	—
Middle Nonmanual	63	80	65	22	18	2%
Low Nonmanual	40	50	67	37	21	10
Skilled Workers	12	19	33	42	25	8
Semiskilled Workers	4	10	13	35	32	10
Agricultural (except Laborers)	5	11	17	24	33	75
Unskilled Workers and Farm Laborers	1	4	5	31	36	25
Total[a]	147%	187%	207%	196%	168%	130%
N	73	235	141	303	111	40

[a] Total percentages exceed 100 because of multiple choices.

occupational composition, cannot objectively include themselves. In a manner of speaking, they are subjectively *of* that class, even though they are not objectively *in* it.

When we go to the Workers, the tendency to extend objective class boundaries reaches even higher proportions. Their most frequent choice was skilled workers. But less skilled workers and lower nonmanuals were selected with almost the same frequency, and, in an impressive display of symmetry, peasants and the middle nonmanuals were included by more than one-fifth of the self-assigned Workers. More important still, if we compare Tables VIII:5 and VIII:6 we find that while in the former objective context self-classification showed a marked propensity toward class realism, in the present subjective context the Workers constructed their class into a veritable social mosaic. This strongly suggests that *feeling of class,* in the Marxian sense, was weak and segmented. It also indicated that when we attempt to assess this phenomenon more directly in the next chapter, the findings will have to be appreciated in the light of the foregoing.

Data for the Powerless Poor also bear witness to the relative lack of class feeling. Although the frequency with which given occupational categories were selected as constituents of this class decreases as the top of the occupational hierarchy is approached, considerable numbers did claim as fellow members people who were far from being either poor or powerless by objective measures. If nothing else, this inclusion can only reflect a lack of predisposition to impute fault for one's poverty and powerlessness to the rich and the powerful. To that extent, the probability of corporate class feeling and action in this, the most apparently proletarian of all the subjective classes, is greatly reduced.

In sum, our data show that perceptions of the range of occupational positions encompassed by self-assigned classes more often tend to be inclusive than exclusive. Some of this diffusion, no doubt, results from an optimism about future life chances that often accompanies personal biographies of social ascent. We shall also see in a moment that downward mobility constitutes another source of this diffusion: by defining the boundaries of his class broadly enough, a person can deny the objective fact of social descent. But regardless of sources and reasons, the degree of class-identity diffusion manifested in our data is one good clue to the low probability of conflict along the dualistic lines traditionally proposed by theories of class conflict.

CLASS MOBILITY AND CLASS IDENTIFICATION

On several occasions, we have referred to the influence of vertical social mobility on class identification. We should expect at an aggregate level certain differences in patterns of class identification according to the mobility history of the study subjects. Table VIII:7 demonstrates this for the skilled blue-collar workers, using information on intergenerational occupational mobility. Similar patterns obtain for other occupational groups, although not always as distinctly as in this illustration. The table shows that, from the achievers to the stationary to the skidders, there was an increasing tendency toward self-placement in the higher reaches of the subjectively constructed class structure. Interestingly, the newcomers from below (the achievers) were most often self-assigned Workers; by comparison, the two-generation old-timers (the stationary) less often designated themselves as Workers and more often as Neither Rich nor Poor; and the newcomers from above (the skidders) still less frequently saw themselves as Workers but more frequently assigned themselves to the Middle Class and to the Bourgeoisie, thereby demonstrating a lingering sentiment in favor of their class of origin. We shall return to this latter finding in Chapter XV.

TABLE VIII:7. VERTICAL OCCUPATIONAL MOBILITY AND SUBJECTIVE
CLASS PLACEMENT AMONG SKILLED WORKERS

| | *Mobility Experience* | | |
Self-Assigned Class	*Achievers*	*Stationary*	*Skidders*
Bourgeoisie	5%	2%	12%
Middle Class	14	18	28
Neither Rich Nor Poor	17	24	16
Workers	55	49	40
Powerless Poor	9	7	4
Peasants	0	0	0
Total	100%	100%	100%
N	64	45	25

Note: "Achievers" are skilled-worker sons of semiskilled, unskilled or agricultural-laborer fathers. "Skidders" are skilled-worker sons of nonmanual fathers.

An analysis of the linkage between mobility and class identification can shed light on questions concerning identification with classes of *destination, origin,* and *reference.* By making new comparisons of data already presented in this chapter, we can build a bridge between observer-defined and participant-defined class structures in such a way as to measure a person's mobility experiences *in his own terms.* From this, we can then determine whether mobile individuals identified with their class of origin, with their class of destination, or with neither, and what differences that kind of identification made in their experiences of solidarity with peers in the self-assigned class. Further, we can determine which nonmobiles identified with a class that was either "too high" or "too low" by their own definition of the class structure. Here we are getting at the notion of class as a reference group (see Bott, 1957; Runciman, 1966).

To avoid confusing the reader with a hasty exposition of this analysis, we should give in some detail the procedures employed. Four sets of data were utilized: (1) the respondent's occupation (the basis for the observer-defined class); (2) the respondent's class self-placement (participant-defined class); (3) his description of the occupational content of his self-assigned class (the bridge from 1 to 2); and (4) his father's main occupation (the referent for the objective mobility comparison). An abbreviated statement of the analysis program is shown in Figure VIII:1.

For each of the subjective classes, compare each respondent's description of his class's occupational content (X) with his own occupation (Z):

1. If different, respondent identifies with a class that is "not his own."
    A. Is Z higher or lower than X?
        a. If higher, was his father an X?
            ____ Yes: Respondent is an achiever who identifies with his class of origin.
            ____ No: Respondent identifies with a class that is lower than his self-assigned class.
        b. If lower, was his father an X?
            ____ Yes: Respondent is a skidder who identifies with his class of origin.
            ____ No: Respondent identifies with a class that is higher than his self-assigned class.
2. If same, respondent identifies with his "own class."
    A. Was his father an X?
        ____ Yes: Respondent is intergenerationally stationary.
        ____ No, higher than X: Respondent is a skidder who identifies with his class of destination.
        ____ No, lower than X: Respondent is an achiever who identifies with his class of destination.

Figure VIII:1. Program of Analysis Used to Generate Table VIII:8.

It must be emphasized that all decisions called for in this program of analysis were made within the context of the *respondent's* definitions of his self-assigned class. Thus, to use an illustration, a respondent who described the boundaries of his self-assigned class in terms of occupations higher than his own, and whose father did not hold one of those occupations, was by his own definition identifying with a class of reference that was "higher" than his own self-assigned class. If, on the other hand, his father did hold one of those occupations, the respondent could be termed a skidder who identified with his class of origin. In the first case, the respondent had no membership experience with the "higher" class, either during his adult career life or during his formative years. In the second case, he had once been a member of that "higher" class (during his boyhood) but was so no longer, yet still identified with it.

The logic of the analysis program may be prototypically summarized as in Figure VIII:2. Taking the respondent's perception of the occupational content (X) of his self-assigned class as the point of reference, we simultaneously compared to it both his father's actual occupational position and his own, thus generating a nine-cell typology. Respondent's occupation may be higher than, the same as, or lower than X; father's occupation may be higher than, the same as, or lower than X.

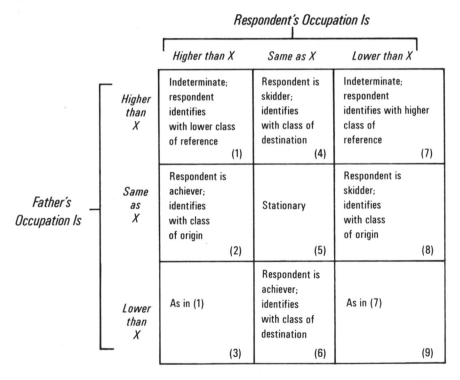

Figure VIII:2. The Relationship of Respondent's Occupation and Father's Occupation to Respondent's Perception of the Occupational Content (X) of Self-Assigned Class

Note that the "father's occupation" dimension of the typology was differentiated three ways in the analysis program only in the case of respondents who identified, by their definitions, with their own class, that is, whose actual occupations were the same as, or were included in, their perceptions of the occupational content of their self-assigned classes. Among the respondents who identified with a class not their own, the second dimension of the typology was merely bifurcated—was father's occupation the same as X or different from X? Although this reduced differentiation introduces a mild contaminant into the analysis program—it means that some of the "class-of-reference" identifiers could have been mobile by their own accounting—it was necessary as a practical matter. By the very circumstance that father's occupation *was* different from X, we have no way of determining whether the respondent whose occupation was also different from X was identifying with a class of origin. If he was being consistent in his definitions, he could not have made such an identification. There is some inferential evidence that he seldom did (as we shall see in Table VIII:8, detectable class-of-origin identifiers were comparatively rare); but the assumption of consistency is nevertheless debatable. At any rate, since we cannot determine the respondent's specific identifications in these cases, we cannot empirically separate into discrete categories the various possibilities contained by the corner cells of the typology in Figure VIII:2. That is, we cannot do so and still remain within the context of subjectively anchored interpretations of class structure and mobility. To accomplish that separation would require at the very least information about respondent perceptions of father's class position, which we do not have. Thus, with the exception of respondents whose occupations were included within the range of occupations they specified as incorporated by their self-assigned classes, for purposes of empirical investigation the vertical dimension (father's occupation) of the typology has been reduced to a dichotomy. The result is a reduction of the typology to seven cells, with the top and bottom cells of the first and third columns collapsed.

With this modification, the typology translates directly into the seven columns of Table VIII:8, which reports the data analysis. Because of size restrictions, two of the subjective classes (Bourgeoisie and Peasantry) were excluded entirely. One other, the Powerless Poor, was included despite the smallness of its subcategories. These data will be examined from two perspectives. The first concerns a cross-class comparison of relative frequencies associated with the different combinations of identifications and mobility experiences (the Total: N rows). The second refers to intraclass comparisons on two variables: expressions of class solidarity and perceptions of hostile class relations.

With respect to the first of these perspectives, class-of-origin identifiers for both upward *and* downward mobility were comparatively rare in all four classes (columns 6 and 7). About equally rare were those respondents who, by their definitions, identified with a class lower than their own self-assigned class (column 3). Although, as noted above, we cannot ascertain their mobility experiences within a subjective framework, most of these people were objectively defined as occupational skidders.

TABLE VIII:8. OCCUPATIONAL MOBILITY, CLASS SOLIDARITY, AND PERCEPTIONS OF QUALITY OF CLASS RELATIONS AMONG FOUR SUBJECTIVE CLASSES

| Self-Assigned Class, Class Solidarity, and Perceptions of Quality of Class Relations | Self-Assigned Class Is Respondent's Class | | | | | | |
| | Of Reference | | | Of Destination | | Of Origin | |
	Stationary (1)	Higher (2)	Lower (3)	Skidder (4)	Achiever (5)	Skidder (6)	Achiever (7)
Middle Class							
Total: N (204)	61	31	9	27	70	4	2
% (99)	30	15	4	13	34	2	1
Percent Who Were Class Solidary	69	61	*	59	60	*	*
Percent Who Perceived Hostile Class Relations	43	36	*	44	34	*	*
Neither Rich Nor Poor							
Total: N (123)	52	19	4	13	31	2	2
% (100)	42	15	3	11	25	2	2
Percent Who Were Class Solidary	75	74	*	86	71	*	*
Percent Who Perceived Hostile Class Relations	39	32	*	54	29	*	*

Workers							
Total: N (273)	134	35	14	28	49	7	6
% (100)	49	13	5	10	18	3	2
Percent Who Were Class Solidary	81	87	*	82	80	*	*
Percent Who Perceived Hostile Class Relations	38	43	*	46	47	*	*
Powerless Poor							
Total: N (93)	44	11	5	19	14	0	0
% (99)	47	12	5	20	15	0	0
Percent Who Were Class Solidary	77	*	*	79	*	*	*
Percent Who Perceived Hostile Class Relations	50	*	*	47	*	*	*

* Too few cases.

Note: Mobility categories and class-of-reference categories are constructed in terms of the respondents' own definitions of self-assigned class (see Figure VIII:2 and the preceding text). The class-solidarity data refer to the interview question recorded in Table VII:1. The question on perceived class relations was, "Judging by your experience, what kinds of relations exist among the various social classes? Would you say that on the whole they are relations of *amity*, *hostility*, or something else?"

By contrast, those who identified with a higher class of reference constitute a sizable category in all four cases: from 12 to 15 percent of the total of each class (column 2). Interestingly, the majority of these respondents were also objectively mobile.[6] For three of the classes, the bulk of the movement was in an upward direction; in the fourth, it was downward, as follows:

	Middle Class	Neither Rich nor Poor	Workers	Powerless Poor
Percentage Upward	48	21	34	27
Percentage Downward	16	42	29	18

These percentages suggest that identifications with a class that is admittedly higher than one's occupational position would warrant is for the most part a consequence either of hopes for the future, based on a personal biography of social ascent, or else of denial that loss of occupational position means descent into a lower class. Those respondents who were father-to-son achievers revealed their optimism about the future by identifying with a higher class of reference. Those who were father-to-son skidders similarly demonstrated their refusal to accept loss of occupational position as an indication of loss of class.

It is noteworthy that nearly half of those who identified with a higher class of reference and who considered themselves Neither Rich nor Poor were objective skidders. That fact may tell us something about their reasons for choosing the specific class label. According to Table VIII:5, nearly two in five of the Neither Rich nor Poor were members of the working class, and another 10 percent were sharecroppers, small-farm owners, or tenant farmers. For those among them who had skidded from bourgeois or petty-bourgeois origins, the use of a "neutral" expression of class location avoids the unwanted alternative of employing a proletarian type of expression, and at the same time it circumvents the possibly unconvincing form of self-description as Middle Class or Bourgeoisie.

Among the class-of-destination identifiers (columns 4 and 5), who as a whole constituted from 28 to 47 percent of the four subjective classes, the achievers were the more frequent in all but the Powerless Poor. This exception could be artificial (in part or in whole), given the circumstance that there were proportionately fewer *potential* achievers below the Powerless Poor than below any of the other classes. (The scheme of subjective classes moderately correlates with the occupational hierarchy.) The same circumstance could also

---

[6]Objective mobility is here measured as movement between any two of twelve occupational categories: (1) large-scale proprietors, entrepreneurs, managers of big firms, politicians, high government officials; (2) university-educated professionals; (3) medium-sized proprietors and merchants, managers of medium-sized firms; (4) other professionals; (5) middle grades of officials in state, industry, and commerce; (6) small merchants and proprietors, artisans with dependent workers; (7) low grades of officials and clerks; (8) skilled workers; (9) semiskilled workers; (10) small-farm owners, sharecroppers; (11) unskilled workers; (12) farm hands.

account for part of the negative relationship between the "rank" of the subjective class and the size of its class-of-destination achiever component. And again, the same argument stated in reverse could apply to the skidders. But even after this artifact is taken into account, it would seem reasonable that the Middle Class should contain a greater proportion of class-of-destination achievers than should the Workers. And, still more to the point, the frequencies for the skidders are *curvilinear* in their variation by class, with the highest proportion occurring for the Powerless Poor and the second highest for the Middle Class. The logic of the argument regarding artificial differences would by itself predict something closer to linearly accelerating proportions. Thus, it may be that the higher subjective classes contained a larger proportion of people who were both self-defined and observer-defined achievers *and* a relatively large proportion who were both self-defined and observer-defined skidders.

Turning now to internal comparisons on a series of "dependent variables" for each of the classes, the reader will recall from the chapter on Marx our proposition that *the probability of class consciousness is directly associated with downward social mobility,* and, by implication, inversely associated with mobility in the opposite direction. Before either of these propositions can be meaningfully subjected to a first test (a more detailed test will appear in Chapter XV), it is necessary to determine the mobile person's class identification. The proposition concerning skidding, for example, can be interpreted in at least three ways: (1) the skidder identifies with his class of destination and is resentful of his loss of position; (2) the skidder identifies with his class of origin and in effect denies the loss of position in the hope of one day regaining it; (3) the skidder identifies with his class of origin but admits the loss of position and is resentful of it. Unfortunately, the second and third interpretations cannot be directly tested here, owing to the small number of class-of-origin identifiers. And since even the class-specific subsamples of skidders who identified with their class of destination are fairly small, any conclusions with respect to the first interpretation will have to be treated as tentative. In a related sense, however, we shall return to this problem in Chapter XV.

When we compare the skidders with the stationary respondents (Table VIII:8, column 1) on class solidarity, and collapse the four classes to one comparison in order to maximize percentage bases, the first interpretation of downward mobility does not receive support from our data. Approximately 77 percent of both the skidders and the two-generation old-timers were class solidary. However, there would appear to be significant variations by subjective class in the hypothesized relationship. Among the Neither Rich nor Poor, the Workers, and the Powerless Poor respondents, the skidders were slightly more likely to exhibit class solidarity. Only among the self-assessed Middle Class did the skidders less often express such sentiments, as compared with the old-timers. In short, *where the material reasons for feeling a sense of resentment and injustice are greatest, class solidarity may be at its highest.* To paraphrase an old aphorism, the difference between 1 foot candle of light and total darkness is subjectively much greater than the difference between 10 and 11 foot candles. In an analogous sense, skidding X units into the Working Class can give more reason for despair and anger than skidding X units into the Middle Class.[7]

The imputed significance of the above-noted percentage differences, which in absolute terms are admittedly quite small, may be enhanced by consideration of another circumstance. Occupational mobility, especially when it is movement down the scale, is attended by general disruptions of established networks of family, friends, work associates, and so forth (see among others Durkheim, 1897; Sorokin, 1959; Blau, 1956; Luckmann and Berger, 1964; Ellis and Lane, 1967). These disruptions are most pronounced when the mobile person identifies with his class of destination, and although their effects eventually decay, in the meantime they may hinder the formation of solidarity and unity with new class peers. One may accept the fact of mobility, and either celebrate or rue it; but the destination class still presents a new world in many important respects, and the adjustments called for do not come immediately. Thus, at an aggregate level residues of those disruptive influences may interfere in the establishment of solidary relations with the destination class. In a manner of speaking, the skidders have a deficit to overcome before they can manifest a stronger tendency toward class consciousness than that displayed by their stationary associates.

Upwardly mobile persons, we have suggested, might in some cases display less class consciousness than either the skidders or the old-timers of their class. The data shown above consistently support this expectation. Furthermore, the percentage differences between achievers and old-timers decline as we move

---

[7]Leggett's (1968:92–94) data on mobility experience and class consciousness for a sample of blue-collar workers show that intergenerational skidders into the working class were *less* prone to class consciousness than were the blue-collar old-timers. Possible reasons for this discrepancy between Leggett's findings and those suggested by our data include the following: (1) It may represent an actual difference between Italian workers and the Detroit residents studied by Leggett. (2) Leggett's measures of class and mobility were entirely observer-constructed, whereas our measures contain both observer and subjective constructions. (3) The measures of class consciousness differ. Whereas Leggett's scale consists of a series of evaluational attitude statements, our measure is based on expressions of perceptions and solidarity. (4) Leggett's intergenerational skidders represent a relatively "pure" category of analysis, in the sense that career skidding was at least partially factored out. We could not perform this refinement because the subsamples were dangerously small. Resolution of the discrepancy in findings will have to await future research. Based on our own experience, we can offer two recommendations in that regard. First, in order to obtain meaningful data, the measures of class and mobility should incorporate respondent definitions in parallel with observer models. Perhaps a bridging device such as that employed above will continue to prove fruitful. Second, and stemming from the first, a purposive sampling plan would seem to be warranted for the initial stages of the investigation. Otherwise, very large total samples will be necessary in order to obtain reliable differences among the several analysis categories, especially for the class-of-origin identifiers.

from the Middle Class to the Workers. In other words, both relative to the stationary members of their own class and in comparison to the other subjective classes, those who had ascended into the Middle Class were the least prone to class consciousness.

At the same time, the achievers were generally less likely to perceive relations of interclass hostility. The difference was most pronounced in the Neither Rich nor Poor class, with 29 percent of the achievers, in contrast to 39 percent of the old-timers and 54 percent of the skidders, indicating that relations among the classes were marked by sentiments of antagonism. Curiously, the only subjective class (of those tested) in which a similar percentage difference did not appear was the Workers. This circumstance seems to be accounted for by the atypically high proportion of *achievers* who perceived conditions of hostility among the classes. Not only were they nearly identical to the skidders in their perceptions; unlike both Bourgeoisie and Middle-Class achievers, they expressed such perceptions more often than even the two-generation-stationary Workers. In short, one could conclude that upward movement into what the respondents termed the Workers class is experienced as a more difficult and tension-ridden task than comparable ascent at subjectively higher levels of the occupational hierarchy. Perhaps the worker achievers have more often confronted animosities and obstacles of various sorts in trying to improve their own lot, which make them ill-disposed to a conception of amiable, harmonious interclass relations. This explanation is all the more plausible since many among the Workers are recent migrants to the cities who have had to suffer the discomforts of uprooting and the pains of settling down to the business of work in an often hostile and highly competitive environment.

Before leaving the data of Table VIII:8, we should briefly explore certain aspects of the self-defined category of two-generation-stationary respondents. We have already noted in other contexts the tendency of many downwardly mobile people to deny objective indications of skidding by manipulating definitions of class boundaries and class content. This tendency was probably operative among many if not all of those objective skidders who identified with what by their own accounting was a higher class of reference. It is conceivable that these same motivations were operative among many of the respondents who defined themselves as stationary. By defining the occupational composition of his class rather diffusely, the actual skidder could include his former position (that is, his social origin) in his present class and thereby camouflage from himself—and presumably from others—judgments of downward mobility. The question is, how often did this camouflage happen?

It must be admitted that any determination of whether a person's definition of his class's occupational composition is "diffuse" involves a degree of intuitive speculation on the part of the researcher. Intrinsic standards for objective comparisons are necessarily lacking. Nonetheless, as a fairly reliable estimation, it appears that from 10 to 20 percent of the self-defined stationaries would have been self-defined skidders had they not extended the boundaries of their classes a considerable distance by including professionals, managers and proprietors of medium and even large establishments, and middle-level bureaucrats in government, commerce, and industry in the Workers and the Powerless Poor classes. Obviously, we do not have data which will allow us to conclude what proportion of the camouflage effect resulted from intentional planning by the respondent. Probably little of it did, if we take "planning" to mean a preconceived and thoughtfully executed scheme. But however conscious the intentions may have been, our data suggest that the phenomenon in question was not absent.

STRUCTURED SELF-PLACEMENTS

In 1945, Centers (1949:76) asked a national cross section of 1,097 white males in the United States the following question: "If you were asked to use one of these four names for your social class, which would you say you belonged in: the middle class, lower class, working class, or upper class?" In our present survey, we raised a corresponding question for purposes of comparative study: "If you were asked to choose one of the following terms to define the social class to which you belong at the present, which would you choose?" Interviewers then showed the respondents a card on which Centers's four class labels were listed. The results were:

Self-Classification	Number	Percent
Upper Class	36	2
Middle Class	542	35
Working Class	873	56
Lower Class	100	6
Other Class	4	—
Denied Class	4	—
Don't Know; No Answer	10	—
Total	1,569	99

The first thing to note is that when the respondents were not required to engage in the complex task of sociologically quarrying their class experiences, only 10 individuals failed to assign themselves to a class. An even smaller number, 4, denied the existence of classes, and another 4 refused to classify themselves according to the proposed scheme, arguing that they belonged to two or more of the given classes or that the class scheme was inappropriate to themselves. The most common self-placement, here as previously in the unstructured context, was in the Working Class, and, again as before, the second most frequent was in the Middle Class. Two percent saw themselves as members of the Upper Class, and about three times as many placed themselves in the Lower Class.

Data on self-classification are virtually meaningless unless a certain degree of congruence can be demonstrated between objective and subjective assignments. Table VIII:9, which again utilizes occupational position as an index of objective class, demonstrates that such congruence is quite considerable. Manual workers of all degrees of skill thought of themselves predominantly as members of the Working Class, just as those engaged in nonmanual occupations were inclined to identify with the Middle Class. The peasants, in turn, who, along with members of the unskilled urban strata, generally represent the poorest and humblest people in Italy, were the most likely to choose one of the bottom classes. But a third placed themselves in the Middle Class.

In all occupationally defined classes, the "deviant" cases were numerous. Note that appreciable numbers of bourgeois and especially petty-bourgeois respondents allocated themselves to the Working Class. In Chapter X, where objective and subjective class positions will be cross tabulated, it will be possible to see whether such discontinuities reflect actual class interests and ideologies. For the time being, the temptation is to agree with Milton Gordon (1958:199) when he argues in his cogent critique of Centers's study that the term "working class" is ambiguous and offers a refuge for those persons of middle-class or higher position who, influenced by egalitarian ideology, are reluctant to verbalize class distinctions. Forced as they are into verbalizing some sort of class identification, they would seem to solve the problem by selecting a label which, in common parlance, is not only shorn of all ideological connotations; it has a redeeming quality to it as well. "Work ennobles man" goes an old Italian saying. People who work belong to the working class; and who does not work?

The case of the petty bourgeoisie is somewhat more problematic than this, however. Although they are in white-collar occupations, many of them greatly resemble certain members of the working class, particularly the skilled strata, in such things as educational background, work responsibilities, and especially income. They perhaps differ most from certain craft groups of manual workers in the relative lack of freedom of their work situation. Compared to the carpenter, who can set his own pace to some extent, the routine clerk in a bureaucracy must cope with the pace of both superior and colleague. In short, many of these petty-bourgeois respondents find themselves in borderline occupations, where they are most susceptible to the pressures of status ambiguity (see Rogoff, 1953b; Lockwood, 1958). At least part of that ambiguity is undoubtedly manifested through self-classification in a diffusely defined "working class." By extending the boundaries of the class so as to include not only themselves but also people from the high bourgeoisie, they manage to lessen some of the pressures of their own ambiguous situation.

It should be emphasized that all in all, this four-fold "Centers-type" class scheme did not correspond to objective class structure as well as the previously examined "spontaneous" scheme of six subjective classes. In discussing Table

TABLE VIII:9. OBJECTIVE CLASS POSITION AND STRUCTURED CLASS SELF-PLACEMENT

Structured Class Self-Placement	Objective Class Position							
	Bourgeoisie			Working Class			Peasants	Total
	Elite	High	Petty	Skilled	Semiskilled	Unskilled		
Upper Class	20%	4%	4%	1%	0%	0%	1%	2%
Middle Class	57	68	55	23	28	9	33	39
Working Class	23	28	39	75	67	72	59	54
Lower Class	0	1	3	1	6	19	7	5
Total	100%	101%	101%	100%	101%	100%	100%	100%
N	35	168	135	145	141	103	112	839

Note: This table refers to the spontaneously class-aware respondents. The discrepancy between this total of 839 and that of previous tables (844) is accounted for by persons who did not locate themselves within one of the above observer-given classes.

VIII:5, we noted in footnote 4 a rank-order correlation coefficient (Kendall's τ_c) of $+ .41$; with the Centers-type scheme of class placement, the corresponding correlation coefficient is $+ .32$.

One other set of data regarding structured class placements should be presented before closing this discussion. From the viewpoint of the student of class structure, a major shortcoming of the Centers question is that it provides the respondent little opportunity to identify with classes that are structured along the classical lines of economic, political, and related differentials. There is evidence to indicate that the phrase "upper class," for example, carries connotations which the rich and the powerful do not care to appropriate for themselves, even after they have spontaneously referred to themselves in terms of wealth and power. To our knowledge, however, no attempt has been made to ask a structured question in which the proffered class labels are strictly descriptive along the dimensions of theories of class conflict.

Immediately following the structured question discussed above, the interview continued with the following query: "And among the following terms, which would you choose to define your social class?" Eight class labels were provided; they consisted of four pairs of dichotomies, two of which emphasized the economic dimension in two distinct ways while the others emphasized the authority or political dimension, again in two different manners. Our assumption was that, by providing respondents with two closely related linguistic variations of each of two class models, we would facilitate their "sociological imagination." The labels provided, along with the frequencies of selection, are as follows:

Self-Classification	Number	Percent
Ruling Class	100	6
Governed Class	517	33
Master Class	106	7
Subordinate Class	162	10
Rich Class	110	7
Poor Class	235	15
Capitalist Class	6	—
Proletarian Class	237	15
Other Class	52	3
No Answer	44	3
Total	1,569	99

It may be seen that in comparison to the responses to the Centers question, there was a rather large increase in the number of those who, for one reason or another, did not classify themselves according to the proposed scheme. Previously there were 18 such individuals; now there are 96. It is hard to say why that change occurred. One can only speculate that, in comparison to such relatively neutral and uncontroversial labels as "middle" and "working," the present class labels are laden with ideological connotations that are more difficult for some to countenance.

Of those who made a class identification, a total of about 20 percent chose the upper side of the four dichotomies. The selections were rather evenly distributed among the "ruling," the "master," and the "rich" classes, but self-placement in the Marxian "capitalist" class was exceedingly rare. The 73 percent who placed themselves in the lower sides of the dichotomies gave a strong preference to the "governed" class, although all four of the under-privileged classes were represented by at least a tenth of the sample.

In conclusion, three observations may be offered. First, a small but appreciable number of the respondents found classical descriptive class labels objectionable enough to refuse self-location. Second, the 20 percent or so who identified with the "ruling," "master," "rich," or "capitalist" class were probably the real representatives of "the people's enemy" and to that extent were the most conservative with respect to the existing power structure. Finally, of the majority who assessed their class position as underprivileged, by far the largest proportion selected the variable of political power as the most descriptive dimension of the class structure. This datum appears to give some credence to the school of class analysis best represented by Vilfredo Pareto.

IX

THE DISTRIBUTION OF SOCIAL CONSCIOUSNESS

In Chapter VII we have seen evidence of inconsistency or "error"[1] in the distribution of responses to the interview questions pertaining to the five conceptual levels of social consciousness. While 61 percent of the sample members identified without assistance two or more specific classes, and another 20 percent did so under conditions of a probe, 89 percent later professed to know the characteristic factors of class membership. We may inquire into such discontinuities in the total distribution of responses and also into the rate of inconsistency of response from one level of awareness to the next on an individual basis, treating the five conceptual levels in the sense of an ordered scale. Because of methodological divergences in the structure and format of the interview questions, we cannot be rigorous in this assumption of ordinality and treat the problem of consistency through conventional scaling techniques. We can, nevertheless, fruitfully assume a certain logical ordering—if a respondent expresses awareness at one level, he should have responded positively at all lower levels—and assess divergences from that assumption simply as a matter of empirical classification. We shall make this assumption and these assessments in this chapter, wherein the specific objectives of analysis are two:

---

[1] "Error" and "inconsistency" will be used interchangeably throughout this discussion and, for the sake of convenience, without quotation marks. It must be emphasized, however, that both terms are relative to the particular model of class-consciousness formation employed, and do not necessarily imply anything "unreal" about represented patterns of consciousness.

(1) to identify *patterns* of internal arrangement and ordering in the distribution of social consciousness; (2) to identify major *structural factors* or observer-defined conditions and contexts which are associated with and at least partially account for variations in the distribution of social consciousness.

PATTERNS OF CONSCIOUSNESS

In order to identify the major patterns of social consciousness, taken within the theoretical context of dispositions toward class consciousness, the frequency distributions recorded in Table VII:1 have been elaborated by the method of tree analysis, results of which are reproduced below in Figure IX:1. A few comments about the construction of this figure will be helpful to the reader.

First, because of sample-size restrictions, it was necessary to simplify the analysis by dichotomizing the response categories in Table VII:1. Two alternatives were possible: (1) separate for each question the unambiguously positive responses from all other responses; (2) collect the unambiguously negative responses into separate categories. We chose the first alternative in order to preserve as much as possible the homogeneity of those kinds of people who expressed awareness at each of the various levels. Thus, each of the "Yes" cells in the figure is relatively homogeneous, while the "No" cells contain both the straightforward negative responses and the residual data ("No answer," "Don't know," or the like).

Second, the tree analysis was constructed from the top downward, so to speak; that is, respondents who displayed class solidarity were first separated from those who did not, then class-placement determinations were made, and so on down the tree. This construction sequence, however, does not prevent reading of the tree in an ascending direction, which is the convenient perspective we shall take in subsequent discussion.

Third, as was shown in Table VII:1 by the category "inapplicable," the class-solidarity and class-placement questions were not asked of the entire sample, on the convenient assumptions that (1) people who are unaware of the existence of classes cannot be aware of belonging to a class and (2) people who are not aware of belonging to a class cannot be class-solidary. Both assumptions carry over into Figure IX:1 and the subsequent analyses.

Fourth, the data on class-awareness and subsequent levels—dimensional awareness, class placement, class solidarity—incorporate the results of *both the initial and the probe questions*. Inclusion of the latter set of data has the disadvantage of decreasing somewhat the spontaneous quality of the classification of positive responses; at the same time, it increases the likelihood of response consistency across the five levels of awareness. Our rationale for making the inclusion is as previously stated: the initial question on class awareness is a fairly demanding one, for it asks not just about the existence

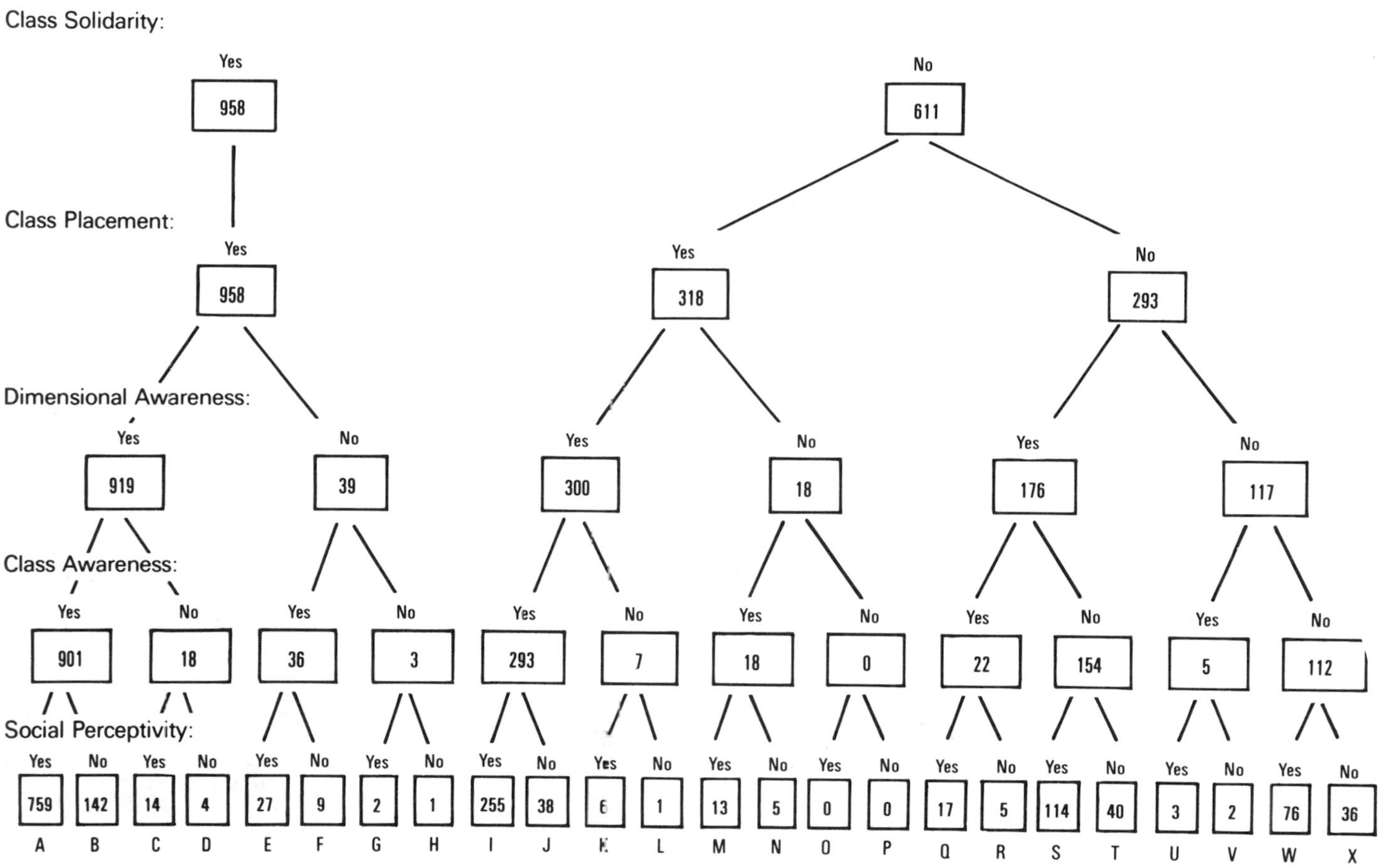

Figure IX:1. Tree Analysis of Patterns of Social Consciousness

of classes but also about the *identity* of classes on a *national* scale. The probe allows for the (here untestable) possibility that some respondents were aware of the existence of classes but could not articulate their identities, or that some were aware of class structure only in a particular region or community and were reluctant to project it into Italian society as a whole.

Considering the complexity of the phenomena under consideration, and the necessarily less than "in-depth" penetration of survey research, the degree to which interviewee responses were consonant from one level to another is remarkably high. Examine, for instance, the proportions of people who evinced awareness at contiguous levels. Of the 1,276 respondents who could place themselves in a particular class, 96 percent (1,219) were also cognizant of the dimensions of class division. These 1,219 constitute about 87 percent of all the dimensionally aware. Again, 87 percent of those who specified factors of class division had previously confirmed the existence of a class structure in their society, at least to the extent of naming two or more distinct social classes (1,216 out 1,395). Or, again, of the 1,275 class-aware individuals, about 84 percent (1,074) observed strong social differences in Italy.

Of the twenty-four cells at the bottom of Figure IX:1, six are of immediate interest to us. These represent the five consistent categories that were conceptually distinguished in Chapter VI (cells A, I, Q, U, and W), plus the sixth category of "total unawareness" (cell X), which will be discussed shortly. We should emphasize again that a pattern of responses is "consistent" if the interviewee uniformly displayed awareness up to and including a given level, after which point he was uniformly *un*aware. These six cells account for a little more than 73 percent of the total sample. The largest by far is cell A, containing 759 individuals who demonstrated consciousness through all five levels. According to the analysis of Chapter VI, these people exhibit the closest approximation to a full consciousness of class. Although we have yet to examine data regarding their images of class structure and their specific self-placements, as a group they may be fruitfully contrasted with other categories of respondents for the purpose of elucidating some of the dynamics of class-consciousness formation.

Between cell A and the next largest of the consistent categories of consciousness lies a rather wide gap in frequencies. Cell I, which represents the terminal level of self-placement as the highest level of consciousness achieved, contains only 255 interviewees or just under a third the number of class-solidary consistents. Still more interesting is the finding that a mere 17 persons terminated at dimensional awareness (cell Q), and only three persons terminated at class awareness (cell U). The rarity of these patterns confirms previous suggestions that the intermediate levels—class awareness, dimensional awareness, class placement—are all very closely interrelated and highly resistent to empirical separation. If a person is cognizant of a class order, he is also quite likely aware of the dimensions of that order; if he is dimensionally aware, the probability that he has located himself within the class structure approaches unity. Finally, the fifth and most elemental level of consciousness—social perceptivity—is represented as an isolated form of consciousness by only 76 persons (cell W). This number is slightly less than 5 percent of the total sample.

In addition to these five cells, the logic of the analysis in Chapter VI calls for recognition of a sixth, the totally "unaware" (cell X). Obviously, our use of this term is relative; few people other than the organically defective are totally unaware of social differences. Still, when a person consistently fails to recognize even the existence of significant social differences, he is revealing a perspective that demands some amount of attention. Accordingly, cell X, containing 36 respondents, will be utilized as a potentially enlightening counterpart to the higher levels of social awareness.

The remaining eighteen cells of Figure IX:1, only five of which are of any size, represent various inconsistent patterns of responses to the interview questions. The largest is cell B, with 142 persons who responded positively at all levels of awareness except the first, social perceptivity. Considering the logic of this response pattern and the number of people associated with it, this cell may be more of an artifact of the question on social perceptivity than an accurate representation of a distinct pattern of social consciousness. That question, it will be recalled, was phrased in terms of *strong* social differences. While we have no way of gauging what constituted "strong"for each of the interviewees, many of those categorized in cell B may have been reacting to the presence of that word in the interview question. If this speculation is correct, cell B respondents diverged from the people in cell A primarily in the judgment of whether class differences were "strong," whatever may be the exact denotation of that adjective.

A preliminary comparison between respondents of cells A and B indicated that they were in fact similarly situated in objective social structure, at least with respect to age, occupation, and educational attainment. Accordingly, in the analysis of structural factors reported later in this chapter, cells A and B will be treated as one. Extending the logic of this combination to the remainder of Figure IX:1, this also means that cells I and J are collapsed, as are cells Q and R, and cells U and V. The last two cells, W and X, are kept distinct, since the distinction between awareness of broad social differences other than class and awareness of neither class nor other social differences is at least theoretically very important.

The next most frequent of the inconsistent patterns is represented by cell S. In our discussion of Table VII:1, we noted that nearly two-thirds of the observed discrepancy between the gross frequencies of class and dimensional awareness could be accounted for by one specific pattern of consciousness. The reference was to these 114 persons, who perceived strong social differences and were cognizant of their underlying dimensions but did not conceptualize them in class terms. In a sense, they were displaying a consistency of their own, but it pertained to a nonclass framework. For purposes of analysis, these 114 respondents can be treated in conjunction with the 40 members of cell T, since once again the major distinction between the two groups seems to be with regard to the "strength" of social differences.

We have no way of determining the nature of the social differences referred to by these 154 sample members, aside from the circumstance that they probably had nonclass or status differentiations in mind. An examination of the kinds of dimensional factors they mentioned suggests that, compared with the total subsample of dimensionally aware respondents, they were somewhat more likely to stress factors of deportment and speech (14 versus 20 percent), but without any particular overtones of morality, honesty, or "uprightness" (5 versus 3 percent), luxuriousness of dress, appearance, or style of life (30 versus 27 percent), or educational background (5 versus 2 percent). Otherwise, they were not distinguishable with regard to dimensional factors.

The most outstanding peculiarity of the 154 respondents in cells S and T was their objective social location. Compared with the total sample, many more were unskilled urban or farm laborers (14 versus 25 percent), and only half as many (27 versus 14 percent) occupied nonmanual positions. Commensurately, they were also less well educated, 46 percent of them having failed to obtain the elementary-school diploma, in contrast to 29 percent of the total sample. These differences reflect not only their own low station in life but also that of their parents, by and large. To the extent that educational attainment levels and the status characteristics of parental origin correlate with variations in the ability to conceptualize complex social structures, these 154 respondents were at somewhat of a disadvantage.

Cells E, F, M, and N are all very similar in the sense that the respondents at least were aware of class (81 percent of them were spontaneously aware) and could locate themselves within their own constructions of the class structure, but could not identify important dimensions of class division and membership. Their inconsistency at this point may simply mean a failure of articulation, resulting in part from what was for them an unfamiliar situation—the formal interview. But it probably also indicates that their awareness and conception of class was a bit more fuzzy than usual. As a group they were indistinguishable from the total sample in both occupational position and educational attainment, hence it seems unlikely that they possessed significantly weaker capabilities of perception and conceptualization than others; rather, they probably had simply thought less about class distinctions. In any case, it would seem preferable to drop them from subsequent analysis, as opposed to combining them with other cells, especially since they constitute a very small portion (3 percent) of the total sample.

Finally, we come to the remaining eight cells (C, D, G, H, K, L, O, and P), which total only 28 cases or less than 2 percent of the 1,569 sample members. These will be treated as irretrievable-error cells and accordingly excluded from future consideration. It should be noted in passing, perhaps, that collectively these 28 respondents were somewhat overrepresented in the upper age brackets and in the poorly educated category (46 percent had not obtained the elementary-school diploma).

TABLE IX:1. IDENTIFICATION OF THE TREE-ANALYSIS CATEGORIES

Analysis Categories	Cells[a]	N	Percent of 1,569
Consistent Categories			
Class Solidarity	A + B	901	57.4
Class Placement	I + J	293	18.7
Dimensional Awareness	Q + R	22	1.4
Class Awareness	U + V	5	0.3
Social Perceptivity	W	76	4.8
Social "Unawareness"	X	36	2.3
Total		1,333	84.9
Inconsistent Categories[b]			
Group I	E, F, M, N	54	3.4
Group II	C, D, G, H, K, L, O, P	28	1.8
Group III	S, T	154	9.8
Total		236	15.0

[a] See Figure IX:1.
[b] Excluded from subsequent analysis.

One of the objects of this chapter is to examine the structural underpinnings of major patterns of social consciousness. Accomplishment of that task requires that each of the analysis categories be reasonably distinct and homogeneous, and yet also large enough to permit a series of statistical manipulations. It should be evident by now that two of the consistent categories pertaining to class consciousness are too small for such operations. This can be appreciated from Table IX:1, wherein the relevant categories of analysis are set forth. In view of this circumstance, there is no choice but to combine class awareness (cells U and V) and dimensional awareness (cells Q and R) with class placement (cells I and J). In addition to providing us with sufficiently large and still relatively homogeneous categories, this tactic has behind it the logic of empirically treating together the three levels of awareness that are most tightly interwoven from a conceptual standpoint. Our analysis of structural factors in the formation of class consciousness will therefore utilize the following comparison groupings: (1) *the socially "unaware"*; (2) *the socially perceptive;* (3) a combination of the class-aware, dimensionally aware, and self-located respondents, who will henceforth be designated as *the class iden-*

tifiers; and (4) *the class solidary.* The three "inconsistent categories" shown in Table IX:1 are excluded from the analysis.

STRUCTURAL FACTORS IN SOCIAL CONSCIOUSNESS

One of the topics on which studies of social stratification converge with those of both political sociology and the sociology of knoweldge concerns the distribution of social consciousness. A basic perspective for understanding phenomena such as class-based political behavior asserts that linkages between the objective conditions of existence, on the one hand, and the consequent behavioral expressions of those conditions, on the other, are mediated by the social consciousness. Conditions of inequality as revealed by the insights of a particular class model, for example, will remain well-nigh ineffectual with regard to political behavior until that model becomes integrated into the general consciousness of a people. Once conditions reach a certain minimum level of intensity, they become "visible," and those who are most subject to them begin to construct practical schemes of explanation regarding causes and consequences. But various factors, including the distribution of conceptual abilities, determine the extent to which particular conceptions are commonly constructed and dispersed throughout the population. In order to understand the political activities of a given population, therefore, it is necessary that we first understand the social structure as it is delineated in the general consciousness. To get this understanding, one must explore the structural factors that underlie the distribution of that consciousness.

It should be evident that the perspective outlined above is what has come to be identified as the Marxian perspective in the sociology of knowledge. Emphasis is placed on existence as a determinant of consciousness, rather than vice versa. But as we have also sought to emphasize in previous discussions, consciousness—especially the highly developed corporate consciousness-as-organizational-form—is not without its own influence on conditions of existence. The behavioral and organizational consequences of a given social consciousness can operate both as stimuli and as limiting conditions to the formation of a new consciousness. Thus, conceptualizations created in man's imagination quite often become objectivated as things of independent existence, which can then exert a subtle but profound influence on his conceptions of current situation and future events, and, through these, on much of his behavior.

In the remainder of this chapter, we shall focus on aspects of the relationship between conditions of existence and the social consciousness by exploring structural factors associated with particular configurations of social consciousness. Later, in Chapter X, the link between social consciousness and political behavior will be examined via an analysis of class interests and attitudes.

Variations in Conceptual Ability

The imaginative feats called for in conceptualizations of the class structure of an entire society require certain accomplishments of perceptual and interpretive skill. There is every reason to believe that such accomplishments are unevenly dispersed throughout the population of any given society. To the extent that a person is lacking in the requisite tools and skills, he will less likely than others display a highly developed awareness of social structure. Furthermore, the same circumstances that create unevenness in the distribution of conceptual skills also produce important variations in verbal abilities. Thus, a person may create a highly complex picture of the social structure of his society but lack the means of effectively articulating it to others.

Sombart (1909:9) observed in his study of the proletariat that "The spread of education and intelligence, to which town life contributes no small share, enables [the proletariat] to think about the . . . cause . . . of the contrast between their own position and that of the rich." Sombart undoubtedly had in mind something more diffuse than formal education, since opportunities for such were still severely limited among the working classes of early twentieth-century Europe. But his observation does suggest that in analyzing data formal schooling might be used as a workable approximation of variations in conceptual ability. It is acknowledged that the development of skills of imagination and mental organization may in any given instance show no connection with the amount of formal schooling—some people develop a degree of conceptual facility after, say, four or five years of formal instruction that others may not acquire after twice the time. For large groups of people, however, the two variables should be sufficiently correlated to permit the use of formal education as a substitute measure of conceptual ability.

If our assessment is adequate, rather definite evidence of the influence of variations in conceptual ability is detectable in the data (Table IX:2). Compare by columns, for example, the sums of the first two rows of the table. This division of the distributions—between the class solidary and class identifiers, on the one hand, and the socially perceptive and socially "unaware," on the other—is theoretically significant with regard to capabilities of perception and concept formation, inasmuch as it discriminates between those who did and those who did not report class maps of social structure. The proportions of the former range from a low of 86 percent among the respondents with less than the elementary-school diploma to highs of 98 to 99 percent among those with the senior-secondary-school diploma, some university training, or a university degree. Indeed, the proportions who were socially "unaware" range similarly from 6 percent to zero. Furthermore, the greatest disparities in level of conceptualization occurred at the lower end of the educational scale, as would be expected. About 15 percent of the people who had attended school not at all or for four years at the most were not aware of classes, in contrast to 8 percent

TABLE IX:2. EDUCATIONAL ATTAINMENT AND SOCIAL CONSCIOUSNESS

Analysis Categories	Less than Elementary Diploma	Elementary Diploma	Secondary		University	
			Intermediate	Senior	Partial	Degree
Class Solidary	69%	68%	70%	62%	50%	71%
Class Identifier	17	23	25	37	48	27
Socially Perceptive	9	6	3	1	2	2
Socially Unaware	6	2	1	0	0	0
Total	101%	99%	99%	100%	100%	100%
N	356	522	185	131	50	59

Note: The elementary-school diploma (licenza di scuola elementare) is normally obtained at the end of the fifth year of study. Senior secondary studies are normally completed after the twelfth or thirteenth year. Cases for which information on educational attainment was unavailable are excluded.

of elementary-school diplomates and only 4 percent of those who had attended intermediate secondary school.

At the same time, however, the data also suggest an effect of objective class position. This shows up most clearly in comparisons of the proportions "class solidary," which fluctuate across the table. For instance, the high rate of solidarity demonstrated by university graduates (71 percent) largely mirrors the sharp awareness of "right-wing" class interests displayed by the economic and (part of) the political elites (compare the preceding discussion in Chapter VII). Similarly, the low rate of solidarity among the senior-secondary graduates (62 percent) and especially among the respondents with a partial university education (50 percent) undoubtedly represents the conventionally described "middle-class" effect of status striving. Predominantly members of the middle and lower reaches of the bourgeoisie, these people are typically aware of class structure and can locate themselves within it, but they do not profess as often as others a personal unity of needs and ideas with their self-assigned class. To this degree, they come somewhat closer to Blalock's (1959:243) description, on a Weberian key, of the person for whom "status considerations are of the utmost importance . . . the essence of social interaction."

Objective Class Location

Given the foregoing points, we should immediately turn to an investigation of the relationship between objective class position and the distribution of social consciousness. Following conventional practice, as in previous chapters, occupation is taken as the key variable in constructing the class scheme, since it includes more class-relevant information than any other single structural variable. Among other things, it is particularly relevant to the upper end of our scale of social consciousness, a circumstance that is most opportune, given the skewed distribution of the total sample on that scale. Both Marx (1867), in Chapters 13 and 14 of the first volume of *Capital,* and Lukács (1923), in his chapter on reification and the proletarian consciousness, for example, devote considerable attention to the work setting as a source of class solidarity. In the workplace a person is most intimately confronted by relations of authority and by the exigencies of superior and subordinate roles. There economic sanctions and deprivations, and a corresponding sense of powerlessness, are most keenly felt. There also a person can best observe a large number of others who share experiences similar to his own and who consequently face a similar fate. It stands to reason, then, that differences in work environments would be reflected in expressions of social consciousness.

In our sample, consciousness of class was most highly developed among the elite, 78 percent of whom expressed solidarity with their self-assigned class, and among the semiskilled and unskilled members of the working class, with 73 and 71 percent, respectively, expressing solidarity (Table IX:3). Members

TABLE IX:3. CLASS POSITION, LEVEL OF EDUCATION, AND SOCIAL CONSCIOUSNESS

Analysis Categories	Bourgeoisie			Working Class			Peasants	Total
	Elite	High	Petty	Skilled	Semiskilled	Unskilled		
Sample as a Whole								
Class Solidary	78%	58%	67%	67%	73%	71%	68%	68%
Class Identifier	22	39	27	22	17	18	23	24
Socially Perceptive	0	2	4	8	6	8	5	6
Socially Unaware	0	0	1	3	4	4	4	3
Total	100%	99%	99%	100%	100%	101%	100%	101%
N	36	180	164	217	216	171	193	1,177
Low Education[a]								
Class Solidary	0	50%	71%	65%	73%	70%	68%	69%
Class Identifier	0	44	23	21	17	18	23	20
Socially Perceptive	0	6	5	10	7	8	5	7
Socially Unaware	0	0	1	4	4	4	4	4
Total	0	100%	100%	100%	101%	100%	100%	100%
N	0	16	75	167	184	164	176	782
High Education								
Class Solidary	77%	60%	66%	72%	73%	*	*	65%
Class Identifier	23	39	31	26	23	*	*	32
Socially Perceptive	0	2	2	2	4	*	*	2
Socially Unaware	0	0	1	0	0	*	*	0
Total	100%	101%	100%	100%	100%	*	*	99%
N	34	159	87	47	26	4	12	369

Note: Cases for which information on occupation or education was unavailable are excluded.
* Too few cases.
[a] Elementary-school diploma or less.

of the "bourgeoisie," as we may have misnamed it, were least likely to be class solidary, although they were at least aware of class nearly as often as the elite. As was previously noted, this circumstance undoubtedly manifests the bourgeoisie's concern with status distinctions both internal to the class and between one class location and another.

Interestingly, among the three skill levels within the working class the semiskilled demonstrated the highest, and the skilled the lowest, rate of solidarity. A number of tentative conclusions are suggested by these distributions, the two most important of which pertain to the alienative quality of different work settings and the thesis of *embourgeoisement* among the so-called "aristocracy of labor" (see, for example, Aron, 1964:205–213; Mackenzie, 1967; Broom, Jones, and Zubrzycki, 1968; Goldthorpe and others, 1968a; 1969). First, the higher rate of solidarity, and cognizance of class in general, among the semiskilled manifests their greater concentration in assembly-line types of jobs. Their intermediate skills enable them to avoid the usually less remunerative but more "holistic" tasks of purely physical labor and yet are insufficient to qualify them for the more "holistic" *and* more remunerative craft and craftlike activities. Instead, they are employed in tedious repetitive activities, of which the assembly line is the fullest expression. As several investigators have demonstrated (among them Chinoy, 1955; Blauner, 1964; but also see Goldthorpe and others, 1969), it is the most alienative, most exploitative work setting. Second, the lower rate of solidarity among the skilled workers may partly constitute evidence in support of the *embourgeoisement* thesis, that is, the notion that certain more "comfortable" members of the skilled stratum think and act more like occupants of white-collar positions than like their own fellow workers. The data so far examined seemingly point in that direction. But because they do not indicate subjective identifications, these data are inadequate to a meaningful test; we must therefore postpone further consideration of the thesis.

The control for differences in education, as shown in the second and third panels of Table IX:3, does not significantly alter any of the aforementioned descriptions and conclusions. The only influences readily interpretable from the presumed control for differences in conceptual ability pertain to the bourgeoisie and to the skilled workers, and these may be accounted for by alternative factors. In the first case, the higher rate of class solidarity among the better-educated members of the bourgeoisie probably derives from the circumstance that a greater portion of them were near elite in objective location, and indeed more often identified themselves as members of the elite. In the latter case, the higher rate of solidarity among the better-educated skilled workers would indicate an influence of superior conceptual abilities, except that if the indication were valid the same differentiation by education should have occurred among the semiskilled workers. The control for education is admittedly crude, and within either of the categories the average attainment was higher for the skilled than for the semiskilled. Nevertheless, as we saw in Table IX:2, the line between elementary and higher schooling was slightly discriminative of class solidarity, and this discrimination did not appear among the semi-skilled. An alternative explanation that may partially account for the lower rate of solidarity expressions among the less well-educated skilled workers is that they more often thought of themselves as located within a class that is more in the nature of a statistical aggregate than a self-conscious collectivity —that is, the Neither Rich nor Poor. Some evidence in support of this possibility is recorded in Table IX:5 below, wherein we find that nearly a third of the skilled workers with low incomes, who were also generally the lowest in education, assigned themselves to the Neither Rich nor Poor.

Taken as a whole, the petty bourgeoisie displayed a pattern of consciousness very similar to that of the skilled stratum of the working class. Once gross differences in educational history are controlled, however, some important divergences appear. The better-educated members of the petty bourgeoisie were more often aware of class structure; but, in contrast to the skilled workers, those petty-bourgeois respondents with lower educational attainments *more* often expressed solidarity. At least with respect to this highest level of measured consciousness of class, then, the control for educational background isolated factors in addition to, and more influential than, variations in conceptual ability. These concomitants of formal schooling pertain largely to differences of work setting within the petty bourgeoisie.

In pursuit of such differences, we may consider the applicability to Italian society of a notion recently explored in the literature on stratification and industrial organization, namely, that changes in social structure attending advanced stages of industrialization have produced what is referred to as a "service class" (Bahrdt, 1958; Crozier, 1960; Dahrendorf, 1964). This "class" (which, as Dahrendorf has pointed out, is hardly a single unified class at all, strictly speaking) comprises the clerical workers, the conveyors of administrative services and materials, and other incumbents of bureaucratic supportive offices and agencies. It can accordingly be deemed, as Dahrendorf correctly argues, an adjunct to the ruling class. But the argument also contends that this "class" is therefore essentially similar to the ruling class in spirit, if not also in privileges; that its political attitudes and images of society are essentially those of the ruling class; that, in short, it may be considered a "class" without its own consciousness.

While our data base is small and imperfectly addressed to this issue, we can nevertheless examine the routine clerical members of the petty bourgeoisie with respect to variations in consciousness. If these individuals had been in fact a class without consciousness, either they would have frequently expressed solidarity, or the focus of their solidarity would have been a self-defined elite or bourgeoisie class. The data do not show that they did either. Nearly two-thirds were class solidary (with the proportion being slightly higher among the better educated); this ratio is not appreciably different from that for the petty bourgeoisie as a whole; and of these class-solidary routine clerks (48 in number), 33 percent identified themselves as Middle Class, 23 percent as Neither Rich nor Poor, and 35 percent as Workers. This latter proportion, indeed, is higher than the proportion who had attained an elementary-school diploma or less; so, even some better-educated routine clerks thought of themselves as Workers. In sum, then, a considerable portion of these low-echelon "bureaucrats" were exhibiting images and attitudes not of the ruling class but of the working class, whatever the objectively defined "contributions" of their work activity.

Dahrendorf's discussion of the "service class" presumes a relative efficiency and freedom of internal circulation of talent among the various echelons of the bureaucratic world. Given these conditions, employees typically encounter a series of opportunities for personal advancement, with each step up the ladder reasonably ordered according to a schedule of promotions and predictably resulting in increments of privilege and prestige. The formal requisites to advancement encompass specific requirements of skill and experience; the informal gatekeeping processes emphasize discoverable qualities of mien and personal attribute. With such anchorages at his service, the aspiring individual knows that with the proper emulations, judiciously but visibly performed, he can succeed to ever higher rungs of the ladder and enjoy increasingly attractive emoluments. Such are the assumptions of an open, efficient bureaucratic structure.

But the bureaucracy in Italy does not fit these assumptions. Hence at this juncture reality parts company with Dahrendorf's expectations regarding the "service class." Few nations have found it necessary to create a separate governmental ministry whose function is to disentangle a sprawling jungle of duplicative offices, inefficient practices, contradictory policies, and a host of appropriative officeholders. Italy has. Obstructionism is rife, not only with respect to clientele services but also in internal matters. The "old monuments of the office," as some interviewees termed bureaucrats, are intensely jealous of the rights and privileges of office, frequently to the extent of *de facto* appropriation, and they tend to neglect their public responsibilities. They are constantly suspicious of ambitious underlings. In consequence, the internal circulation of talent is neither rapid nor widespread (see Rossi, 1954; LaPalombara, 1964). Lower-echelon clerical workers in particular increasingly find themselves in the classlike situation of blocked mobility and exploitation, and they tend to respond to it through essentially working-class conceptualizations of society.

Income Strata

The data of Table IX:3 are not conclusive evidence that specific proportions of occupationally delineated classes in Italy were in any degree class-conscious, for the working sample constitutes only three-quarters of the original repre-

TABLE IX:4. CLASS POSITION, MONTHLY FAMILY INCOME, AND SOCIAL CONSCIOUSNESS

Analysis Categories	Elite	Bourgeoisie		Working Class			Peasants	Total
		High	Petty	Skilled	Semi-Skilled	Unskilled		
Over $325								
Class Solidary	77%	61%	71%	*	*	*	*	66%
Class Identifier	24	37	29	*	*	*	*	31
Socially Perceptive	0	2	0	*	*	*	*	2
Socially Unaware	0	0	0	*	*	*	*	1
Total	101%	100%	100%	*	*	*	*	100%
N	17	43	17	2	2	1	8	90
$165–$325								
Class Solidary	75%	60%	66%	77%	54%	*	66%	66%
Class Identifier	25	39	31	19	29	*	22	29
Socially Perceptive	0	1	2	2	11	*	13	3
Socially Unaware	0	0	2	2	7	*	0	1
Total	100%	100%	101%	100%	101%	*	101%	99%
N	16	94	61	57	28	6	32	294

$85–$164

Class Solidary	*	53%	67%	66%	74%	73%	70%	69%
Class Identifier	*	47	23	23	18	19	23	22
Socially Perceptive	*	0	9	9	5	5	4	6
Socially Unaware	*	0	0	2	3	4	4	3
Total	*	100%	99%	100%	100%	101%	101%	100%
N	2	32	64	129	148	86	82	543

Under $85

Class Solidary	0	*	82%	54%	84%	66%	70%	69%
Class Identifier	0	*	9	25	8	18	19	18
Socially Perceptive	0	*	0	14	5	12	5	9
Socially Unaware	0	*	9	7	3	4	6	5
Total	0	*	100%	101%	100%	100%	100%	100%
N	0	7	11	28	38	76	63	223

Note: Cases for which information on occupation or income was unavailable are excluded.
* Too few cases.

sentative sample and may, therefore, be inadequately representative of the designated universe. But relative comparisons from one class to another can be made with reasonable ease. The elite and the working class, for example, demonstrated the greatest inclination toward a mature class consciousness.

Neither of these two classes nor any other, however, is homogeneous with respect to other objective factors, and the various discernible strata within each class may significantly relate to variations in the disposition toward class consciousness. We have already seen, in fact, that they did so among the working class: skill level—and behind that, at least partly, educational attainment—differentiated among the blue-collar respondents with regard to class solidarity. Other factors may also exhibit differentiating power.

One such factor is income. In Marx's theory of class conflict, one encounters the previously noted proposition that the likelihood of class consciousness among the proletariat increases as wages diminish (for example, in Marx and Engels, 1848:16–17). Of course, the postulated relationship assumes an explicitly historical perspective, which the present data do not possess. Nevertheless, we can treat cross-sectional variations in income as indicators of strata distinctions within the observer-defined classes and relate these to differences in consciousness. Among other things, doing this will afford us an additional perspective for evaluating the thesis of *embourgeoisement* in the context of Italian society.

As the Total column of Table IX:4 shows, the relationship between income and level of consciousness is not uniform. For instance, on the one hand, the proportion of respondents who were class identifiers—that is, people who were aware of class structure and its dimensions and could generally locate themselves within it, but did not give evidence of solidarity—increased with advancing incomes (from 18 to 31 percent). A good part of this relationship stems, of course, from the generally positive association between awareness of class and level of conceptual abilities: the better educated usually command higher incomes.

At the same time, however, the likelihood of class solidarity tended to vary inversely with income. It would seem, thus, from the two findings, that the smaller a person's share of the distributed wealth of society, the less likely he is to be aware of class structure, not because of any direct causal linkage between the two variables but because low income usually also means a complex of other distinguishing characteristics: for example, the lower chances inherited from parental origin to acquire the skills and tools with which complex mental images of social structure are constructed. However, once this inhibition has been overcome and awareness of class achieved, then the smaller a person's share of national income the more likely will he think in terms of a shared unity of needs and ideas with other members of his self-assigned class.

There are, needless to say, important variations in these relationships by occupational class position. We are handicapped in Table IX:4 by the expected correlation of income with class position, which results in inadequate numbers for several columns of the table. Still, some tentative conclusions can be broached. The peasantry, a class we have not directly discussed heretofore, followed the pattern previously described: the poorest among them were more often class solidary, but they were also less likely to be aware of class, or even of strong social differences. More than one in ten did not name any classes, and the socially-unaware category accounted for slightly over 6 percent of them, which is the largest proportion yet encountered. Once again it should be noted that a substantial part of this observed lack of awareness stems from inadequacies of conceptual skill, and perhaps an equally large segment is evidence not so much of a *lack* of awareness—at least of a broad social differentiation—as of an inability to express it verbally.

At the other end of the class scheme, it is notable that differences in income had no appreciable effect on the response patterns of the elite (although it is also possible that our categorization of income does not in this case detect such differences). Among the upper bourgeoisie, by contrast, the likelihood of class solidarity systematically increased with ascending income levels. These income strata very probably correspond with an increasing social-psychological as well as structural proximity to the elite. The well-to-do members of the bourgeoisie probably enjoyed the acquaintance of elite members, participated in overlapping social circles, adopted similar if scaled-down styles of life, and generally tended to assume elite perspectives and attitudes.

Data pertaining to the petty bourgeoisie are not as readily interpretable with regard to class solidarity, though awareness of class seems to follow the expected pattern. The small frequencies at the extremes of the income scale impose a handicap, since we are left with only two categories rather than the minimum of three necessary to a determination of the linearity of relationship. Moreover, the percentages of class solidarity are virtually identical for the two intermediate categories of income. On the basis of the recorded distributions, however, plus the fact that the class-solidary members of the petty bourgeoisie reported considerably lower incomes on the average than did the class identifiers, we may tentatively conclude that the frequency of solidarity expressions varied inversely with size of income.

For the working class as a whole, size of income predictably discriminated between the class-aware and the merely socially perceptive or "unaware" respondents. For instance, only 8 percent of those reporting a family income of more than $165 per month could not name specific classes, in contrast to 15 percent of the workers whose family monthly incomes were less than $85. But when asked if there was "anything in particular that many have but which your family is compelled to deprive itself of?" the class-aware workers were far more likely to say "yes." Or, to approach the matter from another perspective, fewer than one in ten of the self-styled deprived workers were unable to name the classes of their society, whereas nearly one in five of the nondeprived could not do so. The apparent inconsistency of response points to the importance of two factors. First is the importance of "felt" deprivations, as opposed to size of income (see Hamilton, 1967:151ff); the worker's perception of such factors as the *fairness* of his allotted share of available rewards, and not its absolute size, is most crucial. Second, there are important linkages between income strata and skill levels within the working class that must be considered. In general, size of income and level of skill are directly related; but the correlation is far from perfect, and each of these variables relates to the consciousness dimension in different ways.

It was noted earlier that the semiskilled worker exhibited most strongly a disposition toward mature class consciousness. Present data confirm and elaborate that conclusion. Those semiskilled workers engaged in work that was the *least remunerative,* as well as the most tedious, monotonous, and meaningless, were not only the most often class solidary, but also, because of their exceptionally high rate of solidarity, they were the least likely to be unaware of class or of some important form of social differentiation. This pattern of response is particularly marked in view of two circumstances: (1) it runs counter to the pattern typical of the total sample; (2) it runs counter to the postulated influence of variations in conceptual ability on the likelihood of class descriptions of society.

Given the correlation between educational attainment and skill-income strata within the working class, one would predict that, other things being equal, poorly paid semiskilled workers would reveal lower levels of class consciousness than both equally remunerated skilled workers and their own semiskilled but better-paid colleagues, for reasons of differences in the ability to formulate class conceptualizations. As we have just seen, neither aspect of the prediction gains the support of the data. But the prediction assumes that each individual constructs a mental map of the social structure on his own; that, given the required abilities, he formulates an image of society himself, rather than adopt a ready-made image from outside his own unique experience. Clearly that assumption is unrealistic, for each person is continually bombarded with ready-made images of his society—almost from the moment of birth, and with heightened intensity from the time he enters the formal educational process, gains intelligible access to television, becomes a part of the "youth commodity" market, and so forth. These ready-made conceptualizations of social reality may flow from deliberate attempts to manipulate, as in the cases of modern advertising or of religious or political evangelism, or they may constitute an inseparable and well-nigh insensible part of social institutions, as in the case of formal educational processes by and large.

The semiskilled workers of Italy, and of industrial societies in general, constitute the most susceptible clientele of an intense, coordinated effort to bring together a large mass of people under the umbrella of a single coherent image of society: namely, the radical union movement. Represented in 1964 by the *Confederazione Generale Italiana del Lavoro* (CGIL), this movement has had greatest success with the semiskilled worker precisely because of the alienative quality of his conditions of work. His factory labor is servitude to machinery—tedious, demanding, without fulfillment, debasing in general. If he has not been able to put together a unified conception of society based on his own experiences, or if he has been too isolated psychologically to develop a sense of solidarity with similarly situated others, a member of the union's political action committee will eagerly, even insistently, do these things for him. And the conditions of his work situation, combined with a wage so low as to make those conditions and the quality of life in general quite intolerable, produce a frame of mind highly disposed toward the unfolded image. At the least, the offered image rings of plausibility; more often it rings of undisputed truth.

When we examine the skilled stratum of the working class, the fact that radical unionism has registered fewer successes in gaining the allegiance of these more craft-oriented workers probably accounts in part for their failure to respond to the interview questions in the same manner as the semiskilled. For them, both awareness of class and expressions of solidarity varied directly with size of income. The effects of the education correlate of income, in other words, were not counterbalanced by the influence of externally supplied images of class structure, since the skilled work setting was not as susceptible to the programs of radical union organization. Among other things, mechanisms of income mobility within the skilled stratum are usually intrinsic to the tradition of the work activity itself (that is, to the craft tradition of standardized gradations of talent and reward), and the worker does not see the need to adopt the radical-union practice of seeking group income mobility, that is, industry-wide wage increases. For the semiskilled worker, individual income mobility can come only through such group mobility, since (1) alternative mechanisms of ascent are either nonexistent or inefficient, (2) there are fewer gradations of income to begin with, and those that do exist correlate negatively rather than positively with the satisfying nature of the activity performed, and (3) chances of interstratum mobility to the skilled category are limited by deficiencies of work qualification and of the economic resources necessary to support a period of retraining.

The higher rate of class awareness and solidarity among the better-paid skilled workers calls to mind once again the thesis of *embourgeoisement.* Table IX:4 casts doubt upon the applicability of that notion to the Italian case, unless, of course, these class-solidary "aristocrats of labor" were identifying with a class other than the working class, a possibility which can be examined with the aid of Table IX:5.

Of the 42 class-solidary skilled workers who could make a class self-identification and whose family earned $165 or more per month, 45 percent placed themselves in the Workers class and 5 percent among the Powerless Poor. For

TABLE IX:5. OCCUPATIONAL CLASS, MONTHLY FAMILY INCOME, AND SELF-ASSIGNED CLASS AMONG THE CLASS-SOLIDARY RESPONDENTS

Occupational Class and Income	Self-Assigned Class, Percent						Total	N
	Bourgeoisie	Middle Class	Neither Rich nor Poor	Workers	Powerless Poor	Peasants		
Petty Bourgeoisie	15%	28%	27%	31%	0	0	101%	102
Over $325	25	50	17	8	0	0	100	12
$165–$325	21	26	23	31	0	0	101	39
$85–$164	10	26	31	33	0	0	100	42
Under $85	*	*	*	*	*	*	*	9
Skilled Workers	4%	16%	20%	55%	5%	0	100%	137
Over $325	0	0	0	0	0	0	0	0
$165–$325	7	19	24	45	5	0	100	42
$85–$164	4	17	16	59	4	0	100	81
Under $85	0	0	29	57	14	0	100	14

	1%	16%	10%	56%	17%	0	100%	154
Semiskilled Workers								
Over $325	*	*	*	*	*	*	*	2
$165–$325	7	21	7	57	7	0	99	14
$85–$164	1	18	11	55	15	0	100	107
Under $85	0	7	7	58	29	0	101	31
	1%	4%	5%	49%	31%	10%	100%	118
Unskilled Workers								
Over $325	0	0	0	0	0	0	0	0
$165–$325	*	*	*	*	*	*	*	6
$85–$164	2	5	5	59	22	8	101	63
Under $85	0	4	0	37	45	14	100	49

* Too few cases.

the next income category ($85–$164) the proportions were 59 and 4 percent, respectively; for those with the lowest income, 57 and 14 percent. There was, then, a tendency for the high-income substratum of the skilled workers to think of themselves as other than working class. Nearly half of these better-paid upward-looking affiliates described themselves as Neither Rich nor Poor (24 percent of the total) or Middle Class (19 percent). Both labels, as discussed in Chapter VIII, suggest a concern with status distinctions of prestige and social striving.

Several of the percentage bases in Table IX:5 are so small that great caution is warranted when interpreting the distributions, especially with regard to the absolute size of particular values. For instance, the 21 percent of the better-paid semiskilled workers who identified as Middle Class may or may not be significant in itself. Nevertheless, it should be said that nothing in the table challenges any of the foregoing conclusions; if anything, there is much that supports or adds to them.

In general, it may be observed that size of income—and to the degree that it is a concomitant, magnitude of felt deprivation[2]— constituted an important component of stratum formation with respect to the subjective identifications of social location made by members of the various classes. This effect appears most sharply in the petty bourgeoisie and, as a sub-stratum formation, among the unskilled workers. Because of insufficient percentage bases for two of the four income categories in each case, we cannot tell exactly where the major differentiations occurred, but they probably were connected with divergences of work setting. Using the re-stricted comparisons available to us in Table IX:5, and the occupational composition of the classes, the following breakdowns seem most probable: (1) in the petty bourgeoisie there was a threefold division, with better-paid routine clerks and low-income shopkeepers and store merchants identifying predominantly as Middle Class or Neither Rich nor Poor, the better paid shopkeepers and merchants as Bourgeoisie, and the low-income routine clerks as Workers; (2) among the unskilled workers there was again a threefold division, with the better-paid workers identifying predominantly as Workers, the low-income farm hands as Peasants, and the low-income urbanites and better-paid farm hands as Powerless Poor.

Income differentiations of subjective identifications among the skilled and the semiskilled strata were of about the same magnitude, but by and large they ran in opposite directions. Whereas the skilled were primarily divided between the Workers and higher subjective classes, in the latter case discrimination was primarily between the Workers and the Powerless Poor. This difference in the psychological content of substrata has important implications for the cohesion

---

[2]For the total subsample of class-solidary respondents, the median monthly income of those who reported deprivations was $120; for the nondeprived, $185.

of an observer-defined working class. Self-identifying descriptions such as the Workers and the Powerless Poor strongly suggest feelings of collectivity or group cohesion. Moreover, the two labels (and the expressions they represent) do not imply an exclusion of each other; that is, description of a person as a member of the Workers class does not necessarily mean that he could not also be considered a member of the Powerless Poor. By contrast, the distinction between the Workers class and the Neither Rich nor Poor, the Middle Class, or the Bourgeoisie does suggest a rather definite exclusion. Thus, income substrata among the semiskilled and the unskilled workers are unlikely to be damaging to a working-class cohesion, because of the generally affinal psychological content of the substrata. But among the skilled workers the substratum division between the richer and the poorer is paralleled by a differentiation in consciousness between exclusive identities; this division is disruptive of a cohesive working class.

Thus, some evidence of *embourgeoisement* in the Italian working class may be inferred from the foregoing tabulations, but the data also indicate that it probably existed on a relatively small scale. According to Table IX:5, it involved less than 3 to 4 percent of all objectively delineated working-class members who could meaningfully locate themselves within their own conception of the class structure.

Regional Cleavages

Given the sharp historical disparities of economy and polity between the northern and southern regions of Italy, some scholars have written of "the two Italies" (see Rossi Doria, 1958:320). Hence, it is only fitting to expect differences in class consciousness between the two regional divisions. Not only should the content of class conceptualization differ but, considering the relative economic histories of the two regions, one might also reasonably expect a difference in the rate of class awareness and solidarity. In one sense, the North represents a "new" tradition, the industrial-city, while the *Mezzogiorno* represents an "old" tradition, the peasant-village. But perhaps because neither exists in isolation from the other, there is a parallel relationship that can reverse the order of "age." The advantages of the industrial order have grown increasingly if selectively visible to people of the *Mezzogiorno,* and with that visibility both regions become subjectively located on an industrial scale of "age" in which the North is "developed" and the South "developing." Northern affluence now stands in contrast to southern poverty within a single frame of reference; thus the contrast itself can be perceived as "artificial," susceptible of correction, and therefore unjust, rather than as part of the natural scheme of things and therefore outside the realm of human justice. In this sense, it should not be surprising to find greater class consciousness in the developing South than in the developed North.

A number of factors have been responsible for this alteration of social consciousness, including the deliberate efforts of state elites to create a national political community. Very likely the single most important factor has been the heavy migration flow from the South to the industrial cities of the North as well as to foreign countries (see Lopreato, 1967b). More than anything else, this shift has magnified on the one hand the aspirations and expectations of southerners and, on the other, the availability of a radical political education. Old deprivations have acquired new interpretations, and gradually the militancy of southerners in general has grown, that of southern labor in particular (see MacDonald, 1963).

TABLE IX:6. REGION OF RESIDENCE, MIGRATION HISTORY, AND
SOCIAL CONSCIOUSNESS

Analysis Categories	Northern Old-Timers	South-to-North Migrants	Southern Old-Timers	Total
Class Solidary	64%	65%	74%	68%
Class Identifiers	26	25	20	24
Socially Perceptive	6	7	5	6
Socially Unaware	3	3	1	3
Total	99%	100%	100%	101%
N	801	72	447	1,320

Note: The North-to-South migrant category is excluded from consideration because of insufficient numbers.

That long-time residents of the *Mezzogiorno* were more often class aware and class solidary than their northern compatriots is documented in Table IX:6. The large majority of the two categories of old-timers were regional *natives,* and the rest were old-timers of long duration. Thus, the "contaminating effects" of migrants have been factored out, by and large, with the major group of migrants (that is, the South-to-North movers) recorded separately in the middle column of the table.

This distribution is of relevance to an oft-treated hypothesis in the literature on political concomitants of industrialization, namely, the thesis of the "transplanted worker" (see Ulam, 1960:62–69; Maurice Zeitlin, 1967; Leggett, 1968). The usual interpretation, which has received some empirical documentation (for instance, Leggett, 1968), is that because the transplanted worker is torn out of his traditional agrarian setting and thrust unprepared into the demands of life in the industrial world, he is uncommonly susceptible to the proselytizations of radical groups, including left-wing union and party organizations. The data shown above do not seem to indicate applicability of this complex of postulated relationships to the Italian setting, inasmuch as the ex-peasant migrants to the North were indistinguishable from the northern old-timers in frequency of class awareness and solidarity. However, such a conclusion is premature, for a number of refinements are required in the migrant category before an adequate test of the thesis can be made. For example, variations in occupation and educational attainment, in recency of migration, and in type of community of origin (such as size, or degree of industrialization and/or commercialization) should be controlled. With these refinements taken into account, the above-recorded impression of adaptation and resocialization on the part of the migrants might or might not be borne out. Unfortunately, the percentage base is too small to permit reliable testing of this sort, since the existence of selectivity processes in the migration phenomenon necessitates simultaneous control of two or more variables.

There are notable dissimilarities between the occupational structures of northern and southern Italy. In terms of our own class scheme, the elite in the North has become predominantly the economic and political elite of the modern industrial society, whereas in the *Mezzogiorno* it still retains on a larger scale remnants of the old nobility and aristocracy. The bourgeoisie in the North is generally better educated and more fluid, as compared to the South. Workers in the *Mezzogiorno* are typically either artisans or unskilled manual laborers, and the relatively few skilled and semiskilled industrial workers are usually found in very small plants engaged in light or medium production. Peasants in the northern regions are more often mechanized farmers; peasants in the South are peasants in the fullest sense of the word.

Notwithstanding these and related divergences, however, we can still fruitfully apply the objective class scheme to both the North, where it fits rather well, and the South, where its fit is somewhat less accurate (see Lopreato, 1967b:162–195). We may examine the degree to which this regional cleavage in the social body of Italy was manifested in the consciousness of the several classes.

As a concomitant of the South's yearning and often frustrating struggle to enter the industrial world, by the 1960's its class structure was in a state of instability. The factor of large-scale migration alone had contributed substantially to the turmoil. Thus, it is no surprise that class awareness and experiences of class solidarity were more frequent among the southern old-timers, regardless of occupational class, than among northern old-timers. Turning to Table IX:7, we see that despite the fact that educational attainment levels were lower in the South, and despite the fact that visible indicators of class boundaries were confused and disrupted, southerners not only more often identified specific classes and located themselves with respect to them; they also more frequently expressed a solidarity of needs and ideas with other members of their self-assigned class. The breakdown of the old class structure—or, more accurately, the fact that it was being overlain and invaded by new elements—

TABLE IX:7. CLASS POSITION, REGION OF RESIDENCE, AND SOCIAL CONSCIOUSNESS

Analysis Categories	Bourgeoisie			Workers			Peasants	Total
	Elite	High	Petty	Skilled	Semi-skilled	Unskilled		
Northern Old-Timers								
Class Solidary	79%	52%	61%	68%	70%	65%	66%	64%
Class Identifiers	21	45	33	21	20	12	24	26
Socially Perceptive	0	3	6	9	7	14	4	7
Socially Unaware	0	0	1	3	3	9	6	3
Total	100%	100%	101%	101%	100%	100%	100%	100%
N	24	116	104	139	145	66	119	713
Southern Old-Timers								
Class Solidary	*	67%	77%	71%	86%	76%	70%	75%
Class Identifiers	*	33	19	20	10	20	22	20
Socially Perceptive	*	0	2	7	0	4	7	4
Socially Unaware	*	0	2	2	4	1	1	2
Total	*	100%	100%	100%	100%	101%	100%	101%
N	8	49	53	56	49	102	74	391

* Too few cases.

increased the salience of class interests and, concomitantly, the self-conscious struggle of "some" against "others," of "us" against "them." One wonders what was at work here—was it some social force akin to those that typically have produced "Marxist revolutions" in peasant *not* in industrial societies? Did Marx look for the forces of class transformation in the wrong corners of the globe?

An examination of the content of the southerners' class images (Table IX:8) shows that the conflict was still conceptualized to a considerable extent in the terms of the old class structure. North-South differences are not nearly as marked as most Italians and scholars would expect. But new terms of self-placement in the social order, such as the Middle Class, the Neither Rich nor Poor, and even to a small degree the Workers were less often selected by native southerners than by northern old-timers. Exceptions to this general rule can be noted for particular observer-defined classes, but even these exceptions tend to confirm the existence of somewhat stronger disruptions and conflicts in the consciousness of social structure in the *Mezzogiorno*. Thus, for example, the northern petty bourgeoisie, and especially the routine clerks, thought of themselves as Workers primarily and as Middle Class or as Neither Rich nor Poor secondarily. By contrast, the much higher social standing (in the sense of prestige) of the southern petty bourgeoisie relative to their own class structure produced a greater inclination toward adoption of the new terms of class location: 29 percent were Middle Class and another 29 percent Neither Rich nor Poor, while only 22 percent assigned themselves to the Workers class.

Among the working-class respondents, those residing in the North revealed a stronger tendency than their southern counterparts toward self-description as Neither Rich nor Poor, Middle Class, and even Bourgeoisie. The southerners, in turn, tended more toward the Powerless Poor and the Peasants. This pattern was least marked among the skilled workers, primarily because of the inclination of some southern artisans to think of themselves as "above" the Workers. It should be noted, incidentally, that this "self-elevation" on the part of southern artisans is not of the same fabric as the *embourgeoisement* tendency observed among a few skilled workers in the North.

According to Table IX:7, semiskilled and unskilled workers in the South exhibited some of the highest rates of class solidarity of the entire sample (86 and 76 percent, respectively). The preceding tabulations show that the vast majority of these class-solidary people considered themselves to be members of the Workers, the Powerless Poor, or the Peasantry. As was previously noted, the frequency with which these particular respondents were aware of class, in the first place, and then expressive of solidarity is remarkable for a number of reasons, one being the fact that educational levels—and presumably conceptual abilities—were quite a bit lower in the South, especially among these very respondents. Another factor, which was not mentioned earlier, is the lower level of urbanization in the southern regions; as of the early 1960's, for exam-

TABLE IX:8. OCCUPATIONAL CLASS, REGION OF RESIDENCE, AND
SELF-ASSIGNED CLASS AMONG CLASS-SOLIDARY RESPONDENTS

Region of Residence, and Occupational Class	Self-Assigned Class							
	Bour-geoisie	Middle Class	Neither Rich nor Poor	Workers	Power-less Poor	Peasants	Total	N
Northern Old-Timers								
Bourgeoisie	14%	53%	17%	14%	2%	0	100%	58
Petty Bourgeoisie	12	27	20	40	2	0	101	60
Skilled Workers	4	18	21	53	3	0	99	90
Semiskilled Workers	2	20	10	54	13	0	99	98
Unskilled Workers	0	5	12	65	12	7	101	43
Peasants	5	9	17	32	10	27	100	78
Southern Old-Timers								
Bourgeoisie	22%	50%	16%	9%	3%	0	100%	32
Petty Bourgeoisie	20	29	29	22	0	0	100	41
Skilled Workers	3	14	19	58	6	0	100	36
Semiskilled Workers	0	2	7	61	29	0	99	41
Unskilled Workers	0	3	1	43	39	14	100	74
Peasants	8	11	8	28	20	26	101	51

ple, the *Mezzogiorno* contained only two of the six largest cities of Italy, despite the fact that its share of the total national population was about 37 percent.

Marx, it will be recalled, stipulated as one of the factors responsible for a rise in proletarian consciousness the increased concentration of workers in large cities that attends industrialization. He was of course stating a historical relationship, but some of the components of the urbanization process undoubtedly have cross-sectional applicability, at least at a gross level of comparison. Larger cities generally mean higher density of residence and workplace, both of which are associated with enhanced opportunities for the development of large intraclass communication networks and for the formation of such class-based voluntary organizations as mutual-aid associations, burial societies, and recreational groups (see Nordlinger, 1967:181). Moreover, the probability of coming into contact with the political leadership of radical unionism tends to vary in proportion to the size of workplace; thus, class consciousness may be positively associated with *increased* economic development, as this is reflected in degree of urbanization (see Hamilton, 1967:6–7, 132–133 for a related discussion). With respect to these various concomitants of urbanism, then, the class awareness and solidarity of the southern semiskilled and unskilled workers were probably achieved under conditions of handicap, relative to the northern counterparts.

From a broader perspective, the data presented in this section on regional cleavages in the consciousness of class structure allude to the existence of complex interactions between two sets of variables. One can be summarized as the absolute and felt deprivations associated with the juxtaposition of areas of relative poverty and relative affluence; the other, as the availability of an informal, radical, class-based political education. At the time of the interviews, the two sets of variables did not converge very closely geographically. For the most part, the higher political education characterized the North where conditions of life were better rather than the South where they were worse. Since the start of economic recovery following World War II, however, and especially during the late 1950's, the degree of convergence had steadily risen. It has undoubtedly continued to the present time. As the people of the *Mezzogiorno* have grown more sensitive to the existence of regional disparities, through mechanisms such as migration and the mass media, they have also gained access to the political education of radical parties.[3] Assuming that other factors

---

[3]In his discussion of the political consequences of social mobility, Germani (1966) identifies three major requirements for the formation of a radical political opposition to ruling parties: available masses, an available ideology, and available leadership. Of these factors, the third has been traditionally meager in the *Mezzogiorno,* wherefore the salience of the second has been weak in comparison to the North. Lacking the efficient recruiting base of large-scale factories, and facing the deeply ingrained tradition of suspicion and distrust that has long been characteristic of the southern peasant, radical political organization has been largely confined to the more affluent regions of the North. Consequently, the *Mezzogiorno* has rather been without a resident leadership cadre which could complete the synthesis of available masses and available ideology. It is becom-

associated with the distribution of social consciousness do not intrude—and the most likely intruding factor would be an increased rate of upward social mobility—radicalization of consciousness in the *Mezzogiorno* will probably continue to increase, for a while at least.

Social Mobility

As a number of scholars have argued (among them Schumpeter, 1951; Dahrendorf, 1959; Lipset, 1959), where possibilities of individual ascent are structurally present and are made into personal advantage on a sufficient scale, strong forces of *status* concerns are unleashed to mitigate the salience of conditions that might otherwise give rise to a consciousness of *class*. Upward mobility, when it occurs on an individual and not group or stratum basis, tends to atomize the psychosocial bases necessary to class awareness and class feeling

TABLE IX:9. OCCUPATIONAL CLASS, VERTICAL SOCIAL MOBILITY, AND SOCIAL CONSCIOUSNESS

Occupational Classes and Analysis Categories	Respondent's Occupational Position in Relation to Father's Position				
		Higher than Father's		Lower than Father's	
	Same as Father's	Crossed Boundary[a]	Didn't Cross Boundary	Crossed Boundary	Didn't Cross Boundary
Elite					
Class Solidary	80%	*	73%	—	—
Class Identifier	20	*	27	—	—
Socially Perceptive	—	*	—	—	—
Socially Unaware	—	*	—	—	—
Total	100%	*	100%	—	—
N	15	5	15	—	—
Bourgeoisie					
Class Solidary	58%	62%	53%	—	60%
Class Identifier	41	35	44	—	40
Socially Perceptive	2	3	3	—	—
Socially Unaware	—	—	—	—	—
Total	101%	100%	100%	—	100%
N	59	68	34	—	15

ing evident, however, that the physical presence of such leadership is not a totally indispensable element of the formula. The introduction of mass communication, especially television, and a large migration flow between the ends of Italy have expanded the effective audience of a distant radical leadership. If the conditions to which the ideologies and leaders speak are observably present, the potential for radical politics is thereby increased.

TABLE IX:9. (*continued*)

Petty Bourgeoisie					
Class Solidary	71%	61%	—	—	76%
Class Identifier	22	33	—	—	24
Socially Perceptive	7	4	—	—	—
Socially Unaware	—	2	—	—	—
Total	100%	100%	—	—	100%
N	55	84	—	—	17
Skilled Workers					
Class Solidary	63%	—	66%	76%	—
Class Identifier	24	—	20	24	—
Socially Perceptive	9	—	11	—	—
Socially Unaware	4	—	3	—	—
Total	100%	—	100%	100%	—
N	79	—	101	29	—
Semiskilled Workers					
Class Solidary	71%	—	70%	82	71
Class Identifier	14	—	19	15	21
Socially Perceptive	8	—	5	3	8
Socially Unaware	6	—	5	—	—
Total	99%	—	99%	100	100
N	63	—	94	34	24
Unskilled Workers					
Class Solidary	76%	—	69%	*	*
Class Identifier	9	—	22	*	*
Socially Perceptive	9	—	7	*	*
Socially Unaware	7	—	2	*	*
Total	101%	—	100%	*	*
N	91	—	55	2	9
Peasants					
Class Solidary	69%	—	—	*	74%
Class Identifier	21	—	—	*	26
Socially Perceptive	6	—	—	*	—
Socially Unaware	4	—	—	*	—
Total	100%	—	—	*	100%
N	165	—	—	7	19

a "Boundary" refers to the division between the "higher" or privileged strata (the nonmanual) and the working class and peasantry.
* Too few cases.

by inhibiting the development of sentiments of common experience and destiny. Ties with family, friends, former work associates, and similar significant others become less stable, and interests grow increasingly divergent (see Durkheim, 1897, 242 ff; Blau, 1956; Sorokin, 1959; Luckmann and Berger, 1964; Ellis and Lane, 1967; Adams, 1968). In effect, the socially mobile individual often finds that his "stake in the future" is different from that of his old companions.

In Table IX:9, we have cross-tabulated mobility experiences and level of consciousness, controlling for the respondent's occupational class position. The measure of mobility compares respondent's occupation to his father's last occupation; thus, it detects only the net result of intracareer and career-entry movements. The first column in the table contains the nonmobile or stationary respondents; columns two and three represent upward mobility; columns four and five, downward mobility. A partial control for *intensity* and class significance of mobility has been built into the mobile categories, the distinction being between those who did and those who did not cross the boundary between the nonmanual strata and the manual and peasant classes.

Examining first the upward-mobility data, we find that in four of the seven available comparisons of achievers and stationary respondents, the achievers were less often expressive of class solidarity. In one case, the semiskilled stratum of the working class, there was no difference to speak of. The other exceptions are probably interpretable in terms of resistance to resocialization. First, the bourgeois sons of working-class or peasant fathers were more often class-solidary than either their new class peers or their fellow newcomers whose fathers were members of the petty bourgeoisie; but they were less often class solidary than the working class or the peasant old-timers. It would appear, then, that some of these bourgeois newcomers were exhibiting remnants of their previous class culture. The contrast becomes even clearer when we consider the formerly petty-bourgeois newcomers to the high bourgeoisie, who seemed to have fully resocialized. Second, the skilled-worker sons of peasants or of fathers located in lower-skill strata were similarly displaying a residue of their origins. They were more likely to be class solidary than the skilled stationary, but less likely than the old-timers of the semiskilled and unskilled strata and of the peasants.

These interpretations necessarily assume that we know the class identifications of the respondents; or, to be more exact, that we know what their identifications were both before and after the act of mobility. We naturally have no attitudinal information for times prior to the interview. As for present class identifications, we examined them within a mobility context in the previous chapter. Strictly speaking, that information should also be applied to this analysis, but unfortunately we cannot apply it because of restrictions in sample size. Nevertheless, it may be recalled from Table VIII:8 that, given specific class identifications and respondent definitions of the composition of their self-assigned classes, the achievers were generally somewhat less likely to express sentiments of solidarity than were the stationary.

Turning now to the data on downward mobility, we must again consider the question of subjective identifications, since it is critical for selecting from among competing interpretations of the relationship between skidding and variations in social consciousness. It can be argued that the skidder is resentful of what he defines as *external* causes of his descent, that is, of conditions that are extrinsic to himself and over which he has no control. As a corollary, he might tend to perceive society as marked by class exploitations and obstacles to individual success. Such conceptualizations can be particularly useful as mechanisms for the avoidance of personal responsibility for "failure," regardless of their accuracy as evaluations of objective conditions.

A counterargument contends that different mechanisms for the avoidance of "personal failure" definitions are operative, and that because of these the skidder is *less* likely to entertain notions of class structure. Rather than seeking an escape from the conflicts and tensions of downward mobility by invoking the influence of external conditions (for example, class exploitations), he in effect denies the *existence* of failure (see Wilensky and Edwards, 1959). He may accomplish this denial by manipulating his image of the social structure so as to include in his original class or stratum his current lower position. Or he may simply alter his temporal perspective of evaluation and contend that his loss of status is only a momentary anomaly in what will otherwise prove to be a pattern of continued success; given time and patience, he believes, a reacquisition if not a betterment of lost position will inevitably occur. Consequently, he continues his investments in the appropriate emulations and identifications.

In the analysis in the previous chapter wherein we examined mobility within the context of participant definitions (Table VIII:8), the evidence pertaining to skidders who identified with their self-defined classes of destination indicated weak support for the first of the above interpretations. The alternative interpretation could not be directly tested, since very few of the skidders identified with what were, in their own contexts, classes of origin. But this latter circumstance itself provides an element of support for the alternative interpretation—specifically, for that part of it which argues that a skidder may deny what would otherwise be a loss in position by expanding the boundaries of his former self-assigned class so as to incorporate his current lower position. Indeed, we observed some evidence of that tendency in the earlier analysis.

Thus, it would seem that there is a certain amount of support for both interpretations, which is not at all impossible, since they are not mutually exclusive but revolve around differences in the individual's personal identification of class location.

Data presented in Table IX:9, however, would suggest that the interpretation in terms of external causes, exploitations, and resentment is probably the stronger. Let us remember from the analysis in the preceding chapter that most of those who were skidders by their own definitions identified themselves with their classes of destination. Under the circumstances, the finding in Table IX:9 that the skidders more than the stationary expressed class solidarity in four of the comparisons available probably means that these people were reacting against perceived class exploitation and injustice. The exceptions, moreover, do not detract from this reading of the data. One class (the bourgeoisie) is exceptional only to the extent that the skidders and old-timers did not differ in the rate of class solidarity. The other (semiskilled workers) also involves only an absence of difference—and not an unexpected one, inasmuch as it pertains to skidders whose fathers were located in the skilled stratum of the working class. Those respondents who skidded from petty bourgeois, bourgeois, or elite origins to the semiskilled stratum were presumably those who felt the loss of position most. And this feeling was displayed in their high rate of class solidarity. An analogous effect of high intensity of downward mobility could be demonstrated with respect to political-party preferences. (See Saltzman, 1969:178–179.)

The foregoing conclusions from Table IX:9 should be treated as tentative for a number of reasons. One, of course, concerns the relatively small numbers on which many of the percentage distributions are based. These small bases put several already narrow percentage differences in jeopardy. But perhaps more important is the related handicap that small numbers impose, namely, the inability to effect necessary controls on a number of variables that are at least theoretically germane to the interpretations given above. It would be preferable, for example, to interrelate objective and subjective definitions of mobility more directly than we have done. And, ideally, the data on objectively defined mobility should be differentiated according to the respondent's effective career age and the amount of elapsed time since the change in class position was accomplished. Finally, to mention only one more example, our previously noted lack of information on the respondent's subjective identifications preceding his mobility also imposes restrictions.

In spite of these problems, nevertheless, it is significant that the data lent themselves to interpretations that are consonant with the existing body of theory, however rudimentary the theory may be. If nothing more, the findings and interpretations suggest promising lines for future research and elaboration of theory.

OBSTACLES TO CLASS CONSCIOUSNESS

As a way of summarizing this chapter, we may consider various conditions and contexts that impede the formation of class consciousness. In an early paper on this subject, Rosenberg (1953) explored the limiting influences associated with several broadly abstracted structural factors. The effects of some of these appear to be manifested at an aggregate level in portions of our data. Others, for which we have no relevant data, are also germane to the Italian case.

One of the obstacles discussed by Rosenberg concerns the organization of production systems in modern industrial societies. The structure of large-scale industry and the increasing differentiation of skills and tasks that is associated with expansion of the productive system tend to create *inter*class buffers that insulate the major economic interest groups of owner and worker; examples are the various supervisory levels, such as the shop foreman. Recognition of these impediments to the formation of a unified corporate class consciousness is not new. Among others, Weber (1921–1922, I:305) observed that "class-conscious organization succeeds most easily" where it involves "immediate economic opponents."

In terms of our own data, such structural developments are probably reflected at a gross level in the North-South differences in inclination toward class consciousness. Industrial production in the North typically involves a greater number of skill differentiations within the working class and a greater number of intermediate supervisory levels between the machine operator (who is most likely class solidary) and the factory owner. By contrast, industrial production in the *Mezzogiorno*—what little of it there is—is usually conducted on a small scale with relatively few gradations of workers and a shorter "chain of command" from top to bottom. Furthermore, such differences in the organization of production mean corresponding differences in the immediacy of owner-worker relations. And again, the greater the number of skill (and usually wage) differentiations within the working class, the more likely a preemptive concern for intraclass distinctions of status will arise: aspirations and expectations of intraclass (*stratum*) mobility, with all the rivalries and dissensions that these imply.

To the extent that the South's economy still has to go through the earlier stages of industrial differentiation and expansion, its potential for class consciousness may yet increase. Hamilton (1967:132–133) found evidence of this phenomenon in parts of France. As more and more laborers of an "underdeveloped" economy are drawn into industrial production and organized as a labor force for large factories, they are simultaneously drawn into the focus of radical unionism. On the one hand, the conditions of their new work setting as semiskilled machine operators and tenders make them prime candidates for the programs of radical unions—particularly those among them who were formerly artisans and independent craftsmen. On the other hand, their very concentration in large factories provides the union with an efficient base for recruitment and political organization, a base that did not exist previously.

A second obstacle to class consciousness discussed by Rosenberg[4] pertains to membership in multiple groups and to competing forms of group consciousness. The most notable examples in recent history have been self-conscious ethnic, religious, racial, and generational communities of people who define their respective interests as mutually contradictory.[5] Where such forms of group consciousness are strong and allied prejudices rampant, the formation of a unified consciousness of *class* is highly problematic (see Bettelheim and Janowitz, 1964). In its stead, complex patterns of consciousness of "ethclass" (Gordon, 1964), religious-group class, or racial class emerge. Indeed, in the extreme case the salience of socioeconomic-class distinctions may be almost completely submerged in the welter of ethnic, religious, or racial strife. The United States experience has been informative in this regard. In place of the comparatively simple, clear-cut division of rich owner versus exploited worker, the division has as often as not been a more complicated one of rich *"English"* owner versus exploited *"Irish"* laborer, rich *white* owner versus exploited *black* laborer, and the like.

Compared with the United States, Italy is relatively free of the cleavages engendered by large ethnic, religious, and racial minority groups. To that extent, class consciousness in Italy has not been encumbered by competing forms of group awareness and loyalty. There has been one obstacle of a comparable nature in recent Italian history, however, and that is the existence of regional, sectional, and even village loyalties. National unification lies so recently in the past that remnants of older identities can still be found. Among the older generations, consciousness of being a Venetian as opposed to a Florentine, for example, is still present. Northerners in general still look upon themselves as civilized in contrast to "those *terroni*" (earthworms) in the South (Compagna, 1959). These cleavages are reinforced and made even more complicated by the vast number of dialects in Italy, some of which are so distinctly separate from one another as to create barriers to communication. In recent decades the mother language has increasingly spread across the country, in large part through the state's programs of universal education and literacy, but also as a result of mass media like the radio and more recently

---

[4]Others include the territorial organization of political representation, which cuts across class boundaries, and the existence of forms of group consciousness that are more inclusive than class —nationalism for example. See Marshall's (1965) discussion of the role of citizenship in inclusive nationalism.

[5]Note, for example, Schumpeter's (1951) recognition of this in his essay on "Social Classes in an Ethnically Homogeneous Environment." On generational cleavages, see Mannheim (1952), Maurice Zeitlin (1967), Feuer (1969).

especially the television. But these influences are still restricted mostly to the younger generations and to the nonimpoverished. Many of the people of Italy are still characterized by localized dialects and identities.

In consequence of such territorial-cultural divisions as these, the development of a unified consciousness of class on a national scale has probably been somewhat impeded. Just as the presence of ethnically, religiously, or racially specific associations can lead to intraclass cleavages, so can associations that are regionally and linguistically specific (see Eisenstadt, 1966:65–67).

X

CLASS INTERESTS AND SOLIDARITY

We come now to the main goal of our studies in class consciousness: an assessment of the degree to which class position is accompanied by theoretically appropriate expressions of interest and class solidarity. In view of the evidence considered in previous chapters, the findings of this chapter might well be anticipated by the general prediction that expressions of class interest and solidarity will fall somewhat short of expectations based on theories of class conflict. In particular, the working people, "the poor," are not likely to reveal the strong tendency to class conflict that (from the viewpoint of class theory) might be expected from their ranks. Two sets of data are perhaps most relevant to this prediction. First, recalling our discussion of the influence of educational factors, we may argue that many people knew very little about the economic interests that may be theoretically attributed to their class, and are therefore apt to hold contradictory definitions and evaluations of their class situation. Second, there is the multiplicity of class images held by our respondents: an individual's attitudes and definitions of interest are formed within a variety of distributive systems and reward contexts, and in consequence of this fact his awareness of theoretically appropriate *class* interests may be distorted or obscured. Beyond this, as it was stated by Durkheim (a sociologist who transcended Weber's and Pareto's skepticism almost to the point of sanctifying the idea of social solidarity), most people regard the existing social order as just (Durkheim, 1897:252). More recently, a sociologist in Pareto's mold has implied that nineteenth-century reformers were naive not only about human nature but also about politics. Assuming that the poor would pursue their class interest and that the poorest class was the most numerous, they championed universal suffrage in the interest of socialism. But as the poor achieved the suffrage, masses of them also achieved levels of living clearly above subsistence. To many of these, the idea of revolutionary activity must have seemed quite rash because it could be much too costly. Did some cease to vote or act with the poor? In any case, "the poor have got the vote but they no longer have the votes" (Homans, 1961:394).

Still, if classlike behavior is likely to fall short of expectations derived from theories of class conflict, it can also be argued that bourgeois and proletarian ideologies are less moribund in Italy than in such countries as Germany, Great Britain, and the United States, certainly—probably less moribund than in any other country in the North Atlantic community. As we shall presently see, Italy features what is undoubtedly one of the most complex, vigorous, and aggressive political party systems of contemporary industrial society. It hosts one of the strongest socialist movements, and unquestionably the most popular Communist Party, in Western Europe. While some might wish to debate the degree to which Italy exhibits unique residua of the classical age of capitalism and bourgeois ideology, it is clear that in comparison with other industrial societies Italy should display high levels of class consciousness and feeling.

THE SCHEME OF ANALYSIS

One of our basic theses throughout the preceding chapters has been that the usual approaches to the study of class consciousness, which focus on class awareness and observer-circumscribed self-placement, are grossly inadequate. Class consciousness is above all else a *political* phenomenon. In theory as well as in practice, it is derived largely from a political education, and it is articulated as political culture. Even given the limitations of a survey approach to class consciousness, the political nature of class consciousness must be acknowledged and woven into the fabric of specific investigations.

Our concern in this chapter, therefore, is with the manner in which differences in political attitudes and interests correspond to differences in class position. According to the perspective stated in Chapter IX, that correspondence is located in the social consciousness. Political expressions of objective conditions are not linked directly to those conditions; they are linked via subjective conceptions of social structure and subjective definitions of economic and other interests. Consequently, we are concerned with the *interaction* of observer-defined and participant-defined class position, on the one hand, and with political interests and attitudes, on the other.

A fruitful precedent to this approach was established by Heinz Eulau (1956; see also 1962) in his study of political identifications, demands, and expectations. As was noted in our previous review of his findings (Chapter VI), Eulau examined for a national sample from the United States the relationship of objective and self-assessed class position to the elements of political perspective. This type of research scheme will be quite useful to our own investigation, with some major alterations. First, because of the critical importance of interviewee spontaneity to the study of class consciousness, we have restricted the analysis to those respondents who were (1) spontaneously aware of class and expressive of an image of class structure, and (2) capable of self-location within that structure. In assessing subjective class position, therefore, we have relied as much as possible on the *respondent's own definitions and conceptualizations* rather than on a structured question of the Centers variety. Second, because self-placement in the class structure is by itself a poor indicator of class feeling, we have further restricted the analysis to those respondents who were also expressive of sentiments of class solidarity. Although it is sometimes done, one should not use class variations in political interests and attitudes as the primary indicator of class consciousness (Eulau, 1962:11ff; Sartori, 1969:65ff). On the one hand, too many factors are fused in the objective circumstances associated with a given class position to permit such inferences. On the other hand, too many people vote for or otherwise support even classist parties for reasons that subjectively have nothing to do with class interests. The shared consciousness that "black is beautiful," for example, may be more determinative of shared class-linked political interests and attitudes than the shared consciousness of class as such.

Having noted that the restrictions outlined above have reduced substantially the size of our working sample, one might question the validity of the present approach. Obviously we are confining the analysis to a relatively small and, in some respects, select portion of the original sample. Nevertheless, it is equally true that the purpose of the analysis is to investigate *class consciousness,* not a consciousness of status, race, or some other such categorization. Only a few of the original 1,569 sample members displayed a measurable, reasonably consistent disposition toward mature class consciousness. They are the focus of this investigation. The central question is whether differences in their class position, both objectively and subjectively defined, account for differences in their political interests, political expectations, and class-related ideologies and evaluations.

Given the characteristics of contemporary industrial societies, including the characteristics of the social consciousness manifested by members of those societies, it would have been profitable if we could have used a three-class model in our analysis. Since the most prevalent image of society displayed by our respondents was trichotomous, for one consideration, a trivalent construction of both objective and subjective class would have been only logical. But unfortunately, since the small number of respondents at the upper ends of the two scales (the elite objectively defined and the self-proclaimed bourgeoisie) precluded that construction, we are left with the conventional two-class model, constructed according to the manual-nonmanual occupational distinction. In commensurate fashion, the spontaneous self-placements were collapsed into two classes: the Bourgeoisie, the Middle Class, and the Neither Rich nor Poor make up what will henceforth be collectively designated the *Middle Class;* the Workers and the Powerless Poor will make up the *Working Class.* The peasants—both objectively defined (sharecroppers, small farm owners, tenants) and subjectively defined (Peasants)—have been omitted from the analysis. They cannot be categorized into either of the analytic classes without grave theoretical difficulties, and subjectively defined they constitute a class too small to permit separate categorization.[1] As before, however, agricultural day workers have been included in the Working Class, since they are indistinguishable from urban unskilled workers in many crucial respects. Indeed, a large number of those respondents who reported their principal occupation as *braccianti* (farm hands) also reported that they spent a good portion of the year engaged in unskilled labor in small towns and cities. The reason is quite elementary: they needed a supplementary income. Thus, many worked in the city in the winter months and on the fields in the warmer and busier farm season.

One final point regarding construction of the analytic sample should be made. Owing to the fact that they did not report an occupation, 185 respondents lay outside the manual-nonmanual occupational framework. Many of these were retired persons, some were students not yet in the labor force, but a large proportion consisted of the unemployed. Because unemployed persons are among the most manifest "victims" of a capitalist-industrial order, and as such may also be among the most class conscious, it seemed a pity not to include them in the analysis. In such cases, we therefore turned to information on educational attainment as a supplementary indicator of objective class position, since, in Italy as elsewhere, education is a very close correlate of occupation. In our sample, for instance, respondents having no more than five years of schooling were, with few exceptions, engaged in manual occupations, and those with more than five years were engaged in nonmanual employment. This division, then, constituted our criterion for allocating objective class position when data on occupation were missing.

It is now possible to allocate the respondents according to the four-cell arrangement shown in Figure X:1. Thus, we have two classes containing people who "correctly" identified themselves and one offshoot of each containing people who identified with a class that was theoretically not their own. Toward the end of this chapter we will examine these affiliate categories within the context of the notion of "false" consciousness.

---

[1]For a good analysis of peasant politics in Italy, see Tarrow (1967). Also in this connection, see Mitrany's (1951) analysis of the role of the peasant and the "green revolution" in late nineteenth- and early twentieth-century Europe.

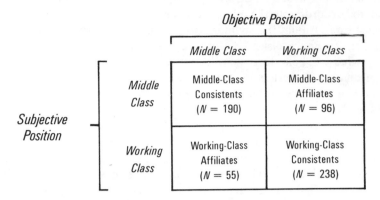

Figure X:1.

Among other things, this scheme of analysis should be of value in clarifying the old and confusing controversy of whether classes are objective or subjective realities. According to some scholars, they are undeniably psychological phenomena. Centers (1949:27), for instance, in seeking to distinguish between "stratum" and "class," argues that

Classes are psycho-social groupings, something that is essentially subjective in character, dependent upon class consciousness (i.e. a feeling of group membership), and class lines of cleavage may or may not conform to what seem to social scientists to be logical lines of cleavage in the objective or stratification sense.

For other scholars, class is primarily an objective phenomenon, and no amount of individual definition or psychological distortion can alter that fact. Thus, an assembly-line worker cannot be a member of the bourgeoisie under any circumstances, just as no businessman can possibly be a member of the working class (see Glantz, 1958:375–376). As Durkheim would say in his celebrated distinction between the *social* fact and the *psychological* fact, an individual can never recruit himself into a class by psychological invention.

To be blunt about it, this entire controversy is totally absurd. *Class is both objective and subjective in nature.* Class is objective by virtue of its status as an observer construction—that is, a collectivity to which particular interests are theoretically attributable. Class is subjective when and if its members become aware of, and act in, the collective pursuit of those interests. The issue is not whether class is a social fact *or* a psychological fact; it is whether a group of people, theoretically delineated as a class, becomes conscious of itself as such. This issue extends to the circumstances under which class consciousness arises, and to how the class consciousness that a participant experiences is related to class as defined by any particular observer model—that is, in what sense can we determine nontautologically whether such class consciousness is "accurate." In terms of the usual concern with class identification, the issue embraces whether subjective identification with a class that is theoretically not one's own constitutes evidence of "false" class consciousness. Fundamentally perhaps, the issue is whether theoretical (objective) classes have sufficient predictive value to be useful scientific devices.

THE PARTY STRUCTURE

The party structure[2] of Italy displays a remarkable heterogeneity. In addition to eight or nine parties of more or less national stature—which span the ideological spectrum—a host of lesser parties and factions is scattered throughout various regions and localities. LaPalombara (1965) has aptly described the Italian political culture as one of "fragmentation, isolation, and alienation." Distrust of party as well as of governmental bureaucracy is rampant; concern for political programs and knowledge of them tends to be rather parochial; "grass-roots" participation in the politics of the nation is generally erratic, despite the existence of mild legal sanctions regarding dutiful exercise of one's suffrage.

A vote for the Communist Party in Italy does not necessarily mean support for a proletarian revolution; such a vote sometimes simply reflects a generic dissent against "the way things are"; in still other cases it represents not even that. A vote for the Christian Democrats does not necessarily mean approval of their governmental record or acceptance of their Church support; sometimes it is merely an instance of the "traditional vote." More generally, and especially in the South and among the male electorate, it represents the citizen's half of an informal exchange of favors. Only votes for one or two of the very small parties (for instance, the Republican Party) can with reasonable certainty be considered committed votes, expressions of deep-seated preference for the party in question. Though such sentiments of genuine commitment are found among the Communists, Socialists, and Christian Democrats, a variety of other motivations are also operative in the support of those parties. We shall have to take this into account in our analyses.

Moreover, suspicion of political matters is so intense that Italians are often reluctant to discuss politics with anyone, even friends and close work associates. With the partial exception of the better educated and those who occupy top-level positions, Italians are convinced, as LaPalombara (1965:290) notes, that

it is safer to keep one's affairs and political views strictly to oneself. This . . . is natural in a society in which jobs are awarded or denied, business with the government expedited or impeded, passports and emigration permits issued or refused, and other values distributed or subtracted in part on the basis of one's political affiliation.

---

[2]What follows refers to conditions as they were in 1964. Since then, they have changed somewhat, and even new labels have been introduced, but the political party structure of Italy remains essentially unchanged.

In political culture, as in many other aspects of Italian life, there is a breach between the institutions of the industrial North and those of the agrarian South. In the northern regions, political structures are generally fabricated out of secondary associational networks, which to some extent insulate political processes from the demands of kinship and other ascriptive factors. In the South, the *Mezzogiorno,* they are greatly based on relations of personal interest, with only a thin veneer of formal organization to give the appearance of mass participation. If one is without the influence of wisely placed friendships and personal obligations, one is essentially powerless. The Weberian *office,* typical of Western-style political structures, is less applicable to southern Italy, where the locus of authority is very often the powerful individual and much less often the abstracted and formalized position that he may occupy.

The personal-interest basis of political interaction in the South describes a relationship of *clientelismo* in which broad functional interests generally lack an effective voice. To a large extent, "politics is nonideological . . . and access to authority can expand only through the further vertical extension of clientele links, [which] lengthens obligation beyond the scope of effective political allocation" (Tarrow, 1967:74). If an individual lacks the personal resources with which to break into the tightly knit scheme of favoritism and patronage, he is immobilized politically. In combatting this system of representation, families that can afford to do so stockpile their collective resources in a concerted effort to gain entrance to the circle of power and privilege. One of LaPalombara's (1964:345) informants, for example, told how

families that wish to prosper will place family members in several of the political parties. Thus, one will go into Christian Democracy, another into the Communist Party, another to the Monarchist Party or the Italian Social Movement as a means of hedging against all of the probable or possible political eventualities of the country.

But relatively few people of the *Mezzogiorno* are successful in such pursuits, simply because they cannot maintain a reservoir of suitable goods for exchange. As a result, resentments against the ruling groups who take advantage of and seemingly perpetuate the system of political control—in particular, the Christian Democrats and the Church—are prevalent and strong. Some of the resentment is expressed as a "committed" leftism; probably more of it is manifested as a "protest" leftism.

Of the eight or nine important parties of Italy, three have been most important: the Communist Party (PCI), the Socialist Party (PSI), and the Christian Democratic Party (DC). Collectively, they attracted nearly four-fifths of the total vote in the national elections of 1963 (see Table X:1).

The PCI, representing the extreme left wing of Italian politics, was formed in 1921 from a small splinter of the *Massimalisti* Socialists, who, under the leadership of Amadeo Bordiga, Palmiro Togliatti, Umberto Terracini, Angelo

TABLE X:1. NATIONAL ELECTION STATISTICS, 1946–1963

Party	1946	1953	1958	1963
Communist	18.9%	22.6%	22.7%	25.3%
Socialist	20.7	12.7	14.2	13.8
Social Democrat	—	4.5	4.5	6.1
Republican	4.4	1.6	1.4	1.4
Christian Democrat	35.2	40.1	42.4	38.3
Liberal	6.8	3.0	3.5	7.0
Monarchist	2.8	6.9	4.8	1.7
Social Movement (Neo-Fascist)	5.3	5.8	4.8	5.1
Other Parties	5.9	2.8	1.7	1.3
Total	100.0%	100.0%	100.0%	100.0%

Source: For 1946–1958, Istituto Centrale di Statistica (ISTAT), 1960:144–148. For 1963, ISTAT, 1965:148–149.

Tasca, and Antonio Gramsci, had become disenchanted with what they deemed the indecisiveness of the old-line Socialists. Almost immediately after its formation, with some 46,000 members, the young PCI encountered the stiff opposition of Mussolini's increasingly powerful Fascists and was driven underground. During the years of the Second World War, however, its steadfast participation in the Resistance movement netted substantial grass-roots support, especially in the central regions of the peninsula, and as the Allied Military Government returned areas to civilian rule the PCI successfully filled the organizational vacuum in a great many places. Since the end of the war its share of the electorate has grown progressively, with the largest proportional gain occuring in the *Mezzogiorno* (see Tarrow, 1967). For the nation as a whole, the PCI won approximately four million votes in the Constituent Assembly election of 1946—just under a fifth of the total, for 104 of the 556 delegates elected. In 1963, it attracted over a quarter of the electorate, for a total of more than seven million votes and 166 seats in the Chamber of Deputies.

For a variety of reasons, not all of them ideological, the PCI draws more support than any other party from unskilled urban workers and agricultural day laborers. Ironically, however, its most concentrated strength lies not in the industrial regions of the Piedmont, Lombardy, or Liguria, nor in the impoverished *Mezzogiorno,* but in the so-called "Red Belt" regions of central Italy: Tuscany, Emilia-Romagna, Umbria, and part of the Marches. From 40 to 50 percent of the vote in these regions went to the PCI in the 1963 elections. The interesting fact is that in the majority of the provinces encompassed within the Red Belt, less than 20 percent of the population was actively employed in industry. The Communist vote here comes not from the central city, as it does in the regions north of the Po Valley, but from the urban periphery and from the rural districts.

Ideologically, the Italian Communist Party is a class party—the "party of the poor, the exploited, the workers," as our respondents stated. And indeed this is largely true in practice, although the motivations of the PCI voter do not always match the doctrinal expectations of the PCI leadership. As previously noted, a sizable proportion of Communist voting represents a generic dissent against existing conditions of life and governmental institutions and policies, rather than a committed support for the party's doctrine. It is a striking fact that at the same time that the PCI's electoral strength has grown in recent years, its membership lists have shrunk.

Nevertheless, the majority of those who vote Communist are among the poorest people of Italy. Of the PCI supporters in our sample, for instance, 62 percent reported a monthly income of less than $120, in contrast to only 45 percent of the total sample. Communist supporters are urban or urban-oriented people, generally the products of effective political education through union organization and mission work in the slums and outlying shanty towns, or, especially in the Red Belt regions, the historical residue of a time when Communist and non-Communist alike valiantly fought as compatriots in the Resistance movement of World War II. On the whole, they are the most sensitive to existing social, economic, and political injustices, and the most disgruntled with the slow pace of constitutional equalitarianism. Perhaps foremost in their list of grievances against existing institutions is the strong influence which religious institutions such as Catholic Action have exerted on postwar politics—despite the fact that the late leader of the PCI, Togliatti, following World War II voted for continuation of the Concordat and Lateran Pact with the Vatican (see Jemolo, 1960; Hughes, 1967:233–237).

To the right of the PCI is the Italian Socialist Party, representative of the survival of a revolutionary Marxism that has experienced both Bolshevik and Social Democratic schisms and the internal disorders of "democratization." Although it has retained enough of the Marxian heritage to incur the suspicion and at times the wrath of the Church—to which it usually replies with acid disdain and anticlericalism—it has nonetheless grown increasingly "respectable" over the years.

Like the Communist Party, the PSI is by historical commitment a working-class party. It draws most of its support from the urban working classes, although these adherents tend to be somewhat better educated, higher in skill level, and more prosperous than their PCI counterparts. In the level of satisfaction with existing institutions and conditions of life, the two parties still resemble one another rather closely—perhaps because they made common cause for so long. More recently, however, they have diverged in their choice of means to social justice, with the PSI taking a more reformist attitude. During the first republican parliamentary elections of 1948, the Socialists and Communists joined to form a "Popular Front"; collaboration had never been greater. While the PSI chose not to repeat the Popular Front coalition in the 1953 elections, ties between the two parties continued to be close. But with the crisis of the Hungarian revolution and subsequent Russian intervention in 1956, Nenni's Socialist party broke ranks with the Communists, deciding that its former strategy of working closely with the PCI, but independently of it, would no longer be effective. From then until 1963, Nenni's PSI and one faction of the Christian Democrats took hesitant steps toward a position of cooperation in the political administration of the nation. The center-left coalition, which had consisted mostly of left-wing Christian Democrats and the Social Democrats, was about to effect *l'apertura a sinistra,* an opening to the left on a grand scale.

The PSI has suffered various splits. The first post-war split occurred in 1947, when a right-wing group (led by Giuseppe Saragat and encouraged by a small faction of middle-class adherents who had found their way into the party during the Resistance years), splintered off to form the Italian Social Democratic Party (PSDI). This latter party has been primarily a northern industrial phenomenon, centering in the Piedmont, Lombardy, and Liguria. An equivalent of various labor parties throughout the continent, it participated in the national government of Alcide de Gasperi in the early 1950's. Following Nenni's entry into the center-left coalition the PSDI returned to the socialist fold, but the reunion had a brief honeymoon. Under the pressure of Italian political life, the two groups split again into distinct parties. The PSDI is now the PSU (Unitary Socialist Party).

L'apertura a sinistra, the opening of the governing coalition to the left to include the PSI, was the outcome of four major factors. First, a majority of the Socialists had moved to the position that structural reforms of the "capitalist system" were both possible and desirable through direct influence and participation "within the system." Second, center parties had become aware of their own inability to form a viable coalition, and since the threat of the Communists loomed very great in their eyes, Socialist support was thus desirable. Third, the Christian Democrats, always the locus of internal dispute and fractionalization, were witnessing the ascending power of the *morotei,* the left-wing group led by Amintore Fanfani and Aldo Moro. And finally, there was an influence still to be fully measured: the political vision or daring of Pope John XXIII. Italians first noted that he smiled more frequently than his ascetic predecessor; belatedly, they came to realize that his humanely political brand of religious leadership had served as a schooling in the realities of the mid-twentieth-century world, including Italy.

Although the Socialists were initially hesitant about collaboration with the left-wing Christian Democrats, Nenni eventually prevailed with the argument that the opening to the left was the Socialists' one hope of achieving their goals. In May, 1963, Nenni assumed the deputy prime ministership in a government headed by Aldo Moro.

The coalition move by Nenni was not without its fractures, however. In 1964, a small left-wing group broke away from the PSI to form the Italian Socialist Party of Proletarian Unity (PSIUP) under the leadership of Tullio Vecchietti. Together with the PCI, the PSIUP represents the major leftist opposition in Italy. It is fair to say that its departure from the PSI, plus the brief reintroduction of the Social Democrats, has to some extent bourgeoisified the Italian socialist movement.

The strongest party in Italy is the Christian Democratic Party (DC). Even though it has never attained a majority, it has achieved a plurality of votes in every election since World War II. In 1963, it won nearly twelve million votes, for about 38 percent of the total, and 260 parliamentary seats.

Christian Democracy in Italy stems from the pre-Fascist Popular Party of Luigi Sturzo, established in 1919 as a "party of national integration" (Einaudi and Goguel, 1952:13). Sturzo, priest and sociologist, intended it as a nonclerical party, feeling that in then monarchist Italy both "cross and Crown" would benefit from the separation. Traditionally, however, the party's power has been geared to a sense of loyalty to the Church and—especially since World War II and the formation of the DC—from a deep fear of the communist movement. Technically, the DC is not a "church party," just as Italy is technically not a "church state." But without the active support of local village priests, Catholic Action, and so forth, the DC would undoubtedly enjoy less strength than it currently demonstrates.

If class considerations are taken as the discriminating variable, the Christian Democrats probably constitute the only party that can reasonably claim a broadly based popularity. Indeed, the range of competing interests encompassed by the DC is so broad, and the factors rending the party so numerous, that it is often referred to as a federation of parties (see LaPalombara, 1964: 96–97; Hughes, 1967:206ff). Its appeal has ranged from big business in the North and "reactionary" landowners in the South to peasants and socialist-minded trade unionists everywhere. Its greatest strength, however, is centered in the northern agricultural and strongly Catholic regions of the Veneto, Friuli-Venezia Giulia, and Trentino-Alto Adige, and in the rural provinces of the *Mezzogiorno*. In the urban-industrial centers, where "literacy is greater and political participation presumably more purposive and meaningful" (LaPalombara, 1964:91), its support is considerably weaker. Finally, the DC has a special appeal to Italian women, who are prone to take their religion more seriously and abide by the village priest's political injunctions. Estimates suggest that the party gains over half of the female vote and that women constitute as much as two-thirds of the party's total electoral following (LaPalombara, 1964:95; Dogan, 1963).

Of the remaining parties of national significance, the Italian Liberal Party (PLI) is the most important. The others—two monarchist groups that attained a degree of unity as the Italian Democratic Party of Monarchical Unity

(PDIUM) for electoral purposes in 1963, the Italian Republican Party (PRI), and the neo-fascist Italian Social Movement (MSI)—are all very small. The Republicans, with a tradition rooted in the ideals of Mazzini, could gain no more than 4.4 percent of the vote during the euphoria that surrounded the dismantling of the monarchy in 1946. Much the same may be said of the Monarchists, who have constituted a regionally isolated phenomenon in the South, especially the Naples area, with major support coming from landowners and members of the aristocracy, plus a few other nostalgic individuals who dream of a return to the "glory of royalty." Just as nostalgic are MSI supporters, the *Missini*—those 1.5 million Italians who are eager to honor "Italian traditions," "the homeland," "social order," the war against the "red menace," and other such metaphysical entities. This party, though essentially fascist in composition, is tolerated as a preferable alternative to a secretive or "underground" movement. It also responds to a deep-seated need in a sizable minority of Italians for the euphoria that cultural braggartry and historical wishful thinking often produce; hence, of the three smaller parties considered here, the MSI is probably the least likely to disappear in the near future.

The Italian Liberal Party (PLI) is the closest approximation to a viable capitalist party in present-day Italy. It is the favorite of entrepreneurs, latifundists, managers and proprietors of larger establishments, upper-level bureaucrats, and a sprinkling of intellectuals from the teaching and liberal professions. Much of its financial support has come from *Confindustria* (Italy's national association of manufacturers, and the creation of Gino Olivetti). Theoretically the party of the philosopher Benedetto Croce—though in practice there was a telling difference between Croce and other Liberals on the importance of *economic* liberalism—the PLI represents the defender of lay culture, moderate nationalism, and private initiative. It very nearly went bankrupt in the early 1950's from a lack of pragmatism and an intransigent purity of "moralism"; but later it gained strength as a mood of reactionary politics surged through the nation following Russian intervention in Hungary. In 1958, the PLI won 3.5 percent of the electorate and 17 seats in the Chamber; in 1963, its share of the vote doubled, giving it 39 seats. The Liberal resurgence, especially strong in the North, combined with Communist gains in the *Mezzogiorno,* gave the opening to the left its first crucial test—and while it was still feeling the pangs of birth.

POLITICAL INTERESTS, EXPECTATIONS, AND EVALUATIONS

The political history and current party structure of Italy is a fascinatingly complex topic of study, one that warrants long hours of attention and an eye for the most detailed of political mosaics. It is appropriately *Italian*—proudly individualistic, independent, pluralistic. Our concern in the above brief review has been merely to give some flavor of the Italian political spectrum, in anticipation of the analyses that follow.

Political Interests

Table X:2 compares the four analysis cells described earlier in this chapter according to the political interests of the respondents. The findings are based on the following question: "In your opinion, which party in Italy best defends the interests of people like you?" It may be noted that this query makes it possible to study not political behavior as such, but rather political interests, and more specifically perceptions of which power group defends the interests of one's own class. To this extent, this type of question seems preferable to another we might have asked on actual party affiliation or voting behavior, for evidence is not lacking that Italians very often do not vote for the party of their choice. This fact partly explains the heavy support drawn by the Communist Party, recently enjoying the good will of seven million voters. Many vote for the Communist Party as a reaction to what they see as "meddling" on the part of the Church. Others vote for that party because it is the most powerful and effective opposition against the traditional interests often only too blatantly represented by the parties in government; in this sense a vote of opposition given to any other party is a vote squandered; this kind of voting seems to be the problem faced by Nenni's Socialist Party, which at election time draws much less support than the PCI. Still others vote for the Communist Party for a related and sociologically quite intriguing reason. In a case we have in mind, an elderly gentleman from the South, a farmer by occupation, presented himself in an interview as a Catholic and Christian Democrat, but then proceeded to reveal that in the previous national election he had voted for the Communists. Upon our inquiring into the reasons for this apparent discrepancy, the wise peasant explained his actions thus:

You see, it's like a game of cards when you choose *"padrone e sotto"* [master and submaster] in order to distribute the wine at stake. If you play the version of the *padrone assoluto,* he is absolutely free to give wine to whichever players he likes most. But if you play the *padrone-e-sotto* version, the *padrone* will have to take the will of the *sotto* into consideration.

For this clever Christian Democrat, his vote for the Communist Party was a vote for a more democratic Christian Democratic Party. It was intended as a means of giving more concrete meaning to the republican constitution and the political institutions it has helped bring into existence.

The eight most important parties as of 1963 have been grouped into the three general interest groups of the "left" (PCI, PSI, PSDI), the "center" (DC and PRI), and the "right" (PLI, PDIUM, MSI). Also recorded are those respondents who gave unclassifiable answers, those who gave no answers, and two categories of respondents who stated either that (1) "No party best defends my interests," or (2) "I'm not interested in politics," "I don't understand politics," or the like. Because of the reluctance of many Italians to openly discuss political matters, especially with strangers, these two categories are very difficult to interpret. We may take some of these interviewees' replies at face value, but not all, and the differentiations are not easy to make. There is some evidence to suggest that the "no-party" respondents tended mostly toward "political alienation," while the category of "not interested, etc." represented "political apathy" (see Almond and Verba, 1963). Certainly the differences in education are aligned with that possibility: regardless of occupation, the "no-party" group was the best educated, the "no-interest" people were the least educated, and those people who selected a specific party orientation were in between. But we lack specific data on such variables as political participation, knowledge of party events, and perceptions of political efficacy; hence, an accurate assessment of those suggested patterns is not possible.

TABLE X:2. DIFFERENCES IN POLITICAL PREFERENCES AMONG CLASS-SOLIDARY RESPONDENTS OF VARYING OBJECTIVE/SUBJECTIVE CLASS POSITION

Political Preference	Objective/Subjective Class Position			
	Middle/ Middle	Middle/ Working	Working/ Middle	Working/ Working
Left	27%	35%	43%	53%
Center	24	22	23	19
Right	14	11	3	4
None	16	7	13	12
Not interested	11	15	9	8
Other answer	5	6	4	3
No answer	3	5	5	2
Total	100%	101%	100%	101%
N	190	55	96	238

The majority of our respondents did state preferences for particular parties; and it is with them that we are here primarily concerned. Theories of class conflict argue that the privileged class defends the *status quo* and is therefore a force against change, while the underprivileged class challenges the existing state of affairs. Concomitantly, parties of the left are considered to be programmatically oriented toward a change in the system, whereas those of the right are viewed as defenders of tradition and as forces of rigidity. The role of center parties is in a sense ambiguous, though in Italy they may be viewed profitably as representing a sort of compromise between left and right—an attempt to build a broad base of electoral strength across the classes and one with appeal to a wide range of the political spectrum. To the extent of their success in establishing this appeal, the center parties are not likely to differentiate very much along class lines, but at close inspection the Christian Democratic Party for one is certainly more "rightist" than "leftist."

In general, our data are compatible with these characterizations. The consistently working-class respondents were much more often leftist and much less often rightist than the consistently middle-class, and there were only minor differences between the classes in relative orientation to parties of the center. We should also note that, consonant with previous comments about the political culture of Italy, considerable numbers in both classes (though more in the middle class than in the working class) and in their affiliate categories either could not distinguish between the parties or stated that their interests were defended by none of the existing parties. It is likely that some of these people displayed neither disaffection nor an intrinsic apathy but simply attributed irrelevance to the party structure, in the sense that they held interests and pursued goals that were deemed unaffected by existing party alignments, or perhaps even by class action of any type. Among other phenomena, however, we have one that has increased in magnitude during the last few years: the "blank ballot" expressing a lack of confidence in the ability of the traditional parties to solve the important social problems rather than a *"qualunquista"* (who gives a damn?) position. This is a rising phenomenon in Europe as a whole. In Italy it is probably connected with disappointment in the failure of the World War II Resistance movement to realize its ideals and with the incapacity of the parties of the Resistance to be the true voices of the protest. Two events can illustrate this point.

A rather spontaneous series of strikes that took place in 1959 among the metal workers left the parties of the working class and the trade unions surprised at their strength and violence. It was the time of the economic boom in the nation, and it must have seemed obvious that the benefits of economic development were not divided equitably. Such spontaneity and violence of protest showed up again in July 1960, when an attempt by Fernando Tambroni to impose an authoritarian government failed because of the furor that broke out in the streets of the major towns.

Support for our point of view may be found in Kogan's (1966) comprehensive analysis of Italian politics. Kogan points out that the Communist Party has always been divided between a politics of compromise with the Christian Democrats and the politics of the traditional revolutionary spirit. Within this dilemma, the PCI has often abandoned the latter, pursuing a dialogue with the Catholics and an alliance with "the middle classes."

If theories of class conflict are generally consistent in predicting the direction of the relationship between class position and political orientation, they have little or nothing to say about the relative influence of objective and subjective definitions of class position in that relationship. It is interesting, however, to consider available data relevant to the matter. Centers (1949: 126–127) found that workers identifying with the middle class were more "conservative" than working-class consistents but more "radical" than middle-class consistents. Middle-class people identifying with the working class similarly bestrode the two consistent positions. Eulau (1956:244–245; 1962:62) and Runciman (1966:171), among others, show analogous evidence. Our own data (Table X:2) demonstrate that the affiliates were rather evenly spaced between the consistent categories, but the nonmanual respondents showed a stronger tendency toward rightist parties while the manual respondents leaned more toward the left. This pattern suggests that while self-assessed class clearly had an effect on political orientation, such effect was not quite as great as that produced by occupational position. By contrast, Runciman found in England and Wales that the relationship between self-rated class and party preference was so strong that it reversed the usual correlation between objective position and party choice. That is, the nonmanuals who described themselves as working-class people were more often Labour and less often Conservative Party supporters than the "middle-class" manuals. As a contingency analysis of his published tabulations verifies, Runciman correctly ascribed this reversal to the predominant influence of the "working-class conservative," who, we might add, is considerably more common in England and Wales than in Italy.

So far we have examined variations in the political interests of class-conscious respondents—both those whose consciousness corresponded with our own working definition of the class structure and those who classified themselves in disagreement with it. At this point we should pause to recall another category of respondents, the "class unconscious," or class unaware, and ask whether the fact of class consciousness alters in any way the linkage between objective position and political interests. The presumption of class-conflict theories is that it does: the manual laborer who is cognizant of his working-class position is likelier to espouse leftist politics than is the laborer who has no awareness of any class location. In an effort to find out whether the presumption of class consciousness as an intervening variable is sound, we turn to Table X:3, wherein the strength of association between objective position and political orientation for different categories of respondents is recorded. The first row of figures gives a summary measure of associational strength (τ_b) for each of the categories. This measure can assume values from zero (a condition of independence between the variables) to unity (a condition of complete covariation), and it is amenable to comparisons across categories (see Blalock, 1960:232–234). The bottom three rows give percentage differences between objective classes (middle minus working) on political orientation.

The Total column of the table records the strength of association between objective position and the dependent variable without regard to class consciousness. It shows that the relationship is actually rather weak. Interpreted strictly, a coefficient of .021 means that knowledge of objective class position

TABLE X:3. STRENGTH OF ASSOCIATION BETWEEN OBJECTIVE
CLASS POSITION AND POLITICAL PREFERENCE,
VARIOUS CATEGORIES OF RESPONDENTS

| | | Class Conscious | | Class |
Statistic	Total	Consistent	Affiliate	Unaware
τ_b	.021	.051	.011	.007
Percentage Difference (Middle−Working)[a]				
Left	−.182	−.275	−.107	−.118
Center	.042	.115	−.009	.020
Right	.141	.161	.117	.098

[a] Columns do not always sum to zero because of rounding errors.

reduces by slightly more than 2 percent the number of errors committed in predicting respondents' party choices. In absolute terms, that prediction is not very efficient. But it is not with absolute values that we are here concerned.

The second and third columns represent people who were cognizant of location in the class structure—respectively in agreement and disagreement with objective position—and the fourth column represents those who were not cognizant of *any* class location, the "class unaware" as defined by the initial interview question on class awareness (see Table VII:1). In short, these three columns reflect a tabular control over the influence of class consciousness on the relationship measured in the first column. A comparison of coefficients across the four categories demonstrates the relative importance of class consciousness as an intervening variable. Whereas the weakest association between the independent and dependent variables occurred among the class unconscious (.007), the strongest was among those people who displayed a "confirmatory" awareness of their objective class location (.051). Indeed, knowledge that such consciousness exists produces a proportional reduction of predictive error on the dependent variable that is nearly 2½ times as great as the reduction stemming from knowledge of the independent variable alone.[3]

Inspection of the percentage differences shown in the lower portion of the table reveals that the intervention of class consciousness (but only of the "confirmatory" variety) does indeed create a greater polarization of political interests. The largest differences between the objectively defined middle and working classes in leftist and rightist choices occurred among those respond-

[3] Incidentally, a recomputation of Runciman's (1966:Table 7) data yields a very similar ratio of coefficients for his English-Welsh sample: namely, .157 versus .066, in comparison to .051 versus .021 for the Italian data.

ents whose self-placements agreed with their objective locations. At the same time, differentiation of the classes on parties of the center increased between the class unaware and the class conscious. Among the class unaware, the middle-class respondents were only 2 percent more likely than the working-class respondents to select a center party (nearly always the DC); among the class-conscious consistents, this discrepancy reaches nearly 12 percent. In sum, then, it would seem that with class consciousness there was a greater politicization of attitudes with respect to the "ambiguous" middle range of the party spectrum.

Class as Party Ideology

Having demonstrated the intervening effect of class consciousness, we must further consider the nature of the linkage represented in Table X:2. According to the theoretical framework herein employed, the conditions associated with objective class position are linked to political attitudes and behaviors via the social consciousness. In principle, as the individual grows increasingly cognizant of his place in the class structure, his consciousness is translated into politically relevant cognitions and evaluations of the distribution of power and rewards in society. Such translation, however, does not take place in a social vacuum. To the contrary, a variety of factors or cues impinge upon the individual with greater or weaker effect to channel the "political" translation in particular directions and in terms of particular contents. Some of these cues are relatively "passive," in the sense of coming from the individual's more or less diffuse observations of the world around him and from "sedimentations" of his personal biography. But others are much more "active" as numerous agents purport to advise him of the "correct" translation—family members, circles of friends and work associates, educators and religious leaders, political party organizations, and so forth.

The political party is usually one of the most important of these influences since, where it exists as a mechanism of conflict regulation, legitimization, and consensus formation, it is engaged in the allocation of values in society; the distribution of such values is both the product of past class structure and the foundation of future class structure. Especially for parties located toward the extremes of the existing political spectrum, class typically becomes an element of ideological persuasion, useful in the recruitment and retention of popular support. Thus, party organizations of the left and the right actively participate in the translation of class conditions into political attitude and behavior by nurturing particular class imageries and by contributing to the "structural cement" of class reality (Sartori, 1969:84). Parties of the center, on the other hand, deemphasize or even reject outright the notion of a class-linked distribution of values in order to widen in both directions their base of popular support. And so it is also with parties in established control of the state apparatus, in order to perpetuate their control. For them, "the utility of presenting one's own society in terms of a nonegalitarian classless society is apparent. . . . such a presentation affords no bases for group solidarity amongst the under-privileged; it inclines them to endeavour to improve their fortunes, and to seek upward social mobility by means of personal effort . . . and not by collective action" (Ossowski, 1963:154).

We cannot accurately determine the extent to which this organizational variable actively influenced our respondents' perceptions and translations of existing class conditions. However, within the limits of ecological analysis a crude assessment can be tendered by making use of the rather sharp regional differences in the strength of leftist party organizations in Italy. As previously noted, Communist and Socialist Party organizations are weaker in the *Mez-zogiorno,* as compared with either the "Red Belt" central regions or the industrial regions of the North. Although a number of other factors are unquestionably intertwined, parallel variations in the strength of the relation-ship between objective/subjective class and political preference, on the one hand, and the strength of leftist party organization, on the other, may be taken as tentative indication of the influence of the organizational variable.

The question, it must be emphasized, is not whether or to what extent party organization is a stimulus to consciousness of class in the first place. It un-doubtedly is a stimulus, particularly if by consciousness of class is meant a coherently detailed and politically implicated class image—although, signifi-cantly, the data examined in Chapter IX show that there was a stronger disposition toward class consciousness in the South, where "classist" parties of the left were weakest, than in the central and northern regions. Rather, the question here is whether the presence of a comparatively vigorous leftist party organization was associated with a translation of class conditions into leftist

TABLE X:4. REGION OF RESIDENCE AND DIFFERENCES IN POLITICAL PREFERENCE AMONG CONSISTENT CLASS-CONSCIOUS RESPONDENTS

Political Preference	North		Central		South	
	Middle	Working	Middle	Working	Middle	Working
Left	35%	72%	55%	84%	45%	61%
Center	44	21	23	16	36	32
Right	22	7	23	0	19	7
Total	101%	100%	101%	100%	100%	100%
N	55	61	22	43	47	74
τ_b	.093		.078		.017	

Note: Distributions represent spontaneously class-aware, self-located, and class-solidary respondents whose self-assigned class was consistent with observer-defined class position.

political attitudes among respondents who were spontaneously aware of a class structure, who located themselves within it in accord with observer definitions of their class position, and who expressed sentiments of unity in needs and ideas with other members of their self-assigned class.

The evidence in Table X:4 suggests that the organizational variable may indeed have been at work. Thus, preferences for left-wing parties were least polarized by class in the *Mezzogiorno* and most polarized in the North. Some of this variation can be attributed to regional differences in the composition of the occupational classes. For example, proportionately more of the middle-class respondents in the central and northern regions were members of the petty bourgeoisie, and on the whole they espoused leftist attitudes more often than did those above them. But such divergences very likely cannot account for all observed variations. Furthermore, only in the North were centrist preferences clearly differentiated by class—a differentiation that partially reflects variations in the impact of the Church on the political attitudes of the classes (see further, below).

Still, it must be noted that even in the South, where leftist party organizations were weakest—but also where relative deprivations, both internal and in comparisons with the "affluent" North, were greatest—the relationship between objective class position and political preference among the class-conscious was stronger than the corresponding relationship among the total category of class-unconscious respondents (see Table X:3).[4]

Religion, Class, and Politics

Stimuli produced and/or expressed in the terms of class are not the only elements that influence political orientation. In Italy, as we have on several occasions suggested, one of the most significant additional factors concerns attitudes toward the predominant religious institution of that society, the Catholic Church. Resentments run very deep in many sectors of the population against the Church's active involvement in political processes—from the role of the village priest at the local level to that of such organizations as the Catholic Action Youth Movement, the National Confederation of Direct Cultivators, and the Italian Confederation of Workers' Unions at the regional and national levels. And to a considerable extent resentment is translated into a protest vote for leftist parties in general and for the PCI, the staunch enemy of the Church, in particular.

The importance of such "religious factors" can be appreciated in part from a comparison of political interests among members of the working class and middle class, according to variations in their levels of participation in the religious life of the Church. For this purpose, we have divided the Catholic members of the sample according to their responses to a question on religious

---

[4]The respective "proportional-reduction-in-error" coefficients were .017 and .007.

beliefs and activities.[5] Those who stated that they attended mass only irregularly or not at all are designated "marginal" participants; those who attended
regularly but did not emphasize communion are "moderate" participants;
those who attended regularly and received communion at least two or three
times a year are "strict" participants.

While the so-called "religious alienation" has been normally interpreted as
a working-class phenomenon in other countries, in Italy it applies to many of
those who occupy middle-class positions (see Hazelrigg, 1970). At least half
of the respondents who were middle-class in both objective and subjective
placement were *marginal* participants, and those who identified themselves as
members of the working class were still more frequently marginal, as the
percentages shown in Figure X:2 on "marginal" participants reveal (total cell
N's in parentheses). These data are hardly indicative of a specifically working-
class disengagement from organized religion.

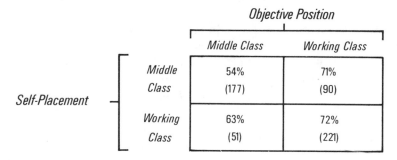

Figure X:2.

The sharpest differentiation of political interests was between the marginal
participants, on the one hand, and the moderate and strict participants, on the
other. Where disengagement from the Church was combined with a working-
class position, both subjectively and objectively defined, leftist political interests were most pronounced (Table X:5). Among those who selected a party
preference, for instance, more than four-fifths of the working-class marginal
participants chose the PCI, PSI, or PSDI (now PSU), in contrast to only
two-fifths of the moderates and one-third of the strict participants. Differences
for the consistently middle-class respondents were of only a slightly smaller
magnitude.

---

[5]"Please observe the statements listed on this card concerning religion. Which statement would
you choose to describe yourself?" The alternatives listed were: (1) I don't believe in any religion.
(2) I am not a Catholic, but a ——. (3) I am a believer, but not a churchgoer. (4) I attend Mass
irregularly, but I believe. (5) I attend Mass regularly. (6) I receive Communion at least two or
three times a year. (7) I receive Communion at least once a month.

TABLE X:5. OBJECTIVE/SUBJECTIVE CLASS POSITION,
RELIGIOUS PARTICIPATION, AND POLITICAL PREFERENCE

Political Preference	Religious Participation of Middle-Class Consistents			Religious Participation of Working-Class Consistents		
	Marginal	Moderate	Strict	Marginal	Moderate	Strict
Left	58%	29%	17%	82%	42%	33%
Center	23	50	56	13	54	62
Right	18	21	28	6	4	5
Total	99%	100%	101%	101%	100%	100%
N	60	38	18	119	26	21

In sum, then, the evidence suggests that linkages between class position and political interest are partly mediated by attitudes and evaluations regarding the Church. Involvement in the Church, as measured by observance of doctrinal expectations concerning ritual participation, exerted enough influence on political preferences to overcome a good part of the usual working-class tendency toward leftist parties, especially the PCI. Avoidance of involvement, at least in part a consequence of resentments against the Church's political activities, was often expressed through an increased emphasis on leftist politics —again, especially the politics of the Communist Party (see Hazelrigg, 1970).

Motivational Bases of Political Interests

In seeking to elucidate further the relationship between class position and political interests, we must examine still other aspects of the assumption that class position *directly* influences a person's party orientation. The assumption is central to theories of class conflict, but it is a sociological fact that people vote for, or are inclined toward, a particular party for a variety of reasons, only some of which pertain to politicized class interests.

If voting for parties of the left is a class-induced phenomenon, then an effort to determine the motivational bases of a leftist orientation should produce direct evidence to that effect. Some scholars (see Glantz, 1958; Leggett, 1968) have found evidence that a working-class position and left-wing voting do indeed go together to a considerable extent, *specifically because of* class considerations. Nevertheless, as we have just seen from the data on religious activity, and as Leggett's (1968) analysis of racial distinctions has also shown, class situations do not exist in a social vacuum. They are criss-crossed by a number of other situations, interests, and forms of group consciousness; some of these undermine the purity of *class* interests, situations, and consciousnesses. After reviewing both historical and public-opinion-survey data, Bernard Barber

(1957:224–225) concluded that the "predominant pattern is one of the recognition of class-structured economic and political interests." But a secondary pattern revealed many other important factors pertinent to the awareness and definition of interests: ethnic origin, race, religion, size of community, regional differences, and so on.

Table X:6. Reasons Given for Political Preferences among Class-Solidary Respondents of Varying Objective/Subjective Class Position

Reasons for Party Preference	Objective/Subjective Class Position			
	Middle/ Middle	Middle/ Working	Working/ Middle	Working/ Working
Classist Party	15%	22%	34%	53%
Progressive Party	41	22	34	19
Popular, Nonsectarian Party	11	19	9	10
Prudent, Nonextreme Party	19	19	14	8
Party Favors Private Initiative	9	8	3	1
Other Answer	5	11	6	9
Total	100%	101%	100%	100%
N	124	37	65	175

Table X:6 classifies the reasons given by our respondents for their particular party preferences on the basis of the interview question: "Why do you think that the [party mentioned] defends the interests of people like you better than other parties?" The data show that just over one-half of the working-class consistents explained their preferences in clearly class-related terms. They chose a particular party because, as they put it, "it is a party of the workers," "it is a classist party," "it is the party of the poor." Of those who selected the Communist Party, 83 percent used a class-related explanation, as did 66 percent of the Socialists. Furthermore, the tendency to use such reasoning was most pronounced in the South (80 percent of the leftists), next highest in the Red Belt (67 percent of the leftists), and weakest in the North (58 percent of the leftists).

For the middle-class consistents, on the other hand, about four in ten said they chose a specific party because it was a party of "reforms," "social progress," "justice," or the like. Their emphasis, it would seem, was on more of the same rather than on a new turn in the road, so to speak. Theoretically, the most appropriate response for a superordinate class would be "private initiative," or something analogous to it. But only 9 percent of our middle-class consistents, all of them oriented toward the PLI or some other rightist party, gave this as the reason for their party choice. The finding is not surprising, in view of our construction of the objectively defined middle class. It contains not only businessmen and entrepreneurs, but also various white-collar categories of people for whom the important point is not the particular mode of economic organization as such but rather the individual opportunities for advancement which that structure provides. Little wonder, then, that middle-class respondents emphasize broad causes such as progress, justice, and equality, as well as the moderateness and nonsectarianism of their preferred parties.

From a wider perspective, it would seem only logical that the working class, inasmuch as it suffers economic detriment, should emphasize the classist nature of political parties—both those which allegedly seek to abolish all disparities in wealth and power and those which allegedly seek to protect those differentials. Conversely, the middle class, which enjoys relative economic privilege, would be guilty of ideological bluster if it accented the class character of its parties, for in doing so it would also flaunt its position of privilege. Moreover, it is quite possible that what is manifested by our middle-class consistents is something other than mere class sedateness. Privileged classes and individuals rarely believe that what they enjoy would not be good for everyone. But they also interpret any alteration of the existing state of affairs as a zero-sum game, with improvements at the lower end of the social scale necessarily resulting in costs to themselves. Hence, their emphasis on the *symbolic* monuments of culture—progress, justice, equality, prudence—as a safe confirmation of their "egalitarianism."

Political Expectations

The nature of class-linked political interests can be observed in yet another way: namely, by assessing the expectations that different classes of people have of the political structures they support. At the time of the present study, an interesting political "experiment" was being conducted in Italy—*l'apertura a sinistra,* the "opening to the left" previously discussed. It now gives us an excellent focus for the issue under consideration.

As was noted, no single party in Italy is powerful enough to administer the affairs of state without the continued cooperation of some other parties. By the early 1960's, the Christian Democrats had drifted without pattern—surely without design—from one center-right coalition to another. In February, 1962, Amintore Fanfani, a Christian Democrat and at the time prime minister of Italy, ushered in a new era in Italian politics by presiding over the opening to the left. Rejecting parliamentary support from the right and the demands of right-wing members of his own party, Fanfani announced a tentative coalition government inclusive of Nenni's Socialist Party (PSI) in addition to the

Republicans, the Social Democrats, and the Christian Democrats. The PSI did not immediately join in a full coalition, nor did it accept a ministry in the cabinet; but it did agree not to oppose the modified policies of Fanfani's government by abstaining from all votes of confidence and by avoiding conflicts on major parliamentary questions. During the next several months the desirability of the center-left formula seemed clearly demonstrated, and, after much debate and dissension in both parties, the Socialists, who had been in opposition since 1947, began to participate fully in the coalition government in 1963.

The point of chief importance to us is that the PSI agreed to join the new government under certain conditions, which, if realized, would net certain advantages to the working people. Among these conditions were promises by the Christian Democrats to extend regional autonomy; to nationalize certain industries; to reform educational, bureaucratic, judicial, and tax structures; to accelerate land reform; to systematically increase workers' wages; and to institute keener safeguards against governmental corruption. It therefore seemed useful to include the following question in the survey, which began just before the center-left government was in full operation: "For some time now there has been talk in Italy of a Center-Left Government, namely, a government that would include Nenni's Socialist Party. In your opinion, what can we expect in the future from such a government?" The responses to this open-ended question are organized in Table X:7.

TABLE X:7. EXPECTATIONS CONCERNING A CENTER-LEFT GOVERNMENT
AMONG CLASS-SOLIDARY RESPONDENTS OF VARYING
OBJECTIVE/SUBJECTIVE CLASS POSITION

	Objective/Subjective Class Position			
Expectations	*Middle/ Middle*	*Middle/ Working*	*Working/ Middle*	*Working/ Working*
Positive consequences	53%	59%	63%	60%
Negative consequences	24	16	18	16
Uncertain	9	5	2	5
No change	7	9	6	8
Don't know	5	12	9	10
Other answer	3	0	1	2
Total	101%	101%	99%	101%
N	190	55	96	238

Far from distinguishing emphatically between the classes, responses to the question revealed that favorable expectations were surprisingly widespread—

despite the fact that both the DC and the PSI had lost votes in national elections held in the spring of 1963, while the Communists and Liberals had gained strength (see Table X:1). In part, these favorable expectations were due to the undoubtedly great support given to the new government by certain groups of Christian Democrats who considered themselves to be middle-class progressives. And partly, no doubt, many citizens of all inclinations had grown weary of the increasing and relatively undisturbed lethargy of the old conservative governments. But as was expected, the working class was somewhat more hopeful about the promises of the opening to the left. The chief expectations concerned economic and political ameliorations such as better employment opportunities and greater social justice.

Differences within the middle class between the consistents and the class "apostates" run in an expected direction: those who identified with the working class were slightly more favorably disposed toward the political "experiment." Within the working class, however, the direction of differences is contrary to simple prediction, inasmuch as the self-styled middle-class individuals were in fact somewhat more often favorable to the center-left coalition than were the working-class consistents. To a degree, this rather peculiar datum may be explained by the operation of an essentially sociological skepticism on the part of some working-class consistents. With reason, they feared that formal participation in the coalition would severely compromise and perhaps irrevocably weaken the Socialists. At best, some were still uncertain about the course of future events; at worst, they were convinced that the only outcome possible would be a cooptation of Socialists' resources, both material and nonmaterial. A composite characterization of this dilemma, as constructed from volunteered statements by interviewees, might be expressed as follows:

The Socialists in government? It's hard to tell what will happen. Maybe they will succeed in making the Christian Democrats more honest and energetic about the needs of the country. And then again, maybe they will sell out for a few choice spots and part of the loot. Look what has happened to the Social Democrats. Once they were Socialists; now they are the errand boys of the Pope. Who knows? Maybe Nenni is a better man. Let's wait and see.

The middle class was slightly more pessimistic about the opening to the left than was the working class, and within each class the affiliates displayed an inclination toward their class of identification. As to the content of expectations, many were simply categorical statements that "nothing good" would come of the coalition government. The most recurrent expectation among the middle-class respondents, however, concerned the question of an alleged "economic setback." Many individuals feared confusion and an end to the recently enjoyed economic boom, either as a consequence of an alleged incompetence of the Socialists or because the rich industrialists, whose Liberal Party was now excluded from the reins of government, would attempt to undermine the venture by withholding economic support.

The making of a center-left coalition was indeed accompanied by a serious economic crisis. Prices rose sharply; employment rates declined abruptly and massively; the stock market fell; the external deficit kept growing, aided by an exodus of capital to Switzerland. In 1962, 500 billion lire left the country; twice that amount was lost the next year. In some measure, the crisis resulted from a thoughtless reaction against *l'apertura a sinistra* by the industrialists. Mostly, however, it was due to an ill-balanced expansion during the economic boom of the preceding years. Italian industry, in its first burning love affair with success, had enlarged the forces of production and started programs of expansion at a pace so vertiginous that it could not avoid going lame at the slightest jolt (see Posner and Woolf, 1967:15–18).

The crisis frightened all—and not least of all the hundreds of thousands of workers who, having recently migrated from the rural areas to discover a future in the city, now found themselves faced with nothing but a long, sad train ride back to the village or farm. Our study came at a time when the crisis was at its peak. Under the circumstances, the predominantly *favorable* expectations held by our respondents are all the more remarkable.

Class Evaluations

What we have found so far demonstrates the existence of a real if not very deep division between blue-collar workers and people in nonmanual occupations, a division that many identified as a class line. Blue-collar support of leftist working-class parties, and especially the stated reasons for their support, constitute evidence supporting that identification. This line of division leads to the conclusion that what we have termed class-solidary people, especially the workers, were characterized by appropriate class attitudes and definitions of interest—that, short of overt corporate action, they displayed a relatively developed form of class consciousness.

Still other tests can be made that increase our confidence in that conclusion. For instance, working-class consciousness, in the Marxian sense, implies not only theoretically appropriate interests but also a feeling that the distribution of power is unequal and unjust. It carries notions of *distributive injustice*. This particular implication has not been totally extraneous to the findings so far produced, but something can now be gained by confronting it directly. Consider the responses, organized in Table X:8, to the following unstructured question: "In your opinion, are there in Italy persons, groups, or categories of people who have special powers or privileges? [If yes] Can you give me an example of such persons or groups?"

TABLE X:8. GROUPS RATED BY CLASS-SOLIDARY RESPONDENTS OF
VARYING OBJECTIVE/SUBJECTIVE CLASS POSITION AS HAVING
SPECIAL POWERS OR PRIVILEGES

Groups with Special Powers or Privileges	Objective/Subjective Class Position			
	Middle/ Middle	Middle/ Working	Working/ Middle	Working/ Working
Economic elite	18%	29%	26%	42%
Political elite	40	26	32	28
Clergy	14	11	12	7
Other	6	20	8	6
None	12	9	12	3
Don't know	10	6	10	13
Total	100%	101%	100%	99%
N	190	55	96	238

On a somewhat related question, which focused on the equity of wages for a list of occupational categories, Centers (1949:141–143) found that middle-class persons were more likely to claim that manual occupations paid excessively high wages, whereas working-class persons more often felt that nonmanual people were excessively remunerated. In both cases, furthermore, a clear majority pointed to big business (owners and executives) and, to a smaller degree, to physicians and lawyers as people who got "too much pay." Again, in their study of 95 textile workers in Paterson, New Jersey, Manis and Meltzer (1954:31) found on a question almost identical to ours that only 4 respondents introduced references to the "wealthy" or to "any of the other familiar class referents." However, 23 workers mentioned politicians or political groups as "a significant element in local community organization."

A number of interesting findings are discernible in our own data. There is indication that subjective identifications more thoroughly differentiated the respondents on economic and sociopolitical matters than did occupational position. Thus, it may be seen that the middle-class identifiers were high in suspicion with respect to the powers and privileges of a political elite; in contrast, the working-class identifiers were more typically suspicious of the entrenched power and privilege of economic elites.[6] Both groups of respondents, it would seem, hoped for the changes that seemed most likely given their view of the high and mighty: if you have inept (or corrupt?) politicians, the most you can hope for is somewhat better living conditions; if, on the other

---

[6]This working-class attitude may in part reflect recognition of the fact that economic elites are considerably less accessible than political elites (see Sartori, 1963; Pizzorno, 1964).

hand, you have grabbing capitalists, only a popular government can curb their greed.

The extremes of this dichotomization of perceptions are most clearly represented by the two consistent classes. The working class tended to respond to concepts of power and privilege in economic terms, while the middle class stressed the political and authority dimensions. It is not difficult to understand why this difference would be present in Italy. Sensitivities to the distribution of authority will be examined in greater detail in Chapter XVII, where we shall argue—in contention with Dahrendorf—that a desire for authority is found in proximity to authority positions and is consequently most pronounced among minor officials of bureaucratic structures. We shall note here only that what we are confronted with in the above data may to some extent be a matter of individual sensitivities to authority. The political, economic, and social reconstruction of Italy has been impeded by the existence of a "paternalistic administration system" which exhibits strong tendencies toward the "protection of the interests of the privileged classes, the negation of private individual rights, and opportunism deprived of justice" (LaPalombara, 1964:340–341). To many Italians, the major problem of their country is not economic inequality of itself but rather what appears to be a permanently crippling *anarchical traditionalism*. The constant quibbling, the frequent scandals, the endless red tape, the omnipresent payoffs, and the innumerable other ills of the national bureaucracy produce political rancors that often transcend class antagonisms. Correlatively, the political structure reflects a constellation of familistic groupings internally knitted by strong relationships of *parentela* (kinship) and communicative with one another on the basis of *agevolazioni,* an exchange of favors. Those who do not possess appropriate goods for exchange are excluded from the distribution of favors. They constitute the vast majority. Many of them still seem unmoved by this morass of neglect and confusion; but many others are growing increasingly antagonized by it. Understandably, that antagonism increases as familiarity with the sources of neglect that affect one personally increases.

Our specific concern in this section is with antagonism as a class phenomenon. To examine it thus, we turn to the data on perceptions of interclass relations (Table X:9). If class consciousness exists in society, then it must be demonstrable that class relations are viewed as marked by animosity, especially by the working-class consistents. Such perceptions would constitute indirect evidence of working-class hostility toward the more privileged class.

Available evidence for contemporary industrial or industrializing societies points just in the opposite direction; that is, it indicates that the level of the interclass antagonism tends to be very low. Manis and Meltzer (1954:33), for instance, reported that their textile workers typically viewed the classes in terms of a "paternalistic relationship" of leaders and followers. Elsewhere they (1963:183) conclude that the definition of class relations in terms of animosity has no predictive power for phenomena supposedly related to class consciousness. Similarly, Tumin (Tumin with Feldman, 1961:194–196) claims to have found "considerable interclass confidence, and relatively very little interclass hostility," among the people of Puerto Rico. The classes were largely concerned with "the good opinion of each other; they feel respected by each other and respectful of each other, and there is mutual trust and value for others' opinions and ideas."

Lorwin (1958) suggests that Marxist predictions have been contradicted by the experience of all Western nations except France and Italy, but that these two countries do not really support them because capitalism here has shown the least sustained dynamism. This is not exactly true, since Italy has had one of the higher annual rates of economic development. What is true is that Italian economic growth is characterized by a great lag between North and South, by exaggerated development in certain sectors while others have been poorly developed, and by unreduced differences in affluence and style of life between the traditionally wealthy and the traditionally poor.

TABLE X:9. PERCEIVED INTERCLASS RELATIONS AMONG CLASS-SOLIDARY
RESPONDENTS OF VARYING OBJECTIVE/SUBJECTIVE CLASS POSITION

Interclass Relations Perceived in Terms of:	Objective/Subjective Class Position			
	Middle/ Middle	Middle/ Working	Working/ Middle	Working/ Working
Amity	31%	15%	28%	24%
Hostility	27	40	47	46
Suspicion, Distance	3	2	4	2
Collaboration, Mutual Interest	11	13	5	9
Indifference	13	11	5	7
Lack of Perception	4	2	4	3
Unclassifiable	11	18	6	9
Total	100%	101%	99%	100%
N	190	55	96	238

Italians are indeed better subjects for theories of class conflict.[7] About

---

[7]At the time of this writing, May 1970—and intermittently for nearly a year—concerted action of all major unions in Italy has paralyzed one big city after another, one week after another, by closing national universities, stopping trains, evacuating hotels, leaving garbage uncollected, and the like. The strikes aim at reform rather than higher wages: they request more low-cost housing, better health services, reform of the tax law, improved public transportation, inflation controls, and such others. What is more important, for the first time the government has truly recognized the unions as a new political force by inviting union leaders to a political dialogue with the prime minister himself. This event is coincidental with two others of equal importance. First, the major labor confederations, heretofore dominated by one political party or another, have now sworn

one-fourth did perceive relations of good will and friendship. But relations of enmity were perceived by both objective classes (disregarding differences in subjective identification) more often than any other type of relations. As would be predicted, moreover, the working-class consistents were significantly more likely to perceive antagonism than were the middle-class consistents. Indeed, only among the latter were perceptions of amity more frequent than perceptions of hostility.

What the middle class lost to the working class in perceptions of antagonism it gained in perceptions of indifference or collaboration and partnership. To put it otherwise, the more privileged class generally de-emphasized feelings of enmity and stressed the reciprocal nature of class interests. That view is hardly surprising. Submission and subservience are always practiced more generously and more peaceably when men think it is to their advantage to defer to their "betters." And fables about the mutual benefit of master and servant are legion within privileged circles. If championed persuasively enough, injunctions of the form "We are all in this together, so let's all pull together!" can produce the most contradictory arrangements of group interests, with the result that factual inequalities may eventually become concealed within a theoretical equality. In short, wherever there is a tendency to efface the distinctness of social inequalities—for whatever reason—we naturally find an inclination to give priority to mutual dependence (see Ossowski, 1963:90).

Summary

We introduced this chapter with the observation that the findings would likely fall short of expectations derived from theories of class conflict. In particular, we did not expect to find a strong tendency among the working class toward sustained class warfare, and we did not. Nor did we find evidence of a fundamental reduction of all lines of cleavage and class conflict to that which runs between people who are in positions of power and authority and people who are not. But we have found substantial evidence that large numbers of Italians were aware of divergent class interests, that the majority of them identified with theoretically appropriate class interests, and that awareness and definition of those interests were often politicized, at least attitudinally.

Yet there is an issue in the foregoing analyses that until now has been only skirted; it demands attention. If nearly three-quarters of the class-solidary respondents recognized and identified with class interests that were, according to our scheme of analysis, theoretically appropriate, one-quarter did not. They

---

independence from political parties and support for each other's programs—apparently some of the political (party) "alienation" revealed by our study in a considerable proportion of Italians has spread to the unions themselves. Second, *Confindustria* (the Italian equivalent of the National Association of Manufacturers) has assumed a new leadership committed to a more progressive approach to labor relations and social reform.

are the affiliates: the working-class respondents who located themselves among the more privileged people, and the nonmanual respondents who placed themselves among the more humble people. Together, they are the focus of a concept that has received more ideological bluster than empirical scrutiny. It is the notion of "false" class consciousness.

"FALSE" CLASS CONSCIOUSNESS

When a particular observer model of class structure is juxtaposed with various participant models, the resulting matrix necessarily contains two or more "consistent" cells and two or more "inconsistent" cells. Inevitably, these will be filled by some number of people. There will be those whose self-definitions of class position agree with the observer's definitions, and there will be cases in which the sets of definitions do not agree. All too often in discussions of class consciousness, the latter are simply labeled cases of "false class consciousness," as if the label itself were sufficient explanation. But, as Geiger (1949:124–125) has cautioned,

Differences in the class consciousness of members of the same class are facts that simply exist; logically, they can be neither true nor false. This is not altered by the circumstance that it is possible to determine an average or normal mode of behavior. We may observe all those who live by the sale of their labor power, for example, and on the basis of mass observation attempt to gain a picture of how they feel, think, react, and behave on the average. We can then make certain conclusions about the psychological structure behind those behaviors, attitudes, and reactions. Similarly, we may be able to identify closely related mentalities for a large, perhaps the greater, proportion of the class members. We may then call this or that structure of feelings, attitudes, ideas, and so on, "typical" for the person who sells his labor power. We have, in other words, constructed a normal type in the statistical sense. However, we are not correct if we then describe deviations from this norm as "false" ideology or "false" consciousness, because the deviations themselves are also psychological facts, just as the norms are. And facts cannot be true or false. They simply exist and, as such, are conceivably the subjects of true or false statements.

Geiger's point is well taken, for it prevents the premature foreclosure of theoretical constructions. Theories must bend to human realities, not vice versa. Thus, he continues, "It *is* possible and desirable to relate the observed deviations in behavior to variations in class position. In this way, one discovers new normal types" (emphasis added).

The notion of false class consciousness also poses an artifactitious problem with regard to the use of any given observer model of class structure. It concerns the detail with which "class situation" and "class interests" are defined. Generally speaking, the greater the detail, the less "false" class consciousness one will find. If we use the definitional criterion of "ownership of the means of production," for instance, very large proportions of the populations of current industrial societies will display a "false" class consciousness.

The reason is simple: the criterion has very low salience for most of the people in those societies, and it therefore plays little part in their conceptualizations of the social order. Conversely, if we base our observer model on a very detailed definition of class situation and class interest—and thereby construct a great number of distinct, homogeneous classes—considerably fewer people will exhibit "false" class consciousness (see Ossowski, 1963:176ff).

Turning to our own data, then, we should make some effort to differentiate variations of objective situation within each of the affiliate categories. Although we cannot hope to resolve all theoretical difficulties inherent in the comparison of competing models of class structure, we *can* examine some of the empirical differences associated with our scheme of observer-defined and participant-defined class placements. We shall begin with the middle-class affiliates.

Of the blue-collar respondents, 29 percent saw themselves as members of the Bourgeoisie, the Middle Class, or the Neither Rich nor Poor class. Common sense would lead us to believe that such people were generally better off than the working-class consistents. They were. Whereas 53 percent of these middle-class identifiers were skilled workers and 30 percent enjoyed monthly incomes of more than $165, the corresponding figures for the working-class faithful were 32 percent and 15 percent, respectively. Similarly, on a measure of consumption patterns, the middle-class affiliates demonstrated greater access to material necessities and pleasures, 35 percent of them indicating that they possessed seven or more of ten consumer items listed in an interview question, in contrast to only 8 percent of the working-class consistents.[8]

But that vindicated expectation tells us only part of what we wish to know. How precisely did these affiliates see themselves in terms of the class models generated by themselves? That is, what variations according to self-placement existed in respondent-defined classes? In comparison to those who were *both* objectively and subjectively middle-class, the affiliates more often chose to describe themselves as Neither Rich nor Poor (28 versus 45 percent) and less often chose the Bourgeoisie self-description (22 versus 6 percent). Furthermore, their statements of membership in either the Middle Class or the Neither Rich nor Poor class did not seem to manifest a great deal of *embourgeoisement*. If we look at their perceptions of the occupational content of their self-assigned classes, for instance, it is not possible to say that they were setting themselves apart from other manual workers to any great extent. More than 94 percent of those who claimed membership in the Neither Rich nor Poor class, and about 80 percent of those in the self-assigned Middle Class, included not only skilled and semiskilled urban workers *but also* unskilled urban workers and farm laborers. Corresponding percentages for the middle-class consistents in our scheme were only 17 and 7 percent. In short, while the blue-collar affiliates

---

[8]The items considered were: automobile, refrigerator, washing machine, television, vacuum cleaner and/or buffer, electric or gas stove, radio, toilet with bath, telephone, running water.

of the middle class were objectively better off than the working-class consistents—they were, in other words, what might be termed the "affluent workers" of Italy (see Goldthorpe, 1964; Goldthorpe and others, 1969)—the majority apparently did not translate that affluence into any great sense of exclusiveness vis-à-vis other, less fortunate blue-collar workers. Moreover, it must be remembered that while they were less often leftist in political orientation than the working-class consistents, the gap between the two was not inordinately large. Among those who stated definite preferences, for example, 62 percent of the affiliates, in contrast to 70 percent of the working-class consistents and 42 percent of the middle-class consistents, gave leftist choices. If these percentages were converted into election statistics, each of the first two would constitute landslide support for parties of the left—primarily the Communist Party and the Socialist Party.

And yet the fact remains that these 96 affiliates—29 percent of the observer-defined working-class respondents in our scheme—described themselves as members of the Neither Rich nor Poor, the Middle Class, or, less frequently, the Bourgeoisie. What meaning may be attributed to this apparent inconsistency? In part, it can be accounted for in terms of differential mobility experience. Whereas only 13 percent of the working-class consistents were sons of nonmanual fathers, more than twice as many (29 percent) of the affiliates were social skidders. Thus, the middle-class identifications of some of the affiliates may be interpreted as a form of political inertia rooted in the fact that they were once members of one of the more privileged classes, wherein they still had close relatives. But this explanation can apply to no more than a third of the affiliates, if that many.

In addition to the mobility factor, we suspect that the case of the middle-class affiliates may represent a reorientation, fostered by middle-class influence, of certain elements of working-class culture away from traditional collectivist perspectives and toward somewhat more individualistic concern (see Goldthorpe and others, 1969). To what extent this phenomenon was *new* we cannot determine. In any case, it would pertain to only about one-quarter of the working-class respondents.

The evidence pointing toward this possible phenomenon comes from the following data. First, as was reported in previous tabulations, the affiliates were slightly more concerned with matters of economic progress, which can be interpreted as having an individualistic focus, than with problems of political and social progress, which have more of a collectivist focus on issues of distributive justice, among others. Second, on a question that inquired into the causes of poverty,[9] 40 percent of the affiliates but only 28 percent of the working-class consistents cited factors of *individual responsibility* such as lack

---

[9]The interview question, results of which will be treated in more detail in Chapter XVI, read as follows: "Throughout Italy, as in many other countries, there are some very poor people. In your opinion, to what is the poverty of these people due most frequently?"

of initiative, laziness, squandering of earnings, negligence, lack of character, immorality, and the like—that is, negative attributes of the person, for which the person himself was to blame. By contrast, 40 percent of the affiliates but 51 percent of the consistents attributed poverty to causes *external* to the individual, for which society as a whole or "the system" was to blame: unfair distribution of wealth, ineptitude of the government, egoism of the wealthy, public waste, class inequality, low wages, and the like. Finally, it is also noteworthy that whereas 63 percent of all objectively defined working-class respondents in our scheme were residents of the industrial North, more of the affiliates (75 percent) than of the consistents (58 percent) resided in the northern regions.

Although this inferred relative emphasis on individualistic orientations among the middle-class affiliates was associated with a decreased preference for leftist politics, it was not severely damaging to leftist party support. Of those who stated a preference, slightly over six in ten chose the Communists, Socialists, or Social Democrats. More important, the affiliates were quite different in their reasons for choosing a left-wing party. Nearly seven-tenths of the leftist working-class consistents said they preferred the chosen party because it was a classist party, a party of the working class. By contrast, less than half of the leftist affiliates gave that reason. Rather, the explanation of their party choices more often emphasized reasons of "progress," "reform," and "prudence." A total of 31 percent of the affiliates, as opposed to 17 percent of the consistents, cited such reasons. Apparently, then, these affiliates saw some benefit in supporting the parties that call for major changes in the structure of society, but the benefits perceived had more of an individual than a class focus. Inasmuch as many middle-class affiliates were downwardly mobile, we are probably confronted here by a phenomenon that pertains specifically to the relation between downward mobility and political orientation. We shall return to this question in more detail in Chapter XV.

In the case of the 55 working-class affiliates—that is, objectively defined middle-class respondents who identified themselves as members of either the Workers or the Powerless Poor classes—we are confronted with a somewhat different pattern of data. As would be expected, these individuals were predominantly petty bourgeois: 60 percent, in contrast to 36 percent of the middle-class consistents, were either small shopkeepers or routine clerks. Materially, they were less well off than those with whom we classified them: 43 percent, versus 68 percent, had seven or more of the ten consumer items mentioned earlier.

More than nine-tenths of these affiliates described themselves as members of the Workers class. Here, however, in contrast to the previous case, there was a noticeable tendency toward an exclusiveness of class definition. On the one hand, the majority (70 percent) accepted low nonmanual and high manual occupations as representative of their self-assigned class. Slightly more than a fifth also included high nonmanual positions. But a mere 3 percent would accept unskilled urban workers and agricultural laborers as class peers.

Lockwood (1958:126–133, 211) has observed that a concern for distinctions of status is especially marked among middle-level occupational groups, because "position" tends to be rather precarious. Thus, he found that despite the convergence of "black-coated" and blue-collar workers in such objective factors as income and literacy, the status ambiguities and rivalries characteristic of the former were an important obstacle to "the mutual identification of clerk and manual worker." Some element of this status rivalry would seem to have been operative among our working-class affiliates. It was not so intense as to prevent them from seeing some commonness of interests with certain blue-collar workers, or from identifying with such groups as members of the Workers class. In this, a mobility effect was probably involved; 34 percent of the affiliates versus 24 percent of the middle-class consistents were sons of working-class fathers. But the status rivalry did apparently lead them to be somewhat selective in their selection of the occupational categories to be included in their own self-assigned class and of the categories to be relegated to the Powerless Poor or some other "inferior" class.

In conclusion of this section we must emphasize that we do not intend to argue that the concept of "false" consciousness is without utility. We merely point out that it is highly susceptible to the oversimplifications and distortions of an uncritical, categorical application. In any instance of empirical research on class consciousness—or any other form of group consciousness, for that matter—one must carefully attend to the difficult problem of distinguishing between what is truly an inappropriate identification of class interest and what is the genuine reflection of a different class situation, and between both of those data and what is simply an artifact of one's analytic scheme. In attempting such distinctions, of course, one eventually runs into the difficult epistemological question of how the "accuracy" of a participant-defined class model can be nontautologically assessed. Nevertheless, the importance of those distinctions cannot be ignored, simply because that question has not yet received a satisfactory answer.

PART THREE

Studies in Job Satisfaction and Alienation

XI

WORK, SATISFACTION, AND ALIENATION*

In the first chapter of the book we reviewed Marx's theory of the role played by work activity in the development of man's capacities. The model of man contained in that theory is probably the most powerful challenge to the fragmentation of job tasks and the impersonality of work relations which has been produced since the advent of industrialization. A portion of Marx's (1844: 98–99) assessment of alienated labor bears repeating here:

What constitutes the alienation of labor? First, that the work is *external* to the worker, that it is not part of his nature; and that, consequently, he does not fulfill himself in his work but denies himself, has a feeling of misery rather than well being, does not develop freely his mental and physical energies but is physically exhausted and mentally debased. The worker therefore feels himself at home only during his leisure time, whereas at work he feels homeless. His work is not voluntary but imposed, *forced labor*. It is not the satisfaction of a need, but only a *means* for satisfying other needs. Its alien character is clearly shown by the fact that as soon as there is no physical or other compulsion it is avoided like the plague.

Our purpose in the present chapter is to pursue the logic of Marx's model of *homo faber* in an investigation of work attitudes. Before proceeding with our investigation, however, it would seem advisable to take an explicit position with respect to certain pertinent debates existing in the literature on job satisfaction.

---

*By Marilyn Bidnick and Joseph Lopreato.

303

ALIENATION AND JOB SATISFACTION

In the twentieth century, interest in the concept of alienation has been keen among both social philosophers and social scientists. While Marx did not originate the notion, his formulation of it with respect to the worker is in large measure responsible for the currency it has enjoyed among scholars. However, the accumulating body of research on alienation has *not* been concerned solely or even predominantly with the topic of human labor. Rather, today's literature on alienation deals with a plethora of disaffections which any man may experience in his relations with specific human institutions or with respect to life in general.[1]

In the meantime, research into the antecedents and consequents of "job satisfaction" has gone pretty much its own way. A number of models of human motivation have competed with that of Marx and with each other for a central position in the emerging portrait of the work experience. From classical economics there remains the "economic man," for whom the only purpose served by work is economic gain. From Elton Mayo and the human-relations school of industrial psychology there emerged the "affiliative man," for whom the most salient motive for work was not to maximize his economic self-interest, but rather to satisfy his need for comradeship and for social recognition.[2] Alongside, and oftentimes in opposition to, these models stood the Marxian view, in which the meaning of work for the worker was primarily neither economic nor social, but rather the maximization of satisfaction forthcoming from work itself. Specifically, man was viewed as having what Thorstein Veblen later termed an instinct of craftsmanship. It was a plastic quality, and with its development went the development of man's own creative energy.

Let us admit at the outset that social, economic, and "intrinsic" factors all have their part in determining the feelings of pleasure and displeasure that men associate with their work. Implicit in this simple admission is the notion that

---

[1] The most successful attempt to identify the various meanings associated with the term "alienation" has been that of Melvin Seeman (1959). His formulation of the five senses in which the term had been used (powerlessness, meaninglessness, normlessness, isolation, and self-estrangement) provided the initial impetus for a body of empirical research whose growth to date shows no signs of abating. Seeman did not tie his definitions of the variants of alienation to the category of work, and the research applications which followed have spanned a large number of disaffections only some of which are directly associated with the work realm. One notable exception to this trend was provided by Robert Blauner (1964), who reformulated Seeman's definitions so as to make them directly relevant to the conditions of work in modern industry, and then proceeded to apply the scheme in a study of four occupations which represent characteristic forms of industrial work organization. Lucid analyses and assessments of the uses to which the term "alienation" has been put by sociologists are presented by Horton (1964) and by Kon (1969).

[2] Bendix (1956:308–340) has traced the initial impact of Mayo's work on modern philosophies of work.

job satisfaction, which varies along several different dimensions, might best be *measured* along several different dimensions. Since the early 1950's a body of research has been accumulating in which job satisfaction is treated multidimensionally.[3] Unfortunately, the fact that such measured dimensions have been shown to admit of a substantial proportion of independent variation has not had an appropriate impact on theoretical formulations of the social and human meanings of work.

Recognition of the multidimensional character of job satisfaction does not, however, preclude the exploration of work attitudes with propositions derived from the Marxian model. It only bids us to be mindful of the kinds of need satisfactions and deprivations which enter the picture so as to qualify the predictions which would be made on the basis of that model standing alone. Behind our use of the term "job satisfaction," then, we shall be interested in exploring, insofar as our data permit, the salience of "alienation" as elaborated by Marx. This alienation is rooted in the idea of self-meaning that flows from work activities and in the social consequences which ensue from the experienced significance of work.

The reader may recall that in a previous chapter on Marx we presented propositions which related differences in job satisfaction to *antecedent* conditions in the work situation and to some attitudinal *consequences* which could be expected on the basis of the Marxian model. This analytical distinction provides the principle of division used in the present chapter. In order to set our sights on the direction to be taken shortly in our exploration of the data, we reiterate at this time those propositions that properly belong to the analytical category of antecedent conditions:

1. *Job dissatisfaction increases as the monotony of work increases.*
2. *Job dissatisfaction increases as exercise of control over one's work and its products decreases.*

MEASURING JOB SATISFACTION

Ideally, a measure of job satisfaction should include a large number of questions that tap a variety of the dimensions along which work attitudes vary. This desideratum springs not only from the analytical purposes to be served by allowing for variation along different dimensions, but also from the require-

---

[3]Survey Research Center studies published in the early 1950's used four dimensions of job satisfaction: intrinsic job satisfaction, financial- and job-status satisfaction, company involvement, and pride in group performance. In one of these studies, Morse (1953:18–20) reported that while the first three indices were significantly interrelated, the relationships were not so strong (correlation coefficients from .35 to .43) as to preclude a sizable amount of independent variation. Similarly, a number of factor-analysis studies of attitudes toward a number of job factors have been published. See Vroom (1964:102–103) for a summary report on this literature.

ments of reliability and validity of measurement. Attitudes associated with work are presumably too closely linked with perceptions of success and failure in the work career, and consequently with self-perceptions and self-feelings in general, to be elicited without evoking a variety of defensive reactions on the part of most individuals. Accordingly, it can be assumed that any interview question is likely to elicit information that is misleading, if not erroneous, in direct proportion as the question tends to be perceived as threatening by the persons of whom it is asked. The best strategy is to use a battery of questions which tap job attitudes, on the assumption that over the long run distortions will tend to cancel one another.

Notwithstanding what has just been said, the fact remains that research has commonly relied on single-question probes to measure job satisfaction. The present effort will not be an exception, and consequently it is appropriate to consider at the outset the limitations which may be expected to accompany this kind of measure.

One single-item probe commonly encountered in the literature is some variant of the question, "All things considered, how do you like your job?" Five response options are offered ranging from "very satisfied" to "very dissatisfied." There is good reason for supposing that the measurement error associated with this type of question will lead to an overestimation of job *satisfaction* in any given population. Arthur Kornhauser (1965:138) and Blauner (1966:474), among others, have commented on this problem. Kornhauser states:

> In the first place, one must ask what it means when workers declare that they are satisfied or have neutral feelings. Most of the men see little likelihood of moving out of their present type of work. This is especially true of the middle-aged. Consequently, they have a strong need to believe, to convince themselves, that the job is at least reasonably satisfying. To admit the opposite, even to themselves, is tantamount to recognizing that in the vitally important sphere of work their lives are irremediable failures.

In our study, the respondents' attitudes toward their jobs were tapped by a somewhat different question. They were asked, "Is there anything in particular that you do not like about your present job? (What?)" Although this question introduces its own kind of response bias, shortly to be discussed, it has two noteworthy advantages over the question inquiring of the worker how he "likes his job." In the first place, because the question is a less direct inquiry into the kind of feeling a man has for his job, it should not be so likely to be perceived as threatening. Consequently, we would expect a greater willingness on the part of respondents to answer the questions forthrightly, which should in turn correct the bias toward an expression of positive feeling for the job. The second advantage of our question is that it allows the respondent to specify a feature of the job which is particularly salient to him. If people are dissatisfied with their work, it is important to know why. Our question does give us a way of investigating what the more important of these reasons are.

The reader will note, however, that the virtues of our question have begotten some vices. Since, presumably, all individuals have some complaints about the day-to-day procedures that constitute their work experience, we must concede that the question has a bias in the direction of *dis*satisfaction. The respondent is not at all required to provide a *summary* assessment of the satisfactions and dissatisfactions that determine his feelings about his job. Thus our type of question may fail to differentiate between rather satisfied workers who are merely complaining and workers who are, on the whole, truly dissatisfied. Some indication of the extent of this possibility is given by a study of white-collar workers in the United States. Nancy Morse (1953:61–62) grouped her respondents into "high," "medium," and "low" categories according to their scores on an index of "intrinsic job satisfaction." She cross-tabulated this distribution with responses to the following question: "What things in particular do you dislike about the work you are doing?" Of those who were "high" on the index of job satisfaction, 34 percent nevertheless voiced a complaint about their job. It is also worth noting that, of those workers who scored "low" in job satisfaction, 35 percent *failed* to voice a specific complaint when invited to do so.[4]

It should be clear, then, that the fact of an individual's expressing a complaint about his job cannot be construed as a sign that he is necessarily dissatisfied with it in general. Specifically, the question which we are using as an indicator of job satisfaction (or, inversely, of alienation) cannot be construed as an adequate measure of the job satisfaction of any one respondent. We would expect, however, that the responses of aggregates of persons can properly be used to gauge differences in the satisfaction or felt deprivation among differing groups. Stating this expectation more formally, we shall assume that *the greater the job satisfaction in a given group of persons, the smaller the probability that any given member of the group will voice a complaint, and accordingly, the smaller the proportion of persons in the group who actually complain about their job.*

The validity of this assumption depends in part on the extent to which group differences other than those which are directly relevant to differences in job satisfaction influence the responses to our question. One factor that might be mentioned at the outset is the existence of differences in *occupational norms* with respect to the expression of work attitudes. Blauner (1966:476) comments with respect to this problem:

The professional is expected to be dedicated to his profession and have an intense intrinsic interest in his area of specialized competence; the white-collar employee is

---

[4]The percentages have been calculated from information given by Morse (1953:56 and 62) in Tables 13 and 19.

expected to be "company" oriented and like his work; but the loyalty of the manual worker is never taken for granted and, more than any other occupational type, cultural norms permit him the privilege of griping.

Katz (1965) offers the intriguing suggestion that it is precisely because the worker's loyalty cannot be counted on that he is allowed the privilege of griping. He notes that the integration of the blue-collar worker into the organization is much more problematic than is the integration of managerial or clerical personnel. This difference exists because clearly limited opportunities for advancement as well as a lower pay scale give the blue-collar worker fewer incentives to commit himself firmly to his place of employment. Katz suggests that the organization copes with the problem of integrating the worker into the organization by allowing him greater *autonomy* in the workplace with respect to those aspects of behavior which do not directly impinge on the performance of work tasks.

A major area in which this autonomy is exercised is that of verbal behavior. Bantering and joking are not defined by management as relevant to the work role so long as they do not interfere with the work process. Katz (1965:204) argues that workers tend to use the freedom allowed them in verbal behavior to "bring their working-class culture into the organization, even though this is alien to the bureaucratic ethos of the higher echelons of the organization." The continuity which is thus introduced between the worker's life inside and outside the organization serves to integrate the worker into the work organization.

The extent to which differences in occupational norms will affect our estimation of the differences in job satisfaction between occupational levels is, we acknowledge, something we do not know. We will, however, be using the proportion of complainers only to provide relative comparisons of "less or more" between occupational categories. Accordingly, it is not anticipated that the effect will be more serious than to make occupational differences appear larger or smaller than is objectively warranted. In line with the remarks made by Blauner and Katz, it might be anticipated that the satisfaction of the nonmanual employees of bureaucratic organizations will be overestimated and that of the blue-collar workers underestimated, making the differences between them appear somewhat larger than they really are.

BASES OF JOB DISSATISFACTION: THE GENERAL CASE

With these limitations in mind, we will now take a preliminary look at the data. We list here the percentage distribution of the complaints given by the 1,374 respondents who were employed at the time of the interview in response to the question, "Is there anything in particular that you do not like about your present job? (What?)":

Complaint about Job	
Low Income	13%
Toilsome, Dangerous, Dirty, Lowly Job; Irregular, Inconvenient, Numerous Hours; Inclement Weather	11
Lack of Security of Stability	4
Lack of Freedom; Incompetent Superiors; the "Attitude" of Superiors	3
The People One Works with; the Contacts	2
Little or No Chance to Get Ahead	1
The Monotony or Boredom of the Job	1
Heterogeneous Complaints	7
Dislike Everything	4
Nothing	54
Total	100%
N	1,374

Although caution is required in interpreting such figures in their absolute sense, it is difficult to resist speculation about the general level of job satisfaction on the basis of the proportion of working respondents who described themselves as having no complaints. Accordingly, note that over half of the interviewees failed to volunteer any complaint about their jobs ("Nothing"). Given the almost casual (and therefore, we tend to assume, relatively unthreatening) fashion in which our respondents were quizzed about their feelings toward their work, it is particularly noteworthy that for a majority of the sample no aspect of their work situation was sufficiently salient to prompt them to voice a complaint.

Taken at face value, on the other hand, this finding suggests the possibility that negative attitudes toward work were more pervasive in Italy than has been found to be the case in some other places, such as in the United States, where the dissatisfied account for 10 to 20 percent of the total employed population. Morse and Weiss (1955) asked a random sample of employed males to give a summary assessment of their satisfaction with their jobs and found that 20 percent were dissatisfied. Cumulative evidence from several hundred studies employing nonrepresentative samples of United States workers has yielded a median of 13 percent dissatisfied (Blauner, 1966:474). In the present study, 46 percent were job dissatisfied. And we could show further that a full 25 percent of the respondents either reported disliking everything about their job, or mentioned a specific complaint about their present job *in addition* to reporting that they had at some time wished they could have had some other job.

While, as we have argued, the wording of our question probably facilitated expressions of job dissatisfaction, it should also be noted that the history of the Italian job market has been such as to have actually discouraged many manifestations of work discontent—and the two factors may have canceled each other out. Work opportunities in Italy have traditionally been so poor that many millions of her citizens have emigrated since the 1880's (see Lopreato,

1970). To this datum we might add a reminder that our respondents were interviewed at a time when most still remembered only too well the joblessness and the hunger of the years immediately following World War II. Under the circumstances, it is in a sense surprising that so many had the temerity, so to speak, to express any negative feelings at all toward their job.

In accordance with the hypotheses stated earlier, our interest lies in occupational differences in job attitudes. Accordingly, we will defer a discussion of the individual job factors listed above until we introduce a control by occupation. For the sample as a whole, however, reasonably comparable findings on the relative importance of such factors are available from the United States, and notice should be taken of the degree of congruence between the present findings and the United States data.

Herzberg and associates (1957:47–48) pooled the data reported in eleven different studies. In each study, respondents had been asked, by means of an open-ended question, to indicate factors which were for them sources of dissatisfaction with their jobs. Mean ranks for the factors reported across the eleven studies, which together encompass a total of 28,000 employees, were computed. The factor that attained the highest rank was "wages," followed by "opportunity for advancement," "social aspects of job," "supervision," "intrinsic aspects of job," and "working conditions," in that order.

As can be seen by reference to our findings, the Italian and United States respondents are agreed in naming wages as the major job complaint. Beyond this agreement, the two lists present three major discrepancies.[5] First, working conditions were second in rank order of mention among the Italians: 11 percent complained about such features of the job as toilsomeness, danger, dirtiness, and the like. The same factor is only sixth on the list reported by Herzberg and his associates. Second, security and stability of employment were third in frequency of mention by the Italians (with, however, a much smaller proportion of respondents mentioning this factor in comparison to that which preceded it). The respondents in the United States failed to mention this factor with sufficient consistency to warrant its inclusion at all. Finally, opportunity for advancement was a concern of only one percent of the Italian sample, while it appeared second on the Herzberg list.

These three contrasts, taken together, would appear to reflect differences in the job markets of the two countries.[6] The greater importance of opportunities

---

[5]The factors employed to organize data differ, however, from study to study, and all interpretation, therefore, is subject to error.

[6]A time factor involved in this Italian-American comparison should be taken into account. Of the 28,000 employees involved in the Herzberg summary, almost 23,000 were contributed by a single study (Brissenden and Frankel) that was conducted in 1922. Accordingly any juxtaposing of these findings with the Italian study must take into account the heavy weighting of the United States results by the prevailing economic and cultural conditions before the Great Depression. The time lapse is one across which the differences between the two nations should be decreased rather than increased.

for advancement to people in the United States highlights a point we made earlier. Until recently at least, conditions in Italy were such that merely having a job was a source of a sense of accomplishment. To a lesser extent, this is true even today. It could be argued that workers in the United States could better afford to entertain expectations of advancement; the Italians were well off if they were secure in the job they had. Little wonder that in Italy there has traditionally been a race for government jobs. It is precisely the desire for security of employment that makes the government bureaucracy attractive to Italian workers. Once in it, they have few worries with job security, in marked contrast to the uncertainties of the highly competitive market outside the government. If the vast and bumbling public bureaucracy in Italy can claim one accomplishment, it is that it has provided a large number of Italians with stable, even if modestly rewarded, employment.

The serious concern of Italians with working conditions reflects in part the fact that industrialization in Italy is a more recent phenomenon, with the result that collective bargaining and whatever enlightened attitudes one may find among modern employers have not had sufficient time to improve the conditions of the work setting to the United States level. In part also, the Italian concern with working conditions reflects the fact that, much more than is the case in the United States, agricultural activities still loom large in Italian society. At the same time, farming continues to be feudal in nature, in much of the country involving little mechanization and a great deal of walking to and from extremely small plots of land over dusty or muddy trails that overtax human energy. As if such conditions were not enough, the mass media of communication display better life conditions in the city, with the result that the peasant's discomfort with his working conditions is greatly intensified (see Lopreato, 1967b).

OCCUPATIONAL DIFFERENCES IN JOB SATISFACTION

Although we are about to look at occupational differences in job satisfaction, it is appropriate at this point to remind ourselves that our theoretical interests lie with a construct—alienation—that is somewhat different in scope from job dissatisfaction as such. The process of making inferences to Marx's construct of alienation from research materials on job satisfaction is attended by certain difficulties. It is clear that Marx was concerned with a set of relationships that, in his view, have their roots primarily in the process of work activity itself. However, as was pointed out above, we have good reason for supposing that job satisfaction varies along a number of dimensions only some of which are clearly and properly classified as "intrinsic" to work in the sense corresponding to Marx's ideas about alienation. The problem is that there is a high degree of intercorrelation among the various kinds of rewards or "profits" associated with work. It is necessary to separate out the effects of these differing kinds of rewards in order to test propositions relating any one kind (such as wages, or social esteem, or a consummatory enjoyment of work tasks) to the subjective satisfactions which are theorized to be associated with them.

The most convincing demonstration of the scientific fruitfulness of the work-alienation construct has come from studies of workers at one extreme of the continuum of autonomy and control in the occupational hierarchy. The automobile assembly line (Walker and Guest, 1952; Chinoy, 1955) has provided a situation in which one can observe the response of men to work situations largely devoid of opportunities for intrinsic rewards. The paced and repetitive tasks that are found in the automotive assembly line require a low level of skill, and consist of but a minuscule fragment of the total production process. In this type of work, the features of work that, according to the Marxian perspective, are critical to human fulfillment are as close to an absolute minimum as is likely to be found in a nonexperimental setting. At the same time, material reward in the form of wages, and social reward in the form of occupational prestige, are not so low as to render the relative salience of these factors and "intrinsic" job characteristics inextricably obscure.[7]

In general terms, two major findings have emerged from the test case provided by automotive workers (see Blauner, 1964: 89–123). First, it has been found that assembly-line workers by and large respond to the "alienating" conditions of their work in much the fashion that Marx said they would. The debilitating effects of work which is monotonous, fragmented, and provides little or no opportunity for the exercise of intelligence or creativity has been documented for workers on automotive assembly lines by Walker and Guest (1952) and by Chinoy (1955), among others. Second, as is true of most generalizations about the behavior of men, there are exceptions to the rule. There are men who report that they do derive satisfaction from work that is "on the line." The fact that a minority of workers appear to adjust well to highly repetitive tasks suggests that Marx's ideas on the importance of creativity in work have to be qualified by appropriate conditional statements. This suggestion means that, if the insights of Marx are to be formalized into a coherent theory, the factors will have to be identified which account for individual

---

[7]The careful reader will note that the portrait of deprivation in work which drew the attention of Marx in his early writings included insufficient wages and low esteem as well as intrinsically alienating work tasks; in his view, deprivation on all dimensions of need was the inevitable lot of the worker in a capitalist economy. While Marx placed a good deal of emphasis on the role of work tasks themselves as determinants of a man's response to his job, it would certainly not be possible to demonstrate from his writings that he ascribed to so-called "intrinsic" satisfactions an importance that was untempered by the claims of other needs. The usefulness of the assembly line as a setting in which Marx's ideas on work can be tested is not that it reproduces precisely the industrial conditions about which Marx wrote, but rather that it allows the researcher to observe the effects of deprivation in the intrinsic satisfactions of work in comparative isolation from the effects of other need deprivations.

differences in the tolerance for monotonous and repetitive tasks.[8]

Studies of automotive assembly-line workers have provided a good deal of empirical support for Marx's ideas on the importance of the intrinsic properties of the work task to the worker. However, automotive assembly-line workers are themselves an atypical rather than a typical case in the sense that they represent only a small fraction of the labor force. Statements about work alienation among such workers cannot be generalized uncritically to all workers.[9] If Marx's model of work motivation is to be useful, investigations are required in more representative occupations and at all levels of skill in the occupational structure.

In what follows, we shall use a more detailed scheme of job levels than was used in previous chapters in order to introduce a more precise control for the general *type* of work represented by each occupational category. Accordingly, in Table XI:1, the "routine clerks" and the "small proprietors" together correspond to the petty bourgeoisie of previous chapters. What was previously the "bourgeoisie" has been divided into its clerical and its executive components, the clerical being shown separately as the "middle clerks," and the executive shown in combination with the previous "elites." In the interest of keeping at least this degree of occupational homogeneity within categories, 13 semiprofessionals are not included in Tables XI:1 and XI:2. This occupational division has the advantage of greatly facilitating comparisons with other studies of job satisfaction.

Job-Satisfaction Hypotheses

We have predicted that job alienation among Italian workers will be *directly related to the monotony of work, and inversely related to the amount of the workers' control over the work process and the products of work.* While monotony of job and work control are in principle distinct and independent properties, we have no data with which to assess them directly. However, it may be noted that both these variables concern the kind of job one performs, and this information we do have. Accordingly, we will use occupational level as a rough measure of these independent variables, and we would expect that

---

[8]It is important to remember that individuals differ in the needs which are relevant to the properties of a work role. While the role of personality in determining job satisfaction has its own body of cumulative research, *interaction* between personal needs and the conditions of work has been given less attention. Morse (1953:27–39) and Vroom (1964:276–288), among others, have offered models of job satisfaction in which personal needs and job characteristics are both taken into account. Argyris (1957; 1964) has formulated the problem in terms of the congruence that can be found to exist between the needs of the individual and the needs of the organization. For a review of the research literature on the role of personality differences, as well as a discussion of the issue of interaction between personality needs and work roles, see Vroom (1964:159–179). The range of problems involved in investigations of job attitudes is given a thorough and helpful airing by Arthur Kornhauser (1946:297–322).

[9]This is a point of which sociologists have had to be reminded before (see Palmer, 1957:18).

TABLE XI:1. JOB SATISFACTION IN SPECIFIC OCCUPATIONAL CATEGORIES

Occupational Category	Job Satisfaction	
	Percent with No Complaints About Job	Total N in Category
Professionals, Large Proprietors, Managers, and Functionaries	70%	81
Middle Clerks	61	138
Small Proprietors	55	111
Routine Clerks	63	78
Skilled Workers	54	261
Semiskilled Workers	54	239
Unskilled Workers	53	95
Small Farmers and Sharecroppers	46	232
Farm Laborers	45	126
All Respondents	54%	1,361

job satisfaction varies directly with position in the occupational hierarchy.

Looking at Table XI:1, it can be seen that this summary expectation is generally upheld. The professional and managerial workers were more job satisfied than lower white-collar workers, who in turn complained proportionately less often than the blue-collar workers. Within these broad ranges of differences, however, the direct relation between job satisfaction and position in the occupational hierarchy is not as clear as might have been expected. For example, the two grades of clerks were not noticeably distinguished from one another; indeed, the differences fail to fall in the direction in which we would expect them.[10]

[10]One variable which is of particular interest in an examination of the relation between occupational level and job satisfaction is income. An adequate exploration of the Marxian model of work motivation would require careful control of variables such as prestige and income at the same time that job characteristics like monotony and control over the work process are allowed as much variation as possible. In the present case, the results produced by introducing a control by monthly income are fragmentary because in each income category only a segment of the occupational levels contains frequencies of any size. However, two sets of comparisons were obtained which were of interest given the performance of our measure of job satisfaction in the white-collar and blue-collar groups. Among those blue-collar workers whose family incomes were up to $120 per month, the proportions of satisfied workers for the skilled, semiskilled, and unskilled categories were 51, 48, and 45 percent, respectively. Among clerical workers whose family income was from $121 to $240 per month, 74 percent of the middle clerks and 70 percent of the routine clerks failed to complain about their jobs.

Two variables which are relevant to the question of differences in the needs and expectations of the workers are age and education. Generally it has been found that *within* relatively homogeneous white-collar and blue-collar occupational groupings, job satisfaction decreases with increasing education (Bruce, Bonjean, and Williams, 1968) and increases with increasing age (Morse, 1953: 58–59). Among our respondents within each occupational grouping shown in Table XI:1, these two relationships were generally confirmed.

Two findings are especially worthy of note. First, there were no differences in job satisfaction among the three grades of urban manual workers. In view of Marx's emphasis on the depression of task skills as a crucial determinant of work alienation, this datum is necessarily puzzling. But recall that our question on job satisfaction is not addressed to a global feeling of alienation but only to specific job complaints. It may be that this circumstance explains the lack of difference we have observed among urban blue-collar workers. At the same time, the finding probably suggests that whatever differences may in fact have existed among these three work categories in terms of a Marxian type of alienation, they were not very great. It should be noted that, strictly speaking, the effective dimensions of work alienation do not concern work skill of itself but such other properties as monotony of work and, perhaps especially, job fragmentation. If this be true, we really should not expect major differences in work alienation among the three levels of urban blue-collar skill because in fact these three categories are *quite similar* in their monotony and task fragmentation. The tool maker in industry often represents the highest level of blue-collar skill. Yet he, like less skilled colleagues, is usually engaged in work tasks that, while requiring a high level of dexterity, are no less fragmented and tedious. The tool room in industry today employs not craftsmen, who individually construct complete tools, but workers who specialize in particular phases of their manufacture.

Second, the level of job dissatisfaction of small proprietors stands out among the nonmanual respondents. There is a good reason for this finding. We suspect that it reflects the precariousness of these people's market situation. A concomitant of Italy's continuing industrialization and modernization is the advent of the big store, like the supermarket. Until the recent past, most of the shopping in Italy, especially in villages and smaller towns, took place in the neighborhood stores. Nowadays, shopkeepers more and more find themselves in competition with the much larger and more affluent corporations not only because these are going up everywhere but also because the people now have better transportation. Thus, shoppers are more easily attracted to the larger stores which offer both a greater variety of goods and also better quality and better prices. Under the circumstances, many small shopkeepers are fighting hard to survive, and their discontent manifests itself in our measure of job satisfaction.

When all is said and done, the fact remains that despite some attenuation, a positive relation between job satisfaction and occupational level exists. This relation has been rather well established in investigations of industrial workers. For example, in a study of the British civil service, Nigel Walker (1961:176) found a positive association between the job levels of his respondents and job satisfaction. In attempting to account for the relation in terms of other job factors, Walker (1961:246) concluded that the respondents' assessments of "estimated status" and "interest of the work" were the crucial ones.

There is evidence which links differences in job satisfaction by job level more directly to differences in the monotony of work and differences in the exercise of control over it. In her study of white-collar workers in the United States, Morse (1953:14–16) used scales to obtain measures of three dimensions of job satisfaction: an index of "intrinsic job satisfaction," an index of "company involvement," and an index of "financial and job status satisfaction." The first index contained four questions which quizzed the respondent on how well he liked his work, whether it gave him the chance to do the things he felt he did best, whether he derived any feeling of accomplishment from his work, and whether he would rate his job as an important one. The second index contained four questions which were directed toward satisfaction with company policies. The third index inquired about satisfaction with salary, with chances of getting a raise, with past history of advancements; it also incorporated a coder rating of the over-all degree of frustration with career advancement. Morse found that only one of these indices was positively and significantly related to the job level of the respondents, and that was the index of "intrinsic job satisfaction."

An additional and interesting piece of evidence on the nature of the link between job satisfaction and job level is provided by Arthur Kornhauser (1965). He developed six indices which together constituted a composite index of mental health. The component indicators were: an index of manifest anxiety and emotional tension, an index of self-esteem, an index of hostility, an index of sociability, an index of life satisfaction, and an index of personal morale (Arthur Kornhauser, 1965:25). The index of mental health was independently validated by a panel of four psychiatrists and two clinical psychologists (Arthur Kornhauser, 1965:323–326). In addition, the interview schedule contained an index of job satisfaction.

In a sample consisting of employed factory workers, Arthur Kornhauser (1965:85) found a strong positive relation, for both younger and older workers, between (1) level of skill and the proportion of workers in each skill category who scored "high" on the index of mental health, and (2) level of skill and job satisfaction. After exploring the effects of personality and background variables on these relationships, he (1965:89) concluded:

The evidence as a whole accords with the hypothesis that gratifications and deprivations experienced in work and manifested in expressions of job satisfaction and dissatisfaction constitute an important determinant of mental health. Our interpretation is that job conditions impinge on working people's wants and expectations to produce satisfactions and frustrations which in turn give rise to favorable or unfavorable perceptions of self-worth, opportunities for self-development, and prospective gratification of needs.

Kornhauser's investigation is obviously quite pertinent to Marx's ideas on the role played by work in the developmental psychology of man. It provides a direct test of the contention that the procedural routines that make up the duties of a job make a critical independent contribution to the psychological well-being of the man who performs them. The findings reported by Arthur

Kornhauser, as well as those reported by Walker (1961) and by Morse (1953), give empirical support to an assumption underlying our own proposition which relates job satisfaction to job level, namely, that differences in job attitudes by occupation can be accounted for in part by concomitant differences in the intrinsic features of work.

OCCUPATIONAL DIFFERENCES IN THE BASES OF JOB SATISFACTION

There is another way in which the relative salience of such factors as variety and control in work can be explored: by observing the kinds of specific complaints that were volunteered by the respondents in answer to the job-satisfaction question. Table XI:2 gives the profiles of job complaints volunteered by each of the nine occupational categories used in Table XI:1. It is immediately apparent that the heavy weight given to wages and working conditions (toilsome, dangerous, dirty, etc.) in the sample as a whole was due largely to the urban manual workers and the agrarians. Among the nonmanual workers, "lack of freedom" and "incompetence of superiors" stand out as major disaffections. Beyond these points, the dominating feature of the table is the gradation by skill level of those proportions of persons who reported they "disliked everything" about their jobs. A person who was a manual worker was at least twice as likely to express this radical kind of disaffection with his job as a person who was a nonmanual worker.

Consistently with previously offered remarks about the relative attractiveness to the Italians of the kinds of jobs represented by the routine clerks, this category of workers was the only one besides the highest occupational category that did not have any members who indicated an intense dislike for their work by reporting that they disliked "everything" about their jobs.

With these preliminary remarks, let us now consider the job complaints of the manual and nonmanual workers taken separately.

Complaints in the Manual Categories

The dominant complaints among the manual workers in Table XI:2 are low income and features of the job such as toilsomeness, danger, irregularity, and inconvenience. This distribution is to be expected, since these are the major deprivations experienced by manual workers anywhere, but perhaps especially in areas where, as in Italy, labor supply exceeds demand. In such cases, employment is not only irregular but also is more than usually subject to managerial definitions of work conditions that are still anchored in nineteenth-century capitalist mentality.

The data in Table XI:2 do not provide much evidence in support of the hypotheses, offered above, which stated that job dissatisfaction varies directly with job monotony and inversely with the amount of control the worker is permitted to exercise over the work process. To the extent that monotony is

TABLE XI:2. DIFFERENCES IN SPECIFIC JOB COMPLAINTS AMONG OCCUPATIONAL CATEGORIES

Complaint about Present Job	Occupational Category								
	Professionals, Large Proprietors, Managers, Functionaries	Middle Clerks	Small Proprietors	Routine Clerks	Skilled Workers	Semi-skilled Workers	Un-skilled Workers	Small Farmers, Share-croppers	Farm Laborers
Low Income	2%	2%	5%	6%	9%	15%	19%	25%	21%
Toilsome, Dangerous, Dirty; Irregular, Inconvenient, etc.	1	6	7	6	15	14	19	9	15
Lack of Security or Stability	2	1	10	1	5	2	*	5	6
Lack of Freedom, Incompetent Superiors, etc.	4	13	3	5	2	5	*	1	*
The People One Works With; the Contacts	5	3	8	3	2	3	*	*	*
Little or No Chance to Get Ahead	*	4	*	3	*	*	*	*	*
Monotony; Boredom	1	3	*	4	2	1	*	*	*
Heterogeneous Complaints	14	7	10	9	7	3	*	9	4
Dislike Everything	*	1	2	*	4	3	9	6	9
Nothing	70	61	55	63	54	54	53	46	45
Total	99%	101%	100%	100%	100%	100%	100%	101%	100%
N	81	138	111	78	261	239	95	232	126

* No cases, with the following exceptions: one skilled worker and one small farm owner complained "Little or no chance to get ahead"; one small farm owner complained of "monotony, boredom."

saliently related to job dissatisfaction, we might expect that the frequency with which this factor is mentioned will increase as the general level of skill and initiative required in the performance of work tasks decreases. As can be seen, this expectation is not borne out among the manual workers. Similarly, the expectation concerning the salience of a sense of control in the execution of work tasks receives little support. Such complaints as "lack of freedom" and "incompetent superiors" are the clearest expression bearing on "sense of control"; yet only for the middle clerks were these complaints salient at all. While these findings are somewhat disappointing from the theoretical perspective taken in the present chapter, they are not entirely surprising.

Maslow (1954) has provided a theoretical statement which formalizes an expectation we would have on an experiential or intuitive basis, namely, that basic physical needs, if unmet, will be more immediately important to a worker than the satisfaction of a desire for interesting and fulfilling work. In a key highly reminiscent of Giambattista Vico, the great Italian philosopher and historian of the seventeenth-eighteenth century, Maslow suggests that there exists a hierarchical ordering of human needs, and that higher-order needs do not become important to a man until lower-order needs are reasonably well met. Maslow suggests this ascending order of importance for the basic categories of human needs: subsistence needs, security needs, and self-actualization needs. Since the needs for the exercise of initiative and creativity in work correspond to the category of self-actualization in Maslow's scheme, while income and features of work such as toilsomeness and danger have relevance primarily to subsistence and security needs, the profile of dissatisfactions found among the manual workers in Table XI:2 could be partially explained by reference to his notion of need hierarchy. This consideration gains in importance by reference to a methodological circumstance. It must be remembered that the respondents were asked to volunteer only one complaint about their jobs. Within this restriction, it is certainly understandable that fundamentally practical matters, particularly wages, came to the minds of the manual workers much more readily than job monotony or the opportunity to exercise initiative and control. Had a more extensive list of sources of dissatisfaction been recorded, a fairer gauge of the importance of these variables would have been possible.

Data which, though not strictly comparable, nonetheless provide an interesting contrast to the Italian case are contained in a study of young Russian manual workers which was reported by Zdravomyslov and Iadov (1965:10). When these researchers asked a sample of 2,665 workers in Leningrad to evaluate some of the features of their jobs, they found systematic differences between the responses of satisfied and dissatisfied respondents. Those factors which received high ratings as causes of satisfaction by satisfied workers, and which were also rated high as bases of dissatisfaction by dissatisfied workers, were earnings, initiative, and opportunities for advancement. It was the opportunity to exercise initiative that most clearly differentiated between the job satisfied and the job dissatisfied.

Lest we be overzealous in our effort to marshall evidence in support of the peculiarly Marxist vision of the human meaning of work, we should point out that not all the evidence reported in the literature confirms that vision. A case in point is the study of affluent British automotive workers conducted by Goldthorpe, Lockwood, Bechofer, and Platt (1968b). These researchers found little evidence for the proposition that the intrinsic characteristics of work were of concern to the subjects of their study. To the contrary, the orientation of the respondents toward work appeared to be fundamentally instrumental; the reasons given for liking the job and remaining on it dealt predominantly with economic considerations (Goldthorpe and associates, 1968b:144). These investigators suggest that it was due to this orientation that the workers were not frustrated or alienated by the paucity of intrinsic or consummatory satisfactions connected with their work. Accordingly, they argue that as determinants of job satisfaction the expectations which were brought to work must be given a weight which is comparable to that assigned to the technological and social organization of work (1968b:182–183).

Complaints in the Nonmanual Categories

Two features of the nonmanual distributions shown in Table XI:2 invite attention. The first and most obvious is the prominence among the middle clerks of complaints about "lack of freedom" and "incompetent superiors." This finding is part of a larger syndrome that will be discussed in some detail in Chapter XVII. Suffice it to say here that the middle clerks are subordinate workers in close proximity to highly authoritative positions, and as such they suffer most from relative deprivation on the one hand, and from the burden of obedience on the other. The second is the fact that the middle clerks and the routine clerks were the only occupational categories in the entire sample in which lack of opportunity for advancement figured as a job complaint. This finding makes good sense, for in Italy career mobility occurs infrequently, as will be seen in Chapter XIII. At the same time, it is exactly the workers in the lower ranks of nonmanual categories that have a good glimpse of higher opportunities. Again, the finding is consistent with the explanation advanced earlier that merely having a job has traditionally been a matter of import in Italy, and that alongside this fundamental desideratum the disadvantages associated with particular jobs are secondary in importance. This relativity is especially manifest among manual workers. Similar evidence is available from a question which asked the respondents whether they had ever wished they had some other job. Only 6 respondents out of the 507 who had so wished gave opportunities for advancement as the primary motivation behind the wish. It might be noted for what it is worth that four out of these six were from the clerical categories.

Sykes (1965:299) reported evidence from a study of clerical and manual workers in Scotland that points to a primary reason why aspirations for promotion are less likely to be salient among manual workers than among white-collar workers. In this study, the 96 clerical workers of the sample were unanimously agreed that prospects for promotion were more important to them than pay, while the 118 manual workers were agreed by a margin of 106 to 12 that pay was the more important job factor. The reason for this difference between the two categories of workers appeared to be a very practical one, namely the objective chances for promotion in the two cases. Thus only 9 workers reported that they had a "reasonable expectation" of being promoted, in contrast to the clerks, among whom only 9 *failed* to report that expectation. In both categories, aspirations had to a large extent been brought in line with expectations of success. All of the clerks reported that they wanted a promotion, while only 12 of the manual workers admitted to the same desire. These findings parallel those of Chinoy (1955:110–111), who reported on the gradual erosion of job aspirations as automobile workers gain in seniority in the plant. Additional evidence with respect to the aspirations of clerks is provided by Dale (1962:17–20). In a sample of highly mobile male clerks in Liverpool (80 percent of whom had changed their jobs), the most frequently given reason for changing jobs was "poor prospects" for advancement.

In summary, the evidence from Tables XI:1 and XI:2 which has been brought to bear on propositions relating job satisfaction to task variety and the exercise of control can be viewed as suggestive only. It may be viewed as an appropriate test of those propositions only insofar as the hierarchy of occupational levels can be accepted as a measure of increasing variety and control of the work task. This is an assumption that neglects the confounding effects of other sources of variation, such as differences in status, which are properly viewed as being of secondary importance from the vantage point of the work-motivation model delineated by Marx.

ATTITUDINAL CORRELATES OF JOB SATISFACTION

Research on job satisfaction, both within and without sociology, has tended to concentrate on identifying the factors which produce job satisfaction. Less attention has been paid to the possible *consequences* of the worker's satisfaction with his job or his alienation from it. Certainly, the full scope of these possible consequences is unexplored. The assumption has for the most part been that psychological deprivation which is work-related has import for the individual and at the most for the employer, but not much effect worthy of attention beyond that. Thus, the worker might suffer frustration, and the employer might lose productive efficiency, but at that the matter is pretty much ended.[11]

This trend stands in marked contrast to theoretical and empirical treatments of "alienation" in the *broader* sense (that is, to treatments not conceived as predicated primarily or necessarily on work) that have enjoyed such popularity in sociology. For example, the Dean scales, which have been used rather widely to measure generalized feelings of "powerlessness," "normlessness," and "social isolation" (conceived as semiindependent components of an alienation syndrome), originated in an investigation of political apathy as a possible consequence of alienation (Dean, 1960;1961). Earlier, alienation had been linked to authoritarianism and prejudice (Adorno and colleagues, 1950), to social conformity (Fromm, 1941), as well as to withdrawal from political participation (Rosenberg, 1951; William Kornhauser, 1959), and to numerous other ills of undisputed sociological import. It bears repeating, however, that these theoretical and empirical treatments of the possible consequences of "alienation" have not been concerned with what we have termed work alienation—that is, with the alienation whose causal nexus is conceived to lie specifically in the interaction between human needs and the conditions of human work. Rather, they have been concerned more generally with the "alienating" qualities of modern life that have been the efflux of industrialization.[12]

All of this is to say that one-half of the portrait of the relationship between *work* and man which was drawn by Marx has seldom been investigated systematically. That the *sociological* implications of Marx's theory of alienation in work often receive little more than perfunctory attention would seem to be most unfortunate. Although the terms employed by Marx leave the discussion at a philosophical level of discourse, with the consequence that the suggested theoretical propositions require elaboration in terms of sociological concepts and observable behaviors, there can be no doubt of the sociological relevance of Marx's portrait of the impact of alienating labor. According to Marx, the alienation of man "from" his work (and therefore the alienation of man from himself, in view of the postulated self-fulfillment in work) would cause him to become alienated from his social milieu as well. What this alienation suggests to the sociologist is that chronic frustration in work may be associated with

---

[11]Actually, the consistent finding in the research literature has been that productivity as such is not related in any direct fashion to job satisfaction. For example, Morse (1953:5) found no relation between productivity and job satisfaction among her sample of clerical workers in the United States. Walker (1961:184–185) failed to discover a relation between efficiency and job satisfaction. For a summary of literature from industrial psychology on this point, see Vroom (1964:175–187).

[12]A notable exception has been provided by Seeman (1967). Focusing explicitly on alienation in work, Seeman tested propositions relating this variable to certain consequences which are frequently attributed to it in the literature, particularly the mass-society and neo-Marxist literature. Using a sample of male workers in a Swedish community, he found little support for hypotheses linking alienation in work to a generalized sense of powerlessness, to anomia, to political awareness, to intergroup hostility, to status seeking, and to a readiness to leave decision making on political and social questions to experts.

attitudes toward other men and toward social arrangements that are potentially "dysfunctional" for the operation of those arrangements.

Of course, drawing inferences between circumstances of work and differences in attitudes and behavior is an undertaking which must always be made with care and circumspection, for a multitude of factors enter into the determination of attitude and behavior, many if not most of which may be only tangentially related to work. This caution is doubly applicable when such inferences are grounded in Marx's theory of work alienation. That theory carries with it certain conditional statements that enunciate relatively extreme conditions which were more fully descriptive of nineteenth-century industrialism than of the present day. Furthermore, the sequences of influences which intervene between the conditions of work and the individual and social consequences flowing from it were not, even in the objective industrial circumstances to which *Capital* was addressed, conceived as either simple or direct. For instance, widespread alienation in work among the members of the proletariat was not sufficient in itself to ensure the emergence of class consciousness and class militancy. Rather, Marx postulated the necessity of certain additional conditions which would have to be fulfilled. These were discussed, it may be recalled, in the previous chapter on Marx.

It is clear that one is given little reason in Marx's writings for expecting bold and readily discernible encroachments upon "bourgeois" ideologies among the much more favored industrial workers of the mid-twentieth century. This caution does not, however, negate the continuing value of the sociological implications of Marx's ideas of the centrality of work to human life. Armed with our measure of job dissatisfaction as an indicator of aggregate differences in work alienation,[13] and with certain attitudinal questions which are relevant to the concerns of a theory of stratification, we will make bold to offer certain propositions which can be inferred from Marx's theory of class conflict or at least are consistent with it. We shall then proceed to explore the extent to which those propositions are supported by the Italian data.

Statement of Hypotheses

The basic notion underlying the Marxian prediction of the formation of a self-conscious and politically viable proletariat was that material and psychological deprivations imposed primarily through the instrumentality of the conditions of employment would lead to the dissolution of the patina of legitimacy that mediates relations between workers and the privileged class. With this dissolution, a redefinition of social reality would occur in which the workers would come to a clearer perception of their own economic and politi-

---

[13]We remind the reader that this indicator is properly conceived as being associated with levels of alienation in aggregates of persons, and is not taken as necessarily an indicator of alienation in any given individual.

cal interests and to a clearer perception of the antagonism between their interests and those of the privileged class. Accordingly, the most direct (and conceptually the most simple) approach to the problem of investigating the correlates of work alienation within a Marxian framework is to compare the responses of the satisfied and the dissatisfied to questions that tap their perceptions of the legitimacy and the desirability of prevailing social arrangements.

We might suspect that if work alienation has relevance to the subject of social change in the way that Marx envisioned, then somewhere along the line it must exercise an effect on people's perceptions of those who wield authority and on their attitudes toward them. Accordingly, we might look for differences between the job satisfied and the job dissatisfied in attitudes expressed toward the authority which is exercised in the workplace. Specifically, we will predict that:

1. Legitimacy-Acquiescence Hypothesis. *The job dissatisfied will be more likely than the job satisfied to perceive the authority of work superiors as illegitimate, and to express a nonacquiescent attitude toward that authority.*

A second locus of authority which should be salient to the worker is political authority written large. In Marx's theory of class, the awakening of class consciousness among the disfranchised members of society is seen as resulting from a process in which increasing dissatisfaction with "things as they are" prepares the way for an acceptance of programs of radical change. Since Marx saw work alienation as one of the factors contributing to this process, we would expect on the basis of his theory that the work alienated are more likely than the nonalienated to voice preferences for leftist political parties. Conversely, we would expect to find a higher proportion of conservative-party preferences among the nonalienated than among the alienated. Accordingly, it might be predicted that:

2. Political-Interest Hypothesis. *The job dissatisfied will be more likely than the job satisfied to voice preferences for political parties of the left and less likely to voice preferences for parties of the center and the right.*

A final proposition can be offered on the basis of the observation that increasing alienation in work should eventually begin to reshape the worker's feelings of resignation toward the circumstances that set bounds on his life chances. Insofar as a worker's satisfaction with his position in society can be taken as an indicator of his satisfaction with those life chances, it might be predicted that:

3. Social-Satisfaction Hypothesis. *The job dissatisfied will be less satisfied with their position in society than the job satisfied.*

These three propositions will now be considered in their turn.

Legitimacy-Acquiescence Hypothesis

There are two principal ways in which the link between feelings toward work and attitudes toward authority can be made within the Marxian theoretical framework. The first is to focus on the efficacy of feelings of dissatisfaction in molding attitudes toward those who exercise authority in the workplace. In this connection it might be noted that the adoption and expression of negative attitudes toward superiors might be added to the list of adaptive mechanisms delineated by Argyris (1964:60–67). This author notes that behaviors such as restricting output, cheating, creating waste, and making errors constitute expressions of aggression by means of which workers can attempt to compensate for feelings of psychological failure, frustration, and conflict that have their source in their work.[14] Complaining about the actions of superiors, calling their competence into question, and the like, is one way (when such behavior is manifested with a modicum of discretion) in which feelings of aggression can be "acted out" symbolically with relatively little risk being taken by the perpetrator. Since, presumably, such behavior facilitates actual changes in basic attitudes toward authority, we can conceive of this behavior as being one way in which alienation from work might exercise an effect on perceptions of the legitimacy of authority and concomitantly on the willingness of the worker to acquiesce to the commands of authority.

The second way in which attitudes toward work and attitudes toward authority can be linked within the context of Marx's theory is to focus on the element of compulsion. For Marx, a critical aspect of the alienating conditions of industrial employment was precisely that the wage system made it impossible for the worker to escape alienating labor. On the one hand, he was compelled to accept meaningless work in order to survive. On the other, the wages provided were insufficient to enable the worker to build that money reserve required to shift occupations and try his hand at another skill. Frustration in the performance of unfulfilling work, combined with the sense of being trapped by the conditions of work laid down by the employer, would lay the groundwork for a revolt against the authority of the owner of the means of production. While Marx's views on alienation in labor apply in their most literal sense to the factory worker, one can see on reflection that they can be validly and fruitfully used with reference to nonmanual employees as well. C. Wright Mills (1951) showed this possibility most convincingly when he applied Marx's alienation framework to white-collar workers.

Table XI:3 reports the distribution of choices of the sample respondents to a question which asked them to choose from a list of four phrases the one that "best describes what you think of your work superiors." As will again be noted, the response options allowed the expression of an opinion on whether the

---

[14]A fuller treatment than is possible here of the usefulness of the alienation concept in job attitude research would have to include an accounting of Argyris's (1957; 1964) efforts to render explicit and specific the generally fuzzy notions that lurk behind such terms as "fulfillment" and "frustration" in work. Although Argyris does not address himself to the problem of "alienation" as such, his formulation of the needs of individuals for "psychological success" and his juxtaposing of these needs with a very different set, the needs of the organization, constitute a fruitful attack on the meaning of work alienation which is particularly suited to the kind of perspective that Marx brought to the subject.

TABLE XI:3. ATTITUDES TOWARD SUPERIORS AND JOB SATISFACTION IN SPECIFIC OCCUPATIONAL CATEGORIES

Attitudes toward Superiors	Elites and Bourgeoisie		Petty Bourgeoisie		Skilled Workers		Semiskilled Workers		Unskilled Workers and Farm Hands		Peasants	
	Satisfied	Dissatisfied	Satisfied	Dissatisfied	Satisfied	Dissatisfied	Satisfied	Dissatisfied	Satisfied	Dissatisfied	Satisfied	Dissatisfied
They Do Their Duty, and I Obey	62%	34%	48%	35%	57%	35%	60%	33%	53%	38%	46%	33%
They Do Their Duty, but It Is Hard to Obey	20	20	18	16	7	10	5	10	6	13	9	6
They Take Advantage of Their Position, but One Must Have Patience	14	37	23	29	24	43	27	40	36	32	38	44
They Take Advantage of Their Position, and That Makes Me Mad	4	9	11	20	12	12	8	17	5	17	7	17
Total	100%	100%	100%	100%	100%	100%	100%	100%	100%	100%	100%	100%
N	110	56	66	49	108	86	115	103	102	104	55	70

respondent's superiors "do their duty" or "take advantage of their position" (legitimacy-illegitimacy dimension), and also tapped the extent to which obeying the commands of those superiors was experienced as being easy or hard (acquiescence-nonacquiescence dimension). Only those respondents to whom the question applied (thus omitting those who were self-employed) and who actually chose one of the proffered responses (thus omitting the "no answer" and "other answer" data) are included in the table. The response distributions are given by occupational level.

Focusing first on the proportions in each occupation-satisfaction grouping who felt that their superiors "do their duty" rather than take "advantage of their position" (the first two rows versus the last two rows of the table), we can see that the satisfied respondents were more likely than the dissatisfied in every occupational category to see the exercise of authority by their superiors as legitimate. Thus, consistent with the first set of expectations expressed in the legitimacy-acquiescence hypothesis, the proportion of workers who perceived the authority of their superiors as legitimate is related to job satisfaction in a positive fashion, and this relation holds at all levels of the occupation hierarchy. This effect exists alongside an effect by occupational level. Among the satisfied, as within the ranks of the dissatisfied, the proportion of respondents who viewed the actions of their superiors as legitimate is in general directly related to ascendancy on the occupational hierarchy.

The first and third rows of Table XI:3, when combined, provide the proportions of workers who, irrespective of their views on the legitimacy-illegitimacy dimension, reported that they either willingly obeyed the commands of their superiors or were willing to exercise patience with their excesses. Perhaps not surprisingly, at least 7 out of 10 respondents in every occupation-satisfaction grouping (except dissatisfied petty bourgeois) expressed an acquiescent attitude toward their superiors. Nevertheless, consistent with our prediction, the proportion of acquiescent responses is positively related to job satisfaction.

The relationship is not, however, nearly so pronounced as was the case for the effects of job satisfaction on perceptions of legitimacy. Only among the semiskilled workers and the combined category of unskilled workers and farm hands was there a substantial difference in the proportions of satisfied and dissatisfied workers who indicated their willingness to accept the commands of superiors with a minimum of questioning. This piece of evidence is consistent with the hypothesis with which we are working, since it is among the semiskilled and unskilled industrial jobs that the most onerous tasks are found. It is also in this segment of the occupational hierarchy that the labor supply is the most captive in the sense that relatively low wages combined with low educational accomplishment make mobility to significantly better jobs improbable.

Table XI:3 shows also that the manual workers were generally *more* likely to express acquiescent attitudes toward the exercise of authority by their superiors than were the nonmanual workers; this tendency held among both the satisfied and the dissatisfied. Needless to say, these differences do not coincide with the view that would be most consistent with Marx's views on alienation in work—namely, that the productive economy is more likely to breed rebellion among the members of the proletarian than among the bourgeoisie or petty bourgeoisie. Nor is the finding predictable from the perspective of Dahrendorf's theory. The greater manifest docility of the manual workers can probably be explained in part as a class difference that is linked to education: while manual workers are probably more likely to indulge in criticism of their superiors as a by-product of their work-culture socialization, they are less prepared than nonmanual workers by virtue of either birth or education to question the exercise of authority itself. In part also greater docility is the statistical result of the fact that the petty bourgeoisie, and particularly the dissatisfied workers therein, are especially nonacquiescent. This is an interesting finding that bears more directly on Dahrendorf's theory, and will be discussed in detail in Chapter XVII.

In summary, the job satisfied were more likely than the dissatisfied at every occupational level to report that their superiors "did their duty" and, especially in the two lowest occupational groupings, to indicate their willingness to obey or at least to have patience with their superiors' excesses. In general, perceptions of legitimacy were positively related to occupational level among both the satisfied and the dissatisfied. On the other hand, willingness to obey was inversely related to occupational level across the manual-nonmanual line. These relationships survive controls by both age and career mobility, although the effects by occupational level are somewhat obscured among the job dissatisfied in certain instances. Thus the data are generally in accordance with the first of the three propositions linking job satisfaction to expressions of attitudes.

Political-Interests Hypothesis

A number of factors besides those that are important to the perspective we have taken can and do intervene to shape political attitudes. Thus, in predicting a greater degree of political "radicalism" (that is, a greater preference for parties of the left) among the job dissatisfied than among the job satisfied, we are dealing with a proposition for which certain rather weighty conditions are appropriate. We know, for example, that preferences for the Communist and the Socialist Parties will be more prevalent among manual than among nonmanual workers, quite apart from variations in job satisfaction. While the logic of our argument does assert that a greater degree of work alienation among manual workers should help to explain this gross difference, it is clear that other factors, such as objective political interests and political socialization, have a larger role to play. What we would expect, however, is for differences in work alienation to reveal differences in party preference which build upon the modal political composition of a category of workers. Specifically, in addition to the effect by occupational class, we would expect the work alienated to be more often leftist and less often conservative than the nonalienated workers. Accordingly, in examining the data we will compare the political preferences of the job satisfied to those of the job dissatisfied *within* each occupational category taken separately. This analytical scheme has the advantage, in fact, of providing a check on any too facile interpretation of the political differences that parallel the satisfaction differences, since it enjoins us to compare them to the differences in political orientation that occur by occupational level.

An additional point is to be noted before we proceed to an examination of the data: an important fact not accounted for by the hypothesis—namely, that a preference for parties of the left is not the only response which can be expected from work alienation. Equally compelling possibilities are apathy, withdrawal, and indifference. Such responses are consistent with Marx's theory, for in that theory the emergence of political alertness is tied to a complex set of factors, and is always somewhat problematic even when industrial exploitation is relatively severe. Furthermore, evidence indicates that alienation in work tends to produce correlates at the psychological level that should constitute effective tension toward political withdrawal. For example, in his study of United States factory workers Arthur Kornhauser (1965:238–239) reported a positive relation between the amount of skill exercised on the job and an index of "purposeful striving." It would seem most likely that an absence of purposeful attitudes, rather than political activism, will parallel political apathy. However, it should also be noted that Seeman (1967), who tested the proposition linking work alienation to political apathy in a study conducted in Sweden, found little evidence to support it.

Table XI:4 reports the responses of the sample respondents, by occupational level and by job satisfaction, to the question, "In your opinion, which party in Italy best defends the interests of people like you?" Responses are grouped according to whether the respondent volunteered the name of a leftist party (Communist, Socialist, or Social Democratic, present in Italy during the period of our field work), a "conservative" party (one of the center or right, such as Christian Democratic, Liberal, Monarchic, or Social Movement), or gave a response suggestive of cynicism or apathy. Respondents were classed as having given a cynical response if they said that "no party" best defended their interests. Those who replied "not interested in politics," "don't know," "don't understand politics," "don't wish to say," or who otherwise gave no response are reported as apathetic. The rubrics of "apathy" and "cynicism" must be taken only as loose descriptions of categories of responses, since they may not constitute accurate interpretations of the detailed meanings behind the specific responses. As was already noted, many people in Italy are quite reluctant to

TABLE XI:4. POLITICAL PREFERENCE AND JOB SATISFACTION IN
SPECIFIC OCCUPATIONAL CATEGORIES

Political Preference	Elites and Bourgeoisie		Petty Bourgeoisie		Skilled Workers		Semiskilled Workers		Unskilled Workers and Farm Hands		Peasants	
	Satisfied	Dissatisfied	Satisfied	Dissatisfied	Satisfied	Dissatisfied	Satisfied	Dissatisfied	Satisfied	Dissatisfied	Satisfied	Dissatisfied
Leftist	22%	38%	30%	40%	46%	42%	51%	55%	42%	40%	14%	21%
Conservative	43	21	24	27	20	24	21	15	33	27	42	45
Cynical	21	22	16	13	15	17	8	19	12	11	12	12
Apathetic	9	14	23	18	15	10	19	9	12	20	25	17
Other Response	5	5	7	2	4	7	1	2	1	2	7	5
Total	100%	100%	100%	100%	100%	100%	100%	100%	100%	100%	100%	100%
N	152	80	110	79	142	119	128	111	107	114	106	126

discuss their party affiliations or preferences, given the prevalence and importance of political patronage, and given their own distrust of the machinations
of political and governmental processes.

Turning now to the data in Table XI:4, it can be seen that the political-
interest hypothesis was given varying measures of support among the nonmanual respondents, the semiskilled workers, and the peasants. The strongest
support came from the elites and bourgeoisie, among whom the satisfied were
more likely than the dissatisfied to voice a political preference for center or
rightist parties, and less likely to choose a party of the left. Among the petty
bourgeoisie, while the dissatisfied were more likely than the satisfied to choose
a party of the left, the two categories of workers were about equally likely to
side with the conservatives. Similarly, among the peasants the expectations of
the hypothesis regarding leftist preferences were fulfilled, while those regarding conservative preferences were not. Among the manual workers, there was
no clear-cut relationship between job satisfaction and political preference.[15]

The meaning of these data becomes clearer when differences in political
preference by occupational category are considered. Looking first at the distribution of preferences for leftist political parties by occupation we can see that
this distribution is curvilinear, taking the form of a rough and inverted U.
Generally speaking, preference for political parties of the left was low among
the elites and bourgeoisie, reached an apex in the political choices of the
semiskilled workers, and from there fell to its lowest point among the peasants.
It can also be seen that, as a general rule, the differences between the job
satisfied and the job dissatisfied within the occupational categories were low
by comparison to differences between those categories. Only in the three
instances pointed out at the top and bottom of the occupational hierarchy, and
especially within the uppermost occupational category, was the effect by job
satisfaction a significant addition to the effect by occupational level. In each
of these three cases, the difference between the satisfied and the dissatisfied lay
in the direction predicted by the political-interest hypothesis.

The inverse of this situation can be observed in the distribution of preferences for conservative political parties. Again the distribution by occupation
is curvilinear, this time the highest values being found at the top and bottom
of the occupational structure, and the minimum being found in the semiskilled

---

[15]The general absence of a consistent relationship between job satisfaction and political preference in the three levels of manual skill has relevance for a methodological problem of which we
have not yet taken explicit note. This is the possibility that party affiliation might itself have a
direct effect on our indicator of job satisfaction. It is possible that leftist, and particularly Communist, party ideology might encourage affirmative answers to a question asking whether there is
"anything in particular" the worker does not like about his job. On the other hand, the Christian
Democratic party, insofar as it serves as a vehicle for Judeo-Christian values with respect to the
meaning of work, might just as plausibly tend to discourage complaining. However, if such an
effect exists, it is not very strong; otherwise, we would expect a greater differentiation between
satisfied and dissatisfied workers in political orientation than is observed in Table XI:4.

workers. The more compelling departures from the observed relationship by occupation are found among the elites and bourgeoisie, the semiskilled workers and unskilled workers. Again, in each of these instances the differences in political preference between the job satisfied and the job dissatisfied lie in the direction predicted by the hypothesis: the job dissatisfied were less likely to opt for a political party of the center or right than were the job satisfied.

It should be noted that the differences in political preference by occupation, although not interpretable directly as support for the hypothesis, are consistent with expectations from the perspective of Marx's theory. The tasks featuring the least variety, the most monotony, and the highest degree of mechanical pacing are found among jobs which are classified technically as semiskilled (for instance, assembly-line work). Although other factors are undoubtedly involved in producing this effect, nevertheless from the perspective of the Marxian theory of class and of work alienation we would expect to find the greatest acceptance of leftist political ideologies and the greatest rejection of conservative ideologies in that area of the occupational spectrum where the most alienating jobs are found.

There is a source of variation that is analytically extraneous to the relationship of our present interest and whose effect on that relationship is worth reporting. That is the factor of geographic region. At first consideration it might be thought that the important regional differences dividing northern (industrial) and southern (agricultural) Italy might be responsible for a sharpening of the expected effect of job satisfaction on party preference in the North and a diminution of its effect in the South. These include specifically the higher level of general education in the industrialized North, the greater degree of political education through secondary associations, the relatively smaller dependence of the population on political favors for things that are required for meeting the basic requirements of living, the greater alienation of the masses from the Church, and concomitantly, the greater organization and appeal of the Communist party; and all of these might be expected to operate in such a fashion as to make the northern and central regions of Italy a more auspicious testing ground for the political-interest hypothesis than the agrarian South.

In point of fact, while the greater conservatism of the South operates on the relationship in expected ways, the predictive efficiency of job satisfaction is enhanced rather than obscured among the southern respondents of the sample. Furthermore, this enhancement occurs most markedly with respect to leftist rather than conservative political preferences. In the South, the job dissatisfied among the elites-bourgeoisie and the petty bourgeoisie were more likely to choose a party of the political left than were the job satisfied by margins of 44 to 25 and 41 to 19 percent, respectively. Furthermore, it is among the southerners that the greatest differences in leftist party preference between satisfied and dissatisfied skilled workers occurred. For instance, 40 percent of the job-dissatisfied skilled workers as compared to 26 percent of the satisfied preferred leftist political parties.

An examination of the distribution of political preferences by occupational level in the South reveals that the greater support given the political-interest hypothesis in that region is due primarily to a markedly decreased preference for leftist affiliations among the satisfied workers rather than to an increased preference on the part of dissatisfied workers. In other words, the primary effect would appear to be the regional difference in the appeal of conservative over leftist party affiliations rather than the effect by job satisfaction. The dissatisfied southern workers were not markedly different from dissatisfied workers in the North in their preference for leftist parties.

In summary, the most consistent support for the political-interest hypothesis was found among the elites and bourgeoisie, for whom differences between the job satisfied and job dissatisfied lay in predicted directions with respect to both leftist and conservative party preference for the category as a whole as well as by region. If we maintain a singleminded perspective through Marx's eyes, we would not look to this place in the occupational structure for such a vigorous affirmation of this particular hypothesis. Indeed, Pareto might better have prepared us for the relatively marked differences in political preference between the job satisfied and the job dissatisfied among the elites and bourgeoisie. Once again, we shall have to return to this finding from a different perspective in Chapter XVII.

In part the differences observed among the elites and bourgeoisie parallel occupational differences between the managerial and professional personnel on the one hand, and the middle clerks on the other, who are combined within the top occupational category in Table XI:4. It has been shown that the middle clerks were more job dissatisfied than the proprietors, managers, and professionals above them. It could also be shown that they account for a sizable proportion of the leftist party affiliates among the elites and bourgeoisie. While this correlation between occupation and party preference helps to explain the strength of the relationship found between job satisfaction and political orientation among the elites and bourgeoisie, it does not account for it entirely, particularly if these differences are juxtaposed with the smaller differences found elsewhere on the occupational scale.

Education might help to explain this finding. A greater intellectual vigor would be expected of persons with more schooling; in a country still deeply rooted in the ways of the past, this vigor in turn should encourage political progressivism among the elites and bourgeoisie. Another explanation concerns occupational and class folkways with regard to political preferences. Among the nonmanual workers, a preference for the political left constitutes a deviation from a subcultural norm, and in this sense provides a means of symbolic protest for the disaffected.

A more compelling substantive explanation might perhaps be found by remembering the content of the job complaints offered by the members of the top nonmanual categories. The most prominent complaint from the middle clerks was the "lack of freedom" and the "incompetent superiors" they found at their jobs. Such disaffections are amply justified by the character of bureaucratic institutions in Italy. Career making comes hard, and the hands of "the old autocrats" of the office bear down heavy on the underlings. To the extent that chafing under the rule of a burdensome authority structure accounts for dissatisfaction among the elites and bourgeoisie, it is perhaps not surprising that the dissatisfied tend to choose the leftist political parties and to reject the conservative with a remarkable consistency that clearly differentiated them from the noncomplainers. In Italy, a preference for the Communist or one of the Socialist political programs may serve nicely as a channel for psychic release from resentment toward authority structures that are relatively static and often corrupt, inefficient, and overbearing.

Social-Satisfaction Hypothesis

The final prediction which was made with respect to work alienation was that the job dissatisfied are less satisfied with their social position in society than the job satisfied—that satisfaction with work is positively associated with satisfaction with the set of circumstances which are externally symbolic of success in life. Comparing the attitudes of a man who is happy with his work and those of a man who is unhappy with it, we would expect the former to be the more likely to feel satisfied with the social position to which his work entitles him. Among the truly work alienated, we would expect to find a loss, not only of satisfaction with one's social position but also of hope of improving that position. A theme that recurs in Marx's treatment of work alienation is that the worker was forced to persevere at alienating labor in order to meet his subsistence needs. Presumably then, the work alienated have no "way out," or they would have taken it.

In Table XI:5 are given the respondents' answers by occupation-satisfaction category to the following question: "Which of these statements best describes what you think of your social position?" Response options ranged from "very satisfied" to "dissatisfied," and probed for the respondents' hopes of improving their social position, as is indicated in the table.

It can be seen that the job satisfied were decidedly more likely than the job complainers to voice satisfaction with their social position, and less likely to voice dissatisfaction, at every level of the occupational hierarchy.[16] Further-

---

[16]Joseph Weitz (1952) has suggested that correlations between measures of general satisfaction and job satisfaction might measure nothing more than systematic differences among individuals in the tendency to complain. With circumstances of job and life held constant, those who have a tendency to complain about one would probably have a tendency to complain about the other quite apart from their composite feelings of satisfaction with the two sets of circumstances. An artificial inflation of the relationship due to the presence of such set toward the "gripe" response is a possibility to which our data on job satisfaction are particularly susceptible, since they were elicited by simply asking the respondents if there was "anything in particular" about their jobs they did not like. We have already taken note of this fact in our discussion of differences in occupational norms with respect to the expression of job complaints.

TABLE XI:5. JOB SATISFACTION AND SATISFACTION WITH SOCIAL POSITION
IN SPECIFIC OCCUPATIONAL CATEGORIES

Satisfaction with Social Position	Elites and Bourgeoisie		Petty Bourgeoisie		Skilled Workers		Semiskilled Workers		Unskilled Workers and Farm Hands		Peasants	
	Satisfied	Dissatisfied	Satisfied	Dissatisfied	Satisfied	Dissatisfied	Satisfied	Dissatisfied	Satisfied	Dissatisfied	Satisfied	Dissatisfied
Very Satisfied	10%	1%	6%	3%	9%	2%	6%	3%	3%	2%	10%	2%
Satisfied but Hope to Improve	61	54	56	37	45	33	55	25	30	10	36	21
Neither Satisfied nor Dissatisfied	16	17	21	31	25	22	23	19	29	26	23	19
Dissatisfied but Hope to Improve	10	24	14	24	20	36	13	40	28	46	23	39
Dissatisfied and Have No Hope of Improvement	3	4	3	5	1	7	3	13	10	16	8	19
Total	100%	100%	100%	100%	100%	100%	100%	100%	100%	100%	100%	100%
N	143	76	107	76	139	111	124	111	107	110	102	122

more, they were also more likely to combine a feeling of satisfaction with their social position with the hope of improving that position. This second effect is particularly marked among the petty bourgeoisie, the semiskilled, the unskilled workers and farm hands, and the peasants.

It might be questioned to what extent the two measures which are cross-tabulated in Table XI:5 really tap differing dimensions. Insofar as work is constitutive of social position, the two are but differing measures of the same thing. However, while a certain amount of overlap unarguably exists between the dimensions underlying the two measures, the degree of analytical as well as methodological independence between the two should be noted. First the job-satisfaction probe did not directly ask for a composite feeling of satisfaction or dissatisfaction with work; it simply asked if there were any particularly salient complaints about work that the respondent might like to volunteer. This request for a specific answer should have minimized the extent to which the two questions carried effectively the same subjective meaning to the respondents. In addition, there is indeed a considerable extent to which job and social position are not completely determinate of one another, particularly in an industrial society. Max Weber's distinction between social class and social status may be fruitfully recalled here.

The point is an important one and deserves explicit attention. Rather different kinds of work are associated with similar positions in the status hierarchy as this is manifested in modes of dress, type and location of housing, and the like. This diversity is particularly present in proportion as industrialization distributes the external badges of affluence further down the occupational hierarchy. Hence the explicit nature of a man's work is not always evident to persons outside the actual place of employment. Concomitantly, a man who is dissatisfied with the "intrinsic" aspects of his work may not have cause for complaint about the social position to which the financial rewards of that job give him access.

A case study suggesting the degree to which job aspirations and satisfaction related to social position can vary independently of one another is given by Goldthorpe and his associates. As we have noted previously, these investigators found a decidedly "instrumental" attitude toward work among a sample of affluent blue-collar workers in England. The aspirations of these workers were centered primarily in the hope of attaining greater consumer power within the subsequent years. Except for a very small minority of respondents, their aspirations were not contingent on complementary hopes of advancement on the job or dreams of starting independently in business. Rather, the objective basis for looking forward to an improvement outside the work situation lay with expectations of an improved rate of remuneration for all the workers with whom they worked (Goldthorpe and others, 1968b:137–138).

Additional evidence of the extent to which satisfaction with social position and satisfaction with work can vary independently was reported by Arthur

Kornhauser (1965:127–131). Kornhauser found very little evidence to support the notion that concerns with prestige and social standing were important determinants of occupational differences in mental-health scores, or by implication, of occupational differences in job satisfaction, since job satisfaction was highly related to differences in mental health. Although the nature of his data demanded that his conclusions be tentative, Arthur Kornhauser (1965: 130–131) noted that his

workers' concern with the social-status aspects of jobs, in the sense of prestige and social standing, is little evidenced in our interviews though ample opportunity was afforded for such interest to manifest itself. Questions pertaining to the pros and cons of factory work, the importance of the man's own job, and his feelings about advancement and what getting ahead means to him elicit responses that only infrequently suggest status considerations. Other aspects of work loom much larger—earnings, agreeable and interesting work, pleasant surroundings, freedom and independence, for example. The several job meanings cannot be completely isolated, of course; unexpressed concern about esteem and social status may be present beneath the surface of other responses. But the assumption is at least open to question.

A point of note in Table XI:5 is the fact that job dissatisfaction, insofar as it is indicative of occupational differences in work alienation, does not seem to be remarkably associated with aspirations for improvement. If the second and fourth rows of Table XI:5 are combined, it can be seen that only among the nonmanuals were there differences worthy of mention between the job satisfied and the job dissatisfied in their hopes of improving their social positions. Whatever the satisfactions and deprivations associated with work and life for our respondents, the outstanding fact remains that for most of them there is hope for better days, and it is a hope that is not noticeably dampened by present deprivations.

CONCLUSION

It is but a short step from a perusal of occupational differences in work-related attitudes to the suggestion that job alienation might be fruitfully considered as a dysfunctional consequence of social stratification. That this perspective was present in the works of Marx there can be no doubt. In Marx's work, alienation in work was tied in large part to what we have come to term the "intrinsic" characteristics of the job. Work which was forced by an external agent, which was performed solely for the fulfillment of extrinsic purposes, and which therefore bore no expression of the creative and free individuality of the worker, was necessarily and intrinsically alienating. The frustration of this inner *work*-predicated creativity provided the fertile soil in which the seeds of revolution might eventually be sown. Thus, for Marx, interaction between a man and his work, if infelicitous in character, formed the kernel of the most radically *dys*functional social phenomenon, namely massive revolt against established institutions.

Marx elaborated a single dysfunction of work roles with an eloquence that is philosophically compelling even when it lacks scientific explicitness. To those who fall under the spell of his ideology of work, it is easy to dismiss as relatively irrelevant all other kinds of profits and costs which determine the impact that the job has on the man, and conversely, the attitudes that the man has toward the job. Marx pays little heed to those characteristics of the interaction between man and his job which are *socially* defined and concern the relation between man and society directly. He makes, for example, but passing and relatively peripheral mention of the variable of social recognition or of prestige. Those who have reacted to the unidimensional quality of the Marxian ethic of work have a point when they protest that work roles are bearers of other salient costs and profits besides those pertaining directly to creativity.

What is of interest from the present perspective, however, is that job morale can be fruitfully admitted as a phenomenon with potentially functional or dysfunctional consequences irrespective of which work-related profits or costs are of immediate concern. Then one need not ask whether intrinsic or extrinsic determinants of job satisfaction are to be given *(a priori)* prominence, but needs rather to investigate fully the gallery of such variables and determine empirically their relative importance. As will be seen in the next chapter, this approach is immediately fruitful, for it allows us to juxtapose two perspectives on social stratification which are at opposite poles in both analytical strategy and ideological position: the Marxian and the Davis-Moore perspectives.

XII

SOME DYSFUNCTIONS OF STRATIFICATION*

Two theories of social stratification which have occasioned a good deal of debate in sociology are Karl Marx's theory of class conflict and the "functional" theory of Kingsley Davis and Wilbert E. Moore (1945; see also Davis, 1948). It would be a difficult task to find two statements which contrast more with each other. Davis and Moore provide a closely reasoned argument for the proposition that the unequal distribution of scarce and valued social commodities is functionally necessary for the operation of social institutions. For Marx, on the other hand, class inequalities reflect gross imbalances in private property and in the social, legal, and political power that is generated by, and in turn generates, private property. Marx, in short, focuses our attention on the dysfunctions that emanate from distributive systems, while Davis and Moore emphasize the positive functions of such systems.

Each of these theories rests in part on a set of assumptions about the motives that govern the actions of men, and traces the consequences of those motives for the operation of the social order. However, the two sets of motivational schemata are seen as interacting in entirely different ways with the same sociological datum, social stratification. Davis and Moore point out that unequal rewards motivate individuals to compete for the more societally important positions, and thereby serve the positive function of encouraging the

*By Joseph Lopreato and Marilyn Bidnick.

339

recruitment of qualified personnel to those positions. Marx focuses on the
psychological and social penalties imposed on less privileged workers by an
unjust system of unequal rewards, and argues that this system provides an
important impetus for social change.

While the flow of criticisms of the Davis-Moore and Marxian theories has
been sustained over the years, the two statements have rarely if ever been
brought together in a single perspective on institutionalized social inequalities
and their significance for the people who bear them. The mutual relevancies
of the two contributions might be profitably utilized in a number of ways. One
approach, which will be taken in the present chapter, is to compare segments
of the population that participate generously in those valued properties that
are central to the Davis-Moore formulation with segments who do not so
participate, focusing on attitudes and values which are of relevance to the
functioning of the social order. More specifically, our attention in the present
chapter will be on certain dysfunctional aspects of social stratification—a
major area of emphasis for Marx—from the vantage point of a scheme articulated in terms of two variables central to the Davis-Moore theory: *functional importance* and *prestige* (as a social reward).

FUNCTIONAL IMPORTANCE, PRESTIGE, AND JOB SATISFACTION

It will be remembered that the Davis-Moore theory pivots on the causes and
the consequences of social stratification for society taken as a unit. There is
little or no concern in it for the personal experiences of individuals who
constitute the society. Differential rewards are necessary, according to Davis
and Moore, as incentives or inducements that motivate individuals to fill
functionally important positions (1945:243). But this relatively uncomplicated
picture of stratification demands elaboration in that one must consider the
response of men who are located in poorly rewarded positions, a response that
is a consequence of stratification and logically independent of those outcomes
suggested by Davis and Moore. In this connection the reader will recall our
earlier contention that Tumin's (1953a) chief contribution to discussions of the
theory lay in his reminder that social dysfunctions may result when social
arrangements wreak violence on individual needs. Among other things, he
suggested that when "favorable self-images" and the "sense of significant
membership" are distributed unequally in a population, the results may include an underdevelopment both of creative potential and of loyalty to the
society. Here focusing on the fact that a man's self-image is likely to be
intimately associated with the kind of work he performs, we find ourselves at
the heart of concerns that are germane to the Davis and Moore theory and can
also be readily articulated from a vantage point that is thoroughly Marxian in
its basic thrust.

We might ask, for example, whether any social dysfunctions stem from the fact that persons occupy positions of differing functional importance. If the positions that must be filled in order for society to function are not equally important, then feelings of making a *significant contribution to the social enterprise* are also likely to be unequally distributed among the incumbents of those positions. To the extent that a sense of making a meaningful social contribution through work integrates individuals into the social order, we would expect to find evidence of alienation from the social order among those workers who find it difficult to derive this kind of meaning from their jobs.

How much functional importance men perceive in their jobs is a datum closely related to how highly they assess their worth as that is reflected in the rewards they receive for the contributions they make through their work. In the light of the basic thrust of the Davis-Moore argument, there is one kind of reward which is particularly relevant to the question of relative contribution, and that is occupational prestige. The prestige conferred on a person is directly interpretable as an affirmation of the functional importance of the job he holds; and indeed there is evidence that conceptions of the relative importance of jobs are highly correlated with the prestige that is typically enjoyed by the occupants of those jobs (Lopreato and Lewis, 1963, 1965; Harris, 1964). We might inquire whether the unequal distribution of prestige, by reflecting in an indifferent or even a negative way on the usefulness of substantial segments of the citizenry, has consequences that are ultimately dysfunctional for the society as a whole. It should be noted that this was one of the major questions recommended for future research by Tumin (1953a) in his critique of the Davis-Moore theory.[1]

The Davis-Moore and the Marxian theories converge most clearly in the domain of work. The possibility suggests itself that the same system of unequal rewards may have paradoxical effects: (1) it may motivate individuals to assume highly important social positions; (2) it may produce alienation from work among the incumbents of less important positions, with the consequence that, in the aggregate, motivation in work is depressed rather than stimulated. Our first application, then, of a perspective that borrows from the Davis-Moore and the Marxian theories will be to study two separate effects on

---

[1]Following his original critique of the Davis-Moore (1945) article, Melvin Tumin produced a statement that related the distribution of scarce resources and ideologies of human equality to social integration and social conflict (Tumin, 1953a; Tumin with Feldman, 1961:467–511). A key variable in this formulation, which was based on insights gained from a study of stratification in Puerto Rico, was the feeling of self-worth which flows from the conviction of being both a valuable and a valued member of society. Briefly, Tumin argued that official pronouncements assuring the Puerto Rican peasant of his own worth and of the value of his contribution to that rapidly industrializing society served the necessary function of toning down invidious comparisons across the immense gap that separated peasants from the emerging business and managerial classes. Tumin, contemplating the societal "problem" of preventing a potentially disruptive degree of inequality in the distribution of positive self-images in a society, cast it as a problem of assuring the maintenance of adequate commitment to roles which are necessary for the proper functioning of system processes but are nevertheless poorly rewarded in terms of scarce commodities.

people's sense of satisfaction with their jobs: (1) the effect of people's perceptions of the social contribution rendered through their work; and (2) the effect of their perceptions of the prestige conferred on them through their work. Then we will look at the effects of these two perceptual variables as they operate conjointly on our measure of job satisfaction. Evidence of work alienation in our sample was reviewed in the preceding chapter and provides a background for the investigation which follows.[2]

Functional Importance and Work Alienation

If we take seriously Marx's conception of the centrality of work to human experience, we would expect individual judgments of the meaningfulness of work (including its social utility) to be operative at every level of the occupational hierarchy as a factor in determining whether people derive a sense of fulfillment from their work or not. Accordingly, we would predict that *the greater the functional importance imputed by a man to his job, the greater his job satisfaction.*

As is so often true of propositions which attempt to delineate a relationship between attitudes toward work and some specific independent variable, certain conceptual difficulties attend the formulation of the proposition offered above, and these should be dealt with before we proceed to the relevant data. Perhaps the most obvious problem concerns the fact that, whereas we have designated job satisfaction as the dependent variable in the relationship, a compelling argument could be made for the claim that a causal link in the opposite direction is also operative. We would expect, in fact, that the relationship is reciprocal; the particular choice of independent and dependent variables in the present case is, however, the appropriate one for the theoretical ideas with which we are dealing.

A more fundamental problem concerns the propriety of using perceptions of social contribution as an independent variable at all. This problem probably rests at least as much with the conceptual biases of contemporary social science as it does with the proposition itself. Because we tend to attribute the greater part of how a man perceives his world, and particularly of how he perceives himself, to the impress of messages which he receives from the social environment, we tend to leave little room for the role of the individual himself in sifting through these social judgments and integrating them selectively into his own definition of the meaning of his experience. To borrow from Allport's (1955: 100) assessment of the behavioral sciences, man as he emerges from the sociological literature can be aptly characterized as "an 'empty organism,' pushed by drives and molded by [social] environmental circumstance." In sociology generally, as Wrong (1961) pointed out, the tendency has been to posit a

---

[2]In particular, the reader is referred to Chapter XI for a discussion of the measure of job satisfaction which was used in that chapter and will also be used in the present chapter.

well-nigh absolute importance to primary socialization on the one hand, and to the influence of social approbation on the other, in molding human perception and human response. In sociological treatments of attitudes toward work, this tendency has in turn encouraged the view that job satisfaction is likely to be a direct reflection of the feelings which are socially defined as appropriate for the reward received in work. Consistent with this mode of thinking, the individual's perception of the social contribution of his work is viewed as being determined by variables, such as pay and prestige, which together constitute the social definition of the value of the work.

There are findings in the literature which bear on the independent influence of perceptions of the contribution of work on job attitudes, and while they certainly do not resolve the issue, it might be worthwhile to consider them briefly. The objective in looking at such research findings is not to argue for the greater importance of perceptions of social contribution as compared to other variables. Our aim, rather, is to adduce evidence which at least indirectly supports the propriety of treating this variable as partly independent of the influence of social definitions of functional contribution, and thus as worthy of study for its influence on job satisfaction.

In his investigation of the correlates of mental health among skilled and semiskilled industrial workers, Arthur Kornhauser (1965:117) found that men who did not feel they were doing "something important" on the job were decidedly poorer in mental health, on the average, than were their more positive fellow workers at the same job level. The difference was found to be greatest among those engaged in routine semiskilled labor. Kornhauser concluded that the poorer mental health of the least skilled workers, as compared to the respondents at higher job levels, was "disproportionately accounted for by workers who feel their jobs are unimportant."

Related evidence is reported by Morse and Weiss (1955:191–194), who asked a national sample of employed persons in the United States whether they would continue to work if they were to inherit enough money to "live comfortably without working." Of the respondents, 80 percent said they would continue. When these were asked *why* they would want to keep working, 12 percent volunteered responses to the effect that work "justifies existence," work gives "feelings of self-respect," and without work they would "feel useless." Similarly, when those who wanted to continue working were asked what they would miss most if they did not work, 9 percent responded that they would miss such things as the feeling of "doing something important, [or] worthwhile," and the "feeling of self-respect."

A final revealing example is provided by Nigel Walker (1961:188–191). In a study of work morale in the British civil service, this researcher used a sample of more than 1,740 workers that included employees of private firms as well as civil servants. Walker asked his respondents to rank the occupations from a prepared list of nine in the order of their "importance and value to the community." Eight of the occupations to be ranked represented a wide range of prestige, from "taxi driver" to "Member of Parliament." The remaining occupation was the respondent's own job. It was found that, out of 1,090 civil servants, 4.2 percent ranked their own occupation first, which meant, of course, that they considered their own job to be of greater importance than that of a Member of Parliament. Another 22.7 percent ranked their own occupation either second or third. Corresponding percentages for the 650 respondents employed in private firms were 3.5 and 8.2, respectively (Nigel Walker, 1961:189).

While Walker found the expected positive association between the rank the respondent assigned to his job and the actual rank of his job in the bureaucratic hierarchy, he also found that there was a good deal of variation within each job grade represented by the respondents. Walker hypothesized that the high degree of variation within job grade was connected with the respondents' feelings about their jobs. To test this hypothesis, he cross-tabulated the rank assigned by the respondents to their jobs with his measure of job satisfaction, and, as he expected, he found a positive association between the two. For example, of the civil servants who ranked their jobs first, 36 percent were "satisfied" with their jobs, 61 per cent were "in between," and 2 per cent were "dissatisfied" with their jobs. Corresponding percentages for the respondents from private firms were 62, 33, and 5, respectively. At the other end of the spectrum, of the civil servants who ranked their own occupation as eighth or ninth in importance to the community, 15 percent were satisfied, 43 percent were in between, and 41 percent were dissatisfied. Corresponding percentages for the employees of private firms were 26, 44, and 30, respectively. Walker noted that job satisfaction seemed more highly correlated with the jobholder's perceived importance of jobs than with the actual job grade. He also observed that for the civil servants, on the basis of a test of partial association, the two relationships were independent of one another (Nigel Walker, 1961:190–191).

The following question was asked of our sample in order to obtain an indication of their own assessment of the "functional importance" of their job relative to other jobs in their society: "In your opinion, the work you do is much more useful, more useful, equally useful, less useful, or much less useful than other types of work for the *welfare of the nation?*" Using the same six-point occupational breakdown that was used previously, the respondents in each occupational category were classified according to whether they viewed their work as "more useful," "equally useful," or "less useful" (the "much more" and "more" combined, likewise the "much less" and "less"), and the percent of workers in each of these three categories who had no complaints about their jobs were computed. The results are presented in Table XII:1.

The findings show that, generally speaking, workers were job satisfied in direct relation to their tendency to judge the utility of their work in favorable terms. There were, however, reversals. The petty bourgeoisie and the peasants

TABLE XII:1. JOB SATISFACTION OF RESPONDENTS IN VARIOUS
OCCUPATIONAL STRATA WHO PERCEIVED DIFFERENTIALLY THE
FUNCTIONAL IMPORTANCE OF THEIR OWN JOBS

	Respondents' Perceived Usefulness of Their Own Jobs Relative to Other Kinds of Jobs					
	More Useful		Equally Useful		Less Useful	
Occupational Stratum	Number of Respondents	Percent Job Satisfied	Number of Respondents	Percent Job Satisfied	Number of Respondents	Percent Job Satisfied
Elites and Bourgeoisie	68	75	126	63	15	27
Petty Bourgeoisie	40	58	126	63	19	32
Skilled Workers	62	63	176	52	18	50
Semiskilled Workers	55	60	149	55	30	33
Unskilled Workers and Farm Hands	55	51	139	52	25	23
Peasants	109	43	113	48	9	56

in the category of high functional importance (more useful) were less job satisfied than their colleagues who judged their work as equally useful with other kinds of work. Also, among the unskilled workers and farm hands, those who saw their work as more useful were not more likely to be satisfied with their jobs than those who judged the contribution of their work as equally useful.

A related and conspicuous feature of Table XII:1 should be noted. Although the base frequencies for some of the recorded percentages are too small to support firm generalizations, the findings do suggest that the critical point on the gradient of self-assessed functional importance lies between those who express a generally positive feeling toward their jobs (by reporting that it is either more useful, or at least as useful as the work of others) and those who express a negative evaluation of the comparative usefulness of their work (by reporting that it is less useful). For example, in no occupational stratum was there more than a 12-percent difference in job satisfaction between those who felt that their work surpassed the work of others in usefulness and those who saw their work as only equally useful. In contrast, in four of the six occupational strata those who took a dismal view of the value of their work were about half or less as likely to be job satisfied as those who had positive conceptions of their jobs' worth. Furthermore, consistent with our expectations, the association between perceptions of the job's social contribution and job satisfaction was operative at all levels of the industrial hierarchy even though the correlative effect of occupational prestige is partially controlled. Among the elites and bourgeoisie, for instance, only about a quarter of those who saw their work as less useful failed to complain about their jobs. By contrast, three-fourths of those who stated that their work was more useful than the work of others were job satisfied.

A most interesting fact comes to light as we move to a different set of data in order to examine the effect of occupational status on the distribution of respondents among the three functional-importance categories. An examination of the proportion of workers at each occupational level who fell in each of the three categories of functional importance reveals that there was rather negligible variation in the self-imputed social value of occupations by occupational level. The proportions of workers who saw their work as more useful are 33 percent for the elites and bourgeoisie combined, 22 for the petty bourgeoisie, 24 for the skilled workers, 23 for the semiskilled workers, 25 for the unskilled workers, and 47 for the peasants. The percentages of those who saw their work as less useful are 7, 10, 7, 13, 11, and 4, respectively. At least five out of ten men in every occupational category declined to categorize their work either as more useful or as less useful than any other kind of work. Most of these proceeded to give reasons for their unwillingness to make invidious comparisons. Typically, they argued that "everybody is useful, really." "Who can say who is more useful and who is less useful?" "Without the humble peasant, for instance, we would die of starvation." One respondent had a particularly interesting twist: "All occupations are useful," said he; "even the beggar is useful to society, because we can teach our children to study and to work in order to avoid falling to that level." It would almost seem that this person's scheme of things was made to order for the "theory" of reference group behavior (see Merton, 1968: Chapter X).

One conspicuous deviant case was provided by the peasants: they were much more likely than other respondents to say that their work was more useful than that of others. It is possible that being involved in activities that are immediately directed to self-sustenance gives one a particularly strong feeling of pride in the value of one's work. However, it is also likely that the peasants' stance was at least as much a matter of protestation as of conviction. It is worth noting that those peasants who reported their work to be more useful than that of others were less job satisfied than their colleagues who said merely that their work was equally useful with that of others.

Prestige and Work Alienation

We have at our disposal two puzzling facts regarding social prestige. On the one hand, as indicated by Harris (1964) and by Lopreato and Lewis (1963), social prestige would seem to be the basis for imputations of the functional importance of occupations by the man on the street. On the other hand, as we have just seen, gradations in occupational prestige have little effect on the kinds of judgments that workers make about the relative functional importance of their *own* work.

In his discussion of the Davis-Moore theory, Tumin (1953a) made a point which is helpful in reconciling these two findings.[3] He noted that any position is functionally important in the sense that the welfare of the community is dependent on having at least some practitioners of each occupation. Thus, even though the engineer in the factory is *relatively* more important than the unskilled worker, in an *absolute sense* the factory cannot function without the services of the workers any more than it can function properly without the

---

[3]Tumin provides a compelling explanation of the capacity of lower-status persons to rank their own job tasks above all others in importance. Three rank orderings are normally extant in a society, he says. As these rank orderings would apply to occupations, they are: (1) ranking by reference to a high priority list of immediate goals; (2) the assignment of equal importance to all tasks; and (3) a derivative of the second ranking which Tumin describes as follows: role players are encouraged, while believing and acting as "if their roles are as important as those played in any other phase of the system," to "ascribe the highest order of system importance, insofar as they personally are concerned, to their roles . . ." (Tumin with Feldman, 1961:489). In this way, Tumin argues, all actors can be motivated to perform their roles properly, even those roles which otherwise are not publicly rewarded. Tumin continues to note "that a role can be both equal and greater in importance presents no difficulty if we realize that it is *equal* from the *overall* point of view, and *more important* from the point of view of the player himself. Not only is there official *permission* for him to conceive his role as more important, but there is official *pressure* and institutional *support* for him to do so" (Tumin with Feldman, 1961:490).

services of the engineer. What may in fact occur is that notions of functional importance in a relative sense (which is the sense in which the concept is used by Davis and Moore) are used by men when they are asked to rank the occupations of others, but importance in the absolute sense becomes more salient when they are quizzed about the contribution of their own jobs. In assessing the usefulness of his own job, a man can avoid invidious comparisons by affirming the importance, in an absolute sense, of his own work. When, in assessing the usefulness of other people's jobs, the same individual shows himself to be quite sensitive to the value implications of differences in prestige, he is perhaps providing himself with a means for coping with the objective fact that others have more (or less) of the scarce goods of the society than he does. Men are better able to accept the fact of unequal rewards if they can correlate them in their minds with notions of unequal contribution. Accordingly, recourse to the relative importance of positions probably serves to further the legitimation of the unequal distribution of rewards.

Assuming for the moment that what we suggest is a fact, we might well ask how workers' perceptions of the social recognition that they receive by virtue of their occupation varies by occupational status. It would seem a little more difficult for a man to ignore or sidestep the reality of the prestige of his occupation than to sidestep the issue of the *relative functional importance* of his work.

The question that was asked of our respondents in order to tap their perceptions of their own status on the occupational prestige ladder was the following: "In your opinion, how much respect do people have for the type of work you do?" The response options formed a five-point scale ranging from "very much respect" to "very little respect," with the central response worded "considerable respect." As was the case in the question on functional importance, the respondents were trichotomized with "considerable respect" providing the middle category.

As a general principle, it may be stated that the probability of perceiving that one's work is respected varies directly with occupational status. Thus, the proportions of workers who reported that they received much or very much respect were 42 percent for the combined elites and bourgeoisie, 34 percent for the petty bourgeoisie, 29 percent for the skilled workers, 22 percent for the semiskilled workers, 11 percent for the unskilled workers and farm hands, and 13 percent for the peasants. The corresponding figures of those who reported they received little or very little respect were: 9, 16, 14, 21, 44, and 50, respectively. As compared to the distribution of responses on the question regarding functional importance, the respondents' perceptions of their place in the prestige hierarchy would seem to have been more predictable. The two sets of findings together lend additional support to the argument referred to in Chapter V that in the people's own sociological laboratory, so to speak, it is prestige rather than notions of functional importance that is the more salient, and therefore the more important, variable.

The distribution of respondents along the three-category gradient of perceived prestige brings us close to the substantive concerns borrowed from Tumin's work which helped to launch the investigation in the present chapter. The unequal distribution of the raw materials needed for a favorable self-image and a "sense of significant membership" is clearly visible in the positive relationship that exists between occupational prestige and the proportions of workers who described the respect they received from others in positive rather than negative terms. Returning to our interest in work alienation as a consequence of stratification, a consequence that is potentially dysfunctional for the social order, we can now predict that *the greater the prestige which a man perceives as being imputed to his occupational role, the greater his job satisfaction.*

Table XII:2 confirms this proposition. It can be seen that the amount of respect that a man perceives as forthcoming to him by virtue of his occupation bears a strong positive relationship to job satisfaction. The single, quite minor, exception to this generalization is that those petty bourgeois workers who placed themselves in the highest of the three prestige categories were not more job satisfied than their peers who said they received only considerable prestige.

Moreover, as was true with respect to the effects of perceived functional importance on job satisfaction, the crucial dividing point is that which separates responses with a positive affective tone (much respect and considerable respect) from those with a negative tone (little respect). With a single exception, the case of the skilled workers, the percentage differences in job satisfaction between respondents who perceived considerable respect and those who perceived little respect are on the order of 15 percentage points or better. Again with the exception of the skilled workers and the peasants, the difference in proportionate satisfaction between those two categories is at least double that which occurs between those who perceived much and those who perceived considerable respect.

DISTRIBUTIVE JUSTICE AND JOB ALIENATION

Reward structures may be viewed as having important consequences for two distinct need systems: on the one hand, they may serve to satisfy *societal* needs; Davis and Moore focus on these. On the other, they may serve to satisfy *individual* needs; Marx focuses on these. Marx's interest in the consequences of social stratification for individual need systems was wedded to a principle that gave the needs of the individual an explicit sociological relevance. The principle, simply stated, is that the survival in any society of the institutions by means of which scarce values are distributed is ultimately dependent on the satisfaction of individual needs.

One way of undertaking an appraisal of stratification from the viewpoint

TABLE XII:2. JOB SATISFACTION OF RESPONDENTS IN VARIOUS OCCUPATIONAL STRATA WHO PERCEIVED DIFFERENTIALLY THE OCCUPATIONAL PRESTIGE OF THEIR JOBS

Occupational Stratum	Respect Accorded by Others to Respondents' Jobs					
	Much Respect		Considerable Respect		Little Respect	
	Number of Respondents	Percent Job Satisfied	Number of Respondents	Percent Job Satisfied	Number of Respondents	Percent Job Satisfied
Elites and Bourgeoisie	89	73	106	61	19	37
Petty Bourgeoisie	61	62	91	64	30	37
Skilled Workers	73	66	145	50	35	40
Semiskilled Workers	49	63	131	56	48	38
Unskilled Workers and Farm Hands	23	65	97	58	95	35
Peasants	29	62	85	52	114	37

of men in the flesh is to ask whether men perceive a reasonable and acceptable *balance* between what society demands of them in their work roles and what society rewards them with in return. For instance, individuals who feel that the social recognition which they receive is less than proportionate to the social contribution which they think they make, or who perceive that recognition to be inadequate in an absolute sense, are perceiving a condition of distributive *injustice:* either the reward does not compensate them fairly, or it does not compensate them adequately, for the investment they make in the collective enterprise (see Homans, 1961:75).[4] Such a situation certainly touches on one aspect, germane to the concerns of Marx, of the impact of unequal rewards on men. Using Marxian terminology, we might say that such persons are being socially exploited or deprived by society; accordingly, we would expect them to be more likely to become disaffected with their jobs and with the social order generally than persons who perceive what might be termed a "fair," or otherwise adequate, amount of social recognition attaching to their work. We can thus predict that:

Individuals who define the functional importance of their productive roles as high, and who perceive the social recognition accruing to those roles as high, are more likely to be satisfied with their jobs than individuals who see an imbalance between those two factors.

An additional proposition is particularly relevant from the vantage point of Marx's theory. Feelings of being a useful and respected member of society address themselves to the individual's need for a positive feeling of self-worth. It is clear that individuals who enjoy neither the satisfaction of feeling useful nor the satisfaction of being respected for their work are seriously impaired in the satisfaction of a basic human need. While from a societal vantage point such a situation may be a situation of balance between contribution and reward, and therefore just retribution, from the vantage point of the individual it is less likely to be perceived as justice than as deprivation.

In this connection, we should remember Davis and Moore's argument that theirs is a theory of how unequal rewards come to be assigned to differing positions, and not of how persons come to occupy different positions (Davis and Moore, 1945:242). This caveat makes recognition of the fact that, while a principle of justice (specifically, relative contribution) governs the distribution of rewards to positions, this does not necessarily mean that a principle of

---

[4]The importance of notions of "equity" between reward and contribution has been discussed by a number of scholars. In a volume on job attitudes, Vroom (1964:167–168), for instance, writes that "A somewhat different starting point is represented in the assumption that persons do not strive to maximize the attainment of desired outcomes like money, but rather strive to obtain an equitable or fair amount. Basic to this position is the belief that individuals are guided by a moral system which has as a basic tenet the fair distribution of rewards. If a person receives less than a fair amount he feels that an injustice has been done him; if he receives more than the fair amount he feels guilty." As Vroom points out, in the job satisfaction literature this perspective has received empirical attention primarily with respect to attitudes toward wages.

justice (such as equal opportunity in the field of social competition) governs the distribution of *persons* to positions, and hence of persons to unequal social rewards.

Insofar as individuals who neither contribute much nor receive much have been constrained to remain in lowly positions by rigidity in the class structure, the deprivation which they experience is clearly not equitable either from their perspective or from the Marxian perspective to which we owe so much in this volume. Furthermore, since such individuals are in a situation of greater deprivation than those who are at least convinced that their contributions are useful, they are preeminently those in whom Marx would predict the emergence of severe alienation. Accordingly, the proposition can be enunciated that:

Individuals who define the functional importance of their productive roles as low, and who perceive the social recognition accruing to their jobs also as low, are less likely to be satisfied with their jobs than individuals who define at least one of these factors as high.

Perceptions of Distributive Injustice

When we cross-tabulate the respondents' reports of the functional importance and the prestige of their jobs we can introduce the question of imbalance between the two factors. Because the critical points on these two perceptual scales are the demarcations between self-supportive or positively toned responses on the one hand (much or considerable respect, more or equally useful) and self-derogatory or negatively toned responses on the other (little respect, less useful), these points will be used to dichotomize each scale into "high" and "low" categories. Cross-tabulating then the two dichotomies, we obtain the scheme and distribution of sample subjects shown in Figure XII:1.

Strictly for convenience, we have designated each cell with a label that roughly describes the individuals therein with at least a bit of fidelity to class theory. Those individuals who perceived as high both their contribution to society and the received social reward were in effect reporting a positive balance between the cost and profit of their work investment, and may be termed *integrated*. Those who reported that their job contributed relatively little to the social good and also reported that they received little respect by virtue of their work were reporting a negative balance between the cost and the profit of their work, and may be defined, balance notwithstanding, as *alienated*.

Those who defined their contribution as high but perceived the respect accorded to their job as low are, by their accounting at least, socially *exploited*. We have here individuals to whom the concept of distributive injustice is perhaps most explicitly applicable. As they saw it, their cost of participation in the social contract, so to speak, exceeded their profit. Conversely, there are

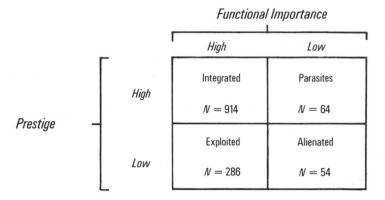

Figure XII:1.

those who, by their own accounting, were *parasites* in the sense that the imbalance perceived between what they contributed and how they were rewarded was one of an excess of reward over contribution. For our purposes, the Integrated and the Alienated are the most crucial categories.

The occupational distribution of respondents within each of the four categories is given in Table XII:3. As we already know from the occupational distributions found in Tables XII:1 and XII:2, each research category is composed of workers from throughout the occupational hierarchy. Representation

TABLE XII:3. OCCUPATIONAL PROFILES OF CATEGORIES RELATING
FUNCTIONAL IMPORTANCE AND PRESTIGE

Occupational Stratum	Categories Relating Functional Importance and Prestige			
	Integrated	Parasites	Exploited	Alienated
Elites and Bourgeoisie	20%	16%	3%	10%
Petty Bourgeoisie	15	21	9	10
Skilled Workers	22	22	11	8
Semiskilled Workers	17	30	13	21
Unskilled Workers and Farm Hands	13	8	26	38
Peasants	12	3	38	13
Total	99%	100%	100%	100%
N	914	64	286	54

from the nonmanual strata accounts for 35 percent of the Integrated, 37 percent of the Parasites, 12 percent of the Exploited, and 20 percent of the Alienated. Skilled and semiskilled workers accounted for the largest proportion of the manual workers in both high-functional-importance categories. Of interest, in view of the high level of job dissatisfaction among the peasants noted in the previous chapter, is the marked tendency of these respondents to consider themselves exploited, according to our terminology. Indeed, 46 percent of the 107 individuals in this occupational stratum saw themselves as exploited. From another perspective, nearly four-tenths of the exploited are peasants.

Job Satisfaction

As we pointed out previously, the respondents characterized as low in functional importance and low in prestige should represent individuals truly alienated from work. By their own admission, not only do they lack a feeling of significant membership as honored members of the social community, but they are also deprived of a self-redeeming feeling of self-worth. The proportion of job complainers computed for each of the functional-importance-prestige categories reveals that, consonant with our prediction, such individuals were in fact the least job satisfied. Only 27 percent of the Alienated could find nothing about their jobs about which to complain. By contrast, rates of job satisfaction for the other three groupings were 61 percent for the Integrated, 44 percent for the Parasites, and 38 percent among the Exploited. It is noteworthy, moreover, that the exploited workers, who deemed their social contribution to be at least as high as that of anyone else, but their social reward to be low, fulfilled both of the expectations we would have of them from a perspective that borrows both from Davis and Moore and from Marx. On the one hand, they were less satisfied with their jobs than either the Integrated or the Parasites, both of whom felt they received more ample reward. On the other, they were more satisfied with their jobs than the Alienated, who were likewise poorly rewarded but did not have the saving conviction of making a worthwhile social contribution through their work.

On balance, it can be seen that two forces are in operation in the job attitudes of the four research categories under consideration. First, those who thought their work contributions to be at least respectable were more job satisfied than those workers who failed to share that conviction. Second, those who perceived themselves to be the recipients of high rewards were more job satisfied than those who perceived their social reward to be meager, *irrespective of their perceptions of the relative functional importance of their jobs.* Consequently, while perceptions of social contribution *are* important, *they are, nevertheless, not so important as perceptions of the honor received as practitioners of a given profession.* The need for social recognition, which has been often

TABLE XII:4. OCCUPATIONAL DIFFERENCES IN JOB SATISFACTION AMONG RESPONDENTS WITH VARYING PERCEPTIONS OF FUNCTIONAL IMPORTANCE AND PRESTIGE COMBINATIONS

Job Satisfaction	*Categories Relating Functional Importance and Prestige*							
	Integrated		*Parasites*		*Exploited*		*Alienated*	
	Nonmanual	*Manual*	*Nonmanual*	*Manual*	*Nonmanual*	*Manual*	*Nonmanual*	*Manual*
No Complaints about Job	67%	58%	46%	42%	46%	37%	—	33%
Some Complaints about Job	33	42	54	58	54	63	100	67
Total	100%	100%	100%	100%	100%	100%	100%	100%
N	327	587	24	40	37	249	10	42

postulated in sociology (see Pareto, 1916; Thomas, 1923), appears to be a powerful human force indeed.

Table XII:4, which gives the job-satisfaction rates for the nonmanual and manual workers within each functional-importance-prestige category, reveals substantially the same relationships. The expected relationships between job satisfaction and perceptions of the degree of balance existing between contribution and reward are present in both occupational groupings. Moreover, the familiar class effect remains: within each functional-importance-prestige category, subjects holding a "middle-class" position were less dissatisfied than "working-class" subjects.

DISTRIBUTIVE JUSTICE, SUCCESS IDEOLOGY, AND ATTITUDES TOWARD AUTHORITY

One question which class-conflict theory brings to the scientific model of social reality proposed by Davis and Moore has great heuristic value: what happens when the demands of one functional necessity eventuate in consequences which are dysfunctional with respect to another, equally important, functional requirement? More specifically, the notion of functional requisite itself bids us examine the consequences of distributive systems as these impinge on other critical properties of the social order.

The foundations of the Davis and Moore theory are constituted by two propositions, one addressed to a "functional requisite" of society, and the other to the nature of human motivation. Specifically, in order for any given society to maintain some form of equilibrium, (1) its important positions must be competently filled, and (2) if this functional requisite is to be met, then the more important positions must be given higher rewards than the less important ones in order to properly motivate adequately talented individuals to train for them.

Beyond these functional requisites, an additional one may be attributed to a society as a going concern from a broader perspective: (3) a sufficient proportion of the population must accept the existing distributive system and its complex authority structure so that at any given time the forces of dissension and conflict will not prevail over the forces of consensus and integration. This may be viewed as the functional requisite of *legitimacy*. Without a substratum of consent and/or resignation to institutionalized inequality and authority, the authority structure and the class structure over which it presides cannot long endure unmolested. Accordingly, it can be said that a proviso which is left implicit is critical to the Davis-Moore theory: namely, that the requisite of legitimacy not be seriously threatened by institutionalized inequality. If it is thus threatened, social stratification quite obviously cannot be as positively functional as Davis and Moore claim. Pursuing our interest in the dysfunctional consequences of unequal reward, it is therefore appropriate that we

Quality Most Important for Getting Ahead in Life	Categories Relating Functional Importance and Prestige							
	Integrated		Parasites		Exploited		Alienated	
	Percent	Rank	Percent	Rank	Percent	Rank	Percent	Rank
Good Education	9%	6	11%	4	12%	4	4%	8.5
Intelligence	12	4	8	5.5	11	5.5	12	3.5
Personal Initiative	19	1	24	1	16	1.5	10	6
Occupational Skill	18	2	13	3	8	8	12	3.5
Honesty	11	5	5	8	10	7	10	6
Subtotal	69%		61%		57%		48%	
Knowing the Right People, "Pull"	6%	8	8%	5.5	11%	5.5	21%	1
Good Fortune	8	7	5	8	13	3	14	2
Servility, Dishonesty	1	10	3	10	1	10	4	8.5
Material Aid of Parents	2	9	5	8	2	9	2	10
Savoir Faire	14	3	18	2	16	1.5	10	6
Subtotal	31%		39%		43%		51%	
Total	100%		100%		100%		99%	
N	874		62		273		49	

investigate the effects of perceptions of distributive injustice on attitudes which have relevance to the question of the legitimacy of prevailing political and economic arrangements.

Distributive Justice and Success Ideology

In all industrialized societies to date, a tremendous expansion and differentiation of the occupational structure has been accompanied by a "secularization" of values. It is generally agreed that this process marks the end of an ancient moral system wherein institutionalized social inequality is legitimized as an ascribed and unalterable condition of life, and marks the beginning of an era when such legitimation is founded on an ideology of achievement.

A possible societal dysfunction of such an ideology of unequal rewards is precisely that it may lead to the erosion of belief in it among those who, by virtue of hard experience, are acquainted with the difficulties of ascending the social ladder. Accordingly, it may be predicted that:

The Alienated are the least likely to accept the ideology of success which typifies industrial societies, and the Integrated are the most likely to accept this ideology.

The following question which was asked of our respondents can be used to test this hypothesis. Upon being presented with a card listing factors—such as education, skill, and family influence—which might figure in the success or failure of career ambitions, they were asked: "Among the alternatives listed on [this card], which one do you consider the most important for getting ahead in life?" The distribution of responses to this question by categories relating functional importance and prestige is given in Table XII:5. The list of alternatives has been grouped into those which are "universalistic" in the criterion for career advancement that they enunciate and those that are "particularistic" in nature. In order to facilitate systematic comparisons between research categories, ranks have been assigned to the items on the basis of their popularity among the members of each category.

A glance at Table XII:5 reveals that the proportions of respondents choosing a universalistic criterion decreases as the table is read from left to right— from the integrated to the alienated workers. Conversely, the tendency to choose a particularistic criterion increases in the same direction. While 69 percent of the Integrated saw success as contingent on factors which bespeak individual merit (education, skill, initiative, and the like), only 48 percent of the Alienated were of the same mind. Furthermore, the latter were outvoted within their own ranks by those who opted rather for such opportunistic or aleatory factors as "pull" or luck.[5] This greater skepticism among the Alien-

---

[5]A similar finding is reported by Dale (1962:51) in his study of 208 male clerks in five industries in Britain. The clerks were asked to choose and rank the three most important determinants of position from a list of five. Weighting each first choice by 3, each second choice by 2, and each

ated with respect to the salience of merit as a factor explaining success gives us additional evidence that we were not far afield in identifying their condition as an aspect of the alienation described by Marx.

There are additional contrasts between the Alienated and the remainder of the sample that come to light. Personal initiative was the most popular choice for all respondent categories except the Alienated; among the Alienated, initiative ranked sixth in popularity. Furthermore, it shared that rank with *savoir faire* and with honesty. Remembering that all the research categories except the Alienated reported that they were high either on functional importance, or on prestige, or on both, it is not surprising that echoes of an ideology of success should appear as the theme of the favorite choice of these groupings. It would seem that where achievement or honor is to be reaped, most human beings would prefer to take credit for it themselves rather than to write off their success to luck or to such factors as education, which imply an initial position of advantage. Conversely, whether by way of ego-defense or worldly wisdom, those who are completely "down and out," like the Alienated in the present scheme, selectively perceive the fortuitous and the particularistic factors in the structure of opportunity. Thus, the Alienated gave their highest number of votes to "pull" and the second highest number to good fortune in explaining the distribution of achievements in their society.

It is also instructive to observe the assessments given to the education factor. It will be shown in a subsequent chapter that education beyond the five years of primary school greatly increases chances of social mobility. Yet to gauge from their own testimony, our respondents were relatively insensitive to the importance of education in underwriting the success or failure of their own careers. Education was the sixth most frequently mentioned item among the integrated respondents, and had a rank of 8.5 on the basis of its popularity among the Alienated. For both intermediate categories it placed fourth in order of frequency of mention. By contrast, another variable which has rather direct relevance to the concept of functional importance, namely occupational skill, ranked second (after initiative) among the Integrated, third among the Parasites, and shared third place with intelligence among the Alienated. The Exploited, for reasons which can perhaps be inferred from the functional-importance-prestige category in which they placed themselves, relegated occupational skill to a rank of eighth; we have here concrete evidence of the feeling on the part of these workers that others do not appreciate sufficiently the value of their work activities. Finally, the proportion of Alienated respondents who

---

third choice by 1, he obtained a composite score for each factor. "Merit" led the field with a composite score of 375, followed by "influence" with 232, and "personality" with 192. "Seniority" and "luck" were given composite ratings of 183 and 96, respectively. Although the comparability of these figures with our own is limited by the smaller number of options allowed by Dale, it can be seen that the universalistic criteria included by each investigator were perceived as being the most important determinants of advancement in both studies.

chose "pull" as the factor most important for getting ahead was larger than the proportions who chose education and occupational skill combined. Of the Alienated, 1 out of 5 saw opportunity for advancement as being predicated on "pull"; more than 1 out of 3 chose either "pull" or good fortune.

It is clear that the most telling differences in Table XII:5 lie between the Alienated and the remaining respondents. It was among those who admitted to less than the average degree of usefulness as well as to less than "considerable" social recognition that belief in achievement took a severe battering. An examination of the responses of nonmanual and manual workers taken separately revealed nothing which would substantially alter these conclusions.

Distributive Justice and Attitudes toward Authority

In testing the final proposition to be offered shortly, we shall have occasion to bring evidence of a more direct nature to one of the propositions offered by Tumin (1953a:393) in his critique of the Davis-Moore theory: "To the extent that loyalty to a society depends on a sense of significant membership in the society, social stratification systems function to distribute loyalty unequally in the population." Although we have no direct index of "loyalty," we do have information which relates in a rather important fashion to it. Specifically, we can inquire into the extent to which our respondents' perceptions of their place in the productive-distributive system of their society was related to their perceptions of (1) the legitimacy of authority in their work context, and (2) the willingness to acquiesce to the imperative demands of that authority. Pursuing the same reasoning that guided our earlier formulation of hypotheses linking contribution and reward to job attitudes, we offer the following proposition:

The Alienated are the least likely to view the exercise of authority by their superiors as legitimate, and to express an acquiescent attitude toward the commands of their superiors; and the Integrated are the most likely to manifest such behavior.

We are guided by the assumption that recalcitrance or rebelliousness with respect to work-authority structures—that is, the persons or agencies that execute societal functions—injures those societal functions. Hence we are looking beyond the issue of loyalty on the job as such to the social dysfunctions that its opposite implies.

The question relating to authority which was addressed to the respondents is by now familiar: "Which of these phrases best describes what you think of your work superiors?" As may be recalled, the response options allowed the respondents to indicate whether or not they accepted as legitimate the actions taken by their superiors in their formal capacities, and also to indicate whether or not they were of a mind to obey or to reject the commands flowing from that authority. Table XII:6 shows the findings on this basis.

TABLE XII:6. ATTITUDES TOWARD AUTHORITY ASSOCIATED WITH
CATEGORIES RELATING FUNCTIONAL IMPORTANCE AND PRESTIGE

Attitude toward Superiors	Categories Relating Functional Importance and Prestige			
	Integrated	Parasites	Exploited	Alienated
1. They Do Their Duty, and I Obey	47%	39%	29%	18%
2. They Do Their Duty, but It Is Hard to Obey	11	12	6	13
3. They Take Advantage of Their Position, but One Must Have Patience	26	35	38	40
4. They Take Advantage of Their Position, and That Makes Me Mad	8	10	16	27
5. No Response	5	4	6	—
6. Unclassifiable Response	3	—	5	2
Total	100%	100%	100%	100%
N	745	51	238	45

Note: Respondents to whom the question did not apply (that is, respondents who were self-employed) have been excluded from the analysis.

It can be seen that if the four functional-importance-prestige groupings were taken to constitute a scale on a "sense of significant membership" and on loyalty, ranging from a low score among the Alienated to a high score among the Integrated members of the sample, then this variable would bear a strong relation to attitudes toward authority. Focusing first on the proportions from each of the four categories who said of their superiors that "they do their duty," we see that these range from a high of 58 percent among the Integrated to a low of 31 percent among the Alienated. Alternatively, combining those proportions of each category who, whatever their opinion on the legitimacy of their superiors' commands, nevertheless expressed a willingness to obey (options 1 and 3), a similar though less marked gradient appears: 73 percent of the Integrated, as contrasted to 58 percent of the Alienated, thus expressed an acquiescent attitude toward their superiors. Contrary to one prediction contained in our hypothesis, no significant difference appears between the proportion of the Integrated and the proportion of the Exploited who expressed acquiescence toward superiors.

Two conclusions emerge from Table XII:6. The first is that, while substan-

TABLE XII:7. OCCUPATIONAL DIFFERENCES IN ATTITUDES TOWARD
AUTHORITY AMONG PERSONS IN CATEGORIES RELATING FUNCTIONAL
IMPORTANCE AND PRESTIGE

Attitude toward Superiors	Categories Relating Functional Importance and Prestige							
	Nonmanual				Manual			
	Integrated	Parasites	Exploited	Alienated	Integrated	Parasites	Exploited	Alienated
1. They Do Their Duty, and I Obey	46%	47%	12%	11%	48%	36%	31%	19%
2. They Do Their Duty, but It Is Hard to Obey	16	27	12	22	9	6	6	11
3. They Take Advantage of Their Position, but One Must Have Patience	19	13	32	56	29	44	39	36
4. They Take Advantage of Their Position, and That Makes Me Mad	7	13	20	11	8	8	15	31
5. No Response	7	—	8	—	3	6	6	—
6. Unclassifiable Response	4	—	16	—	3	—	4	3
Total	99%	100%	100%	100%	100%	100%	101%	100%
N	258	15	25	9	487	36	213	36

tial proportions of all four functional-importance-prestige categories were likely to question the propriety of at least some of the commands of their superiors (options 3 and 4), fewer were ready to take an insubordinate posture toward that authority (options 2 and 4). In the sense that the rejection of the legitimacy of authority would for most persons precede the rejection of the authority itself, this finding is not surprising. However, it should be noted that a full 40 percent (options 2 and 4) of the Alienated, in contrast to much smaller proportions of the other three groups, were willing to verbalize this extreme position. This fact points up the second major conclusion, namely, that the tendency to view as illegitimate *and* to reject imperative demands is negatively related to perceptions of adequate reward and functional contribution, thus giving support to our research proposition.

In Table XII:7 we observe the responses to the authority question for nonmanual and manual respondents considered separately. It can be seen that, if the data for the 9 nonmanual Alienated is ignored, the proposition regarding perceptions of legitimacy and acquiescence is generally upheld among both categories of workers. The nonmanual workers were, however, *less* likely than manual workers to subscribe to the statements that one must obey superiors, or at least bear patiently their commands (options 1 and 3). Among the integrated nonmanual workers, 65 percent advocated acquiescence, while the corresponding proportion among the integrated manual workers is 77. The percentage difference between nonmanual and manual workers among the Exploited is even more pronounced; 70 percent of the manuals but only 44 percent of the nonmanuals reported a submissive mood. This lower incidence of acquiescent attitudes toward authority on the part of the nonmanuals probably concerns the heavy burden of authority for those underlings who were in close proximity to those highly endowed with authority functions. We have come up with this type of finding repeatedly; it will be discussed in detail in the final chapter.

Our evidence so far indicates that feelings of distributive injustice and alienation are powerful incentives toward attitudes, and implicitly toward actions, which, at least from the vantage point of the more privileged, are dysfunctional to "societal" needs. As noted in Chapter III, the differential access to, and exercise of, authority in modern industrial societies has recently received attention by Ralf Dahrendorf (1959). This scholar has suggested that the sources of class conflict in industrial societies may be found in the unwillingness of those in positions of complete subjection to accept their subordination to those in positions of domination. To the extent that acquiescense to the exercise of authority may be expected to characterize "loyal" members of society, those members who perceive the authority structure as illegitimate in the first place are less likely to acquiesce when confronted by it, and therefore represent potentially "disruptive" elements in society.

In conclusion, we submit that a more nearly complete theory of stratification will have to take into account the "dysfunctional" as well as the "functional" aspects of social inequality. Ultimately, the fundamental problem, from a societal as well as an individual point of view, concerns the opportunities that are available for the members of a society. For Marx, as for Davis and Moore, the ultimate stability of a society depends upon the existence of adequate opportunities for its members. The existence of high rewards in a society in no way indicates that they are equally accessible to all members of society. For those who can take advantage of the opportunities available, there is probably no problem; for those who cannot, a system of differential rewards and the ensuing institutionalized social inequality symbolize their inferior status. The resulting material and psychological deprivation—and the perception of injustice—that is the lot of many such individuals is not likely to have an integrative influence in the collectivity.

In sum, while the dimensions of functional importance and prestige, as conceived by Davis and Moore, may help to explain *why* societies are stratified, they have significance for men in the flesh that emphasizes the maladaptive aspects of a system of differential rewards. In particular, these concepts have proved fruitful as subjective dimensions that distinguish some members of society from others in terms of their apparent willingness to accept the institutional arrangements of their society. In this achievement, Marx's work has proved very useful.

PART FOUR

Studies in Social Mobility

XIII

Social Mobility: Rates and Comparisons

The study of social mobility is fundamentally the study of class behavior viewed from the vantage point of the *structure* and *composition* of classes. The student who is sensitive to the Marxian tradition of class theories is apt to be interested in social mobility for the particular relation it bears to class consciousness. Although explicit recognition of this relationship is usually lacking in the literature, social mobility—especially the ascending variety—is a source of dissociative influence on class behavior. As was noted in Chapter VI, unlike class consciousness, which directs attention to the *formation* of classes, social mobility quite clearly refers to the *disruption* of classes.

The present chapter makes no effort to examine the aforementioned relationship. But it sets the stage for a later effort in this regard. Specifically, our present concern is to determine the rate and volume of vertical mobility in Italy and in various occupational sectors therein. The utility of this focus is not bound to descriptions of changing class structure; the focus also entails the study of relative opportunities in society. This latter concern is particularly appropriate to an undertanding of Italian society, since in recent decades this country has experienced a major expansion of its opportunity structure. We naturally wish to know in what ways and to what extent the distribution of new opportunities has been influenced by the prior system of inequalities.

PROBLEMS OF MEASUREMENT

Vertical social mobility is conventionally specified in occupational terms, on the assumption that position in the occupational structure is the best single indicator of the distribution of opportunities and rewards in society. Whatever the accuracy of that assumption—and it is certainly not beyond challenge— it ignores the possibility that for given categories of occupational mobility changes in status on other dimensions of stratification (such as education, participation in voluntary associations, income) can have important ramifications for the opportunity structure. One would not expect in most cases, for example, a high-school-educated assembly-line worker to hold the same evaluations of relative opportunities as his primary-school-educated father who performed similar assembly-line tasks.

The preceding clearly implies the existence of certain methodological problems in the study of social mobility. Before moving to the analysis of data, it would therefore be useful to highlight some of these problems. A variety of them have been discussed in the literature—some of the best presentations appear in Duncan (1966), Jackson and Curtis (1968), Blau and Duncan (1967) —and future study surely promises the isolation of still others. For present purposes, we shall limit ourselves to problems associated with (1) conceptual types of vertical occupational mobility, (2) measurement statistics, and (3) international comparisons.

Types of Mobility

Our focus here is on the conventional distinction between *intergenerational* and *intragenerational* mobility. The former refers to the degree of similarity between an individual's occupational position and that of his father, while the latter refers to occupational changes within an individual's work career. This distinction is important, since, in terms of satisfaction with a status quo, for instance, even an intergenerationally "successful" person may be quite dissatisfied if his position in the occupational structure remains constant throughout his career.

One of the problems associated with the conventional distinction pertains to the points in time at which the occupations of fathers and sons are to be compared for purposes of assessing intergenerational movement. This, in turn, relates to a more basic issue: in comparing the occupational distributions of the son and father generations, how shall we assess the relative significance of the son's advancement which results from opportunities connected with his father's occupation in relation to that which results from the independent efforts of the son himself? Obviously, the points in time on which the comparison is based will influence the amount of mobility observed, and any divergencies between scholars on this selection will result in disparate mobility rates, even for the same country.

In most studies of intergenerational mobility it has been customary to compare the respondent's present occupation with his father's *main* occupation. This approach entails some serious pitfalls, however. Some scholars (see Glass and Hall, 1954:179; Carlsson, 1958:78; and Lenski, 1958) have pointed out that the son's present occupational status has not reached its probable maximum if he is still very young, and it is often lower than that maximum if he is very old. In either case, the measurement is faulty to the extent of seriously misconstruing the degree of difference between father-and-son occupational distributions (see also Allingham, 1967). In one attempt to solve the difficulty, Glass and Hall (1954) have proposed that the analysis should be confined to a comparison between father's "last main occupation" and the present occupation of respondents 50 years of age or more, who alone may be expected to have achieved their own last main status.[1] But this suggestion does not address itself to the problem of distinguishing between intergenerational and intragenerational mobility; occupational changes after the son's first-held job are still to some extent a function of the son's own *career* mobility.

Other scholars have asked the respondent to give his father's occupation when he was the same age as the son's "age at time of interview." This method of inquiry represents some improvement over techniques that do not control for age at all, but it still leaves unsolved the basic problem of differentiating mobility within and between generations. As Lipset and Bendix (1959:183) point out, depending on the respondent's age, this method is apt to result in either an underestimation or an overestimation of the advantages accruing from the father's position, since the father's position at the time his son is in high school or begins his own occupational career is the one that will most likely influence the son's future career opportunities. These authors therefore suggest that what is needed is a complete career history of both generations. This is probably an unattainable goal, inasmuch as neither father nor son is likely to give valid information about the other's entire occupational career. Failing this desideratum, Lipset and Bendix propose using the "principal" occupation of father and the entire career pattern of son.

In one of the most rigorous discussions on the methodology of social mobility, Yasuda (1964) proposes that we compare the subject's first job with the job held by his father at the time the subject began his career.[2] On logical grounds, Yasuda's comparison is indeed appropriate, for by and large at that point in time, or cumulatively until that point in time, the status of the father

---

[1] A point very similar to this was subsequently made by Lenski (1958:518), who sought to control for the effects of intragenerational mobility by comparing the father's occupation during the time the son was growing up with the occupation of the son in his "fifth decade of life," by which time "occupational stability has been achieved in the lives of most men." A variation of this has been used by Jackson and Crockett (1964), who have compared respondent's present occupation with father's occupation while the son was growing up, by age cohorts.

[2] This approach is similar to one used by Rogoff (1953a), who compared males' occupations at the time of marriage with the occupations of the fathers.

totally establishes the status of the son. After that time, the son usually becomes an independent adult, and his own career efforts influence his status. Yet serious problems remain to be solved, indicating the great technical difficulties which, as Lipset and Bendix (1959) note, may not be soluble in any absolute sense. For instance, Yasuda's suggestion neglects the fact that *even after* an individual has become an "independent adult," his family background may still influence his subsequent career in a "hidden effect." Thus, Perrucci (1961:881) found that within the engineering profession the sons of fathers in high-status occupations were overrepresented in high-prestige positions, while the sons of fathers in low-status occupations were underrepresented in those positions. Similarly, there is reason to believe that of two equally competent college graduates who enter the banking business at an equally low level of employment—one the son of a banker and the other the son of a skilled worker —the former has the greater chance of "reaching the top."

Perhaps part of the difficulty of selecting appropriate points of reference for the measurement of mobility stems from a lack of conceptual clarity with regard to use of the notion of an "intergenerational" status comparison. At least two analytically separate meanings can be distinguished in that notion, and, although these meanings are related to each other, they do not isolate identical phenomena (see Lopreato and Hazelrigg, 1970).

The first has to do with social inheritance, that is, with the effect of the subject's social origin on his career entry (and residually on his subsequent career). As Yasuda indicated, it requires a measure based on the relationship between the son's first occupation and the occupation of the father at the time the son began his career (in the terms of Figure XIII:1, u' in relation to w). This measure gives us one estimation of how "open" the opportunity structure is. If there is a high (positive) correlation between the two distributions, the opportunities for individual achievement are undoubtedly lower than if the correlation approaches zero. The comparison to the father must be the son's first occupation and not some other, such as present occupation, because the measure of social inheritance must be free of the influence of the son's career success or failure. The reverse of that—that the son's career success is independent of social inheritance—need not be true, as Perrucci's study reveals. But this is a problem that, in the measurement of *intra*generational mobility, can be circumvented by standardizing the occupational distribution of the parent generation. Indeed, an important question in the study of career mobility is the strength of influence of social inheritance on subsequent career experience.

The second meaning of "intergenerational" mobility, on the other hand, refers to the retrospective comparison of the son's *current* occupation to an occupational position held by his father at some point in the father's career (in the figure, z' in relation to $u, x, w,$ or z). Thus what is called "intergenerational" by this operation encompasses two components of potential status change: changes that take place at career entry (that is, differences between

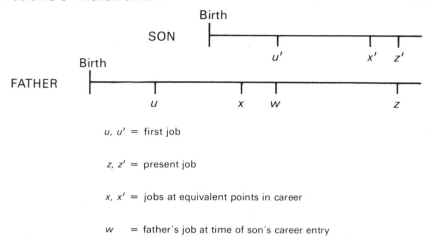

u, u' = first job

z, z' = present job

x, x' = jobs at equivalent points in career

w = father's job at time of son's career entry

Figure XIII:1. Relationships between Career Patterns of Father and Son Generations

u' and w), and within-career or *intra*generational changes (that is, differences between u' and z'). By this meaning of "intergenerational" mobility, a person labeled an intergenerational achiever (or skidder) may have ascended (or skidded) at career entry, after which time he remained stationary; on the other hand, he may have inherited his career-entry status and experienced the status change *during career only*. These two patterns of mobility are sufficiently distinctive, theoretically at least, to warrant separate treatment (see Lopreato and Hazelrigg, 1970).

What point in the father's career (*u, x, w,* or *z,* in Figure XIII:1) should be selected as the comparison to the son's current occupation? The answer is that the choice will depend ideally on the nature of the theoretical issues under consideration. As a matter of general rule, we may reject the father's first job *(u)* and current job *(z)*. But that rule leaves such possibilities as the father's job when he was at a point in elapsed career time equivalent to that of the son (for example, x in relation to x') and the father's job at the time of the son's career entry *(w)*. Again as a general rule, if the theoretical issues under examination are concerned with such phenomena as socialization and resocialization, the latter alternative comparison *(z' to w)* is preferable. If the issues incorporated assumptions of social-comparison behavior on the part of the son with respect to his father, however, the former measure is preferable because it standardizes for *both* distributions the amount of elapsed career time. To the extent that the son does compare himself to his father for purposes, say, of assessing his own fortunes (see Wilensky, 1966), he is constrained toward a reasonably fair test, and this means in part some rough standardization of career age. A son young in career would not always find it very satisfying to juxtapose his current status to that of a father who was at the height of his career; if he did (because of ascent at career entry, probably), he would likely find the comparison even more satisfying by making it age-standardized. In short, the query the son asks of himself in such instances of success estimation is of the form, "How well am I doing in comparison to my father when he was my career age?"

Finally, we come to intragenerational or career mobility, which is generally subject to less confusion. It represents the change in the occupational distribution of a population from one point in time (for example, first job) to another (for example, present job). As was noted above, the effects of social origin can extend beyond the first job to the subsequent development of career patterns. But the bulk of these effects can in part be "partialed out" through the insertion of a statistical control for social origins, thereby leaving a relatively "pure" measure of intragenerational mobility.

There is, however, a qualification to the notion of *intragenerational* mobility that should be mentioned. In national surveys of stratification, the population under study includes all adults (or adult males) of labor-force age; or at least it encompasses people from a wide range of ages. Thus, it does not represent a single generation in the conventionally accepted sense of that term. In fact, a significant proportion of the population can consist of a second generation (fathers of the younger respondents), and if the average age of labor-force entry is relatively low, a certain part of the population can consist of a third and even a fourth generation (grandfathers and great grandfathers). This wide dispersion of ages has important practical consequences for comparisons of career mobility rates between different populations or, for that matter, within one population at different points in time.[3] Since not all members of a given population have had an equal opportunity to attain their own destined pinnacles of success (or depths of failure) simply as a function of differential age, the fact that two populations seldom have identical age distributions confounds cross-sectional and longitudinal comparisons (see Hammel, 1969). Other things being equal, for example, we should expect a lower rate of career mobility for a population in which 17.6 percent of the male labor force is under 25 years of age (the United States in 1960) than for a population in which this proportion is smaller. Comparative analyses of career-mobility rates therefore include some provision for the standardization of age.

Measurement Statistics

Acute testimony to the conceptual complexity of social mobility can be gathered from a survey of attempts to develop measures that will adequately

---

[3]This problem also characterizes many studies of "intergenerational" mobility, wherein its complication is even greater. As Figure XIII:1 illustrates, the actual generations represented in a sampled population variously overlap, and it is entirely possible that some of the respondents in a large sample are not only "sons" but also the fathers of other "sons" in the sample (see Blau and Duncan, 1967:82–84).

express the volume or rate of vertical mobility. Little improvement in such measures has been registered over the past several years. In what follows we do not offer a complete survey of these attempts;[4] nor do we make any substantial contribution to the researcher's current bag of tools. We must instead content ourselves with brief considerations of some of the available statistics and techniques, especially as these relate to our later analyses of data.

The techniques of measurement may be conveniently divided into two major categories: those that directly compare tabular distributions and those that result in summary statistics. The latter approach has the important advantage of facilitating cross-sectional and longitudinal comparisons, since it is easier to contrast single values than entire matrices. However, the summary statistics currently available contain flaws of one sort or another that restrict their usefulness.

Major examples of the technique that directly compares tabular distributions are the transition matrices of inflow and outflow rates employed by Lenski (1958) and Miller (1960). Inflow matrices consist of the proportions of respondents in given current occupations who came from specific origins, either parental or career entry. They describe the patterns of recruitment into and current composition of a series of occupational categories. Although this type of analysis has some utility for examinations of the consequences of mobility patterns, it is generally unsuited to an analysis of mobility rates, since it is the distribution of sons and not fathers that has been sampled. That shortcoming is especially handicapping in comparative studies. Outflow analysis, on the other hand, is not subject to this limitation, since the proportions are of respondents from a given origin (parental or career entry) who are in specific current occupations. The advantages of this mode of analysis have made it a very popular approach, followed by Lipset and Bendix (1959), Miller (1960), and Blau and Duncan (1967), among others.

One statistical application to outflow analysis that facilitates comparisons in time or place is Feldmesser's (1955:223–225) "index of equality of opportunity." Essentially, for each origin stratum in a distribution this index standardizes the frequency of social inheritance as unity and then expresses deviations as percents of that standard. The lower the index value for a particular cell in a mobility matrix, the less likely it is that people with those origins will enter the specified destination stratum, in comparison with the "inheritors" of that stratum. Recent use of this measure of relative opportunity can be found in Fox and Miller's (1965) intercountry comparisons.

Among the summary-statistics techniques, the second major method of measurement mentioned above, the simplest is the ratio of the number of respondents not in their stratum of origin (career or parental) to the total

---

[4]Technical discussions of many of them can be found in Duncan (1966), Yasuda (1964), Blau and Duncan (1967), and Jackson and Curtis (1968), and in some sources cited therein.

number of respondents in the sample. In an r-by-k contingency table, where r is the origin distribution and k is the destination distribution, this ratio is the sum of all cells lying outside the positive diagonal divided by the total N of the table; it is commonly referred to as the rate of *total observed mobility*. It can be expressed in its separate directional components, with those cells lying above and to the right of the diagonal representing downward mobility and those in the lower left corner of the table representing upward mobility.

The utility of this measure is restricted by the fact that it fuses the various sources of potential mobility in society. To borrow an illustration from Jackson and Curtis (1968:140), is a high rate of total observed mobility "associated with urbanization, for example, because viable industrial economies must allocate crucial roles on the basis of achievement criteria or because the relative demand for clerical and managerial work increases with size and complexity of the labor force?" If we are interested in the answers to such questions, a refinement in the total observed rate is in order. We must distinguish between the component which is due to *structural demand*—that is, quantitative changes over time in the distribution of occupations—and the component which results from the "free" *circulation* of individuals up and down the occupational hierarchy. This point was made by Pareto (1916:2046) over half a century ago and more recently by numerous others (such as Kahl, 1953: 252–262; Jackson and Curtis, 1968). Unfortunately there does not appear to be any way of translating this important conceptual distinction into an unambiguous empirical operation. The conventional approach has been to factor out that proportion of a transition matrix that can be accounted for by the index of dissimilarity of marginal distributions, call it the "structural-demand" component, and then treat the remainder of the observed mobility as "free circulation" and an estimation of the "openness" of the occupational structure. However, as Blau and Duncan (1967:25–26) caution, that operation does not yield routinely interpretable values. The difference between the total observed rate and the structural-demand value includes not only the free interchange of individuals but, as well, an unknown number of moves that represent "indirect repercussions of changes in demand."[5]

---

[5]Consider the following comparison of two hypothetical matrices, for example. In matrix A, all of the observed mobility is accounted for by the dissimilarity of marginal distributions; thus, the rate of structural-demand mobility equals the rate of total observed mobility, and the circulation rate is zero. In matrix B, only half of the total observed rate is attributable to "demand," and the other half is therefore labeled "circulation." But, *given exactly those matrix constraints,* it is entirely possible to construct the cell frequencies of matrix B in such a way that one-half of the total observed mobility is interpretable as the demanded movement of manual-origin sons into nonmanual positions and the remaining half as demanded movement of agrarian-origin sons into the vacancies left by the upwardly mobile manual-origin sons. In other words, the summary rate of circulation mobility that was given by the conventional measure refers in this case to phantom people. Of course, the assumption that allows this complete contradiction between the transition rates and the summary rate of circulation is the assumption of no downward mobility—an empirically unrealistic assumption. The notion of a free circulation of individuals implies both

In comparing two or more societies, or in comparing one society at different points in time, one could relate measures of total observed mobility. But in general this comparison would not be very useful, since two societies with identical total observed rates could well be vastly different in their structural-demand rates and, hence, in their free-circulation rates. Consider, as an example from Pareto, that in a society "where there is little industry and little commerce, the supply of individuals possessing in high degree the qualities requisite for those types of activity exceeds the demand." In such a society, mobility rates would be low *even if* there were perfect equality of opportunity in it. "Then industry and commerce develop and the supply, though remaining the same, no longer meets the demand" (Pareto, 1916:2045); in this society, mobility (of the *structural, forced* type) is now very high *even though the society be antiegalitarian.*

Unless one is interested only in questions regarding the total volume of actual movement, some control for structural demand must be effected. In order to control for structural demand in a comparative setting, a benchmark has to be established. Two possibilities are: (1) the *model of perfect or full equality* and (2) the *model of maximum stability.* The first constructs a hypothetical matrix for a given population under the assumed condition of equal opportunity of circulation, whereas the second constructs a matrix under the assumed condition that *no* circulation has occurred. Both take the structural-demand factor (that is, the marginals of the contingency table) as given; therefore, both yield ambiguous conclusions, for reasons already stated.

In the maximum-stability model, the *expected* total rate of mobility is equivalent to the observed rate of structural demand. Cross-national comparisons, then, are made between ratios of structural demand to total observed mobility. In the full-equality model, calculation of the expected total rate of mobility involves an intermediate step. Given an r-by-k table of observed frequencies, an expected value for each nondiagonal (positive slope) cell is computed, following procedures of standard contingency analysis. These values are then summed—they may be divided into the upward and downward components—to give the total expected rate of mobility. Ratios of this index to the total observed rate form the basis for comparisons across populations (see Carlsson, 1958: Chapter 5; Glass, 1954:218–259; Rogoff, 1953a: Chapter 2; Duncan, 1966; Blau and Duncan, 1967:90–97; Jackson and Curtis, 1968: 141–143).

A technique for collapsing the outputs of these two models into a single statistic has been presented by Durbin (1955) and Yasuda (1964). This index

upward and downward movements. The point is, however, that the conventional summary measure of this phenomenon does not yield *in any case* an unambiguous meaning. Similarly, the conventional measure of structural demand gives only a *minimum* estimate of the amount of movement that can be attributed to direct or indirect consequences of change in the supply and demand characteristics of the occupational structure.

is given by the following procedure: (1) for the observed matrix, calculate the number of status changes from each origin (row) that are due to circulation, and summate down the rows; (2) repeat the first step for the hypothetical matrix resulting from application of the full-equality model; (3) compute the ratio of the summation of the first step to that of the second.

As we mentioned several paragraphs earlier, these summary statistics are handicapped by certain flaws. The simple measure of total observed mobility may be statistically sound, but it yields very little information. The available techniques for isolating the structural demand and circulation components of observed mobility, a theoretically important distinction, are not sound. The comparative analysis of mobility across occupational structures requires the use of a standard such as the full-equality or maximum-stability model; and these, as Blau and Duncan (1967:93–94) have illustrated, yield an index which possesses a questionable property: a matrix of index values for a given mobility table "rigorously imply the marginals" of that table—that is, the origin and destination distributions—and therefore "it is difficult to see in what sense the 'effect' of [structural demand] has been 'controlled'. . . ." In view of these circumstances, for purposes of later analyses of data we can only adopt the course that Blau and Duncan, among others, have followed and use a variety of measurement techniques and statistics.

International Comparisons

A single set of mobility rates, even after it has been standardized against some theoretical model, is enhanced in its meaning when it is compared with at least one other set. Basically, such comparison can be conducted in one of two ways or in a combination of the two. One involves longitudinal comparisons of a given population over time, preferably by the careful techniques of a panel study or those of cohort analysis, but more frequently by simply contrasting the results of independently executed—and usually not quite comparable—studies (see, for example, Jackson and Crockett, 1964; Blau and Duncan, 1967: Chapter 3).

A second and increasingly popular method of enhancing the meaningfulness of mobility rates is by comparing measures across populations, usually nations, at a given point in time. Ideally, though seldom in practice, the comparisons are truly synchronic. Assuming the individual measures are reasonably accurate and comparable, this second method allows one to rank the populations in terms of various mobility components, such as degree of "openness" of societies; such ranking in turn becomes an independent and/or dependent variable in subsequent analyses. The foregoing assumptions are not easy to establish, however, given the current state of mobility research. We have already examined the question of accuracy from the standpoint of statistical measures as such; another, equally important aspect of that question, which we shall only mention, concerns the skills of the researcher himself. In what follows we turn to the comparability of the individual measures.

In 1960, S. M. Miller cogently summarized the state of international comparisons with this observation:

> It is impossible to make a comparison between even two nations without inflicting some violence upon the data in order to make the comparisons. And, of course, the basic data in almost all cases are less than satisfactory. The renowned economist, John Maurice Clark, unfortunately little read by sociologists, has stated that we must choose between using shaky data or no data. Anyone making international comparisons, whether a Simon Kuznets or a Max Weber, puts himself down on the side not of the angels, but on the side of the foolhardy and/or courageous (Miller, 1960:18).

Over the past decade nothing that substantially alters this evaluation has happened. Comparative studies are still ruled by the availability rather than by the validity of data.

A number of difficulties can be briefly summarized here (see Carlsson, 1958:114–116; Lipset and Bendix, 1959; Miller, 1960; Wilensky, 1966; Blau and Duncan, 1967:432–435). First, since such studies are typically secondary analyses of available national studies, the summary measures or indices are not always identical for all countries. When they are not, the analyst must fall back upon the original frequency tabulations, but unfortunately these are not always published or otherwise made available.

A more complicated problem concerns the similarity, or lack thereof, in the occupational classifications used in the original studies. (1) The detail of the classification schemes must be identical, or nearly so, since this factor will undoubtedly influence the amount of mobility observed. In most cases, a population which has been divided into a large number of categories will by that circumstance alone show more mobility than a population divided into a few. (2) The content of categories must be defined in comparable ways across the various populations—an exceedingly difficult task to accomplish (see, for example, Duncan, 1966). For example, category A should have the same relation to the entire occupational structure of one society that it has to the occupational structures of the other societies. But meeting this requirement entails at least potentially the consideration of countervailing factors. (3) We want to compare mobility rates that are anchored in some scheme of ranked occupations, and that scheme must be similar for all populations. Simultaneously, we are interested in comparisons of movements between groupings on the basis of intrinsic characteristics such as type of work performed, relations to superiors, or the amount of discretionary time associated with workplace activities. But the relationship between the two schemes may not be the same for all countries. To use Miller's (1960:19) illustration, a skilled laborer who moves into a low nonmanual position may be deemed ascendant in one society but downwardly mobile in another. Yet in both instances he may undergo similarly important shifts in the objective circumstances of workplace. If we homogenize the definitions of mobility direction by standardizing the prestige rankings of the two occupational distributions, we may simultaneously destroy the comparability of workplace factors. In the end, our choice of strategies will depend on the kinds of questions we propose to answer.

Variations in the construction of classificatory schemes can introduce yet another obstacle to comparability. In all likelihood the rate of movement between contiguous occupations is seldom if ever equivalent at all points in an occupational structure. Some occupations, that is, are "closer" to their "neighbors" than are others (especially, oftentimes, those just to each side of the manual-nonmanual boundary). Furthermore, some occupations more likely than others possess "bridging attributes" which provide, "through work experience, the conditions and opportunities for movement from one occupation . . . to another" (Broom and Smith, 1963:322). The problem is that such clusters and bridges may not be commonly located in the occupational structures of various societies. If, for example, the occupations comprising category A form a high-mobility cluster in one country but not in another, an artificial bias has been introduced into the comparison, even though the classificatory scheme had been standardized in other respects (see Carlsson, 1958:116).

Other defects in the comparability of international data include differences in sampling frame and techniques, in the accuracy of data collection, in the rates of immigration and emigration, and in the fertility rates of the various origin strata (see Matras, 1961; Blau and Duncan, 1967:429–431). The point of our discussion has not been to supply an enumeration of the problems involved, however. We are more concerned to stress the caution that must be taken when comparing rates and making interpretations of their similarities and differences. At best they are crude estimations, and only the most tenuous of conclusions can be drawn from them.

INTERGENERATIONAL MOBILITY AND SOCIAL INHERITANCE

In their well-known comparative analysis of occupational-mobility patterns, Lipset and Bendix (1959:13, 24–26, 73) have pointed out that "the social mobility of societies becomes relatively high once their industrialization, and hence their economic expansion, reaches a certain level." This observed fact, they reasoned, supports the hypothesis that "mobility patterns in Western industrialized societies are determined by the occupational structure" rather than by political institutions, historical legacies, and other such factors. Specifically, these authors concluded that "the countries studied are characterized by a high degree of mobility. From one generation to another, a quarter to a third of the non-farm population moves from working class to middle class or vice versa." There appeared to be one major exception to this finding—namely, Italy, a country that, while almost surely at that "certain level" of industrialization and economic expansion, showed an over-all mobility index of only 16 percent, according to a reexamination of 1949 data presented by the Italian economist Livio Livi (1950). These data quite properly arrested the attention of students of social stratification. For if it is true that, as Colin Clark (1957:-554) put it in a similar context, "Italy is [intrinsically] a society of much greater hereditary stratification than any of the other countries examined," the Lipset and Bendix hypothesis cannot be considered as conclusively validated.

We should now point out that Livi's findings were misleading as an indication of mobility rates in Italy—and not surprisingly so, since Livi's (1950:76) stated intention was *not* to accurately gauge the rate of mobility but *"seulement de proposer une méthode"* of statistically measuring such phenomenon. It is crucial to note that he worked with a sample of 636, which is probably too small as a national survey, and that the occupational distribution of the sample was somewhat skewed, according to the 1951 census data. Furthermore, the occupational categories were so arranged as to systematically produce a low rate of upward mobility. The typical study of mobility measures it across the agrarian-manual-nonmanual axes. But in Livi's study, farm and urban manual occupations are treated together. This procedure tends to depress mobility rates, for, as many studies have confirmed, mobility rates into nonmanual occupations are everywhere lower from agrarian than from manual positions. Livi's measure was especially depressive in this respect, since farm occupations in 1949 still encompassed a comparatively large proportion of the total labor force of Italy.

Data from the present survey rectify the impression given by Livi's study that Italy exhibits a considerably lower rate of vertical mobility than other industrial societies for which data are available. Let us first look at the evidence of Table XIII:1, which cross-classifies father's "last main" occupation and son's "present" occupation on a simple nonmanual-manual-agrarian scheme.[6]

Focusing first on the urban portion of the table, that is, on movements across the manual-nonmanual axis, the data reveal that one-quarter of the respondents with manual backgrounds were in nonmanual positions at the time of the interview. Conversely, 24 percent of those with nonmanual backgrounds had declined to manual occupations.[7] As a crude index of total mobility in the urban occupational structure, we may add the numbers of upwardly and downwardly mobile sons and express this sum as a percent of the total: 179 out of 703, or more than 25 percent. This index compares favorably with corresponding indices from several other countries, as reported

---

[6]It should be noted that we are here using a comparison of occupational distributions that defines a crude intergenerational mobility. That is, choice of son's present occupation means that we are measuring not just social inheritance but also at least some portion of the son's career experience. This choice is dictated for the present analysis by the need for comparability with other studies.

[7]These findings update data previously reported in Lopreato (1965). In that paper, small shopkeepers and proprietors and artisans with dependent workers were included in the manual category. In the present assessment, we are following existing convention.

Table XIII:1. Father-to-Son Mobility

Father's Occupational Level	Respondent's Present Occupational Level			
	Nonmanual	Manual	Agrarian	Total
Nonmanual	73.3	23.6	3.1	100.0%
	(233)	(75)	(10)	(318)
Manual	24.9	69.6	5.5	100.0%
	(104)	(291)	(23)	(418)
Agrarian	11.8	35.2	53.1	100.1%
	(71)	(212)	(320)	(603)
Total[a]	30.5	43.2	26.4	100.1%
N	(408)	(578)	(353)	(1,339)

[a] Note that the percentages in the column totals of an r-by-k (origin by destination) mobility matrix are also the *expected* percentages for origin strata under conditions of full equality of opportunity. For this reason, column totals will be shown in all subsequent mobility matrices.

$\tau_c = .543.$

by Lipset and Bendix (1959:25): West Germany, 31; United States, 30; Sweden, 29; Japan, 27; France, 27; Switzerland, 23. Although closer to the bottom than to the top of this list, the Italian index of 25 is neither the lowest nor more than six points below the highest. For the time being, at least, this comparison eliminates the one major evidence previously recorded as adverse to Lipset and Bendix's conclusion.

Turning to farm occupations, the data continue to be highly comparable to corresponding findings for other countries. According to the comparisons of Lipset and Bendix (1959:19–21), mobility *into* farm occupations from nonmanual or manual origins ranged from a low of zero to a high of 10 percent, with averages around 3 and 4 percent. These fit almost perfectly the pattern in Italy, which shows total movements into farm occupations of 6 percent from manual positions and 3 percent from the nonmanual category.

Mobility *from* the agrarian level, on the other hand, was very high; but it largely involved movement into manual occupations. Thus, only 12 percent of the agrarian-origin sons had achieved nonmanual positions as compared to three times as many (35 percent) who were in urban manual occupations when interviewed. This rate is somewhat lower than the corresponding rates for the six other countries, wherein the percentages of agrarian fathers claimed by nonmanual sons ranged from a low of 12, according to a German study, to a high of 28 in Japan (Lipset and Bendix, 1959:19–21). One may speculate that the relatively low chance of sons of Italian farmers to achieve nonmanual positions was due to the low educational standards of Italy in general and of her agricultural workers in particular. As a consequence, when farmers' children left the farm to pursue urban occupational activities, their occupational shifts tended to go no higher than the lowest urban occupations. This point receives substantial support from the relatively large number of farm workers whose sons achieved manual positions. The percentage of 35 falls within the range of corresponding figures from the six other countries, reported by Lipset and Bendix, which vary from a high of 46 for the United States, according to one study, to a low of 13 for France. Our finding reflects also the heavy flow of labor from Italian farms since the end of World War II. From November, 1951, to October, 1963, the number of employed agricultural workers decreased from 8,261,000 to 5,457,000—that is, from 42 percent of the labor force to a mere 27 percent (*Istituto Centrale di Statistica,* 1964). This decrease in turn attests to the rapid economic expansion undergone by Italy within the period in question; the "rural exodus" has, in part, occurred in response to an industrial "pull."

Further International Comparisons

How did Italy compare with other societies in terms of such measures as "minimum mobility" (that mobility accounted for by the index of dissimilarity between father and son distributions), "excess over minimum" (what is conventionally but ambiguously termed "free circulation"), and "expected mobility" (that is, assuming independence of father and son distributions). Table XIII:2 supplies one set of answers, according to which Italy ranked relatively low in her rates of observed and "excess over minimum" mobility and in the ratio of observed to expected mobility. But the rates are certainly not totally incomparable to those of other countries. For example, Italy ranked somewhat above France and Hungary, and only slightly below West Germany on the mobility ratio, with total observed movement being 55 percent of what would have been expected under the assumption of independence.

These comparisons, we must again emphasize, are very tenuous and should be treated as only crude estimations. For reasons already noted, they do not do what sociologists would like them to do. Blau and Duncan (1967:432), moreover, have recently questioned the significance of Lipset and Bendix's thesis that mobility rates in industrial societies are about equally "high," arguing that "a meaningful study of national differences in opportunities must take into account differential chances of achieving elite status in one of the top strata" (see also Jones, 1969, who challenges Lipset and Bendix's conclusion). Movement between the upper echelons of the manual category and the lower levels of the nonmanual category says little about the availability of the most meaningful opportunities in a society. Accordingly, Blau and Duncan have used most of the comparative data assembled by another scholar of mobility (Miller, 1960) in order to investigate national differences in such opportunities. The Italian data were taken from a preliminary report of the present survey (Lopreato, 1965:314). Blau and Duncan's table is here reproduced as Table

TABLE XIII:2. VERTICAL SOCIAL MOBILITY:
SOME INTERNATIONAL COMPARISONS

Country, and Date	Total Observed	Minimum Mobility	Excess over Minimum	Total Expected	Ratio, O/E
Australia, 1965[a]	41.6	10.1	31.5	61.6	67.5
Finland, 1958[b]	49.6	28.1	21.5	58.5	84.8
France, 1948[c]	34.4	3.5	30.9	65.3	52.7
Hungary, 1949[d]	29.4	14.2	15.2	56.3	52.2
Italy, 1964[e]	37.0	18.6	18.4	67.3	55.0
Norway, 1957[f]	44.1	18.6	25.5	67.2	65.6
Puerto Rico, 1954[g]	51.1	33.3	17.8	65.2	78.4
Sweden, 1950[h]	46.8	20.0	26.8	66.0	70.9
United States, 1962[i]	48.5	23.1	25.4	64.6	75.1
West Germany, 1955[j]	37.3	11.9	25.4	63.6	58.6

Note: All measures were computed from nonmanual-manual-agrarian classifications. Because published matrices did not always contain cell frequencies, some of the above measures may involve small rounding errors.

Sources:
[a] Broom and Jones, 1969a:335.
[b] Pesonen, 1968:42, 376. Sample restricted to Tampere, Finland.
[c] Bresard, 1950:539. Reported in Miller, 1960:70.
[d] Reported in Miller, 1960:72. Census data.
[e] Present study.
[f] Special tabulations by Stein Rokkan, reported in Miller, 1960:75.
[g] Tumin with Feldman, 1961:430.
[h] Carlsson, 1958:93.
[i] Blau and Duncan, 1967:496.
[j] Janowitz, 1958:10.

XIII:3. It will be noted that there are two entries for Italy. The one in brackets refers to findings previously published by Lopreato (1965) and used by Blau and Duncan. The second entry for Italy shows findings from the present analysis; they have been added to those reported by Blau and Duncan for two reasons. First, our present data bring up to date those previously reported by Lopreato (1965). Second, Blau and Duncan's treatment of the previously reported Italian data is somewhat misleading. What Blau and Duncan term "elite" refers to what had been termed in Lopreato's preliminary report as the "ruling class," consisting of a very small number of top professionals, officials, executives, and entrepreneurs. For the United States entry in Blau and Duncan's table, the elite is equivalent to "professional, technical and kindred" workers; for the other countries, the elite refers to Miller's "Elites I and II" (Blau and Duncan, 1967:434). In all these cases, "elite" encompasses a wider occupational range than Lopreato's original "ruling class."

Recognizing the difficulties flowing from these differences, Blau and Dun-

Country	Percent of All Men in Elite	Working Class into Elite		Manual Class into Elite		Middle Class into Elite	
		Percent	Mobility Ratio	Percent	Mobility Ratio	Percent	Mobility Ratio
Denmark	3.30	—	—	1.07	.32	4.58	1.39
France I (Bresard)	8.53	4.16	.49	3.52	.41	12.50	1.46
France II (Desabie)	6.12	1.99	.33	1.56	.25	10.48	1.71
Great Britain	7.49	—	—	2.23	.30	8.64	1.15
[Italy]	[2.77]	[.48]	[.17]	[.35]	[.13]	[5.76]	[2.08]
Italy	5.90	2.23	.38	2.15	.36	10.04	1.70
Japan	11.74	—	—	6.95	.59	15.12	1.29
Netherlands	11.08	—	—	6.61	.60	11.55	1.04
Puerto Rico	13.79	11.42	.83	8.60	.62	23.17	1.68
Sweden	6.66	4.43	.67	3.50	.53	18.09	2.72
United States	11.60	10.41	.90	9.91	.85	20.90	1.80
West Germany	4.58	1.55	.34	1.46	.32	8.28	1.81

Source: Blau and Duncan (1967:434) except for second Italy entry.
Note: "Working Class" equals urban blue-collar workers; "Manual Class" refers to urban blue-collar workers plus farmers; "Middle Class" consists of nonmanuals.

can employed "mobility ratios that standardize for size." But their effort does not solve the problem at issue here, because standardizing for size is an artificial operation unless the margins of the elite are actually widened. The problem concerns not merely the size of the Italian elite but also its breadth: the wider apart the "borders" of the category, the lower the *social distance* between it and the low categories and, consequently, the greater the possibility of access to it from below. Hence, if we increase our previous "ruling class" to include all major professionals and all top and middle-range officials, executives, and entrepreneurs, we have not only a larger "elite" but also a less socially distant one. The Italian elite will then more nearly (though probably still not fully) resemble the other national elites as used by Blau and Duncan. We have introduced this change into Table XIII:3.

According to Blau and Duncan's comparisons, Italy had the second lowest ratio of mobility from the middle class into the elite. This ranking suggests in effect a very low degree of equality of opportunity for the society as a whole, since the middle class is the most immediate social neighbor of the elite. Italy also showed the lowest ratio of mobility into the elite from the manual class and from the working class.

The corrected data (second Italy entry) reveal a different picture. In all three instances, despite a still relatively small elite, the Italian mobility ratio is closer to the middle of the various national ratios. When all is said and done, nevertheless, mobility into the elite from the manual class (especially the farmers, as we could show) still leaves much to be desired. The Italian data reflect a rather low level of what Blau and Duncan term "opportunity and democracy."

The point may be made otherwise by turning to Table XIII:4, which elaborates the previous analysis of Table XIII:1 by utilizing a seven-point occupational scale that, in our opinion, is particularly appropriate for assessing major changes in the distribution of occupations in Italy.[8] The ranking was suggested not only by a social-historical appreciation of Italian society but also by a comparative examination of these seven categories in terms of such fundamental factors of stratification as income, education, prestige, self-assigned power, and consumption patterns.[9]

---

[8]The major exception concerns the two strata of subproletariat and farm hands, which are highly similar, as witnessed by the fact that individuals active in one category are often at least temporarily active in the other. It is useful to keep the two strata separate, however, so as to facilitate the work of other scholars who may wish to compare the present data to their own while keeping all agricultural occupations separate.

[9]Information obtained on all of these factors suggested that conventionally used occupational scales are, for Italy at least, grossly deficient. Such categories as "professional," "business," "white-collar," and "farmer" are particularly crude, since they too often bring together occupational groups that are greatly heterogeneous. The same can be said of such other frequently employed categories as "middle classes," "working classes," and so on. For a critical discussion of occupational classifications, see Duncan (1961).

Father's Occupational Level	Son's Present Occupational Level							
	I	II	III	IV	V	VI	VII	Total
I. Elite	_40.0_ (16)	40.0 (16)	7.5 (3)	10.0 (4)	2.5 (1)	0.0 (0)	0.0 (0)	100.0% (40)
II. Bourgeoisie	10.4 (12)	_55.7_ (64)	15.7 (18)	15.7 (18)	2.6 (3)	0.0 (0)	0.0 (0)	100.1% (115)
III. Petty Bourgeoisie	2.5 (4)	21.5 (35)	_39.9_ (65)	31.3 (51)	3.1 (5)	1.2 (2)	0.6 (1)	100.1% (163)
IV. Proletariat	0.6 (2)	12.6 (45)	14.6 (52)	_62.7_ (224)	3.1 (11)	4.8 (17)	1.7 (6)	100.1% (357)
V. Peasantry	0.7 (3)	6.5 (29)	5.8 (26)	24.9 (111)	_45.3_ (202)	6.5 (29)	10.3 (46)	100.0% (446)
VI. Subproletariat	0.0 (0)	1.6 (1)	6.6 (4)	39.3 (24)	1.6 (1)	_42.6_ (26)	8.2 (5)	99.9% (61)
VII. Farm Hands	0.0 (0)	0.0 (0)	8.3 (13)	34.4 (54)	4.5 (7)	11.5 (18)	_41.4_ (65)	100.1% (157)
Total N	2.8 (37)	14.2 (190)	13.5 (181)	36.3 (486)	17.2 (230)	6.9 (92)	9.2 (123)	100.1% (1,339)

Note: We are following no one particular terminology; for example, the distinction between "Elite" and "Bourgeoisie" and the label "Subproletariat" are dictated by mere convenience of language or analysis.

A cell-by-cell calculation shows 677 cases of observed mobility out of a total *possible* of 1,339, that is, 51 percent. The full-equality model, however, predicts mobility for 1,076 of the sons, or 80 percent of the total. In short, actual mobility was a little more than six-tenths of what it would have been if the opportunities of all sons had been equally good.

Some of the observed mobility was *forced* by structural demand. The extent to which actual mobility was the result of changes in the occupational structure can be conventionally estimated as follows. With the small exception of the elite stratum (which we shall here ignore), the number of sons in each urban occupational category was larger than the corresponding number of fathers. For the two agrarian categories, the reverse was true. Although sampling errors are undetermined and for the distribution of fathers are undoubtedly large, we will attribute the greater part of this discrepancy between father and son distributions to the national expansion of urban occupations and the accompanying demise of agricultural occupations. Given this change in occupational structure, it can be argued that while all sons of urban fathers could conceivably have inherited their fathers' level, a total of 250 sons of agrarians —that is, $(446 - 230) + (157 - 123)$—or 19 percent of the sample would have been forced by a reduction of farm positions to enter newly developing urban occupations. In short, under conditions of maximum stability or inheritance, 81 percent of the respondents would have been stationary and 19 percent would have been mobile. This refinement means that of the total observed mobility rate of 51 percent, at least 19 percent can be attributed to structural changes and the remaining "excess over minimum"—up to 32 percent—to individual circulation.

Social Inheritance

As was noted earlier in this chapter, the foregoing analyses were based on comparisons of occupational distributions that combine in varying degrees the effects of social inheritance with those of career effort. This compounding of effects occurred because the comparisons to sons were to their present and not their first jobs. Let us now turn to a consideration of social inheritance alone. Later we shall examine separately career mobility.

The data (Table XIII:5) indicate that for every stratum of origin but one, the most common destination was the occupational stratum of the father.[10] Rates of inheritance range from a low of 36 percent for the elite to a high of 67 percent for the proletariat. A total of 645, or 45 percent, of the 1,429 respondents moved from their fathers' strata. Mobility at career initiation was therefore appreciable, involving nearly one-half of the sons. Of the 645 mobile sons, 53 percent (345) moved up the occupational scale and 47 percent moved

---

[10]The discrepancy between the total N of this table and those of Tables XIII:1 and XIII:4 $(1,429 - 1,339 = 90)$ is due to those sons who had once been in the labor force (first job) but were no longer in it at the time of the interview. Of these people, 80 percent were over 60 years of age, and 94 percent were over 50 years old.

TABLE **XIII**:5. SOCIAL INHERITANCE: MOBILITY FROM
SOCIAL ORIGINS TO CAREER ENTRY

Father's Occupational Level	Son's First Occupational Level							Total
	I	II	III	IV	V	VI	VII	
I. Elite	36.4 (16)	27.3 (12)	18.2 (8)	13.6 (6)	2.3 (1)	2.3 (1)	0.0 (0)	100.1% (44)
II. Bourgeoisie	10.1 (12)	41.2 (49)	31.9 (38)	10.9 (13)	5.0 (6)	0.8 (1)	0.0 (0)	99.9% (119)
III. Petty Bourgeoisie	1.7 (3)	13.9 (25)	39.4 (71)	39.4 (71)	1.7 (3)	2.8 (5)	1.1 (2)	100.0% (180)
IV. Proletariat	0.3 (1)	6.1 (23)	11.9 (45)	67.2 (254)	2.9 (11)	8.2 (31)	3.4 (13)	100.0% (378)
V. Peasantry	0.4 (2)	4.9 (23)	5.5 (26)	13.6 (64)	59.9 (282)	5.9 (28)	9.8 (46)	100.0% (471)
VI. Subproletariat	0.0 (0)	0.0 (0)	6.1 (4)	40.9 (27)	1.5 (1)	45.5 (30)	6.1 (4)	100.1% (66)
VII. Farm Hands	0.0 (0)	0.0 (0)	2.9 (5)	24.6 (42)	13.5 (23)	11.1 (19)	48.0 (82)	100.1% (171)
Total N	2.4 (34)	9.2 (132)	13.8 (197)	33.4 (477)	22.9 (327)	8.0 (115)	10.3 (147)	100.0% (1,429)

$\tau_c = .439$

down. Not infrequently such movement was to nonadjacent (but still near) strata, invalidating in effect a part of Pareto's argument on circulation. For instance, 32 percent of the sons of elite fathers dropped to petty-bourgeoisie positions or to the proletariat. Nearly a third of the respondents of bourgeoisie origins skidded to the petty-bourgeoisie stratum, but 11 percent declined even farther to the proletariat. At the other end of the occupational hierarchy the rates of movement were even greater. Thus, 41 percent of the subproletariat fathers and 25 percent of the agricultural-worker fathers had sons who moved to the proletariat, leaving the intervening strata relatively empty. This movement not only reflects the predominant rural-to-urban migration flow; it suggests that both the urban unskilled workers and the agricultural laborers had common work orientations. Contrary to the expectations of some (for instance, Redfield, 1963:77), movement to what has been called a "stable" peasantry was rare among the farm hands.

It is interesting to note that upward mobility from the bourgeoisie nearly exhausted the volume of elite inflow, this providing support for another Pareto-inspired hypothesis: that elite circulation is almost exclusively a phenomenon of the upper levels of society.[11] This pattern of elite circulation indirectly supports also Pizzorno's (1964) argument that, although the chances for attaining political power have improved in recent years for Italians belonging to the middle and lower strata, the influence of social background is still strongly felt when "governing group" is considered in the strictest sense—those at the very summit of power. At this level, self-perpetuation is still very nearly complete. According to Pizzorno, elite mobility is more restricted within the economic sphere, where despite the "considerable" mobility at "intermediate levels," or "even at a fairly high level which remains outside the circle where the ultimate decisions are made," "the group wielding the economic power remains exclusive and virtually inaccessible."[12]

Of those sons who originated in the petty bourgeoisie, 16 percent moved up,

---

[11]This finding is in close agreement with the result of another study of the "ruling class" in Italy, according to which only very small percentages of the elite originated in categories below what we here refer to as the bourgeoisie (see Inchiesta SHELL No. 3, 1961:34). On the other hand, focusing on the Piedmont candidates to the 1958 Italian Parliament, Barbano (1961:181–189) found that a large number of the candidates originated in the middle and lower classes. This origin was particularly characteristic of members of the Communist and Socialist parties, among whose fathers the occupations of laborer, skilled or semiskilled worker, and farmer reached, respectively, for the two parties, 45 percent and 55 percent of the totals.

[12]This argument, however, is subject to some debate, depending on how elites are defined, among other things. Thus, in discussing the previously cited SHELL study, Touraine (1964:314) argues instead that "the rapid and thorough transformation of the economy has diminished the importance of heredity in the choice of senior executives." The disagreement may be merely definitional in nature. Pizzorno (1964:214) admits "considerable" mobility right up to "the circle where the ultimate decisions are made." Whether or not this circle is coterminous with, or, perhaps, more restricted than, the "senior executives" to which Touraine makes reference cannot be inferred from the latter's discussion. However, Touraine confesses that the category to which he refers is "too broad, since it includes both economic and administrative leaders." This statement may indicate that the two sources do not contradict each other.

nearly always into the bourgeoisie, and 45 percent declined, mostly into the proletariat. Movement from this origin stratum, then, generally involved contiguous strata, indicating the heavy emphasis on status that is typical of the Italian *ceto medio inferiore* (petty owners and office workers) and also the closed nature of the elite groups.

Mobile sons of the proletariat, of whom there were relatively few, more often moved up than down. Two-thirds of the ascenders moved into petty bourgeoisie positions, while the skidders were concentrated in urban unskilled occupations.

About one-quarter of the sons of peasants attained positions in higher strata, generally in skilled and semiskilled urban occupations, whereas 16 percent declined into the lower strata—partial testimony to the very inadequate education and the poverty of the Italian peasantry. However, although peasants' sons did not move to nonmanual jobs as often as sons of skilled and semiskilled urban workers, they were more likely to do so than the sons of urban unskilled and farm-hand fathers. As we observed previously, large numbers of respondents with farm-hand and subproletarian backgrounds acquired first jobs in a higher stratum; but only 3 percent of the first group and 6 percent of the second, as contrasted to 11 percent for the peasantry, attained positions above the ranks of the proletariat.

Before leaving Table XIII:5, we should explore its meaning in terms of available models of mobility analysis. A total observed rate of 45 percent may be considered appreciable, but in the last analysis any characterization of it as "high" or "low" depends on how closely it approaches what it *could be* if inheritance did not operate. Also, how much of the 45 percent can be accounted for as "minimum mobility" (that is, the dissimilarity index)? The following figures are pertinent:

Observed Mobility:	
Up	24.1%
Down	21.0
Total	45.1
Minimum Mobility	12.6
Excess over Minimum	32.5
Expected Mobility:	
Up	42.3
Down	37.2
Total	79.5

It appears that at least 13 percent of the 1,429 respondents moved as a result of structural changes. However, according to the model of independence, the rate of total observed mobility was roughly only six-tenths of what it would have been without social inheritance (45.1/79.5). Whereas fewer than half of the sons were in fact mobile at first job, just under 80 percent of them would have been, under the assumption of independence. Upward and downward movements contributed rather equally to this discrepancy: the first is 57.1

percent of its expected value; the second, 56.5 percent.

In terms of full-equality expectations, the highest rate of social inheritance occurred in the elite stratum of origin, by a ratio of 16 to 1, while the lowest was among the sons of proletarian fathers (about 2 to 1). This difference forms an interesting comparison to our earlier observation that the elite stratum contained the lowest rate of *actual* immobility and the proletariat showed the highest. The conclusion to be drawn from it is that inheritance among the former was *sixteen times greater* than would have occurred under conditions of equal opportunity, whereas among the latter it was "only" twice as great. Social inheritance, especially in the higher reaches of the opportunity structure, was indeed quite pronounced.

Nevertheless, upward mobility at first job exceeded theoretical expectations in four of the seven origin strata, two of them toward the top of the occupational scale. Although sons of bourgeois and petty bourgeois fathers entered the next higher strata only 10 and 14 percent of the time, respectively, these rates were larger than they "should" have been by factors of about 4 and 1.5, respectively. Similarly, sons of urban unskilled workers jumped to proletariat positions slightly more often than expected, and sons of farm hands moved to the subproletariat at a rate in excess of equal opportunity.

In the case of downward mobility, actual rates were greater than expected in three origin strata: the elite stratum to the bourgeoisie by a factor of 3, and to the petty bourgeoisie by a factor greater than 1; the bourgeoisie to the petty bourgeoisie by a factor of more than 2; and the petty bourgeoisie to the proletariat by a factor slightly larger than 1. Downward movement from skilled and semiskilled urban occupations, on the other hand, was generally lower than expected.

To reiterate and summarize the findings, while the amount of inheritance at the top levels of the occupational hierarchy was comparatively small in terms of observed rates, it was still indicative of an "excessive" social inheritance. About the only sons who gained access to the elite were those with bourgeois backgrounds; and if a person fell from the elite category, his social origins worked a substantial "braking effect" on the intensity of his fall, increasing his chances threefold that he would not slide below the bourgeois level. At the middle of the occupational hierarchy, on the other hand, observed inheritance was frequent, but in terms of theoretical expectations it was not nearly so frequent as among the elite. Only 12 percent of the sons of proletarians moved up to the petty bourgeoisie, and only half of that proportion made it a step higher to the bourgeoisie stratum; but in neither case was the percentage far below what would have been expected under conditions of equal opportunity (factors of .9 and .7, respectively). Finally, among the subproletariat and the agricultural laborers actual inheritance again declines and the mobility ratio increases. In both cases, however, there are instances of slightly greater-than-expected mobility: among the former, ascent to the proletariat; among the latter, movement to the subproletariat.

Trends in Time

Is social inheritance increasing or decreasing in Italy? One attempt to answer this question is shown as Table XIII:6, which records a number of summary measures of mobility yielded by a cohort analysis of rates of inheritance at career entry. The matrices on which this analysis was based utilized the nonmanual-manual-agrarian classification of occupations. This, as opposed to the larger seven-point scheme, was dictated by the total sample size. While the smaller scheme may result in some loss of information, it also minimizes possible variations over time in the ranking of occupations.

The cohorts are actually birth cohorts and are recorded as such in the table. But, on the assumption that the average age at first job has not changed very much over the years, the cohorts may also be interpreted as "career-entrance" cohorts. By using this interpretation we can achieve a series of temporal comparisons in the rate of social inheritance. Assuming an average range of from 15 to 20 years of age at entry into the labor force, the five birth cohorts of post-1932, 1923–1932, 1913–1922, 1903–1912, and pre-1903 give overlapping career-entrance cohorts of post-1947, 1938–1952, 1928–1942, 1918–1932, and pre-1923.

TABLE XIII:6. COHORT VARIATION IN SOCIAL INHERITANCE

Summary Measures	Birth Cohort				
	Post-1932	1923–32	1913–22	1903–12	Pre-1903
Observed Mobility:					
Up	21.8%	21.7%	21.2%	13.5%	13.3%
Down	12.2	10.5	8.7	9.1	9.6
Total	34.0%	32.2%	29.9%	22.6%	22.9%
Minimum Mobility	12.3	10.2	14.6	10.5	7.8
Excess over Minimum	21.7	22.0	15.3	12.1	15.1
Expected Mobility:					
Up	37.4%	39.0%	38.2%	34.5%	33.5%
Down	28.6	27.7	26.9	29.1	28.9
Total	66.0%	66.7%	65.1%	63.6%	62.4%
Ratio:					
Up	58.3%	55.6%	55.5%	39.1%	39.7%
Down	42.7	37.9	32.3	31.3	33.2
Total	51.5%	48.3%	45.9%	35.4%	36.7%
N	147	382	391	275	218

Examining first the observed rates, we find that the rate of inheritance has diminished considerably since the early part of the century, though not as much during recent years as in the earlier periods. The proportion of sons who moved up from their fathers' occupational category increased from 13 percent among the oldest respondents to nearly 22 percent among the youngest. At the same time, the frequency of downward mobility grew, although at a somewhat slower pace, from just under 10 percent to just over 12 percent.

Although we should not place too much weight on the capabilities of the measure used, the rate of movements attributable to alterations of the occupational structure (that is, "minimum mobility") apparently underwent a substantial increase during the career-entrance years of 1918 to 1942 (the 1903 to 1922 birth cohorts). Assuming that this relative increase (if not the absolute values of minimum mobility) is reasonably accurate, it may be interpreted as a reflection of the period of recovery following World War I, especially the years up to 1926, and to some extent also the transformations wrought by Mussolini in the economic structure of Italy (see Clough, 1964: Chapter 7).

The pattern of change in the mobility ratios parallels that for the observed-mobility rates. Again the biggest increase occurred between the second and third cohorts—among those sons who first entered the labor force during the Mussolini years. Previously, the rate of mobility had been only a little more than one-third of theoretical expectation. Now it was very nearly one-half of the expected value, and subsequent increases were to be proportionately smaller. Moreover, the bulk of that major growth was contributed by enlarged ratios of upward mobility. Among the respondents who gained first jobs during the 1918–1932 period, ascent was only 39 percent of what the full-mobility model would have predicted; the corresponding figure for the next younger cohort was 56 percent. By contrast, the ratio of observed to expected downward movement remained essentially constant during this period—about 32 percent. Only later did the nonmanual-manual boundary become more permeable to skidding.

Three Generations

Mobility trends can also be evaluated roughly by contrasting the experiences of multiple generations, a procedure which permits an assessment of the *stability* of mobility patterns (for examples, see Mukherjee, 1954; Svalastoga, 1959:340–344; Allingham, 1967:442–449). In the present case, we make use of occupational data on three generations—sons (that is, our respondents), fathers, and paternal grandfathers—as recorded in Table XIII:7. As a general rule—and the present case is certainly not an exception—such three-generation comparisons must be viewed as highly questionable, because of problems of inestimable sampling error. In father-son comparisons we are usually handicapped by an unknown sampling error with respect to the distribution of fathers; in father-grandfather comparisons *both* distributions are so characterized, and if the unknown error for the parent generation is appreciable (and in most cases it probably is), the unknown error for the grandparent generation will surely be considerably greater. However, to repeat a point made earlier, we must choose between using shaky data and using no data at all.

In the present case, comparisons between the older two generations concern distributions not of "first job" but of later positions in career-life; thus, we are assessing the results of varying amounts of career effort as well as social inheritance. In order to make the occupational distributions of sons and the older generations as much comparable as possible, we have selected "present job" as the point of reference. Also, because the points of reference for fathers and grandfathers probably lie well into their respective career spans, we have excluded the youngest cohort of sons. Born after 1932, they may not have had as much time, relative to labor-force entry, to achieve their maximum occupational level as had their fathers and grandfathers.

TABLE XIII:7. OCCUPATIONAL MOBILITY ACROSS THREE GENERATIONS (EXCLUDING SONS BORN AFTER 1932)

Grand-father's Level	Father's Level	Son's Present Occupational Level			
		Nonmanual	Manual	Agrarian	Total
Nonmanual	Nonmanual	78.5	18.8	2.8	100.1%
		(113)	(27)	(4)	(144)
	Manual	30.0	66.7	3.3	100.0%
		(9)	(20)	(1)	(30)
	Agrarian	20.0	40.0	40.0	100.0%
		(1)	(2)	(2)	(5)
	Total	68.7	27.4	3.9	100.0%
	N	(123)	(49)	(7)	(179)
Manual	Nonmanual	58.3	41.7	0.0	100.0%
		(21)	(15)	(0)	(36)
	Manual	21.0	72.9	6.1	100.0%
		(38)	(132)	(11)	(181)
	Agrarian	0.0	78.6	21.4	100.0%
		(0)	(11)	(3)	(14)
	Total	25.5	68.4	6.1	100.0%
	N	(59)	(158)	(14)	(231)
Agrarian	Nonmanual	64.0	26.0	10.0	100.0%
		(32)	(13)	(5)	(50)
	Manual	20.6	70.1	9.3	100.0%
		(22)	(75)	(10)	(107)
	Agrarian	10.9	31.8	57.3	100.0%
		(55)	(161)	(290)	(506)
	Total	16.4	37.6	46.0	100.0%
	N	(109)	(249)	(305)	(663)

On the assumption that the farther back we go into Italian history the lower the level of industrialization—and, thus, the lower the chances of occupational mobility—we would expect greater mobility rates between fathers and sons than between grandfathers and fathers. The data support these expectations. Comparisons of the older two generations show a total movement of only 22 percent among the sons of manual grandfathers, of whom about seven-tenths moved up to nonmanual positions. Again, 22 percent of the sons of nonmanual grandfathers were mobile, nearly all of them skidding into manual positions. Finally, 24 percent of the sons of agrarian grandfathers were mobile, about two-thirds of them to the manual stratum.

By contrast, the rate of mobility between the younger two generations was somewhat greater. The outflow percentages corresponding to the previous set, for example, were 29, 28, and 44, respectively. Moreover, when computed against the total mobility possible under conditions of full equality, the statistics reveal a record of considerable improvement. Between the fathers and grandfathers the total rate of observed mobility was about 38 percent of the expected rate; between sons and fathers, it was 54 percent of expectation. However, it must be emphasized again that these comparisons are tenuous, owing to the unknown magnitude of sampling error for the distribution of fathers. For example, fathers who, in comparison to their own origin levels (that is, the grandfather's position), had been upwardly mobile may have had fewer children and were therefore underrepresented in the distribution of fathers. In that case, the observed-to-expected mobility ratio of 38 percent for the grandfather-to-father comparison would be an underestimation.

Table XIII:7 also provides a basis for answering the question about the stability of attained mobility from one generation to the next. That is, how great were the chances that a son would retain his manual social-origin status, for example, if his grandfather had been an agrarian, as compared to the son whose grandfather had been a manual worker? In this specific example his chances seem to have been relatively quite high. Among the respondents with both manual fathers and manual grandfathers, 73 percent "retained" their manual location. Among those respondents with manual fathers but agrarian grandfathers, the percentage was only slightly lower: 70 percent; the remainder of 3 percent had skidded back to their grandfathers' agrarian status. At the same time, however, the probability that a son would remain in a manual occupation if his father had skidded from nonmanual origins was almost as great as that for the son who possessed a consistent background (67 percent versus 73 percent). In short, stability of mobility experiences at this level of the occupational scale was relatively high for both upward and downward movements.

For movements across the nonmanual-manual boundary, the data indicate that families which began in the nonmanual category (the grandfather's generation) but then at the father's generation fell to the manual category, about one-third (30 percent, to be exact) regained a nonmanual position at the son's generation. Conversely, for those families that experienced upward mobility from grandfather to father, about two-fifths (42 percent) did not retain their nonmanual location in the third generation.

As for the manual-agrarian boundary, relatively few families suffered a decline in position from the first to the second generation; and of those that did, nearly four-fifths (79 percent) were once again in the manual stratum by the time of the son's generation. In short, reacquisition of lost nonmanual status was much more problematic than reacquisition of a former manual status. On the other hand, it was much easier for "originally" agrarian families to keep a newly won manual location than it was for the once manual families to retain a second-generation nonmanual status. In the latter case, as we just found in the preceding paragraph, 42 percent dropped back to the first-generation level; in the former case, only 9 percent did so.

CAREER MOBILITY

Comparisons between the occupational distributions of sons and fathers have traditionally commanded the lion's share of attention in empirical studies of social mobility. Yet at least equally germane to questions regarding the "openness" of a society is information about its rates of intragenerational or career mobility. If father-son comparisons tell us something about the ascriptive basis of occupational recruitment and selection, the scrutiny of longitudinal variations in the career statuses of people tells us something about the achievement basis of individual occupational success. *Both* sets of information are important to an assessment of the occupational fluidity of a society's population and of the distributive justice which it experiences.

We have already had occasion to observe indirect evidence of career mobility, namely, in the preceding section when we compared the father's occupation to the son's present occupation and then to the son's first occupation. The differences between those two matrices (Tables XIII:4 and XIII:5) can be attributed to within-career movements, a more detailed picture of which is given in Table XIII:8.

Over all, the evidence suggests a lower volume of total or gross mobility and a greater inequality of opportunity within work careers than between one generation and the career-entry distribution of the succeeding generation. This difference in turn suggests (and we shall later examine other evidence in support of this point) that entry inheritance exerted a stabilizing effect on career opportunities, especially against skidding, in the sense that when a person entered the labor force at origin level he was unlikely to experience subsequent mobility. This effect can be appreciated summarily from a comparison of the mobility ratios for Table XIII:8 with those for Table XIII:5.

TABLE XIII:8. CAREER MOBILITY: CAREER ENTRY TO PRESENT OCCUPATION

Son's First Occupational Level	Son's Present Occupational Level							
	I	II	III	IV	V	VI	VII	Total
I. Elite	96.9 (31)	3.1 (1)	0.0 (0)	0.0 (0)	0.0 (0)	0.0 (0)	0.0 (0)	100.0% (32)
II. Bourgeoisie	5.3 (7)	85.6 (113)	4.5 (6)	2.3 (3)	2.3 (3)	0.0 (0)	0.0 (0)	100.0% (132)
III. Petty Bourgeoisie	0.0 (0)	25.7 (48)	57.8 (108)	12.3 (23)	2.1 (4)	1.1 (2)	1.1 (2)	100.1% (187)
IV. Proletariat	0.0 (0)	4.8 (22)	11.6 (53)	75.9 (346)	2.6 (12)	3.5 (16)	1.5 (7)	99.9% (456)
V. Peasantry	0.0 (0)	1.9 (6)	3.9 (12)	21.0 (65)	62.3 (193)	4.5 (14)	6.5 (20)	100.1% (310)
VI. Subproletariat	0.0 (0)	0.9 (1)	5.5 (6)	37.3 (41)	2.7 (3)	48.2 (53)	5.5 (6)	100.1% (110)
VII. Farm Hands	0.0 (0)	0.7 (1)	2.8 (4)	13.3 (19)	11.9 (17)	7.0 (10)	64.3 (92)	100.0% (143)
Total N	2.8 (38)	14.0 (192)	13.8 (189)	36.3 (497)	16.9 (232)	6.9 (95)	9.3 (127)	100.0% (1,370)

$\tau_c = .676$

Whereas upward mobility between father and son's first job was 57 percent of the value expected under the assumption of independence, in the present matrix it was 52 percent—only slightly less. But the corresponding ratios for skidding were 57 and 23 percent, respectively—different by a factor of two.

Observed rates of career mobility were 23 percent up and 8 percent down, for a total of 31 percent (of which at least one-fourth can be accounted for by differences between entry- and current-job distributions). Thus, over two-thirds of the respondents occupied the same positions in 1964 that they held at career entry. (The rank-order correlation τ_c was .676, in contrast to a coefficient of .436 for the origin-to-entry matrix.) An unknown proportion of these nonmobiles, of course, could have changed strata a number of times between the two points in career. They very doubtfully comprised more than a handful of cases, however, as some subsequently examined data will testify.

One question that must be entertained before proceeding with a discussion of the foregoing matrix is the question of age variations in observed career mobility rates. Sons born after 1933 or so had perhaps not yet attained the heights of their careers, whereas middle-aged respondents were possibly at their peaks and the oldest respondents past theirs. Unfortunately, given the relatively small number of career mobiles, our sample is not large enough to permit reliable age standardizations of the seven-strata matrix. We can compare nonmanual-manual-agrarian mobility rates for categories of respondent's age (21–30, 31–40, 41–50, 51–60, and over 60), the results of which indicate no age variations in the rate of total observed mobility (only unordered fluctuations between a low of 19 percent and a high of 22 percent). There were small increases in the rate of ascent, and corresponding decreases in skidding, with decreasing age of respondent, but the variations were neither systematically ordered nor of appreciable size. However, the three-strata matrix is not a very suitable basis for testing age effects. Especially the nonmanual-manual boundary, it would seem, should be rather impermeable to movements that are a direct function of career aging.

An alternative approach to the problem is to restrict the matrix and rate calculations to the intermediate cohorts—that is, to exclude respondents who for reasons of age are either least likely to have experienced career ascent or most likely to have experienced career skidding. In this instance we excluded those born after 1932 and those born before 1903, and then computed indices for the remaining sample members (aged 31 to 60 at the time of interview). Interestingly, the net result of this operation was a reduction in the rate of total observed mobility (from 31 to 23 percent), nearly all of which reduction was due to a lower rate of career ascent (23 percent versus 14 percent). This decrement, in turn, must be attributed almost entirely to the exclusion of the respondents 30 years of age and younger. In other words, a substantial proportion of the upward career movement revealed by the seven-strata matrix of Table XIII:8 (something on the order of half of the 315 cases of ascent) was contributed by the slightly more than one in ten respondents who were between 21 and 31 years old. This finding could be indicative of a secular change in the rate of upward career mobility; we rather think it means simply that career movement across those stratum boundaries takes place within the first 12 or 15 years of career, by and large, or not at all.

Returning to Table XIII:8, we find, not surprisingly, that the greatest rate of immobility occurred, first, among the elite and, second, among the bourgeoisie entry stratum. Of the sons who began career at the elite level, 97 percent retained their position; at the bourgeoisie level, 86 percent. These observed rates are, respectively, about 31 and 6 times their expected values. The next highest observed rate of immobility was among those with proletarian entries —76 percent—which is a little more than twice its expected value. These conclusions apply also to the age-restricted matrix discussed above.

The highest probability of upward movement was exhibited by sons who began their careers as unskilled urban workers. According to both the age-restricted and the unrestricted matrix, a total of 46 percent moved up, the vast majority of them making it to skilled or semiskilled positions. Since the job qualifications at higher skill levels can usually be met through apprenticeships or other forms of on-the-job training, the subproletarian can more easily advance in the occupational world than can the proletarian, who faces a quite different kind of skill acquisition (both occupational-technical and social skills) if he aspires to move into the nonmanual ranks. In contrast to the United States, unskilled first jobs in Italy seem more likely to be "distributor occupations" than do skilled or semiskilled first jobs (see Blau and Duncan, 1967: 42–48).

Men who started career-life in the peasant or petty-bourgeoisie stratum improved their locations about equally often—about 26 percent in the first case and 27 percent in the second. However, there was a vast discrepancy between the two groups in their mobility ratios, a discrepancy that well illustrates the differential opportunities for social ascent at various levels of the occupational hierarchy. The 26 percent of the respondents who moved up from petty-bourgeoisie entry was in excess of the theoretical expectation by a factor of 1.5. (Again the notion of a "distributor" stratum of occupations is pertinent; and, in that regard, it is significant that these career achievers were disproportionately represented in the 21–30 age group.) In contrast, the socially ascendant respondents who began career as peasants represented only 40 percent of expectations. So the very fact that approximately equal proportions of the two entry strata achieved higher occupational positions constitutes evidence of the inequality of opportunities for career achievement from those entry strata.

Son's Present Occupational Level	Occupational Categories Other than Present One							
	I	II	III	IV	V	VI	VII	Total
I. Elite	—	18.4 (7)	0.0 (0)	0.0 (0)	0.0 (0)	0.0 (0)	0.0 (0)	18.4% (7)
II. Bourgeoisie	1.0 (2)	—	26.8 (52)	12.4 (24)	1.0 (2)	1.0 (2)	0.0 (0)	42.2% (82)
III. Petty Bourgeoisie	0.5 (1)	3.2 (6)	—	30.2 (57)	4.2 (8)	1.6 (3)	2.1 (4)	41.8% (79)
IV. Proletariat	0.0 (0)	0.8 (4)	8.0 (40)	—	8.8 (44)	10.2 (51)	3.4 (17)	31.2% (156)
V. Peasantry	0.0 (0)	0.9 (2)	3.4 (8)	6.9 (16)	—	1.7 (4)	6.0 (14)	18.9% (44)
VI. Subproletariat	0.0 (0)	0.0 (0)	4.2 (4)	18.9 (18)	15.8 (15)	—	10.5 (10)	49.4% (47)
VII. Farm Hands	0.0 (0)	0.0 (0)	1.6 (2)	4.0 (5)	18.3 (23)	7.9 (10)	—	31.8% (40)
Total N	0.2 (3)	1.4 (19)	7.7 (106)	8.7 (120)	6.7 (92)	5.1 (70)	3.2 (45)	33.0% (455)

Note: Career data concern (1) present occupation, (2) occupation before present occupation, (3) occupation before the last one mentioned, and (4) first occupation.

Previously we noted that the comparisons on which all of the preceding statistics are based involved only two points in career time—namely, first and present occupations—and therefore may significantly underestimate the rate of career mobility. Table XIII:9, which represents most or all of the career experiences for the great majority of our respondents, reports data relevant to this question: the percentage of sons who had previously worked in occupational categories other than those held in 1964.

It should be noted that, whereas previous tables report outflow rates, the percentages shown above are in the nature of *inflow* rates. In effect, they tell us where the respondents had been rather than where they were going. Therefore, in order to evaluate the amount of additional mobility uncovered by Table XIII:9, we must transform the matrix of Table XIII:8 into inflow rates. Once we have done so we find that, generally speaking, the two-point comparison of first and present jobs did not in fact significantly underestimate career mobility. To put it otherwise, once a person set out in a particular direction from his entry occupation, either upward or downward, he generally continued in that direction up to the point of his present occupation. Taking the matrices as a whole, for example, data on respondents who had ever been in an occupational category other than their present categories reveal a total mobility rate of just over 33 percent, whereas the corresponding value for the two-point comparison is 31 percent.

Nearly all of the discrepancy between these rates was contributed by three destination strata: in decreasing order of contribution, the subproletariat, the farm hands, and the peasants. The *inflow* values for the other strata were very nearly identical; for the elite, in fact, they were exactly the same. Apparently, then, to the extent that the two-point comparison has understated the rate of mobility, it has been only among the lower levels of the occupational hierarchy that circulations from one stratum to another went undetected. In the case of the unskilled urban workers, for instance, roughly 44 percent did not begin their careers at that level; 5 percent did, but then temporarily moved into another occupational category, probably a contiguous one, only to return later into the subproletarian stratum; 51 percent started and continued uninterruptedly in the subproletarian stratum. Similarly, 28 percent of the farm hands were not farm hands at first job; 4 percent were, but temporarily moved into another stratum, probably into the ranks of the unskilled urban workers, only to return into the farm-hand category; the remaining 68 percent were farm hands from the time of career entry to the time of the interview. Finally, 17 percent of the peasants were mobile in relation to first job; 2 percent were stable in that comparison but had experienced some mobility during the intervening period; 81 percent were peasants throughout their career spans.

TABLE XIII:10. PERCENTAGE OF RESPONDENTS WHO HAD PREVIOUSLY
CROSSED THE NONMANUAL-MANUAL-AGRARIAN BOUNDARIES

Son's Present Occupational Level	Percentage Who Crossed to:			
	Nonmanual	Manual	Agrarian	Total
I. Elite	—	0.0 (0)	0.0 (0)	0.0% (0)
II. Bourgeoisie	—	13.4 (26)	2.6 (5)	16.0 (31)
III. Petty Bourgeoisie	—	33.9 (64)	6.3 (12)	40.2% (76)
IV. Proletariat	8.8 (44)	—	16.8 (84)	25.6% (128)
V. Peasantry	5.2 (12)	7.7 (18)	—	12.9% (30)
VI. Subproletariat	0.0 (0)	—	26.3 (25)	26.3% (25)
VII. Farm Hands	2.4 (3)	11.9 (15)	—	14.3% (18)
Total N	4.3 (59)	9.0 (123)	9.2 (126)	22.5% (308)

Another impression of inflow mobility is given in Table XIII:10, namely,
the proportion of respondents who had ever crossed one or both of the nonmanual-manual-agrarian boundaries. There was no crossing at all on the part
of the elite, and only 16 percent of the bourgeoisie had ever experienced
something other than a nonmanual status. Major shifts were heavier among
the petty bourgeoisie, two-fifths of whom had at one time or another worked
in manual or farm occupations. Urban manual workers were somewhat less
mobile, only one-quarter of them having crossed at least one of the two
boundaries. After the elites, peasants and farm hands were least likely to have
shifted.

International Comparisons

Now that we have gained some picture of the volume and rate of mobility
within occupational careers in Italy, we should try to interpret it from the
broader perspective of international data. Unfortunately, the number of countries that can be contrasted here is much smaller than was true of the father-to-

son comparisons. National surveys of career mobility have been conducted for very few countries.

TABLE XIII:11. CAREER-MOBILITY RATES:
INTERNATIONAL COMPARISONS

Country and Date	Total Observed	Minimum Mobility	Excess over Minimum	Total Expected	Ratio, O/E
Australia, 1965[a]	31.8%	8.5%	23.3%	57.9%	54.9%
Italy, 1964[b]	20.3	6.9	13.4	65.6	30.9
Puerto Rico, 1954[c]	61.7	19.1	42.6	66.2	93.2
United States, 1962[d]	36.9	12.4	24.5	59.2	62.3

Note: All measures were computed from nonmanual-manual-agrarian classifications, without adjustments for variations in the age composition of the samples.
Sources:
  [a] Broom and Jones, 1969b:653.
  [b] Present study.
  [c] Tumin with Feldman, 1961:366–367. Estimated from Table 24.1.
  [d] Blau and Duncan, 1967: 498.

According to the comparisons shown in Table XIII:11 (all of which are based on the nonmanual-manual-agrarian classification and are unadjusted for variation in age composition), career mobility was substantially lower in Italy than in other industrial or industrializing societies. In Australia, for instance, Broom and Jones (1969b) found a total observed rate of 32 percent, at least one-quarter of which was attributable to changes in occupational structure. The observed rate was about 55 percent of what would have obtained under conditions of the full-equality model. Blau and Duncan's (1967:498) data for the United States indicate that the total observed rate for that country (37 percent) was just over 62 percent of the expected value. At least a third of the actual movement was contributed by structural changes. The evidence published for Puerto Rico (Tumin with Feldman, 1961:366–367) indicates an inordinately large rate of career movement, greater even than the movement between father's occupation and son's present occupation. These scholars (1961:365) report that "roughly 62 percent of the total population" had different first and present jobs. That observed rate constituted over 93 percent of full-equality expectations. The Puerto Rican data admittedly represent a period of very pronounced industrial development and deagriculturalization of the island's economy, and would therefore understandably show a high rate of change between first and present occupational distributions. Nevertheless, a mobility ratio of .93 would still seem to warrant a degree of skepticism; taken at face value, it shows an almost perfectly egalitarian society.

In comparison with any one of these three countries, Italy demonstrated a considerably lower rate of career mobility. It was most nearly similar to Australia, but even in that comparison the differences were substantial: its mobility ratio was only a little more than half the size of Australia's, and slightly less than half of that for the United States. Among other things, these comparisons suggest that the restrictive influence of social origins on subsequent career opportunities was perhaps relatively more extensive in Italy. In terms of the direction of career movements, such influence could have meant either or both of two consequences: (1) a degree of protection against future skidding; (2) an impediment to future advancement. Previous information (Table XIII:8) has already implied that the first consequence was the predominant one. The mobility ratio for upward career mobility was .519, which is close to that for father-to-son ascent; it also compares rather favorably with corresponding ratios from the other countries listed in Table XIII:11—for example, it is nearly two-thirds of Australia's. The mobility ratio for downward career mobility, on the other hand, was only .230, which is only one-half of that for father-to-son skidding, and is also considerably smaller than comparable ratios for other countries (only about two-fifths of Australia's). It would appear that the great gap in mobility rates between Italy and other industrial (or industrializing) countries, as recorded in Table XIII:11, was largely the result of its lower rate of career *skidding*. Some part of this unusually low downward mobility ratio, in turn, was undoubtedly due to the stabilizing effects of entry inheritance. How much can be attributed to that factor we shall see momentarily.

Social Inheritance and Career Mobility

An important question in studies of vertical social mobility concerns the degree to which social origins exert a *direct* effect on later career opportunities —that is, an effect that is unmediated by the level of entry into the labor force. Other investigators (such as Perrucci, 1961; Blau and Duncan, 1967:49; also see Allingham, 1967) have shown that such "delayed effects" do indeed exist. How strong were they in Italy?

Let us rephrase the question and ask, how strong was the direct effect of social origin on current occupation, within given career-entry strata? It will be recalled from Table XIII:1 that the rank-order correlation τ_c between origin and current occupation without controls is .543. How much is that correlation reduced by controlling for differences in entry level? The answer is, according to the matrices of Table XIII:12, that the correlation is reduced substantially. The τ_c values for each of the entry strata are: nonmanual, .074; manual, .161; and agrarian, .043. Thus, the bulk of the impact of social origin occurred at entrance into the labor force.

TABLE XIII:12. FATHER-TO-SON MOBILITY BY
STRATUM OF SON'S CAREER ENTRY

Son's First Occupation	Father's Occupation	Son's Present Occupational Level			
		Non-manual	Manual	Agrarian	Total
	Nonmanual	93.1%	5.6%	1.4%	100.1%
		(201)	(12)	(3)	(216)
Nonmanual	Manual	83.3	15.3	1.4	100.0
		(60)	(11)	(1)	(72)
	Agrarian	82.0	8.0	10.0	100.0
		(41)	(4)	(5)	(50)
	Total	89.3	8.0	2.7	100.0
		(302)	(27)	(9)	(338)
	Nonmanual	31.5	68.5	0.0	100.0
		(28)	(61)	(0)	(89)
Manual	Manual	13.2	84.3	2.5	100.0
		(42)	(268)	(8)	(318)
	Agrarian	7.6	80.0	12.4	100.0
		(11)	(116)	(18)	(145)
	Total	14.7	80.6	4.7	100.0
		(81)	(445)	(26)	(552)
	Nonmanual	18.2	18.2	63.6	100.0
		(2)	(2)	(7)	(11)
Agrarian	Manual	7.4	40.7	51.9	100.0
		(2)	(11)	(14)	(27)
	Agrarian	4.4	22.7	72.9	100.0
		(18)	(92)	(296)	(406)
	Total	5.0	23.6	71.4	100.0
		(22)	(105)	(317)	(444)

The "delayed effects" of social origin were small; but they were not quite uniformly small for the three entry categories. As a comparison of columns in Table XIII:12 will show, the influence of origin level was somewhat greater in the case of sons with manual first jobs than among those sons with either nonmanual or agrarian entries. About 89 percent of all nonmanual-entrant sons were still in nonmanual positions when interviewed; while their origin characteristics did make some difference in that percentage, it was a relatively small difference: 93 percent for those with nonmanual fathers versus 82 percent for those with agrarian fathers. By contrast, 81 percent of the 552 manual-entrant sons were still in blue-collar jobs at the time of interview, but that average percentage conceals a range from 84 percent among the 318 whose fathers were also in blue-collar jobs to 69 percent among those 89 sons who were manual-entry skidders. At the time of interview, about twice as many of those 89 sons were in nonmanual positions as would have been the case had origin level exerted no direct influence on career chances. In a sense, the delayed effects of social origin assisted in their reacquisition of lost status. Similarly among the agrarian entrants, the only notable instance of a direct effect of origin level on career experience appears to have been the greater than "expected" rate (by a factor of nearly two) at which sons who had skidded from a blue-collar origin to an agrarian first job later regained manual status. Some of this movement, it should be noted, consisted of shifts between the agricultural-laborer and the urban-unskilled stratum.

Once again we see demonstration of the considerable significance of career beginnings (see Blau and Duncan, 1967:48-58). Insertion of the tabular control for entry level very nearly obliterated an otherwise fairly strong correlation between social origin and current occupation. An alternative demonstration, stated in terms of mobility frequencies, can be accomplished by visually re-arranging the rows of Table XIII:12 so as to contrast first job and present job within origin categories, and then comparing these distributions with the corresponding (uncontrolled) father-to-son distributions reported in Table XIII:1. For example, we found in the earlier table that 73 percent of all sons of nonmanual origin were themselves nonmanually occupied when inter-viewed; the pertinent data in the table just above show what great variation in that proportion may be attributed to differences in the entry levels of the sons. Thus, whereas 93 percent of those who also began career in white-collar jobs retained their origin status, only 32 percent of the manual entrants and 18 percent of the agrarian entrants were in white-collar jobs at the time of interview. Or, to take a different comparison, 24 percent of all nonmanual-origin sons had skidded to a blue-collar current job; but of these 75 respond-ents, 61 (or about four-fifths) had incurred the status decline at career entry. Similarly, 104 of the 418 manual-origin sons (or 25 percent) reported non-manual current jobs, but more than half of them (58 percent) had started their careers at the nonmanual level.

Earlier we found that, in comparison to some other countries, Italy exhib-ited a low rate of career skidding. In a sense, part of this can be interpreted as a consequence of the delayed effects of social inheritance. If a person entered the labor force at the level of his father's occupation, he was comparatively more immune to future losses of status than was the career-entry achiever. Take the case of sons who inherited a nonmanual entry, for example. Only 7 percent were career skidders when interviewed; by contrast, 17 percent of those who attained a nonmanual career entry from manual origins were career skidders, and 18 percent of those entering the labor force as nonmanuals from an agrarian parentage were career skidders. This and similar comparisons suggest that entry inheritance exerted a dampening effect on the rate of career skidding. But such effect was not large; the more important observation is that once a person entered the labor force, the chances were quite good that he would not subsequently fall below that level of entry, *whatever* his family background.

Trends in Time

It is extremely difficult to assess changes in the rate of career mobility from only one set of survey data. In the case of social inheritance, trends can be estimated through the use of cohort analysis. But, obviously, the longer a person has been in the labor market, the better his chances to take advantage of whatever opportunities for upward mobility there may be (and also, the greater the chances that he will skid); so, a cohort analysis of career data cannot be used with the same effectiveness.

Given these limitations, we shall not attempt an estimation of trends in career mobility with the data at hand. However, we may point to certain factors that are relevant to changes in the rate of career movement. Two in particular should be considered: (1) changes in the distribution of entry occupations in Italy; (2) the altered importance of educational attainment to career mobility in industrial societies in general. As Table XIII:13 reports, nonmanual occupations have accounted for an increasingly large proportion of first jobs over the years. Initially, the change was fairly small, but since the 1930's the proportion has nearly doubled, mostly at the expense of agricultural occupations. Consequently, the distribution of first jobs for the post-1932 cohort was significantly different in its implications for future career mobility, in comparison to that of, say, the 1913–1922 cohort.

TABLE XIII:13. Cohort Variations in Entry Occupations

Occupational Level	Birth Cohort				
	Post-1932	1923–32	1913–22	1903–12	Pre-1903
Nonmanual	36.7%	32.2%	20.0%	19.6%	15.9%
Manual	40.3	40.3	43.9	42.0	25.0
Agrarian	17.4	26.6	34.6	35.1	34.5
Unknown	5.6	1.0	1.5	3.2	24.7
Total	100.0%	100.1%	100.0%	99.9%	100.1%
N	161	399	405	308	296

In industrial society, upward mobility from one nonmanual occupation to another increasingly means additional formal training, often of a quite specialized nature. Whereas a general education would suffice for a wide range of occupations a generation or two ago, the requirements of a great many nonmanual positions today are rather narrowly defined, and often an adequate training for one type of work ill prepares a person for another type. Since in all but a very few societies—and Italy is not yet one of them—an adult only rarely returns to school after career entry, the education he takes with him into his first job establishes the broad limits of his future mobility. Moreover, if his first job is that of a blue-collar worker, he may experience upward mobility from one skill level to another, and more often within the same industry than across industry lines (see Blau and Duncan, 1967:37). But he is not very likely to move into the ranks of the white-collar world. Thus, since the occupational structure of Italy has grown disproportionately at the nonmanual level, we would expect that the rate of upward *career* mobility both *into* and *within* that category has declined somewhat in recent years. To put it simply, if the son of a blue-collar or agrarian father aspires to a nonmanual position, or if the son of a petty-bourgeois father aspires to a bourgeois or elite position, the chances are rather great that his ascent will come at career entry or not at all.

XIV

EDUCATION, MIGRATION, AND SOCIAL MOBILITY

Among the many variables that are known to be associated in one degree or another with vertical mobility, educational attainment and migration certainly occupy a central position. Generally speaking, the better educated a person is, the more likely he is to either experience mobility from a lower to a higher occupational position or retain a high initial occupation position. Similarly, as a general rule, migrants more often experience upward mobility than nonmigrants.

We are being advisedly cautious in saying that these two variables are associated with occupational mobility. Without specifying a number of other variables and constructs, such as the respondent's age, the mobility experiences of the parental family, the occupational structure of the community of residence, and so forth, it is specious to assert what is clearly determinant and what is clearly consequent. Of the two correlates considered here, this caution pertains especially to migration. It is quite difficult to determine at an aggregate level how much of the observed migration is due to occupational mobility, how much of the observed rate of occupational mobility stems from migration, how much each change is due to their likely interdependence, and what portion of both changes is the consequence of some common third factor or set of factors.

With these introductory comments in mind, we turn to a consideration of our data: first, those on the relationship between educational attainment and occupational mobility; second, and more briefly, those on migration.

EDUCATION AND SOCIAL MOBILITY

In comparison to many other Western European countries, Italy has until very recently paid little attention to the development of its educational system as a national resource. Prior to 1963, for example, the universal requirement was only five years of schooling; and many, especially in the rural districts, found it only too easy to escape the official obligation. Where conscious efforts at further education were made, the training was usually obtained in workshops and was oriented toward the inculcation of practical skills, such as those required by the various arts and crafts. Secondary schools and universities primarily served as preparatory agencies for the select few, the "elites," who would one day assume privileged places in the educational, economic, and political orders.

Even as late as 1955, Italy expended the fourth lowest percent of public funds for educational purposes among eighteen Western European nations— namely, $9.30 per capita (United States equivalent), or about half of the Western European average. In turn, this expenditure constituted only 2 percent of the gross national product of Italy, also the fourth smallest figure for the eighteen nations (Dewhurst and others, 1961: Table 10–1). Investments in education, both current and capital, had not changed appreciably since the end of World War II, despite the fact that Italy's economy began to register notable gains during the decade of the 1950's. The prewar (1938) proportion of the GNP allotted to education was 1.7 percent; in 1950 it had increased to more than 2 percent, but for the next several years the percentage remained more or less constant. By contrast, comparable proportions for the United Kingdom as a whole increased from 3.7 percent at the start of the decade to 4.2 percent in 1956 (Edding, 1958: Appendix, 143–144; for more recent comparisons, which indicate relative gains in Italy vis-à-vis other countries, see Poignant, 1969:236–253).

In view of this record, it is little wonder that Italy has long suffered one of the highest illiteracy rates of Western Europe. Since the turn of the century, true, significant inroads have been made: in 1900 nearly half of the population aged 15 and over was classified as illiterate; by 1910 the proportion was 39 percent, and succeeding efforts saw the rate dwindle to 21 percent in 1930, 14 percent in 1950, and 9 percent in 1960 (UNESCO, 1957; Istituto Centrale di Statistica, 1968: Table 1). Much of this accomplishment was due to a certain emphasis on adult education, which cost the state little (for example, television literacy programs), and did even less to eliminate functional illiteracy in contrast to official illiteracy. In any case, illiteracy is still more prevalent in Italy than in most other Western countries. Furthermore, the national average conceals enormous variations by region. In the Trentino (the Trento area), for example, illiteracy characterized less than 1 percent of the population in 1956 and about ½ percent in 1960; among the predominantly peasant population of Calabria, the corresponding rates were 31.8 percent and 21.4 percent (Istituto Centrale di Statistica, 1957a:397; 1968: Table 9).

Formal education in Italy is roughly divided into six levels of instruction. At the bottom are the primary and postprimary levels, consisting respectively of five and three years. Until 1963, few people went beyond the first five years. According to the General Census of 1961 (Istituto Centrale di Statistica, 1968: Table 1), for example, slightly more than 15 percent of the population aged 21 and over had attained more than the primary-school diploma *(licenza di scuola elementare)*. In October of 1963, however, Italy took a significant step toward transforming her public instruction from an elitist to a popular orientation by extending the universal requirements through the postprimary level, that is, to eight years of school.

Secondary education comprises the intermediate or junior (ninth and tenth) years and the final or senior (eleventh through twelfth or thirteenth) years of instruction. Commencing to some extent with postprimary curricula but especially at the intermediate-secondary level, students are channeled into different courses of study. At postprimary this channeling involves a distinction between the preparatory "general" course of study and the terminal "vocational training" programs. At the junior-secondary level a much wider range of alternative curricula is available, with the terminal programs divided into several vocational schools and a series of technical institutes—agricultural, industrial, nautical, commercial, teacher-training, and so on. Until a few years ago, college-preparatory programs were offered almost exclusively by the lyceum *(liceo),* of which there are two types, the "scientific" and the "classical." Of the 80,165 students who obtained a senior secondary diploma in 1957–1958, two-thirds received their training in one of the technical institutes, one-quarter came from the classical lyceums, and the remainder were graduates of the scientific lyceums. Of the technical-institute graduates, 42 percent received instruction in teacher-training curricula and 31 percent received commercial training. Less than 10 percent graduated from the industrial institutes (Central Institute of Statistics, 1963: Table 36).

Higher education typically begins with the fourteenth year of study, although for some courses it may commence a year earlier. Curricula are divided into a variety of degree programs. With the exception of students in the physical-science and engineering programs, who sometimes continue through the eighteenth year of study, and the medical students who remain still another year, higher education generally ceases at the end of the seventeenth year. The distinction between graduate and undergraduate training (the fifth and sixth levels) is not clearly made, and to the extent that graduate training exists, it is usually continuous with the undergraduate program.

Before the reforms of 1963, Italy ranked near the bottom among Western European countries in the proportion of school-age children enrolled at the various grades. In his comparative study, Poignant (1969: Table 103) gives for each of 9 countries the total full-time schoolgoing population over 5 years of age as a percentage of the total "at risk" population (aged 5–24 years), about 1961. These figures in descending order are: United States, 77 percent; France, 65 percent; Belgium, 64 percent; Netherlands, 63 percent; England and Wales, 61 percent; Soviet Union, 56 percent; Luxembourg, 54 percent; Italy, 48 percent; West Germany, 46 percent. Again, Italy ranked near the bottom.

Increasingly in recent years, the Italian state has attempted to improve its educational training, especially at the secondary and university levels, in order to meet the technical manpower needs of an industrial economy. A SVIMEZ (1961a:61,73) report undertaken at the request of the Ministry of Public Instruction, for instance, argued that the annual output of university graduates should be more than doubled as quickly as possible. More generally, it concluded that "the educational system will have to pay close attention to the development of our economic structure so as to adapt itself, both from the point of view of general education and from that of professional training, to the ever growing requirements of society for specialized and differentiated technical skills and functional education." An annual crop of 20,000 to 22,000 university graduates is hardly sufficient for an industrial society of over 50 million people, especially when as few as a third of them attained their degrees in areas most essential to economic growth—in the "scientific," engineering, and agricultural groups of degree courses (Central Institute of Statistics, 1963: Table 39).

One of the most formidable obstacles to improvements in the educational composition of Italy's population has been the traditionally high cost to individual families of keeping their children in school after the fifth year of study. The cost comes not only from current expenditures of capital, which very often does not exist in sufficient quantity in the first place, but also from the loss of potential income in the short-range future. For a great many families in Italy, especially in the South, a teen-age son employed outside the home is a valuable asset to the household economy. So, even if the state assumed the burden of *current* expenditures for sending children to school beyond the obligatory point, the family would still in many cases stand to lose an important part of its earning power.

One impression of the strong link between family economic resources and the likelihood of extended schooling is shown in Table XIV:1, which reports for two levels of students information about their social origins. Nearly a quarter of the students who obtained a senior-secondary diploma from one of the various technical institutes during 1957–1958 were from blue-collar families, and another third were from families in which the father was a self-

employed, independent, or "own-account" worker. By contrast, less than a
tenth of the students graduating from the preparatory lyceums had wage-
earner fathers, and about one-fourth had "own-account" fathers. More important still, over 60 percent of the lyceum diplomates and university
postbaccalaureate students came from middle- and upper-echelon nonmanual
families.

TABLE XIV:1. SOCIAL ORIGINS OF SENIOR SECONDARY AND UNIVERSITY
POSTBACCALAUREATE STUDENTS, 1957–1958 ACADEMIC YEAR

Occupation of Father	Senior-Secondary Diploma[a]			University Post-baccalaureate Students[b]
	Technical Institutes	Lyceums		
		Scientific	Classical	
Entrepreneur, Professional	7.7%	14.0%	16.0%	16.5%
Director, Manager,				
Salaried Employee	34.9	48.7	48.4	44.4
Own-Account Worker	30.7	25.2	24.3	25.8
Wage Earner	23.7	9.8	8.9	7.4
Unpaid Family Worker	0.3	0.3	0.1	0.2
No Occupation	0.6	0.3	0.7	1.3
Unknown	2.2	1.8	1.5	4.3
Total	100.1%	100.1%	99.9%	99.9%
N	52,344	6,837	20,984	19,251

Source: Central Institute of Statistics, 1963: Tables 36 and 39.
[a] Students who obtained a senior-secondary diploma in 1957–1958.
[b] Postbaccalaureate students enrolled in 1957–1958.

Indirectly, these data tell us something about what have been called the
"class chances" of educational attainment (see Floud and others, 1957:42ff;
Duncan and Hodge, 1963; Fürstenberg, 1968:165; Tilford and Preece, 1969:
53–59), that is, about the likelihood that a child from one social class, as
compared with those from a higher or lower class, will attain a given level of
schooling. Consider as a case in point the distribution of lyceum diplomates
in Table XIV:1. Even a superficial glance suggests that children of blue-collar
families had much lower chances of attaining that level of education. But this
comparison tells only a portion of the story. In the first place, the number of
wage-earner families in Italy is considerably larger than the number of families
with fathers in entrepreneurial, professional, managerial, or salaried-employee
occupations. Second, wage-earner families tend to be somewhat larger, on the
average, than those higher up the occupational scale. Consequently, the disparity in class chances between the two groups of children is greater by far than
the above comparison would imply. Even if family size were uniform, by rough

estimate the wage-earner children should account for something over half of the lyceum diplomates, *if class chances were approximately equal.* In other words, measured against the assumption of equal opportunity, the wage-earner children successfully completed the lyceum requirements for a senior-secondary diploma about one-fifth as often as they "should" have. The remaining four-fifths either failed to remain in the senior secondary schools until completion or, in the majority of cases, terminated their formal education before they even got to the senior-secondary level. The junior secondary grades are a major gatekeeper in the process of class selection: they filter out those lower-class children who presumably cannot benefit from higher education (see Barbaglia and Dei, 1969).

Whether or not one agrees with Lenski's (1966:391) assumption that there is a notable "egalitarian tendency inherent in modern educational system,"[1] the family is a very powerful impediment to the equalization of life chances through education. Social-origin status determines the financial possibilities of continued schooling; just as important, it is also critical in the encouragement of requisite interests and perspectives and in the provision of an environment that is conducive to curiosity, quiet study, and the informal exchange of ideas. By its operation through these variables, as well as by its unmediated "delayed effects" (see Glass, 1954:98–140, 291–307; Carlsson, 1958:124ff), social-origin status exerts strong limitations on the choice of career-entry occupations; and since, as we found in Chapter XIII, it is at labor-force entry that upward mobility is most frequent, the level of educational attainment is an important determinant of achievement in the world of occupational activity (see Eckland, 1965).

EDUCATIONAL ATTAINMENT AND MOBILITY

A more detailed picture of the relationship between social-origin status and educational attainment, on the one hand, and between educational attainment and occupational mobility, on the other, is presented in Table XIV:2. The education variable has been dichotomized between those respondents with a primary-school diploma or less (5 years or less), which was the legal requirement when our interviewees were of school age, and those who attained higher levels. Percentages shown in the second through sixth columns of the table are outflow rates computed as percents of immediately preceding base figures. Reading across the top as illustration, 68.5 percent of the 390 respondents from nonmanual families acquired more than five years of schooling (high). In turn, 73 percent of these 267 respondents entered the labor force at the nonmanual level. Finally, the next three columns give standard outflow rates of career mobility; the percentages here, however, are based not on the frequencies

---

[1] For a contrasting view, see Young (1959).

TABLE XIV:2. SOCIAL ORIGINS, EDUCATION, SOCIAL INHERITANCE, AND CAREER MOBILITY: OUTFLOW RATES

Social Origins	Education	Career Entry		Present Occupation			
				Non-manual	Manual	Agrarian	N
Nonmanual (390)	High 68.5% (267)	Nonmanual	73.0%	36.1	63.9	0.0	184
		Manual	13.5	*	*	*	36
		Agrarian	1.9	95.7%	3.8%	0.5%	4
		Total		85.3%	13.4%	1.3%	224
	Low 27.4% (107)	Nonmanual	26.2%	72.7%	18.2%	9.1%	22
		Manual	53.3	26.5	73.5	0.0	49
		Agrarian	6.5	*	*	*	7
		Total		38.5%	52.6%	9.0%	78
Manual (473)	High 24.3% (115)	Nonmanual	48.7%	85.5%	12.7%	1.8%	55
		Manual	41.7	28.3	71.7	0.0	46
		Agrarian	1.7	*	*	*	2
		Total		58.3%	39.8%	1.9%	103
	Low 74.4% (352)	Nonmanual	4.5%	75.0%	25.0%	0.0%	16
		Manual	82.4	10.8	86.2	3.0	268
		Agrarian	7.7	8.0	40.0	52.0	25
		Total		13.9%	79.3%	6.8%	309
Agrarian (661)	High 10.0% (66)	Nonmanual	53.0%	90.9%	3.0%	6.1%	33
		Manual	19.7	30.8	69.2	0.0	13
		Agrarian	19.7	23.1	23.1	53.8	13
		Total		62.7%	22.0%	15.3%	59
	Low 88.2% (583)	Nonmanual	3.6%	64.7%	17.6%	17.6%	17
		Manual	23.5	5.4	80.6	14.0	129
		Agrarian	70.5	3.9	23.1	73.0	386
		Total		6.2%	36.8%	57.0%	532

Note: Percents in the "Education" and "Career Entry" columns do not total 100, since a small number of respondents did not report their educational attainments and others who reported their educational attainments did not report career-entry occupations.

* Too few cases for useful percents.

recorded (as percentage distributions) in the "Career Entry" column but on those in the last column of the table. The discrepancy between these two sets of frequencies results from the number of interviewees who reported labor-force experience but were not employed at the time of the interview.[2]

These data also offer testimony to the disparity in class chances of educational attainment. Whereas nearly seven out of ten sons of nonmanual fathers attended school beyond the fifth year, only one-quarter of the sons of manual workers and one-tenth of those of agrarian fathers did so. The rank-correlation coefficient (τ_c) between social-origin status, based on the seven-point occupational scale employed in Chapter XIII, and educational attainment, using the seven-point scale recorded below in Table XIV:4, was .421.

Furthermore, the table demonstrates the power of education as an intervening variable in social inheritance. Thus, 73 percent of the "high"-education sons of nonmanual fathers retained their social-origin status at career entry, in contrast to only 26 percent of those with no more—and often less—education than the legal minimum. Again the "low"-educated sons of agrarian families inherited that lowly status at first job nearly four times as often as their better-trained counterparts. Among the sons of blue-collar workers, upward movement to nonmanual occupations was nearly *eleven times more frequent* if they had continued in school beyond obligation, and skidding to an agrarian job was less than one-fourth as frequent. Similarly, given an agrarian background, the acquisition of more than five years of school increased the chances of ascent at career entry (either into manual or into nonmanual positions) almost threefold. Indeed, over half of the better-educated sons made it all the way to white-collar positions, and another one-fifth entered the urban world of manual workers, mostly at the skilled level. But the vast majority of sons from agrarian families did not enjoy such opportunities for education, and for them the prospects of beginning adult career-life as anything other than an agrarian were quite bleak; more than 70 percent remained agrarians, while fewer than one in twenty-five gained entrance to the white-collar world, and about one in four began their careers as blue-collar workers (rather equally divided among the skilled, semiskilled, and unskilled levels).[3]

---

[2]Note also that there is a small loss of information between the social-origin and educational-attainment and between the educational-attainment and career-entry distributions. Thus, the percentage distributions in the second and third columns of the table do not total 100.

[3]Another way of demonstrating the influence of educational attainment on origin-to-entry mobility is to examine the direct effects of origin level on entry level within categories of educational attainment. Using the nonmanual-manual-agrarian occupational classification and the "high" versus "low" division of educational attainment, we find rank correlations (τ_c) of .455 for the low-education category and .214 for the high-education category. These contrast with a coefficient of .603 for the uncontrolled origin-to-entry relationship. Thus, among the better-educated respondents (nearly six in ten of whom were of nonmanual origin) the impact of origin level on the son's chances of entering a particular occupational category was relatively weak; most of the mobility observed among these respondents was upward. Among those sons who attained a primary-school diploma or less, on the other hand, the impact of origin level on entry level was greater. Moreover, the difference between the coefficient for this low-education category of re-

In terms of conventional summary measures of mobility, the benefits of education beyond the primary-school years produced an absolute increase of 9 percentage points in the total rate of observed mobility (27 percent versus 36 percent). Nearly all of this increment was due to a higher rate of upward movement: 18 percent of the low-education respondents, in contrast to 25 percent of the better-educated, were career-entry achievers. Moreover, when measured against the full-equality benchmark, the experience of those respondents who acquired "high" levels of education came much closer to theoretical expectations. For them, upward mobility was 78 percent of the expected value, and downward mobility was 53 percent of what it would have been under conditions of equal opportunities; comparable figures for the respondents with less education were 52 percent and 39 percent, respectively.

Returning to Table XIV:2, the matrices for career mobility indicate that the importance of education applied not only to recruitment and selection processes at labor-force entry but also to subsequent chances of advancement. Consider, for instance, the sons of nonmanual fathers: almost all of them retained a nonmanual entry if they had more than the primary-school diploma behind them; if they did not, their chances of skidding were about one in four. As for upward movement, about 36 percent of the better-educated advanced from a blue-collar entry, versus 27 percent of those who had dropped out of school on or before attainment of the primary-school diploma.

Ignoring differences in social-origin status, the relationship between education and career mobility is essentially the same: the higher the level of educational attainment, the lower the rate of immobility and downward mobility and the higher the rate of upward mobility. Components of this relationship can be summarized, as before in the case of social inheritance, by using the conventional summary statistics. However, because of the strong connection between education and career entry, an additional procedural step in computing these measures is called for. A high level of schooling produces a top-heavy distribution of nonmanual first jobs, while low attainment levels channel proportionately more people into the agrarian and manual categories. As a result of these excessive "loadings" at the extremes of the occupational scale, the "ceiling" and "cellar" effects of an occupational classification are magnified. People in the top category at career entry cannot by definition be registered as upwardly mobile; if the great majority of the members of a particular subsample enter the labor force at the top, there can be little evidence of career ascent for that subsample. Conversely, if the members of a different subsample predomi-

---

spondents and the zero-order coefficient (.455 versus .603) is attributable largely to the "excess" skidding of nonmanual-origin sons who did not attend school beyond the fifth year, at most; 62 percent skidded to the manual level, and another 8 percent skidded to the agrarian level.

nantly enter the labor force through low-status jobs, there can be little evidence of career skidding.

These circumstances describe very well the career mobility profiles of our two educational subsamples. In the case of respondents with more than the primary-school diploma, for example, 71 percent held nonmanual first jobs, 24 percent began as blue-collar workers and 5 percent started in agrarian positions. Among those with a primary-school diploma or less, on the other hand, only 7 percent entered the labor market at the nonmanual level, while 49 percent began as manuals and 45 percent as agrarians. The extremes of the occupational scale were thereby loaded so heavily—especially at the top of the scale for the better-educated respondents—that there was seemingly a direct relationship between the likelihood of career ascent and low educational attainment (see the "Actual Values" columns of Table XIV:3). Indeed, according to the full-equality model, upward mobility for the better educated respondents was only 36 percent of expectation, whereas for the less well educated it was 52 percent.

Although it is not entirely inconceivable that the low-education subsample should have exhibited the higher mobility ratio on career achievement, the

TABLE XIV:3. EDUCATIONAL DIFFERENCES IN CAREER MOBILITY:
ACTUAL AND ADJUSTED VALUES

| Mobility Statistics | Educational Level | | | |
| | Actual Values | | Adjusted Values[a] | |
	Low	High	Low	High
Observed:				
Up	18.2%	7.7%	13.1%	23.6%
Down	4.6	5.1	11.6	2.3
Total	22.8%	12.8%	24.7%	25.9%
Minimum Mobility	9.5	1.6	9.1	15.3
Excess over Minimum	13.3	11.2	15.6	10.6
Expected:				
Up	34.7%	21.5%	33.3%	56.5%
Down	22.8	19.7	33.4	23.4
Total	57.5%	41.2%	66.7%	79.9%
Ratio, Observed/Expected:				
Up	52.4%	35.8%	39.3%	41.8%
Down	20.2	25.9	34.7	9.8
Total	39.7%	31.1%	37.0%	32.4%

[a] Based on hypothetical career-entry populations distributed equally among the nonmanual, manual, and agrarian categories (see text for procedures).

magnitude of the difference is rather startling. Undoubtedly some part of the discrepancy can be attributed to the "distortion" in career-entry distributions that resulted from the statistical control for education; the question is, how much?

We can nullify the "loading" effects of educational attainment on the two career-entry distributions by proportionally adjusting those distributions in such a way as to equalize the number of respondents located in each occupational category, and by applying then the outflow rates of the original matrices to the adjusted distributions. In effect, we are simply applying the actual outflow rates to a hypothetical career-entry population that is composed of equal numbers of nonmanuals, manuals, and agrarians. Since the outflow rates are stated in tenths of percents, a thousand people in each occupational category of the entry distribution is a convenient number. This procedure, then, will enable us to assess the relationship between educational attainment and career mobility relatively independently of the prior linkage of education and social inheritance. It must be emphasized that the *absolute* values of the resulting summary measures (the "Adjusted Values" columns of Table XIV:3) apply to the hypothetical population and not to the actual respondents. But the relative size of the measures gives meaningful information; for example, a larger rate of upward mobility in the "high-education" category indicates a positive correlation between level of educational attainment and the probability of career ascent.

The results of our procedure quite clearly show that, independent of its influence on status changes between social origin and career entry, education acted as a selective screen to movements along the career dimension. The chances of advancement were greater among the better educated, while the likelihood of skidding was about five times larger among those who ended their formal education with no more—and often less—than the primary-school diploma.

However, when we compare the mobility ratios for social inheritance and career mobility, the impact of education appears to have been different for the different periods in which the status changes occurred. Career movements up the occupational scale were less affected by educational attainment than were status gains between social origin and first job. Thus, the greatest occupational benefit derived from continued schooling was manifested through the selection processes of labor-force recruitment. Once a person had entered the labor force, the chances of advancement were comparatively small, and the amount of schooling he had behind him made very little difference in his chances. A "high" level of schooling did constitute a degree of insurance against career skidding. For instance, a person who had attained more than the primary-school diploma and then entered a nonmanual occupation very likely retained that occupational level during his career, regardless of his social origin; if, on the other hand, he had not gone to school beyond the fifth grade of instruction, his chances of downward mobility were much greater. But a "high" educational level (which often meant no more than eight years of schooling) was *not* always enough to insure that a son of nonmanual origin could begin his career at his father's level. Indeed, referring back to Table XIV:2, about 15 percent of such respondents did not have nonmanual career entries. Of these, more than a third later regained their social-origin status via career effort.

In terms of the *actual* career experiences of our interviewees, of course, the better educated were less often upwardly mobile. But as we pointed out earlier, the difference in actual rates reflects the impact of education on career entry as well as on career mobility. By virtue of their superior qualifications, presumably, the better educated disproportionately acquired (or inherited) nonmanual status when they began their adult work lives. In a manner of speaking, they thereby exhausted their opportunities for upward mobility the minute they entered the labor force, in contrast to their less educated fellow citizens who had to start lower on the occupational scale and then try to work their way up.

The Differential Risks of Education

In their analysis of education and occupational mobility, Blau and Duncan (1967:156ff) found that while the benefits of education (in the sense of improved chances for social ascent) were relatively uniform for men of different family backgrounds, the risks of skidding were differentially distributed. The likelihood of upward mobility rather systematically increased with increasing levels of schooling; and, in general, downward mobility negatively correlated with educational attainment. But men who had college experience short of degree requirements exhibited disproportionate rates of skidding. That is, compared with their fathers' occupational position, these men were more likely to have skidded in status to their present jobs than either those who had more education or those who had less. The reason, Blau and Duncan suggest, is that they in effect failed to acquire the educational prerequisites typical of their own social origins. Inasmuch as their fathers could afford to send them to college in the first place, they generally came from higher-status families. And their one, two, or three years of college was not enough to overcome the greater risks of downward mobility that inhere in a high origin status. Not only did they fail to "inherit"; they were also unable to regain their origin status through career striving.

Our data also display evidence of such differential risks of educational attainment, albeit the greatest risk of skidding occurred somewhat lower on the educational scale (Table XIV:4). Specifically, those respondents who dropped out of school after completing the junior-secondary level of instruction were the most likely to have skidded from their social-origin status (in

Educational Level	Social Origin				N	Mobility Rates[a]		
	Non-manual	Manual	Agrarian	Total		Up	Stable	Down
No Education	1.6%	20.6%	77.8%	100.0%	63	12.7%	82.5%	4.8%
Some Primary School	4.1	26.6	69.3	100.0	316	27.5	66.1	6.3
Primary-School Diploma	11.8	39.1	49.1	100.0	542	32.8	58.5	8.7
Junior Secondary	46.0	36.9	17.0	99.9	176	27.8	54.5	17.6
Senior-Secondary Diploma	59.8	23.9	16.2	99.9	117	35.9	60.7	3.4
Some University	77.3	11.4	11.4	100.1	44	20.5	79.5	—
University Degree	78.8	11.5	9.6	99.9	52	17.3	82.7	—

[a] Mobility rates based on comparisons of father's occupation to son's present occupation.

most cases, the nonmanual level). As a group, moreover, they exhibited a lower rate of upward mobility than either of the neighboring categories, and their rate of inheritance was the lowest of the seven attainment categories. By contrast, the interviewees who obtained at least the senior-secondary diploma were the least likely to have experienced downward movement, despite the fact that statistically they had the highest risk of skidding, since from 60 to 79 percent of them came from nonmanual families. There was no difference in the rate of skidding between those who attended but did not complete college and those who were awarded a degree. In Italy, then, as compared to the United States, the premium placed on one, two, or three years of college—or, for that matter, on the senior-secondary diploma—was very nearly as high as the value of a college degree. There is a good reason for this finding: school teachers in Italy do not need a university degree, even though they are considered professional workers. Likewise, many diplomates from the various technical institutes occupy professional or semiprofessional positions without a university degree.

Blau and Duncan (1967:161, 158) argue within the context of their data for the United States that, because "the relative deprivation of social status implicit in downward mobility is suffered most often by men in the intermediate educational brackets . . . their exposure to this greater risk . . . may well make them a potentially explosive force in periods of economic crisis." Citing the work of Lipset (1959:134ff), among others, they suggest that these circumstances might "help to explain why, as has often been alleged, the lower middle class generally," and the stratum skidders in it in particular, show a heightened sensitivity to the appeals of authoritarian and totalitarian doctrines and to various kinds of prejudice. Denying personal responsibility for their failure to inherit, they tend to lash out at convenient scapegoats.

There is also the peculiar manner in which the process of formal education supports the existing order of society (see Lenski, 1966:394–395). It would seem that, other things being equal, increased education through the primary and secondary levels of instruction tends to exert a conservative influence on the sociopolitical attitudes of people. Curricula at these levels, after all, generally reflect an unquestioned acceptance and even glorification of basic political arrangements, a circumstance that is often consciously manipulated by the state in order to construct and preserve an integrated political community (see for example, Coleman, 1965: especially Part II). Beyond the secondary level, on the other hand, formal education often has somewhat more of a "liberalizing" tendency, at least to the degree that curricula stimulate independent critical thinking. To be sure, universities are not always or uniformly free of conscious efforts to disseminate "appropriate" political ideologies, and conduct celebrations thereof. But, by and large, the assumption has been that by the time a person enters tertiary education he is safely indoctrinated with "correct" beliefs and values, and that, accordingly, the "civics function" is less important in the university.[4]

If this distinction in the political implications of formal education is as sharp as it appears to be, it has potentially important class-linked consequences. The children who, by virtue of objective conditions of existence, are most apt to display leftist political attitudes—children of working-class and peasant families—are also those most likely to end their formal schooling before they have gone beyond the civics and history textbooks of primary school. Thus, the leftist influence commonly associated with working-class parentage is potentially counteracted by the political education offered in state-supported classrooms. The higher and often "liberalizing" grades of instruction are traditionally populated by children of the privileged class. In contrast, the person who skids from the privileged class because of inadequate schooling has not had the opportunity to learn the alternative perspectives often found in the university setting and is therefore left with the perspectives taught by his parents and in the primary and secondary schools. In other words, as Blau and Duncan suggested, in his understandable status frustration he may well be a promising candidate for authoritarian-totalitarian reactions and prejudices.

In Italy, however, such linkages between class and the political implications of formal eductaion are still mostly potential, for two reasons. First, in many ways the political-integration function of the public-school system has never operated very effectively; in part, this ineffectiveness has been due to the abbreviated nature of compulsory attendance. Perhaps more crucially, classroom experience is as often as not a window upon the ineptness, corruption, and self-serving of the state bureaucracy. Hence, instead of molding sentiments of loyalty and trust toward the state and its captors, much that is characteristic of public instruction in Italy has exactly the opposite consequence.

Second, an informal, "popular" political education is widely available in Italy, and it is predominantly leftist. Because it is given openly and insistently, it is also generally more effective than the political education offered by the state through the public schools. This education, combined with the realities of a working-class or peasant life, does much to nullify any conservative influences that primary- and secondary-school instruction might have on working-class or peasant children.[5] It can have a comparable, though some-

[4]Recent student riots in Italian universities, as in those other countries, cast appreciable doubt on the veracity of this assumption.

[5]In Italy such nullification has typically been greater among the working-class than among the peasant children. On the one hand, the popular leftist political education has been targeted mainly at the urban working class and in part at the agricultural day laborers. The peasantry has not been ignored completely, but socialist and communist doctrines are primarily attuned to life in the urban-industrial world, and only in that larger context do they usually address the peasant's problems of day-to-day living. For their own part, moreover, the peasants have long harbored a suspiciousness toward all politics—whether left, center, or right—and this attitude tends to separate them from the countervailing influences of the popular political education (see Lopreato,

what less substantial, effect on the political perspectives of the person who has skidded from a privileged family, depending on whether he has accepted the status loss as representative of something more than a temporary circumstance. In any case, in Italy, where the state has a reputation of ineptness and corruption, if he is angry he is more likely angry toward the state than toward some scapegoated minority group. And in the present juncture, leftist parties support that anger.[6] We will return to the topic of skidders' politics in the chapter next following.

EDUCATION AND ECONOMIC DEVELOPMENT

Economic productivity in industrial society is in some measure tied to the educational quality of its labor force. At a bare minimum, it requires a literate population, one that can sensibly interpret instruction manuals, regulations, and other written documents, and can complete various official forms and work records, and so forth. In addition, ever larger pools of technically and professionally skilled manpower are needed, and this need in turn implies a supply of competent teachers, physical facilities, instructional equipment, and curricula designed to meet the demands of industrial and bureaucratic machinery. According to one recent study (Harbison and Myers, 1964:40), the correlation between values of gross national product and enrollment ratios at the secondary level of instruction for seventy-five countries was .817; between GNP and the number of teachers per 10,000 population, .755; between GNP and the number of scientists and engineers per 10,000 population, .833; and between secondary-school enrollment and percentage of the labor force engaged in agriculture, a high *negative* correlation of −.835. "Hence," as Lenski (1966:390) put it, "the privileged classes have a vested interest in providing

---

1967b:255). On the other hand, because of the surveillance of rural priests, peasant children are more often subject to the pressures of the Church, both through their more easily influenced mothers and through direct associational involvement. Though the parents may not intend or even be cognizant of such consequences, this involvement tends to increase susceptibility to and acceptance of whatever state-supported (and in recent times church-supported) political education the child comes in contact with.

[6]The importance of the skidder's evaluation of the status loss as temporary or permanent was discussed in Chapters VIII and IX. In brief, if he has accepted the fact of skidding as a probably irreversible event, he more likely identifies with working-class interests and is therefore open to working-class political perspectives. Although the relevant frequencies are small—only 27 interviewees with a junior-secondary education skidded from nonmanual origins to manual status at present occupation—our data do not reveal any significant differences in political attitudes between the aforementioned skidders and other nonmanual-to-manual skidders. That is, the level at which they terminated their formal education did not seem to differentiate them in any significant manner. However, because of the small frequencies involved, we were not able to control for class identifications. It is conceivable that those nonmanual-to-manual skidders who had terminated at the junior-secondary level *and* who, after skidding, continued to identify with their class of *origin* were prone to adopt reactionary perspectives of authoritarianism and scapegoating as explanations of status loss and failure of re-acquisition.

educational opportunity for all—a situation radically different from that in agrarian societies."

Perhaps because the dominant northern interests in Italy found it advantageous for so long to keep the *Mezzogiorno* an essentially agrarian society—a commercialized but nonindustrialized market for its own industrial production—southern Italy has traditionally suffered from underdevelopment of its educational resources.[7] Since the end of World War II, it is true, the state has variously exerted itself to further the cause of education in the South, both directly through the Ministry of Public Instruction and via agencies such as the *Cassa per il Mezzogiorno,* a corporate fund chartered by the Italian Parliament for the financing of public works in the South. But very often in the South, given the absurdly complicated and inefficient nature of the state bureaucracy, intentions have a way of becoming sidetracked along the road to actual deed. Lopreato (1967b:138), for example, reports that a few years ago in the small Calabrian village of "Franza," a public school was planned and construction begun through the resources of the *Cassa.* "But for various unfathomable reasons, adequate funds were not forthcoming, and the initiated building has been serving since as a public latrine." Schachter cites another instance of government efforts gone askew (see also Dolci, 1968). The mayor of Santa Maria Salina, Sicily, wrote in a letter to *Mondo Economico* the following:

On the basis of the Tupini Law (for school construction), I obtained permission to build additional classrooms to the existing school. Thus far I have been unable to have the classrooms built because the Government Commission has not found time to come here to choose the proper location. I emphasized (to the higher scholastic authorities) that the location presents little problem. A school building previously built under the Tupini Law exists. Additional classrooms can be constructed in one place only, that is, as an extension of the existing school. Nothing to be done. The Commission must come first. Since December 1955, the Commission has not been able to come to S. Maria Salina (cited in Schachter, 1965:79).

The mayor's letter was dated February, 1963.[8]

We have already noted briefly the North-South disparity in illiteracy. According to the general census of 1961 (Istituto Centrale di Statistica, 1968: Table 9), the regions north of the Po Valley averaged 22 illiterates per thousand population aged 6 and over, while the central "Red Belt" regions averaged 68

---

[7]Submitting this possibility does not discount the fact that the general populace itself is often resistant to changes in the educational system, especially when such changes result in a lengthened universal requirement. A poll conducted in West Germany in 1965, for example, found that 52 percent were opposed to raising the school-leaving age, and only 5 percent were explicitly in favor of the change (cited in Tilford and Preece, 1969:51). The point is, the ruling interest sometimes takes advantage of such resistances and perpetuates them.

[8]Failures by the state to successfully develop educational resources, particularly in the South, have been one of the major criticisms of the Left Opposition (see, for example, LaPalombara, 1966b:67–68).

per thousand and the region of Latium, of which Rome is the capital, 64 per thousand. The average rate in the *Mezzogiorno,* by contrast, was 160 per thousand, with extremes of 132 for Abruzzi-Molise and 214 for Calabria. Similarly, proportionately fewer people in the South attend school, not only at the higher levels of instruction but even through the constitutionally mandated primary years. In the late 1950's, "of two million pupils who entered the first grade of elementary school, only one tenth registered at high school" (Schachter, 1965:80–81). A third of these matriculated in a college or university, but, again, "only one tenth eventually graduated." Census data for 1961 (Istituto Centrale di Statistica, 1968:Table 9) show that 4.7 percent of the people aged 6 and over in the North had obtained the senior-secondary diploma and 1.4 percent had a college degree; respective proportions for the South were 3.5 and 1.2 percent; in Calabria, 3.1 and 0.9 percent.[9] Further, college education in the South very frequently means training in disciplines not the most suited to economic development. Schachter (1965:81) notes, for instance, that of a total of about 60,000 full-time university students in southern Italy in 1960, "11,498 were in science and engineering, 5,584 in medicine, 1,320 in agronomy, and *40,703 in letters, social sciences, and law"* (emphasis added).

Since educational attainment and occupational position correlate very closely, it is sensible to examine regional differences in education within categories of occupation before attempting a comparative analysis of mobility experiences. As expected, the North still exhibits superior patterns of attainment. Thus, 76 percent of the northern nonmanuals in our sample, versus 69 percent of the southern nonmanuals, attained "high" levels. Among manual respondents, the respective proportions were 17 and 11 percent; for the agrarians, 6 and 2 percent.

Moreover, a "high" level of attainment was "higher," so to speak, in the northern regions than in the *Mezzogiorno.* That is, proportionately more of the "high" attainers in the North had at least some university experience. In contrast, the "low" attainers in the South were much more often without formal education (especially the peasants), and less often had successfully completed primary school. The regional differences at the top of the educational scale are fairly small, but those within the "low" category of attainment are sizable enough to be kept in mind during the mobility analysis.

An investigation of the consequences of educational attainment for career-entry occupations in different economies must take into consideration both supply and demand components of the labor market. The immediate demand for better-educated people may be lower in an underdeveloped economy—such as the *Mezzogiorno*—than in one which has reached an advanced level of

---

[9]A difference of two-tenths of one percent may not seem to be very much, but it represents several *thousands* of people.

industrial technology and production; the occupational structure of the former is less expansive at the nonmanual end, particularly in the broad middle range of nonmanual positions. But if the supply of trained personnel is *even lower,* proportionately speaking, in the underdeveloped economy, the premium placed on such training—whether senior-secondary, partial college, or college degree—will often be higher in comparison to the advanced industrial economy. The educational system of the industrial society may be producing annual crops of graduates that are more or less adequate to the "needs" of the economy, possibly to the extent that selection processes at career entry are based not simply on the presence or absence of a certain number of years of schooling but rather upon a more incisive measure of skill. In the under-developed economy, the gap between supply and demand is often such that the keepers of the gates to various high-status occupations can less afford the luxuries of additional tests of skill, personality evaluations, and the like. It is, in the common phrase, a "seller's market."[10]

These differing circumstances fairly well describe the economies of "the two Italies," especially for the period of time during which the majority of our respondents terminated their formal schooling and entered first jobs. Within that context the mobility patterns shown in Table XIV:5 are to be interpreted. In general, rates of upward mobility at career entry were higher in the South than in the North, and the difference by level of education was greater in the South than in the North. Comparing outflow rates from manual origins to nonmanual first jobs, for example, the better-educated respondents of northern regions were less successful as a group than their southern counterparts (50 versus 59 percent), and the difference between educational categories was smaller in the North than in the *Mezzogiorno* (46 versus 54 percent).

Correspondingly, the rate of skidding was higher in the northern regions —but only for those who had attended school beyond the fifth year. Apparently, this difference reflects the difference in criteria of selection at labor-force entry: in the North, number of years of school *plus* other measures of ability, like practical training; in the South, more often simply the number of years of school.[11] Also, it should be remembered that "low" education in the *Mezzogiorno* represented on the average a substantially lower attainment level than in the North.

If, as the data in Table XIV:5 have implied, the supply-demand ratio of educated people in the South was such that it created a "seller's market" for

---

[10]As Carlsson (1958:123) figuratively stated it, "because education is more widespread [in the advanced industrial economy] it might take more education to 'buy' a given type of occupation" than in the poorer economy.

[11]Anderson (1961) and Carlsson (1958) argue that for the United States and Sweden, respectively, both of which boast relatively highly industrialized economies, ability is a more important factor of occupational selection than amount of formal schooling as such. However, see also Eckland (1965).

TABLE XIV:5. EDUCATIONAL ATTAINMENT AND SOCIAL INHERITANCE, BY REGION: OUTFLOW RATES

Region	Educational Level	Social Origin	Career Entry				N
			Non-manual	Manual	Agrarian	Total	
North	High	Nonmanual	81.1%	16.0%	2.9%	100.0%	175
		Manual	50.0	48.6	1.4	100.0	74
		Agrarian	53.3	24.4	22.2	99.9	45
		Total	69.0%	25.5%	5.4%	99.9%	294
	Low	Nonmanual	35.2%	57.4%	7.4%	100.0%	54
		Manual	4.4	88.2	7.5	100.1	228
		Agrarian	3.6	27.2	69.2	100.0	334
		Total	6.7%	52.4%	40.9%	100.0%	616
South	High	Nonmanual	86.9%	13.1%	—	100.0%	61
		Manual	59.4	34.4	6.3	100.1	32
		Agrarian	68.8	12.5	18.8	100.1	16
		Total	76.1%	19.3%	4.6%	100.0%	109
	Low	Nonmanual	23.7%	68.4%	7.9%	100.0%	38
		Manual	5.7	84.8	9.5	100.0	105
		Agrarian	3.8	19.6	76.6	100.0	235
		Total	6.3%	42.6%	51.1%	100.0%	378

people with at least a secondary-level education, in the North it produced a greater turnover of manpower during careers. This difference is manifested most clearly in rates of career skidding. Consider Table XIV:6, which summarizes regional differences in the impact of educational-attainment levels on the probability of career mobility (along with a summary of the social-inheritance matrices of Table XIV:5). The values shown in this table are percentage differences between the two educational categories in outflows from specified origin strata to specified destinations.

TABLE XIV:6. DIFFERENCES BETWEEN CATEGORIES OF EDUCATIONAL ATTAINMENT IN OUTFLOW RATES FROM SPECIFIED ORIGIN TO SPECIFIED DESTINATION, BY TYPE OF MOBILITY AND REGION

| Type of Mobility and Region | Differences in Outflow Rates ("High" — "Low" Education) | | | | | |
| | Upward Mobility | | | Downward Mobility | | |
	Agrarian to Manual	Manual to Non-manual	Agrarian to Non-manual	Manual to Agrarian	Non-manual to Manual	Non-manual to Agrarian
Career Mobility:						
North	− 2.8	45.6	49.7	−6.1	−41.4	−4.5
South	− 7.1	53.7	65.0	−3.2	−55.3	−7.9
Social Inheritance:						
North	− 3.0	19.2	*	−5.6	−21.8	−7.1
South	−11.6	21.3	*	−6.0	− 2.7	−8.7

Note: Negative values indicate that the rate of specified mobility was higher for the "low"-education than the "high"-education category.
* Too few cases for useful percents.

The North-South differences in rates of career skidding were quite small, *except* in the case of skidding from a nonmanual entry to manual status at the time of the interview. That is, of the three groups of skidders, the impact of different levels of schooling on the likelihood of manual-to-agrarian and non-manual-to-agrarian movements was virtually the same for both regions of economic development. But for nonmanual-to-manual skidding, it was substantially different: without a "high" attainment level, retention of a non-manual career entry was much more problematic in the industrial North. Thus, 27.3 percent of the interviewees with a nonmanual entry and "low" education, in comparison to 5.5 percent of the better-educated entrants, had dropped to manual status by the time of the interview, for an absolute difference of 21.8 percent. Comparable values for the *Mezzogiorno* were 8.7 and 6.0

percent, for an absolute difference of 2.7 percent. Because of the barrier to downward mobility into agrarian occupations that generally characterizes Italy, very few of the nonmanual entrants for either region fell below blue-collar status; this barrier probably also accounts for the regionally uniform effect of education on manual-to-agrarian skidding. But given the narrower gap between supply and demand factors of quality manpower in the northern industrial economy, people who managed to begin their careers in nonmanual occupations without having first attained more than a primary-school diploma were not very secure in their positions. As compared to the corresponding group in southern Italy, where the supply of better-educated manpower was so much lower than the demand, they were rather more likely to have been replaced by superiorly qualified individuals.

The evidence contained in Table XIV:6 suggests elements of the distinction between "contest" and "sponsored" forms of mobility (Turner, 1960). In the South, possession of the senior-secondary diploma or a university degree, which itself usually reflects superior family resources and status, was generally enough to insure a nonmanual first job. Once a person was "in," the probability of staying in was very high; according to our data, only one in twenty subsequently dropped out of the nonmanual category. In effect, then, the better-educated southerner was sponsored in his social ascent. Conversely, in the North, he may have been sponsored by his family to the extent of obtaining the diploma or college degree, but beyond that his potential for advancement into a nonmanual career entry was assayed by recruitment and selection processes that were somewhat more in the nature of a contest among prospective entrants. The very fact that the supply of such candidates was relatively more favorable in relation to demand means that nonmanual occupational selection in the northern industrial economy was less often between the "high" and "low" educational attainers and more often among different grades and qualities *within* the "high" attainment category.

To continue with Turner's distinction, the divergent implications of sponsored and contest mobility for social-control mechanisms parallel reasonably well aspects of social structure in the South and in the North, especially the social structures that were extant when most of our respondents were first entering the labor force. Traditionally, the privileged class in the South has done precious little to illuminate for the peasant masses the mystery of "the skills and manner of the elite"; indeed, it has felt comfortable in fostering the "illusion of a much greater hiatus of competence" in the skills of statecraft "than in fact exists." Further, although conditions are rapidly changing (Lopreato, 1967b), early selection for elite status occurred and continues to occur by default in the South, since few families can afford to send their children to school for more than five or six years, if that long. The earlier the selection in a system of sponsored mobility, the more likely class disparities in opportunity are perceived as part of the "natural" order.

In northern Italy, on the other hand, popular norms of ambition, achievement, and individual responsibility, and the ideologies of equal opportunity and success are more often cultivated by the privileged class, in order to disarm the "nonsuccessful" of any societally targeted resentments. Occupational selection processes typically occur later in life, generally during the late teens and early-to-middle twenties, and at no absolute points. This timing gives the impression that everyone enjoys an equal opportunity to win the contest; and if someone does not win, it is because of personal failure.

Finally, northern and southern Italy have traditionally differed in the mechanisms of control exerted by the privileged classes over their new recruits. In the *Mezzogiorno,* the newcomers are restrained from taking undue advantage of their superior position, and thereby jeopardizing the security of the entire class, by inculcating in them "a norm of paternalism toward inferiors"— *noblesse oblige.* In contrast, in the North, control over recruits more often occurs as an "impersonal" function of the market situation itself, that is, in characteristics of the contest form of mobility. The "principal regulation" tends to be found in the "insecurity of elite position." Indeed, as the data of Tables XIV:5 and XIV:6 testify, there were fewer "final arrivals" and fewer "safe seats" awaiting the northern high-school and college graduates.

Education, Opportunity, and Democracy

Increasingly, twentieth-century industrial culture has become imbued with the notion that if a person fails to attain a certain level of education, he should not expect too much future success, in the sense of occupational advancement, periodically improved financial rewards, a steadily more comfortable style of life, and so forth. Perhaps nowhere is this notion more pronounced or so widely accepted as "obvious" than in the United States. But it also characterizes other industrial societies, including Italy, and under the aegis of the "developed" fraction of the world it is rapidly growing roots among the less developed majority.

To be sure, there is basis in concrete experience for the stated relationship: the probability of upward mobility *is* substantially correlated with educational attainment. But there is more than mere empirical relationship in the aforementioned notion; it also serves as a legitimizing ideology, and the moral element of that ideology hides a half-truth—namely, that "equal opportunity is assured through education." It is only right and proper, according to the ideology, that people who acquire certain educational credentials should be upwardly mobile and otherwise successful; they have earned it. The argument, it may be noted, is implicit in the theory of Davis and Moore discussed in our Chapter V. Tumin (1953a), however, would argue that it was not earned at all, since it was paid with the financial rewards reaped from society by their parents. Conversely, those who do not acquire the credentials deservedly remain enmeshed in their lowly circumstances; they cannot justifiably expect anything different, for, after all, they too had their opportunities for education.

In fact, however, these people often did not have "their opportunities," at least not their share of them. Educational opportunity structures are still governed in fairly large measure by social inheritance, especially in the developing economies but certainly also in the advanced industrial societies such as the United States (see Blau and Duncan, 1967:152–161). The child of high-status parentage has significant advantages, both material and intangible, with respect to his educational possibilities, and thus he will more likely "achieve" a high-status career entry. As the quotation marks have just intimated, educational attainment and its implications for career entry are often much more in the nature of ascriptive than achieved status. Consequently, the ideology of "equal opportunity through education" legitimizes what is in fact, to a large extent, an occupational inheritance; and its moral component thereby implies a *personal* responsibility for failure, as if the child could enter the family of his choice.

In the Italian *Mezzogiorno* as in other developing economies, and to some extent also in the more advanced industrial states, regulation of human traffic into and out of the educational process is left mainly to the operation of simple market mechanisms. In some instances, this process may operate mostly by default; in others, it stems more from conscious efforts to retain the veil of "free-market" principles, beneath which the actual regulation of traffic may be manipulated by the captors of the state. But certainly for the economy that is struggling to break fully into the industrial order, it is not sufficient to "let the market set the traffic." In the *Mezzogiorno,* and in many other societies like it, great numbers of children are denied the benefits of extended education precisely because a free-market situation does not exist. Their chances of educational attainment are closely circumscribed by class considerations— ultimately by the biological "accident" of being born into a working-class or peasant family. In order to reverse this inefficiency, it may well be necessary for the state to intervene massively in the educational process, even to the extent of equalizing "class chances" by imposing restrictions on the number of children of high-status families who may remain in school. The alternative is a continuation and, perhaps, intensification of the class-linked division between a small highly trained elite and the great ignorant masses.[12]

MIGRATION AND SOCIAL MOBILITY

Because occupational structures typically differ from one place to another, the country, region, and locality in which a person is born potentially influence his chances of occupational advancement. The influence is *potential* because the individual often has open the alternative of physically moving to a different

---

[12]See the relevant discussions by Young (1959) and Carlsson (1963) of "meritocratic" systems of inequality. Both point out that under certain conditions, education can actually increase inequalities and the rigidity of the class structure.

area, with different opportunities. He may relocate from a locality of high unemployment and depressed pay scales to one in which the possibilities of growth and improvement are greater. Of course, a good many factors besides differential occupational opportunities are involved in the migration of populations, and the potential influence of which we just spoke may become *actual;* that is, the person may remain in his locality of birth. There are indeed "pushes" from the community of origin, such as a glutted labor market for particular skills, and "pulls" from possible communities of destination, such as favorable supply-demand ratios. But these pushes and pulls are not the whole; also operating are a series of "anchoring" factors, such as the presence of extended networks of family and friends in the home town, and, from the other direction, a series of "repelling" factors, perhaps the most important of which is simply the unknown quality, so to speak, of a new home. Migration, then, can be conceived as one possible outcome of a more or less delicate balancing of numerous countervailing factors.

People do move from one community to another, however, and when they do so, *occupational* mobility is a frequent concomitant (see, for example, Bell, 1968:44ff). As Blau and Duncan (1967:243) concisely stated it, "Migration provides a social mechanism for adjusting the geographical distribution of manpower to the geographical distribution of occupational opportunities." In the adjustment, some individuals usually move up the occupational scale and others down.

Although massive migration as an exceptional phenomenon has been a historical occurrence from the time nomadic life styles were replaced by sedentary communities, the connection between migration and occupational mobility is a fairly new wrinkle of importance in the stratification of societies. Until the advent of urban and industrial economies, occupational structures were neither expansive nor flexible enough to allow much ascent (although perhaps a bit more descent) by physically moving from one place to another. Migration did act as an adjustive mechanism of sorts, especially during endemic crises —famine, disease, invasion, or the like—but at best the migrant typically moved from a particular branch of work in one locality to the same activity in another locality. If he was less fortunate than usual, he fell to baser work or perhaps to no regular employment at all.

An early example of an adjustive mechanism which succeeded to a degree in combining on a large scale both geographic and social mobility was the great exodus from the manorial system in Europe which coincided with the rebirth of city life as well as commerce and craftsmanship toward the beginning of the second millennium A.D. A more recent example was provided by the "tramping system" of nineteenth-century England (Hobsbawm, 1964:34–63). This was a more or less regularized arrangement whereby the apprenticed worker usually, though sometimes the journeyman also, could leave the locality of his particular trade society in search of more fruitful employment elsewhere. Social ascent by this means was relatively infrequent, and seldom involved more than very small gains. But with its way-stations, meal tickets, and letters of introduction, the tramping system did enable artisans to move from low-wage areas to areas somewhat more profitable in remuneration. To the artisan himself, such small gains were indeed quite significant.

Migration in Italy

For the past seven or eight decades, the predominant pattern of geographic mobility in Italy has been from the *Mezzogiorno* outward, both to the urban industrial North of Italy itself and to other countries—other European countries, North and South America, Australia.[13] During the 80 years from 1871 to 1951, the South had a net loss of 4.5 million people due to migration (SVIMEZ, 1961b: Table 107). Between 1906 and 1915 alone, Basilicata, Calabria, and Abruzzi-Molise each would have lost about two-fifths of their inhabitants, had some of them not returned later (Vannutelli, 1961:572). The exact proportion who returned cannot be determined, but it was unlikely more than half of them.

TABLE XIV:7. NET-MIGRATION STATISTICS: DISTRIBUTION OF RESIDENCE OF BIRTH AND RESIDENCE IN 1963–1964, BY REGION

Region[a]	Residence of Birth	Residence in 1963–1964
North		
Piedmont	8.4%	10.2%
Liguria	2.6	3.7
Lombardy	13.1	15.2
The Venetias	10.7	10.2
Emilia, Romagna	7.7	7.6
Marches, Umbria, Tuscany	11.4	10.0
Latium	4.9	7.6
South		
Campania	10.1	8.7
Abruzzi-Molise	3.4	2.9
Apulia	13.5	11.9
Basilicata, Calabria	10.3	9.4
Sicily	2.5	2.5
Total	98.6%	99.9%
N	1,569[b]	1,569

a Val d'Aosta and Sardinia were not included in our survey.
b Of the 1,569 respondents, 22 were born outside of Italy.

[13]We will not attempt in this volume a detailed analysis of geographic mobility and its effects on the stratification of the Italian South; in part, this analysis is already available in Lopreato (1967b).

Since 1951, proportionately more of the southern exodus has been to the Italian North. While accurate counts of this internal stream are unavailable, a conservative estimate for the 1952–1963 period puts it at about 5 million people. The increased attractiveness of the northern regions, relative to other and more distant lands, has stemmed in large part from the postwar "economic miracle" of industrial development. Between 1954 and 1960, in the regions indigenously known as the *Settentrione* (from Emilia-Romagna northward), the proportion of the active male labor force engaged in the industrial sector increased from 40.4 percent to 48.1 percent; in the tertiary sector, from 24.0 to 27.6 percent (SVIMEZ, 1961b: Table 341).

In addition to the major internal flow of people from the *Mezzogiorno* outward, other patterns of migration have developed. Disregarding for the moment the large flow across the South-North boundary, certain differences of geographical mobility appear *within* each of the two geographical partitions. In the North, interprovince migrants have outnumbered intraprovince movers in the agricultural sector (by a factor of more than two to one in 1958, for instance; SVIMEZ, 1961b: Table 351), but not in the industrial sector. This indicates that the experienced or potential industrial worker generally moved only as far as the major industrial center of his province, whereas his compatriot who migrated from one agricultural job to another usually had to move a greater distance. In the internal population movement of the South, on the

Table XIV:8. Net-Migration Statistics: Distribution of Residence of Birth and Residence in 1963–1964, by Size of Community

Size of Community	Residence of Birth	Residence in 1963–1964
Up to 2,000	10.9%	8.3%
2,001–3,000	6.3	3.4
3,001–5,000	12.7	10.6
5,001–10,000	17.7	14.9
10,001–20,000	11.0	10.8
20,001–30,000	7.0	7.8
30,001–50,000	6.0	5.3
50,001–100,000	10.4	11.7
100,001–250,000	3.5	4.4
250,001–500,000	5.0	7.4
500,001–1,000,000	1.7	2.6
1,000,001 or more	6.4	12.7
Total	98.6%	99.9%
N	1,569[a]	1,569

[a] Of the 1,569 respondents, 22 were born outside of Italy.

other hand, intraprovince moves predominated even within the agricultural sector. This predominance reflects the fact that farm jobs are about equally ill paid throughout the southern regions, and a long-distance move from one plot of land to another within the South will generally avail the migrant very little if any real gain. Moreover, there is a selectivity factor operating here. Long-distance moves cost more money, often borrowed money, and if the southern peasant undertakes such a venture, his intended destination is typically the North, where the promise of payoff appears to be greater.

Among our sample members, Table XIV:7 suggests, the three regions of the "Industrial Triangle" (Piedmont, Liguria, Lombardy) and the Roman region of Latium were the most frequent destinations of our migrant respondents. The more agricultural regions of central Italy generally experienced net losses of population, as did the *Mezzogiorno*. Commensurately, Table XIV:8 shows a net shift of residence from rural areas, villages, and small towns to communities of greater size. Net losses were heaviest for communities of 10,000 or fewer inhabitants, while cities of more than 50,000 population experienced net gains. The biggest growth was among the metropolitan areas of a million or more people (+6.3 percent).

Migration and Occupational Achievement

To the extent that migration patterns take the form of rural-to-urban, agrarian-to-industrial population transfers, we may reasonably expect a correlation between geographic and occupational mobility. The peasant enters a world of possibly greater opportunity for himself, and at the same time he replaces some of the native industrial workers on the lower rungs of the occupational hierarchy, thereby "pushing" them upward. But there are typically other patterns of migration, too, such as the farm-to-farm, city-to-city, factory-to-factory movers, and for them occupational mobility may be more problematic. We must therefore examine in some detail evidence pertaining to the question, "To what degree and under what conditions are migration and occupational achievement associated?"

The usual conclusion from studies of geographic and occupational mobility is that migrants tend to enjoy "superior occupational achievement, regardless of place of birth or destination" (Blau and Duncan, 1967:250; also Scudder and Anderson, 1954; Lopreato, 1967b: Chapter 7; Svalastoga, 1959:394–399; Lipset and Bendix, 1959: 213ff). However, as Blau and Duncan also pointed out, the linkages underlying that statistical association are not altogether simple and straightforward. These scholars conclude from their examination of data for the United States that migration is both selective of persons "with higher potential for occupational achievement" and representative of a complex of factors, not all of them specifiable, that additionally enhance an originally higher potential.

With these foregoing conclusions in mind, we examine the Italian data. Table XIV:9 records summary statistics from the social-inheritance and career-mobility matrices of migrants and nonmigrants. In this instance, migration is defined as difference in community of residence between birth and 1963–1964, the time of the interview. It should be noted that the "migrant" category includes men who moved from place of birth not as adults but as the children of migrating families. Similarly, the "nonmigrant" category contains an unknown number of respondents who left and then returned to community of birth. Occupational mobility is measured according to the seven-point scale previously described.

TABLE XIV:9. SUMMARY TABLE: SOCIAL INHERITANCE, CAREER
MOBILITY, AND MIGRATION STATUS

Mobility Statistics	Social Inheritance		Career	
	Migrant	Nonmigrant	Migrant	Nonmigrant
Observed:				
Up	25.9%	23.2%	27.6%	24.3%
Down	23.5	19.6	9.2	15.3
Total	49.4%	42.8%	36.8%	39.6%
Minimum Mobility	15.2	10.8	15.0	7.9
Excess over Minimum	34.2	32.0	21.8	31.7
Expected:				
Up	43.2	41.7	44.2	43.6
Down	37.2	44.5	33.2	36.1
Total	80.4%	86.2%	77.4%	79.7%
Ratio, Observed/Expected:				
Up	60.0	55.6	62.4	55.7
Down	63.2	44.0	27.7	42.4
Total	61.4%	49.7%	47.5%	49.8%
N	498	932	467	902

Note: Migration is defined as a difference in community of residence between birth and 1963–1964.

These statistics suggest that the migrants experienced upward mobility, both from social origin to career entry and during career, slightly more often than the nonmigrants and, with the exception of the social-inheritance measure, experienced descent slightly less often. The career-mobility statistics, for example, show that 28 percent of the migrants were achievers and 9 percent were skidders, compared with 24 and 15 percent, respectively, for the nonmigrants. About two-fifths of the occupational change among the migrants, as opposed to one-fifth among the nonmigrants, could be attributed to adjustments from the origin to the destination occupational distributions.

The expected rates show the same pattern. If the origin distributions (either social origin or career entry) and the destination distributions (career entry or present occupation) had been independent of one another, the migrants still would have enjoyed a higher probability of ascent and a lower probability of skidding than the nonmigrants. The pattern is consistent for both measures of mobility.

TABLE XIV:10. MIGRATION STATUS AND EDUCATIONAL LEVEL

Education	Migrants	Nonmigrants
None	3.1%	5.9%
Some Primary School	23.1	25.9
Primary-School Diploma	36.2	41.7
Junior Secondary	15.7	12.2
Senior-Secondary Diploma	11.5	8.2
Some University	3.8	3.5
University Degree	6.6	2.5
Total	100.0%	99.9%
N	549	985

There is some evidence that migration was selective of persons with better achievement potential. At least the migrants were slightly better educated, as Table XIV:10 indicates. Moreover, as a group they had higher career entries: 4 percent into the elite, 12 percent into the bourgeoisie, 15 percent into the petty bourgeoisie, 36 percent into the proletariat; by contrast, the nonmigrants showed values of 2, 8, 13, and 32 percent, respectively. However, it would also appear that the fact of migration had separate effects on career achievement, such that for specific career entries the migrants still outperformed the nonmigrants. By way of illustration, 11 percent of the movers who began in the bourgeoisie and 36 percent of those who entered at the petty-bourgeoisie level were subsequently upwardly mobile; among the nonmigrants, the corresponding proportions were 1 and 19 percent. For entrants at the urban unskilled level, 52 percent of the migrants but only half as many of the nonmigrants later climbed at a higher position. Furthermore, if we standardize the career-entry distributions and recompute on that basis the mobility statistics, we find again a somewhat greater rate of achievement among the migrants: 29 percent upwardly mobile, in contrast to 26 percent of the nonmigrants.

Additional evidence bearing on the matter can be gained by focusing on career mobility and separating those who migrated *during career* from those who changed residence *before they entered the labor market* (Table XIV:11).

Because dates could not be exactly matched in some cases, this division is only approximately defined; but at most, the precareer category of migrants is contaminated only by cases in which geographical movement occurred very early in career.

TABLE XIV:11. TYPE OF MIGRATION EXPERIENCE, AGE, AND
CAREER-MOBILITY RATES

Migration Experience and Present Age of Respondent	Career Mobility				
	Up	Stationary	Down	Total	N
Nonmigrant:					
21–40	19.7%	73.8%	6.5%	100.0%	325
41+	20.1	72.0	7.9	100.0	492
Total	20.0	72.7	7.3	100.0	817
Migrant, before Career:					
21–40	32.4	59.2	8.5	100.1	71
41+	26.1	63.9	10.0	100.0	180
Total	27.9	62.5	9.6	100.0	251
Migrant, during Career:					
21–40	25.9	63.3	10.9	100.1	147
41+	24.5	65.4	10.1	100.0	159
Total	25.2	64.4	10.5	100.1	306

Note: Career mobility is defined in terms of first and present jobs.

Keeping in mind that limitation, the tabulations suggest the following points. First, migration experience coming after adolescence (that is, during career) was associated with higher rates of occupational mobility, in comparison to the nonmigrants. One-quarter of the former, as opposed to a fifth of the latter, were career achievers, and the corresponding rates of skidding were 11 and 7 percent. Second, the respondents who had changed residence only during or before adolescence—that is, while they were still within the parental household, in most cases, and not regularly employed—also exhibited higher rates of mobility than the nonmigrants. Indeed, their rate of achievement was even higher than that of the respondents who migrated only after career entry, a difference contributed largely by the *younger* precareer migrants. In sum, then, the likelihood of occupational achievement was influenced by physical relocations that had occurred prior to the respondent's entrance into the adult work life, as well as by those that took place subsequently as part of that life. To a degree, this difference manifests the greater opportunities of preparatory or anticipatory socialization afforded the children of parents who move from the rural to the urban world, from the small town to the large city. Educational opportunities are better, schools are of better quality, and supplemental resources such as libraries are more accessible. The everyday world is more varied, which means among other things that a greater number of alternative occupational roles are visible to the child for vicarious practice.

While the tabulations in Table XIV:11 indicate that people who moved from one place to another as working adults were more successful in career than the natives, we still cannot rule out the possibility that "migration is selective of men with higher potential for occupational achievement" (Blau and Duncan, 1967:259). Undoubtedly a series of social-psychological variables were operating in conjunction with such structural variables as urbanization, so that geographic and occupational mobility were to some degree complementary effects. Factors of "aggressiveness," of a willingness to invest in uncertain future payoffs, of social attitudes that are at least partially free of the traditional indrawing toward the multigenerational family home and web of friendship, and so forth, some or all of which are themselves differentially linked to origin class—all these factors distinguish both between migrants and nonmigrants and between the occupationally mobile and the nonmobile.

We can here do no more than note the probable importance of such vaguely defined social-psychological variables, since appropriate data for our respondents are lacking. However, we can examine in some greater detail the structural effects of the urbanization factor. The great bulk of population movement in Italy, whether from the *Mezzogiorno* outward to the northern regions, or within regions and even provinces, has fitted the general historical pattern characteristic of industrial society, namely, transfers from rural to urban areas and from small to large cities. Most of these migrants, especially the ex-peasant migrants, have been in the younger age ranges. Typically either young sons who left the farm early in career in search of better opportunities in the city, or sons who went to the city initially in order to acquire further education and then remained, as a group they more likely experienced occupational mobility subsequently in career than did the nonmigrants. Furthermore, there is some evidence that this linkage between urban migration and occupational advancement has slightly increased in strength over the past several years. At a gross level, the data of Table XIV:11 suggest that migrants who were less than about twenty years into career (that is, the 21–40 cohort) were more likely to be upwardly mobile than the older migrants. The differences are small; but it is significant that the relationship is reversed among the nonmigrants, that is, the younger nonmigrants were slightly *less* likely to have experienced career advancement. In addition, the small age differences in the mobility rates of the migrants persist regardless of when the physical relocation occurred, that is, before or during career.

There is still the question of internal variations in the general relationship between migration and mobility as complementary structural effects of urbanization, however. Were the migrants consistently more successful in career, whatever the type of community of destination and/or origin, or did this latter variable exert important influences on the probabilities of occupational advancement? Indirectly, of course, we are asking about variations of opportunity structure in different types of communities.

TABLE XIV:12. MIGRATION AND CAREER MOBILITY, BY SIZE OF COMMUNITIES OF ORIGIN AND DESTINATION

Migration Pattern by Size of Community	Career Mobility				
	Up	Stationary	Down	Total	N
Village (up to 5,000)					
Nonmigrant	18.7%	73.5%	7.8%	100.0%	230
From Another Village	19.1	66.0	14.9	100.0	47
From a Larger Community	25.0	67.9	7.1	100.0	28
Small City (5,001–50,000)					
Nonmigrant	18.8	73.7	7.5	100.0	362
From Another Small City	29.3	58.5	12.2	100.0	82
From a Village	38.3	61.7	—	100.0	47
From a Larger Community	12.1	69.7	18.2	100.0	33
Large City (50,001–500,000)					
Nonmigrant	24.5	68.8	6.7	100.0	208
From Another Large City	16.0	76.0	8.0	100.0	25
From a Smaller Community	29.1	63.3	7.6	100.0	79
From a Metropolis	12.5	87.5	—	100.0	8
Metropolis (over 500,000)					
Nonmigrant	26.0	64.4	9.6	100.0	104
From Another Metropolis	28.6	50.0	21.4	100.0	14
From a Smaller Community	32.2	63.2	4.6	100.0	87

Note: Migration was measured with reference to community of residence during adolescence. See the text for a discussion of this measure.

Table XIV:12 reports some pertinent comparisons, in which size of community of residence for the nonmigrants, and of communities of origin and destination for the migrants, is controlled. Because the frequencies in several cases are rather small, we should not place too much stock in the accuracy of particular mobility rates. But the consistency of patterns is often noteworthy.

In comparison to the nonmigrants, movement from one type of community to another of the same type was, with one exception, associated with higher rates of achievement (and also higher rates of skidding). The exception—the large-city migrants—may be a function of the small number of cases, or it may represent certain selectivity mechanisms; we cannot tell which. At the same time, migration to communities of greater size than the community of origin was associated with still higher probabilities of occupational ascent, and, conversely, with somewhat lower probabilities of skidding. In other words, for each of the three possible comparisons, the opportunity structure was more "open" for in-migrants from smaller communities than for the native population. This agreement reflects rather clearly the selectivity of geographical mobility. The in-migrants, despite the possible handicaps of coming from communities with different styles of life, perhaps poorer formal and informal educational facilities, and different labor-market characteristics, were nevertheless better prepared to compete in the new opportunity structure.

The more detailed tabulations on which Table XIV:12 is based provide additional source of support for the foregoing conclusion, namely, comparisons based on the *degree* of dissimilarity between community of origin and community of destination. The superiority in career chances of migrants into larger communities, as compared with both the natives of the destination communities and those respondents who moved between communities of the same size, holds true not only if the upward migration was between contiguous categories on the community-size scale—for example, from a village to a small city, or from a small to a large city, and so on. If the move was between localities more widely divergent in size, the migrants to the larger localities still exhibited superior career chances of advancement, indicating that the selectivity mechanism of migration was even more pronounced for them, since their communities of origin were generally less well equipped to prepare them for the transition.

We may also infer from Table XIV:12, however, the existence of structural differences in opportunity between the various communities. If the occupational careers of the nonmigrants are any guide, opportunities for advancement increased with increasing community size. Among the four types of community delineated in the table, for example, the village nonmigrants were the least likely to have experienced upward mobility during career, while the metropolitan nonmigrants were the most likely. Furthermore, the data suggest a fairly pronounced pattern of dichotomization, with the dividing line occurring roughly between communities with more and communities with less than 50,000 population. Rates of career ascent were about equally "low" for the village and small-city nonmigrants and similarly "high" for the long-time residents of large cities and metropolitan areas. This difference pattern reflects the concentration of industrial development in the more populous urban areas of Italy.

XV

CLASS MOBILITY AND CLASS CONSCIOUSNESS*

In Chapter XIII the point was made that class consciousness and class mobility are the fundamental concepts of class theory. They refer to the two chief dynamics of class structure. They are also antithetical: while consciousness is the indispensable condition for the formation of classes as politicized groups and hence serves an *associative* function, mobility keeps the classes demographically open to each other, thereby promoting the diffusion and fragmentation of internal ideologies—hence, mobility serves a *dissociative* function in the evolution of class phenomena.

The "anticlass" character of mobility is the focus of the present chapter, and, in part, of the chapter next following. Specifically, concern now is with what are loosely known as the political "consequences" of social mobility. We speak cautiously of mobility consequences because our data, like all other known to us in this area, are cross-sectional rather than longitudinal. The strategy of our inquiry will be to compare, within a two-class scheme, the socially mobile to the class of origin on the one hand and to the class of destination on the other, in terms of political preferences held at *one point in time only*. We shall, therefore, have to accept with reservation the usual assumption that differences in political preference between the socially mobile

---

*Part of this chapter consists of an elaboration and reformulation of a paper previously published by the senior author with Janet S. Chafetz (1970). We are grateful to Dr. Chafetz for permission to rework this material here.

and their class of origin are the results of mobility itself. Clearly, this assumption is problematic, for it is indubitable that some individuals move out of a given class *because* they hold values and ideas (reflected in their political orientations, *inter alia*) that are "inappropriate" to that class and facilitate membership in another. The tale of the successful emulator is of all times and places. There is change in class position here, but no change in political behavior accompanies the class change.

It is equally certain, however, that some individuals do change their political behavior *after* they have changed class position. New occupational associates and modified interests often encourage shifts in political position. Hence, although we do not have the (ideal) data on the politics of the mobile for periods both before and after their mobility, we can safely hold that a substantial, though indeterminate, number of the socially mobile exhibited a political orientation that was the direct result of their change in class position.

A BRIEF REVIEW

A few introductory remarks concerning the role played by social mobility in the theories considered in Part One will help sustain the theoretical coherence of the argument. Recall that Weber focused on the descriptive aspects of social stratification, pointing to the plethora of "classes," "status groups," and "parties" and to the attendant variety of interests and styles of life. He was also sensitive to the occupationally expanding nature and the fluidity of industrial society. As a result, even without Weber's specific discussion of the issue here in question, the message flows unmistakably from his general argument that movement among stratification units is commonplace and that, moreover, with a shift in class position, social status, or political power there occur also shifts in interests, values, and ideologies. A further point of interest with regard to Weber's position concerns his emphasis on status groups and the salience of "social honor" in social relations. Man is, among his many qualities, what more recently has been referred to as a "status-seeker." Hence, it is possible to predict on the basis of Weber's work that matters of social honor and recognition play an important role among the socially mobile; and we should not be surprised, for example, to find among them a certain tendency to emulate the political behavior of the "socially superior."

Davis and Moore are even less emphatic about the role of social mobility in social stratification, but the phenomenon is important to their theory as well. In a nutshell, it may be said that the validity of their theory is to a large extent dependent on the openness of the stratification system. The theory revolves around a theoretical idealization which postulates, among other things, a direct correspondence between "social position" (as a reward phenomenon) and the "functional importance" of roles *only in a state of free competition*. To this extent, here as in Weber's argument, social mobility must have what we may term a conservative effect, for mobility is a sort of reminder, however feeble, that a certain amount of free competition in fact exists in society— hence, the individual is not likely to breed resentment against the social order.

Mobility is more central to the theories of Marx, Pareto, and Dahrendorf. Under Pareto's influence, and in recognition of recent findings, Dahrendorf has not only pointed to the rather "high" rates of intergenerational mobility in industrial society, but argued also that where mobility rates are high, and hence mobility expectations are "legitimate," people are likely to jockey for a place in the sun *as individuals* rather than as members of classes. The theme of the conservative effects of mobility thus recurs.

In Pareto's work, social mobility—especially the unhindered "velocity in circulation"—is the indispensable condition for social "stability" and for what he conceived of as "true democracy." More important still, mobility from one class to another may be higher in some periods and under some forms of sociopolitical organization than others; but it is everywhere an inevitable and ever-present fact of life. There has always been in all societies a certain amount of "circulation of the elite," whereby skillful lower-class individuals have risen to the top to replace individuals who have degenerated in biological or intellectual capacity and have not been replaced from within their class. What is the sociological function of such individuals who leap the gap, as it were, between the humble and the mighty? What goals, interests, and values ("residues," Pareto termed them) do they bring into their new class? What changes does their abstraction from the lower class bring about in the ideological temper of the masses? These are some of the questions that occupied Pareto's attention. For us it may suffice here to note that, whatever else their role, the social climbers have always constituted what, from the perspective of theories of class conflict, may be termed *a safety valve* for the resentments and antagonisms continuously generated in the masses. Not only do they withdraw their possibly effective leadership from the masses, but they also bear witness to the fact that the top *can* be reached. They provide the basic support for the Horatio Alger complex. Thus, Pareto (1916:2179) argued that it is

in the highest degree difficult to overthrow . . . a [governing] class when it successfully assimilates most of the individuals in the subject class who show the same [governing] talents, are adept in those same arts, and might therefore become the leaders of such plebeians as are disposed to use violence.

What is equally important is that even when rising individuals bring to their new position interests and aims that are agreeable to those from among whom they originated, soon they will become like those whom they have recently joined. Selfishness sets in. Power corrupts—if not power, then the proximity to power, or merely the newly gained honor of living in the shadow of the mighty. The interests of the "aristocracy" are absorbed. Success renders conservative.

The case for mobility in Marx's sociology is somewhat less clearcut, although insofar as he was concerned with the political effects of the phenomenon his emphasis was on the associative aspects of it. To be sure, in attempting to explain the difficulty of class formation in the United States of his time, he did espouse the idea that social mobility was somehow a prime preventive of class formation (Marx, 1852b:18). Again, at one point in *Das Kapital* (1867, III:650) he anticipated Pareto's argument above in noting that the greater the success of a ruling class in absorbing the best men of the "oppressed" class, the more solid and dangerous is its rule. But in general, perhaps because Marx paid so little attention to social ascent, he tended to see this class dynamic as a force not antithetical to class consciousness but largely productive of it.

There are three major types of mobility in Marx's work. A first kind may be observed during the period in which a newly arising governing class entrenches itself and consolidates its power. This is social ascent that clearly portends conservative (or self-perpetuating) politics. A second type concerns the migration, so to speak, of sections of the dominant class—especially those intellectuals who have a theoretical understanding of the historical process— downward into the ideological ranks of the working class. The third and most important type entailed the proletarianization, or downward mobility, of the petty bourgeoisie, namely, those who were being pushed out of the bourgeoisie by unrestrained capitalistic competition.

Like other reformers who tend to stress the real or imagined revolutionizing elements of social process, Marx emphasized *downward* mobility and the allegedly revolutionizing effects of this phenomenon, and he paid little attention to upward mobility and its conservative effects—the *embourgeoisement* of the economically successful. History and the facts of human psychology suggest that this neglect was probably one of his more glaring errors, and in this respect the data from Italy will reveal some extremely interesting findings. For the present, we may conclude these introductory remarks by noting, in the words of Lipset (1959:257), that "perhaps the most important effect of mobility on politics which should be noted is that the bulk of the socially mobile, whether their direction be upward or downward, vote for the more conservative parties." In what follows, we shall discuss political behavior first in relation to upward mobility and then in relation to downward mobility. To facilitate comparative analysis, we shall conceive of the stratification system as a class dichotomy and concentrate on father-son comparisons across the manual-nonmanual line.

UPWARD MOBILITY AND POLITICAL BEHAVIOR

Table XV:1 compares in terms of political party choice the upwardly mobile (the *newcomers*) of the "middle class" to the *old-timers* of that class, on the one hand, and to the urban manuals (the "working class"), on the other.

Agrarian respondents and those cases for which information on occupation was not available are excluded. The working class is further reduced by excluding 75 individuals who were downwardly mobile in order to clean out the possible influence of downward mobility on political orientation.

TABLE XV:1. DIFFERENCES IN POLITICAL PREFERENCE BETWEEN THE UPWARDLY MOBILE AND THEIR CLASSES OF ORIGIN AND DESTINATION

Party Preferred	Occupational and Mobility Status		
	Stable Nonmanuals	Upwardly Mobile	Stable Manuals
Communist, Socialist, Social Democratic	27%	39%	46%
Christian Democratic, Republican	20	19	17
Liberal, Monarchic, Social Movement	15	4	2
None[a]	20	14	16
Not Interested[b]	9	12	12
No Response	9	12	7
Total	100%	100%	100%
N	233	104	291

[a] Respondent rejected all political parties.
[b] Includes those who answered with "do not know," "do not understand politics," and "not interested in politics."

The findings present the upwardly mobile in a stance of political consciousness that clearly bestrides the two social worlds between which they live. Thus, the class of origin was most frequently oriented toward parties of the left and least toward those of the center and right. Conversely, the class of destination was the most conservative and "moderate," the least leftist. The newcomers were located somewhere between the two classes, and to that extent appear to have achieved a sort of political compromise between the two cross-pressures, although the pull of the class of origin was clearly the stronger.

The only fairly clear lack of difference between the upwardly mobile and both class of origin and class of destination concerns the failure or unwillingness to show a political preference. In all three cases, nearly two-fifths of the respondents either stated directly that existing parties lacked the ability to "defend" their interests, or merely failed to make a party choice. This finding is at odds with most others reported on this question. Lipset and Bendix (1959:68–69) have noted that according to most studies, the mobile, who as such are subject to "cross-pressures," are more likely than stable fellow citizens to abstain from voting or to otherwise show low levels of political interest. Presumably this "withdrawal from involvement" is their way of resolving the internal conflict which results from exposure to varying appeals and pulls in different political directions.

Before even tentatively accepting the above data as indicative of mobility effects in political orientation, we should consider alternative explanations. It may be that the observed differences in preference for leftist parties were due not to upward mobility in itself but to other factors. The data may be indicative of variations in the structural characteristics of the three mobility categories, for example.

One possibility is that the observed differences manifest discrepancies between the occupational distribution of the nonmanual old-timers and the destination distribution of occupations among the achievers, on the one hand, and between the occupational distribution of the manual old-timers and the origin distribution of occupations among the achievers, on the other. After all, the nonmanual category is a rather diverse one, both occupationally *and* politically, and the manual category is less than perfectly uniform (see Dogan, 1967). In the former case, members of the petty bourgeoisie, especially the routine clerks among them, were more often leftist than other nonmanuals. In the latter, skilled workers were less often leftist than other working-class strata, particularly the semiskilled stratum. Thus, if the strata of two-generation skilled workers and petty bourgeoisie were only insignificantly different in preferences for leftist parties, and if the bulk of our achievers were upwardly mobile only within the limits of these two strata, then very little or no resocialization need have occurred. The percentage differences recorded in Table XV:1 would be simply a function of the heterogeneity of the nonmanual and manual categories.

Neither presumption is probably correct, however. The stable members of the skilled-worker and petty-bourgeoisie strata were substantially divergent in leftist orientation (42 versus 28 percent), and not the "bulk" but only one-fifth of the achievers were petty-bourgeois sons of skilled-worker fathers.

More generally, detailed comparisons show that the differences observed in Table XV:1. cannot be attributed entirely to occupational variations in origin and destination strata. Consider the percentages of leftist party preference according to specific social strata and mobility status (next page). With one exception, the achievers stood between their old and their new social peers with respect to the frequency of leftist party preferences. The exception, it may be noted, was part of a systematic variation between leftist preferences and the "intensity" of mobility. Newcomers to the petty bourgeoisie, who accounted for 60 percent of all manual-to-nonmanual achievers, were more like their former peers in party choice, whereas newcomers to the elite or the high bourgeoisie were very similar to their new peers. But, although it is still possible that as *individuals* of particular and politically heterogeneous classes

PERCENT OF RESPONDENTS PREFERRING LEFTIST PARTIES

Respondent's Father's Stratum	Respondent's Stratum				
	I, II	III	IV	V	VI
I, II: Elite, High Bourgeoisie	29				
III: Petty Bourgeoisie	NA	28			
IV: Skilled Worker	33	39	42		
V: Semiskilled Worker	28	45	NA	49	
VI: Unskilled Worker	*	43	NA	NA	44

Achiever cells underscored.   * Too few cases.   NA = Not Applicable.

the achievers had *not* changed their politics as a result of mobility, what we have just observed does not damage the inference that in general the achievers probably had altered their political perspectives away from those of the class of origin and toward those of the class of destination. Rather, it may suggest that the greater the intensity of mobility, the more likely the achievers took on almost exactly the political orientation of the old-timers in their class of destination.

A second alternative interpretation of Table XV:1 suggests that what we have witnessed is simply the result of a "political generationalism" (see Lipset, 1959: Chapter 8; Sears, 1969:382ff). It is possible, in other words, that the younger sample members were disproportionately leftist in orientation and that most of our achievers were within the younger age cohorts. As data shown below will testify, however, this interpretation is not supportable either. Indeed, if anything the likelihood of a leftist orientation increased with age up to about age 50.

At this point we may anticipate a subsequent explanatory argument of our own and consider the important question of "decay effects" in the leftist orientation of manual-to-nonmanual achievers. Generally speaking, findings of the sort displayed in Table XV:1—that achievers bestride the classes of origin and destination in leftist preferences—are explicated in terms of political resocialization. Upwardly mobile people shift their allegiances and attitudes so that they better align with the allegiances and attitudes of their new peers. But, just as they do not execute these modifications at the same rate or to the same degree, they do not execute them overnight. Whether the changes are made anticipatorily or after the fact, they are nonetheless made more or less gradually. According to this argument, therefore, the greater the length of time since the transition in class position, the more likely is the achiever to exhibit political perspectives that are indistinguishable from those of his new class peers.

We may test the foregoing hypothesis by comparing across mobility categories the frequency of leftist-party choices, controlling for elapsed time since the mobility event. Exact data on this control variable are unavailable; but by restricting the mobility categories to career-stable respondents, we can use respondent's age as a substitute measure, on the assumption that all respondents initiated career at about the same age. In short, we are comparing within age cohorts (1) career-stable nonmanual sons of nonmanual fathers, (2) career-stable manual sons of manual fathers, and (3) career-stable nonmanual sons of manual fathers. (Respondents who were achievers only within career—that is, nonmanuals who inherited manual position at career entry—are separately considered in the "Achievers—Career" column, below.) Given these specifications, then, the hypothesis is that the older the achiever, the less likely he stated a preference for leftist parties. Results of the analysis are as follows (percentage leftist):

| Age of Respondents | Stable Nonmanuals | Achievers | | Stable Manuals |
		Noninheritors	Career	
Under 31	23	——— 31 ———		33
31–40	27	39	31	53
41–50	32	47	44	48
Over 50	19	24	53	47

Although we have had to collapse the two categories of achiever for the "Under 31" cohort in order to obtain an acceptable percentage base, it is clear that the data do not support the hypothesis. Indeed, the age patterning of leftist preferences was substantially uniform across all mobility categories: an increase from the youngest to the middle cohorts and then (for all but the career-only achievers) a decline.[1] With that one exception, the upwardly mobile respondents in each cohort were less often leftist than the stable manuals but more often leftist than the stable nonmanuals. In the absence of properly longitudinal measures, we may therefore conclude that there were no major "decay effects" in the leftist preferences of our manual-to-nonmanual achievers. A possible implication of this conclusion is that most of the resocialization that took place was anticipatory. In any case, it would seem that it takes two generations before the distribution of political preferences among a population of achievers fully corresponds to that of the destination population.

A further explanation of the observed differences in Table XV:1 concerns

---

[1] A plausible interpretation of this curvilinearity holds that disproportionately large numbers of both the youngest and the oldest age cohorts are less interested in party politics and do not express preferences for any party. But the argument does not fit the present case, for the curvilinearity persists when the leftist respondents are tabulated as percentages of only those respondents who stated party preferences.

the political orientation of the respondent's father. Rokkan (1967:431ff; see also Hyman, 1959; Butler and Stokes, 1969:98), for example, found in his Norwegian study a consistency in party preferences across father and son generations even among the upwardly mobile sons: nonmanual sons of left-oriented manual fathers were more likely to be leftist themselves than were nonmanual sons of nonleftist manual fathers. Thus, controlling for presumably different political socializations in the parental home attenuated the over-all relationship between mobility experience and the likelihood of leftist preferences; but it did not destroy it.

It is possible that the distribution of party preferences among the fathers of our upwardly mobile respondents was such that these achievers were not in fact manifesting any alteration of political perspective. Unfortunately, we do not have the required data with which to test this possibility. But, while variations in the political orientation of the parental home may account for some of the disparity in leftist choices shown in Table XV:1, we strongly suspect that, as in the case of Rokkan's study, substantial differences in party preference between the achievers and the nonmobile would still remain.

Other alternative interpretations of Table XV:1 involve consideration of such factors as educational attainment, migration experience, size of community, and geographical region. All of these have been tested and rejected. We are led to conclude that the differences recorded in Table XV:1 are largely indicative of mobility effects—that along with social ascent goes a transformation of political ideology away from those parties that are traditionally considered advantageous to the interests of the working class. The class skepticism of Pareto and Weber appears to be amply vindicated. What people seem to want is not "social justice" and equality, but equality for themselves in relation to those who are already better off. The degree to which the political socialization undergone in the family of orientation is often unlearned, and a new political culture acquired in contact with people of the more privileged class, is somber evidence of the prevalently individualistic character of "class" experiences, the largely individualistic nature of "social" interests, the prevalence of emulation tendencies in social behavior, and the pervasiveness of the age-old need for social recognition invidiously understood. Lipset (1959:258) hits a realistic chord when he proposes that findings such as the above "illustrate the pervasive influence of contact with superior status on attitudes and behavior." Human beings tend to understand class phenomena more readily as individuals than as members of classes. They are more likely to be interested in their own individual betterment than in "collective justice." They are more attracted toward rich and awe-inspiring styles of life than toward life styles in which the very concepts of wealth and power would be irrelevant.

Some Prior Findings

Cross-national comparisons suggest that the conservative tendency of the upwardly mobile varies from country to country. In both Western Europe and the United States, the upwardly mobile are more frequently conservative than their class of origin. But whereas in European countries the achievers are more often leftist (Socialist or Communist) than their class of destination,[2] evidence for the United States indicates that they are more often *conservative* (Republican) than even the nonmanual old-timers.[3] The national data, which report leftist preferences as a percentage of all respondents who stated a preference, summarize some available comparisons.[4]

	Stable Nonmanuals	Upwardly Mobile	Stable Manuals
Finland, 1949	6%	23%	81%
Finland, 1958	17	38	78
Germany, 1953	20	32	64
Italy, 1964	44	64	71
Norway, 1957	19	48	88
Sweden, 1960	25	49	83
United States, 1948	39	35	82
United States, 1952	30	22	62
United States, 1960	40	38	58

It is conceivable, of course, that comparing these or other countries at different points in time and at different political junctures would produce different, perhaps more comparable, findings. Furthermore, there are serious problems involved in the comparison of party politics from one country to another, particularly in comparisons of most Western European countries with the United States. It is inexcusable, for instance, to equate a member of the Democratic Party in the United States with a Finnish or Italian Communist. These individuals are all "leftist" only in a manner of speaking. It may even be that "mainstream" party politics in the United States is so lacking in ideological diversity that social and personal strains which seek a "political" expression are more likely to lead to "margin politics," represented by in-

---

[2]See Lipset and Zetterberg (1966: Tables 2 and 3). Milne and Mackenzie (1956:58) present similar findings for Great Britain.

[3]Recent work by Thompson (1967; 1971) considers additional studies and, using data on female as well as male repondents, seeks to prove false the United States exception. However, when he considers only male respondents—as did the previous studies referred to—he, too, finds that achievers in the United States tend to be Republican more often than the nonmanual old-timers.

[4]Sources for these data are as follows. Finland, 1949; Germany, 1953; United States, 1948 and 1952, are from Lipset and Bendix (1959:67). Finland, 1958, is from Pesonen (1968: Table 5:13); the data refer to the city of Tampere only. Norway, 1957, is from Rokkan (1967: Table 27). Sweden, 1960, is from Anderson (1963: Table 2); the data refer to the city of Märsta only. United States, 1960, is from Thompson (1971); the data refer to male respondents only. The Italian data are from the present study.

dividuals at the fringe of either party, than to either of the two major national parties.

There is, in short, serious doubt about the comparability of United States and European data on political-party preference. Certain findings based on questions related to, but different from, questions on party preference make the doubt all the more compelling. For example, dividing respondents participating in public attitude surveys carried out in 1945–1947 into "radical," "intermediate," and "conservative" types on the basis of their score on a battery of questions concerning *various economic and political issues,* Richard Centers (1949:180) produced for the United States findings that are comparable to those from Europe. The upwardly mobile were considerably less "radical" and more "conservative" than their class of origin, but they were somewhat more radical and less conservative than their class of destination.[5]

Again, on the basis of a nationwide survey of about 10,000 college graduates made by *Time* magazine in 1947, Patricia West (1953) reported that men who had earned at least half of their expenses while attending college were less likely to be Republican later in their work career than those who had not worked while attending college. West, however, did not study mobility directly but merely assumed that those working while in college were of working-class background and later, therefore, were upwardly mobile individuals. This assumption may have had its utility, but it was questionable.

The picture that can be drawn from West's findings is not totally lacking in support for the previous conclusion that achievers in the United States tend toward ultraconservatism. West noted, for instance, that the conservatism of previously low-status individuals increased as they grew older and reached the highest levels of success. Considering the politically relevant question of support for, or opposition to, government planning, West (1953:478–479) found that men who had worked their way through college were noticeably less opposed to government planning while they were still in the lower income brackets. When they had risen to the higher brackets, "they were, if anything, *more* opposed to government planning than the originally privileged group." In short, in the absence of more data, it is still reasonable to adhere to the position that, while achievers in both the United States and Europe are more rightist than their class of origin, the Europeans remain more leftist than their class of destination while their North American counterparts become even more conservative than their new class peers.

Why such variations? Barring vague suggestions to the effect that both rightist and leftist political orientations may represent "alternative reactions" to the "status discrepancies" entailed by the experience of mobility (Lipset and

---

[5]In other, related respects, upwardly mobile people in the United States again have been observed to take a midcourse position. Blau (1956), for instance, finds in a study of interpersonal relations that many beliefs and practices of the upwardly and of the downwardly mobile are intermediate between those of the "stationary highs" and those of the "stationary lows."

Zetterberg, 1966:571–572),[6] no serious attempt to explain them has been made. The tendency has rather been to take the United States case as given, assume it to be the normal case, and then seek to explain the several European instances by reference to the findings from the United States. Lipset (1959:254) has speculated, for instance, that upward mobility in European countries entails greater status discrepancies, and hence greater difficulties in class readjustment, than in the United States. Specifically,

Given the much wider discrepancy in consumption styles between the European and American middle and working class, one would expect the upwardly mobile European of working-class origin to have somewhat greater difficulties in adjusting to his higher status, and *to feel more discriminated against* than his American counterpart . . . (emphasis added).

All conceptual and theoretical difficulties notwithstanding, it is happily true that the present is one of the few areas in social stratification where development has reached a point when at least a quasi-formal statement of theory can be essayed. Some work in this formalization has already been done (see Lopreato, 1967a). We shall continue the effort in this chapter. The argument in which the preceding comments are rooted yields the following set of propositions:

1. Men are positively influenced by "superior status"; that is, they tend to emulate the behavior of "superiors."
2. If men experience upward mobility, they (the "achievers" or "newcomers") are likely to emulate the political behavior of the "old-timers"—the more prestigeful—of their class.
3. However, if men experience upward mobility, they also suffer status discrepancies. Specifically, the newcomers are likely to: (a) encounter difficulties in raising a working-class consumption style to a middle-class level; and (b) feel discriminated against by the old-timers of the class.
4. The effect of status discrepancies is to weaken the influence of the emulation factor.
5. Status discrepancies are greater among middle-class Europeans of working-class origin than among their counterparts in the United States.
6. Therefore, middle-class Europeans of working-class origin are more likely to retain a working-class political orientation, and hence are more leftist than their United States counterparts.

Note that whatever the validity of the above theory, it still leaves unanswered the interesting question of why upwardly mobile people in the United

---

[6]Strictly speaking, of course, they are not alternative reactions but different degrees of the same "consequence" of mobility: political conservatism. Stated otherwise, the difference is that upwardly mobile Europeans maintain a political link with their class of origin more frequently than do their United States counterparts.

States are even more conservative than those whose middle-class position is of long standing. European achievers—it argues—are more likely to feel rejected by their new class peers than are their United States counterparts. That may well be so. But can the lesser status difficulty of upwardly mobile people in the United States in itself explain the fact that they are even more conservative than the old-timers of their own class? Obviously not. In short, Lipset has argued as if the European instances were to be explained away as many exceptions to the United States rule. The opposite, however, more nearly does justice to the logical structure of the above theory.

The normal case to which the theory addresses itself is one in which its two fulcrums—"status discrepancies" and "emulation of superior status"—are both operative in producing a given political stance. In Europe the known facts are indeed consistent with their logic: the upwardly mobile bestride class of origin and class of destination in their political behavior. The case is different in the United States, where the strength of the emulation factor seems to be so overpowering as to produce political "overconformity." Why?

On this question, in this book, we can only speculate (see also Lopreato, 1967a). The answer may lie in an alleged characteristic of United States society widely discussed in the literature. In his essay on "Social Structure and Ano-mie," Merton (1957) discusses some interesting implications of the "American Dream." This ethos is presumably built on certain cultural axioms enjoining individuals to recognize that success can always be realized if one but has the requisite abilities and the perseverance to strive. By implication, the citizen ought not to blame anyone but himself in case of failure. According to Merton (1957:139),

the culture enjoins the acceptance of three cultural axioms: First, all should strive for the same lofty goals since these are open to all; second, present seeming failure is but a way-station to ultimate success; and third, genuine failure consists only in the lessening or withdrawal of ambition.

The point we wish to make here is this: Given the extreme emphasis on success, combined with the individual responsibility for nonfulfillment, the fear of failure is likely to be a constant threat to one's sense of security. Conversely, the experience of social success will give the achiever enormous satisfaction and a deep sense of relief. "God bless America for sparing me the tragedy of failure!" So profound indeed is the sense of relief, so great the joy of having avoided personal disaster, that the achiever is quite likely to develop what Melvin Tumin (1957) has termed a "cult of gratitude," namely, an attitude of deep appreciation toward the social order for making the present pleasures possible. Such gratitude, we suggest, is then expressed through an overconformity to the prescribed political behavior of the middle class, specifically, by voting disproportionately for the party that is loudest in proclaiming the reality of the "American Dream" and the old American virtues: self-reliance, individualism, faith in the existing social order.

The fact that the United States has not fully digested the immense intake of European immigrants may, of course, add to this possible consequence of the cult of success. Handlin (1951) has suggested that most immigrants have accepted the United States as the land of opportunity. And so it has been— for them especially; whatever their difficulties of acculturation, in the New World they have found economic conditions that far excelled those in the old country.

The above comments must for the time being remain at the level of speculation. There is, however, an aspect of the theory stated so far that can be examined directly with the data from Italy. The "status-discrepancies" variable is highly suggestive and deserves empirical examination. We may have no way of demonstrating that upwardly mobile Italians suffer greater status discrepancies than their North American counterparts. But if the notion of status discrepancies is to be generally relevant to an explanation of the political orientation of the upwardly mobile, it must be demonstrated that our upwardly mobile respondents suffered greater status discrepancies than those in their class whose position was of long standing. This aspect of the work can be readily undertaken with the data at our disposal, and the next section of this chapter is devoted to that task.

Confirmation of Theory

In returning to the theory, our first job is to isolate the elements in terms of which *status discrepancies* is explicable. A close examination of the theory reveals that by itself this factor has very little meaning. Indeed, it is obviously shorthand for certain other, more specific, variables. Three come immediately to mind: (1) *difficulties in personal adjustment to a middle-class position,* (2) *discrepancies in consumption styles between the classes,* and (3) *feelings of discrimination.* Of the three, the second and third are by far the most manageable. They will be the focus of two sets of propositions designed to guide the following research.

With respect to *discrepancies in consumption styles,* we are led to predict that within the middle class:

I. The newcomers have a lower consumption style than the old-timers.

II. As the newcomers attain the consumption level of old-timers, they become comparable to them in political orientation.

We shall refer to these two propositions as *Life-Style Hypotheses* I and II.

With respect to *feelings of discrimination,* the approach will necessarily be more circuitous. It is predicated on the assumption that people who suffer status rejection are likely to interpret it as an expression of a tendency in the stratification system to restrict interclass relations. With this in mind, it is predicted that:

I. The newcomers are more likely than the old-timers to perceive restrictions in interclass relations.

II. Among the newcomers, those who perceive obstructions to interclass relations are politically more leftist than those who do not perceive such restrictions.

III. Finally, those who do not perceive impediments to interclass relations are politically alike—whether old-timers or upwardly mobile.

These propositions will be termed *Class-Closure Hypotheses* I, II, and III.

Life-Style Hypothesis I

Our data regarding variations in consumption style show that those middle-class respondents whose fathers were themselves in the middle class did indeed enjoy a significantly higher style of life than middle-class individuals of working-class origin. Thus, considering a list of ten consumer items,[7] we note marked differences between the two groups: while 40 percent of the old-timers owned at least nine of the items in question, only 25 percent of the newcomers were so fortunate. Again, 11 percent of the former and 16 percent of the latter owned fewer than five of the items. The evidence would seem to indicate that the upwardly mobile were having some difficulty in raising their style of life to a middle-class level, and our first prediction is therefore upheld.

TABLE XV:2. POLITICAL PREFERENCE OF MIDDLE-CLASS RESPONDENTS, BY NUMBER OF ITEMS OWNED AND POSITION IN THE MIDDLE CLASS

Political Preference	0–8 Items Owned		9–10 Items Owned	
	Old-timers	*Newcomers*	*Old-timers*	*Newcomers*
Left-wing[a]	49%	68%	32%	61%
Conservative[b]	51	32	68	39
Total	100%	100%	100%	100%
N	84	47	60	18

[a] Includes Communist, Socialist, and Social Democratic parties.
[b] Includes Christian Democratic, Liberal, Monarchic, and Neo-Fascist parties.

[7]The items considered were: automobile, refrigerator, washing machine, telephone, television, radio, vacuum cleaner and/or buffer, electric or gas stove, toilet with bath, running water.

Life-Style Hypothesis II

The second prediction reasons that if differences in consumption patterns are to be taken as indicative of the causes of differences in political orientation, it must be demonstrated that as middle-class individuals of working-class origin attain the consumption level of the old-timers of the class, they become comparable to these in political orientation as well. Some evidence to this effect has already been presented in a Swedish study by Zetterberg (reported in Lipset and Bendix, 1959:68).

Our information (Table XV:2) casts doubt on the alleged influence of style of life in itself on the political orientation of the upwardly mobile. Contrary to expectation, the achievers in the middle class still surpassed the old-timers of the class in left-wing party preferences even after a comparable level of consumption style had been achieved. To note this fact is not to say, of course, that variations in style of life left political orientation totally unaffected. Among both newcomers and old-timers, an enriched consumption level was associated with a certain conservative tendency. However, such improvement was more likely to reduce left-wing orientation within the more established section of the middle class than among the new arrivals, with the result that the upwardly mobile actually increased their leftist lead over the old-timers.

It is evident that, although the upwardly mobile did not enjoy the high life style of the old-timers of their class, differences in consumption patterns do not account effectively for differences in political orientation between the two middle-class categories. After controls for consumption level, the achievers were still politically more left-wing than their new class peers.

This finding is supported by a set of data previously considered. If differences in consumption level correlated with differences between the newcomers and old-timers in political orientation, it would be reasonable to expect a "decay effect" in the leftist preferences of the achievers. The newcomer, no matter how strongly inclined to adopt the more luxurious style of life characteristic of his new position, can seldom attain the higher consumption level over any short time span. The process is typically one of a gradual accretion of commodities and habits. It could be reasoned, then, that the further back in time the achiever changed from a manual to a nonmanual position, the higher his current level of consumption and, hence, the less likely he is to prefer left-wing parties. But, as we found on the previous occasion, such decay effects in the probability of a leftist political orientation were not observable. In fact, the likelihood of leftist preferences among the achievers—as among the nonmanual and manual old-timers—was apparently greater among those who had been in the nonmanual category for some time than among the recently arrived.

Taken together, the findings in the present section suggest that if the status-discrepancies variable is relevant to an explanation of political orientation among the upwardly mobile in Italy, consumption level is too crude an indicator of it. It is more likely that the significant status discrepancies of the upwardly mobile consist of a gap between their class position and a set of cultural *intangibles* that are expected of that position. Put otherwise, it would seem that the *social distance* between the once-proletarians and the old-timers of the middle class is not easily bridged through occupational achievements and objective aspects of life style. Apparently, not even higher levels of formal education constitute a very effective bridge; it may be recalled, for instance, that variations in educational attainment did not account for the findings of Table XV:1.

Perhaps in consequence of a long national tradition of aristocracy, Italian —and very likely European—middle classes are even today heavily permeated by an atmosphere of *hauteur*. As a result, they are keenly sensitive to the nuances of "class" behavior, and the occupationally successful children of the working class may find it particularly trying to gain the social recognition and acceptance that their economic achievement would warrant. Whatever their present education, position, or wealth, one fact is not easily concealed: they were socialized within the working class. From the working class they are likely to have brought into their new class situation evident traces of a "vulgar" upbringing that must be distasteful to the old-timers of the class, devoted as they are to the art of what a historically minded journalist once termed *"domenichino* snobbery."[8]

Mixed with whatever class consciousness we may have glimpsed within the context of a brief formal interview, Italians of the middle class and its aspirants have a hypersensitivity to status factors and a style of life that brazenly expresses it. A "middle-class cesspool," a disappointed and angry traveler termed it (Rowdon, 1963). It is manifested in countless ways, small and big. Take their fashions. Italians are in the aggregate the best-dressed people in the world, and they have in various periods of history contributed a great deal to international styles. But what sharpens this esthetic sense is not their genius for yet another art form, as some might think. It is their extreme preoccupation with *fare buona figura* (literally, to make a good figure—to show up well). Often such preoccupation reaches impractical proportions, as when a mother sends her little child to play in the park properly attired in jacket, white shirt and tie, and hat. Very often the child is accompanied to the park by the family maid, who, because the Italian poor now "are getting ideas," is increasingly a vanishing institution but still one of the highest aims of all good middle-class families—even if employing a maid entails paying her as much as one-fourth of her employer's meager salary of $200 per month. And while the lady of the

---

[8] *Domenichino* is the Italian word for that peculiar type of servant who in past centuries enjoyed the privilege of accompanying his lord on his Sunday *(domenica)* walk. This unusual honor was the source of grotesque ostentation of the part of the *domenichino* in relation to other members of the populace.

house spends much of her time staring out of the window or talking about this and that, the maid spends much of her time, when she is not at the park, dry-cleaning the child's other suit of clothes, which was soiled during his last outing. In February, during the *Carnevale* period (the Italian *Mardi Gras),* middle-class children can be seen by the thousands on the streets of a city like Rome dressed in facsimiles of the genteel costumes of an era long gone by.

We could multiply such examples. But so much may suffice to suggest that the newly arrived in the middle class are not easily "accepted." After all, they remind many others of an unfortunate and painful past of their own that had best be forgotten. Under the circumstances, the postulated tendency to imitate superior status is somewhat weakened among new arrivals, early political socialization asserts itself the more forcefully, and political affiliation with the class of origin is more readily retained.[9]

Class-Closure Hypothesis I

The findings and discussion so far highlight the possible importance of *feelings of discrimination* as an influence on the political orientation of the upwardly mobile. Consider data which compare the achievers to the old-timers of the middle class on the basis of the following question: "In your opinion, do those who belong to a given social class tend to avoid relations with persons belonging to another social class?" The findings bear out the prediction of the first class-closure hypothesis. Despite their actual experience of mobility, the upwardly mobile were significantly more likely than the old-timers of their class to perceive a tendency toward closure in the stratification system (68 percent versus 57 percent).

It may be noted that the research question was broadly stated. It did not single out any particular class, such as "the middle class" or the "higher classes," for assessment concerning a possible tendency to restrict out-class relations. Our underlying assumption is that the perceptions produced by the present question reflected personal experiences. This query, it would seem, is not one that can be answered in the abstract. Again, it it is hardly likely, although conceivable, that a higher class would feel excluded by a lower class. Hence, it is reasonable to assume that the achievers' responses reflected their experiences of discrimination suffered at the hands of the old-timers of their new class, both while moving from a working-class position to their position at the time of questioning, and also in the process of adjusting to the new position.

Class-Closure Hypothesis II

Table XV:3 examines data relevant to the second class-closure hypothesis and further shows the pertinence of feelings of discrimination for explaining

---

[9]For the influence of early political socialization on political orientation, see Hyman (1959) and Dawson and Prewitt (1969).

TABLE XV:3. POLITICAL PREFERENCE AMONG NEWCOMERS, BY
PERCEPTION OF INTERCLASS RESTRICTIONS

	Class Restrictions Perceived	
Political Preference	Yes	No
Left-wing	73%	40%
Conservative	27	60
Total	100%	100%
N	41	15

the political orientation of the upwardly mobile. In keeping with the prediction, the table demonstrates that those newcomers who perceived impediments
in class intercourse were also significantly more leftist in political orientation
than those who viewed social contact as unhindered by class differences.
Among those who attested to class closure, preferences for parties of the left
were almost three times as frequent as conservative preferences. Conversely,
three-fifths of those who perceived free interclass contact also favored the
conservative side of the political spectrum.

Class-Closure Hypothesis III

Finally, our data also uphold the third class-closure hypothesis, demonstrating that when the newcomers did not perceive hindrances to interclass
relations—in other words, when they did not feel themselves to be the objects
of social rejection, according to our interpretation—they were almost exactly
like the old-timers of their class in political preference. In both groups, about
two-fifths (40 and 42 percent, respectively) showed a preference for parties of
the left, while the other three-fifths chose conservative parties.

A Theory of Upward Mobility and Political Behavior

The evidence presented above lends plausibility to *one aspect* of the theory
as it was briefly stated earlier in the chapter. The concept of status discrepancies, explicated in terms of *feelings of discrimination*,[10] does indeed help explain

---

[10]It should be noted here, in connection with an important issue current in sociological
controversies, that this finding lends considerable support to those sociologists who argue that
truly explanatory variables entering a theoretical construct must be "psychological" in nature. A
case in point in recent years is represented by Homans's argument in favor of "bringing men back
in" the theoretical constructs of the sociological enterprise. Homans's argument is a complex one
—or at least refers to a complex question. Briefly, however, he insists that the "general propositions" of sociology—like those of sister disciplines—can only be "psychological," in the sense that
they refer to the actual behavior of men and not to structural or processual conditions of societies
or other collectives. They are general in the sense that "they appear in many, and I think in all,
of the deductive systems that will even begin to explain social behavior." In the present study,

the political orientation of upwardly mobile individuals in one European country.[11] We can now return to the previously stated theory and amend it in keeping with the arguments and findings encountered since then. The lessons we have learned require several major premises as introduction to the theory. We may proceed as follows:

Premise A: Men seek social recognition.

Premise B: Men tend to emulate their social superiors.

Premise C: Upward mobility constitutes a social experience which incorporates both the search for recognition and the tendency to emulate social superiors.

Premise D: Political behavior among adults is in part determined by early political socialization.

1. If men experience upward mobility, they suffer status discrepancies and difficulties in gaining social recognition from the old-timers in the class of destination—that is, the newcomers feel discriminated against by the old-timers.

2. If men experience upward mobility, then they are likely to emulate the behavior of the old-timers—thus the more prestigeful members—of their class.

3. Emulation varies directly with the emphasis on social achievement in society and with the degree of social recognition received.

4. The likelihood of retaining political links with the class of origin (avoiding resocialization)

   (a) increases with the degree of status discrepancies, namely, rejection—real or imagined—by the old-timers in the class of destination; and

   (b) decreases with the strength of *(p)* the emphasis on achievement, *(q)* the tendency toward emulation, and *(r)* recognition received.

Assuming now that

---

it should be noted, we began with the structural concept of "status discrepancies" as the crucial variable. It was then discovered, however, that this variable made sense and became useful for explanation only when articulated in the social-psychological terms of "feelings of rejection." For a brief discussion, see Homans (1961; 1964). An analogous and much earlier statement is found in Pareto's review of Durkheim's *Suicide* (see Pareto, 1966).

[11] In the absence of empirical data, Miller (1960:16) has argued that it is uncertain whether the upwardly mobile are "the most resentful, frustrated groups in society." Although the present findings are far from providing an answer to this question, they do suggest that middle-class Italians of working-class origin feel rejected by those whose middle-class position is of long standing, and that such feeling may be strong enough to retard their political socialization into their new class.

W. the middle class as a whole prefers conservative parties to leftist parties;
X. status discrepancies (experienced social rejection) are greater among middle-class Europeans of working-class origin than among their North American counterparts;
Y. the emphasis on success and achievement is "excessive"[12] in the United States but not in Europe; and
Z. emulation of higher status can be as disproportionate as the emphasis on success and achievement;

then it follows that:

5. Middle-class Europeans of working-class origin are more leftist than their new class peers and more conservative than their class of origin.
6. Middle-class North Americans of working-class origin are more conservative than both their class of origin and their class of destination.

DOWNWARD MOBILITY AND POLITICAL BEHAVIOR

Most of the work done on the political "consequences" of social mobility concerns *upward* mobility; the study of downward mobility is an underdeveloped area of social stratification. The remainder of this chapter represents an effort to add substantially to our present knowledge of sociopolitical aspects of class descent.

Some Prior Findings and Explanations

A few studies have consistently found the downwardly mobile in an intermediate position between the class of origin and the class of destination. For instance, Lipset and Bendix (1959:67–72) cite evidence from Norway, Germany, Finland, and the United States to demonstrate that intergenerational skidders prefer left-wing parties more frequently than members of the middle class, but less often than their stable manual peers.[13]

The explanation generally advanced for this finding employs some of the same variables utilized to explain the political orientation of the upwardly mobile. On the one hand, *emulation* of the higher-status group that the skidder hopes eventually to rejoin, or refuses to believe he has left, is thought to buttress the beliefs and behaviors, including political conservatism, with which he was socialized in a middle-class family. Particularly in a society where success values are stressed and the belief in an open class structure is widespread, many a skidder will, as Wilensky and Edwards (1959:217) put it,

---

[12]In the sense that it represents a "threat to one's sense of security."

[13] Additional or related corroborative evidence may be found in Lipset, 1959:272–273; Wilensky and Edwards, 1959; Stacey, 1966; Sorokin, 1959:510; Blau, 1956:291; Lipset and Zetterberg, 1966:572; Janowitz, 1956; Kornhauser and others, 1956:43; Centers, 1949:179–180; Maccoby and others, 1954:34–35; Pesonen, 1968: Table 5.13; Anderson, 1963: Table 2.

"resist the status implications of downward mobility by denying failure and striving to succeed."

On the other hand, the reality of a working-class status is conducive to some adult *resocialization* into this class, whose normal behavior generally includes a left-wing political orientation. Blau (1956:294) has observed that if the skidder associates with members of his former class, his inability to honor the social obligations proper to that class keeps alive his feelings of deprivation and occupational failure. In contrast, if he ceases to associate with them in favor of people of his own standing, "he is socially permitted to forget how much more fortunate he could have been, and his occupation is not a sign of failure in this group." As his associations shift, so does his political orientation. This process takes place over time, and it is not surprising, therefore, that Wilensky and Edwards (1959:227) found older skidders to be less conservative than younger ones. In any case, the skidder experiences a sort of tug-of-war between the above two factors—emulation and resocialization—that presumably results in a political orientation falling somewhere between the two social classes.

The Italian Finding

Just as achievers in the United States appear to represent an exception to the usual finding on upward mobility and political orientation, so Italian skidders constitute a remarkable exception to the usual finding. Again in keeping with widespread practice, downward mobility is measured by father-son comparisons across the nonmanual-manual line, excluding the agrarian respondents of both generations in addition to those sons not in the labor force at the time of interview and those who did not give the necessary information on father's occupation.

Table XV:4, which compares the skidders to the classes of their origin and destination, shows that skidders in Italy did not exhibit the sort of political compromise that elsewhere finds them bestriding these two social classes. Quite to the contrary, the skidders surpassed the old-timers of the working class in the frequency with which they preferred parties of the left. Furthermore, the skidders were far less likely than either the nonmanuals or the manual old-timers to be politically ignorant or disinterested. From one viewpoint at least, this latter finding is somewhat surprising. As has been noted, Lipset (1959:208–209), for instance, argues that both upward and downward social mobility should increase political cross-pressures which are then resolved by a reduced interest in politics. Indeed, data from election surveys in several countries indicate that individuals in the social class of their fathers are more likely to vote than those who are socially mobile (Allardt and Bruun, 1956). In a related area, it has been found that the mobile are less likely than the stable to belong to, or be active in, trade unions (Lipset and Gordon, 1953:493; Tannenbaum and Kahn, 1958:142–148).

TABLE XV:4. DIFFERENCES IN POLITICAL PREFERENCE BETWEEN THE
DOWNWARDLY MOBILE AND THEIR CLASSES OF ORIGIN AND DESTINATION

Party Preference	Occupational and Mobility Status		
	Stable Nonmanuals	Downwardly Mobile	Stable Manuals
Communist, Socialist, Social Democratic	27%	55%	46%
Christian Democratic, Republican	20	17	17
Liberal, Monarchic, Social Movement	15	4	2
None[a]	20	16	16
Not Interested[b]	9	5	12
No Response	9	3	7
Total	100%	100%	100%
N	233	75	291

[a] Respondent rejected all political parties.
[b] Includes whose who answered with "do not know," "do not understand politics,"
and "not interested in politics."

Some Anticipations of the Exception

We shall return to the above point presently. In the meantime, we must
inquire whether available theory makes any provision at all for the empirical
exception represented by Italian skidders. From the chief theoretical perspective of this book, an affirmative answer comes immediately to mind. If we look
at the Italian finding from the Marxian viewpoint, the finding is no surprise
at all. In appearance at least, it is a direct reflection of the postulated political
consequences of proletarianization and pauperization. The chapter on Marx,
it may be recalled, predicted that the skidders would indeed manifest "revolutionary politics." We shall return to this point toward the end of the chapter.
In the meantime, we should also take into account contradictory theoretical
positions. As it happens, they are directly or indirectly rooted in the arguments of one or more of the other theorists dealt with in Part One of the
book.

Wilensky and Edwards (1959:229) suggest that under certain "structural
and cultural conditions," skidders may be disposed to "more radical political
adjustments" than those characteristic of their sample of factory workers in
the United States. Among such conditions are: (1) the insecurities of early
industrialization, entailing "painful transformations from peasant to
proletarian, rural to urban, alien to citizen"; (2) economic slump accompanied
by "a wide-spread sense of declining opportunity"; and (3) cultural values

which put a low emphasis on an open class structure and the urgency of success.

Elsewhere, Wilensky (1966:124–125) posits the idea that downward mobility in poor or newly developing nations is apt to be conducive to political radicalism. Rich and highly developed societies, he argues, include a plurality of status hierarchies that provide "consolation prizes" for the downwardly mobile. Not so in the poorer nations. Moreover,

in rich countries [there] are the cultural correlates of economic growth, particularly a success ideology which accents personal responsibility for work performance and job fate. Poor countries usually lack this ideology, so that the response to intergenerational or worklife "skidding" is externalized; it is readily channeled into collective political protest. In rich countries the same skidding leads to self blame. . . .

Relatedly, Lipset (1959:253) argues that when the stratification system is seen as providing the means for individual success, the discontented will attempt to work their way up the social ladder within existing structures. Conversely, when the discontented hold an image of a "closed" society, they are impelled to act for change through collective efforts, as provided by such interest groups as unions and leftist parties.

The sizable body of literature concerning status inconsistency, patently a Weberian and Paretian area, also has implications for the political behavior of skidders. Social mobility, regardless of direction, tends to intensify discrepancies among an individual's various rank positions in given status hierarchies. This fact in turn implies a number of social and psychological problems for the mobile individual (Blau, 1956:290; Jackson, 1962; Durkheim, 1897:252–254; Sorokin, 1959:522–526). The resulting stress and uncertainty are manifested in many ways, one among them being extreme political behavior. Although the precise nature of the political correlates of status inconsistency has been subject to lively debate, it has been often observed that swings to both extremes of the political spectrum are possible (see Lenski, 1954, 1967; Rush, 1967). It would follow that where the discomforts of status inconsistency are compounded by the conviction or fear that status retrieval is not possible through individual effort, skidders are especially apt to support political parties that advocate radical social changes. With respect to the Italian case in particular, it might be added that, given the fascist debacle in the not too distant past, the probability of right-wing extremism is lower than that of left-wing extremism.

Explicit or implicit in all the above arguments concerning the possibility of radical politics on the part of the downwardly mobile are two basic assumptions: (1) *skidders wish to regain a middle-class status;* (2) *they see no way in which this goal can be accomplished through the existing social and economic structures.*

From this perspective, it now seems possible to comprehend not only the

Italian skidders' frequent preference for left-wing parties but also their conspicuous interest in the politics of their society. Their relatively low frequency of political apathy and ignorance, like their heavily leftist orientation (see Table XV:4), would seem to reflect deep grievances against the existing opportunity structures and an inclination to invoke the help of parties that specialize in attacks on those structures to redress their grievances. An alternative explanation—that the skidders' political alertness was due to their possibly high education—quickly comes to mind, but can be just as quickly dismissed. While on the average the skidders had more years of schooling than their stable peers, they were far behind their class of origin in this respect. Specifically, 66 percent of the skidders had attained no more than the elementary-school diploma, 34 percent claimed some secondary-school training, and none had attended a university. The corresponding figures for the class of destination are 87, 13, and 0 percent; for the class of origin, 14, 52, and 34 percent, respectively.

Our interpretation is sustained by a school of thought which interprets low rates of political interest and participation as evidence of basic satisfaction with the status quo. Tingsten (1937:225–226), for instance, has interpreted a high vote turnout as a symptom of the decline of consensus, and others (see Hogan, 1945:275ff) have suggested that interest in politics varies inversely with pleasure experienced in other worthwhile activities. Our reasoning is also in accord with some studies of status inconsistency which reveal individuals suffering from status inconsistencies to be "activitistic," particularly where political issues are concerned (see Lenski, 1954).

Confirmation of Theory

The arguments presented so far suggest a number of fruitful possibilities for research. Aside from such intricate "structural" factors as level of industrialization and state of the economy, a number of attitudes (or "feelings") are indicated as possibly determining the heavily leftist political orientation of skidders. They concern perceptions about: (1) *the possibility of individual success;* (2) *the possibility of fulfilling personal needs within existing structures;* (3) *the presence or absence of distributive justice in society;* and (4) *the closedness or openness of the class structure.*

Here, as in the case of upward mobility, the logic of the case would ideally call for cross-national analysis. The most basic problem is to determine whether one society's skidders, who may be overwhelmingly leftist, differ appropriately from another society's skidders, who are largely conservative, in terms of those factors which allegedly induce left-wing political behavior. Unfortunately, the data for this ideal procedure are not available at the present. However, a close approximation to it is possible. It entails an intranational comparison between skidders on the one hand and their classes of origin and destination on the other. This comparison we are about to make. If such factors as a feeling of hopelessness with respect to individual success and a feeling that personal needs are not being satisfied by the existing structures are to be taken as causes of left-wing political preference, then it follows that the skidders, who were more often leftist than either their class of origin or their class of destination, should exceed both classes also in the frequency with which they hold those feelings. Further, we should expect those skidders who exhibit such feelings to be more frequently left-wing than those who do not.

In keeping with this reasoning, we shall proceed to examine the validity of the following propositions, all of which are related to what is generally termed a "success ideology" or to what may be antithetically termed a "limited-opportunity ideology":

I.

1. Skidders are more likely than either the class of origin or the class of destination to feel that their chances to get ahead in life are not as good as those of other people. (We shall consider this a measure of perception of the possibility of individual success.)
2. Skidders perceiving little possibility of individual success are more leftist than skidders perceiving a high possibility of success.

II.

1. Skidders are more likely than either the class of origin or the class of destination to feel that in recent years there has been little or no progress in their society. (This will be taken as a measure of the degree to which one's personal needs are thought to be fulfillable within existing structures.)
2. Skidders who feel that their needs are not being satisfied within existing structures are more leftist than skidders who consider such structures adequate to their needs.

III.

1. Skidders are more likely than either the class of origin or the class of destination to feel that when "things go well" in their society, the people to profit most are the rich and the powerful (the elites) rather than the people as a whole. (This is our measure of distributive justice.)
2. Skidders who do not perceive distributive justice are more leftist than skidders who do.

IV.

1. Skidders are more likely than either the class of origin or the class of destination to feel that people belonging to different social classes tend to avoid relations with one another. (We shall consider this a measure of the closedness or openness of the class structure.)
2. Skidders who perceive a closed class structure are more leftist than skidders who perceive an open class structure.

TABLE XV:5. SOCIOPOLITICAL ATTITUDES OF SKIDDERS AND THEIR
CLASSES OF ORIGIN AND DESTINATION

Sociopolitical Attitude	Response	Stable Nonmanuals	Skidders	Stable Manuals
I. 1. Respondents' Chances to Get Ahead in Life, Compared to Others'[a]	Better	32%	24%	25%
	Same	59	53	56
	Worse	9	24	19
	Total	100%	101%	100%
	N	133	55	180
II. 1. Recent Progress in Society[b]	Good	55%	30%	44%
	Some	35	39	32
	None	10	32	24
	Total	100%	101%	100%
	N	142	57	186
III. 1. Who Profits from National Prosperity[c]	Everybody	42%	12%	37%
	The Elites	58	88	63
	Total	100%	100%	100%
	N	134	50	163
IV. 1. Perception of Class Structure as[d]	Open	46%	22%	27%
	Closed	54	78	73
	Total	100%	100%	100%
	N	129	49	165

Note on "No Answers": Panel I—11 among Stable Nonmanuals, 2 among Skidders, and 10 among Stable Manuals. Panel II—2 among Stable Nonmanuals and 4 among Stable Manuals. Panel III—10 among Stable Nonmanuals, 7 among Skidders, and 27 among Stable Manuals. Panel IV—15 among Stable Nonmanuals, 8 among Skidders, and 25 among Stable Manuals. Sample Total: 391.

[a] "In comparison to others you know, your chances to get ahead in life are . . . ."

[b] "In your opinion, which of the following phrases best describes the social and economic progress of Italy during the last ten years?" The choices offered were "rapid progress" and "encouraging progress" (shown in this table together under "good"); "some progress, but it could have been better" (herein shown under "some"); and "very slow progress," "no progress at all," "we have gone backwards" (all combined under "none").

[c] "In your opinion, when things go well in Italy, who stands to profit most?" "Elites" includes the following spontaneous answers: capitalists, industrialists, entrepreneurs, merchants, bankers, employers, the masters, the rich, the upper classes, the government, the ruling class, the politicians, the politicians' protegés.

[d] "In your opinion, do those who belong to a given social class tend to avoid relations with persons belonging to another social class?" This question was open-ended and yielded a variety of "yes" answers (treated under "closed") and "no" answers (shown under "open"). Strictly read, this is not a question concerning the openness or closedness of the class structure. However, it may be argued that in practice this is one way in which the phenomenon is personally experienced.

The findings in Tables XV:5 and XV:6, wherein the sample has been reduced to comprise only those who in Table XV:4 gave specific party preferences, show that in varying degrees all eight of these propositions hold true. (The panels of the tables have been arranged to facilitate reference to our research propositions.) Beginning with Table XV:5, we may note that the downwardly mobile consistently exceeded both the class of origin and the class of destination in the frequency of responses that reflect relatively limited opportunities. Thus, in the first place, they more likely than stable manuals and nonmanuals felt that their relative chances to get ahead in life were poor (panel I). Assuming, as earlier theoretical statements suggested, that the skidders were particularly anxious for success in order to recover their lost status, it is little wonder that they turned for help to parties advocating radical social change. As they saw it, only a major transformation of the opportunity structure could retrieve them from the unwanted position to which they had fallen.

It is fair to surmise, moreover, that the skidders blamed "the system," if not exactly for their fall, then at least for their continued presence in the working class. It may be argued that merely perceiving one's own chances for achievement as relatively poor is not sufficient to promote leftist political behavior if the chances of attainment are deemed adequate for everyone in an absolute sense. In other words, it must be determined whether skidders perceived their opportunities as absolutely as well as relatively limited. If the opportunity structure itself were perceived in a favorable light, it would be logically consistent for a person to maintain both that his chances are worse than those of other people *and* that they are nonetheless adequate. Indeed, this type of thinking appears to be typical of people imbued with a strong success ideology. As such it leads not to political dissension but rather to self-blame, or if that is too painful, to an emphasis on the "more mystical and less sociological" workings of Fortune, Chance, and Lady Luck (Merton, 1957: 147–148; Foster, 1962:66–68).

The findings in panels II and III clearly show that, much more often than either category of old-timers, skidders perceived an absolute inadequacy of opportunities in their society, as well as a relative disadvantage for themselves. In an era of rapid economic expansion, the downwardly mobile were the most apt to minimize or altogether negate all progress in their society (panel II). Even more telling are the differences between the skidders and the two other groups in their tendency to view the profits of their society as accruing overwhelmingly to those who already possess wealth, power, and prestige (panel III).

These findings put teeth in the assertion that skidders blamed their society for their ill fortune—that, as Wilensky put it earlier, under some conditions the response to skidding is externalized. The country, they seemed to be saying, has not "progressed" very much in the first place; in the second place, the new riches, such as they are, have fallen into the coffers of those whose coffers were overflowing to begin with; the social structure is lacking in distributive justice.

Leftist parties make this notion central to their programs. Predictably, skidders were attracted to them.

Finally, the findings in panel IV show that the skidders perceived the class structure as closed much more frequently than did the old-timers of their class of origin, and even somewhat more often than the old-timers of their class of destination. Their frustrations have come full circle, so to speak. As was previously noted, a basic assumption of the theory here at work states that skidders wish to regain a middle-class status. But now they are telling us that their desire is being thwarted. All this highlights the likelihood that skidders in Italy are disquieted by a strong sense of hopelessness and dissatisfaction with respect to existing structures and opportunities.

TABLE XV:6. PERCENTAGE OF STABLE NONMANUALS, SKIDDERS, AND STABLE MANUALS WHO WERE LEFT-WING,[a] BY VARIOUS SOCIOPOLITICAL ATTITUDES

Sociopolitical Attitude	Response	Stable Nonmanual	Skidders	Stable Manuals
I. 2. Respondents' Chances to Get Ahead in Life, Compared to Others'	Better	42%	62%	58%
	Same or Worse	42	74	76
II. 2. Recent Progress in Society	Good	41	65	67
	Same or None	45	75	76
III. 2. Who Profits from National Prosperity	Everybody	23	67	55
	The Elites	59	75	81
IV. 2. Perception of Class Structure as	Open	42	64	53
	Closed	49	74	73

[a] See Table XV:2 for specific party preferences included in the left-wing category.

Table XV:6 presents the findings required to show that an image of limited opportunities is more frequently associated with a leftist political orientation than is a success ideology. This part of the inquiry is critical, for it is a central point of the theory under examination that left-wing politics build upon discontent with existing opportunities. Given our particular focus on downward mobility, the four research propositions previously stated in this connection concern the relationship between *political orientation* and *perception of the opportunity structure* in the case of skidders only. The logic at work, however, could have been employed to state the same relationship regardless of class or mobility status. To clarify the point, the basic logic argues that: (1) a perception of limited opportunities disposes to a leftist political orientation; (2) such perception is more frequent among skidders than among stationary members of the classes of origin and destination; hence, (3) skidders are more frequently left-wing than the old-timers of these two social classes.

Accordingly, Table XV:6 reports the relationship between political preference and perception of the opportunity structure for the classes of origin and destination as well as for the skidders. The table shows a rather complex but enlightening picture. It may be roughly summarized by several brief statements. First, the trend is consistently in the direction predicted by the four research hypotheses: skidders who conceived of limited opportunities were indeed more likely to be left-wing than those who did not have such conception. Second, with a single exception—stable nonmanuals in I.2—the same relationship obtained also in the classes of origin and destination, and thus vindicates the underlying logic of the basic argument. Third, generally speaking, the relationship was strongest among stable manuals, somewhat weaker among skidders, and a great deal weaker among stable nonmanuals. This finding probably indicates an unspecified class component of the relationship. That is, it is working-class people as a whole who are both more likely to have a conception of limited opportunities and more likely to react to it with remonstrative political behavior. The somewhat stronger relationship between a left-wing orientation and a limited-opportunity ideology among stable manuals than among skidders is a fact whose possible explanation escapes us here and which, unless it is accidental, can hopefully be explained by others in the discipline.

The most important point about Table XV:6, however, is that findings therein are fully comprehensible only in strict conjunction with those in Table XV:5. Specifically, the findings in the two tables suggest an interaction between a social-psychological set of factors (what we have conveniently termed "social attitudes") and a specifically unknown set of factors (say, "situational" factors) with "hide,"[14] as it were, under the label of "downward mobility." This interaction produces an additive effect, an effect which shows up in the fact, presented in Table XV:5, that skidders most frequently held an image of limited opportunities, and in the further fact, shown in Table XV:4, that they were the most frequently left-wing in political orientation. In short, a perception of limited opportunities disposed the respondents to left-wing politics, the more effectively so within the context of the working class. Such perception, however, was more frequent among the downwardly mobile than among mem-

---

[14]This point concerns the broader problem of causality in sociology. Our position, in brief, is that being or not being mobile *in itself* is irrelevant to political behavior. What is relevant is the *personal experience* of mobility, which is to say that the mobile individual must first "interpret" his mobility before it becomes a factor in his political behavior. Needless to say, this experience is rich and varied, while our assessment of it in terms of four "sociopolitical attitudes" is obviously only partial. In this sense, we speak of "situational" factors which "hide" under the label of mobility.

bers of the two classes they bestrode because, as skidders, the former had more to be frustrated about.

This interpretation is supported by a number of additional facts, directly or indirectly bearing on the issue in question. For instance, if we elaborate our two-class scheme into a four-class one, the logic of the foregoing argument and findings invites the prediction that *the greater the distance skidded, the greater the likelihood of holding a left-wing political preference.* Our data, though limited, uphold the prediction. If we compare the political preferences of skidder sons of lower-stratum nonmanual fathers (that is, petty bourgeoisie) and the skidder sons of higher-stratum nonmanual fathers (that is, all remaining nonmanual categories) with the political preferences of stable lower- and upper-stratum nonmanuals, we find the following percentages of left-wing preferences (base frequencies in parentheses):

Skidders from upper nonmanual origin	87	(15)
Skidders from lower nonmanual origin	67	(42)
Stable upper nonmanuals	40	(94)
Stable lower nonmanuals	48	(50)

Two findings are especially worthy of note. First, each origin level of skidders was more often left-wing than the corresponding group of stable nonmanuals. Second, and more important, the rank order of the two levels with respect to left-wing political preference is reversed between nonmanuals and skidders. Contrary to expectations based on the political differences between the two nonmanual strata, the skidder sons of upper nonmanuals were more often left-wing than the skidder sons of lower nonmanuals. Hence—though in the absence of data on the politics of fathers we cannot be certain about it—it would appear that the "high skidders" manifested a much greater departure from the political norm of their parents' stratum than did the "low skidders."

These findings, concerning the *intensity* dimension of mobility, add considerable weight to the contention that left-wing political behavior among skidders reflects personal frustration, disappointment, and resentment against the existing order. Those whose frustrations may be presumed to have been the greatest—namely, those who catapulted downward most dramatically—were most readily inclined to support radical changes in the *status quo.* The point can be seen more directly by further partialing the analysis of the above data for subjects with different sociopolitical attitudes (Table XV:7).

Although one must now proceed with special caution due to the all too scant numbers in some cells, Table XV:7 presents data that add to our confidence in the interpretation of the preceding data. The table shows that high skidders holding an image of limited opportunities were more likely to be left-wing than their counterparts among the low skidders. For example, among high skidders 92 percent of those who acknowledged little or no recent progress in society were left-wing; the corresponding figure among low skidders

TABLE XV:7. PERCENTAGE OF HIGH SKIDDERS AND LOW SKIDDERS
WHO WERE LEFT-WING, BY VARIOUS SOCIOPOLITICAL ATTITUDES

Sociopolitical Attitudes	*High Skidders*	*Low Skidders*
Respondents' Chances to Get Ahead in Life, Compared to Others:		
Better	100%	58%
Same or Worse	85	69
Recent Progress in Society:		
Good	67	64
Some or None	92	68
Who Profits from National Prosperity:		
Everybody	—	67
The Elites	92	75
Perception of Class Structure as:		
Open	75	57
Closed	100	68

Note: "No Answers" on skidders as a whole are reported in Table XV:5. Totals of High Skidders and Low Skidders are 15 and 42, respectively.

was only 68. In short, status frustrations rose with the magnitude of status fall. As a result, those who skidded the most had the greatest preference for left-wing parties even when data are controlled for perception of the opportunity structure.

"Revolutionary Politics" and Middle-Class Aspirations

We have now come to a good point at which to return to the Marxian perspective on the political behavior of the downwardly mobile. Contrary to the theory stated earlier, which views the individual as essentially a "loner" —one who judges "class" phenomena in terms of "what's in it for him" as an individual rather than as a member of a class—Marx viewed the pauperization of the "middle strata" (downward mobility) as a crucial ingredient in the allegedly rising corporate consciousness of the working class.

The finding from Italy, which shows an apparently proletarianized "skidder," might now be interpreted as support for Marx's thesis. Such interpretation, however, would not be warranted. Our finding alters the form but not the substance of previous findings: man continues to display a highly individualistic inclination. Consider the relationship between political orientation and class identification, as measured by the Centers-type question requiring self-placement in one of four classes: upper, middle, working, and lower. In the first place, skidders were significantly less likely than their stable peers to identify with the working and lower classes. Whereas 63 percent of the downwardly mobile so identified themselves, the corresponding figure for the manual old-timers was 75 percent. But even more important is the finding that,

whereas the correlation between political preference and subjective class placement is in the expected direction among the stable nonmanuals and the stable
manuals (that is, in each case the self-assigned working-class, or lower-class,
respondents were more often leftist), those skidders who assigned themselves
to the middle class held an edge in leftist political preference over those
identifying with the working (or lower) class—76 versus 69 percent.

To us, this apparently peculiar finding strongly suggests that, far from being
induced by considerations of class solidarity, apparently the "revolutionary"
politics of skidders represents an individualized, pragmatic, and self-seeking
calculation. The finding conveys, loud and clear, an old message about "the
psychology of classes." It forcefully echoes that well-engineered *tour de force*
against Marxian idealism that the skeptical Pareto produced around the turn
of the century. People, Pareto (1916:1220–1226) argued, do not engage in
"class behavior" for abstract reasons. They do so because it is to their selfish
interest. People do not wish equality. They are merely "bent on escaping
certain inequalities not in their favour, and setting up new inequalities that will
be in their favour, this latter being their chief concern." In the process, they
will support those parties that offer the greatest promise, but will offer whatever explanations are "fashionable" for their actions.

More recently, Lipset (1959:240) has restated the above notion on a broader
plane. "It seems logical to assume," he argues, "that men will arrange their
impressions of their environment and themselves so as to maximize their sense
of being superior to others." This tendency appears indeed to be an important
component in the Italian skidders' interest in leftist politics. The following data
are especially revealing in this respect. When asked, in conjunction with an
open-ended question on self-placement, what occupational categories they
would include in their own social class, skidders manifested a far stronger
tendency than their stable peers to deny membership to those occupations in
the lowest reaches of the status hierarchy and to extend it, instead, well up the
top of the hierarchy to managerial and professional positions.

In conclusion, relative to the United States and many other western European countries, Italy is fairly new to the industrialization experience. As a
result, though current opportunities in that country, as measured by mobility
rates, are roughly comparable to, though somewhat lower than, those in other
industrial societies, Italians appear to suffer from what might be termed a lag
in perception concerning the richness of opportunities in their society. Moreover, as LaPalombara (1964:31) has noted,

changes which in many other countries required several decades of evolution have
taken place in Italy in just a few years. These changes . . . brought in their wake the
kinds of social transformations and problems that now have a greater impact on Italian
society than did previous centuries of gradual development.

One of these problems is no doubt an impatient expectation, fostered and strengthened in the masses by very active political ideologies, that changes could in fact be faster and more equitable. To many, the "economic miracle" which began in the mid-1950's has been tarnished by too many enduring deficiencies. Among these are: (1) the persistent tendency of employers to treat workers in a condescending and paternalistic fashion, together with their continuing refusal to accept labor unions as legitimate bargaining equals (LaPalombara, 1964:40); (2) persistent poverty and underemployment, if not unemployment, "in the midst of plenty"; (3) tenaciously high prices for many modern essentials, which must, therefore, continue to be treated as luxuries; (4) frequent public scandals involving enormous graft; (5) a blunderous or inept public bureaucracy that obstinately refuses to be "reformed" despite ministerial efforts to that effect; and above all (6) a long series of residential, legal, and occupational abuses against millions of people uprooted by an expanding economy from rural surroundings and transplanted in the teeming industrial cities of the North.

Under such conditions, public suspicion and resentment are rampant, and political attacks against established structures and powers continue to flourish. Skidders were especially frustrated by the privations and strains of their situation. The fact that, as was previously noted, their society was undergoing an economic slump at the time of our study added to their strains. As a result, they were readily attracted to parties of the left, which specialize in attacking existing structures and in promising better opportunities for the less fortunate. The skidders' aim, however, was highly individualistic rather than being an expression of class consciousness.

A Theory of Downward Mobility and Political Behavior

We shall now proceed to state concisely the logical structure of what may properly be termed a middle-range theory of downward mobility and political behavior (see also Lopreato and Chafetz, 1970). Until such time as new findings and new advances in general theory will suggest a reformulation, the following construct seems both adequate and rich in promise for further research:

Given a middle-class-working-class structure in which conservative political behavior is normal to the middle class and leftist political behavior is normal to the working class:
1. Associated with a status in each class are pressures to espouse political ideologies appropriate to the class. That is, if men experience downward mobility, then they are likely to be subject to political resocialization into the class.
2. Men, however, are influenced by superior status, in the sense that they tend to emulate behavior that gives them a sense of superiority over others.

Thus, skidders are likely to emulate the political orientation of the more prestigeful class of origin, thereby mitigating the force of resocialization to which they are subjected as members of the working class.

3. Therefore, the normal political behavior of skidders is intermediate between the behavior of persons in the class of origin and the class of destination.

4. However, the efficacy of the resocialization factor varies inversely with the strength of the success ideology which (a) underscores individual responsibility for both failure and success; (b) promotes the hope of class re-ascent by accentuating the reality of existing opportunities; and (c) asserts the reality of distributive justice.

5. It follows that: (a) If skidders hold a strong success ideology, they are likely to resemble their class of origin in political behavior; (b) conversely, if they have an image of limited opportunities, they are likely to resemble politically their class of destination.

A Theory of Social Mobility and Political Behavior

In concluding the chapter, an effort should now be made to theoretically combine upward and downward mobility in relation to political behavior. The following sacrifices some details and is, therefore, briefer than either subtheory presented so far. However, it fairly adequately expresses the essential logical structure of both:

1. Men are more easily influenced by superior-status individuals and groups than by inferior-status individuals and groups.

2. Hence, given social mobility within a middle-class-working-class structure, both the upwardly mobile and the downwardly mobile are likely to take on, or retain, the normally conservative political behavior of the (superior) middle class.

3. The tendency toward the political emulation of the middle class is, however, weakened by: (a) the difficulty with which newcomers in the middle class are socially accepted by the old-timers of the class, and (b) the degree to which skidders perceive the existing opportunity structure as being incapable of redeeming their previously superior position.

4. Therefore: (a) the more easily upwardly mobile individuals are accepted socially by the old-timers of their class, the more likely they are to exhibit the political behavior appropriate to their new social class; (b) the greater the opportunity perceived for social re-ascent, the greater the likelihood that skidders will exhibit the political behavior normal to their class of origin.

XVI

SOCIAL-PSYCHOLOGICAL CORRELATES OF INTRAGENERATIONAL MOBILITY

In the preceding three chapters we have dealt with questions concerning the rate of vertical occupational mobility; the relationships of educational attainment on the one hand and migration on the other to social inheritance and career mobility; and differences in political perspective and interest in relation to occupational mobility. There are other aspects of mobility, however, which, though only infrequently discussed in the literature, are of theoretical importance. It is to some of these that we turn in this final chapter of Part Four. They concern the "subjective," as they are sometimes denoted, or social-psychological correlates of mobility.

A wealth of interesting questions lies within this realm. For example, in what significant respects do achievers differ from skidders? And each of these from the nonmobile? What are the subjective experiences of the mobile, and in what ways do they vary? How does one who is occupationally mobile perceive that fact? Is it, in the first place, a fact by his own reckoning? How does mobility experience influence one's sense of economic security, one's satisfaction with present social position and the distribution of opportunities in society, one's confidence in the future for self and children, and so forth?

As early as 1927 Pitirim Sorokin cogently speculated about such matters. Among other things, Sorokin (1927: Chapters XXI and XXII) argued that mobility tends to encourage "more plastic and versatile" behavior; to increase

477

mental strain and disease, superficiality and the "psychology and attitude of a tourist"; to favor "skepticism, cynicism, and misoneism" as well as isolation, loneliness, and restlessness. Conversely, it serves to reduce narrow-mindedness and "occupational and other idiosyncrasies"; to prevent lasting identification with a particular group or class; to diminish intimacy in social relations. These few examples do not exhaust the fruits of Sorokin's pen.

Systematic investigation has advanced this entire range of postulated problems very little beyond Sorokin's challenging imagination. (Indeed, some of Sorokin's conclusions have been forgotten at times, only to be embarrassingly rediscovered later.) Nevertheless, the student of social stratification is not totally lacking in empirical road markers and beacons when making his explorations. There is some evidence, for instance, to demonstrate Sorokin's "dissociative hypothesis" (for example, Ellis and Lane, 1967). Other investigators have sought to show that upward mobility increases aspiration level and the concern for various symbols of social importance, such as luxury items, which in turn positively affect further chances for ascent (e.g. Rosen, 1959). Still others have addressed themselves to the relationship between mobility and mental disorder (e.g., Hollingshead and Redlich, 1958:368–370; Kleiner and Parker, 1963), interpersonal relations (for instance, Blau, 1956), and racial or ethnic prejudice (among others, Bettelheim and Janowitz, 1950:60–61; Greenblum and Pearlin, 1953). But much more work needs to be done in this general area of research if we are to achieve anything near a systematic theory of mobility (see Tumin and Feldman, 1957). The present chapter, we hope, will make some contribution in that direction.

Two preliminary decisions face us, both of them pertaining to the manner in which we shall measure mobility. In the first place, we must consider the alternative of using an intragenerational or a social-inheritance framework. In the second place, we must decide upon a scheme of occupational classification on which to construct the mobility categories.

With respect to the former decision, we have selected the *intragenerational* or career framework as the more appropriate to our concerns. A number of scholars (including Janowitz and Curtis, 1959; Wilensky and Edwards, 1959; Dahrendorf, 1959:59, 219–223) have variously argued that the alteration of status *during* adult career-life is the more important context for assessing attitudinal and behavioral changes linked to mobility, essentially because it is more nearly a direct function of the individual's own personal investments of commitment and aspiration, and because it is less routinized, in comparison to status alterations between generations. Mobility as measured from social origin to career entry is increasingly linked in industrial society to a set of educational-attainment factors as an institutionalized avenue of occupational achievement. Not only has this avenue become a more or less routinely "expected" *means for* and *requirement of* occupational success; in contrast to intracareer achievement, it is somewhat more representative of what Turner

(1960) described as "sponsored mobility": the investments in education for future success are often made by the individual's parents, with or without state subsidy. Moreover, in an indirect sense, the individual is further subsidized by the society in general, through the machinery of the state, to the extent that chances for obtaining a high occupationally qualifying educational attainment are class-linked. The son of elite or bourgeois parentage, in other words, is additionally sponsored by the resources of others.

As we have shown elsewhere (Lopreato and Hazelrigg, 1970), resolution of the issue of whether the intragenerational context is in some sense the more significant dimension of social mobility depends upon the manner in which mobility is conceptualized. The conventional treatment of intergenerational mobility—namely, a comparison of son's current status with his father's status at some previous point in time—is often inadequate for purposes of *ex post facto* analyses of mobility correlates and consequences. It confuses what is status change between active generations (that is, change from social origin to career entry) and what is status change within career. It is entirely possible, then, that some of the conclusions regarding mobility correlates and consequences that have been based on this conventional measure of intergenerational mobility were actually the products of career experience and *not,* in any concrete sense, of intergenerational status change. Moreover, in our previous examination of this issue (Lopreato and Hazelrigg, 1970), we found some evidence to suggest that intragenerational mobility, exclusively conceived, does exhibit exceptional characteristics, for it is associated with at least certain resistances against resocialization into the attitudinal framework of the class or stratum of destination. That is to say, in the particular data examined there, people who had experienced a transition from the manual to the nonmanual category *during career only* were insignificantly different in political perspectives from the nonmobile manual workers. But those people who had moved from the manual to the nonmanual category at the point of career entry (that is, between social-origin status and first job) did give evidence of resocialization into the political perspectives of the white-collar world, thereby indicating that their transition was a much smoother, less discordant experience.

The extent of the effect of any mobility experience on the individual's psychology is contingent upon his choice of evaluational referents. The individual assesses his own success or failure—necessarily so, given characteristics of the success notion—by reference to some significant others, whether these be his own previous selves or some physically separate "others"; and according to such assessment, and the prevailing normative standards of what is justly expected, he forms appropriate attitudes. We agree with Wilensky (1966:103), among others, that family background—though far from unimportant in an objective sense—supplies a less potent frame of reference for a man's success evaluations than the meaningfulness of his own career experiences in relation to those of people he encounters in his daily work.

With respect to the second decision facing us—namely, the occupational classification to be used in constructing mobility categories—our choice has been partly dictated by the relative paucity of intragenerational mobility in Italy. Movement across such broad occupational categories as the nonmanual, manual, and agrarian is predominantly an "intergenerational" phenomenon in Italy, for it occurs primarily in conjunction with educational-attainment experiences and at first entry into the labor force. In order to have a sufficient number of career achievers for purposes of even the simplest analysis, then, we have utilized exclusively the seven-point scale earlier described: elites, bourgeoisie, petty bourgeoisie, proletariat, peasantry, subproletariat, farm hands. With the possible exception of the subproletariat-farm-hands axis, movement between any two of these categories is indeed subjectively significant, given the Italian social structure; there is no doubt about that. The feeling of disappointment which the reader may sense in our decision stems solely from the fact that, given the size of the sample and the seven occupational categories, we cannot control for equally specific origin and/or destination occupational categories. Instead we have divided each of the three mobility subsamples into their manual and nonmanual destination components only.

The resulting percentage distribution for the 1,369 sample members for whom necessary information on career-entry and current occupations was available is listed with cell frequencies.

The Achievers	23.0%	315
Nonmanual	11.6	159
Manual	11.4	156
The Stationary	68.4	937
Nonmanual	18.4	252
Manual	50.0	685
The Skidders	8.5	117
Nonmanual	.5	7
Manual	8.0	110
Total	99.9%	1,369

These rates correspond to those previously recorded in Chapter XIII, wherein the rate of career ascent was calculated as 23 percent and the rate of career skidding as about 8 percent (Table XIII:8).

EVALUATIONS OF THE OPPORTUNITY STRUCTURE

A number of scholars have pointed to the importance in society of belief systems concerning the "openness" or "closedness" of opportunity structures. In discussing mobility in the United States, for example, Tumin (1957:33) observes that a crucial factor in the management of conflicts stemming from reward allocation is the presence of a set of "ideal" values which insist upon the fundamental justice of "things as they are," values which assert that avenues of success are plentiful, fair, and open to everyone. Given the will to strive, a persistence of conviction, and just a dash of patience, anyone can succeed, says the American Dream; and numerous cultural heroes and romanticized models are engrained in the public mind to prove the point.

Education, Ambition, and Success

There is a variety of different success ideologies, of which the American Dream is only one. But the latter is a particularly highly developed version with a major emphasis on tangible, consumable symbols of success and on an intensely personal etiology of success ("if one fails, it's one's own fault"). Our present concern is with the question, "What kind of success ideology has been engrained in the Italian social consciousness, and to what extent?" A first approximation to an answer comes from interviewee responses to the question, "In your opinion, can any educated and willing person reach positions of high importance in Italy, *even if he is of humble origin?*"

The data tell of a quite marked belief in the possibility of success; two-thirds of the total sample replied with a positive certainty, and another near-fifth gave a qualified "Yes" ("with sacrifice," "with luck," "with pull," or the like). Moreover, there were no significant variations by mobility experience in such perceptions of opportunity; whether achiever, stationary, or skidder, whether nonmanual or manual, roughly two-thirds were convinced that one could succeed to a high position, given education and ambition, whether his father was a street cleaner, tenant farmer, clerk, or entrepreneur. Further, it could be shown that neither age nor education of the respondent was related to this belief. In short, it would seem that this perception of the opportunity structure was rather generally dispersed throughout the adult male population.

The Causes of Poverty

Our only caveat concerns the possible fact that different occupational strata in the sample had varying conceptions of "positions of high importance." For the son of a successful magistrate, for example, positions of high importance might have begun with positions of national political administration. For the son of a peasant, on the other hand, they might have begun with teaching positions in the prestigeful classical lyceum of the nearby town. In short, while our research question was probably adequate for purposes of assessing a success ideology in the general sense, it may not have been appropriate enough for assessing the different degrees in which this ideology may have been held among our respondents. Consequently, we should not be surprised to find significant differences in success ideology among our occupational and mobility categories as our interview queries become less general and more specific, less abstract and more immediate in their relevance.

A somewhat different story, for instance, is provided by Table XVI:1, which organizes responses to the following question, still rather abstract: "Throughout Italy, as in many other countries, there are some very poor people. In your opinion, to what is the poverty of these people due most frequently?" The interviewees' responses have been classified into *factors inherent in the individual* and *forces external to the individual.* Within each of these two rubrics we further distinguished between those factors for which the respondents were inclined to express censure of either the individual or the society and those factors for which no imputation of blame was made. In this fashion, we have in effect categorized two forms of reaction directed to either the individual or to forces external to him: one, in which either the individual or some external agency is blameworthy for his poverty; the other, in which the respondent limits himself to merely singling out the causes of poverty. The specific factors mentioned within each of these four response categories may be summarized as follows:

1. An individual locus
   (a) Blameworthy: lack of initiative; laziness; lack of character; immorality; vices; "poverty of spirit"; negligence; squandering of savings; and similar factors.
   (b) Blameless: bad luck; family origin; large family; low intelligence or education; lack of skill; and similar factors.
2. An external locus
   (a) Blameworthy: unfair distribution of wealth; low wages; egoism of the wealthy; class inequalities; ineptitude, negligence, egoism of government or society; public graft or waste; inadequate social legislation; and similar factors.
   (b) Blameless: overpopulation; lack of work; natural poverty; and similar factors.

Turning to the findings, we note that in the majority of responses, whether we focus on manuals or nonmanuals, all three mobility categories looked to the individual himself for the causes of his poverty. Furthermore, with the exception of the stationary nonmanuals, the greater tendency was to single out factors through which the individual was actually censured for his poverty. On the other hand, causes external to the individual were much less frequently mentioned, and then the greater tendency was to absolve the external agents of any guilt by focusing most frequently on such considerations as natural poverty, overpopulation, and the consequent lack of work.

There is in these data, however, an important education linkage to perceptions of the etiology of poverty. In general, but especially among the nonmanuals, the greater the level of educational attainment, the less likely personal responsibility was invoked as a cause of poverty and the more likely external *and* blameworthy factors were cited. For instance, 58 percent of the non-

TABLE XVI:1. CONCEPTIONS OF THE OPPORTUNITY STRUCTURE: PERCEIVED CAUSES OF POVERTY

Mobility Category and Present Occupation	Personal Factors		External Factors		Total	N
	Blame-worthy	Blame-less	Blame-worthy	Blame-less		
Achiever	32.8%	24.3%	19.5%	23.4%	100.0%	329
Nonmanual	35.3	24.6	18.6	21.6	100.1	167
Manual	30.2	24.1	20.4	25.3	100.0	162
Stationary	37.6	25.5	16.3	20.6	100.0	964
Nonmanual	29.3	32.4	17.2	21.1	100.0	256
Manual	40.5	23.0	16.0	20.5	100.0	708
Skidder	31.7	20.8	24.2	23.3	100.0	120
Nonmanual	*	*	*	*	*	7
Manual	31.0	19.5	24.8	24.8	100.1	113
Total Sample	36.0%	24.8%	17.7%	21.5%	100.0%	1,413

* Too few cases.

manual achievers with less than an elementary-school diploma, as opposed to 28 percent of those who attended secondary school and 24 percent of those with university experience, mentioned factors that fit within the personal-blame category. This educational linkage, incidentally, accounts for most of the anomalous comparison between nonmanual and manual stationaries in the first column of Table XVI:1. Very few of the former, but many of the latter, had acquired less than five years of schooling; this fact skews the nonmanual stationaries away from, and the manual stationaries in the direction of, blaming the individual for his poverty.

In short, then, what we might call an "Italian Dream" appears to have been a real and active phenomenon among our respondents. According to it, the individual, in the abstract, is enjoined to strive for success and to blame only himself if that success is not forthcoming. Lacking longitudinal data on this question, one cannot determine whether or not these ideological axioms were of recent vintage, associated with recent social and economic developments. It would be difficult to believe that the axioms comprised an aspect of a society that until recent decades maintained a rigid system of stratification and a social-economic organization in which continued success was largely a prerogative of the already successful, while the masses were continuously dependent upon the good will and charity of the gentry, clergy, and employers in order to avoid slipping further to the most abject levels of poverty, helplessness, and submission.

Our guess is that some version of the American Dream is a cultural peculiarity of industrial and industrializing societies. But there is some evidence that the humble man's capacity for self-flagellation, coupled with upward-directed humility, servility, and even identification with the aggressor, is an elastic quantity. The long, tortuous, and humiliating journey of the successful man who knocks, full credentials in hand, upon the doors of social superiors in search of "the final bestowals of grace," as Tumin (1957:33) colorfully puts it, amply attests to this human capacity. The continued support of much of the Italian masses for political parties which, whatever their spoken ideology and their present labels, continue to incorporate in their ranks and their operative platforms groups, interests, and ideologies that are basically oriented to a feudal form of social and economic organization, is additional confirmation of that capacity. The "passive snobbery" of the noble's servant, the *domenichino,* the "devoted," "attached," "faithful," for whom "a nobleman's most fugitive smile was enough to flood an entire day with sun" further corroborates that human capacity. Such "passive snobbery" has often been documented as an especially pronounced quality of the Italian workingman. Di Lampedusa (1961:120, 126), famed novelist from whom the preceding quotation was taken, brilliantly illustrated it in the person of Don Ciccio, devoted servant to the Prince Salina; having sought without success to prevent the marriage of the prince's noble nephew to the wealthy and beautiful daughter of an enriched commoner, the servant "bent his head and longed in anguish for the earth to open under his feet" (see also Silone, 1961:75–76, for a parallel description of the *domenichino*).

It is likely that this quality, already deeply engrained in the desperate sense of survival of the peasantry, has lately reached a high peak as a result of the economic expansion, increased opportunities, and "democratization" of Italian society. As a result, it is possible that the accentuated tendency to hold the individual, in the abstract, responsible for the causes of his poverty represents what Tumin (1957:35), as was previously noted, has termed "a cult of gratitude" toward the social order. According to Tumin, social mobility—and he might better have said the *perception* of the *possibility* of mobility—leads to such cult whereby individuals tend to "lose sight of the history of effort and struggle which have been required for past mobility. . . . They organize their perspectives around a sense of gratitude to the social order for making the present pleasures possible."

Returning to our findings in Table XVI:1, we note also, however, that the greatest tendency to look for personal causes of poverty and the least tendency to look for external causes were found not among the achievers who, as we previously argued, suffered a history of hardships and discriminations on their way up, but among the stationary, especially those who were engaged in manual occupations. Understandably, it was the skidders who blamed the individual the least, and factors external to him the most. The explanation of this finding may lie in the fact that while the skidders may have participated in principle in the cult of success and gratitude, a considerable number of them could not but have been cognizant of the fact that all their trials had come to nought—or, indeed, had resulted in a decline of life conditions.

Likewise, while the achievers had the most reason to adhere to a cult of gratitude, they were like the skidders in being able to appreciate the waste, the pain, the hardships inherent in the obstacles against the person in his attempt to get ahead in life. Many achievers clearly expressed this feeling in verbal asides, when they stated (in the words of a former semiskilled worker turned successful shopkeeper) that "the road to my present position was strewn with thorns. God only knows how many enemies I had to battle, how many unjust laws I had to honor, and how many filthy hands I had to kiss."

The greater "conservatism" of the stationary is largely attributable to the conservatism of the manual old-timers, the vast majority of whom were either traditional peasants or artisans. The success ideology of the artisan can rather easily be explained: he moves directly, at an early age, from the status of apprentice to that of a full-fledged craftsman—a status that carries, in the smaller communities at least, a considerable degree of prestige and gives the individual good cause for pride.

The case of the peasants is more difficult to explain. We might begin by noting, however, that the research question posed dealt not with poverty in general but with *extreme* poverty ("very poor people"). While the Italian peasant has been traditionally and notoriously poor, he has been relatively better off in comparison to the particular sense in which many urban workers have understood and experienced poverty. Even though deprived of capital, luxury, even the most basic conveniences of the home, and of anything like a varied and rich diet, he has nevertheless been able to avoid real hunger. To the traditional peasant, extreme poverty probably evokes images of the pangs of starvation that the urban subproletariat, as well as a few others above it, has had to endure during periods of national crises and economic difficulties. Such a form of poverty is not known to the peasant, for when conditions reach rock bottom he can always feast on a dish of wild herbs, on the fruit of the trees growing on the land he works, and on such seasonal availabilities as snails, mushrooms, and the like. Thus, bringing a different perspective to bear on our query because they felt themselves relatively well-off, the peasants conveyed probably the message that no one need go hungry, unless he is indolent, lazy, or altogether depraved.

Whatever the frames of reference, however, and whatever the levels of aspirations from which our respondents passed judgment on the opportunity structure of their society, the prevailing tendency in all classes of people and in all categories of success and failure was to acknowledge the existence of reachable opportunities and to put pressure on the individual himself for achieving such opportunities.

Educational Opportunities

Thus far, however, we have been dealing with this question only at an *abstract* level of cognition. We have not asked people to explain to us their own advantages or disadvantages, but to pass judgment on the causes of the extreme poverty of "some people." What happens if we become less abstract and more personal in our inquiry? It is one thing to assess the distribution of opportunities in general terms; it is an entirely different matter to be put in the position of having to assess one's own opportunities in a specific area of social life. In the first instance, the individual is in effect left free to make favorable or unfavorable, realistic or unrealistic assumptions about his own situation. In the second, he is influenced by the researcher to have a more particular understanding of his own situation. Ask a peasant to explain the extreme poverty of "some people," and he is likely to assume that he is comparatively well-off and, therefore, to find fault with those less fortunate than himself. Ask him to explain *his* "failure" to own the land on which he works, and he is likely to have sobering afterthoughts about the causes of "poverty." We suspect that he will be less likely to adhere to the cult of success and gratitude and less likely to express faith in the opportunities of his society. The findings in Tables XVI:2 and XVI:3 confirm our suspicion.

TABLE XVI:2. RESPONDENTS' PERCEPTIONS OF EDUCATIONAL
OPPORTUNITIES FOR THEIR CHILDREN

Mobility Category and Present Occupation	Sending Children to School beyond Eight Grades Is				
	Easy	Neither Easy nor Difficult	Difficult	Total	N
Achiever	29.4%	20.6%	50.0%	100.0%	306
Nonmanual	46.4	21.6	32.0	100.0	153
Manual	12.5	19.6	68.0	100.1	153
Stationary	28.2	21.0	50.7	99.9	914
Nonmanual	65.0	20.7	14.3	100.0	246
Manual	14.6	21.1	64.2	99.9	668
Skidder	18.0	13.5	68.4	99.9	111
Nonmanual	*	*	*	*	7
Manual	15.4	13.5	71.2	100.1	104
Total Sample	27.7%	20.3%	52.1%	100.1%	1,331

* Too few cases.

Table XVI:2 reflects our inquiry into the respondents' perceptions of the ease or difficulty with which people in their own position could continue their children's formal schooling beyond the eight grades legally required in Italy since 1963. Not surprisingly, of course, the greatest perceptual differences paralleled occupational differences; that is, nonmanuals more frequently saw better possibilities of extended schooling for their children than did manual workers. This divergence was especially marked within the stationary category, which brings us to an interesting comparison with Table XVI:1: the manual old-timers were the most inclined of all groups to blame the individual for his poverty within an abstract context; but in the concrete, they were among the least hopeful about educational opportunities for their children.

The significance of mobility experience for such perceptions was also class-linked. Manual achievers—that is, men who succeeded to higher levels of the blue-collar world during career—were little different from their stationary counterparts in viewing the structure of educational opportunity. On the other hand, nonmanual achievers, who numbered among themselves also people who had crossed from the blue-collar to the white-collar world, much more often than the nonmanual old-timers took the view that sending their children to school after the mandatory period would be (or was) a difficult task. This attitude was manifested most frequently by the nonmanual achievers with blue-collar career entries; their own background and career experiences suggested to them that it would not be easy to provide a high-school or college education for their children. An indication of this difference in attitude among the nonmanual achievers is given by a comparison of their own educational attainments with their conceptions of future educational opportunities. About one in ten of the nonmanual achievers had acquired at least some university training, entered directly into the nonmanual category, and then moved up the ladder; of these, 88 percent believed it was relatively easy for people in their position to send children to high school and perhaps beyond. Conversely, about one in twelve of the nonmanual achievers had not obtained the elementary-school diploma but achieved a nonmanual position—typically a very low one—only after having begun their career in the ranks of the manual workers; of these, only 42 percent thought it was easy to give their children more than eight grades of instruction.

Finally, with respect to the occupational skidders, we now have strong evidence of a more concrete basis for the discontent manifested by them in the preceding chapter. Note that they were much less likely than either the achieving or the stationary respondents to express optimism with respect to the future educational opportunities of their children. The solid stance of political protest previously observed among them continues to reveal its specific bases.

The Distribution of Rewards

We cannot reasonably read into the data of Table XVI:2 a major reaction of protest, or even a great lack of confidence in the society's opportunity structure. Considering Table XVI:3, however, we discover a different set of conclusions. First of all, a majority in all mobility and occupational categories were explicit in stating that the conditions of "the good life" in Italy tended to be preempted by those who were already privileged and powerful; the economic elites were especially emphasized for their much better life chances. Second, and predictably, skidders were the most likely and achievers the least likely to single out national categories which took the lion's share of new opportunities in the nation. Finally, individuals in manual occupations predominantly expressed what may surely be termed a protest against the existing social order. These responses, we should emphasize, were spontaneous in the sense that interviewees produced such categories themselves rather than selecting them from a prearranged list of alternative expressions.

To what can we attribute the radical shift from the previous apparent adherence to an ideology of individual responsibility to the present readiness to admit a clear handicap on the part of most in the struggle for the appropriation of national profits? The answer to such a query is not an easy one. We can only speculate.

We begin by observing that the average man's capacity for stretching "the bottom of the bottom" is great—whether the phenomenon under considera-

TABLE XVI:3. PERCEPTIONS OF THE DISTRIBUTION OF
REWARDS IN SOCIETY

Mobility Category and Present Occupation	Who Profits Most from National Prosperity?			Total	N
	Everybody, the People	Economic Elite	Political Elite		
Achiever	40.6%	39.9%	19.4%	99.9%	278
Nonmanual	46.4	34.8	18.8	100.0	138
Manual	35.0	45.0	20.0	100.0	140
Stationary	38.5	43.8	17.8	100.1	811
Nonmanual	43.3	37.5	19.2	100.0	224
Manual	36.6	46.2	17.2	100.0	587
Skidder	30.6	49.0	20.4	100.0	98
Nonmanual	*	*	*	*	4
Manual	28.7	50.0	21.3	100.0	94
Total Sample	38.3%	43.3%	18.4%	100.0%	1,187

Note: The question read, "In your opinion, when things go well in Italy, who stands to profit most?" The Economic Elite category includes such spontaneously given categories as capitalists, monopolists, industrialists, entrepreneurs, merchants, employers, banks, the masters, the rich, and the upper classes. The Political Elite includes the government, the revenue service, the ruling class, politicians, and politicians' protégés.

* Too few cases.

tion be sin, immorality, illegality, poverty, or the reward structure. The most destitute in a given community can point to numberless others more indigent than he. The worst public thief has no difficulty in comparing himself favorably to any number of others who, really or not, made their money by fleecing the poor and the public treasury. The prostitute will point with the greatest of ease to the most respected woman and "reveal" about her all manner of indecencies and illicit behavior. The lowliest citizen—homeless, hungry, and totally at the mercy of others for his daily bread—can mention with the most virginal earnestness countless others, not infrequently his own "benefactors," as examples of still lower levels of prestige that one could reach. The Italian has a long tradition of submission and subjugation to foreigner, aristocrat, state, employer, landlord, tax collector, priest and physician, merchant and pharmacist, baron and overseer, *mafioso* and "fixer," policeman and informer, ingratiator and meddling neighbor. Under these circumstances, the pursuit of life has naturally followed a precarious, often devious, and always individualistic course. The struggle for survival has been a bitter one, at best propelled by the most dubious hope of final success. The elements, a niggardly land, and the unchecked coercion of those above, endlessly rotating to substitute for one another, have sapped the common citizen's strength, courage, and resolve to organize a meaningful protest. In consequence, he has pursued his own salvation, his own sense of self-respect, by fostering and thriving in a context of social chaos in which all but the closest of kin are potential foes.

Having come to recognize the inadvisability of striking back at the high-placed source of his misfortune, he has turned to his equals for an account of his difficulties, thus creating infinite gradations of power and prestige, worth and dignity, wealth and poverty, rights and obligations (see Lopreato, 1967b; 1968). *Cà nisciuno è fesso*—We are no fools here—is the proudest boast of the Neapolitan. There is always someone worse off than one's self; someone who has not been *furbo* (clever) enough to avoid rock bottom; someone who has lost battle, war, armor, weapons, and the courage to initiate his own personal guerilla warfare. The man suffering from "extreme poverty," however this may be defined, is one such individual. He is a despicable example of what is likely to happen to the timid and the meek. He has given up. A public football, he is all too often incapable of safeguarding the "honor" of his wife and daughters. He no longer curses in his hat against the hand that charitably feeds him. He is not an Italian! He is contemptible and blameworthy.

This *modus operandi,* this creed of internecine popular belligerence, this extreme plasticity of the offended heart—these are the facts of life that every-where confuse all theories of class conflict: the "oppressed," the "governed," the "subjected" masses learn easily to cope with their oppression and subjection by reconstructing in their very midst the structure that rests on their shoulders. They do so not only because, often deprived by their "oppressors" of effective leadership through what Pareto termed the "circulation of the elite," they are left incapable of aiming revenge upward—but also because the might, arrogance, and incontestable right of the superiors illustrate the need for power and superiority in themselves. Unable to achieve power and superiority where they face the more powerful and the well-protected, they turn to one another for the gratification of that need. Hagen (1962:71–74) has characterized the "simple folk of traditional societies" as having an "authoritarian personality," in which there is "satisfaction in yielding to the judgment and wishes of superiors and satisfaction in dominating inferiors." The Italian masses may no longer be properly considered "simple folk," nor industrializ-ing Italian society exactly a "traditional society." But the unsevered umbilical cord to a very recent feudalism, coupled with the particular history of the people, makes that characterization especially apt for a great many Italians.

The radical shift between Tables XVI:1 and XVI:3 can be explained in terms of a continuing awareness on the part of the people that there is indeed a "class" of "oppressors" situated above, and that it is this class which reaps the best fruit of the Italian vineyard. That class is not conceived of as a unified entity, for at the top too each individual follows a *modus operandi* and a social creed that are analogous to those followed at the bottom. The "class" consists roughly of "those above." Our distinction into an economic category and a political one is for our own theoretical interest. For the people, the two come together in the same package. Their greater emphasis on the economic category is explained by the fact that, being more visible in everyday life, "the wealthy" constitute the more obvious frame of reference. The Italian masses have no particular sensitivity to the analytical distinction, so dear to the sociologist, between economic power and political power. For them, the one easily reduces to the other, and indeed the two are very often combined in the same individual. As one particularly articulate respondent put it,

The good things of life go first to those who already have an abundance of them. Don't ask me how they got them. Everybody steals in this country. The craftiest are naturally the most successful. Many made their money on the black market [reference to World War II conditions]; others by intimidating the poor peasant; still others by converting a simple trade into industrial and construction empires at the expense of the workers, who are ill-paid or not paid at all. Having become rich, their next step is to enter politics and win positions of great power and authority. From here they continue their looting on a much larger scale.

The corruption and selfishness of those high above is notorious among the Italian masses. The political alienation of the Italian, as pointed out in previous chapters, is to a large extent due to his belief that politicians are untrustworthy individuals full of the unlimited desire for self-enrichment and aggrandizement at the expense of the public.

To be sure, in a society in which suspicion is rampant, exaggerations are as natural as the suspicion itself. The fact remains, however, that the insensitivity of the Italian ruling classes to the public need has been well documented in the intellectual history of the country. Pareto himself devoted much of his scientific energy to measuring it and censuring it. Indeed, his occasionally jaundiced view of "democracy" and the "parliamentary system," as it is revealed throughout his writings, was to a large extent colored by his basic contempt toward such political phenomena as they were embodied in the excessively corrupt Italian politician (see especially Pareto, 1950; also 1916, 1921, 1960). Public scandals have been and are still the order of the day. Newspapers of all colors and inclinations carry almost daily stories of high functionaries, ministers, directors of public institutes and other such notables who have embezzled millions of dollars. Some of the most qualified and internationally famous economists point out that billions of dollars remain unaccounted for in the operation of mammoth public institutions. Occasionally, the legal machinery is set in motion on the trail of such perpetrations; names of accomplices who are located at the very apex of the political structure are suggestively mentioned in public debate; ministers, former prime ministers, and other high government functionaries are publicly invited to give an explanation; such explanation is awaited indefinitely or is given in obviously poor arithmetic; the parties excluded from the governmental exercise yell for punishment and redress. Years go by, and the public forgets—or so it seems. Everyone remembers to forget.

Medicines, butter, fruit, oil, cheese, and all manner of public goods are *"sofisticati"*—adulterated—at great damage and expense to the collectivity; the public and the newspapers again scream for justice. The law is stern, but . . . where is the law? Roads, hospitals, schools, aqueducts, bridges, reforestation projects, industrial loans to "enterprising private citizens," agricultural loans to modernizing farmers, all have been built or consummated—on paper; but in many cases the people are still waiting for the roads, the schools, and the hospitals to be completed. And in the meantime they use them, one-quarter finished, as trails for oxcarts, as public latrines, and the like.

The development of the South is an old promise in Italy, and signs of it do indeed exist. But intentions in this respect are the basis of a hope whose realization is far in the future. Capital disappears through excessive salaries—when it does not disappear *di sana pianta,* that is, totally and without explanation. Roads built five years ago are nearly impassable now. Schools and bridges mysteriously collapse. New funds are allocated; years later they are distributed. By then contractors raise their bids. The people wait. Their leaders proudly enumerate their public achievements; but the people wait; they have learned that development goes on mostly in the form of hope and promise. Squandering, grafting, and above all no unseemly zeal—these seem to be the laws of development in southern Italy, as almost any citizen will readily inform you (see Rossi, 1954, and Bocca, 1963, for two vivid accounts of the manner in which things get done in Italy).

"Everything changes in order, one might say, to reproduce itself"—said Bocca (1963:358–359), speaking of the South. "It is the old face under the new mask." To a lesser extent, these heavy pronouncements are valid also for the country as a whole. As a result, many of the people are bitter and resentful. Whatever their behavior with one another, their recognition of the privilege and power of those above is readily expressed, as we saw in Table XVI:3.

SELF-PERCEPTIONS AND EVALUATIONS

Study of the social-psychological correlates of occupational mobility necessarily begins with an examination of general conceptions of the opportunity structure of society as a whole. The foregoing has provided us with some pertinent insights into such conceptions. Given that general context, we may now ask further, how does the individual perceive his *own place and experiences* within the opportunity structure of his society? To what degree do his perceptions and associated evaluations correspond with objectively defined or inferred positions and experiences? Despite, curiously, sociology's historical sensitization to the fact that man as a social being is forever engaged in an informal calculus of self-evaluation in the everyday world, which is in some way reflective of the perceived judgements of the self made by "significant others," the relationship between objective contexts and participant definitions of success has been a seriously neglected focus of mobility research. Durkheim's classic work on suicide, and especially his concept of "altruistic suicide," is a milestone in this general area of inquiry, notwithstanding accentuations of the "social fact" and the "collective representation" as the allegedly proper subject matter of sociology. Still more apposite are the works of George H. Mead and Charles H. Cooley. Merton's (1957: Chapters VIII and IX) more recent effort at codification of the thinking in the area, through the "theory of reference group behavior," brought important and influential recognition to the fact that success and failure have both absolute and relative dimensions. A person who has achieved some considerable level of success (upward mobility) by one framework might well lament his lack of fortune when he appraises his own accomplishments against those of an even more successful "significant other"—a boyhood friend, a close associate, a brother, a neighbor. Yet, until recently, little systematic attention has been given to the "personality" components of social mobility—the perceptual, cognitive, motivational, and evaluational elements of what is collectively designated "subjective mobility" (see Inkeles, 1959; Lipset and Bendix, 1959:255–259).

Although perhaps more often professed as an ideal than integrated into the actual practice of mobility research, it is now generally agreed that social-psychological variables mediate between the fact and the "consequence" of mobility, objectively conceived. Among these are aspiration levels, perceptions of accomplishment, and the associated balance of gratification-frustration; the "historical" (or life-history) calculus of that balance and the resulting conceptions of relative deprivation; and the degree of resocialization and identification accompanying movement through the status structure. Each of these, in turn, is influenced by a series of contextual variables, which have their own subjective dimensions: for example, the historical structure of stratification and the prevailing conditions of economic development and individual conceptions of orderly career advancement (see Wilensky, 1961).

To some extent, the concepts of reference-group behavior have been taken over by investigators of social structure and mobility. One recent systematic application of certain of these notions to the study of occupational mobility in an entire society is found in the work of Tumin with Feldman (1961:379ff) on Puerto Rico. There they employ a measure which involves the comparison of an individual's status history with the corresponding status histories of his peer group, wherein the peer group is standardized in terms of equivalent social origins (in the case of "intergenerational" mobility) or in terms of equivalent labor-force entries (in the case of career mobility). The resulting "score tells how any individual has done, by way of job movement, compared to all other individuals" who have the same starting point. Because the measure combines "the initial social capital" of parental position (either directly or via career-entry position) and peer position, the authors feel their measure gives a realistic basis for examining mobility with respect to its subjective, experiential dimensions.

A second express effort to utilize reference-group concepts in systematically relating objective structures and participant meanings is Runciman's (1966) analysis of "attitudes toward inequality in the twentieth century." Using both historical and cross-sectional survey materials for England and Wales, Runciman carefully investigates the evidence of relative deprivation and grievances within the context of measured inequalities, which he then relates to a particular theory of social justice. Among other things, Runciman is intent on demonstrating that discrepancies between feelings of relative deprivation and measured inequalities can be adequately assessed by positing a genuine set of just entitlements.

Mobility Perceptions

The operation of reference-group behavior appears to be at work in Table XVI:4, where we present findings yielded by a question that asked the respondent to compare his present social position to the position he held at the time of his marriage, a time roughly equivalent to his career entry. Assuming that our measure of mobility is adequate, we would expect the subjective definition of mobility or immobility to closely reflect actual experience, unless some factors in the nature of reference-group comparisons were operative.

Table XVI:4. Perceived Mobility: Respondent Comparison of Present Social Position to Social Position at Time of Marriage

Mobility Categories and Present Occupation	Present Position Is			Total	N
	Higher	Same	Lower		
Achiever	71.9%	22.7%	5.4%	100.0%	278
Nonmanual	74.1	23.0	3.0	100.1	135
Manual	69.9	22.4	7.7	100.0	143
Stationary	57.5	33.7	8.8	100.0	826
Nonmanual	59.4	37.1	3.6	100.1	197
Manual	56.9	32.6	10.5	100.0	629
Skidder	58.6	27.0	14.4	100.0	111
Nonmanual	*	*	*	*	7
Manual	56.7	27.9	15.4	100.0	104
Total Sample	60.9%	30.5%	8.6%	100.0%	1,215

* Too few cases.

In fact, we see that 28 percent of the achievers either denied any change in position at all or claimed that they had been downwardly mobile. Among the stationary, a small percentage felt that they had actually skidded, whereas a majority believed their present locations were improved over those held at the time they married. From the viewpoint of reference-group behavior, the "deviant" achievers may be telling us in effect, "it could have been better." A similar motivation—"it could have been worse"—may have underlain the responses of those stationary respondents who perceived improvements of position, as well as the stated belief of more than half of the skidders that they had been upwardly mobile.

On the other hand, the optimistic nonmobiles and skidders were also very likely giving testimony of a systemic change in the occupational structure, in the sense of group or *stratum mobility*. Particularly among the older respondents, for whom the elapsed time between marriage and the time of the study encompassed considerable transformation of the Italian economy and social structure in general, present social positions *were* often better—indeed, much better—in terms of "absolute" material conditions, even though the respondents had not changed occupations (see Nowak, 1969:242–243, for analogous evidence regarding Poland). Conditions in Italy have certainly improved in a general sense, so that very few are not better off today than they were in the past, whatever their occupational changes. Public corruption, waste, and foot-dragging notwithstanding, industrialization brings higher salaries, if nothing else.

A life-style or stratum-mobility explanation would reasonably account for a good part of the discrepancy of perceived achievement among the objectively stationary in our sample and also, perhaps, for the favorable self-evaluations of the skidders. In this latter case, however, an additional factor is probably operative, although to what degree we cannot determine. It concerns mechanisms of "denial of failure," whereby the individual struggles to retain the social networks, beliefs and attitudes, consumption patterns, and various other symbols of his original position in an effort to camouflage to himself and to others the social implications of, say, a less "prominent" job (see Wilensky and Edwards, 1959). Such tendencies, we strongly suspect, are most pronounced among those who skid either within or, particularly, from the nonmanual category. However, we detected very few skidders within the nonmanual category, and a comparatively small proportion of the manual skidders had nonmanual career entries (that is, most of our downwardly mobile respondents had dropped from one blue-collar job to another). Hence, this "denial of failure" factor, while of theoretical importance in the general case, probably accounts in this instance for relatively little of the discrepancy between objective and participant definitions of mobility.

We should not leave our present data with the impression of great disparity between objective and participant definitions. When all is said and done, there was an observable tendency toward correspondence, especially with regard to upward mobility versus immobility. This parallels findings reported by other investigators—for example, Tumin and Collins (1959). Similarly, achievers were generally the most often satisfied, and skidders the least often satisfied, with respect to present social position, regardless of whether an objective or a subjective measure of mobility was used.

Self-Comparison to Significant Others

Earlier we suggested the possibility that, in assessing their experiences of career mobility, some of the respondents may have been guided more by a sense of "what might have happened" than by what actually happened. Perceptual frameworks of this sort would seem to be based on two major considerations: first, the thought that things would have been different (better or worse) if this or that had happened—perhaps a timely recommendation, an illness, or some similar event; second, the realization that in view of what apparently happened to others, things could well have been better (or worse) for oneself. With this latter consideration in mind, we were led to inquire of our respondents, "In comparison to others you know, your chances to get ahead in life are ——?" The response options provided to the interviewees, and their choices, may be seen in Table XVI:5.

Table XVI:5. Perceived Chances to Get Ahead in Life, Compared to Significant Others

Mobility Category and Present Occupation	Relative Chances Are			Total	N
	Better	Same	Worse		
Achiever	32.0%	56.1%	11.9%	100.0%	294
Nonmanual	38.5	53.4	8.1	100.0	148
Manual	25.3	58.9	15.8	100.0	146
Stationary	26.4	55.6	18.0	100.0	874
Nonmanual	31.0	57.8	11.2	100.0	232
Manual	24.8	54.8	20.4	100.0	642
Skidder	12.5	67.0	20.5	100.0	112
Nonmanual	*	*	*	*	7
Manual	12.4	66.7	21.0	100.1	105
Total Sample	26.5%	56.7%	16.8%	100.0%	1,280

* Too few cases.

The findings demonstrate significant and linearly patterned differences among the major categories: the achievers perceived their chances of success to be better, and the skidders as worse, than those of known others. To this extent, the subjective definition of the situation bore a high correspondence to already consummated opportunities.

At the same time, however, it is important to note that four-fifths of the skidders nevertheless felt that their chances to get ahead were at least as good as those to whom they compared themselves. In short, it would seem that while the objective circumstances of movement on the occupational hierarchy carried sufficient influence to distribute the mobility categories along a certain "realistic" tendency, the subjective outcomes of self-comparisons to others were also such that objectively defined "failures" were led to assume an essentially optimistic and contented stance.

Whereas success produces an intensification of aspiration along with a marked tendency to appraise one's conditions with reference to people in whom greater possibilities of success are manifest, failure, as represented by actual skidding, leads to the adoption of a perspective that presumes at least a modicum of self-esteem and a positive self-image. The frame of reference takes into account those people in whom evidence of failure is even greater and more frightful, in comparison to one's own biography. It is on the dynamics of such phenomena that an existing system of inequalities rests at any given time. According to the logic involved, in extreme form, the more one has the more one wants; and conversely, the less one has the less one is content with.

This matter is relative—relative to the level of satisfaction that would be expected of the achievers and the skidders if they responded solely on the basis of objectively defined circumstances. We are not saying, in other words, that the skidders were more optimistic than the successful but instead that, given the relative degree of success achieved, they showed a greater optimism than would be expected on objective grounds alone, while those for whom optimism would be more "realistic" manifested a less than expected amount. In this specialized and restricted sense, then, it may be said that the skidders were *relatively more satisfied* than the achievers.

With respect to the question of satisfaction, we found on the basis of a specific query that dissatisfaction with one's position was usually qualified by the hope that things would be better in the future. This futuristic vision applied not only to those who were dissatisfied (with the exception of the self-defined failures among the achievers, who exhibited what was apparently an intense feeling of relative frustration and deprivation). It was also manifested by respondents who expressed satisfaction with present position. This reflects not only a "perennial optimism in the future" but, as well, a guarded confidence in the developments of society as a whole—a faith that the "economic miracle" of postwar Italy will continue in some measure into the indefinite future.

PERCEPTIONS OF CHANGING OPPORTUNITIES: THE PAST AND THE FUTURE

So far, we have focused largely on perceptions and evaluations within a static context. It is perhaps more important, however, to examine the respondents' perceptions and evaluations within a context of change, so that we may consider the variable correspondence of subjective to objective definitions as concomitants of recent economic and sociopolitical developments in Italy.

TABLE XVI:6. RESPONDENTS' PERCEIVED CHANGE IN THEIR
FAMILIES' LEVEL OF LIVING DURING THE LAST TEN YEARS

Mobility Categories and Present Occupation	One's Family's Level of Living Has				
	Improved	Remained Constant	Declined	Total	N
Achiever	75.2%	17.1%	7.6%	99.9%	315
Nonmanual	81.8	14.5	3.8	100.1	159
Manual	68.6	19.9	11.5	100.0	156
Stationary	68.5	20.5	11.0	100.0	937
Nonmanual	81.0	15.1	4.0	100.1	252
Manual	63.9	22.5	13.6	100.0	685
Skidder	50.4	28.2	21.4	100.0	117
Nonmanual	*	*	*	*	7
Manual	47.3	30.0	22.7	100.0	110
Total Sample	68.5%	20.4%	11.1%	100.0%	1,369

* Too few cases.

Table XVI:6 shows that among the achievers, and to a less extent the nonmobiles, whether currently of white or blue-collar position, there was substantial agreement that their families were living better in the early 1960's than they had been a decade earlier. The major departure, as was predictable, is represented by the skidders; but a simple majority of these respondents also perceived improvements. The fact is that in the decade in question Italian society had made measurable progress in providing more work opportunities, higher wages, more freedom of movement for the labor force, more educational opportunities, more mass production of consumers' items (such as automobiles and refrigerators) that in past decades were considered luxuries available only to the rich and influential. In general, there had been a certain tendency toward some economic, political, and cultural rapprochement between the rich and the poor, the rulers and the governed, the elites and the masses.

As in previous sections of this chapter, we see here, too, that both mobility experience *and* high status govern attitudes of optimism and satisfaction toward the opportunity structure of society (see Tumin with Feldman, 1961: 423). There were genuine and concrete differences between the nonmanual and manual occupations, on the one hand, and between the achievers and the skidders, on the other.

TABLE XVI:7. ANTICIPATED FEELINGS OF SECURITY TEN YEARS HENCE, IN COMPARISON TO PRESENT

Mobility Category and Present Occupation	Ten Years Hence Respondent Will Feel				
	More Secure	Like the Present	Less Secure	Total	N
Achiever	61.5%	21.0%	17.5%	100.0%	286
Nonmanual	59.3	22.8	17.9	100.0	145
Manual	63.8	19.1	17.0	99.9	141
Stationary	55.0	20.9	24.1	100.0	813
Nonmanual	57.3	20.1	22.6	100.0	234
Manual	54.1	21.2	24.7	100.0	579
Skidder	51.9	20.4	27.8	100.1	108
Nonmanual	*	*	*	*	6
Manual	51.0	20.6	28.4	100.0	102
Total Sample	56.3%	20.9%	22.9%	100.1%	1,207

* Too few cases.

Our respondents' essentially positive definitions of recent changes in their society should naturally be reflected in their vision of the future, a question to which we shall now turn. Looking at Table XVI:7, which presents data pertaining to the level of security anticipated ten years hence, we find some support for this expectation. Roughly between 50 and 60 percent in each mobility category expected to be better off in the near future than at the present, and about one-fifth in each category anticipated no change at all (see also Tumin, 1957:34). It is worth noting, however, that in keeping with expectations, the achievers were most optimistic about the future, and the skidders the most pessimistic.

Somewhat different findings were yielded by a question which inquired into the respondents' assessments of future "opportunities for young people." Again there were no great differences among the three mobility categories, but two interesting data among present findings depart markedly from the previous table and merit further consideration. In the first place, those who anticipated improved opportunities now constitute about three-quarters of the individuals in each mobility category. What explains the greater inclination to view the future so favorably? In part, the answer lies in the fact that in the present instance the future was assessed not in terms of what it held in store for the respondents themselves, deeply caught up in the realities and difficulties of the present as many of them were, but rather in terms of its promise for the younger generation. Despite the economic and political difficulties that were brewing in Italy at the time of our study (see Chapter X), a great many people harbored the expectation, born of hope for the children, that the "economic miracle" of the late 1950's and (to a lesser extent) of the early 1960's would continue, and perhaps even improve.

In the second place, the skidders who were located in manual occupations were among the most optimistic of all respondents. About two-fifths of these individuals were skilled and semiskilled workers, some of whom had declined from lower nonmanual occupations, while the remaining three-fifths were unskilled workers who had fallen mostly from skilled and particularly semi-skilled positions. Their optimism in this connection therefore seems a bit peculiar, unless—contrary to the considerable literature on the "apathy" or "fatalism" of the lower classes (see Hyman, 1953; Kahl, 1953:207ff)—a con-siderable portion of them had not resigned themselves to a state of poverty and demoralization but had rather continued to strive for a place in the sun. This possibility is entirely in keeping with our argument in the preceding chapter, where the radical political behavior of skidders was interpreted as a reflection of their great desire to redeem their previous position, possibly through a restructuring of the existing political framework. Of course, inasmuch as future opportunities are assessed with respect to the younger generation, it is likely that what we are faced with here is the oft-documented type of vicarious success wherein the unachieved aspirations of the parent are transferred onto the children for future gratification (see Lipset and Bendix, 1959:262–263; Kahl, 1953:203). Indeed, such vicarious gratification might well be one of the main defense mechanisms which those who have gone down in social competi-tion develop in order to cope with their social descent and retain their self-respect.

In general, then, we may conclude by noting that Italians of all walks of life, whatever their past successes and failures in the occupational structure, were remarkably optimistic about possibilities of success and, in particular, prone to envision a future state of affairs in which the good life would be more readily attainable, either for themselves or for their children. This optimism and the resilience of spirit that characterized the skidders in particular were no doubt founded, as we have noted, on the faith that the greater opportunities already introduced in their society would be multiplied still further in the years to come. In this faith, if the findings of the previous chapter are kept in mind, the desired activities of the center-left government in general and perhaps of the leftist parties in particular were probably expected to play a major role. The people's behavior, then, is basically a question of the economic development of their country and of the willingness and ability of their political structure to flex and guide that development. It would seem that, given their particular social and economic history, the people of Italy are often ambivalent in their feelings toward the executive structures and processes of their society, and uncertain as well about the desire and ability of their leaders to engage in actions that would maximize the chances of satisfying public needs. Still, they are a hoping people; the present chapter has revealed in no uncertain terms their hopes.

PART FIVE   **The Continuing Marxian Legacy**

XVII

AUTHORITY RELATIONS, CLASSES, AND CLASS CONFLICT

In this, the last chapter of our volume, we shall return to an issue posed by Dahrendorf's theory of classes, a rich formulation that was intended as a rectification and "supersedure" of Marx's theory. Our immediate aim is to assess the plausibility of limited aspects of Dahrendorf's theory at a point in time by broaching certain perceptions and attitudes that are intrinsically connected to the basic issues of the theory. It would be inordinately ambitious, if not altogether pretentious, to hope to test exhaustively Dahrendorf's complex construct with the data at our disposal. In its full expression, this formulation speaks to certain broad problems of social stratification and political sociology that transcend the scope of the present endeavor.[1]

Our effort, moreover, has ulterior motives: we wish to (1) determine the extent to which Dahrendorf's intended supersedure of Marx's class theory meets with success and (2) tie together Dahrendorf's theory and the "elite theory" of Vilfredo Pareto. As has previously been suggested, Dahrendorf's work represents an intriguing intellectual cross between the brilliant German

---

[1]As in Chapter III, we shall not consider in this chapter the implications that Dahrendorf's subsequent work have for his *Class and Class Conflict in Industrial Society* (1959). It is noted that Dahrendorf himself (for instance, in 1967a) has suggested that certain weaknesses exist in his theory; it is also worth noting that Dahrendorf did not make use of the 1959 theory in his later analysis of *Society and Democracy in Germany* (1967b).

master of class analysis and the great Italian cynical observer of political processes. Like Marx, Dahrendorf focuses on the struggle between a "have" class and a "have-not" class as a crucial force of structural change in society. Unlike Marx, but like Pareto, Dahrendorf theorizes that the bone of contention between the two classes is not property but authority, a subspecies of political power. This perspective, moreover, is highly reminiscent of an argument presented in 1962 by the Polish Wesołowski (1966) who, in an argument against the Davis-Moore theory, contended that if there is a functional necessity for social stratification it must be found in the ubiquity of authority relations rather than in the phenomena singled out by Davis and Moore.

PRELIMINARY NOTES

Dahrendorf's Theory Briefly Revisited

It may be recalled that in Marx's theory, conflict between the classes arises out of a clash of interests over the ownership of the means of production. An examination of various developments in the structure of industrial society since Marx's time leads Dahrendorf to take issue with this heavily economic interpretation of conflict. Predominant among the industrial changes is what has come to be known as "the separation of ownership and control," whereby the economic organization of today increasingly comprises "capitalists without function" or stockholders, and "functionaries without capital," the managers. It follows, according to Dahrendorf (1959:136–137), that a theory of class conflict based on the division of society into owners and nonowners of the means of production lacks analytical value. Moreover, he argues, what is property if not a form of authority? Indeed, authority is "the more general social relation," for wherever there is property allegedly there is authority, but not every form of authority implies property. Hence, to the extent that class conflict exists, it is more likely to be produced by relations of authority; it arises in imperatively coordinated associations, namely, those structures within which "some positions are entrusted with a right to exercise control over other positions in order to ensure effective coercion" (Dahrendorf, 1959:165).

For Dahrendorf the authority structure of any association is dichotomous. However difficult it may be to identify the borderline between "domination" and "subjection," in every association there is a "plus-side" of authority, consisting of those who participate *to any degree* in its exercise, and a "minus-side," comprising those who are *completely subjected* to it (Dahrendorf, 1959: 171). The actual conflict which may exist between these two aggregates, Dahrendorf (1959:176) attributes to their conflicting

interests in the maintenance or modification of a *status quo*. . . . of the two aggregates of authority positions to be distinguished in every association, one—that of domination —is characterized by an interest in the maintenance of a social structure that for them conveys authority, whereas the other—that of subjection—involves an interest in changing a social condition that deprives its incumbents of authority.

These are designated as two sets of "latent interests," and as such they are represented by two "quasi-groups." Under certain conditions, the latent interests may become "manifest interests," which are then represented by two "interest groups," namely the classes in conflict (Dahrendorf, 1959:179–182). Briefly, to reiterate the presentation of Chapter III, the chief conditions— "structural conditions of organization"—are, first, the "technical conditions" (charter, personnel, material requirements, and the like); second, the "political conditions" (freedom of association, and the like); and third, the "social conditions" (ease of communication, and the like).

Since these structural conditions are in the nature of necessary conditions for the applicability of Dahrendorf's theory, it is important to note that all three are reasonably well satisfied in Italy. Indeed, given the high degree of democratic institutionalization, the pronounced and heterogeneous trade-union activity, the freedom of association and coalition exemplified by highly diverse and active political parties, the availability of leadership, and numerous other characteristics, the conditions of class formation and conflict—in the sense specified by Dahrendorf—are probably particularly advantageous in Italy. One other structural contingency, less firmly considered by Dahrendorf, concerns the rate of *intragenerational* mobility *between* the classes. But here again, though Italy is certainly not unique in this regard (see for instance, Lipset and Bendix, 1959:180), the contingency is met. As we observed in Chapter XIII, intragenerational or career mobility, *especially* that across the nonmanual-manual boundary, was relatively infrequent in Italy.

A Note on Power and Authority in Italian Society

Among the industrial nations of Europe, Italy is unequaled in presenting a picture of institutional arrangements and human relations that emphasizes the "ugly face of society." This country came late to industrialization. She is currently a developing society for the most part, and her economy has experienced major periods of instability and uncertainty. Large-scale experiments in the separation of economic interests from political power have been introduced only very recently, and there has not been sufficient time for the establishment of general principles of collective well-being and popular equity that have for many decades been commonplace in some other nations. Political unification likewise came late, and then only after deep, tortuous, and manifold internal divisions combined with baleful experiences of exploitation, economic and political disasters, heterogeneous invasions, devastations, and submissions. Survival in Italy has for centuries been a hazardous enterprise in the face of countless obstacles, adversities, and enemies. To survive is to have power, or at least access to it. As a corollary, one's right is also his might. To a pitifully large extent, authority is recognized as a license to decide and appropriate at will; notions of equality, justice, freedom, fair play are deemed childish principles, real and honorable only in the eyes of visionaries and chronic losers. As Barzini (1964:216) puts it,

In Italy even the Law, any law, changes meaning and purpose according to the power of the person who applies or violates it; taxes tend to become milder and more easily evaded for the powerful and the well-connected (the terms were synonymous with the rich and well-born; they now mean mostly people personally controlling many votes). Everything, in short, turns out to be, in the end, not a balancing of legal rights but a confrontation of pure power.

Little wonder that "the Machiavellians" have flourished in Italy. The phenomena they have studied are so glaring that they could hardly be overlooked. Indeed, they lent themselves to such vivid description that the social scientist, working in the grand manner of the Italian ultrarealist, not infrequently has left himself open to all manner of ideological accusations.[2] The student of politics well remembers Guicciardini's apothegm that to be open, truthful, and frank is a noble and generous thing, but, given the evil nature of man, often harmful; hence, dissimulation and deception are useful and often indispensable.

The solution of common problems, the development of citizenship rights, the emergence of mutual understanding sufficient to graft relations of cooperation onto basic cleavages nowhere totally eradicable, all naturally require a modicum of trust and faith in one's fellows and leaders, as well as a healthy sense of civic responsibility on the part of the latter. Where these ingredients are lacking, cleavages remain open and class conflict and hatred are rampant.

Lorwin (1958:342–344) has characterized Italy, like France, as a nation of noneconomic problems created by wars, religious tensions, social distance, and the relations between the individual and the state, as well as by a sense of injustice growing, "in part, out of the qualities of economic growth: the character of entrepreneurship, the distribution of income, and—even more—the nature of employer authority." The bourgeoisie has demanded protection against labor together with protection against competition, and naturally it has been "niggardly and tardy in concessions to their workers." On their part, the workers have "doubted the ability of their superiors to fulfill their economic functions as an entrepreneurial class," and such doubts have "deepened their feelings of both the injustice and the fragility of the social and political order."

Comparative studies of the attitudes and behavior of entrepreneurial strata suggest that the managerial groups in Italy have been the most resistant to yielding their "historic autocratic and paternalistic view of the role of management" (Lipset, 1964:277). It is interesting to note that still today in Italy the

---

[2]One of the best examples of this is Vilfredo Pareto, who has often been accused of fascist orientations. For a discussion of the absurdity of this indictment, see Lopreato and Ness (1966).

most common term for employer is *padrone* (master). LaPalombara (1964:40) points out that all too frequently management's attitude toward labor is at best condescending. The factory is viewed as personal, inviolable property, while trade unionists are considered social upstarts and dangerous revolutionaries. A rigid discipline over workers is upheld as the sanest and most efficacious means of conducting industrial enterprise. Even where the unions have been successful in obtaining concessions from management, "the latter often view these changes as paternalistic largesse rather than a *quid pro quo* from negotiations among bargaining equals." LaPalombara (1964:42) continues:

It is reasonably clear that most of Italy's industrial workers, concentrated north of Rome, continue to be exposed to work situations that reflect the class structure and conditions of a pre-industrial society, and of authoritarian family enterprises. In this kind of situation both the managers and the workers have a strong belief in, and a commitment to, class war and differentiation.

The nature of industrial relations in Italy can be grasped when we inquire into the workers' accounts of their influence on the affairs of the enterprise. In this connection, Almond and Verba (1963:342) found in their cross-cultural study of five countries (United States, United Kingdom, Germany, Italy, and Mexico) that Italian workers were heavily overrepresented among those who claimed that they were "rarely or never" consulted about job decisions.

In conclusion, from all available evidence it would seem that associations in Italy are not organized as rational bureaucracies effectively engaged in the discharge of collectively desirable functions. The solution of common problems in Italian associations is all too often marred by various intervening variables such as superordinate arrogance, narrow self-interest, job inertia, paternalism, and the familiar forms of purposive "pathological" obstacles commonly known as favoritism, graft, and corruption. Moreover, the Italian bureaucrat operates within what we have termed a context of *anarchical traditionalism*. Even when willing to act, he is unable to find clearly articulated official rules of behavior to follow. What is far worse, in an authority structure characterized by anarchical traditionalism there is a tendency for the bureaucrat, in direct proportion to his rank, to act as if his position were the locus of a set of personal prerogatives and privileges to the relative exclusion of the legally concomitant duties and obligations. In short, there is in Italian associations a particularly marked tendency to convert authority into power—legal right into personal privilege.

Research Hypotheses

We concluded our discussion of Dahrendorf's theory in Chapter III with a number of research hypotheses. In order to refresh the reader's memory, we shall restate some of them (in slightly modified form). If we divide a societal population into what may be termed a *command class* and an *obey class* according to Dahrendorf's own specifications, his theory leads us to the following predictions:

1. The command class will be more likely than the obey class to accept the existing authority structure as *legitimate* and to *acquiesce* with its control system.

The outcome of this prediction will provide the basis on which to judge Dahrendorf's assumption that the two classes have divergent latent interests with respect to the authority structure.

2. To the extent that nonacquiescence and perceptions of illegitimacy are present within the command class, they will not reflect class differences *within* that class.

The outcome of this prediction will constitute the grounds on which to assess Dahrendorf's proposition that in any imperatively coordinated association the class structure is dichotomized just above the zero point of the authority gradient.

These two hypotheses, concerning the nature of authority relations and the locus of class conflict, provide a basis from which to assess directly the validity of central features of Dahrendorf's theory. In addition, other hypotheses can be devised that will make possible a somewhat less direct assessment. It may be noted that the theory is basically intended as a tool for the analysis of conflict in specific imperatively coordinated associations. Each association features two potential classes or "conflict groups." It follows that the number of potential classes exhibited by a given industrial society is equal to the number of imperatively coordinated associations in that society, multiplied by two. In fact, however, this extreme scattering of conflicts and conflict groups is rarely the reality. Empirical evidence shows that different conflicts are often "superimposed," so that the multitude of possible conflict fronts is reduced to a few dominant conflicts (Dahrendorf, 1959:213). Indeed, in principle it is quite conceivable that, in some instances at least, the various conflict fronts are reducible to one. As a result, Dahrendorf's model lends itself to the study of more comprehensive social phenomena. One of these concerns the "images" of the social structure that may exist in a society taken as a political association. In this connection, the logic of Dahrendorf's argument would seem to suggest that, given the tendency toward the superimposition of class interests in society, in the absence of severe hindrances to class consciousness, there would be a general tendency in an industrial society toward a dichotomous image of the class structure as an expression of a basic class cleavage in that society. Dahrendorf (1959:280–289) appears to be under the influence of this particular implication of his argument when he discusses the problem of "how people see society."

When confronted with certain findings, however, one must depart from the logical implications of this argument, as indeed Dahrendorf himself does. Thus, faced with the finding that among those who hold a class image of society, only a few, most of whom are working-class people, visualize society as a dichotomous entity (Dahrendorf, 1959:288), he surprisingly suggests that

> *In terms of our theory of conflict* . . . it would seem that the dominant groups of society express their comparative gratification with existing conditions *inter alia* by visualizing and describing these conditions as ordered and reasonable; subjected groups, on the other hand, tend to emphasize the cleavages that in their opinion account for the deprivations they feel. . . . The integration model, the hierarchical image, lends itself as an ideology of satisfaction and conservation; the coercion model, the dichotomous image, provides an expression for dissatisfaction and the wish to change the *status quo* (Dahrendorf, 1959:284; first emphasis added).

Taking all of the above arguments into consideration, it seems reasonable to generate the following predictions, which concern *images of society* and *class conflict* and whose joint validity will be considered evidence of at least the partial validity of Dahrendorf's theory:

3. There is an "appreciable" tendency within a population at large to view the class structure of its society in dichotomous terms.
4. A dichotomous image is reflective of a perception of conflict-ridden class relations, and, conversely, a hierarchical image corresponds to a perception of harmonious "class" relations.
5. The dichotomous image is more pronounced among those occupying positions deprived of authority (the obey class) then among those partaking of the exercise of authority (the command class).
6. To the extent that class conflict exists, such conflict can be traced to relations of authority in the society.

The Working Sample

Before proceeding with the analysis, it should be noted that Dahrendorf's theory imposes certain limitations on the type of sample we may use for our work. In the first place, the theory is intended to apply only to industrial societies. Although there are no societies where agricultural occupations are entirely lacking, since the peasantry in Italy still constitutes a considerable portion of the entire labor force, we shall be on the safe side of methodological propriety if we exclude from our sample all individuals engaged exclusively in agricultural occupations.

Second, short of considering the entire nation as an imperatively coordinated association, Dahrendorf's theory applies to people actually employed in those associations in which there are dichotomous industrial relations. This restriction means that the sample must include only people employed in associations wherein may be found both those manifestly endowed with authority functions and those who are clearly excluded from such functions.[3] According to Dahrendorf (1959:296), such "dichotomous" organizations make class conflict possible. Purely bureaucratic organizations, on the other hand, "typically display continuous gradations of competence and authority and are hierarchical." Within such associations, *class* conflict is not possible. It would be possible to argue against this standpoint; if authority is defined in terms of a "right to exercise control" over others in "continuous gradations" in order to insure obedience, those at the bottom of the gradations —where the chain of command exhausts itself—*have no authority.* However hierarchical a bureaucracy may be, it too must have a bottom. The distinction between the "industrial" and the "bureaucratic" organizations would hence seem to rest on mere considerations of handy doctrine. Nevertheless, while in the second major section of this chapter we will find it proper to neglect the present stricture and expand the sample somewhat, at this point we shall endeavor to follow Dahrendorf's sample specifications to the letter.

Finally, the sample must also exclude the unemployed, the independent workers, and certain other occupational categories that, according to Dahrendorf (1959:255, 287), "stubbornly resist allocation" to one or the other authority class—"staff" members, routine clerks, foremen, and the like.[4]

Making all possible efforts to approximate Dahrendorf's specifications, we have thus constructed the two classes as in the following scheme, where it is worth noting that the two totals reflect Dahrendorf's (1959:195) assertion that "in many modern industrial enterprises almost one-third of all employees exercise superordinate functions":

	Percent	N
I. Command Class		
1. Proprietors and managers of larger firms	5	8
2. Proprietors and managers of medium-sized firms	18	27
3. Middle grades of officials	76	111
Total	99	146
II. Obey Class		
1. Skilled workers	38	192
2. Semiskelled workers	43	218
3. Unskilled workers	18	92
Total	99	502

---

[3]Our interview schedule did not contain items specifically designed to obtain such information, but with few exceptions the information can be gleaned by inferences from the interviewees' responses to several existing questions.

[4]Dahrendorf (1964:227) also has some doubts as to whether the southern regions of Italy may be considered under the rubric of "the industrial society." His doubts are indeed well-taken, as previous chapters of this volume have shown. However, preliminary comparisons between the northern and southern regions in terms of the major factors relevant to our analysis show that such differences as existed were not destructive of our findings and conclusions.

The Applicability of Survey Data

One last remark before we present our findings concerns Dahrendorf's position on the value of survey data for testing his theory. As was noted, our intention is to determine whether certain propositions flowing from Dahrendorf's theory are supportable in terms of the pertinent *attitudes* of a sample of people at work in imperatively coordinated associations within one particular industrial society. The author of the theory, however, is reluctant to accept survey data as "conclusive" evidence of the validity of his theory. He (1959: 281) is explicit in stating that his theory "refers not to what people think but to what they do; and while it may often be difficult to separate the two, the validity of [his] theory is in no way dependent on whether a representative sample thinks that it is valid." In a limited sense, this claim may be taken as correct. Nevertheless (and disregarding pointless debates about "conclusive" evidence), it cannot be taken to mean that the data of participant attitude and perception are irrelevant to his theory, to the extent that the theory is concerned with class behavior.

It is worthy of note that, despite Dahrendorf's aversion to survey data as evidence of the validity of his theory, he finds it quite convenient to "illustrate some points" of his theory with precisely that kind of data. For instance, his general argument draws strength from certain survey findings that (1) "As a way of seeing society . . . the dichotomous view [the coercion or "conflict model"] is a solid and, probably, powerful social fact"; (2) for those who visualize society as dichotomous, "the upper part of the dichotomy begins not far from the bottom layer of social stratification and includes all those who have even a minimal share in the exercise of authority" (Dahrendorf, 1959: 280–289).

More to the point, let us imagine for a moment that a study of *actions* following the specifications of Dahrendorf's theory discovers conflict in an association—say, the U.S. Rupper Company—along the class lines suggested by Dahrendorf. What evidence is there that the observed conflict flows from the relations to the authority structure and not from some other source—for instance, the relations to the means of production? When all dubious occupational categories have been omitted from the sample, the two classes proposed by Dahrendorf are remarkably similar to those singled out by Marx. Why then did the conflict arise? Short of the dogma that "it's got to be so," we are confronted with the task of determining the basis of class consciousness and concerted class action. We can think of no one better qualified than the employees of the U.S. Rupper Company to reveal to us that basis. They may or may not exhibit attitudes and conceptions that agree with Dahrendorf's evaluation of the sociolegal implications of the "separation of ownership from control."

The weight of Dahrendorf's argument that his is a theory of actions, and not of attitudes, is on thin ice when he (1959:176) suggests that "empirically, group conflict is probably most easily accessible to analysis if it be understood as a conflict about the *legitimacy* of relations of authority." (Emphasis added.) In itself, this is a perfectly sensible statement. Indeed, it evinces a recognition of possible fundamental forces at work in the organization and change of social orders. It is sometimes argued that there is no greater force of conflict and change in a social structure than a condition which, as Marshall (1965:189) puts it, "renders contract a sham." Then "the system must be changed." A crisis of legitimacy is usually a crisis of change (Lipset, 1959:78). But, the moment Dahrendorf introduces the concept of "legitimacy" into his formulation, his caveat about the validity of what "people think" has no basis, for, as Weber (1921–1922:I, 31, 214) suggested, the *Geltung* or *validity* of social order is not independent of the *Vorstellung* or *belief* of actors in the existence of a valid or legitimate order. Nor is their conduct independent of such belief. In short,

the legitimacy of a system of domination may be treated sociologically only as the probability that to a relevant degree the appropriate *attitudes* will exist, and the corresponding practical conduct ensue. (Emphasis added.)

AUTHORITY RELATIONS AND CLASS CONFLICT

The above considerations imply that we find ourselves with the task of reinterpreting a theory whose validity can indeed be ascertained, at least in part, with the type of data at our disposal. The present section addresses itself to the first two hypotheses stated above. The prime source of data for our argument is the following interview question: "Which of these statements best describes what you think of your work superiors?" The query provided the interviewees with the following four choices:

1. I know that they do their duty, and I obey.
2. They do their duty, but it is hard to obey.
3. They take advantage of their position, but one must have patience.
4. They take advantage of their position, and that makes me mad.

Two dimensions of authority relations are revealed by the responses to this query. One concerns perceptions of the authority structure of their work association as "legitimate" or "illegitimate." The first two response alternatives define the structure as legitimate, whereas the last two present it as illegitimate. We shall refer to this dimension as the *perception of the nature of authority*. The other dimension concerns variations in *attitude toward authority*. The first and third alternatives exhibit an attitude of "acquiescence" to the authority structure, and the second and fourth indicate an attitude of "nonacquiescence."

Table XVII:1 examines differences between an authority-endowed com-

TABLE XVII:1. PERCEPTIONS OF THE NATURE OF AND ATTITUDES
TOWARD AUTHORITY, BY AUTHORITY CLASS

Percentage of Respondents Who	Authority Classes	
	Command Class	Obey Class
Perceived Authority as Legitimate	72	54
Displayed an Attitude of Acquiescence	73	80
N	146	502

mand class and an authority-deprived obey class in terms of these two dimensions. The data uphold part of the first of the hypotheses stated earlier by showing that the authority-endowed class was significantly more inclined to perceive existent authority relations as legitimate. It would seem, in other words, that those who were excluded from the exercise of authority were more often characterized by an interest in changing the authority structure.

Before we draw any definite conclusions, however, other important questions must be examined. In the first place, does the command class represent a homogeneous entity with regard to the manner in which the nature of authority was perceived? In the second place, although a perception of illegitimacy with respect to the authority structure may be taken as an indication of an interest in changing that structure, what does the more direct evidence pertaining to the acquiescence dimension reveal? A person who defines the authority structure as illegitimate may then rebel against it in attitude and behavior; but he may also respond to it with compliance, despite the perceived absence of legitimacy.

Taking this latter question first, we were led by Dahrendorf's theory to predict that the command class would be more likely than the obey class to acquiesce with the control system of the existing authority structure. Our data show that the opposite was true (Table XVII:1). Although the vast majority in both classes manifested attitudes of either conformity or compliance, the command class was considerably less acquiescent than the obey class (73 versus 80 percent). What accounts for this finding, which is totally unexpected from the vantage point of Dahrendorf's theory?

An answer to this question lies in the answer to our query of a moment ago concerning the homogeneity of the command class. If the command class is divided into an upper stratum, containing the first two occupational categories as shown in the previous discussion of our sample, and a lower stratum, consisting of the third category, and if these two strata are then compared with respect to the perceived nature of and attitudes toward the existing authority structure, the findings show that the command class was indeed not a homogeneous entity. The lower stratum defined authority relations as legitimate appreciably less frequently than did the upper stratum (68 versus 83 percent, respectively). Interestingly, the lower stratum was in this respect intermediate between the obey class and the upper stratum of the class in which Dahrendorf's theory places it.

Similarly, there was a remarkable difference between the two strata of the command class with respect to attitudes toward authority, with the lower stratum being markedly less acquiescent (68 percent versus 86 percent of the upper stratum). Indeed, it was this much lower rate of acquiescence within the lower stratum of the command class that accounted for the greater rebelliousness of the class as a whole, as compared to the subjected class (Table XVII:1). To put it differently, of the three aggregates examined here, the lower stratum of the command class, not the obey class, was the *least* likely to display an attitude of conformity or compliance toward the authority structure.

A "False" Command Class

There is an implication of this finding that deserves serious attention. Dahrendorf never claims that those in the authority-endowed class either are completely at peace with their superiors or have no superiors in the first place. Had either been the case, the question we posed to the entire sample would have been meaningless to the authority-endowed section of it, the command class. Dahrendorf merely argues that, regardless of the continuous nature of authority within social organization, *class-based conflict* can appear only in terms of the dichotomy between those who are totally deprived of authority and those who possess *any* degree of it. It is incumbent upon us, therefore, to determine whether the perceptions of illegitimacy and the attitudes of nonacquiescence with regard to authority which have been uncovered within the ranks of the dominant class can be taken as evidence of *divergent class interests within that class,* rather than of simple "intrafamilial" stresses and tensions. If the former be the case, our second prediction will not be substantiated, and a fundamental weakness of Dahrendorf's theory will have been singled out.

Consider, in that connection, differences between the two strata of the command class in their respective *self-placements* in the authority structure, as revealed by the interview question, "On almost every job, some command and others obey. On the whole, you: (1) command more than obey; (2) obey more than command?" Based on the number of respondents in the command class who gave classifiable responses,[5] 67 percent of the members of the upper stratum but only 31 percent of those in the lower stratum thought of themselves as being in the command class. That is, nearly seven-tenths of the lower-stratum individuals considered themselves *de facto* members of the subordinate class. It is possible to conclude, therefore, that the discord and "rebelliousness" that have been evidenced within the dominant class repre-

---

[5]For the upper stratum, $N = 24$; for the lower stratum, $N = 105$.

sented real class cleavages *within* that class. It may well be true that in many modern industrial enterprises about "one-third of all employees exercise superordinate functions" (Dahrendorf, 1959:195). But this would not appear to justify the theoretical decision to attribute to all such persons a common class orientation. If the concept of authority is indeed theoretically relevant to an analysis of *interclass* conflict, then, a more realistic definition of "effective command" would seem to be in order. Unfortunately, the size of our sample does not permit further subdivisions within the plus side of the authority structure. With a larger sample, cutting points could conceivably be established between an *actual* dominant class and one or more *apparent* ones. Nevertheless, our data are sufficient to show that an effective authority-wielding class is much smaller in composition than Dahrendorf has maintained.

TABLE XVII:2. DIVERGENCES WITHIN THE COMMAND CLASS BY
SPECIFIED FACTORS

	Command Class	
Differentiating Factors	*Upper Stratum*	*Lower Stratum*
Education above Senior-Secondary Diploma	49%	25%
	(35)	(111)
Income above $250 per Month	71	45
	(34)	(109)
Age above 40 Years	63	41
	(35)	(111)
Political Preference: Left-wing[a]	24	53
	(29)	(79)
Class Identification with Governed-Proletarian Class	29	86
	(34)	(107)

Note: Base frequencies in parentheses; unclassifiable and nonresponse cases are excluded.
[a] Includes the Communist, Socialist, and Social Democratic Parties.

That there is fundamental cleavage within the dominant class as conceptualized by Dahrendorf can be further shown by reference to a number of other crucial factors (Table XVII:2). Thus, the lower stratum of the class was considerably less educated, poorer, and younger than the upper stratum. The lower stratum was also significantly more likely to prefer parties of the political left, among which structural change is a programmatic specialty, and vastly more inclined than the upper stratum to identify with either a "governed" or a "proletarian" class, taking the society as a whole. Such pronounced differences between the two levels of superordination give us still more reason to believe that the conflict previously isolated within what had been defined as *the* dominant class represents an *inward* orientation.

Before we proceed to a testing of our remaining four hypotheses, we should note that, whatever else may be said of Dahrendorf's theory of class conflict, the conclusion is inescapable that his attempt to reinforce interest in problems of social conflict is on solid grounds. His formulation has provided a tool of analysis which, in Italy at least, reveals social conflict to be a real and prominent property of social relations. The reader inclined to see in it an oversimplified view of the authority phenomenon might indeed entertain the saving thought that Dahrendorf's first and foremost aim has been to buttress interest in the continuing reality of social conflict in industrial societies.

It is no accident that he has projected his theory of class conflict against a broader sociological background, wherein two major "meta-theories" of social structure and social change are seen emerging: one, a theory of consensus, integration, and basic stability; the other, a theory of conflict, coercion, and ever-present change (Dahrendorf, 1959:157–165). His position is that the first has dominated by far the interests and activities of present-day sociologists. In this, he may have erred by overstatement. But very few sociologists would deny that much, though by no means all, of current sociology is lacking at least in the *temperament* required to make the analysis of social conflict an *unavoidable* step in the construction of social theories. Dahrendorf's own work, whatever its over-all scientific validity, is a forceful reminder of the necessity for that step.

With respect to the systematic validity of that part of Dahrendorf's theory which has been of concern to us in this section, it is necessary to point out that the real issue is not the extent to which conflict between the classes actually arises, for he himself does not assert that a given authority structure necessarily results in the full formation of organized conflict groups. On the whole, therefore, we should refrain from taking issue with Dahrendorf solely on the basis of the particular degree of conflict found existing between the two social classes specified by him. The real question concerns Dahrendorf's particular delineation of the two classes. Our most considered doubt about the validity of his theory concerns the finding that internally directed conflict *within* the command class, totally unaccounted for by Dahrendorf, is often more pronounced than conflict between the two classes. To this extent, his revamped model of class conflict leaves something to be desired.

Close scrutiny develops that what Dahrendorf has offered is a theory of organizational conflict in which the class dichotomy is so broad that it differs but slightly from the rough dichotomy of nonmanuals and manuals, a convenience very frequently adopted by students of social stratification. This crude division, however, becomes particularly problematic the moment it is burdened with the concept of authority for purposes of assessing interclass conflict, for authority is patently a continuous phenomenon. So graduated and so broad is it, in its spectrum of probabilities for effective coercion, that for some incumbents of authority positions having a little authority is more like having none than like having a great deal. Indeed worse: having a little authority seems to be a greater source of dissatisfaction with the existing authority structure than having no authority at all (a dynamic long recognized in the realm of material poverty). This circumstance is bound to create class schisms *within* the plus side of the authority structure.[6]

All this implies that Dahrendorf's theory of conflict is more useful in explaining conflict among those in *close proximity* to positions of authority than for understanding interclass conflict as such. The finding provides an interesting parallel to the sort of finding that may be predicted on the basis of Pareto's theory of conflict. We may recall that according to Pareto's formulation the struggle occurs not between the classes but *within* the elite, namely within the group of usually already privileged individuals. Similarly, while Dahrendorf's theory predicts conflict between a privileged class and a deprived one, the reality of the case shows the struggle to be more frequently among those already endowed with authority functions. Pareto claimed that "history is a graveyard of aristocracies" in continuous struggle with each other. Dahrendorf could be reinterpreted as arguing that history is a graveyard of bureaucracy echelons in continuous contention with one another.

Our data suggest forcefully that what we might call a "need for power" increases with the "first taste" of power enjoyed. Such a need may take various forms. Authority may be viewed, for instance, as an instrument for mobility, wealth, or merely a less tedious job. When held to a sufficient degree, authority also makes it possible to avoid the excessive, persistent, and not always edifying demands made upon the authority-endowed individual of the "understructure" by his more powerful superordinates. Comments offered by some of the lower-level superordinates concerning their superiors richly testify that subjection to greater authority by those who already have a little can be a painful experience. Thus, they sometimes volunteered statements that pointed to the "stupidity," "obduracy," "primitiveness," "injustice," "selfishness," and "arrogance," of the "old guard," the "big shots," the "tyrants," and the "old bureaucrats."

Analogous evidence can be recorded from considerations of data regarding job satisfaction. Job dissatisfaction was expressed more frequently in the obey class than in either stratum of the command class: 44 percent of the former as compared to 19 and 33 percent for the upper and lower strata of the latter, respectively. It is of more than passing interest, however, that the sources of dissatisfaction among incumbents of authority positions, the lower-level

---

[6]It is interesting to note that in a different context Hunter (1953:42) found it necessary to point to the hostility on the part of the "understructure" toward the "upper leaders." Similarly, see Dahl's (1961:97–100) discussion of points of conflict between "leaders" and "subleaders."

superordinates especially, comprised most frequently the "incompetence of superiors," "their attitudes," the "lack of freedom," and other such factors at least remotely connected to problems of authority distribution. Those excluded from the exercise of authority, in turn, selected this category of responses much less frequently, emphasizing instead such factors as a low income, the monotony, the danger, the arduousness of their work, and the lack of security. Contrary to Dahrendorf's thesis, then, a preoccupation with authority was far more pronounced within the command class than within the obey class.

It is an ironic truth that those who are entirely excluded from the exercise of authority are often insulated from the most unpleasant effects of effective coercion. To a large extent, they are protected from them because they come into meaningful contact with the authority structure less frequently and for shorter durations. Many a worker keeps busy in the routine of his daily task with little or no interference on the part of his superiors. Little wonder that, as Bendix (1956:249) has pointed out, the distribution of authority between managers and workers is by and large accepted, despite the ambivalence of ideas and feelings, and despite the conflict about the distribution of rewards.

Persons in positions of authority, on the other hand, have more frequent and more intense contact with one another. And the lower they are in the authority structure, the more likely they are to suffer from the effective coercion that it entails. Consequently, the lower-stratum members are more likely to develop tensions, hatreds, and resentments (as well as a desire for greater authority as a means of escape) toward their superiors—conflicts that are based in part upon what Aubert (1963:41) terms "a feeling of distributive injustice between the competitors," which concerns a possible discrepancy between merit and reward. Marx was well attuned to such schisms and conflicts when he advisedly set off the petty bourgeoisie from the capitalists proper.

In conclusion of this section, it may now be said that—again conceding the likelihood that authority relations are relevant to an explanation of class conflict—Dahrendorf must face one of two major tasks: either (1) the command class needs reduction to a more compact and unified size, or (2) the theory of dichotomous class division needs amplification to specify (a) additional strata within the plus side of the authority structure, and (b) the conflict-producing as well as the integrative factors operating among the various layers of authority incumbency.

In the latter alternative, the end result would be a theory of strata which, despite its anchorage in the concept of authority, would be one more in a series of what Dahrendorf terms "descriptive theories of stratification," which, as studies of prestige, he considers quite alien to class theory. Given the focus of his theory on phenomena of social conflict, it might prove to be a corrective influence on such descriptive theories. It would also bring a measure of realism into his own thinking. As an antidote to the multitude of studies of prestige and status seeking that pass for studies of class, Dahrendorf's interpretations of class as a vehicle of social conflict and change is a welcome reminder that what he terms "the ugly face" of society may be elaborately wished away in the vineyard of sociological naiveté, but is never quite done away with. But as a construct designed to represent and explain the realities of systems of structured inequality, Dahrendorf's theory falls far afield of the facts.

On the other hand, should Dahrendorf consider a reduction in the size of the superordinate class, he would arrive at a theory that in its essential elements would hardly depart from the sort of class theory advanced by Vilfredo Pareto—or Gaetano Mosca (1939) and Robert Michels (1914), among others. Dahrendorf (1959:193, 196) himself concedes that these earlier conceptions resemble his own in several points. But he chooses to take issue with them on the ground, among others, that their "thesis of a small ruling minority requires correction" in the direction of enlarging the "dominant class." Our evidence indicates the contrary: if there is validity to Dahrendorf's theory, it is in fact dependent on precisely that thesis, and on the argument—germane especially to Pareto's thesis—that conflict occurs not between classes but between sections of the elite (or the elites of the classes).

IMAGES OF SOCIETY AND CLASS CONFLICT

In this section, we shall pursue our empirical scrutiny of Dahrendorf's theory and address ourselves to the remaining four hypotheses stated earlier. In Dahrendorf's theory, the broadest imperatively coordinated association is the entire society viewed as a political community. This unit of analysis enables us, by taking some license, to focus on some important considerations of "images of society"—in particular, on what such images tell us about subjective conceptions of and attitudes toward class structure. Given Dahrendorf's particular construction of the class structure, and also his (1959:289) conclusion from previous studies that as a way of seeing society the dichotomous class view is "a solid and, probably, powerful social fact," we were led to predict that the dichotomous image is prevalent or at least "appreciable," that this image is reflective of perceived interclass conflict, that it is more often held by those who are deprived of authority (the obey class), and that such reflected conflict is an outgrowth of authority relations in society. Matters of this general sort have been examined already in Part Two; we must return briefly to them with an eye specifically toward Dahrendorf's conception of class structure.

The change in unit of analysis has implications for the kind of sample we can use. To be on the safe side of methodological propriety, we shall continue to use the restricted sample drawn earlier in the chapter, with two exceptions: the command class will now include all individuals above the ranks of routine clerks, whether or not they are employed in industrial, dichotomous associations. Similarly, the obey class is increased by the inclusion of a few self-employed urban workers. As a result, the working sample is now as follows:

I. Command Class	Percent	N
1. High functionaries, proprietors and managers of larger firms	4	9
2. Professionals	15	31
3. Proprietors and managers of medium-sized firms	18	39
4. Middle grades of officials	63	132
Total	100	211
II. Obey Class		
1. Skilled workers	42	238
2. Semiskilled workers	41	236
3. Unskilled workers	17	95
Total	100	569

Class Images

As was previously observed (Chapter VII), our data offer little support for the hypothesized frequency of dichotomous images. In Italy, the dichotomous view was indeed a fact; but it was not terribly imposing in its frequency: less than 11 percent of the 780 interviewees represented in Table XVII:3 held such an image. The most frequent view of the class structure, in *both* authority classes, was a trichotomous one. Moreover, if only those who held a specific image are considered, the trichotomy was slightly more prominent in the obey class than in the command class (53 versus 51 percent).

TABLE XVII:3. THE COMPLEXITY OF CLASS IMAGERY, BY
AUTHORITY CLASS

Class Structure Perceived as	Authority Classes	
	Command Class	Obey Class
Dichotomous	15%	9%
Trichotomous	45	30
Tetrachotomous	12	10
Polychotomous	15	8
Lack of Awareness[a]	9	41
Unclassifiable	4	2
Total	100%	100%
N	211	569

[a] With reference to Chapter VII, these respondents were class unaware; that is, they did not name specific classes in response to the initial question on class awareness.

What is even more surprising is that, contrary to still another hypothesis, a dichotomous view of society was almost twice as frequent in the dominant class as in the subordinate class (15 versus 9 percent). Even if we restrict the comparison to only those respondents who held specific class images, the proportion of dichotomous conceptions in the obey class increases to 16 percent, which still does not surpass the comparable figure of 17 percent for the command class. This finding is in keeping with the previous observation (Chapter VII) that the political-ideological images, which were often expressed in dichotomous terms, were characteristic of the better educated. It is at odds with Dahrendorf's position, however, which argues that the dominant group's satisfaction with their position leads them to view society in hierarchical terms —this view of society being one that is conducive to the rationalization and maintenance of the *status quo*. Conversely, the subjects are understood, by that argument, to hold more readily a dichotomous and hence conflict-ridden image of society, because they are dissatisfied with their location within it.

It remains to be seen whether a dichotomous image in fact represented a conflict-laden view of society that is predicated on considerations of the distribution of authority. Data previously examined (Chapter VII) have discounted the proposition of an equation between a dichotomous class image and a conflict-laden view of society; the comparisons shown in Table XVII:4 further confirm that verdict. But, we may ask, to the extent that conflicts *are* expressed in dichotomous terms—and they often are—does the twofold division of class structure follow problems of authority distribution? That is, in view of Dahrendorf's intention to offer an alternative to Marx's theory, which theory is better supported by the data?

Before we propose an answer, some preliminary points from Chapter VII should be reiterated. The class criteria used by the respondents in their expressions of class imagery have been grouped into four specific categories, plus a residual "Other." The *economic* model, referring to such expressions as "the rich and the poor" and "the rich and those who have to work," is most closely representative of Marx's conception of classes in terms of relations to the means of production. The *occupational* model, suggested by such expressions as "white-collar workers and manual workers" and "those who work in offices and those who work with their hands," is more difficult to attribute to either Marx's or Dahrendorf's theory, for obviously it can be claimed by both. Accordingly, we shall avoid considering it as evidence in support of either. Likewise, the *political-ideological* model presents evidence in support of both theories. It comprises class images expressed in such terms as "the bourgeoisie and the workers" and "the powerful and the poor." The fourth model, *political and work dependency,* is the clearest expression of the Dahrendorfian conceptualization, and on it, therefore, must fall the burden of proof in favor of that formulation. It is represented by such class images as "the rulers and the populace" and "the *dirigenti* (managers) and the workers." The residual category encompasses various class dichotomies that follow neither Marx's nor Dahrendorf's line of thought. It is also the category that is inappropriate to any theory of class conflict. It includes prestige-connoting expressions, such as "those who command respect and the rest of us"; moralistic notions, such as "the smart ones and the *cretini* (fools)"; and "intellectual" expressions, such as "the educated class and the masses" or "the intelligent and the common people."

It is worth noting that the number of respondents falling within the residual category was quite appreciable, in fact comparable to all other models except the economic or Marxian dimension. This finding constitutes direct evidence that not all dichotomous images of society are expressive of class conflict. Whether the other types of dichotomies shown in Table XVII:4 represent in fact conflict-ridden images of society is a question that cannot be answered with the present findings. However, Table XVII:5, as we shall presently see, provides some basis for a direct answer to that query.

TABLE XVII:4. DISTINGUISHING CONTENT OF DICHOTOMOUS
CLASS IMAGES, BY AUTHORITY CLASS

	Authority Classes	
Class Model	Command Class	Obey Class
Economic	35%	45%
Occupational	10	8
Political-Ideological	29	8
Political and Work Dependency	10	25
Other	16	15
Total	100%	101%
N	31	53

Concerning the question of whether the findings at this point provide any basis of support for Dahrendorf's theory of class conflict, it may be seen that only relatively small numbers in both classes expressed an image of society bearing clearly, and perhaps exclusively, authority connotations, as reflected by the category of responses that has been termed "political and work dependency." On the other hand, omitting from consideration those class images which, as we have suggested, do not lend themselves to unequivocal allocation, support is more substantial for Marx's theory of classes, as represented specifically by the economic model, which accounted for more than one-third of the command class and nearly one-half of the workers.

Where have these findings taken us so far? Two observations are in order. In the first place, if the maintenance of the existing authority structure and, conversely, a change of such structure constitute, as Dahrendorf proposes, a basic bone of contention among members of social structures, it appears that the people themselves are not particularly aware of the fact. Their spontaneous definition of the situation is at variance with the theoretical definition of it. It is not difficult now to see why Dahrendorf looks askance at any attempt to determine the validity of his theory on the basis of the type of data at our disposal. There is always the danger that people are "falsely conscious" of their theoretically appropriate goals. What is worse, the sociologist has no sure way of knowing whether consciousness with respect to a theoretically defined issue *is* "false." Nevertheless, everything suggests that the historical record fits more faithfully the changing products of human psychology than the theoretical wishes of historical forecasters.

In the second place, Dahrendorf's position that the dominant class is interested in maintaining the *status quo* begs a simple but crucial question: *Why?* Also, why does the subject class want to change it? For the sake of having authority, or for some other reason? Put otherwise, is the change in the existing authority structure an end in itself or an end that is instrumental to another, perhaps more basic one? Dahrendorf gives no clear answer to this question, although he sometimes comes perilously close to arguing that the subject class competes with the dominant class for the distribution of authority as such. Thus, Dahrendorf (1959:176) argues that the class excluded from positions of authority has "an interest in changing a social condition that deprives its incumbents of authority." For a theory that purports to explain "structural change," this is a most peculiar position to take. What is envisioned here is not structural change at all, not a new social order, but a mere *circulation of personnel* across the command-obey axis. Structures remain as they are. In the language of the logician, only the place holders change. Again we note how close Dahrendorf comes to repeating Pareto's formula of the circulation of the elites. The difference between the two scholars is that, unlike Dahrendorf, Pareto made it almost annoyingly clear that such circulation leaves the existing social order essentially intact.

Moreover, if the distribution of authority is specifically and only at stake, then little wonder that the understratum of the command class is in contention with the overstratum, not the obey class with the command class as a whole. After all, most workers may be expected to be realistic enough to consider themselves by training poorly equipped to assume positions of authority. It is those who already have *some* authority who are the likely aspirants for an even greater share of it. On the other hand, if the entire social order is at stake, then the problem of determining the specific goals of a revolutionary ideology remains an open question. It is conceivable, however, that the attainment of authority is but a means through which other, more basic, goals may be obtained. Pareto (1896–1897:117) recognized this possibility in his discussion of the class struggle. This phenomenon, he argued, takes two forms. "One is plainly and simply economic competition." The other is "that whereby each class endeavors to get control of the government so as to make it an instrument for spoliation."

In a brilliant analysis of Dahrendorf's theory, Alessandro Pizzorno (1963:xxxviii—the translation from the Italian is ours) points out that Dahrendorf ill understands the "revolutionary ideology": "Practically speaking, the revolutionary ideology postulates the abolition of inequalities generated by the existing power [in the broad sense] relations: not a demand for positions of authority, but a different social order." We would argue that a theory of conflict that postulates the distribution of authority as *the* bone of contention between classes without pointing to more specific causes of the contention is liable to two alternative errors: it is likely either to leave out of consideration the masses, for whom the attainment of authority as such must necessarily be low on the hierarchy of values, or to be subject to easy demonstration of its error by any theory that contains a more specific etiology. In any case, it is quite unlikely that such a theory will take roots as a "supersedure" of Marx's great synthesis. It is especially unlikely since Marx gave himself considerable latitude in his so-called economic interpretation of the class struggle. As Dahrendorf (1959:21) rightly notes in his reconstruction of Marx's unwritten theory of classes, it is not clear whether by "relations of property" Marx understood the relations of factual control and subordination in the industrial enterprise, or merely the authority relations insofar as they are based on the legal title to property. It is not improbable that for Marx the distinction was irrelevant inasmuch as property, as an instrument of general power in the hands of the capitalist, was at one and the same time power *and* wealth. Indeed, it may have been an insight into this crucial fact that led Marx to leave his definition of property unclearly specified.

Perceptions of Class Relations

Concern so far has been with the problem of determining whether relations of conflict obtain in the Italian class structure. However, we have not been in a position to observe conflict directly. Its existence has had to be inferred from our theoretical understanding of the sociological substance of certain linguistic expressions. Thus, although not all dichotomous class images can be taken to be expressions of class conflict, the assumption has been that a person who divides his society into "the rulers and the populace" is in fact expressing an experience of conflict somehow connected with that particular class division. Justifiable as this assumption may be, a somewhat more direct approach to this question is now advisable. The findings organized in Table XVII:5 represent a step in this direction. They have been obtained on the basis of the following question, already encountered elsewhere: "Judging by your own experience, what kinds of relations exist among the various social classes? Would you say that on the whole they are relations of amity, hostility, or something else?"

We should begin by reiterating two observations made in a similar context in Chapter VII. First, although what we are about to measure is not relations of hostility, strictly speaking, but only perceptions of it, it is reasonable to assume that in this case perceptions of hostility were very probably representative of actual relations of hostility. After all, the question posed to the interviewees required them to answer it on the basis of personal experience. Second, conflict and hostility are not synonymous, so that what we are about to assess is not conflict as a distinctive form of actual interaction, but only a predisposition to it. As was noted in Chapter VII, the two phenomena are theoretically independent of each other. But again it may be said that we are essentially on the right track. Where there is a predisposition to a given action, there is often also an occurrence of that action.

TABLE XVII:5. PERCEPTION OF INTERCLASS RELATIONS, BY
AUTHORITY CLASS

| Types of Relations Perceived | Authority Classes | |
	Command Class	Obey Class
Amity	22%	22%
Hostility	29	45
Suspicion, Distance	9	4
Collaboration, Mutual Interest	15	8
Indifference	14	8
Lack of Perception	3	7
Unclassifiable	8	6
Total	100%	100%
N	211	569

Glancing now at Table XVII:5 we note that even without taking account of kindred expressions suggesting "suspicion" and "distance," perceptions of hostile class relations were more frequent than any other type of perception in both classes. To this extent, the abovementioned predisposition toward conflict was real enough, and it constitutes rather substantial support in favor of theories of conflict, though not specifically of Dahrendorf's theory. Moreover, such support predictably comes more from those in the obey class, that is, from the poorer and governed strata of society which as such may be expected to more readily harbor resentment and animosity.

The next most frequent response after hostility was that of amity, with 22 percent in each class perceiving this type of class relations. This finding provides partial support also for scholars of "consensus theory" and at the same time makes it all too obvious that a more mature sociology, shorn of platitudinous provincialisms and unharnessed political ideologies, must develop a sensitivity to problems of consensus and of conflict as equally real properties of social relations.

In point of fact, as already noted in an analogous context (Chapter VII),

the data point to still a third major form of social relations which is distinct
from relations of either consensus or conflict, though it is not always so treated
in the literature. It may be noted that a considerable number of respondents,
particularly within the command class, perceived a form of class relations
("collaboration, mutual interest") which is based essentially on conditions of
potential conflict; but the conflict is regulated in a sort of "antagonistic cooperation" because the parties in potential contention find it mutually convenient.
It is worth noting again that this particular perception of social relations is
considerably more marked among the dominant groups than in the working
class. As Bendix (1956:13) points out, in discussing this question in historical
perspective, all ideologies of management have in common "the effort to
interpret the exercise of authority in a favorable light." Such ideologies "interpret the facts of authority and obedience so as to neutralize or eliminate the
conflict between the few and the many in the interest of a more effective
exercise of authority."

At the inception of industrialization in England, the appeal to the masses
for managerial legitimacy was of a form that Bendix (1956:435) refers to as
"traditionalism." The term is well-chosen. The phenomenon in question is
deeply rooted in the Christian morality and *Weltanschauung*. It is an ideology
based on the principle that the head gives substance and meaning to the body
—that human beings are essentially sinful children, dangerously laden with
problems and erroneous notions from which only "God," "the Father," "the
Head" can rescue them. At a time when abandoned and rejected feudal masses
were being thrust, dumbfounded and frightened, from a Dark Ages mentality
into an industrial world, God, the Father, the Head was naturally the capitalist
and the entrepreneur. The "theory of dependence," as John Stuart Mill termed
it, reached a ridiculous pitch in Anglo-American civilization when, with the
American War of Independence just over, the argument on behalf of the
stewardship of the wealthy came to be advanced by the ruling group through
the good offices of the clergy. Max Weber's famous thesis notwithstanding,
God had created existing class divisions and His providence presided over the
affairs of men, "to preserve the various orders, ranks and conditions in society." Hence the poor were exhorted to practice "submission, patience, forti-
tude, industry, frugality, and temperance," for a "pious, virtuous and grateful
behavior, a humble and becoming deportment" would best commend them "to
the charity of others" (Prince, 1806:552).

This view was soon effectively challenged, and managerial ideology changed
from the "theory of dependence" to "laissez-faire," to "social Darwinism,"
and finally to the "human relations" approach (Bendix, 1956:436). At the
present time, we have reached a point where personal industry and success are
to a very large extent tied, ideologically at least, to the success of the enterprise.
The present-day enterprise is also a big family, but the authority of the Head

—in part because the Head has multiple brains and in part because of the demonstrated power of its occasionally naughty and violent children—depends in large measure on the intelligence of the workers to understand that cooperation is the best road to the common good. As has often been pointed out, the most powerful single imperative imposed on corporate management today is to conduct itself so that it retains the confidence of its customers, its labor, its suppliers, and the sector of the public with whom it deals. This imperative is the economic equivalent of the principle of the "consent of the governed" obtaining in the political society.

Returning to Table XVII:5, the reader will note that the number of respondents who perceived relations of hostility among the social classes far exceeded the number of those who, as reported in Table XVII:3, held a dichotomous image of society. This finding is proof of our earlier suggestion that, contrary to a general assumption, a hierarchical image of society is not evidence that class relations are perceived as harmonious. More detailed calculations show, for instance, that 94 individuals in positions of superordination and 171 in the obey class perceived three classes in society. Of these respondents, 25 and 51 percent, respectively, characterized the relations among the three classes in terms of hostility.

But how about the relationship between a dichotomous image of the social structure and perceptions of the nature of interclass relations? On an earlier occasion some doubt was raised concerning the widespread assumption that dichotomous class perceptions reflect conflict-ridden class images. In Chapter VII we uncovered evidence that demonstrated the soundness of that doubt. We are again in a position to question the assumption directly. Among the respondents of Table XVII:3, 32 in the command class and 51 in the obey class held a dichotomous image of their society. Of these, 35 and 53 percent, respectively, perceived hostility in interclass relations. In short, the difference in perceptions of class hostility between those who held a dichotomous image of society and those who had a hierarchical view is hardly noticeable. The critical, distinguishing factor is class position. Working-class people were much more likely than their middle-class fellow citizens to define class relations as being fraught with animosity.

CONCLUSIONS: CLASS, PROPERTY, AND AUTHORITY

In conclusion, data from Italian society indicate that conflicts, to the extent they existed, followed the articulation of heterogeneous interests. Even when dichotomous class images, central to the logical implications of Dahrendorf's theory, were scrutinized with a view to ascertaining the interest basis of such images, concern with the distribution of authority in society appeared to be minimal, while sensitivity to the economic basis of society, central to Marx's theory of class conflict, came more heavily into view. It follows that, whatever evidence exists to substantiate a theory of conflict based on a dichotomous class division, it is more favorable to Marx's theory of classes than to Dahrendorf's. Thus, Marx's theory persists—partly valid and partly not, but quite useful in a heuristic sense. Above all, it is sustained by an observation encountered in the data in more than one place in this volume, namely, that when the masses look upward in anger it is likely to be their bellies that cause the snarl.

Dahrendorf's construct, moreover, cannot be judged as a theory of progressive validity. Like any other theory of class conflict, it properly distinguishes between class, class consciousness, and class conflict. In this conceptual trinity, class consciousness plays a crucial role: it is the psychological process through which one class gradually becomes aware of its interests, and ready and willing to engage another class in combat. Marx's famed theory rested its case hopefully on this precarious "come-tomorrow" notion. As such, it was a theory of progressive social organization, consciousness formation, and eventual structural transformation. Dahrendorf, on the other hand, has no interest in this sort of theory. His analysis of changes in the structure of industrial societies since Marx's time made him keenly aware of the frequent failure of historical processes to follow a theoretically marked course. Indeed, Marx's concern with "the chronological development of conflict groups" is viewed by Dahrendorf as "an error of hypostasis." Dahrendorf's concern is with the present, with the here and now. For him, a *Klasse an sich* becomes a *Klasse für sich* anywhere and at all times *provided* that "no variables not contained in [his] model intervene" (Dahrendorf, 1959:183).

What further may be said of the logical structure of Dahrendorf's theory of class and class conflict vis-à-vis Marx's? The basic point of contention between the two is with regard to the structural determinants of class. Dahrendorf argues that Marx's criterion of "effective private property in the means of production" is not appropriate, since this limits the applicability of class theory to at most a few centuries of European history. Rather he proposes that the determinant of class should be conceived of as the "exercise of, or exclusion from, authority," which he interprets as a more general relational category than property. This supplantation is not free of confusion, however, in part because Dahrendorf misconstrues Marx's concepts of class and property, and in part because he does not carefully attend to a question that, while seldom the recipient of explicit and sustained attention from any quarter, has great importance to his own theory: what precisely *is* "authority" (Hazelrigg, 1972)?

That Marx tended to restrict property to the legal relationship of "ownership" in his class analyses of nineteenth-century European society is, of course, indisputable. No doubt he did not fully appreciate, even in his slightly enamored discussion of the joint-stock company, the future (and now sometimes exaggerated) significance of the so-called "separation of ownership and control." But it is nevertheless evident that for Marx the central feature was *de facto* control, that *de jure* control was simply part of a historically developed "superstructure" of political theory and legalism that at a particular point in time was more or less synonymous with factual control.

Labor, says Marx (1867, I:178ff)—by which he means human creative activity the result of which "already existed in the imagination of the labourer at its commencement"—

is, in the first place, a process in which both man and Nature participate, and in which man of his own accord starts, regulates, and controls the material re-action between himself and [the rest of] Nature. He opposes himself to Nature as one of her own forces. . . . By thus acting on the external world and changing it, he at the same time changes his own nature. . . .

The labor process, Marx continues, consists of three "elementary factors": (1) "the personal activity of man"; (2) "the subject of that work"; and (3) the "instruments" of work. Some of the "subjects" of labor are "spontaneously provided by Nature," that is, are "all those things which labour merely separates from immediate connexion with their environment." Others are raw materials that have already "undergone some alteration by means of labour." The instruments of labor, in turn, are the things that man "interposes between himself and the subject of his labour," ultimately between himself and the rest of the natural world. These instruments are part of man's technology; and, along with his physical capability of labor, they constitute man's means of production—production in the sense of both labor that "merely separates" raw materials from their immediate connections and labor that further modifies materials already humanly altered. They describe man's ecological relationship to the rest of nature. Or as Marx (1867, I:372n) himself put it: "Technology discloses man's mode of dealing with Nature, the processes of production by which he sustains his life, and thereby also lays bare the mode of formation of his social relations and of the mental conceptions that flow from them."

The development or evolution of a societal population can be understood, Marx contends, only in terms of this fundamental ecological relationship. The crucial feature of the relationship is that the population is internally divided into natural ecological units (classes), such that certain of these units—in high abstraction, only one side of a dichotomy—stand in positions of dominance with respect to the instruments and thus the "subjects of the labor process." In short, the determinant of the ecological unit is nothing less concrete than *effective control over the means of production:* that is, *private property,* which may become elaborated as a "right" in some legal or formalized sense, but which is before that simply the ability to exclude others from access to and utilization of the instruments and materials of production and, hence, from the product itself. Whether the source of that ability is partly or even primarily in authority makes no fundamental difference in the *fact* of control, although it does of course have a significant impact on social relations and at the level of consciousness. The matter of first importance for Marx is not the particular historical form of property, which can be understood only within its historical context. Indeed, in *The Poverty of Philosophy* he reserved some of his most scathing words for the classical political economists, who elevated bourgeois property to the level of absolute standard.

Dahrendorf's argument that authority refers to a *more* general phenomenon than does property, and for that reason is preferable as the conceptual basis of class, is troubled by an ambiguity resulting from two circumstances. One of these has just been examined: his failure to carefully distinguish in Marx's usage of the term between property as a legal relationship ("ownership") and property as simply the fact of control. The other is his insufficient conceptual distinction between authority and control or domination. He (1959:166ff) borrows his definition of authority from Weber's (1921–1922, I:53) conceptual treatment of *Macht* and *Herrschaft,* wherein the latter term is defined as "the probability that a command with a given specific content will be obeyed by a given group of persons." Contrary to Dahrendorf's apparent presumption, this is *not* Weber's definition of authority, strictly speaking. For all his extensive discussion of authority and its "types," Weber unfortunately tends to leave implicit the *differentia specifica* that distinguishes authority from other particular forms of domination and control. It is nevertheless evident from his stress on the element of compliance irrespective of source or motive that, while the lexical meaning may indeed be rendered as either "domination" or "authority," he intends the above definition as applicable only to *Herrschaft* in the generic sense of domination (see Roth's editorial comment in Weber, 1921–1922, I:62n). "The sociological concept of *Herrschaft,*" according to Weber, "can only mean the probability that a command will be obeyed," regardless of whether the obedience results from considerations of expediency, from nonreflective habituation, from unexamined beliefs, or whatever. For Weber, authority refers to something more specific than the factual relation of dominance and subjection.

The general phenomenon of dominance and subjection can be divided analytically into relations of control based on coercion and—the category with which we are here concerned—relations of control based on assent. Assent may be acquired in a number of ways, only one of which constitutes authority. It may, for instance, be attained as the consequence of a rational calculation of advantages accruing from submission to the perceived capabilities of another person, a calculation resulting in the recognition that in terms of particular goals it is rational to submit to the commands of a perceived competence with regard to the accomplishment of those goals. This is assent to expertise, in principle an implicitly contractual relation between allegedly free agents who possess unrestricted capacities of reason.[7] Assent may also be attained in another manner, namely, by appeal to the nonrational—to beliefs or "values" or, simply, faith assumptions. It is this latter that peculiarly constitutes authority: the instrumentalization of the nonrational to the service of relations of control or dominance. Appeals to the nonrational are useful, of course, only to the degree that others are convinced by them. And in any case the basis of domination may revert to coercion. Nevertheless, the "assent" that is authority is not strictly one of voluntarism or the effusion of reason, for the ideal to which appeal is directed must have some prior acceptance among the potential subordinates, that is, a "validity" *(Geltung)* that is rooted in the "belief" *(Vorstellung)* of actors (Weber, 1921–1922, I:31).

Weber points to this determinant of authority in his discussion of its "types." In each case the source of the assent to dominance rests in belief in some objectivated "thing-in-itself"—something that is conceived as independent of and superior to (above) any individual or collectivity of individuals. In the rational-legal it is Law and the idea of the Rational; in the traditional, the idea of a sanctified Heritage; in the charismatic, the personification of various ideals in the Exemplar, the Revelator, or the Hero. To be sure, Weber's conceptualization of the rational-legal "pure type" of "imperatively coordinated association" *(Herrschaftsverband)* incorporates notions of competency or expertise. But it is important to recognize that Weber is here describing rationality as *form*—a rational network of social positions and roles, organized according to such criteria as a specified sphere of goal activity, a set of rational rules (enacted laws) or procedures, rationalized means of membership recruitment and promotion, and so forth (Weber, 1921–1922, I:217ff). The question of the source of obedience (assent) in relations of control within that organizational form is an analytically separable question, which concerns rationality as *reason*. An actor may submit to a perceived competence as the result of a reasoned calculation of advantages with respect to his interests. This submission defines a relation of domination and subjection, certainly—one, moreover, that is deemed acceptable by the participants and that is a function of position in social structure (that is, of the status of "expert" within the status hierarchy of knowledge and technical skill); but such submission to expertise does not define the particular relation of control that is authority. In a relation of authority within the rational organizational form, the force of obedience comes not from the potential subordinate's reasoned calculation of advantage but from successful appeal to the nonrational, in other words, to the actor's uncritical *belief* in the ideal of rationality. What the person who obeys authority obeys "is only 'the law' " (Weber, 1921–1922, I:217; see also III:953–954); he obeys the enacted laws of the association precisely because they *are* "the

---

[7]See Weber's (1921–1922, III:943) roughly parallel discussion of authority and "constellation of interests." Also in this regard see Pareto's (1916) discussion of "Class II" derivations.

law"—even though such obedience might be inconsistent with the verdict of an unrealized reasoned calculation of advantage.

The foregoing considerations of property, domination, and authority may be summarized as follows:

1. Authority is a particular mode of assent in relations of domination and subjection that are based upon assent. It is, in other words, a second-order subcategory of the general phenomenon of domination.

2. Property in the most basic sense of *factual* control refers to nothing more than the control by an individual or collectivity over some object(s), skill(s), or both. Assuming a cultural scarcity of the object and/or skill, the fact of control places the individual or collectivity in a position of dominance vis-à-vis others, the force of which lies in coercion, actual or potential.

3. Property strictly defined—in the sense of ownership or *rights* of control over something—places the individual or collectivity in a relation of dominance vis-à-vis others (again assuming scarcity), the force of which lies in assent (though it may revert to coercion). The assent may constitute authority, but it may also be a consequence of reasoned calculation of advantage.

Property is in neither sense a type of authority and therefore cannot be established from that logical standpoint as a less general category than authority. Indeed, only in its strict construction does property in any way relate to authority, and in that case authority is the logically *less general* category, since it is only one of the bases on which the element of assent in relations of dominance can be gained. The sole manner in which one can say that authority is more general than property is by restricting the latter to a particular realm of objects and skills (for instance, property in the means of production)—a useless, if logically valid, proposition.

This brings us full circle to the initial criticism in our evaluation of Dahrendorf's intended supplantation of property by authority as the determinant of class, namely, that he did not fully appreciate Marx's fundamental concern with property as factual control. Ironically, one of the grounds for Dahrendorf's rejection of the property determinant stems from the circumstance that Marx often speaks of property as ownership, which includes *inter alia* authority as a mode of assent—the very concept that Dahrendorf proposes as the replacement of the property determinant. The most appropriate means of "salvaging" this aspect of Marx's theory, of course, would have simply been to distinguish carefully the two analytic senses of property.

At the very least, then, it may be said that whatever the internal consistency and fructiferous capacity of Dahrendorf's formulation, it is of a character significantly different from Marx's theory of class. In principle, of course, nominalistic license in the choice of referents for any concept, such as "class," may be unassailable; in practice, such license often tends toward a confusion of meanings and toward the subversion of previously formulated theoretical constructs incorporative of the particular concept. There is a fine but highly consequential line between replacements of the major referents of a concept and efforts toward the improvement of their precision. But Dahrendorf (1959: 138) explicitly has in mind something more than nominalistic license: he seeks to refine the concept of class by reducing its referent to an allegedly more basic element of social structure, namely, authority.

It is difficult to determine exactly what meaning Dahrendorf attaches to the word "authority," and whether in fact his analysis contains only one meaning or a number of possibly inconsistent meanings. In general, however, his usage seems to refer to a relation of control or domination that has received some manner of common justification—but without adequate specification of the means by which the justification is made. "Legitimate power" is a phrase Dahrendorf (1959: e.g., 166) employs from time to time, for example, although he also engages in the apparent redundancy of the phrase "legitimate authority." If Dahrendorf includes within this conceptualization the strictly defined sense of the authority concept—that is, the instrumental use of beliefs, including the more or less loosely constructed political "theories" that are a part of social consciousness (and there is no evidence that he does not)—then his theory of class and class conflict is based in *justifications* (the Marxian category of "ideology") and not in the prior arrangements that are the target of justification. It is a theory of conflict between groups who, according to the prevailing political "theories," *have justification for asserting commands and demanding obedience* and those groups who have the corresponding *obligation of obedience.* The emphasis has shifted from the locus of conflict as the inherent emission of fundamental, "pre-justification" social arrangements (the Marxian emphasis) to the locus of conflict as the emission of multiple and imperfect consensuses. Whatever else Dahrendorf's theory may be, it is *not,* properly speaking, a theory of classes, not a supersedure of Marx's theory. It does not address the same issues.

When all is said and done, no intellectual praise is sufficient for Dahrendorf's work, our above strictures notwithstanding. In the midst of the current tendency in studies of social stratification to lack explicit awareness of the continuing relevance of Marx's great synthesis, Dahrendorf's work hits our scene as a veritable breath of fresh air. Sensitivity to the value of Marx's theory and to the ever-blooming reality of class conflict has no doubt been enhanced in sociology by virtue of Dahrendorf's work. This work represents perhaps the most noteworthy challenge to Marx's thought since the generation of scholars who boasted Weber and Pareto in their midst. If Dahrendorf's theory does not add a new chapter to the Marx-inspired legacy of that era, at least it provides the tools which add credibility to that legacy. In the meantime, Marx's thought remains fruitfully challengeable.

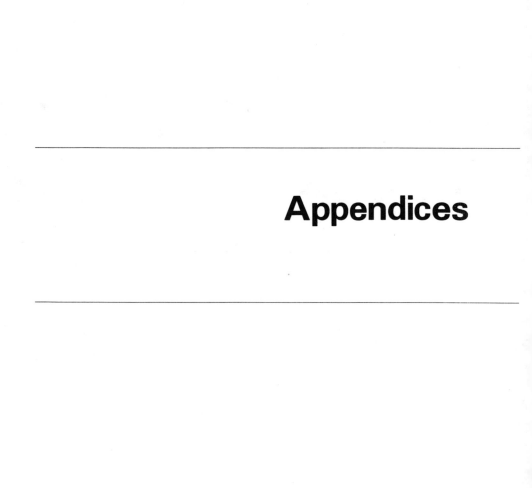

Appendices

APPENDIX I

THE INTERVIEW SCHEDULE*

1. In your opinion, the level of living of your family in the last ten years has:
    1. improved greatly
    2. improved a little
    3. remained the same
    4. become a little worse
    5. become much worse
       other: *(specify)*

2. It is not easy to foresee the future, but do you think that, in comparison to today, ten years from now you will feel:
    1. much more secure
    2. more secure
    3. like today
    4. less secure
    5. much less secure
       other: *(specify)*

3. On the whole, do you think that in the course of your life you have been:
    1. very lucky
    2. lucky enough
    3. neither lucky nor unlucky
    4. unlucky

*All questions marked by an asterisk were open-ended.

     5. very unlucky
       other: *(specify)*

4. In your opinion, which of the following phrases best describes the social and economic progress of Italy during the last ten years?

     1. rapid progress
     2. encouraging progress
     3. some progress, but it could have been better
     4. very slow progress
     5. no progress at all
     6. we have gone backward
       other: *(specify)*

5.* During the last ten years, many things have happened in Italy. In your opinion, what single thing that has happened during this period can we be most happy about?

6.* And what single thing that has happened in the last ten years should we be most unhappy about?

7. In your opinion, in comparison to today, opportunities for young people ten years from now will be:

     1. much better
     2. better
     3. same as today
     4. worse
     5. much worse
       other: *(specify)*

8. Please observe this card. Among the alternatives listed on it, which one do you consider the most important for getting ahead in life? And which do you consider the least important?

     1. *savoir faire*
     2. a good education
     3. the material aid of parents
     4. knowing the right people, "pull"
     5. intelligence
     6. personal initiative
     7. good fortune
     8. honesty
     9. personality
     10. dishonesty
     11. servility
     12. occupational skill

9. In comparison to others you know, your chances to get ahead in life are:

     1. better
     2. the same
     3. worse
       other: *(specify)*

10.*In your opinion, are there strong social differences in Italy?

11. During the last ten years, social differences in Italy have:
    1. increased greatly
    2. increased slightly
    3. remained the same
    4. diminished slightly
    5. diminished greatly
       other: *(specify)*

12. When a person is trying to get ahead in life, he is hindered by other persons:
    1. very much
    2. considerably
    3. a little
    4. not at all
       other: *(specify)*

13. [*Interviewer: If answer to above is 1, 2, or 3*] In your opinion, which of the following is the *greatest* impediment for one who is trying to get ahead in life?
    1. those who are already ahead
    2. those who are at the same level
    3. those who are below
       other: *(specify)*

14.*In your opinion, can any educated and willing person reach positions of high importance in Italy, *even if he is of humble origin?*

15.*Throughout Italy, as in many other countries, there are some very poor people. In your opinion, to what is the poverty of these people due most frequently?

16. Please observe the statements listed on this card concerning religion. Which statement would you choose to describe yourself?
    1. I don't believe in any religion
    2. I am not a Catholic, but a *(specify)*
    3. I am a believer, but not a church-goer
    4. I attend Mass irregularly, but I believe
    5. I attend Mass regularly
    6. I receive Communion at least two or three times a year
    7. I receive Communion at least once a month
       other: *(specify)*

17. On the whole, do you feel a greater sense of kinship with the workers or with the employers and managers?
    1. with the workers
    2. with the employers and managers
       other: *(specify)*

18.*For some time now there has been talk in Italy of a Center-Left government, namely, a government that would include Nenni's Socialist Party. In your opinion, what can we expect in the future from such a government?

19.*In your opinion, which party in Italy best defends the interests of people like you?

20.*[*Interviewer: For those who indicated a party*] Why do you think that the ―――― party defends the interests of people like you better than other parties?

21. On almost every job, some command and others obey. On the whole, you:
    1. command more than obey
    2. obey more than command
       other: *(specify)*

22. Which of these statements best describes what you think of your work superiors?
    1. I know that they do their duty, and I obey
    2. they do their duty, but it is hard to obey
    3. they take advantage of their position, but one must have patience
    4. they take advantage of their position, and that makes me mad
       other: *(specify)*

23.*Nowadays there is frequent talk of social classes. In your opinion, what are the social classes in Italy?

24.*[*Interviewer: Only if interviewee has answered "don't understand," "don't know," or has given no answer to Question 23, ask the following question*] By social classes we usually mean social categories that differ from one another in terms of importance, power, style of life, wealth, privileges, etc. Tell me please, what social classes are there in Italy?

25.*[*Interviewer: Only if the interviewee has indicated some classes in response to Question 23 or 24*] In which of these classes would you put your own family?

26.*To decide whether a given person belongs to your class, what single factor do you have to consider most? That is, by what in particular can you recognize a person belonging to your own class?

27. Here is a list of occupational categories. Which of them do you include in your own social class?
    1. politicians, large-scale proprietors, entrepreneurs, managers of big firms, high government functionaries
    2. university-educated professionals (doctors, lawyers, engineers, artists, etc.)
    3. medium-sized proprietors and merchants, managers of medium-sized firms
    4. other professionals (land surveyors, bookkeepers, etc.)
    5. middle grades of officials in state, industry, and commerce
    6. small merchants, small proprietors, artisans with dependent workers
    7. low grades of officials in state, industry, and commerce
    8. artisans without dependent workers, skilled workers
    9. semiskilled workers
    10. small farm owners, sharecroppers, etc.
    11. unskilled workers, farm hands, etc.
        other: *(specify)*

28. Which of these statements best describes what you think of your social position?
    1. I am very satisfied
    2. I am satisfied and hope to improve
    3. I am neither satisfied nor dissatisfied
    4. I am dissatisfied but hope to improve
    5. I am dissatisfied and have no hope of improvement
       other: *(specify)*

29. Do you think that your present social position is higher, the same as, or lower than the position held by your father when you got married?

> [*Interviewer: If the father was not then alive*] . . . or lower than your father's last position?
> [*Interviewer: If a bachelor*] . . . or lower in comparison to your father's position when he was the same age as you today?

    1. much higher
    2. a little higher
    3. about the same
    4. a little lower
    5. much lower
       other: *(specify)*

30. [*Interviewer: Only if married*] In comparison to your social position at the time you got married, your present social position is:

    1. much higher
    2. a little higher
    3. about the same
    4. a little lower
    5. much lower
       other: *(specify)*

31. Do you think that today, *in comparison to ten years ago,* it is much easier, easier, about the same, more difficult, much more difficult for a person to improve his social position?

    1. much easier
    2. easier
    3. about the same
    4. more difficult
    5. much more difficult
       other: *(specify)*

32.*[*Interviewer: If answer to above is 1, 2, 4, or 5*] Why do you think that today it is easier *(or more difficult)* to improve one's social position?

33.*[*Interviewer: For those who classified themselves in Question 25*] You said that you belong to class —— [*Interviewer: Repeat answer given to Question 25*]. Do you feel a sense of unity with that class? That is, do you think that your needs and your ideas are similar to or different from the needs and ideas of other persons in your class?

34. In your opinion, wealth augments the prestige of a person:

    1. very much
    2. considerably
    3. a little
    4. not at all
       other: *(specify)*

35. The skill of a person's occupation augments his prestige:

1. very much
2. considerably
3. a little
4. not at all
   other: *(specify)*

36. The utility of a person's job augments his prestige:

    1. very much
    2. considerably
    3. a little
    4. not at all
       other: *(specify)*

37. Family origin, that is, family name, augments the prestige of a person:

    1. very much
    2. considerably
    3. a little
    4. not at all
       other: *(specify)*

38.*In your opinion, when things go well in Italy, who stands to profit most?

39.*Is there anything in particular that many have, but which your family is compelled to deprive itself of? [*Interviewer: If Yes*] What?

40.*In your opinion, are there in Italy persons, groups, or categories of people who have special powers or privileges? [*Interviewer: If Yes*] Can you give me an example of such persons or groups?

41.*In your opinion, do those who belong to a given social class tend to avoid relations with persons belonging to another social class?

42.*Judging by your experience, what kinds of relations exist among the various social classes? Would you say that on the whole they are relations of *amity, hostility,* or something else?

43. For persons of your position, sending children to school beyond the eighth grade is:

    1. very easy
    2. easy
    3. neither easy nor difficult
    4. difficult
    5. very difficult
    6. impossible
       other: *(specify)*

44. In your opinion, the work you do is [*Interviewer: Read off the five options*] than other types of work for the *welfare of the nation?*

    1. much more useful
    2. more useful
    3. equally useful
    4. less useful
    5. much less useful
       other: *(specify)*

45. In your opinion, how much respect do people have for the type of work you do?

    1. very much respect
    2. much respect
    3. considerable respect
    4. little respect
    5. very little respect
       other: *(specify)*

46. If you were asked to choose one of the following terms to define the social class to which you belong at the present, which would you choose?

    1. lower class
    2. upper class
    3. working class
    4. middle class
       other: *(specify)*

47. And among the following terms, which would you choose to define your social class?

    1. ruling class
    2. governed class
    3. master class
    4. subordinate class
    5. rich class
    6. poor class
    7. capitalist class
    8. proletarian class
       other: *(specify)*

48.*Let us now suppose that there are four classes in Italy, namely, the upper class, the lower class, the middle class, and the working class. In your opinion, by what single fact or condition above all others can an upper-class family be recognized? That is, what single fact or condition most helps us classify a given family in the upper class?

49.*In your opinion, by what single fact or condition above all others can a lower-class family be recognized?

50.*In your opinion, by what single fact or condition above all others can a middle-class family be recognized?

51.*And by what single fact or condition above all others can a family of the working class be recognized?

52.*What do you think would have to happen in Italy in the next few years in order for you or your family to feel truly content?

DATA ON THE INTERVIEWEE

53. Region of the interview:

54. Size of place of interview:

55. How long have you lived in *(city, town, etc., where the interview takes place)?*

> 1. 2 years or less
> 2. 3 to 5 years
> 3. 6 to 10 years
> 4. 11 to 15 years
> 5. 16 to 20 years
> 6. more than 20 years
> 7. since birth

56.*[*Interviewer: If answer to previous question is .other than "since birth"*]
Where did you live before you came to *(specify locality and province)?*

57. Population of that place:

58. How long did you live in *(place indicated in Question 56)?*

> 1. 2 years or less
> 2. 3 to 5 years
> 3. 6 to 10 years
> 4. 11 to 15 years
> 5. 16 to 20 years
> 6. more than 20 years
> 7. since birth

59.*[*Interviewer: If answer to previous question is other than "since birth"*]
Where were you born? *(specify locality and province)*

60. Population of that place:

61. Please observe this card: (a) Among the occupations listed here, which corresponds to your present occupation? (b) Which corresponds to your father's last main occupation? (c) Which corresponds to your paternal grandfather's last main occupation? (d) Which corresponds to your father-in-law's (if married) occupation? [*Interviewer: Detailed data needed.*]

> 1. politicians, large-scale proprietors, entrepreneurs, managers of big firms, high government functionaries
> 2. university-educated professionals (doctors, lawyers, engineers, artists, etc.)
> 3. medium-sized proprietors and merchants, managers of medium-sized firms
> 4. other professionals (land surveyors, bookkeepers, etc.)
> 5. middle grades of officials in state, industry, and commerce
> 6. small merchants, small proprietors (except farm), artisans with dependent workers

4. junior secondary-school diploma
5. senior secondary-school diploma
6. university, without a degree
7. university degree
   other: *(specify)*

Which of the following does the family have?

1. car
2. refrigerator
3. washing machine
4. television
5. vacuum cleaner and/or buffer
6. electric or gas stove
7. radio
8. toilet with bath
9. telephone
10. running water

Marital status:

1. single
2. married
3. separated
4. divorced

Age:

1. up to 20 years
2. 21 to 25 years
3. 26 to 30 years
4. 31 to 35 years
5. 36 to 40 years
6. 41 to 45 years
7. 46 to 50 years
8. 51 to 55 years
9. 56 to 60 years
10. 61 to 65 years
11. 66 to 70 years
12. over 70 years

And here is the last question. To which of these classes of income would you say your family belongs? [620 lire = $1.00]

1. up to 25,000 lire per month
2. 26,000 to 50,000 lire per month
3. 51,000 to 75,000 lire per month

    7. low grades of officials in state, industry, and
    8. artisans without dependent workers, skilled w
    9. semiskilled workers
  10. small farm owners, sharecroppers, etc.
  11. farm hands
  12. unskilled workers, except farm hands
     other: *(specify)*

71.

62.*[*Interviewer: If interviewee is unemployed*] Why dic

63. [*Interviewer: To all except students and others who h
employed*] Please observe this card again: (a) What
the present one? During what period did you have t
before that job, what kind of work did you do? Du
you have that job? (c) And what was your very first j
you when you entered this job?

    1–12. *Occupations as listed above for Question*

64.*Have you ever wished that you had some other kinc
(specify)

72.

65.*[*Interviewer: If answer to Question 64 is positive*] V
preferred this other job?

66.*[*Interviewer: If answer to Question 64 is positive*] Wha
doing this other job?

73.

67.*[*Interviewer: To all employed*] Is there anything in p
not like about your present job? What?

68.*[*Interviewer: Obtain the following information for a

  (a) How many children do you have?
  (b) What ages are your children?
  (c) What sex are your children?
  (d) How many years of school have they comple
  (e) Are they still in school (or will they enter in
  (f) [*If Yes*] Until what grade do you intend to s

69. [*Interviewer: To those with sons*] Do your sons work?
oldest son's job?

    1–12. *Occupations as listed above for Question*

74.

70. What is the last grade of school you completed?

  1. no education
  2. elementary education, without a diploma
  3. elementary education, with a diploma

4. 76,000 to 100,000 lire per month
5. 101,000 to 150,000 lire per month
6. 151,000 to 200,000 lire per month
7. 201,000 to 300,000 lire per month
8. 301,000 to 500,000 lire per month
9. above 500,000 lire per month
other: *(specify)*

INTERVIEWER'S COMMENTS

1. Interviewee's involvement in the interview session:
    1. excellent
    2. good
    3. average
    4. poor
    5. nil

2. Interviewee's attitude:
    1. very favorable
    2. favorable
    3. average
    4. poor
    5. hostile

3. Interviewee's comprehension:
    1. excellent
    2. good
    3. average
    4. poor
    5. very poor

4. Name of interviewee:

5. His address:

6. Name of interviewer:

APPENDIX II

REFERENCES

Abrams, Mark. 1964. "Party Politics after the End of Ideology," in Erik Allardt and Yrjö Littunen, eds., *Cleavages, Ideologies, and Party Systems. Transactions of the Westermarck Society.* vol. X. Helsinki: Academic Bookstore.

Adamic, Louis, 1931. *Dynamite: The Story of Class Violence in America.* New York: Viking Press.

Adams, Bert N. 1968. *Kinship in an Urban Setting.* Chicago: Markham Publishing Company.

Adorno, T. W., Else Frenkel-Brunswik, Daniel J. Levinson, and R. Nevitt Sanford. 1950. *The Authoritarian Personality.* New York: Harper and Brothers.

Allardt, Erik. 1964. "Patterns of Class Conflict and Working Class Consciousness in Finnish Politics," in Erik Allardt and Yrjö Littunen, eds., *Cleavages, Ideologies, and Party Systems. Transactions of the Westermarck Society,* vol. X. Helsinki: Academic Bookstore.

Allardt, Erik, and Kettil Bruun. 1956. "Characteristics of the Finnish Non-Voter," *Transactions of the Westermarck Society,* 3, 55–76.

Allingham, John D. 1967. "Class Regression," *American Sociological Review,* 32 (June), 442–449.

Allport, Gordon W. 1955. *Becoming: Basic Considerations for a Psychology of Personality.* New Haven: Yale University Press.

Almond, Gabriel A., and Sidney Verba. 1963. *The Civic Culture.* Princeton: Princeton University Press.

Anderson, Bo. 1963. "Some Problems of Change in the Swedish Electorate," *Acta Sociologica,* 6 (fasc. 4), 241–255.

Anderson, C. Arnold. 1961. "A Skeptical Note on the Relation of Vertical Mobility to Education," *American Journal of Sociology,* 66 (May), 560–570.

Argyris, Chris. 1957. *Personality and Organization.* New York: Harper and Brothers.

Argyris, Chris. 1964. *Integrating the Individual and the Organization.* New York: John Wiley and Sons.

Aron, Raymond. 1957. *The Opium of the Intellectuals.* London: Secker and Warburg.

Aron, Raymond. 1960. "Social Class, Political Class, Ruling Class," in Reinhard Bendix and Seymour M. Lipset, eds., *Class, Status, and Power,* 2nd ed. New York: Free Press, 1966.

Aron, Raymond. 1964. *La Lutte de Classes.* Paris: Gallimard.

Aron, Raymond. 1965. *Main Currents in Sociological Thought.* New York: Basic Books, 2 vols.

Aron, Raymond. 1968. *Progress and Disillusion.* New York: Frederick A. Praeger.

Aubert, Vilhelm. 1963. "Competition and Dissensus: Two Types of Conflict and of Conflict Resolution," *Journal of Conflict Resolution,* 7 (March), 26–42.

Bahrdt, Hans P. 1958. *Industriebürokratie.* Stuttgart: Ferdinand Enke.

Barbaglia, Marzio, and Marcello Dei. 1969. *Le Vestali della Classe Media.* Bologna: Società Editrice il Mulino.

Barbano, Filippo. 1961. *Partiti e Pubblica Opinione nella Campagna Elettorale.* Turin: Edizioni Giappichelli.

Barber, Bernard. 1957. *Social Stratification: A Comparative Analysis of Structure and Process.* New York: Harcourt, Brace and Company.

Barzini, Luigi. 1964. *The Italians.* New York: Atheneum Press.

Becker, Ernest. 1968. *The Structure of Evil.* New York: George Braziller.

Bell, Colin. 1968. *Middle Class Families.* London: Routledge and Kegan Paul.

Bell, Daniel. 1960. *The End of Ideology.* Glencoe: Free Press.

Bell, Daniel. 1962. "The Debate on Alienation," in Leopold Labedz, ed., *Revisionism: Essays on the History of Marxist Ideas.* London: George Allen and Unwin.

Bendix, Reinhard. 1956. *Work and Authority in Industry.* New York: John Wiley and Sons.

Bendix, Reinhard. 1960. *Max Weber: An Intellectual Portrait.* Garden City: Doubleday and Company.

Bendix, Reinhard, and Seymour M. Lipset. 1966. "Karl Marx's Theory of Social Classes," in Reinhard Bendix and Seymour M. Lipset, eds., *Class, Status, and Power,* 2nd ed. New York: Free Press.

Berle, A. A., Jr. 1957. *Economic Power and the Free Society.* New York: Fund for the Republic.

Berle, A. A., Jr., and Gardiner C. Means. 1932. *The Modern Corporation and Private Property.* New York: The Macmillan Company.

Bettelheim, Bruno, and Morris Janowitz. 1950. *Dynamics of Prejudice.* New York: Harper and Row.

Bettelheim, Bruno, and Morris Janowitz. 1964. *Social Change and Prejudice.* New York: Free Press.

Birnbaum, Norman. 1968. "The Crisis in Marxist Sociology," *Social Research,* 35 (Summer), 348–380.

Blackburn, Robin, and A. Cockburn, eds. 1967. *The Incompatibles: Trade Union Militancy and the Consensus.* Harmondsworth: Penguin Books.

Blalock, Hubert M., Jr. 1959. "Status Consciousness: A Dimensional Analysis," *Social Forces,* 37 (March), 243–248.

Blalock, Hubert M., Jr. 1960. *Social Statistics.* New York: McGraw-Hill Book Company.

Blalock, Hubert M., Jr. 1967. *Toward a Theory of Minority-Group Relations.* New York: John Wiley and Sons.

Blau, Peter M. 1956. "Social Mobility and Interpersonal Relations," *American Sociological Review,* 21 (June), 290–295.

Blau, Peter M., and Otis Dudley Duncan. 1967. *The American Occupational Structure.* New York: John Wiley and Sons.

Blauner, Robert. 1964. *Alienation and Freedom.* Chicago: University of Chicago Press.

Blauner, Robert. 1966. "Work Satisfaction and Industrial Trends in Modern Society," in Reinhard Bendix and Seymour M. Lipset, eds., *Class, Status, and Power,* 2nd ed. New York: Free Press.

Bober, M. M. 1927. *Karl Marx's Interpretation of History.* Cambridge: Harvard University Press. Revised edition 1948.

Bocca, Giorgio. 1963. *La Scoperta dell' Italia.* Bari: Editori Laterza.

Bott, Elizabeth. 1957. *Family and Social Network.* London: Tavistock.

Bottomore, T. B. 1964. *Elites and Society.* New York: Basic Books.

Bottomore, T. B. 1966. *Classes in Modern Society.* New York: Random House, Pantheon Books.

Bresard, M. 1950. "Mobilité sociale et dimension de la famille," *Population,* 5, 533–566.

Briefs, Goetz A. 1937. *The Proletariat.* New York: McGraw-Hill Book Company.

Briffault, Robert. 1936. *Reasons for Anger.* New York: Simon and Schuster.

Brissenden, P. F., and E. Frankel. 1922. *Labor Turnover in Industry.* New York: The Macmillan Company.

Broom, Leonard, and F. Lancaster Jones. 1969a. "Father-To-Son Mobility: Australia in Comparative Perspective," *American Journal of Sociology,* 74 (January), 333–342.

Broom, Leonard, and F. Lancaster Jones. 1969b. "Career Mobility in Three Societies: Australia, Italy, and the United States," *American Sociological Review,* 34 (October), 650–658.

Broom, Leonard, F. Lancaster Jones, and Jerzy Zubrzycki. 1968. "Social Stratification in Australia," in J. A. Jackson, ed., *Social Stratification.* Cambridge: Cambridge University Press.

Broom, Leonard, and J. H. Smith. 1963. "Bridging Occupations," *British Journal of Sociology,* 14 (December), 321–334.

Bruce, Grady D., Charles M. Bonjean, and J. Allen Williams, Jr. 1968. "Job Satisfaction among Independent Businessmen: A Correlative Study," *Sociology and Social Research,* 52 (April), 195–204.

Buchanan, William, and Hadley Cantril. 1953. *How Nations See Each Other.* Urbana: University of Illinois Press.

Buckley, Walter. 1958. "Social Stratification and the Functional Theory of Social Differentiation," *American Sociological Review,* 23 (August), 369–375.

Buckley, Walter. 1959. "A Rejoinder to Functionalists Dr. Davis and Dr. Levy," *American Sociological Review,* 24 (February), 84–86.

Bukharin, Nikolai. 1925. *Historical Materialism, A System of Sociology.* New York: International Publishers.

Burnham, James. 1941. *The Managerial Revolution.* New York: The John Day Company.

Butler, D. E., and Richard Rose. 1960. *The British General Election of 1959.* New York: St. Martin's Press.

Butler, David, and Donald Stokes. 1969. *Political Change in Britain.* London: Macmillan and Co.

Carlsson, Gösta. 1958. *Social Mobility and Class Structure.* Lund: Gleerup.

Carlsson, Gösta. 1963. "Sorokin's Theory of Social Mobility," in Philip J. Allen, ed.,

Pitirim A. Sorokin in Review. Durham, N.C.: Duke University Press.

Case, Herman M. 1955. "Marxian Implications of Centers' Interest-Group Theory: A Critical Appraisal," *Social Forces,* 33 (March), 254–258.

Centers, Richard. 1949. *The Psychology of Social Classes.* Princeton: Princeton University Press.

Central Institute of Statistics. 1963. *Italian Statistical Abstract 1962.* Rome.

Chinoy, Ely. 1955. *Automobile Workers and the American Dream.* Boston: Beacon Press.

Clark, Colin. 1957. *The Conditions of Economic Progress.* London: Macmillan and Company.

Clough, Shepard B. 1964. *The Economic History of Modern Italy.* New York: Columbia University Press.

Cole, G. D. H. 1950. "The Conception of the Middle Classes," *British Journal of Sociology,* 1 (December), 275–290.

Coleman, James S., ed. 1965. *Education and Political Development.* Princeton: Princeton University Press.

Compagna, Francesco. 1959. *I Terroni in Città.* Bari: Editori Laterza.

Coser, Lewis A. 1956. *The Functions of Social Conflict.* New York: Free Press.

Coser, Lewis A. 1957. "Social Conflict and the Theory of Social Change," *British Journal of Sociology,* 8 (September), 197–207.

Cox, Oliver C. 1950. "Max Weber on Social Stratification: A Critique," *American Sociological Review,* 15 (April), 223–227.

Crozier, Michel. 1960. "Classes sans conscience ou préfiguration de la société sans classes," *European Journal of Sociology.* 1 (No. 2), 233–247.

Curtis, Richard F. 1961. "Conceptual Problems in Social Mobility Research," *Sociology and Social Research,* 45 (July), 387–395.

Dahl, Robert A. 1961. *Who Governs?* New Haven: Yale University Press.

Dahrendorf, Ralf. 1958. "Out of Utopia: Toward a Reorientation of Sociological Analysis," *American Journal of Sociology,* 64 (September), 115–127.

Dahrendorf, Ralf. 1959. *Class and Class Conflict in Industrial Society.* Stanford: Stanford University Press.

Dahrendorf, Ralf. 1964. "Recent Changes in the Class Structure of European Societies," *Daedalus,* 93 (Winter), 225–270.

Dahrendorf, Ralf. 1967a. *Conflict after Class.* New York: Humanities Press.

Dahrendorf, Ralf. 1967b. *Society and Democracy in Germany.* Garden City: Doubleday and Company.

Dahrendorf, Ralf. 1968. *Essays in the Theory of Society.* Stanford: Stanford University Press.

Dale, J. R. 1962. *The Clerk in Industry.* Liverpool: Liverpool University Press.

Davies, A. F. 1967. *Images of Class.* Sydney: Sydney University Press.

Davies, A. F., and S. Encel. 1965. "Class and Status," in A. F. Davies and S. Encel, eds., *Australian Society.* Melbourne: F. W. Cheshire.

Davis, Kingsley. 1948. *Human Society.* New York: The Macmillan Company.

Davis, Kingsley. 1953. "Reply," *American Sociological Review,* 18 (August), 394–397.

Davis, Kingsley. 1959. "The Abominable Heresy: A Reply to Dr. Buckley," *American Sociological Review,* 24 (February), 82–83.

Davis, Kingsley, and Wilbert E. Moore. 1945. "Some Principles of Stratification," *American Sociological Review,* 10 (April), 242–249.

Dawson, Richard, and Kenneth Prewitt. 1969. *Political Socialization.* Boston: Little, Brown and Co.

Dean, Dwight G. 1960. "Alienation and Political Apathy," *Social Forces,* 38 (March), 185–189.

Dean, Dwight G. 1961. "Alienation: Its Meaning and Measurement," *American Sociological Review,* 26 (October), 753–758.

DeGré, Gerard. 1950. "Ideology and Class Consciousness in the Middle Class," *Social Forces,* 29 (December), 173–179.

Dewhurst, J. Frederic, John O. Coppack, P. Lamartine Yates, and Associates. 1961. *Europe's Needs and Resources.* New York: Twentieth Century Fund.

Di Lampedusa, Giuseppe. 1961. *The Leopard.* New York: Signet Books.

Djilas, Milovan. 1957. *The New Class.* New York: Frederick A. Praeger.

Dogan, Mattei. 1963. "La Stratificazione Sociale dei Suffragi," in A. Spreafico and Joseph LaPalombara, eds., *Elezione e Comportamento Politico in Italia.* Milan: Comunità.

Dogan, Mattei. 1967. "Political Cleavage and Social Stratification in France and Italy," in Seymour M. Lipset and Stein Rokkan, eds., *Party Systems and Voter Alignments.* New York: Free Press.

Dolci, Danilo. 1968. *The Man Who Plays Alone.* London: MacGibbon & Kee.

Dubin, Robert. 1957. "Industrial Conflict and Social Welfare," *Journal of Conflict Resolution,* 1 (June), 179–199.

Dufty, N. F. 1960. "Occupational Status, Job Satisfaction and Levels of Aspiration," *British Journal of Sociology,* 11 (December), 348–355.

Duncan, Otis Dudley. 1961. "Properties and Characteristics of the Socioeconomic Index," in Albert J. Reiss, Jr., ed., *Occupations and Social Status.* New York: Free Press.

Duncan, Otis Dudley. 1966. "Methodological Issues in the Analysis of Social Mobility," in Neil J. Smelser and Seymour M. Lipset, eds., *Social Structure and Mobility in Economic Development.* Chicago: Aldine Publishing Company.

Duncan, Otis Dudley, and Robert W. Hodge. 1963. "Education and Occupational Mobility: A Regression Analysis," *American Journal of Sociology,* 68 (May), 629–644.

Durbin, J. 1955. "Appendix Note to a Statistical Question Raised in the Preceding Paper," *Population Studies,* 9 (July), 101.

Durkheim, Emile. 1897. *Suicide: A Study in Sociology.* Translated by J. A. Spaulding and George Simpson; edited by George Simpson. Glencoe: Free Press, 1951.

Eckland, Bruce K. 1965. "Academic Ability, Higher Education, and Occupational Mobility," *American Sociological Review,* 30 (October), 735–746.

Edding, Friedrich. 1958. *Internationale Tendenzen in der Entwicklung der Ausgaben für Schulen und Hochschulen.* Kieler Studien, No. 47.

Einaudi, Mario, and François Goguel. 1952. *Christian Democracy in Italy and France.* Notre Dame, Ind.: University of Notre Dame Press.

Eisenstadt, S. N. 1966. *Modernization: Protest and Change.* Englewood Cliffs: Prentice-Hall.

Ellis, Robert A., and W. Clayton Lane. 1967. "Social Mobility and Social Isolation: A Test of Sorokin's Dissociative Hypothesis," *American Sociological Review,* 32 (April), 237–253.

Engels, Friedrich. 1850. "Introduction" to Karl Marx, *The Class Struggles in France (1848–1850).* New York: International Publishers, 1934.

Engels, Friedrich. 1874. "On Authority," in Lewis S. Feuer, ed., *Marx and Engels, Basic Writings on Politics and Philosophy.* Garden City: Doubleday and Company, Anchor Books, 1959.

Eulau, Heinz. 1956. "Identification with Class and Political Perspective," *Journal of Politics,* 18 (May), 232–253.
Eulau, Heinz. 1962. *Class and Party in the Eisenhower Years.* New York: Free Press.

Faunce, William A. 1968. *Problems of an Industrial Society.* New York: McGraw-Hill Book Company.
Feldmesser, Robert A. 1955. *Aspects of Social Mobility in the Soviet Union.* Unpublished Ph.D. thesis, Harvard University.
Feuer, Lewis S., ed. 1959. *Marx and Engels, Basic Writings on Politics and Philosophy.* Garden City: Doubleday and Company, Anchor Books.
Feuer, Lewis S. 1966. "Alienation: The Marxism of Contemporary Student Movements," in Milorad M. Drachkovitch, ed., *Marxist Ideology in the Contemporary World—Its Appeals and Paradoxes.* New York: Frederick A. Praeger.
Feuer, Lewis S. 1969. *The Conflict of Generations.* New York: Basic Books.
Floud, J. E., A. H. Halsey, and F. M. Martin. 1957. *Social Class and Educational Opportunity.* London: William Heinemann.
Fortunato, Giustino. 1926. *Il Mezzogiorno e lo Stato Italiano, Discorsi Politici, 1880–1910.* Florence.
Foster, George M. 1962. *Traditional Cultures.* New York: Harper and Row.
Fox, Thomas, and S. M. Miller. 1965. "Occupational Stratification and Mobility: Intra-Country Variations," *Studies in Comparative International Development,* 1, No. 1.
Fromm, Erich. 1941. *Escape from Freedom.* New York: Rinehart and Company.
Fromm, Erich. 1961. *Marx's Concept of Man.* New York: Frederick Ungar.
Fürstenberg, Friedrich. 1968. "Structural Changes in the Working Class," in John A. Jackson, ed., *Social Stratification.* Cambridge: Cambridge University Press.

Geiger, Theodor. 1949. *Die Klassengesellschaft im Schmelztiegel.* Cologne: Kiepenheuer.
Geiger, Theodor. 1969. "Class Society in the Melting Pot," in Celia S. Heller, ed., *Structured Social Inequality.* New York: The Macmillan Company.
Germani, Gino. 1966. "Social and Political Consequences of Mobility," in Neil J. Smelser and Seymour M. Lipset, eds., *Social Structure and Mobility in Economic Development.* Chicago: Aldine Publishing Company.
Glantz, Oscar. 1958. "Class Consciousness and Political Solidarity," *American Sociological Review,* 23 (August), 375–383.
Glass, David V., ed. 1954. *Social Mobility in Britain.* London: Routledge and Kegan Paul.
Glass, David V., and J. R. Hall. 1954. "Social Mobility in Britain: A Study of Inter-Generation Changes in Status," in David V. Glass, ed., *Social Mobility in Britain.* London: Routledge and Kegan Paul.
Goldthorpe, John H. 1964. "Social Stratification in Industrial Society," in Paul Halmos, ed., *Sociological Review Monograph No. 8: The Development of Industrial Societies.* Keele, Staffordshire: University of Keele.
Goldthorpe, John H. 1966. "Attitudes and Behavior of Car Assembly Workers: A Deviant Case and a Theoretical Critique," *British Journal of Sociology,* 17 (September), 227–244.
Goldthorpe, John H., David Lockwood, Frank Bechhofer, and Jennifer Platt. 1968a. "The Affluent Worker and the Thesis of *Embourgeoisement:* Some Preliminary Research Findings," in Joseph A. Kahl, ed., *Comparative Perspectives on Stratification.* Boston: Little, Brown and Company.
Goldthorpe, John H., David Lockwood, Frank Bechhofer, and Jennifer Platt. 1968b.

The Affluent Worker: Industrial Attitudes and Behavior. Cambridge: Cambridge University Press.

Goldthorpe, John H., David Lockwood, Frank Bechhofer, and Jennifer Platt. 1969. *The Affluent Worker in the Class Structure.* Cambridge: Cambridge University Press.

Gordon, Milton M. 1958. *Social Class in American Sociology.* Durham, N.C.: Duke University Press.

Gordon, Milton M. 1964. *Assimilation in American Life.* New York: Oxford University Press.

Greenblum, Joseph, and Leonard I. Pearlin. 1953. "Vertical Mobility and Prejudice: A Socio-psychological Analysis," in Reinhard Bendix and Seymour M. Lipset, eds., *Class, Status, and Power,* 1st ed. Glencoe: Free Press.

Gross, Llewellyn, 1949. "The Use of Class Concepts in Sociological Research," *American Journal of Sociology,* 54 (March), 409–421.

Gross, Neal. 1953. "Social Class Identification in the Urban Community," *American Sociological Review,* 18 (August), 398–404.

Haer, John L. 1957. "An Empirical Study of Social Class Awareness," *Social Forces,* 36 (December), 117–121.

Hagen, Everett E. 1962. *On the Theory of Social Change.* Homewood, Ill.: Dorsey Press.

Hamilton, Richard F. 1967. *Affluence and the French Worker in the Fourth Republic.* Princeton: Princeton University Press.

Hammel, Eugene A. 1969. *The Pink Yo-Yo: Occupational Mobility in Belgrade, ca. 1915–1965.* Berkeley: University of California, Institute of International Studies.

Handlin, Oscar. 1951. *The Uprooted.* New York: Grosset and Dunlap.

Harbison, Frederick, and Charles A. Myers. 1964. *Education, Manpower, and Economic Growth.* New York: McGraw-Hill Book Company.

Harris, Edward E. 1964. "Prestige, Reward, Skill, and Functional Importance: A Reconsideration," *Sociological Quarterly,* 5 (Summer), 261–264.

Harris, Edward E. 1967. "Research Methods, Functional Importance, and Occupational Roles," *Sociological Quarterly,* 8 (Spring), 255–259.

Hazelrigg, Lawrence E. 1970. "Religious and Class Bases of Political Conflict in Italy," *American Journal of Sociology,* 75 (January), 496–511.

Hazelrigg, Lawrence E. 1972. "Class, Property, and Authority," *Social Forces,* 50 (June), forthcoming.

Henderson, Lawrence J. 1935. *Pareto's General Sociology: A Physiologist's Interpretation.* Cambridge: Harvard University Press.

Herkner, Heinrich. 1911. "Problems of Worker Psychology," *Verhandlungen der Generalversammlung des Vereins für Sozialpolitik, Nürnberg, 1911. Die Schriften des VfS.* Berlin: Duncker and Humblot, 1912.

Herzberg, Frederick, Bernard Mausner, Richard O. Peterson, and Dora F. Capwell. 1957. *Job Attitudes: Review of Research and Opinion.* Pittsburgh: Psychological Service of Pittsburgh.

Himmelstrand, Ulf. 1962. "A Theoretical and Empirical Approach to Depolitization and Political Involvement," in Stein Rokkan, ed., *Approaches to the Study of Political Participation.* Copenhagen: Munksgaard.

Hobsbawm, E. J. 1964. *Labouring Men: Studies in the History of Labour.* London: Weidenfeld and Nicolson.

Hodge, Robert W., and Donald J. Treiman. 1968. "Class Identification in the United States," *American Journal of Sociology,* 73 (March), 535–547.

Hodges, Donald C. 1965. "Engels' Contribution to Marxism," *The Socialist Register.*
London: Merlin Press.

Hodges, Harold M., Jr. 1964. *Social Stratification.* Cambridge, Mass.: Schenkman
Publishing Company.

Hogan, D. N. 1945. *Election and Representation.* Cork: Cork University Press.

Hollingshead, August B. 1949. *Elmtown's Youth.* New York: John Wiley and Sons.

Hollingshead, August B., and Fredrick C. Redlich. 1958. *Social Class and Mental
Illness.* New York: John Wiley and Sons.

Homans, George C. 1961. *Social Behavior: Its Elementary Forms.* New York: Harcourt, Brace and World.

Homans, George C. 1964. "Bringing Men Back In," *American Sociological Review,* 29
(December), 809–818.

Homans, George C. 1967. *The Nature of Social Science.* New York: Harcourt, Brace
and World.

Hook, Sidney. 1955. *Marx and the Marxists: The Ambiguous Legacy.* Princeton: D.
Van Nostrand Company.

Hook, Sidney. 1965. "Pareto's Sociological System," in James H. Meisel, ed., *Pareto
and Mosca.* Englewood Cliffs: Prentice-Hall.

Horton, John. 1964. "The Dehumanization of Anomie and Alienation: A Problem in
the Ideology of Sociology," *British Journal of Sociology,* 15 (December), 283–300.

Huaco, George A. 1963. "A Logical Analysis of the Davis-Moore Theory of Stratification," *American Sociological Review,* 28 (October), 801–804.

Huaco, George A. 1966. "The Functionalist Theory of Stratification: Two Decades of
Controversy," *Inquiry,* 9 (Autumn), 215–240.

Hughes, Serge, 1967. *The Fall and Rise of Modern Italy.* New York: The Macmillan
Company.

Hunter, Floyd. 1953. *Community Power Structure.* Garden City: Doubleday and Company, Anchor Books.

Hyman, Herbert H. 1953. "The Value Systems of Different Classes: A Social Psychological Contribution to the Analysis of Stratification," in Reinhard Bendix and
Seymour M. Lipset, eds., *Class, Status, and Power,* 1st ed. Glencoe: Free Press.

Hyman, Herbert H. 1959. *Political Socialization.* Glencoe: Free Press.

Inchiesta SHELL No. 3. 1961. *La Classe Dirigente Italiana.* Genoa: Agis-Stringa.

Inkeles, Alex. 1959. "Personality and Social Structure," in Robert K. Merton, Leonard
Broom, and Leonard S. Cottrell, Jr., eds., *Sociology Today.* New York: Basic
Books.

International Labour Office. 1966. *Year Book of Labour Statistics.* Geneva.

Istituto Centrale di Statistica. 1957a. *Annuario Statistico dell Istruzione Italiana 1956.*
Rome.

Istituto Centrale di Statistica. 1957b. *IX Censimento Generale della Popolazione, 4
novembre, 1951: Volume IV, Professioni.* Rome.

Istituto Centrale di Statistica. 1960. *Annuario Statistico Italiano.* Rome.

Istituto Centrale di Statistica. 1964. *Rilevazione Nazionale delle Forze di Lavoro, 20
ottobre 1963.* Rome.

Istituto Centrale di Statistica. 1965. *Annuario Statistico Italiano.* Rome.

Istituto Centrale di Statistica. 1967. *10° Censimento Generale della Popolazione, 15
ottobre 1961. Volume VI, Professioni.* Rome.

Istituto Centrale di Statistica. 1968. *10° Censimento Generale della Popolazione, 15
ottobre 1961. Volume VII, Istruzione.* Rome.

Jackson, Elton F. 1962. "Status Consistency and Symptoms of Stress," *American Sociological Review,* 27 (August), 469–480.

Jackson, Elton F., and Harry J. Crockett, Jr. 1964. "Occupational Mobility in the United States: A Point Estimate and Trend Comparison," *American Sociological Review,* 29 (February), 5–15.

Jackson, Elton F., and Richard F. Curtis. 1968. "Conceptualization and Measurement in the Study of Social Stratification," in H. M. Blalock, Jr., and A. B. Blalock, eds., *Methodology in Social Research.* New York: McGraw-Hill Book Company.

Janowitz, Morris. 1956. "Some Consequences of Social Mobility in the United States," *Transactions of the Third World Congress of Sociology,* 3, 191–201.

Janowitz, Morris. 1958. "Social Stratification and Mobility in West Germany," *American Journal of Sociology,* 64 (July), 6–24.

Janowitz, Morris, and Richard F. Curtis. 1959. "Sociological Consequences of Occupational Mobility in a U.S. Metropolitan Community," Working Paper One, submitted to the Fourth Working Conference on Social Stratification and Social Mobility, International Sociological Association, December.

Janowitz, Morris, and David R. Segal. 1967. "Social Cleavage and Party Affiliation: Germany, Great Britain, and the United States," *American Journal of Sociology,* 72 (May), 601–618.

Jemolo, A. C. 1960. *Church and State in Italy, 1850–1950.* Oxford: Basil Blackwell.

Jones, F. Lancaster. 1969. "Social Mobility and Industrial Society: A Thesis Re-Examined," *Sociological Quarterly,* 10 (Summer), 292–305.

Kahan, Michael, David Butler, and Donald Stokes. 1966. "On the Analytical Division of Social Class," *British Journal of Sociology,* 17 (June), 122–132.

Kahl, Joseph A. 1953. *The American Class Structure.* New York: Rinehart and Company.

Kahl, Joseph A., and James A. Davis. 1955. "A Comparison of Indexes of Socio-Economic Status," *American Sociological Review,* 20 (June), 317–325.

Katz, Fred E. 1965. "Explaining Informal Work Groups in Complex Organizations: The Case for Autonomy in Structure," *Administrative Science Quarterly,* 10 (September), 204–223.

Kleiner, Robert J., and Seymour Parker. 1963. "Social Striving, Social Status, and Mental Disorder: A Research Review," *American Sociological Review,* 28 (April), 189–203.

Kogan, Norman. 1966. "Italian Communism, the Working Class, and Organized Catholicism," *Journal of Politics,* 28 (August), 531–555.

Kolko, Gabriel. 1962. *Wealth and Power in America.* New York: Frederick A. Praeger.

Kon, Igor S. 1969. "The Concept of Alienation in Modern Sociology," in Peter L. Berger, ed., *Marxism and Sociology: Views from Eastern Europe.* New York: Appleton-Century-Crofts.

Kornhauser, Arthur. 1946. "Psychological Studies of Employee Attitudes," in Schuyler Dean Hoslett, *Human Factors in Management.* New York: Harper and Brothers.

Kornhauser, Arthur. 1965. *Mental Health of the Industrial Worker: A Detroit Study.* New York: John Wiley and Sons.

Kornhauser, Arthur, H. L. Sheppard, and A. J. Mayer. 1956. *When Labor Votes—A Study of Auto Workers.* New York: University Books.

Kornhauser, William. 1959. *The Politics of Mass Society.* Glencoe: Free Press.

Lampman, Robert J. 1962. *The Share of Top Wealth-Holders in National Wealth, 1922–1956.* Princeton: Princeton University Press.

Land, Kenneth C. 1970. "Path Models of Functional Theories of Social Stratification as Representations of Cultural Beliefs on Stratification," *The Sociological Quarterly,* 11 (Fall), 474–484.

Landecker, Werner S. 1963. "Class Crystallization and Class Consciousness," *American Sociological Review,* 28 (April), 219–229.

Lane, Robert E. 1959. *Political Life.* New York: Free Press.

Lane, Robert E. 1965. "The Politics of Consensus in an Age of Affluence," *American Political Science Review,* 59 (December), 874–895.

LaPalombara, Joseph. 1964. *Interest Groups in Italian Politics.* Princeton: Princeton University Press.

LaPalombara, Joseph. 1965. "Italy: Fragmentation, Isolation, Alienation," in Lucian W. Pye and Sidney Verba, eds., *Political Culture and Political Development.* Princeton: Princeton University Press.

LaPalombara, Joseph. 1966a. "Decline of Ideology: A Dissent and an Interpretation," *American Political Science Review,* 60 (March), 5–16.

LaPalombara, Joseph. 1966b. *Italy: The Politics of Planning.* Syracuse, N.Y.: Syracuse University Press.

Lasswell, Harold D., and Abraham Kaplan. 1950. *Power and Society.* New Haven: Yale University Press.

Leggett, John C. 1968. *Class, Race, and Labor.* New York: Oxford University Press.

Lenin, V. I. 1902. *What Is To Be Done?* New York: International Publishers, 1929.

Lenski, Gerhard E. 1950. "Prestige, Status, and Wealth." Unpublished Ph.D. dissertation, Yale University.

Lenski, Gerhard E. 1952. "American Social Classes: Statistical Strata or Social Groups?" *American Journal of Sociology,* 58 (September), 139–144.

Lenski, Gerhard E. 1954. "Status Crystallization: A Non-Vertical Dimension of Social Status," *American Sociological Review,* 19 (August), 405–413.

Lenski, Gerhard E. 1958. "Trends in Intergenerational Occupational Mobility in the United States," *American Sociological Review,* 23 (October), 514–523.

Lenski, Gerhard E. 1966. *Power and Privilege.* New York: McGraw-Hill Book Company.

Lenski, Gerhard E. 1967. "Status Inconsistency and the Vote: A Four Nation Test," *American Sociological Review,* 32 (April), 298–301.

Levitsky, Serge L. 1965. "Introduction" to Karl Marx, *Das Kapital.* Chicago: Henry Regnery Company, Gateway Editions.

Lewis, Lionel S. 1965. "Class Consciousness and Inter-Class Sentiments," *The Sociological Quarterly,* 6 (Autumn), 325–338.

Lewis, Lionel S., and Joseph Lopreato. 1963. "Functional Importance and Prestige of Occupations," *Pacific Sociological Review,* 6 (Fall), 55–59.

Lipset, Seymour M. 1959. *Political Man.* Garden City: Doubleday and Company.

Lipset, Seymour M. 1964. "The Changing Class Structure and Contemporary European Politics," *Daedalus,* 93 (Winter), 271–303.

Lipset, Seymour M., and Reinhard Bendix. 1959. *Social Mobility in Industrial Society.* Berkeley: University of California Press.

Lipset, Seymour M., and Joan Gordon. 1953. "Mobility and Trade Union Membership," in Reinhard Bendix and Seymour M. Lipset, eds., *Class, Status, and Power,* 1st ed. Glencoe: Free Press.

Lipset, Seymour M., and Hans L. Zetterberg. 1966. "A Theory of Social Mobility," in Reinhard Bendix and Seymour M. Lipset, eds., *Class, Status, and Power,* 2nd ed. New York: Free Press.

Littunen, Yrjö. 1964. "Social Restraints and Ideological Pluralism," in Erik Allardt and Yrjö Littunen, eds., *Cleavages, Ideologies, and Party Systems. Transactions of the Westermarck Society,* vol. X. Helsinki: Academic Bookstore.

Livi, Livio. 1950. "Sur la mesure de la mobilité sociale," *Population,* 5 (January-March), 65–76.

Lloyd, Barbara B. 1966. "Education and Family Life in the Development of Class Identification among the Yoruba," in P. C. Lloyd, ed., *The New Elites of Tropical Africa.* London: Oxford University Press.

Lockwood, David. 1958. *The Blackcoated Worker.* London: George Allen and Unwin.

London, Ivan D., and Miriam B. London. 1966. "A Research Examination of the Harvard Project on the Soviet Social System: I, The Basic Written Questionnaire," *Psychological Reports,* Monograph Supplement 6.

Lopreato, Joseph. 1965. "Social Mobility in Italy," *American Journal of Sociology,* 71 (November), 311–314.

Lopreato, Joseph. 1967a. "Upward Social Mobility and Political Orientation," *American Sociological Review,* 32 (August), 586–592.

Lopreato, Joseph. 1967b. *Peasants No More.* San Francisco: Chandler Publishing Company.

Lopreato, Joseph. 1968. "Animi avviliti e terre spopolate: perchè emigrano i contadini," *Quaderni Calabresi,* 4 (June-July-August), 3–23.

Lopreato, Joseph. 1970. *Italian Americans.* New York: Random House.

Lopreato, Joseph, and Letitia Alston. 1970. "Ideal Types and the Idealization Strategy," *American Sociological Review,* 35 (February), 88–96.

Lopreato, Joseph, and Janet S. Chafetz. 1970. "The Political Orientation of Skidders: A Middle-Range Theory," *American Sociological Review,* 35 (June), 440–451.

Lopreato, Joseph, and Lawrence E. Hazelrigg. 1970. "Intragenerational versus Intergenerational Mobility in Relation to Sociopolitical Attitudes," *Social Forces,* 49 (December), 200–210.

Lopreato, Joseph, and Lionel S. Lewis. 1963. "An Analysis of Variables in the Functional Theory of Stratification," *Sociological Quarterly,* 4 (Autumn), 301–310.

Lopreato, Joseph, and Lionel S. Lewis. 1965. "Researchers Versus Research Exhorters Apropos of the Davis-Moore Theory," *Sociological Quarterly* 6 (Spring), 175–178.

Lopreato, Joseph, and Robert C. Ness. 1966. "Vilfredo Pareto: Sociologist or Ideologist?" *Sociological Quarterly,* 7 (Winter), 21–38.

Lorwin, Val R. 1958. "Working-Class Politics and Economic Development in Western Europe," *American Historical Review,* 63 (January), 338–351.

Luckmann, Thomas, and Peter Berger. 1964. "Social Mobility and Personal Identity," *European Journal of Sociology,* 5 (November), 331–344.

Lukács, Georg. 1923. *Geschichte und Klassenbewusstsein,* Berlin: Malik Verlag.

Lutz, Vera. 1962. *Italy: A Study in Economic Development.* New York: Oxford University Press.

Lynd, Robert S., and Helen Merrell Lynd. 1929. *Middletown.* New York: Harcourt, Brace and Company.

Macaulay, Frederick R. 1922. *The Personal Distribution of Income in the United States.* New York: Harcourt, Brace, and Company.

Maccoby, E. E., R. E. Matthews, and A. S. Morton. 1954. "Youth and Political Change," *Public Opinion Quarterly,* 18 (Spring), 23–39.

MacDonald, John S. 1963. "Agricultural Organization, Migration and Labour Militancy in Rural Italy," *Economic History Review,* 16 (August), 71–75.

MacIver, Robert M., and Charles H. Page. 1959. *Society: An Introductory Analysis.* London: Macmillan and Company.

Mack, Raymond W. 1965. "The Components of Social Conflict," *Social Problems,* 12 (Spring), 388–397.

Mackenzie, Gavin. 1967. "The Economic Dimensions of Embourgeoisement," *British Journal of Sociology,* 18 (March), 29–44.

MacPherson, C. B. 1962. *The Political Theory of Possessive Individualism.* London: Oxford University Press.

MacRae, Donald G. 1958. "Class Relationships and Ideology," *Sociological Review,* 6 (December), 261–272.

Manis, Jerome G., and Bernard N. Meltzer. 1954. "Attitudes of Textile Workers to Class Structure," *American Journal of Sociology,* 60 (July), 30–35.

Manis, Jerome G., and Bernard N. Meltzer. 1963. "Some Correlates of Class Consciousness among Textile Workers," *American Journal of Sociology,* 69 (September), 177–184.

Mannheim, Karl. 1936. *Ideology and Utopia.* New York: Harcourt, Brace and Company, Harvest Books.

Mannheim, Karl. 1952. "The Sociological Problem of Generations," in *Essays on the Sociology of Knowledge.* London: Routledge and Kegan Paul.

Marshall, T. H. 1950. *Citizenship and Social Class, and Other Essays.* New York: Cambridge University Press.

Marshall, T. H. 1965. *Class, Citizenship, and Social Development.* Garden City: Doubleday and Company, Anchor Books.

Martellaro, Joseph A. 1965. *Economic Development in Southern Italy, 1950–1960.* Washington, D.C.: Catholic University of America Press.

Martin, F. M. 1954. "Some Subjective Aspects of Social Stratification," in David V. Glass, ed., *Social Mobility in Britain.* London: Routledge and Kegan Paul.

Marx, Karl. 1844. *Economic and Philosophical Manuscripts,* in Erich Fromm, ed., *Marx's Concept of Man.* New York: Frederick Ungar, 1961.

Marx, Karl. 1845. *Theses on Feuerbach,* in Lewis S. Feuer, ed., *Marx and Engels, Basic Writings on Politics and Philosophy.* Garden City: Doubleday and Company, Anchor Books, 1959.

Marx, Karl. 1847. *The Poverty of Philosophy.* New York: International Publishers, 1963.

Marx, Karl. 1850. *The Class Struggles in France (1848–1850).* New York: International Publishers, 1934.

Marx, Karl. 1852a. "The Chartists," *New York Daily Tribune,* August 25, in T. B. Bottomore, *Karl Marx: Selected Writings in Sociology and Social Philosophy.* New York: McGraw-Hill Book Company, 1956.

Marx, Karl. 1852b. *The Eighteenth Brumaire of Louis Bonaparte.* New York: International Publishers, 1963.

Marx, Karl. 1867. *Capital.* New York: International Publishers, 3 vols., 1967.

Marx, Karl. 1875. *Critique of the Gotha Program,* in Lewis S. Feuer, ed., *Marx and Engels, Basic Writings on Politics and Philosophy.* Garden City: Doubleday and Company, Anchor Books, 1959.

Marx, Karl. 1904. *A Contribution to the Critique of Political Economy.* Chicago: Charles Kerr.

Marx, Karl, and Friedrich Engels. 1844. *The Holy Family.* Moscow: Foreign Languages Publishing House, 1956.

Marx, Karl, and Friedrich Engels. 1845–1846. *The German Ideology.* New York: International Publishers, 1947.

Marx, Karl, and Friedrich Engels. 1848. *Manifesto of the Communist Party,* in Lewis

S. Feuer, ed., *Marx and Engels, Basic Writings on Politics and Philosophy.* Garden City: Doubleday and Company, Anchor Books, 1959.

Marx, Karl, and Friedrich Engels. 1955. *Selected Works.* Moscow: Foreign Languages Publishing House, 2 vols.

Maslow, A. H. 1954. *Motivation and Personality.* New York: Harper and Brothers.

Matras, Judah. 1961. "Differential Fertility, Intergenerational Occupational Mobility, and Change in the Occupational Distribution," *Population Studies,* 15 (November), 187–197.

Mayntz, Renate. 1958. *Soziale Schichtung und Sozialer Wandel in einer Industriegemeinde.* Stuttgart: Ferdinand Enke.

Meade, J. E. 1964. *Efficiency, Equality, and the Ownership of Property.* London: Allen and Unwin.

Meek, Ronald L. 1954. "The Scottish Contribution to Marxist Sociology," in John Saville, ed., *Democracy and the Labour Movement.* London: Lawrence and Wishart.

Merton, Robert K. 1957. *Social Theory and Social Structure,* 2nd ed. Glencoe: Free Press.

Merton, Robert K. 1968. *Social Theory and Social Structure,* 3rd ed. New York: Free Press.

Michels, Robert. 1914. *Political Parties.* New York: Dover Publications, 1959.

Millar, John. 1803. *An Historical View of the English Government,* vol. IV., in William G. Lehmann, *John Millar of Glasgow.* New York: Cambridge University Press, 1960.

Miller, S.M. 1960. "Comparative Social Mobility," *Current Sociology,* 9 (No. 1), 1–89.

Mills, C. Wright. 1951. *White Collar.* New York: Oxford University Press.

Mills, C. Wright. 1959. "On Intellectual Craftsmanship," in Llewellyn Gross, ed., *Symposium on Sociological Theory.* Evanston: Row, Peterson and Company.

Milne, R.S., and H. C. Mackenzie. 1956. *Straight Fight.* London: Hansard Society.

Mitrany, David. 1951. *Marx Against the Peasant.* Chapel Hill: University of North Carolina Press.

Morse, Nancy C. 1953. *Satisfactions in the White-Collar Job.* Ann Arbor: University of Michigan.

Morse, Nancy C., and Robert S. Weiss. 1955. "The Function and Meaning of Work and the Job," *American Sociological Review,* 20 (April), 191–198.

Mosca, Gaetano. 1939. *The Ruling Class.* New York: McGraw-Hill Book Company.

Mukherjee, Ramkrishna. 1954. "A Study of Social Mobility between Three Generations," in David V. Glass, ed., *Social Mobility in Britain.* London: Routledge and Kegan Paul.

Nordlinger, Eric A. 1967. *The Working-Class Tories.* Berkeley: University of California Press.

Nowak, Stefan. 1969. "Changes of Social Structure in Social Consciousness," in Celia S. Heller, ed. *Structured Social Inequality.* London: Macmillan and Company.

Oeser, O. A., and S. B. Hammond. 1954. *Social Structure and Personality in a City.* London: Routledge and Kegan Paul.

Ollman, Bertell. 1968. "Marx's Use of 'Class'," *American Journal of Sociology,* 73 (March), 573–580.

Orwell, George. 1946. *Animal Farm.* New York: The New American Library. (First published 1945.)

Ossowski, Stanislaw. 1956. "La vision dichotomique de la stratification sociale," *Ca-*

hiers Internationaux de Sociologie, 20 (January-June), 15–29.
Ossowski, Stanislaw. 1963. *Class Structure in the Social Consciousness.* New York: Free Press.

Pagani, Angelo. 1960. *Classi e Dinamica Sociale.* Pavia: Istituto di Statistica della Università di Pavia.
Palmer, Gladys L. 1957. "Attitudes toward Work in an Industrial Community," *American Journal of Sociology,* 63 (July), 17–26.
Pareto, Vilfredo. 1896–1897. (Excerpts from) *Cours d'Economie Politique,* in Vilfredo Pareto, *Sociological Writings.* Selected and introduced by S. E. Finer. New York: Frederick A. Praeger, 1966.
Pareto, Vilfredo. 1901. *The Rise and Fall of the Elites.* Edited and introduced by Hans L. Zetterberg. (First published in Italian as "An Application of Sociological Theories.") Totowa, N.J.: Bedminster Press, 1968.
Pareto, Vilfredo. 1902–1903. *Les Systèmes Socialistes.* Geneva: Librairie Droz, 1965, 2 vols. (reprinted).
Pareto, Vilfredo. 1906. *Manuale di Economia Politica.* Rome: Edizioni Bizzarri, 1965 (reprinted).
Pareto, Vilfredo. 1916. *A Treatise on General Sociology* (first published in Italian and translated into English in 1935 under the title of *The Mind and Society*). New York: Dover Publications, 1963.
Pareto, Vilfredo. 1921. *Trasformazione della Democrazia.* Milan.
Pareto, Vilfredo. 1950. *The Ruling Class in Italy before 1900.* New York: S. F. Vanni.
Pareto, Vilfredo. 1960. *Lettere a Maffeo Pantaleoni, 1890–1923,* ed. Gabriele De Rosa. Rome: Banca Nazionale del Lavoro, 3 vols.
Pareto, Vilfredo. 1966. " 'Il Suicidio': Uno Studio Sociologico di Emile Durkheim," in Giovanni Busino, ed., *Scritti Sociologici di Vilfredo Pareto.* Turin: Unione Tipografico-Editrice Torinese.
Parsons, Talcott. 1953. "A Revised Analytical Approach to the Theory of Social Stratification," in Reinhard Bendix and Seymour M. Lipset, eds., *Class, Status, and Power,* 1st ed. Glencoe; Free Press.
Perlman, Selig. 1922. *A History of Trade Unionism in the United States.* New York: The Macmillan Company.
Perrucci, Robert. 1961. "The Significance of Intra-Occupational Mobility: Some Methodological and Theoretical Notes, Together with a Case Study of Engineers," *American Sociological Review,* 26 (December), 874–883.
Pesonen, Pertti. 1968. *An Election in Finland.* New Haven: Yale University Press.
Petrović, Gajo. 1967. *Marx in the Mid-twentieth Century.* Garden City: Doubleday and Company, Anchor Books.
Pizzorno, Alessandro. 1963. "Le organizzazioni, il potere e i conflitti di classe," (introduction to) Ralf Dahrendorf, *Classi e conflitto di classe nella società industriale.* Bari: Editori Laterza, 1963.
Pizzorno, Alessandro. 1964. "The Individualistic Mobilization of Europe," *Daedalus,* 93 (Winter), 199–224.
Poignant, Raymond. 1969. *Education and Development in Western Europe, the United States, and the U.S.S.R.* New York: Teachers College Press.
Popitz, Heinrich, Hans P. Bahrdt, Ernst A. Jüres, and Hanno Kesting. 1961. *Das Gesellschaftsbild des Arbeiters,* 2nd ed. Tübingen: J. C. B. Mohr.
Posner, M. V., and S. J. Woolf. 1967. *Italian Public Enterprise.* Cambridge: Harvard University Press.
Prince, Rev. John. 1806. *A Discourse Delivered Before the Salem Charitable Society,*

September 17 (reported in Norman Jacobson, "Class and Ideology in the American Revolution," in Reinhard Bendix and Seymour M. Lipset, eds., *Class, Status, and Power,* 1st ed. Glencoe: Free Press, 1953).

Redfield, Robert. 1963. *Peasant Society and Culture.* Chicago: University of Chicago Press, Phoenix Books.

Reissman, Leonard. 1959. *Class in American Society.* Glencoe: Free Press.

Rogoff, Natalie. 1953a. *Recent Trends in Occupational Mobility.* Glencoe: Free Press.

Rogoff, Natalie. 1953b. "Social Stratification in France and in the United States," *American Journal of Sociology,* 58 (January), 347–357.

Rokkan, Stein. 1967. "Geography, Religion, and Social Class: Crosscutting Cleavages in Norwegian Politics," in Seymour M. Lipset and Stein Rokkan, eds., *Party Systems and Voter Alignments.* New York: Free Press.

Rosen, Bernard C. 1959. "Race, Ethnicity, and the Achievement Syndrome," *American Sociological Review,* 24 (February), 47–60.

Rosenberg, Morris. 1951. "The Meaning of Politics in Mass Society," *Public Opinion Quarterly,* 15 (Spring), 5–15.

Rosenberg, Morris. 1953. "Perceptual Obstacles to Class Consciousness," *Social Forces,* 32 (October), 22–27.

Rosenfeld, Eva. 1951. "Social Stratification in a 'Classless' Society," *American Sociological Review,* 16 (December), 766–774.

Rossi, Ernesto. 1954. *Il Malgoverno.* Bari: Editori Laterza.

Rossi Doria, Manlio. 1958. *Dieci Anni di Politica Agraria nel Mezzogiorno.* Bari: Editori Laterza.

Roth, Guenther. 1968. "Introduction" to Max Weber, *Economy and Society.* Edited by Guenther Roth and Claus Wittich. New York: Bedminster Press, 3 vols.

Rowdon, Maurice. 1963. *Italian Sketches.* London: Victor Gollancz.

Runciman, W. G. 1966. *Relative Deprivation and Social Justice.* Berkeley: University of California Press.

Rush, Gary B. 1967. "Status Consistency and Right-Wing Extremism," *American Sociological Review,* 32 (February), 86–92.

Salomon, Albert. 1945. "German Sociology," in Georges Gurvitch and Wilbert E. Moore, eds., *Twentieth Century Sociology.* New York: Philosophical Library.

Saltzman, Janet E. 1969. *Social Mobility and Political Orientation: An Intensive Analysis of the Italian Case.* Unpublished Ph.D. Dissertation, The University of Texas at Austin.

Sargent, S. Stansfeld. 1953. "Class and Class-Consciousness in a California Town," *Social Problems,* 1 (June), 22–27.

Sartori, Giovanni. 1963. *Il Parlamento Italiano, 1946–1963.* Naples: Edizioni Scientifiche Italiane.

Sartori, Giovanni. 1969. "From the Sociology of Politics to Political Sociology," in Seymour M. Lipset, ed., *Politics and the Social Sciences.* New York: Oxford University Press.

Schachter, Gustav. 1965. *The Italian South.* New York: Random House.

Schaff, Adam. 1970. *Marxism and the Human Individual.* New York: McGraw-Hill Book Company.

Schreiber, E. M., and G. T. Nygreen. 1970. "Subjective Social Class in America: 1945–1968," *Social Forces,* 48 (March), 348–356.

Schumpeter, Joseph A. 1951. "Social Class in an Ethnically Homogeneous Environment," in *Imperialism and Social Classes.* New York: Augustus M. Kelley.

Scudder, Richard, and C. Arnold Anderson. 1954. "Migration and Vertical Occupational Mobility," *American Sociological Review,* 19 (June), 329–334.

Sears, David O. 1969. "Political Behavior," in Gardner Lindzey and Elliot Aronson, eds., *Handbook of Social Psychology,* vol. V., 2nd ed. Reading: Addison-Wesley Publishing Company.

Seeman, Melvin. 1959. "On the Meaning of Alienation," *American Sociological Review,* 24 (December), 783–791.

Seeman, Melvin. 1967. "On the Personal Consequences of Alienation in Work," *American Sociological Review,* 32 (April), 273–285.

Shils, Edward. 1955. "The End of Ideology?" *Encounter,* 5 (November), 52–58.

Silone, Ignazio. 1961. *Fontamara.* New York: Dell Publishing Co. (First published in Zurich, 1930.)

Simpson, Richard L. 1956. "A Modification of the Functional Theory of Social Stratification," *Social Forces,* 35 (December), 132–137.

Simpson, Richard L., and Ida H. Simpson. 1960. "Correlates and Estimation of Occupational Prestige," *American Journal of Sociology,* 66 (September), 135–140.

Sjoberg, Gideon. 1960. *The Preindustrial City.* Glencoe: Free Press.

Soares, Glaucio A. D. 1967. "The Politics of Uneven Development: The Case of Brazil," in Seymour M. Lipset and Stein Rokkan, eds., *Party Systems and Voter Alignments.* New York: Free Press.

Sombart, Werner. 1909. *Socialism and the Social Movement.* London: J. M. Dent and Company.

Sorokin, Pitirim. 1927. *Social Mobility.* New York: Harper and Brothers.

Sorokin, Pitirim A. 1959. *Social and Cultural Mobility.* Glencoe: Free Press.

Spiro, Melford E. 1956. *Kibbutz: Venture in Utopia.* Cambridge: Harvard University Press.

Stacey, Barrie. 1966. "Inter-generation Mobility and Voting," *Public Opinion Quarterly,* 30 (Spring), 133–139.

Stanley, Manfred. 1968. "Nature, Culture, and Scarcity: Foreword to a Theoretical Synthesis," *American Sociological Review,* 33 (December), 855–870.

Stinchcombe, Arthur L. 1963. "Some Empirical Consequences of the Davis-Moore Theory of Stratification," *American Sociological Review,* 28 (October), 805–808.

Stinchcombe, Arthur L. 1965. "Social Structure and Organizations," in James G. March, ed., *Handbook of Organizations.* Chicago: Rand McNally and Co.

Strachey, John. 1956. *Contemporary Capitalism.* London: Gollancz.

Sumner, William G. 1906. *Folkways.* New York: Ginn and Company. 1940.

Surace, Samuel J. 1966. *Ideology, Economic Change, and the Working Classes: The Case of Italy.* Berkeley: University of California Press.

Svalastoga, Kaare. 1959. *Prestige, Class and Mobility.* Copenhagen: Gyldendal.

SVIMEZ. 1961a. *Trained Manpower Requirements for the Economic Development of Italy.* Rome.

SVIMEZ. 1961b. *Un Secolo di Statistiche Italiane: Nord e Sud,* 1861–1961. Rome.

Sykes, A. J. M. 1965. "Some Differences in the Attitudes of Clerical and Manual Workers," *Sociological Review,* 13 (November), 297–310.

Tannenbaum, Arnold, and Robert Kahn. 1958. *Participation in Union Locals.* Evanston: Row, Peterson and Company.

Tarrow, Sidney G. 1967. *Peasant Communism in Southern Italy.* New Haven: Yale University Press.

Tawney, R. H. 1920. *The Acquisitive Society.* New York: Harcourt, Brace and Company.

Thomas, W. I. 1923. *The Unadjusted Girl.* Boston: Little, Brown and Company.

Thompson, E. P. 1963. *The Making of the English Working Class.* New York: Random House, Vintage Books.

Thompson, Kenneth. 1967. *Class Change and Party Choice: A Cross-National Study.* Unpublished Ph.D. Dissertation, Department of Political Science, University of Wisconsin.

Thompson, Kenneth H. 1971. "Upward Social Mobility and Political Orientation: A Re-evaluation of the Evidence," *American Sociological Review,* 36 (April), 223–235.

Tilford, R. B., and R. J. C. Preece. 1969. *Federal Germany: Political and Social Order.* London: Oswald Wolff.

Tingsten, Herbert. 1937. *Political Behavior: Studies in Election Statistics.* London: P. S. King and Son.

Touraine, Alain. 1964. "Management and the Working Class in Western Europe," *Daedalus,* 93 (Winter), 304–334.

Tucker, Charles W. 1968. "A Comparative Analysis of Subjective Social Class: 1945–1963," *Social Forces,* 46 (June), 508–514.

Tumin, Melvin M. 1953a. "Some Principles of Stratification: A Critical Analysis," *American Sociological Review,* 18 (August), 387–394.

Tumin, Melvin M. 1953b. "Reply to Kingsley Davis," *American Sociological Review,* 18 (December), 672–673.

Tumin, Melvin M. 1957. "Some Unapplauded Consequences of Social Mobility in a Mass Society," *Social Forces,* 36 (October), 32–37.

Tumin, Melvin M., and Ray C. Collins, Jr. 1959. "Status, Mobility and Anomie: A Study in Readiness for Desegregation," *British Journal of Sociology,* 10 (September), 253–267.

Tumin, Melvin M., and Arnold S. Feldman. 1957. "Theory and Measurement of Occupational Mobility," *American Sociological Review,* 22 (June), 281–288.

Tumin, Melvin M., with Arnold S. Feldman. 1961. *Social Class and Social Change in Puerto Rico.* Princeton: Princeton University Press.

Turner, Ralph H. 1960. "Sponsored and Contest Mobility and the School System," *American Sociological Review,* 25 (December), 855–867.

Ulam, Adam B. 1960. *The Unfinished Revolution.* New York: Random House.

UNESCO. 1957. *World Literacy at Mid-Century.* Monographs on Fundamental Education, No. XI. Paris.

United States Bureau of the Census. 1960. *United States Census of the Population 1960. Occupational Characteristics.* Final Report PC(2)–7A.

Vannutelli, Cesare. 1961. "Occupazione e Salari dal 1861 al 1961," in Bibblioteca della Rivista "Economia e Storia," *L'Economia Italiana dal 1861 al 1961.* Milan: Dott. A. Giuffrè Editore.

Veblen, Thorstein. 1899. *The Theory of the Leisure Class,* in Max Lerner, ed., *The Portable Veblen.* New York: Viking Press, 1948.

Vroom, Victor H. 1964. *Work and Motivation.* New York: John Wiley and Sons.

Walker, Charles R., and Robert J. Guest. 1952. *The Man on the Assembly Line.* Cambridge: Harvard University Press.

Walker, Nigel. 1961. *Morale in the Civil Service: A Study of the Desk Worker.* Edinburgh: Edinburgh University Press.

Wallerstein, Immanuel. 1967. "Class, Tribe, and Party in West African Politics," in

Seymour M. Lipset and Stein Rokkan, eds., *Party Systems and Voter Alignments.* New York: Free Press.

Ward, Lester. 1897. *Dynamic Sociology,* 2nd ed. New York: D. Appleton and Company.

Warner, W. Lloyd, and Associates. 1949. *Democracy in Jonesville.* New York: Harper and Row, Harper Torchbooks, 1964.

Warner, W. Lloyd, and Paul S. Lunt. 1941. *The Social Life of a Modern Community.* New Haven: Yale University Press.

Waxman, Chaim I. 1968. *The End of Ideology Debate.* New York: Funk and Wagnalls.

Weber, Max. 1904. " 'Objectivity' in Social Science and Social Policy," in Max Weber, *The Methodology of the Social Sciences.* Glencoe: Free Press, 1949.

Weber, Max. 1904–1905. *The Protestant Ethic and the Spirit of Capitalism.* New York: Charles Scribner's Sons, 1958.

Weber, Max. 1920–1921. *The Religion of India.* Translated and edited by Hans H. Gerth and Don Martindale. Glencoe: Free Press, 1958.

Weber, Max. 1921–1922. *Economy and Society.* Edited by Guenther Roth and Claus Wittich. New York: Bedminster Press, 3 vols., 1968.

Weitz, Joseph. 1952. "A Neglected Concept in the Study of Job Satisfaction," *Personnel Psychology,* 5 (Autumn), 201–205.

Wesołowski, Włodzimierz. 1966. "Some Notes on the Functional Theory of Stratification," in Reinhard Bendix and Seymour M. Lipset, eds., *Class, Status, and Power,* 2nd ed. New York: Free Press.

West, James. 1945. *Plainville, U.S.A.* New York: Columbia University Press.

West, Patricia S. 1953. "Social Mobility among College Graduates," in Reinhard Bendix and Seymour M. Lipset, eds., *Class, Status, and Power,* 1st ed. Glencoe: Free Press.

Wilensky, Harold L. 1961. "Orderly Careers and Social Participation: The Impact of Work History on Social Integration in the Middle Mass," *American Sociological Review,* 26 (August), 521–539.

Wilensky, Harold L. 1966. "Measures and Effects of Social Mobility," in Neil J. Smelser and Seymour M. Lipset, eds., *Social Structure and Mobility in Economic Development.* Chicago: Aldine Publishing Company.

Wilensky, Harold L., and Hugh Edwards. 1959. "The Skidders: Ideological Adjustments of Downward Mobile Workers," *American Sociological Review,* 24 (April), 215–231.

Willener, Alfred. 1957. *Images de la société et classes sociales.* Bern.

Wrong, Dennis. 1961. "The Oversocialized Conception of Man in Modern Sociology," *American Sociological Review,* 26 (April), 184–198.

Yasuda, Saburo. 1964. "A Methodological Inquiry into Social Mobility," *American Sociological Review,* 29 (February), 16–23.

Young, Michael. 1959. *The Rise of the Meritocracy.* New York: Random House.

Zdravomyslov, A. G., and V. A. Iadov. 1965. "An Attempt at a Concrete Study of Attitude toward Work," *Soviet Sociology,* 3 (Spring), 3–14.

Zeitlin, Irving M. 1967. *Marxism: A Re-Examination.* Princeton: D. Van Nostrand.

Zeitlin, Maurice. 1967. *Revolutionary Politics and the Cuban Working Class.* Princeton: Princeton University Press.

Index